# Biological Approaches to the Study of Human Intelligence

Philip A. Vernon, *Editor*

Department of Psychology
The University of Western Ontario

ABLEX PUBLISHING CORPORATION
NORWOOD, NEW JERSEY

**Library of Congress Cataloging-in-Publication Data**

Vernon, Philip A.
   Biological approaches to the study of human intelligence / Philip
A. Vernon, editor.
     p.    cm.
   Includes bibliographical references and index.
   ISBN 0-89391-798-2 (cloth)
   1. Intellect—Physiological aspects.   I. Title.
QP398.V47    1992
612.8'2--dc20                         92-23462
                                             CIP

Ablex Publishing Corporation
355 Chestnut Street
Norwood, New Jersey 07648

# Contents

# Preface

Biological approaches to the study of human intelligence have been slow to develop and slower to gain acceptance. Yet, as the chapters in this volume demonstrate, much information about the underlying biological bases of intelligence has been amassed. That which is now known in this area is both intriguing and challenging to many traditional notions about the nature of intelligence. To be sure, some of the biological findings are based on small samples and require further study and attempts at replication. Others, however, rest on more solid ground and are sufficiently well-replicated that they deserve serious consideration in any future theories regarding the prime contributors to and causes of individual differences in mental abilities.

In Chapter 1, Hans Eysenck, a long-time advocate of the biological approach, draws parallels between psychology, biology, chemistry, and physics and argues for the need to place the measurement of intelligence, and theories of intelligence, on a more scientific basis. In his summary of research investigating the biological basis of intelligence, Eysenck mentions the study of evoked potentials, cerebral glucose metabolism, and the biochemistry of the brain, each of which is afforded a thorough and detailed discussion in the later chapters by Deary and Caryl (Chapter 6), Haier (Chapter 7), and Naylor, Callaway, and Halliday (Chapter 8), respectively.

Following Eysenck's chapter, Bouchard (Chapter 2) elucidates the roles of genetic, chromosomal, and environmental influences on intelligence, and Thompson (Chapter 3) describes the application of behavioral genetic designs to the study of cognitive development (including general and specific abilities, information processing, scholastic achievement, reading disabilities, and mental retardation) in infancy and childhood. Each of these two chapters provides a convincing demonstration of the value and potential of behavioral genetic methodologies.

In Chapter 4, Jensen and Sinha provide a comprehensive survey of virtually the entire literature on physical correlates of mental abilities in humans. The topics they discuss include height and weight; head and brain size measurements (including the very recent *in vivo* brain size study by Willerman, Schultz, Rutledge, & Bilger, 1991); physical growth rate; myopia; blood types and blood serum chemistry; and a variety of other less-studied physical features. Following this, in Chapter 5, Lynn discusses the effects of nutrition on brain growth and intellectual development and considers the possible contribution of nutritional changes to the large increases in intelligence that have been observed in several economically advanced nations over the past 50 years. He also suggests that nutritional differences may account for a significant proportion of the difference in the mean IQ scores of whites and blacks in the United States—a hypothesis which, if borne out and acted upon, could have immediate favorable consequences. Finally, Kimura and Hampson—in Chapter 9—consider sex differences in mental abilities and the neural and hormonal mechanisms which mediate these. Their chapter identifies a number of biological mechanisms that make substantial contributions not only to observed sex differences in cognition but also to individual differences within each of the sexes.

The purpose of this book is to bring together the results of the many different studies that have investigated and identified biological correlates of intelligence and to suggest that these now constitute a sufficiently large and important body of information to merit considerably greater attention than they typically have been afforded by those interested in the measurement and the theory of intelligence. As readers will hopefully discover, recent biological approaches to the study of intelligence and mental abilities have made many advances, although continuing technological developments make it likely that their potential has only begun to be realized. It will indeed be satisfying if the material presented here stimulates new research which, within 10 or 15 years, has generated an equally large body of results with which to supplement those obtained to date.

# Chapter 1

# The Biological Basis of Intelligence

## H. J. Eysenck

*Professor Emeritus of Psychology*
*University of London*

## INTRODUCTION

### The Concept of Intelligence

The word "intelligence"—like most scientific concepts—began life as a descriptive term used in everyday life to characterize certain aspects of behavior, or of personality. "Intelligentia," as understood by Cicero and other ancient writers, had two rather divergent meanings that can still be found in our dictionaries. On the one hand, the noun may refer to quickness of understanding, sagacity (the Concise Oxford Dictionary), or the capacity for understanding—ability to perceive and comprehend meaning (the *Collins Dictionary*). On the other hand, it may refer to acquired knowledge—"information, news," according to the *Concise Oxford Dictionary*, or the *Collins Dictionary*. Common speech also acknowledges this dual meaning of the term (Derr, 1989). Equally, science has embraced a similar distinction in Cattell's (1963) differentiation

1

between "fluid" ($g_f$) and "crystallyzed" ($g_c$) intelligence. Clearly the two concepts are not unrelated; the first refers to a capacity or disposition that enables us to acquire knowledge, remember things, solve problems, and so on, but the second deals with the results of using that capacity under certain environmental conditions. As a scientific concept, clearly that of intelligence as *capacity* is more fundamental, while that of intelligence as *acquired knowledge* may be of greater practical importance.

From this point of view of measurement, of course, it is much easier to measure acquired knowledge than capacity. Fortunately, under certain circumstances (universal education, similar exposure to books, newspapers, and so forth, the presence of free libraries, etc.) the amount of knowledge acquired may be a good measure of capacity. In spite of the fairly high correlation between $g_f$ and $g_c$ in those populations mostly frequently investigated (North American, Canadian, Australian, British, European) the distinction is an important one that should never be forgotten. Many pointless arguments have been caused by failure to remember it.

It is possible, and may be useful, to extend this notion of different meanings of intelligence, taking into account scientific investigations of the concept. Figure 1.1 shows the three major concepts of intelligence that have been widely used in the past. At the one extreme we have biological intelligence, that is, a concept referring to the *biological* basis of all cognitive behavior. Biological intelligence is conceived of as being largely determined by genetics, which in turn influences the physiology and the biochemistry of the brain. It may be investigated through the use of the EEG, the averaged evoked potential, the galvanic skin response, the contingent negative variation, and possibly through the use of reaction time and inspection time measurements. It is not asserted that biological intelligence is wholly innate, and cannot be influenced by environmental factors; such biological factors as nutrition and sensory experience almost certainly influence the physiology and biochemistry of the brain. It is only in recent years that interest in biological intelligence has come to the fore, although Galton (1883, 1892) had already advocated views emphasizing the biological nature of intelligence.

Strongly determined by biological intelligence is psychometric intelligence or IQ; ever since the days of Binet psychologists have been much more concerned with IQ measurements and psychometric investigations than with biological intelligence and its determination. While IQ is clearly dominated by biological intelligence (as shown by the strong genetic component of IQ), there can be no doubt that environmental factors are also important. Education, socioeconomic status, family upbringing, and cultural factors have been shown to be significantly related to IQ, the degree depending to some extent on the nature of the tests used (Eysenck, 1979). Psychometric intelligence has had considerable practical applications, but has always lacked a solid scientific foundation.

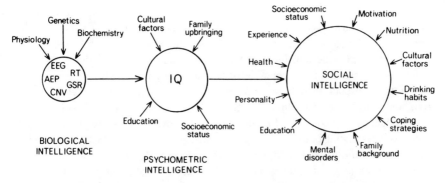

**Figure 1.1.   Three different meanings of "intelligence."**

If psychometric intelligence is an uncertain mixture of capacity and acquired knowledge, then the third concept of intelligence, social or practical intelligence, while largely determined by IQ, is even less unitary. The term refers essentially to the more or less successful way in which people use their cognitive abilities in everyday life (Sternberg, 1985; Sternberg & Wagner, 1986).

We may suggest that IQ, because of its close relationship with biological intelligence, may be an acceptable definition of intelligence (provided its weaknesses are kept in mind), but this is not true of social or practical intelligence. The concept is far too inclusive to have any kind of scientific meaning. Sternberg (1985) acknowledges that this concept "is certainly highly inclusive in the sense that it includes within the realm of intelligence characteristics that typically might be placed in the realms of personality or motivation . . . for example, motivational phenomena relevant to the purpose of adaptive behaviour—such as motivation to perform well in one's career—would be considered part of one's intelligence broadly defined" (p. 55).

It is difficult to assign scientific meaning to such a very broad concept. Scientific advances are based on analysis, and analysis means that artificial compounds should be shunned, and that we should insist on reducing them to their unitary constituents. To bring together dispositional ability factors, personality, motivation, health, experience, and nutrition into one concept simply means that this concept is scientifically meaningless and cannot be measured. Even personality is obviously too vague a concept in this context; you may be able to measure certain aspects of personality, such as extraversion or neuroticism (Eysenck & Eysenck, 1985), but no measurement of personality as such is conceivable. The same applies to motivation. To bring together all these and many other constituents in one concept of practical intelligence is to move it out of the field of scientific investigation and theory altogether. What we must do is to measure each of the variables in question separately and then, if we wish, define social or practical intelligence by means of a formula including each of the variables as a term. Whether this is or is not a meaningful process is questionable, but it is not an issue of interest for the moment.

It is of course true that intelligence and personality can *combine* to produce behavior that is socially acceptable or not, and may prove advantageous to the individual. Eysenck (1979) has summarized some of the literature which shows that both in the high IQ group of Terman's follow-up study, and in low IQ groups of retardades a high degree of neuroticism is disadvantageous, regardless of IQ, and produces social failure. It is specific studies of this kind that are needed to give any meaning that it may have to the concept of social or practical intelligence. Even then, of course, the use of the term "intelligence" is misleading and confusing. In this chapter we will not be concerned with it any further.

What we are concerned with in this chapter is an attempt to place the measurement of intelligence, and the theory of intelligence, on a more scientific basis. Such an attempt at objective analysis has in recent years been frequently declared impossible by writers who have advocated what is sometimes called the "sociology of knowledge." This is based on the belief that it is the relations of production in a society that constitute the basis for the superstructure of ideas in a particular cultural group. Social, political, and intellectual processes within a given society were determined by the *mode of production* in the material sphere, and the attendant social relations. Marx suggested that in relating ideas to a sociological basis, it was the *class structure* that was paramount. The ideas of the ruling class became dominant in a society, and these dominant ideas were nothing more than the mental expression of the dominant material relationships. Thus ideologies emerge which serve the purpose of legitimizing the existing class structure. The measurement of intelligence, and particularly theories concerning the genetic determination of intelligence, are frequently used to exemplify these Marxist notions which, if accepted, would make any scientific study of intelligence impossible.

Recently, Buss (1975) has attempted to apply some such scheme to what he calls "the sociology of psychological knowledge." Following the writings of Berger and Luckman (1966) and Stark (1958), he conceived of his task as being broadly concerned with the social basis of the psychological academicians' ideas. His thesis is based on the belief that "there are no absolute truths in the social sciences, where the 'facts' are embedded in a particular theoretical framework which in turn rests upon certain epistemic and metaphysical presuppositions" (p. 991). In his view there is an intimate relationship between statements of value and statements of fact; "normative statements do have implications for existential statements and vice versa" (Buss, 1975). And he goes on to say that "one of the practical aims of a sociology of psychological knowledge would be to emphasize the relationship between fact and value within psychology and thereby help to make psychologists more self-conscious of the implications their research has with respect to creating a specific image of man in society'' (Buss, 1875).

One of the examples of a sociology of psychological knowledge chosen by Buss is differential psychology. He argues that the growth of capitalism depended on a growing division of labor, and specialization of human talent therefore came to replace the universal man. ''The rise of the scientific study of individual differences may be seen as a new development spurred on by a climate of quantification, where the manifest individual differences promoted by a capitalistic class society became amenable (like its material products) to strict measurement'' (p. 993). He goes on to say that the prevailing political ideology of liberalism *demanded* a strictly genetic interpretation of individual differences in mental abilities. ''Because there were individual differences in abilities as reflected by the existent class structure, such differences must reflect innate differences given the belief that each individual theoretically has the freedom and opportunity for full development'' (Buss, 1975).

Kamin (1974) applied a similar kind of argument to the American continent, and Buss comments: ''Of particular importance in the present context is the idea that a genetic interpretation of individual differences in mental ability served well to legitimise political decisions concerning the restriction of immigration from certain European countries during the 1920s and 1930s'' (p. 993). These ideas coincide with the attempted demonstration by Pastore (1949) that belief in genetic causes went with right-wing political attitudes, and belief in environmentalism with left-wing political attitudes. This whole approach was criticized by Eysenck (1976) on general philosophical grounds, but recent events behind the Iron Curtain suggest a new look at the specific example chosen by Buss (1975).

Let us note, first of all, that the widespread notion that the belief in the (partial) determination of individual differences in intelligence by genetic causes is ''un-Marxian'' and right-wing, is completely false. Mehlhorn and Mehlhorn (1981), speaking as representatives of the communist government of East Germany, explicitly condemn any such interpretations as ''unmarxistisch,'' because they contradict the clearly different positions of Marx, Engels, and Lenin (p. 7). They quote other East German and Russian psychologists in support of this view, and go on to quote Marx and Engels in some detail to the effect that genetic causes are very powerful with respect to differences in mental and artistic ability. These ideas are of course clearly explicit in the Communist Manifesto, as the Soviet psychologist Krutezki (1974, p. 140) points out: ''When it is said, from each according to his abilities, then it is clearly stated that men in this respect are not equal. . . .'' (The best sources for an understanding of Marx's position are his *Kritik des Gothaer Programmes* and the *Deutsche Ideologie* by Marx and Engels.)

Even more explicit is the statement by Lenin (1965, p. 137) that ''when one says that experience and reason testify that men are *not* equal, then one understands under equality the equality of *abilities* or the equivalence of bodily strength and mental capacities of men. It is quite obvious that in this sense men are not equal. No single reasonable man and no single socialist ever forgets this.'' Lenin goes on to characterize as an ''absurdity'' the idea of extending equality into these spheres and concludes by saying: ''When socialists speak of equality, they understand thereby *social* equality, the equality of social position, but not at all the equality of physical and mental abilities of individual persons'' (1965, p. 140).

As Guthke (1978), writing from a communist country, points out: ''Marxist psychology does not by any means deny the importance of genetic factors in the causation of individual differences in intelligence . . . [F]rom the beginning Marx and Lenin have emphasized the biological and psychological inequality of man'' (p. 69). Few Westerners, unfortunately, are familiar with the large-scale work done in the USSR using the twin methods, along lines similar to those adopted in the West (e.g., V. B. Schwartz, K. Grebe, L. Dzhedda, Y. Mirenova, M. Ishidoia, M. Rubinov, B. Nikityuk, V. Yelkin, S. Khoruzheva, N. Annenkov, and many more).

It would seem that historically, communism and capitalism give rise to similar ideas, derived from Darwin, about the importance of genetic factors for differences in human abilities; it would be difficult for any kind of sociological interpretation of psychological knowledge to suggest that the very divergent industrial and social relations obtaining in these two kinds of cultures would necessitate the arbitrary invention of such concepts. It was the brief aberration of Stalinism, with its encouragement of the Lysenko heresy, that gave the erroneous impression to many people unversed in Marxism that environmentalism found some support in the works of Marx, Engels, and Lenin; it is clear from the quotations cited here that this is not so, and indeed these quotations could be multiplied at will.

What is more, recent work in Russia, Poland, and elsewhere have very powerfully supported the view that the influence of genetic factors in differences in IQ is overwhelmingly strong. Thus Lipovechaja, Kantonistowa, and Chamaganova (1978) have recently reported a study in Moscow of 144 pairs of MZ and DZ twins, who were given the various subtests of the WISC, and whose scores were analyzed using Falconer's formula. They found a heritability of these Russian schoolchildren of 0.78 (uncorrected for attenuation), that is, an heritability in excess of that reported by Eysenck (1979) from a reanalysis of all available Western data, excluding Burt's. Similarly the extensive work of Firkowska et al. (1978; Firkowska-Mankiewicz & Czarkowski, 1981) in Poland has shown that in spite of the attempts of the communist government to introduce complete egalitarianism into the school system, the health system, and every other aspect of the individual's life, variance of IQ and correlations between IQ and social-intellectual status of the parent were similar to those found in capitalist countries. The authors rightly argued for the prime importance of genetic factors in producing the observed differences. The important work of Weiss and Mehlhorn (1980) and Weiss (1982) on genetic factors in intelligence and mathematical ability, carried out in East Germany, is too well known to require discussion. Other important references to recent empirical studies and theories in socialist countries are: Mehlhorn and Mehlhorn (1985), Friedrich and Kabatvel Job (1986), Krylow, Kulakowa, Kantonistowa, and Chamaganova (1986) and Ravich-Shaherbo (1988).

We thus arrive at a position which seems to be in exact opposition to that taken by Buss. When he says that "unfortunately (or fortunately) there are no absolute truths in the social sciences," he seems to be arguing a case which cannot be supported by the facts. Both Russian communist and English and American capitalist psychologists arrive at a figure for the heritability of intelligence which is very similar indeed, and Polish, American, and English psychologists all arrive at relationships between the child's IQ and achievement in school, and the intellectual caliber of his parents, which are similar if not identical. Thus regardless of political regime, findings in capitalist and communist countries with respect to this prime example of alleged determination of ideas by the mode of production in the material sphere and the attendant social relations, give rise to identical conclusions which must be said to have a considerable degree of approximation to the "absolute truths" which Buss denies are to be found in the social sciences.

The arguments concerning the sociology of knowledge and the possibility that work on intelligence may be influenced by political ideas have been discussed in some detail because much of the hostility to modern views on intelligence, and many of the arguments against the theories, has arisen from these ideological concepts, rather than from scientific concerns, and it seems desirable to lay this particular ghost to rest once and for all. Our concern in this chapter will be entirely with scientific arguments, although of course the question of what is and what is not scientific is one not as easily settled as might appear at first (Cohen, 1985; Suppe, 1974). The next section will review some of the arguments concerning this problem insofar as it deals with the measurement of intelligence specifically.

## Science and Intelligence: Some Misconceptions

Many critics of the concept of intelligence base their rejection on the grounds that this concept is not scientific; this notion is widespread among many scientists and academics who have little direct knowledge of the research that has been undertaken to make the concept meaningful in scientific terms. Inevitably such criticisms are based on philosophical grounds, and although we shall see that they have little substance, we need to discuss them in some detail, particularly as they are quite relevant to the main contention of this chapter—namely that research into the biological foundations of intelligence is a prerequisite for the scientific acceptance of the concept.

The first criticism to be discussed asserts that theorists in this field reify intelligence, and assert its existence, whereas the critic clearly disbelieves the existence of something called "intelligence." Thus, Keating (1984) has argued that those who believe in the usefulness of the concept of intelligence appear to assume "that *it* is a thing that exists in the head of a person" (p. 2). He and many others argue that intelligence does not exist and that, hence, all efforts to measure it must be useless. This is not a tenable argument. In the first place, none of the leading proponents of the concept of intelligence has postulated its *existence* in any physical shape or form; Galton, Spearman, Burt, Cattell, Wechsler, Horn, Thorndike, Thurstone, and this writer have always regarded it as a scientific *concept*, analogous to such concepts as gravitation, humidity, society, or atoms. Scientific concepts like these do not carry an implication of existence; neither does intelligence. They may be useful or useless as far as scientific description and investigation are concerned. Their main purpose is to bring together in a meaningful shape a large variety of individual events that constitute the blooming buzzing confusion that is reality. There obviously is no such thing as "society"; there are large numbers of individuals interacting in many different ways, and assuming many different roles. These individuals exist, and their interactions (educational, criminal, marital, political, social, etc.) might be considered to exist (although even there some philosophers might express doubts), but society as such is a concept that may or may not be useful in comprehending the totality of these interactions, and cannot be predicated to "exist."

Discussions on the nature of concepts, and the question of existence, will be found in Suppe's (1974) edited book on *The Structure of Scientific Theories*. It is interesting to look at concepts like "ether," "caloric," or "phlogiston," and so forth for which existential claims were made at one time, but which clearly were concepts which, while mistaken, did help to advance the discovery of more useful concepts. Philosophical problems of this kind are somewhat intangible, and a more detailed discussion would not be appropriate here. Let us merely note that criticisms along these lines would have to be much better documented in order to carry any weight. Certainly the claims to be made in this chapter are not that intelligence exists in the same sense as tables and chairs exist, or people, or buildings. It is a concept that unifies many empirical findings in a unique fashion, and has hence been found useful. It is perfectly possible that more useful concepts will be found to describe reality, and in that case intelligence will be displaced by some other concept. What does exist, of course, is the individual brain, with its network of cells, axons, dendrites, and synapses, as well as a multitude of activities governed and regulated by the brain. These "exist" in a very real sense; intelligence does not, and in that sense it shares this quality of "nonexistence" with all other scientific concepts. To argue that intelligence is useless, and cannot be measured, because it does not "exist" is to commit an elementary philosophical error.

A second criticism is often made of the concept of intelligence, namely that there is no agreed-upon definition of the term. Consult such books as *What is Intelligence?* (Sternberg & Detterman, 1986), or its forerunner, the classic symposium published in the *Journal of Educational Psychology* 65 years ago under the title of "Intelligence and its Measurement," and one can see indeed that there is some disagreement on definition. However, as Snyderman and Rothman (1987, 1988) have shown, there is a considerable unanimity among psychologists currently concerning what is *meant* by intelligence. It is easier to recognize an elephant than to describe it!

It is important, in this connection, to realize the difference between a scientific definition, and the identification of important elements or consequences of a given concept. Thus Snyderman and Rothman found that among the 600 plus experts they consulted, there was almost unanimity concerning the importance of abstract thinking or reasoning, problem-solving ability, and capacity to acquire knowledge as important elements of intelligence. But of course these are not definitions, and neither are the many putative definitions given in the Sternberg and Detterman book. To take as an example the concept of gravitation, what would we think of a physicist who attempted to *define* it in terms of the apple falling on Newton's head, planetary motion, the movement of the tides, the bulging of the earth's equator, the falling of the moon toward the earth, "black holes," the formation of the galaxies, the shape of the planets, the paths of comets or asteroids, and the numerous other consequences that follow from positing the concept of a force that acts according to the product of the masses of the bodies interacting, and the inverse square of their distance? Clearly, intelligence is *involved* in abstract thinking, reasoning, problem solving, the acquisition of knowledge, memory, mental agility, creativity, and so on, but these are the *consequences* of applying intelligence in certain directions; they cannot be used to *define* intelligence. The fact that psychologists, when asked to define intelligence, often choose different *examples* of intelligent activity does not mean that we cannot in due course achieve a proper definition of intelligence. Perhaps in the absence of a general theory all that can be done by way of definition would be by way of a descriptive formula, such as the inverse square law of distance in the case of gravitation. Thus one might define intelligence as that which is responsible for producing matrices of unit rank when a large number of dissimilar cognitive problems is administered to a random sample of a given population, and their intercorrelations calculated. The main point to note, however, is that disagreement, so often observed by critics discussing the definition of psychology, does not usually refer to *definitions* at all, but to *examples* of intelligent activity. Here we have a wide choice, and diversity is not really disagreement.

A third objection is often put, pointing out the complete lack of an agreed-upon theory concerning intelligence. In the absence of such a theory, it is argued, is it possible to regard intelligence as a useful scientific concept? Such a view would certainly run counter to anything that the history of science can teach us. Concepts develop for centuries before agreed-upon theories arise, and often the theories on which they are based are known from the beginning to have faults. Gravitation is a good example. Newton's Action at a Distance theory was already known by him to be absurd, but it served a very useful purpose. Even now, 300 years later, there is no agreed-upon theory of gravitation. What we have are two quite dissimilar theories between which it is impossible to make a rational choice. On the one hand, we have Einstein's view according to which gravitation is a distortion of the space-time continuum, and on the other, we have the quantum mechanics interpretation in terms of particle interaction (gravitons).

Much of the same may be said about the theory of heat, where we have the thermodynamic and the kinetic theories side by side. Thermodynamics deals with unimaginable concepts of a purely quantitative kind: *temperature*, measured on a thermometer; *pressure*, measured as a force exerted per unit area; and *volume*, measured by the size of the container. Nothing is said in the laws of thermodynamics about the nature of heat. This, on the other hand, is the foundation stone of the kinetic theory of heat, using Bernoulli's view that all elastic fluids, such as air, consist of small particles that are in constant irregular motion and that constantly collide with each other and with the walls of the container, their speed of motion creating the sensation of heat. Many formulae are quite intractable to kinetic interpretations even today but yield easily to a thermodynamic solution. The unified theory here, as elsewhere, eludes physics, after centuries of endeavor. Should we expect psychology to do better? The unified theory appears at the end, not at the beginning, of scientific search, and to demand such a theory before a concept is taken seriously is to make impossible all scientific research.

However that may be, there is in any case no final, correct theory in science; what we have is a constant improvement in theory that may show considerable differences from one stage to another. Consider the very important notion of an element in chemistry. Boyle gave the first precise definition: "No body is a true principle or element . . . which is not perfectly homogeneous but is further resolvable into any number of distinct substances how small so ever." This insight into the nature of elements unfortunately was unable to furnish him with techniques that could decide in any but a few cases whether a given substance was or was not an element; Boyle's criterion remained inapplicable for another 100 years. Finally, of course, Boyle's definition and the work of the next few centuries resulted in that great monument of classification, Mendeleev's periodic table of the elements, in 1869. This appeared to be a final step in classification for a time, but then came the discovery that the atom was not after all indivisible, and since then we have had a whole shower of long-lived elementary particles and antiparticles, as well as resonances, isobars, and excited states—so much so that few except professional physicists can find their way about among the fermions and bosons, the leptons, baryons and mesons, the nucleons and hyper-ons and the neutrinos, neutrettos, muons, lambdas, sigmas, pions, kaons, and so on and so forth—not forgetting the quarks! Obviously another classification was required, and now that we have the theory of *unitary symmetry* known as SU(3) we have gone some way toward achieving a more satisfactory state, particularly since the discovery of the omego-minus particle has seemed to verify the principles on which the theory of unitary symmetry was based. Modern as all these recent advances may seem, many of them had been foreseen already by Newton, who had evolved a theory of the atom composed of a shell within a shell of parts held together successively more firmly. All these anticipations of future developments by Boyle and Newton were of little use in the development of chemistry because, as Bernal (1969) points out: "In the seventeenth century chemistry was not yet in a state in which the corpuscular analysis could be applied. For that it needed the steady accumulation of new experimental facts that was to come in the next century. Chemistry, unlike physics, demands a multiplicity of experiences and does not contain self-evident principles. Without principles it must remain an 'occult' science depending on real but inexplicable mysteries."

This is an important limitation which applies to psychology just as much as it did to chemistry. The cry is often heard for a Newton to rescue us from the avalanche of facts, and to remedy the lack of self-evident principles in psychology. Yet even Newton, who worked at chemistry for much longer than he worked at physics, did not in fact succeed in advancing that science to any particular degree. Both in the matter of classification and in the matter of the creation of a genuine science of psychology we simply have to live within our means, and realize the bounds set by the nature of the material to the development of the laws we would all like to see develop.

A fourth point of criticism often relates to the accuracy of measurement, contrasting unfavorably the precision of measurement in the physical sciences with that achieved in psychology. It is true that certain measures in physics are extremely accurate. Thus the measurement of time is now accurate to a second in a million years, using the Caesium Time Base at Rugby. Even more recent advances, using "ion traps" to measure time, have improved accuracy from one part in $10^{13}$ to one part in $10^{15}$; at the National Physical Laboratory, the element ytterbium is used as a standard for optical transition methods. But of course this accuracy was achieved only after 2,000 years of constant improvement, using originally devices like the sun dial, or the hourglass in which sand or water ran through a narrow opening at a more or less even rate. (The rate of course was not even because pressure varies with the amount of water or sand in the upper compartment.) Accuracy of measurement of IQ tests does not compare badly with the accuracy of measurement of time intervals prior to the invention of mechanical devices, and Galileo's demonstration of the laws governing the pendulum (Bernal, 1969). A similar lengthy period of development from very primitive types of measurement attended the use of scales to measure weight (Kisch, 1965), the measurement of temperature (Baker, Ryder, & Baker, 1975) and the measurement of mass and length (Feather, 1959). Accurate measurement is the outcome of a long period of evolution, in which practice, theory, measurement, and invention interact in a complex manner to improve accuracy.

It is in any case quite wrong to imagine that all measurements in physics approach the accuracy of the measurement of time. Measurement of the cosmological constant, for instance, has given constantly changing results over the past 50 years, and even now resists accurate determination. To take another quite fundamental measurement, we may look at the half-life of the neutron, which has proved notoriously difficult for physicists to measure. This is an important quantity for both particle-physicists and cosmologists. The former need to know this quantity accurately, because it allows them to determine the so-called "coupling constants" of the weak force of nuclear measure, while the latter need to know because accurate knowledge would allow them to determine the proportion of neutrons and protons that existed soon after the Big Bang. In 1951, the best estimate available of the half-life was 768 seconds, with an error margin of 150 seconds. Recent measures suggest a duration of 615 seconds, a difference from former estimates even beyond the error margin suggested originally!

To take another example, concerning errors in radio-carbon dating, recent studies have shown that errors with this technique may be two to three times as great as practitioners of the technique had claimed previously. Here, as in IQ measurement, there are many unaccounted-for sources of error that occur during the processing and analysis of samples. These are more realistic examples of the fact that all measurement involves error, and that the error, even in physics and astronomy, can be very large indeed. It is not the size of the error that determines whether a measurement is scientific; we could never undertake any scientific measurement if this measurement had to be accurate from the beginning within very narrow limits. What is important is to be able to have some estimate of the *size* of the error variance and some ideas about the *factors* that affect measurement to make it less accurate than it ought to be. On all these grounds measurement can be remarkably accurate under appropriate conditions—even in psychology.

It is important to emphasize the qualification contained in the last sentence, because a fifth objection often made relates to the practical application of IQ measurement and the errors that frequently occur. The use of IQ tests for more practical purposes should not be confused with its use as a scientific measure in experimental studies. The practical application is often constrained by financial considerations, administration is often by untrained personnel, and interpretation is often undertaken by nonpsychologists. Furthermore, tests are often chosen for reasons that have little to do with the accuracy of IQ measurement, but relate to the practical purposes of the investigator. Many so-called IQ tests are really measures for the prediction of scholastic achievement, and combine items of verbal and cultural knowledge with items more properly designed to measure $g_f$. This may be reasonable from the point of view of the administration, but such a test is not a proper IQ test, and the measurement of IQ should not be criticized because such tests fall short of ideal requirements.

But, and this is a sixth objection frequently raised, is it not true that there are many different types of IQ tests, and that these do not always give identical results? This is true, but equally there are many different types of measures of temperature, and these also do not give identical results. There is for instance a mercury-in-glass thermometer depending on the change in volume of the mercury with increase in heat; the constant-volume gas thermometer, depending on the reactance of the welded junction of two fine wires; resistance thermometers, depending on the relation between resistance and temperature; and thermocouples, depending on the setting up of currents by a pair of metals with their junctions at different temperatures. Nelkon and Parker (1965), in their Advanced Level Physics, point out that temperature scales differ from one another, "that no one of them is any more 'true' than any other, and that our choice of which to adopt is arbitrary, though it may be decided by convenience" (p. 186). Thus when a mercury-in-glass thermometer reads 300°C, a platinum resistance thermometer in the same place and at the same time will read 291°C! There is no meaning attached to the question of which of these two values is "correct" any more than to the question of whether an IQ of 120 on the Wechsler Scale is more "true" than an IQ of 125 on the Raven's Matrices!

One further objection may require a brief answer. It is often said that the ordinary measurement of IQ disregards important aspects of human life, such as creativity. That is true, in one sense, but it makes the assumption that creativity is essentially a cognitive variable. The empirical evidence seems to suggest, however, that creativity is a function of personality variables, particularly psychoticism, interacting with cognitive variables, namely IQ (Eysenck, 1983). For great achievement, high IQ is required, but high IQ does not necessarily lead to creativity. A certain element of psychoticism seems to be required, as shown both in real-life studies of highly gifted artists, and in experimental studies using traditional creativity tests. The objection, therefore, does not seem to be a serious criticism of IQ testing.

## Biometric Intelligence: A Problem in Taxonomy

All sciences have a dual problem, in that they are concerned with both *taxonomy* and *causal analysis*. Taxonomy or classification usually precedes attempts at causal analysis. Classification of animals preceded Darwin's theory of evolution, to take but one classical example. Without taxonomy, causal analysis is difficult if not impossible. Of course there is no absolute distinction; there is an interaction, in the sense that advances in the causal analysis will help taxonomy, and vice versa. But in essence there is a very important difference, and unfortunately this difference has been neglected far too much by psychologists working in the fields of intelligence.

Classification is thus one of the classic methods of science and is fundamental in all fields of study. This is equally true in biology as in physics. Systems of classification are always at first simple, governed by common-sense appearances, and far removed from the complexities of later developments. Thus, Thales, the first of the Greek philosophers to think about the constitution of the world and its elements, held the theory that everything was originally water, from which earth, air, and living things were later separated out. Later on Anaximander and Anaximenes modified this hypothesis to include earth, air, and fire as well as water as the main elements. These of course were mere prescientific guesses of little value in the actual development of chemistry and physics, but at least they served to pose a problem.

More fruitful was an approach that appears to have originated with the Chinese. In chemistry we are dealing with a fundamental duality which is exemplified by metals and nonmetals; this we now know to be due to a shortage or excess of electrons. There is evidence for tracing the first appreciation of this duality to the Chinese, who already in prehistoric times used red cinnabar as a magic substitute for life blood and had resolved it into its elements, sulphur and mercury. From these notions the Taoist sect developed a system of alchemy from which it is probable that first Indian and then Arabic alchemy was derived. To these two opposites of sulphur and mercury a third element was added by Philipus Aureolus Theophrastus Bombastus von Hohenheim, who called himself Paracelsus to show his superiority to Celsus, the great doctor of antiquity. By adding the neutral *salt* he established the so-called *tria prima* as a foundation of his "spagyric" art of chemistry (Bernal, 1969).

Curious as these ancient methods of classification seem to us yet there is good modern justification for this spagyric system of mercury, sulphur, and salt. We have here a reasonable prevision of three of the four subfields into which the general field of chemistry is now subdivided: that of the rare gases, where all electrons remain attached to atoms; that of metals, where there is an excess of electrons; that of nonmetals, where there is a lack of electrons; and that of salts, where exchanges have taken place between the metal and the nonmetal ions. Even the analogy from external appearance on which the spagyric art was originally based has now found an explanation in terms of quantum theory.

There are certain important lessons to be learned from this brief excursion into ancient chemical history. One of them is that progress in classification is ultimately dependent on, and in turn central to, general development of the science of which it forms a part. Another important idea is this: The principles of classification based on analogies from external appearance may incorporate very important insights without which the development of a science would be very much slower, although of course it is not suggested that we should rest content with arguments from external appearances.

Psychologists who work in the field of classification, whether that of normal or abnormal personality or of intelligence, seldom concern themselves with the history of classification in physics and chemistry. This may be explained in terms of the obvious differences between animate and inanimate matter. However, they also very rarely seem to show any interest in the history of biological classification or *taxonomy*, and this is rather more difficult to understand because most of the problems that occur in psychology have also been dealt with by biologists and botanists at various stages, and a knowledge of their experiences may be of considerable use in dealing with our own problems.

This is not to say that biological taxonomy has been an unqualified success, or has failed to develop problems of its own. Consider the following quotation from Singer (1959):

> We would stress the fact that, from the time of Linnaeus to our own, a weak point in biological science has been the absence of any quantitative meaning in our classificatory terms. What is a class, and does class A differ from class B as much as class C differs from class D? The question can be put for the other classificatory grades, such as order, family, genus and species. In no case can it be answered fully, and in most cases it cannot be answered at all . . . until some adequate reply can be given to such questions as these, our classificatory schemes can never be satisfactory or natural. They can be little better than mnemonics—mere skeletons or frames on which we hang somewhat disconnected fragments of knowledge. Evolutionary doctrine, which has been at the back of all classificatory systems of the last century, has provided no real answer to these difficulties. Geology has given a fragmentary answer here and there. But to sketch the manner in which the various groups of living things arose is a very different thing from ascribing any quantitative value to those groups.

Similarly, Sokal and Sneath (1963) in their classic book on *Principles of Numerical Taxonomy* have this to say:

> It is widely acknowledged that the science of taxonomy is one of the most neglected disciplines in biology. Although new developments are continually being made in techniques for studying living creatures, in finding new characters, in describing new organisms, and in revising the systematics of previously known organisms, little work has been directed towards the conceptual basis of classification—that is, taxonomy in the restricted sense of the theory of classification. Indeed, the taxonomy of today is but little advanced from that of a hundred, or even two hundred, years ago. Biologists have amassed a wealth of material, both of museum specimens and of new taxonomic characters, but they have had little success in improving their power of digesting this material. The practice of taxonomy has remained intuitive and commonly inarticulate, an art rather than a science.

Sokal and Sneath give the following definition of classification: "Classification is the ordering of organisms into groups (or sets) on the basis of their relationships, that is, of their associations by continuity, similarity, or both." They go on to point out that there may be confusion over the term "relationship." As they say, "This may imply relationship by ancestry, or it may simply indicate the overall similarity as judged by the characters of the organisms without any implication as to their relationship by ancestry." The second of these meanings is the one they prefer, and they give it the special name of "phenetic relationship," using this term to indicate that relationship is judged from the phenotype of the organism and not from its phylogeny. In psychology too there is an important distinction corresponding to this, although the alternative to a phenetic relationship is not one based on ancestry but one based on genotypic consideration. We shall take up this point in some detail later on.

In setting up systems of classification we may follow one of two alternative routes named by Sneath (1962) "polythetic" and "monothetic" (from *poly*: "many," *mono*: "one," *thetos*: "arrangement"). As Sokal and Sneath point out:

> The ruling idea of monothetic groups is that they are formed by rigid and successive logical divisions so that the position of a unique set of features is both sufficient and necessary for membership in the group thus defined. They are called monothetic because the defining set of features is unique. Any monothetic system (such as that of Maccacaro, 1958, or in ecology that of Williams and Lambert, 1959) will always carry the risk of serious misclassification if we wish to make natural phenetic groups. This is because an organism which happens to be aberrant in the feature used to make the primary division will inevitably be removed to a category far from the required position, even if it is identical with its natural congeners in every other feature. The disadvantage of monothetic groups is that they do not yield "natural" taxa, except by lucky choice of the feature used for division. The advantage of monothetic groups is that keys and hierarchies are readily made.

Sokal and Sneath go on to list the advantages of polythetic arrangements. Such arrangements, they say, "place together organisms that have the greatest number of shared features, and no single feature is essential to group membership or is sufficient to make an organism a member of the group." They credit Adamson (1727–1806) with the introduction of the polythetic type of system into biology. He rejected the a priori assumptions of the importance of different characters; he correctly realized that natural taxa are based on the concept of "affinity"—which is measured by taking all characters into consideration—and that the taxa are separated from each other by means of correlated features.

It is important to realize that the distinction between polythetic and monothetic methods of classification has important consequences for our definition of intelligence, and our search for a means of adequate measurement. A *monothetic* approach would be that of defining intelligence a priori in terms of learning, or problem solving, or memory, or inductive reasoning; by adopting such a definition, and only using tests of that character, we would arbitrarily prejudge the issue and make it impossible to ever arrive at a more complex and more decisive definition and measurement of intelligence. *Polythetic* methods are indicated and, as we shall see, these imply the use of correlational and factorial analyses.

The analysis by *phenetic relationship* which had become all but universal in biology received a setback when *analysis by relation through ancestry* was reinstated after the publication of *The Origin of Species*. Suddenly Darwin's theory seemed to suggest the basis for the existence of natural systematic categories: Their members were related because of descent from a common ancestry. Unfortunately, history has shown that this enthusiasm could only be short-lived; we cannot make use of phylogeny for classification since in the vast majority of cases phylogenies are unknown. Inviting as the argument from ancestry may appear, therefore, in its Darwinian guise, nevertheless it has to be rejected for reasons given in detail by Hennig (1957), Remane (1956), and Simpson (1961), as well as in *Principles of Numerical Taxonomy* by Sokal and Sneath already quoted.

An exciting recent development has led to the construction of phylogenetic trees by biochemists, who use quantitative estimates of variance between species as regards substances such as DNA and cytochrome c. Fitch and Margoliash (1967), for instance, have succeeded in constructing such a tree, based on data relating to the single gene that codes for cytochrome c, which is very similar to the "classical" phylogenic tree. The method is based essentially on the appropriate "mutation distances" between two cytochromes, which is defined as the minimal number of component nucleotides that would need to be altered in order for the gene for one cytochrome to code for the other. This number is considered proportional to the number of mutations that have taken place in the descent from the apex of one cytochrome as compared with another. Thus, it is claimed that this new method, which gives a quantitative measure of the event (mutation) which permits the evolution of new species, must give the most accurate of phylogenetic trees. In this way it may be possible to overcome the difficulties in the evolutionary method of classification by descent noted above; it is reassuring that even when based only on a single gene the phylogenetic scheme is remarkably like that obtained by classical methods.

How in fact does a biologist proceed? Sneath (1962) has set the procedures out according to the following four steps:

1.  The organisms are chosen, and their characters are recorded in a table.
2.  Each organism is compared with every other and their overall resemblance is estimated as indicated by all the characters. This yields a new table, a table of similarities.
3.  The organisms are now sorted into groups on the basis of their mutual similarities. Like organisms are brought next to like, and separated from unlike, and these groups or *phenons* are taken to represent the "natural" taxonomic groups whose relationships can be represented in numerical form.
4.  The characters can now be reexamined to find those that are most constant within the groups that have emerged from the analysis. These can be used as diagnostic characters in keys for identifying specimens.

The last paragraph will make apparent the relevance of this discussion to the study of intelligence. We are faced with a very large number of behaviors, measured by means of tests, questionnaires, observations, or experiments. It is obviously impossible to build separate concepts on each of these variables, and we are faced with the problem of taxonomy. Translating the prescription given by Sneath in the above paragraph, but tracing his steps into the field of psychological measurement, we would say:

1. The tests are chosen, and their characters are recorded in a table.
2. Each test is compared with every other, and their overall resemblance is estimated (by means of correlation coefficients).
3. The tests are now sorted into groups on the basis of their mutual similarities. Like tests are brought next to like, and separated from unlike; in these groups all factors are taken to represent the "natural" taxonomic groups where relationships can be represented in numerical form. Factor analysis is the preferred method to carry out this step.
4. The tests can now be reexamined to find those most constant within the factors that have emerged from the analysis. These can be used as diagnostic characters for identifying abilities. Factor analysts have frequently been criticized for using a methodology that is unlike anything in the natural sciences. Our rather roundabout discussion has been undertaken to indicate that such an accusation is not in fact accurate, and that in taxonomy psychologists who use factor analysis are simply following the identical path that has been prescribed for them by experts in the biological field. The taxonomic analysis of the cognitive field begun by Spearman in 1904, and continued by Thurstone, Thomson, Cattell, Guilford, Vernon, and many others has certainly brought a great deal of clarification into this field, and has helped us to a meaningful classification of mental tests.

I have discussed the outcome of this taxonomic effort many times (Eysenck, 1992), and will not do so again here except to summarize the major agreements:

1. The most important finding is that all cognitive tests correlate positively together, to create what is often called the "positive manifold."
2. The first and the most important factor to emerge in the correlations between any variegated set of tests is the general factor of intelligence or $g$. (Tests differ in their $g$ loadings, indicating that some are better measures of intelligence than others.)
3. The nature of tests with high as opposed to low $g$ loadings enable us to formulate and test hypotheses concerning the nature of intelligence.
4. In addition to $g$, all tests measure factors specific to each test.
5. In addition to $g$, and specific factors, each measurement carries with it an error factor, as indeed do all scientific measurements.
6. Tests which are similar in content (i.e., verbal, numerical, visual-spatial, memory, etc.) define group factors or primary abilities which are indepen-

dent of $g$. We have no choice but to attempt to postulate and test the importance of such factors.

7. Estimates of $g$ are remarkably stable across different batteries of mental tests, even when batteries consist of as few as nine tests. Thorndike (1987) demonstrated this by making up six short nonoverlapping batteries of nine tests each. The tests in each battery were randomly sampled from a large pool of extremely diverse cognitive tests used by the U.S. Air Force, including a great variety of tests from discrimination reaction-time to vocabulary. Seventeen highly diverse "probe" tests were interlocked one at a time into each battery, and the average correlation of the $g$ loadings of the 17 probe tests across the six batteries calculated; it turns out to be .85. $g$ emerges with a high degree of robustness and consistency for mental test batteries of a very varied character which in this case were for the most part not even good tests of $g$.

8. The prescription that the $g$ tests in a battery should be as varied as possible is not very precise, but we now have enough evidence available to enable us to follow this prescription with considerable accuracy. This means that $g$ factors obtained from different test batteries can be considered as a statistical estimate of a *true* $g$, a distinction made by measurement theory between an *obtained* measurement and a *true* measurement. We can estimate the degree to which an obtained measure of $g$ approximates a true measure by using a formula given by Kaiser (1968). This indicates that if we determine a $g$ from a sample of 20 tests correlating only to a degree of .20, the resulting measure of $g$ would have a validity of .91.

The major result of such taxonomic studies is a hierarchical structure much like Figure 1.2, which is taken from the work of Jäger (1967) and his colleagues (Jäger & Tesch–Römer, 1988; Jäger & Hörmann, 1981). Unlike Guilford's (1967) model of the intellect, Jager incorporates the vital $g$ factor in his model, which has much greater empirical support than Guilford's.

It is always possible in taxonomic work to argue for alternative methods of classification, if only because causal derivation is difficult or impossible, and because the reasons for classification may be varied. Thus to the biologist the whale may be a mammal, but to the Ministry of Agriculture and Fisheries it may be a fish, for obvious reasons. Hence, there have been many attempts to deny the existence of $g$, and to suggest complex patterns of intercorrelated primaries, or even independent primaries (Guilford, 1967). Improbable as these alternative suggestions are, they are not always mathematically impossible, as it is clearly feasible to rotate factors in any manner whatsoever, thus giving an infinite number of possible solutions. However, as Thurstone (1947) was the first to point out, there are certain preferred solutions (simple structure) which, when they occur in a clear-cut manner, ought to be given preference. This suggestion has been widely accepted, but it is clearly not a mathematical absolute, and may be disregarded if analysts want to do so.

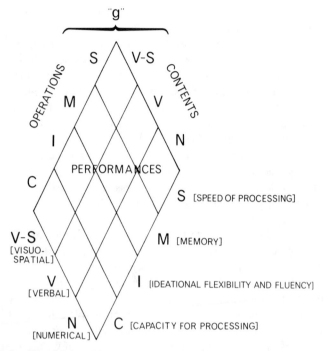

**Figure 1.2.   The hierarchical structure of intellect (Jager et al., 1988).**

This slight degree of subjectivity in taxonomy in general, and factor analysis in particular, makes it necessary to look for causal factors in order to obtain a more universal agreement. There are of course many other reasons for looking at causal factors, and indeed even the earlier workers like Spearman and Thomson attempted to set up theories which might explain the observed phenomena. Thus Spearman (1927) suggested some form of energy as a causal factor for differences in *g*, while Thomson (1939) favored a theory of "bonds," a theory that has been fairly decisively disproved (Eysenck, 1987a). If we take seriously the notion of these rather divergent forms of intelligence suggested in Figure 1.2, then clearly we must look for a causal factor in the biological field, as indeed Galton had already suggested. It is to this search that we now turn. Before doing so, however, it may be useful to point out that most writers looking for a causal theory have adopted good measures of *g* as criteria for such a theory. With all its faults, the psychometric analysis of intelligence has given us very solid results, and has given us excellent measures of *g*; any causal theory that does not account for the psychometric results we have obtained in the past would clearly not be acceptable. Thus it is reasonable to regard *g* as our criterion for judging the adequacy of any biological theory.

## The Biological Basis of Intelligence

The major outcome of the taxonomic investigation into the concept of intelligence results in a hierarchical model specifying four types of factors. By far the most important is a general factor, followed by group factors, followed by specific factors, followed by error factors. The nature of a general factor, whether determined by confirmatory factor analysis (Gustafsson, 1984) or multidimensional scaling (Snow, Kyllonan, & Marshalek, 1984) is most closely defined by tests of $g_f$, such as Raven's Matrices; $g_c$ tests appear at the lower level. This alone should be sufficient to disprove the widely held belief that IQ measures are simply measures of educational achievement and verbal knowledge, a belief still widespread in spite of the strong evidence against it (Sternberg, 1982; Wolman, 1985). But as previously pointed out, taxonomic arguments are impossible to make definitive, and it is usually possible by making arbitrary assumptions of one kind or another to come to a desired conclusion. More impressive are direct tests that require specific theories and experimental studies directed toward a causal analysis of the phenomenon. It is only in recent years that efforts have been made in that direction.

There have been two major lines of attack. The first of these relates to the implementation of the suggestion by Galton, to the effect that reaction times might be a fairly direct measure of biological intelligence. This suggests, and should be supplemented by a theory, that speed of mental processing may be a major causal factor in producing differences in IQ (Eysenck, 1967). The literature has been reviewed by Eysenck (1987b), and more recent advances discussed in other chapters in this book. Here I only summarize the major findings as far as these are relevant to our problem.

1. Measures of DT (decision time) correlate negatively with $g$.
2. Measures of MT (movement time) correlate negatively with $g$.
3. Measures of *variability* of DT correlate negatively with $g$.
4. The more complex the stimulus for RT, the higher the correlation with $g$, as long as total RT is below 1000 millisecs. Simple RT has quite low correlations with $g$, choice RT somewhat higher ones, complex RT, like the odd-man-out paradigm (Frearson & Eysenck, 1986), have the highest.
5. Multiple correlations between different RT measures and $g$ are much higher than individual measures, and can be in excess of .70.
6. The correlation between IQ measures and RT is not mediated by speeded IQ tests, but applies equally to so-called power tests.

All these findings, replicated many times over, favor some sort of "speed of mental processing" theory, except number 3 which cannot easily be accommodated by such a theory. There is, of course, a contingency relation between speed and variability of RT (great variability implies the presence of long as well as short RTs, and this precludes very low RTS on the average), but the contingency is such that RTs should correlate higher, rather than lower, with $g$, as compared with variability. We will return to this anomaly in connection with an alternative theory later on.

Of equal interest and importance as work on RT has been the study of IT (inspection time) (see Eysenck, 1986, and the symposium following this reference). Here, importance attaches to *speed of perception* rather than *speed of reaction*, and the evidence may be summarized by saying that there are correlations averaging around .5 between IT and $g$. It is not yet known whether *variability* of IT is highly correlated with $g$, but clearly this is an important question requiring elucidation. However that may be, IT is an important contributor to any $R^2$ involving measures of DT and MT.

It is unfortunate that most experimenters have used the traditional stimulus in IT studies (comparing a long with a short line); it seems reasonable to expect that a slightly more complex stimulus would correlate more highly with IQ. Thus we might ask subjects to compare two circles, containing different numbers of dots, the task being to identify the circle containing the most dots. Provided the task was easy enough for even retardates to do successfully, if given enough time, and did not last for more than 300 msec. to 500 msec. for average IQ subjects to do, it does seem likely that correlations with IQ exceeding 0.50 would be obtained. Systematic variation of stimuli should in any case throw much light on the mechanics of the phenomenon in question. Correlations between different versions of the IT paradigm could also be used to calculate multiple correlations. A factor analysis of different DT, MT, and IT test scores would be an important contribution to the IQ literature.

A "speed of mental processing" theory would predict most of the results actually found. Cognitive processing must begin with perception (IT), go on to central processing of the information gained (DT), and finally issue in some form of action (MT). The main reasons the mental chronometry involved is relevant to IQ have been spelled out by Jensen (1982a, 1982b).

Essentially, it has been well established in cognitive psychology that the conscious brain acts as a one-channel or *limited capacity* information processing system. As such, it can deal simultaneously only with a very limited amount of information, and this limited capacity also restricts the number of operations that can be performed simultaneously. Speediness of mental processing is advantageous in that more operations per unit of time can be executed without overloading the system. Such operations may involve information entering the system from external stimuli, or from retrieval of information stored in short-term or long-term memory (STM or LTM).

Another advantage is that there is rapid decay of stimulus traces and information, so that there is a clear advantage to speediness of any operations that must be performed on the information while it is still available. Other advantages involve the fact that in order to compensate for limited capacity and rapid decay of incoming information, individuals resort to rehearsal and storage of the information into intermediate or long-term memory, which has relatively unlimited capacity. But this process itself takes time, and therefore uses a general capacity, involving a tradeoff between the storage and the processing of incoming information. Total amount stored and processed is limited by the speed with which these acts are accomplished.

We thus have a fairly coherent theory of speed of mental processing underlying essentially varied accomplishments of $g$. This theory, and the facts on which it is based, are quite incompatible with Binet-type theories emphasizing education, scholastic knowledge, and similar achievements as basic to our conception of intelligence. Inspection time, decision time, and movement time in response to extremely simple stimuli are obviously highly related to differences in $g$-loaded tests, but they cannot be regarded as in any sense measures of crystallized ability, of school learning, or similar types of achievement. The tests are quite novel for practically all subjects, requiring no former knowledge of any kind, and the tasks involved are so simple that even low retardates can carry them out *given enough time*. Yet multiple correlations between tests of this kind and IQ tests are almost as high as are correlations between different IQ tests. This is a fact that requires explanation, and it is difficult to see how one can arrive at such an explanation in terms of orthodox theories emphasizing learning and educational achievement.

It could be argued, and it has been argued, that perhaps reaction and inspection time experiments do not give us a direct insight into brain function. If this is true, different forms of EEG measurement may be used to gain some more insight into the psychophysiology of intelligence (Eysenck, 1982; Eysenck & Barrett, 1985). The study of the EEG itself has proved relatively disappointing, until recently, when computer methods of analysis became available. Gasser and his associates (Gasser, Lucadon-Müller, Verleger, & Bacher, 1983; Gasser, Mocks, Lenard, Bacher, & Verleger, 1983; Gasser, Mocks, & Bacher, 1983) have been most successful in demonstrating that correlations of the order of .5 can be obtained in this field, using variables the choice of which was predicted in terms of a genuine theory. However, most work has been done in relation to evoked potentials, following the early work of Ertl (1973) and Ertl and Schafer (1969). These studies have been extensively reviewed elsewhere (Eysenck & Barrett, 1985) and Eysenck (1986b). The essential breakthrough occurred when the Hendricksons (A. E. & D. E. Hendrickson, 1980; A. E. Hendrickson, 1982; D. E. Hendrickson, 1982) put forward a novel theory to account for existing facts, and predict novel ones. Based on a physiological theory of information processing through the cortex, the Hendricksons argued that individuals with neuronal circuitry that can best maintain the integrity of stimuli will form accessible memories faster than those individuals whose circuitry is more "noisy." In addition, for individuals of low neural integrity, it will be impossible to acquire complex or lengthy information, as the total information content can never be stored in a meaningful way, and no accessible memory can be formed. The integrity of neuronal circuitry is essentially dependent on errorless information processing; the more errors occur (possibly at the synapse) the "noisier" will be the circuitry. IQ, on this hypothesis, should be a function of the integrity of the circuitry, or the absence of errors; the fewer errors, the higher the IQ.

Two measures were derived on the basis of this reasoning, which should correlate with psychometric test intelligence scores, given that such test performance is related to neural transmission integrity. The first measure would be the *complexity* of the waveform, assessed by measuring the contour perimeter of the AEP waveform, a measure originally called the "string" measure, after an early way of measuring this contour perimeter. The second measure would be the *variance* at each point across a number of stimulus waveform epochs. The more intelligent the individual, the longer the contour, and the lower the variance. These two measures would be expected to correlate reasonably well, since they both derive from the same fundamental property of errors in transmission. We thus have a rational measure that can be objectively quantified and correlated with intelligence.

The results of a large-scale study of 219 schoolchildren, using the WAIS as a measure of IQ, gave very positive results which are shown in Table 1.1. The correlations among the WAIS IQ and string, variance, and composite AEP measures are .72, − .72, and − .83, respectively. These data are impressive, but

### Table 1.1.  Relationship between the EEG Measures and the WAIS Subtests

| WAIS test | Variance | String | Variance minus string | Full WAIS IQ (current study) | Full WAIS IQ (published data) |
|---|---|---|---|---|---|
| Information | −.64 | .55 | −.68 | .80 | .84 |
| Comprehension | −.50 | .53 | −.59 | .74 | .72 |
| Arithmetic | −.57 | .56 | −.65 | .79 | .70 |
| Similarities | −.69 | .54 | −.71 | .84 | .80 |
| Digit span | −.54 | .49 | −.59 | .71 | .61 |
| Vocabulary | −.57 | .62 | −.68 | .79 | .83 |
| Verb total | −.69 | .68 | −.78 | .95 | .96 |
| Digit symbol | −.28 | .32 | −.35 | .45 | .68 |
| Picture completion | −.47 | .52 | −.57 | .67 | .74 |
| Block design | −.50 | .45 | −.54 | .70 | .72 |
| Picture arrangement | −.36 | .45 | −.46 | .54 | .68 |
| Object assembly | −.32 | .45 | −.44 | .55 | .65 |
| Peformance total | −.53 | .53 | −.60 | .69 | .93 |
| WAIS total | −.72 | .72 | −.83 | 1.00 | 1.00 |

*Note:* From *A Model for Intelligence* (p. 205) by H. J. Eysenck, 1982, New York: Springer. Copyright 1982 by H. J. Eysenck. Reprinted by permission.

even more important is a calculation reported by Eysenck and Barrett (1985). What is claimed in the Hendrickson theory is that the combined (variance minus string) measure of AEP is a physiological *cause* of differences in IQ. A factor analysis was carried out, using the 11 WAIS scales and the composite AEP score; only one general factor was extracted to represent, in a direct form, the *g* factor common to all the tests. On this factor, the AEP measure has a loading of .77. We argued that if the general factor obtained from the intercorrelations between all the subtests of the Wechsler is our best index of intelligence, and if the AEP composite measure represents a good measure of intelligence, so defined, then we would expect the factor loadings on the 11 WAIS subtests and the correlations of the subtests with the AEP composite measure to be proportional. Using measures uncorrected and corrected for attenuation, we found that as far as the correlation between factor loadings and composite measure are concerned, the correction makes little difference; rho is .95 for the uncorrected values and .93 for the corrected values. Proportionality, therefore, is almost perfect and strongly supports the view that the AEP is a true measure of intelligence.

The Hendrickson paradigm, which has been replicated successfully several times, is not the only one in the field. Another is the Schafer paradigm (Schafer, 1982). On the basis of well-established facts, he argued that there is a modulation of AEPs, manifested as a tendency for unexpected or "attended" stimuli to produce AEPs of larger overall amplitude, compared with those generated using stimuli, the nature and timing of which is known by the individual. Schafer has extended the scope of this empirical phenomenon, hypothesizing that individual differences in the modulation of amplitude (cognitive neuroadaptability) will relate to individual differences in intelligence. The physiological basis of this relationship is hypothesized to be neural energy as defined by the number of neurons firing in response to a stimulus. A functionally efficient brain will use fewer neurons to process a known stimulus, whereas for a new, unexpected stimulus, the brain will commit large numbers of neurons. This theory has received good support, with correlations with IQ ranging into the eighties.

It is interesting to note that Schafer's hypothesis and results can be explained in terms of the Hendricksons' theory. Processing errors would be expected to delay recognition of repetition essential to adaptation; hence, the loss of AEP amplitude with repetition (adaptation) would be less in low IQ than in high IQ subjects. The evidence suggests this is indeed so, and that the two hypotheses make similar predictions.

Also successful has been a theory of Robinson (1982), which is based on a complex theoretical analysis of the role of the diffuse thalamocortical system, believed to act as a mediator of Pavlovian excitation. The theory is too complex to be reviewed here, but it has given results that again show the dependence of IQ measures on cortical events.

We now seem to have two hypotheses furnishing us with causal theories relating to differences in IQ. The first is the speed of information processing theory, the second the integrity of circuitry hypothesis. It may be suggested that the results leading to the former theory may be explained even better by the second theory; in other words, speed of processing is a function of circuitry integrity. The argument may be developed along these lines. It is well known that information is not processed along one channel, but along a large number, and Sokolov (1960) has argued for the existence of a comparator which acts to assess the incoming information and give the signal for the start of a reaction. If the incoming information is incongruent, due to errors of information processing, the comparator will have to wait for more information to come in, thus delaying the process of reaction. Thus, speed of reaction is essentially a function of errorless processing of information. It would be difficult to reverse the argument; errorless processing cannot be explained in terms of speed of processing.

Even more important is a consideration of the facts that cannot be explained in terms of speed of mental processing, particularly the importance of variability in RT experiments. This is analogous to the variability in AEP experiments, and can easily find the same explanation in terms of errors of processing. It is not argued that the theory is necessarily correct, but merely that it seems to explain all the available facts in a reasonable manner, and generates predictions that can be tested; no more can we ask of any theory.

The Hendricksons argued that the locus of the transmission errors would be the synapse, but recent unpublished evidence from our laboratory seems to negate that hypothesis. Barrett, Daum, and Eysenck (1990) studied the speed of transmission in the ulnar nerve, and while not finding any correlation between IQ and speed, we did find a highly significant negative correlation between variability of transmission speed and IQ. As there are of course no synapses involved, it must be some other property of the neuromechanism that is responsible. Clearly the whole theory is in a very early stage of development and will require much detailed experimental work to make it more specific.

The fact that the positive results of Hendrickson (1982) and Blinkhorn and Hendrickson (1982) have been replicated several times (Haier, Robinson, Braden & Williams, 1983; Robinson, Haier, Braden & Krengel, 1984; Caryl & Fraser, 1985; Stough, Nettelbeck, & Cooper, 1990) is impressive, but two points deserve mention. The first is that while positive overall results have been reported, there are marked differences in particular findings. Thus, Blinkhorn and Hendrickson (1982) found significant correlations only for the Matrices test, but not for verbal tests; Hendrickson (1982) found higher correlations for verbal than for nonverbal tests. Stough et al. (1990) found significant correlations only for verbal and nonverbal Wechsler scales, not for the Matrices test. These and other discrepancies may be due to the very variegated choice of tests, populations, stimuli, and methodologies used by different investigators; this variety makes the positiveness appear particularly promising (positive results can be obtained almost regardless of changing conditions) suggesting considerable *robustness* for the paradigm. But contradictory findings, for example, that there is a significant relationship between IQ and the N140-P200 amplitude (Haier et al., 1983; Robinson et al., 1984) or that there is not (Stough et al., 1990) require some explanation. Clearly a more theory-oriented approach is required, with special attention paid to paradoxical results like those mentioned.

A second point to be stressed is the suggestion that different periods of the AEP may be differentially related to IQ, as shown by Stough et al. (1990). As they point out, "that correlations vary from .38 to .86 when measured over different durations of time suggests that there may be different events occurring at different but precise times, with each resulting in different effects on the string length–IQ correlation. If this is the case, then future research will need to break the string lengths into smaller components (especially within the lengths 100–200 msec.) so that underlying processes can be isolated." To which may be added the suggestion that brain stem evoked potentials may be of particular importance theoretically; they have been found in some unreported studies to have quite high correlations with IQ.

One unfortunate feature of all this work is that most of the studies have relied on small and unrepresentative samples (with the honorable exception of the Hendrickson study). Correlational analyses require hundreds of subjects in order to give manageable standard errors. Restricted range samples (e.g., students) are easily available, but corrections are of doubtful value unless samples are very large indeed—with small samples errors multiply. These are all diseases of early childhood, but they do make more difficult a proper understanding and interpretation of the results obtained thus far.

An important aspect of biological intelligence often neglected is the biochemistry of $g$ (Weiss, 1986). This is concerned with glucose and its uptake by the brain; as is well known, glucose is an almost exclusive source of energy as far as the brain is concerned. De Leon et al. (1983), Sinet, Lejenne, and Jerome (1979), Soininen, Jolkkonen, Reinihainen, Halonen, and Riekkinen (1983), and others have shown interesting relations, often quite close, between IQ and glucose uptake. This is an important area deserving attention and development, and which is discussed in Chapter 7 of this book.

## DISCUSSION

It will be clear why we may regard the recent work on the physiology of intelligence as producing a revolution in both theory and measurement of intelligence (Eysenck, 1983). Whether we accept the particular theories discussed in this chapter or not, it is clear that the results are quite incompatible with traditional theories of intelligence, and that something new is required, more in line with Galton's original theories than with Binet's.

One interesting and important consequence that would follow from the theory would be that if we seek to improve IQ, it is unlikely to be accomplished by educational and other similar methods; the poor effects of the Head Start program are, of course, well known. One obvious way of influencing the brain directly is by vitamin and mineral supplementation, and Benton and Roberts (1988) have recently shown that such supplementation, comparing the therapy group with a control group, resulted in a significant increase in $g_f$, but not in $g_c$, just as would be expected on a biological hypothesis. Similar results are being reported from the United States (Schoenthaler et al., 1986, 1991), suggesting that increases in IQ of between 10 and 20 points can be obtained even in children not obviously undernourished. These are important consequences of a biological theory of intelligence (Eysenck & Eysenck, 1991).

For a proper appreciation of this new model, a detailed consideration of the empirical evidence is of course required, and the other chapters in this book are devoted to such a consideration. The present chapter was intended to present theoretical backgrounds of these recent developments, and present them in a theoretical setting, to emphasize their importance for a better understanding of the concept of intelligence. Just as the concept of the atom has changed drastically over the past 100 years, so the concept of intelligence has been changing, and will no doubt continue to change. Such change does not mean that the concept is scientifically valueless; quite the opposite. It is only if a concept remains stationary that it loses interest; new discoveries will constantly produce changes in our conceptions of the Universe and our place in it, and there are large numbers of new empirical findings that need to be tested and brought together in order to improve our conception of intelligence. No doubt the next few years will continue to provide us with many problems and, we hope, with some solutions as well.

## REFERENCES

Baker, H. D., Ryder, E. A., & Baker, N. N. (1975). *Temperature measurement in engineering*. Stamford, CT: Omega Engineering.

Barrett, P. T., Daum, I., & Eysenck, H. J. (1990). Sensory nerve condition and intelligence: A methodological study. *Journal of Psychophysiology, 4*, 1–13.

Benton, D., & Roberts, G. (1988, January 23). Effect of vitamins and mineral supplementation on intelligence of a sample of schoolchildren. *The Lancet*, pp. 140–143.

Berger, P. L., & Luckman, T. (1966). *The social construction of reality: A treatise on the sociology of knowledge*. New York: Doubleday.

Bernal, J. D. (1969). *Science in history*. London: C. A. Watts.

Blinkhorn, S. F., & Hendrickson, D. E. (1982). Average evoked responses and psychometric intelligence. *Nature, 298*, 596–597.

Buss, A. R. (1975). The emerging field of the sociology of psychological knowledge. *American Psychologist, 30*, 988–1002.

Caryl, P. G., & Fraser, I. C. (1985, September). *The Hendrickson string length and intelligence: A replication*. Paper presented at the Psychophysiology Society Scottish Conference.

Cattell, R. B. (1963). Theory of fluid and crystallized intelligence: A critical experiment. *Journal of Educational Psychology, 54*, 1–22.

Cohen, J. B. (1985). *Revolution in science*. Cambridge, MA: Harvard University Press.

De Leon, M. J., Ferris, S. N., George, A. E., Christman, D. R., Fowler, J. S., Gentes, C., Reisberg, B., Gee, B.,.Emnierich, M., Yonekura, W., Brodis, J., Kricheff, I., & Wolf, A. P. (1983). Positron emission tomography studies of aging and Alzheimer's disease. *American Journal of Neuroradiology*, *4*, 568–571.

Derr, R. L. (1989). Insights on the natural intelligence from ordinary discourse. *Intelligence*, *13*, 113–114.

Ertl, J. (1973). IQ, evoked responses and Fourier analysis. *Nature*, *241*, 209–210.

Ertl, J., & Schafer, E. (1969). Brain response correlates of psychometric intelligence. *Nature*, *223*, 421–422.

Eysenck, H. J. (1967). Intelligence assessment: A theoretical and experimental approach. *British Journal of Educational Psychology*, *37*, 81–98.

Eysenck, H. J. (1976). Ideology run wild. *American Psychologist*, *31*, 311–312.

Eysenck, H. J. (1979). *The structure and measurement of intelligence*. New York: Springer.

Eysenck, H. J. (1982). The sociology of psychological knowledge, the genetic interpretation of the IQ, and Marxist-Leninist ideology. *Bulletin of the British Psychological Society*, *35*, 449–451.

Eysenck, H. J. (Ed.). (1982). *A model for intelligence*. New York: Springer.

Eysenck, H. J. (1983a). Révolution dans la théorie et la mésure de l'intelligence. *La Révue Canadienne de Psycho-Education*, *12*, 3–17.

Eysenck, H. J. (1983b). The roots of creativity: Cognitive ability or personality trait. *Roeper Review*, *5*, 10–12.

Eysenck, H. J. (1986a). Inspection time and intelligence: A historical introduction. *Personality and Individual Differences*, *7*, 603–607.

Eysenck, H. J. (1986b). The theory of intelligence and the psychophysiology of cognition. In R. J. Sternberg (Ed.), *Advances in the psychology of human intelligence* (Vol. 3, pp. 1–34). Hillsdale, NJ: Erlbaum.

Eysenck, H. J. (1987a). Thomson's "bonds" or Speaman's "energy": Sixty years on. *Mankind Quarterly*, *27*, 253–274.

Eysenck, H. J. (1987b). Speed of information processing, reaction time, and the theory of intelligence. In P. A. Vernon, (Ed.), *Speed of information-processing and intelligence* (pp. 21–67). Norwood, NJ: Ablex.

Eysenck, H. J. (1992). Intelligence: The one and the many. In D. K. Detterman (Ed.), *Current topics in human intelligence* (Vol. 2). Norwood, NJ: Ablex.

Eysenck, H. J., & Barrett, P. (1985). Psychophysiology and the measurement of intelligence. In C. R. Reynolds & P. C. Willson (Eds.), *Methodological and statistical advances in the study of individual differences* (pp. 1–49). New York: Plenum Press.

Eysenck, H. J., & Eysenck, M. W. (1985). *Personality and individual differences: A natural science approach*. New York: Plenum Press.

Eysenck, H. J., & Eysenck, S. B. G. (Eds.). (1991). Improvement of IQ and behaviorism as a function of dietary supplementation. *Personality and Individual Differences*, *12*, 329–365.

Feather, N. (1959). *Mass, length and time*. Edinburgh: University Press.

Firkowska, A., Ostrowska, A., Sokolowska, M., Stein, Z., Susser, M., & Wald, I. (1978). Cognitive development and social policy. *Science*, *200*, 1357–1362.

Firkowska-Mankiewicz, A., & Czarkowski, M. P. (1982). Social status and mental test performance in Warsaw children. *Personality and Individual Differences, 3*, 237–247.

Fitch, W. M., & Margoliash, E. (1967). Construction of phylogenetic trees. *Science, 3760*, 279–284.

Frearson, W., & Eysenck, H. J. (1986). Intelligence, reaction time (RT) and a new "odd-man-out" RT paradigm. *Personality and Individual Differences, 7*, 807–817.

Friedrich, W., & Kabat vel Job, O. (Eds.). (1986). *Zwillingsforschung international.* Berlin: Deutscher Verlag der Wissenschaften.

Galton, F. (1883). *Inquiries into human faculty and its development.* London: Macmillan.

Galton, F. (1892). *Heredity genius: An enquiry into its laws and consequences.* London: Macmillan.

Galton, F. (1985). *Inquiries into human faculty and its development.* London: Macmillan.

Gasser, T., Lucadon-Muller, R., Verleger, R., & Bacher, M. (1983). Correlating EEG and IQ: A new look at an old problem using computerized EEG parameters. *Electroencephalography and Clinical Neurophysiology, 55*, 493–504.

Gasser, T., Mocks, J., & Bacher, P. (1983). Topographic factor analysis of the EEG with applications to development and to mental retardation. *Electroencephalography and Clinical Neurophysiology, 55*, 445–463.

Gasser, T., Mocks, J., Lenard, H. G., Bacher, P., & Verleger, R. (1983). The EEG of mildly retarded children: Developmental, classification, and typographic aspects. *Electroencephalography and Clinical Neurophysiology, 55*, 131–144.

Guilford, J. P. (1967). *The nature of human intelligence.* New York: McGraw-Hill.

Gustafsson, J. E. (1984). A unifying model for the structure of intellectual abilities. *Intelligence, 8*, 179–203.

Guthke, J. (1978). *Ist Intelligenz messbar?* Berlin: Deutscher Verlag der Wissenschaften.

Haier, R. J., Robinson, D. L., Braden, W., & Williams, D. (1983). Electrical potentials of the cerebral cortex and psychometric intelligence. *Personality and Individual Differences, 4*, 591–599.

Hendrickson, A. E. (1982). The biological basis of intelligence—Part 1: Theory. In H. J. Eysenck (Ed.), *A model for intelligence* (pp. 151–196). New York: Springer.

Hendrickson, A. E., & Hendrickson, D. E. (1980). The biological basis for individual differences in intelligence. *Personality and Individual Differences, 1*, 3–33.

Hendrickson, D. E. (1982). The biological basis of intelligence—Part 2: Measurement. In H. J. Eysenck (Ed.), *A model for intelligence* (pp. 197–229). New York: Springer.

Hennig, W. (1957). *Grundzüge einer theorie der phylogenetischen systematik.* Berlin: Deutscher Zentralverlag.

Jäger, A. O. (1967). *Dimensionen der intelligenz.* Gottingen: Hogrefe.

Jäger, A. O., & Hörmann, H. J. (1981). Demonstrationen von "*g*" (der allgemeinen Intelligenz) und zur Bedeutung des Variablenkomtextes bei exploratorischen Faktorenanalysen. *Psychologische Beiträge, 23*, 408–420.

Jäger, A. O., & Tesch-Römer, C. (1988). Replikation des Berliner Intelligenzstruktur Modells (BIS) in dem "List of Reference Tests for Cognitive Factors" nach French, Ekstrom & Price (1963). *Zeitschrift fur Differentielle und Diagnostische Psychologie, 9*, 77–96.

Jensen, A. R. (1982a). Reaction time and psychometric *g*. In H. J. Eysenck (Ed.), *A model for intelligence* (pp. 93–132). New York: Springer.

Jensen, A. R. (1982b). The chronometry of intelligence. In R. J. Sternberg (Ed.), *Advances in research on intelligence* (Vol. 1, pp. 242–267). Hillsdale, Erlbaum.

Kaiser, H. F. (1968). A measure of the average intercorrelation. *Educational and Psychological Measurement, 28,* 245–247.

Kamin, L. J. (1974). *The science and politics of IQ.* London: Wiley.

Keating, D. P. (1984). The emperor's new clothes: The "new look" in intelligence research. In R. J. Sternberg (Ed.), *Advances in the psychology of human intelligence* (Vol. 2, pp. 1–45). Hillsdale, NJ: Erlbaum.

Kisch, B. (1965). *Scales and weights: A historical outline.* New Haven, CT: Yale University Press.

Krutezki, W. A. (1974). Die Entwicklung Leninscher Ideen in der suwjetischen Psychologie der Fähigkeiten. In W. A. Kratezki (Ed.), *Lenins philosophisches Erbe und Ergebnisse der sowjetischen Psychologie.* Berlin: Deutscher Verlag der Wissenschaften.

Lenin, W. I. (1965). Ein liberaler Professor über die Gleichheit. In W. I. Lenin (Ed.), *Werke* (Vol. 20). Berlin: Deutscher Verlag der Wissenschaften.

Lipovechaja, N. G., Kantonistowa, N. S., & Chamaganova, T. G. (1978). The role of heredity and environment in the determination of intellectual function. *Medicinskie Probleing Formirovaniga Livenosti,* pp. 48–59.

Maccacaro, P. A. (1958). La Misura delle informazione contennta nei criteria di classificatione. *Annuals of Microbiology 8,* 232–239.

Mehlhorn, G., & Mehlhorn, H. G. (1981). *Intelligenz.* Berlin: Deutscher Verlag der Wissenschaften.

Mehlhorn, G., & Mehlhorn, H. G. (1985). *Begabung, Schöpfertum, Persönlichkeit.* Berlin: Akademie Verlag.

Pastore, V. (1949). *The nature-nurture controversy.* New York: Columbia University Press.

Ravich-Shaherbo, I. V. (Ed.). (1988). *Role of the environment and heredity in the formation of human individuality.* Moscow: Pedagogica.

Remane, A. (1956). *Die grundlagen des natürlichen systems.* Leipzig: Geest & Portig.

Robinson, D. L. (1982). Properties of the diffuse thalamocortical system, human intelligence and differentiated or integrated modes of learning. *Personality and Individual Differences, 3,* 393–405.

Robinson, D. L., Haier, R. J., Braden, W., & Krengel, M. (1984). Psychometric intelligence and visual evoked potentials: A replication. *Personality and Individual Differences, 5,* 487–489.

Schafer, E. W. P. (1982). Neural adaptability a biological determinant of behavioral intelligence. *International Journal of Neuroscience, 17,* 183–191.

Schoenthaler, S. J., Amos, S. P., Eysenck, H. J., Peritz, E., & Yudkin, J. (1991). Controlled trial of vitamin–mineral supplementation: Effects on intelligence and performance. *Personality and Individual Differences, 12,* 351–362.

Schoenthaler, S., Doraz, W., & Wakefield, J. (1986). The impact of a low food additive and sucrose diet on academic performance in 803 New York City public schools. *International Journal of Biosocial Research, 8,* 401–406.

Sinet, P-M., Lejenne, J., & Jerome, H. (1979). Trisomy 21 (Down's syndrome), glutathione peroxidase, hexose monosphate shunt and IQ. *Life Sciences, 24,* 29–33.

Singer, C. (1959). *A history of biology.* London: Abelard-Schuman.

Sneath, P. H. G. (1962). The construction of taxonimc groups. In *Microbiological classification* (pp. 287–332). New York: Cambridge University Press.

Snow, R. E., Kyllonen, P., & Marshalek, B. (1984). The topography of ability and learning correlations. In R. J. Sternberg (Ed.), *Advances in the psychology of human intelligence* (Vol. 2, pp. 47–104). Hillsdale, NJ: Erlbaum.

Snyderman, M., & Rothman, S. (1987). Survey of expert opinion on intelligence and aptitude-testing. *American Psychologist, 42*, 137–144.

Snyderman, M., & Rothman, S. (1988). *The IQ controversy.* Oxford: Transaction Books.

Soininen, H. S., Jolkkonen, J. T., Reinihainen, K. J., Halonen, T. O., & Riekkinen, P. J. (1983). Reduced cholinesferase activity and somatostatic-like immunoreactivity in the cerebrospinal fluid of patients with dementia of the Alzheimer type. *Journal of Neurological Science, 63*, 167–172.

Sokal, R., & Sneath, P. (1963). *Principles of numerical taxonomy.* London: W. H. Freeman.

Stough, C., Nettlebeck, T., & Cooper, C. (1990). Evoked brain potentials, string length and intelligence. *Personality and Individual Differences, 11*, 401–406.

Sokolov, E. N. (1960). Neuronal models and the orienting reflex. In M. A. Brazier (Ed.), *The central nervous system and behavior.* New York: Macy.

Spearman, C. (1927). *The abilities of man.* London: Macmillan.

Stangel, C. K., Nettelbeck, T., & Cooper, C. J. (in press). Evoked brain potentials, string length and intelligence. *Personality and Individual Differences.*

Stark, W. (1958). *The sociology of knowledge.* London: Routledge & Kegan Paul.

Sternberg, R. J. (1982). *Handbook of human intelligence.* New York: Cambridge University Press.

Sternberg, R. J. (1985). *Beyond IQ.* London: Cambridge University Press.

Sternberg, R. J., & Detterman, D. K. (Ed.). (1986). *What is intelligence?* Norwood, NJ: Ablex.

Sternberg, R. J., & Wagner, R. K. (1986). *Practical intelligence.* Cambridge: Cambridge University Press.

Suppe, F. (Ed.). (1974). *The structure of scientific theories.* Chicago: University of Illinois Press.

Thomson, G. H. (1939). *The factorial analysis of human ability.* London: University of London Press.

Thorndike, R. L. (1987). Stability of factor loadings. *Personality and Individual Differences, 8*, 585–586.

Thurstone, L. L. (1947). *Multiple-factor analysis.* Chicago: Chicago University Press.

Weiss, P. (1982). *Psychogenetik: Humangenetik in psychologie and psychiatrie.* Jena: Fischer.

Weiss, V. (1972). Empirische untersuchung zu einer hypothese über den autosomal-rezessiven erbgang der mathematisch-technischen begabung. *Biologisches Zentralblatt, 91*, 429–435.

Weiss, V. (1986). From memory span and mental speed towards the quantum mechanics of intelligence. *Personality Individual Differences, 5*, 737–749.

Weiss, V., & Mehlhorn, M. G. (1980). Der hauptgenlocus der allgemeinen intelligenz. *Biologisches Zentralblatt, 99*, 297–310.

Williams, W. T., & Lambert, Z. M. (1959). Multivariate methods in plant ecology: Association-analysis in plant communities. *Journal of Ecology, 47*, 83–101.

Wolman, B. B. (1985). *Handbook of intelligence.* London: Wiley.

# Chapter 2

# The Genetic Architecture of Human Intelligence*

*Thomas J. Bouchard, Jr.*

*Department of Psychology*
*University of Minnesota, Minneapolis*

## INTRODUCTION

### The Nature of Human Intelligence

The goal of this chapter is to elucidate the role of genetic and environmental factors on human intelligence. The problem of understanding human intelligence has been approached from several different perspectives (Sternberg, 1985). The analysis that follows is based on the trait (individual difference) approach to

* Preparation of this chapter was supported by grants to the Minnesota Center for Twin and Adoption Research (MICTAR) from The Pioneer Fund and The Seaver Institute. I would like to thank Mathew McGue and Nancy L. Segal for a critical reading of this manuscript and Greg Carey for suggesting the use of Figure 2.2. Correspondence should be sent to Thomas J. Bouchard, Jr., Department of Psychology, Elliott Hall, 75 East River Road, University of Minnesota, Minneapolis, MN 55455.

intelligence. There are four major reasons for this choice. First, the bulk of the evidence regarding genetic and environmental influence on intelligence has been collected from this point of view. This body of data thus represents the equivalent of a broad and deep research program (Eaves, Last, Martin, & Jinks, 1977; Urbach, 1974a, 1974b). Second, the research program has been enormously successful in explaining a wide range of phenomena about human mental abilities. Third, none of the findings from the other approaches contradict or refute this approach. In some instances the other approaches provide alternative perspectives on common questions, and in other cases they provide more detail regarding the nature of underlying mechanisms. For example, the information-processing approach to intelligence (Hunt, 1983; Sternberg, 1983; Vernon, 1987) is sometimes proposed as a replacement for the psychometric approach because it supposedly explains away the problem of intelligence. This is incorrect. Individual differences in information-processing mechanisms are subject to precisely the same kind of study as ordinary mental ability measures (cf. McGue & Bouchard, 1989); they simply represent a different level of analysis within a broad reductionistic framework. Finally, the individual difference approach to psychological traits is highly consistent with evolutionary theory and is amenable to all methods of quantitative analysis, forms of reasoning, and general conceptual analysis that have been discovered by biological scientists attempting to understand the biological world. Put simply, the individual difference approach assumes that human behavioral traits are largely subject to the same determinants as are the traits and behaviors of other biological organisms. The individual difference approach to intelligence takes the theory of evolution seriously.

There is still considerable controversy over specifics, but there is also a widely shared view that mental abilities are best characterized in terms of a hierarchy of abilities that can be approximated by higher-order factor analysis (Carroll, 1988; Gustafsson, 1984; Marshalek, Lohman, & Snow, 1983). The Gustafsson model probably incorporates the consensus more than does any other and is shown in Figure 2.1.

This model is based on 16 tests given to some 1,000 sixth-grade children. A series of a priori models, including oblique primary factors as suggested by Thurstone, and second-order factors of the sort suggested by Cattell and Horn (cf. Horn, 1985) were tested using LISREL. Gustafsson found that two orders were necessary for a satisfactory fit and that a third-order factor was identical with the second-order factor of fluid intelligence (thus the correlation of 1.00 from G to Gf). The two remaining second-order factors dealt with verbal and figural content respectively. These factors were very similar to the Gc—crystalized intelligence—and Gv—general vizualization—factors of Cattell and Horn (cf. Horn, 1985). Factors at the next level represent primary factors of the kind recommended by Thurstone and Guilford, such as Vizualization (Vz), Spatial Orientation (S), Flexibility of Closure (Cf), Speed of Closure (Cs), Cognition of Figural Relations (CFR), Induction (I), Memory Span (Ms), Vo-

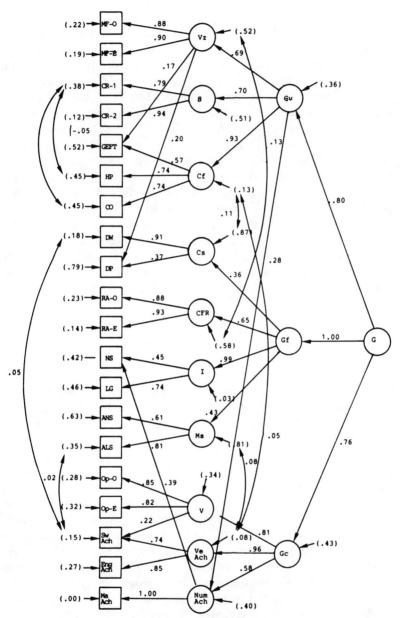

**Figure 2.1.    Three-level model of the structure of cognitive abilities suggested by the work of Gustafsson. (From Gustafsson, 1984; Reprinted with permission of Ablex Publishing Corp.)**

cabulary (V), Verbal Achievement (Ve Ach), Mathematics Achievement (Ma Ach). The numbers on the straight arrows can be read as standardized factor loadings. The bidirectional arrows represent correlations between factors necessary to achieve an acceptable fit, but do not necessarily represent assumptions about causation. Numbers in parentheses represent residual variances.

Ordinary higher-order factor analysis forces levels and it may in fact be the case that factors actually fall along a continuum of referent generality (Marshalek, Lohman, & Snow, 1983). Any realistic model will have complex links between factors, as shown in Figure 2.1. Only a structure of this form would be consistent with biological knowledge about the brain (Gazzaniga, 1989) and knowledge of evolutionary processes. Biological structures are fortuitous adaptations that build upon available resources. New structures do not arise anew in response to novel problems. It should also be recognized that mental ability data can be analyzed in a number of ways and that mathematical criteria alone cannot answer the question "what are the fundamental human abilities." This question may not need to be answered in order to develop a reasonably comprehensive understanding of the genetic and environmental architecture of human abilities. The majority of this chapter deals with findings relevant to the general cognitive factor, or "g."

## Behavior Genetic Methods

In the last 20 years there has been a striking change in the attitude of the scientific community toward behavior genetics, and the comprehensive body of evidence that has accumulated in support of the conclusion that most, if not all, human individual differences are to some degree under genetic influence (Plomin, 1989, 1990; Snyderman & Rothman, 1988). That war has been won with respect to the construct of intelligence (Scarr, 1987) and only a few skirmishes remain with respect to the other domains of individual differences. There has not, however, been sufficient recognition by nonbehavior geneticists that research on environmental influences on behavior is most productively pursued in the context of a genetic analysis. In the domain of developmental psychology, for example, almost every interesting question can be more productively investigated in the context of an adoption or a twin study (Plomin, 1986). Overwhelming evidence now demonstrates that almost all personality traits are more significantly influenced by genetic factors than by any single or group of environmental factors. More interestingly, the critical environmental factors appear to be quite different from those that personality psychologists traditionally emphasized (Loehlin & Nichols, 1976; Tellegen et al., 1988). In addition, the genetic and environmental architecture of personality differs from trait to trait (Eaves, Eysenck, & Martin, 1989). There is also striking evidence that psychological interests are influenced by genetic factors (Nichols, 1978; Grotevant, Scarr, & Weinberg, 1977). Finally, recent evidence supports the conclusion that social attitudes are influenced by genetic factors (Eaves et al., 1989; Martin et al., 1986; Waller, Kojetin, Bouchard, Lykken, & Tellegen, 1990). The lesson is absolutely clear; behavior genetic methods should become the norm in psychological research, not the exception (cf. Lykken, 1982).

Path analysis is a powerful and relatively straightforward tool for illustrating the logic underlying behavior genetic methodology (Loehlin, 1987, 1989). Figure 2.2 shows five different path diagrams. The notation is as follows: Items in circles indicate underlying latent variables, items in boxes indicate measurable phenotypes (scores) for the kinships indicated (i.e., $MZ_1$ is the score, on the trait under consideration, for the first member of a twin pair), G = genotype, E = environment, UE = Unique (unshared) environment, CE = Common (shared) environment, h, c, e = genetic, shared environmental and unshared environmental paths.

Diagram (2a) shows two unrelated individuals reared apart (URA). The phenotype of each individual is influenced both by their genotype and by their environment. That is, the single-headed arrows denote causal influences, with

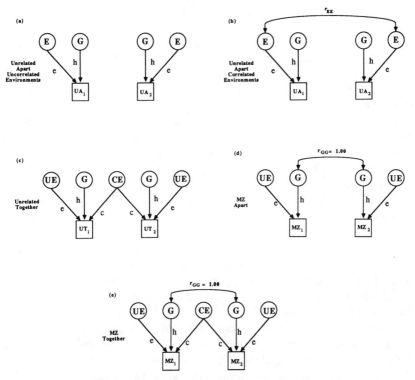

**Figure 2.2.   Path diagrams for unrelated individuals reared in uncorrelated and correlated environments, unrelated individuals reared together and identical twins reared together and apart.**

lower-case letters representing the degree to which the phenotypic standard deviation is a function of the variability in the latent causal entities. On the assumption that genotypes and environments are uncorrelated, the variance for a population of unrelated individuals would be the sum of the environmental deviations from the mean squared and the sum of the genetic deviations from the mean squared. These two individuals are reared apart; consequently there are no arrows connecting any of the causal forces. For a randomly selected group of such individuals the correlation between their phenotypes must therefore be zero.

Diagram (2b) displays a modified version of the situation discussed in diagram (2a). In this instance, the reared-apart individuals have been placed in correlated environments, as shown by the two-headed arrow. Note that the environmental variable for which there is a correlation must be trait-relevant. That is, the environmental variable must be causally linked to the phenotype. The correlation expected between the phenotypes of these unrelated individuals reared apart, but placed in (trait-relevant) correlated environments, is estimated by the equation

$$r_{ua} = r_{EE} * e^2.$$

Diagram (2c) shows the path diagram for unrelated individuals reared together (URT). In this instance the two individuals are linked only by a shared environment. The correlation between the phenotypes of these unrelated individuals estimates the shared environmental variance ($r_{ua} = c^2$). Note the use of the term *shared* rather than family environmental influence. Siblings and/or twins reared in the same family will, on average, share a variety of influences from outside the home (e.g., schools, neighborhoods, etc.) by virtue of having been raised in the same family. These influences are not, however, familial. All familial effects need not be shared.

The two equations that have been presented illustrate some of the rules of path diagrams. A path can be drawn from one phenotype to another through a common cause in only one direction and the terms of the path are multiplied.

Diagram (2d) shows the path diagram for monozygotic twins reared apart (MZA). The correlation between such twins estimates the variance due to heredity $r_{mza} = (h * h)$ or more conventionally $r_{mza} = h^2$. In the case of dizygotic twins (DZ), the correlation between genotypes is .5 (in place of 1.00) and $r_{dza} = .5h^2$. Thus, the correlation between identical twins reared apart directly estimates the heritability of a trait.

Diagram (2e) shows the path diagram for MZ twins reared together (MZT). The correlation for such twins estimates the variance due to both heredity and common environment as $r_{mzt} = (1 * h^2) + (c * c)$ or more conventionally $r_{mzt} = (h^2 + c^2)$. In this case, the correlation is the sum of two paths. In the case of DZ twins, the correlation between genotypes is .5 (in place of 1.00) and $r_{dzt} = (.5h^2 + c^2)$.

If enough kinships are available a model becomes overdetermined, with more observed correlations than free parameters. This allows sufficient degrees of freedom for maximum likelihood or least squares tests of the goodness-of-fit of the observed data to the model.

### Principal Issues in the Causes of Variation in Intelligence

If behavior genetic methods are to become the norm a broad frame of reference for guiding research would be useful. Eaves (1982) has provided such a general framework for behavior genetics. Table 2.1 is an expanded and modified version of the one provided by Eaves (1982) and attempts to reflect the current consensus on these issues. This chapter is to some extent organized around this table. The table is quite rich in content. What was once the primary question involved in the genetics of intelligence "Is the trait influenced by genetic factors?" is no more that a prolegomenon. Indeed, no investigator should carry out a research project solely aimed at determining if a trait is under genetic influence. If the design does not attempt to throw light on a more complex question regarding the genetic and environmental architecture of the trait it probably should not be executed. Well

**Table 2.1.   Major Questions Regarding Sources of Variance in Intelligence (modified from Eaves, 1982).**

A.  Genetic sources of variation
1.  To what extent is the trait influenced by genetic factors?
2.  What kind of gene action is involved?
    a.  Additive?
    b.  Dominant?
    c.  Epistatic?
    d.  How many loci are involved?
3.  Is there sex-limitation or sex-linkage?
B.  Environmental sources of variation
1.  Is the environmental variation social or physical?
2.  Is the environmental variation largely due to chance?
3.  Is the environmental variation due to shared familial factors or is it largely due to idiosyncratic factors?
C.  Joint genetic and environmental influences
1.  What is the role of developmental factors? Does the role of genes change over time?
2.  Are there any genetic x environment interactions?
3.  Are there any gene - environment correlations?
D.  Assortative mating
1.  Is assortative mating due to active phenotypic assortment or is it due to social homogamy?
2.  Are there sex differences in mate preference?
E.  Selection
1.  What sort of selective forces were at work on our primate ancestors during the evolution of the homonid line?

executed designs will allow a test of the question "is it genetic?" as a part of the exploration of more detailed issues.

A strikingly successful example of the implementation of the research program outlined in Table 2.1 in the domain of personality can be found in Eaves et al. (1989).

## SOME PRELIMINARIES

### Meta-analysis of the Evidence

The focus of most of the data presentation in this chapter is on aggregated data— that is, groups of studies of the same type are aggregated in order to enhance empirical cumulativeness (Hedges & Olkin, 1985). The alternative is to carry out a nitpicking evaluation of each study separately. Individual studies must each be evaluated, but an overemphasis on the idiosyncrasies of individual studies is not an informative enterprise (see the pseudoanalysis of placement bias below). The emphasis must be on replications and evaluation of error and bias in a systematic manner, rather than on an idiosyncratic basis (Bouchard, 1983). Psychologists and behavior geneticists have been loath to discard data or trim distributions. This may prove to be a mistake (Hedges, 1987). One of the best examples of a metaanalysis of the IQ and genetics literature is the evaluation of sibling and parent–offspring correlations by Caruso (1983). The data analyzed by Caruso are shown in Figure 2.7 which appears later in this chapter. Both sets of correlations exhibit considerable variability. Following Glass, McGaw, and Smith (1981) and Hunter, Schmidt, and Jackson (1982), Caruso corrected the variance in these correlations for sampling error, test reliability, and range restriction. For the parent-offspring correlations all variation about the mean of .57 could be accounted for by sampling error, test reliability, and range restriction. The sibling correlations yielded a mean value of .51 with a S.D. of .11 when similarly corrected. All variation could *not* be explained by these three factors. Exploration of the effects of sample mean IQ, mean sample age, and racial composition did not provide an explanation of the remaining variability. We are left with some interesting questions. Why should parent–offspring correlations be higher than sibling correlations? Siblings are raised contemporaneously, whereas parents and offspring belong to different cohorts and have often been measured with different tests. What additional factors moderate sibling correlations, but not parent–offspring correlations? Answers to these questions might involve inadequate or biased sampling of populations, developmental effects, and so on.

### Placement and other Biases

Adoption studies are one of the most important sources of evidence of genetic influence on IQ. Placement bias is probably the most widely cited criticism of adoption studies. Prominent examples of such criticisms can be found in Farber (1981), Kamin (1974, Chapter 3); Lewontin, Rose, and Kamin (1984, pp. 106–114) and Taylor (1980). As discussed later, the claim of placement bias is often brought against the evidence provided by studies of twins reared apart. A detailed treatment of the logical structure underlying this criticism is useful.

Critics who cite the possibility of placement bias as an artifact in adoption studies write as if they had disproved the findings being reported, or had explained them away, and that the burden of proof has now shifted to the investigator claiming a genetic effect. Given the available evidence, however, the situation is quite different. If we unpack the assumptions underlying the placement bias argument they prove to be quite demanding and highly unlikely to be met. Consequently, it is not a surprise that, when examined carefully, placement is much less of a problem than has been assumed. Figure 2.3 below shows the effect of selective placement on the MZA correlation for trait-relevant environments with three different levels of effect, under the assumption of zero heritability. It is simply a graphic representation of the path model in Figure 2.2b. The three coefficients that have been plotted reflect three possible levels for the $e$ path or the power of the variable to influence the trait. Three values (.3, .4 and .5) are shown. *The true value of this coefficient must be established in an adoption context where heredity and environment are unconfounded.* The degree of placement is shown along the horizontal axis. The most striking feature of the chart is the modest MZA correlations expected even when there is considerable placement on a trait suspected to have causal influence (at least as evaluated by

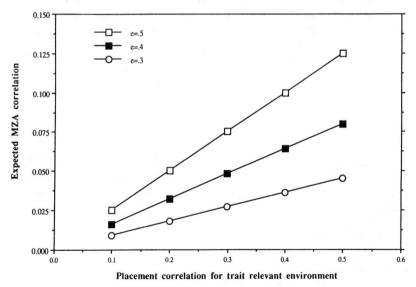

Figure 2.3.    Effect of selective placement on MZA correlations on the assumption of zero heritability.

current standards). Thus, even if e = .5 and the placement is .5 (both high values by current standards) the expected MZA correlation is .125. Bouchard, Lykken, McGue, Segal, and Tellegen (1990) have published placement coefficients for MZA twins on a number of environmental variables for the Minnesota sample of twins reared apart, as well as measures of the trait relevance of these variables and their contribution to the MZA correlations for WAIS IQ. The data are shown in Table 2.2.

There are three measures of parental status (Father's Education, Mother's Education, and Father's SES), Four measures of Physical Facilities of the home (Material Possessions, Scientific/Technical Possessions, Cultural Possessions, and Mechanical Possessions) and two measures of self-reported child rearing. The placement coefficients (corrected for age and sex) are displayed in the first column. The trait relevance of each characteristic is shown in the second column. There are some strong placement effects. However, only two of the environmental factors are trait-relevant. The third column shows the contribution of placement to the MZA correlation. The largest value is .032. A similar analysis of the contribution of placement to MZA and DZA similarity in special mental abilities can be found in McGue and Bouchard (1989). The message here is that both placement and the effect size must be very substantial before the observed correlation between reared-apart relatives is increased beyond a trivial level. Criticisms of the twin and adoption literature advanced by Kamin, Taylor, and others thus require a substantial burden of proof before they can be taken seriously.

**Table 2.2.  Placement Coefficients for Environmental Variables, Correlations Between IQ and the Environmental Variables and Estimates of the Contribution of Placement to Twin Similarity in WAIS IQ**

| Placement Variable | MZA Similarity $(R_{ff})$ | Correlation between IQ and Placement variable $(r_{ft})$ | Contribution of Placement to the MZA Correlation $(R_{ff}*r^2_{ft})$ |
|---|---|---|---|
| **SES Indicators** | | | |
| Father's Education | .134 | .100 | .001 |
| Mother's Education | .412 | −.001 | .000 |
| Father's SES | .267 | .174 | .008 |
| **Physical Facilities** | | | |
| Material Possessions | .402 | .279* | .032 |
| Scientific/Technical | .151 | −.090 | .001 |
| Cultural | −.085 | −.279* | −.007 |
| Mechanical | .303 | .077 | .002 |
| **Relevant Moos Scales** | | | |
| Achievement | .11 | −.103 | .001 |
| Intellectual Orientation | .27 | .106 | .003 |

*$r_{ft}$ significantly different from zero at $p < .01$.
From Bouchard et al. 1990; Reprinted with permission of the American Association for the Advancement of Science.

Consider another related criticism that has repeatedly surfaced regarding the similarity of MZA twins in IQ. It is asserted that ''people treat children as more or less bright and capable according to whether they look bright or not and this treatment affects the child's actual performance (the Pygmalion effect).'' Since MZA twins look so much alike, this effect is purported to explain why they have similar adult IQs. If we unpack the assumptions of this claim, we find that (a) there must be high interrater agreement in judging the brightness of young children from their appearance (otherwise the two sets of adoptive parents would not treat both twins in the same way); (b) adoptive parents will persist in evaluating their adoptive child's brightness on the basis of his or her looks, in spite of growing acquaintance with his/her behavior; (c) identical twins reared apart are sufficiently similar in appearance so that they are treated in a highly similar manner; and (d) differential treatment based on such assessments can move the IQ of individual twins up or down over the entire normal range of IQ variation. If any one step in the chain is weak the overall effect is highly attenuated. Unless all four of these hidden assumptions can be quantitatively substantiated at a rather high magnitude, they carry little force. Thus the critic who proposes such an explanation carries a considerable burden of proof and should cite all the evidence necessary to make the case. Burks and Tolman (1932) long ago showed that physical resemblance in sibling pairs was unrelated to resemblance in IQ.

## The Pseudoanalysis of Kinship Data

An entire industry has evolved up around the reanalysis of kinship data, particularly the large body of published data on identical twins reared apart. Some typical conclusions based on these analyses are given below.

> To the degree that the case for a genetic influence on IQ scores rests on the celebrated studies of separated twins, we can justifiably conclude that there is no reason to reject the hypothesis that IQ is simply not heritable. (Kamin, 1974, p. 67; cf. also Kamin in Eysenck & Kamin, 1981, p. 154; Lewontin, Rose, & Kamin, 1984, pp. 106–110)

> My own evaluation, particularly of the allegedly scientific analyses of the IQ data, is more caustic. Suffice it to say that it seems that there has been a great deal of action with numbers but not much progress—or sometimes not even much common sense. (Farber, 1981, p. 22)

> In sum, given the available methods and data, there once again appears to be no compelling reason to postulate the existence of any genes ''for'' intelligence. (Taylor, 1980, p. 111)

These conclusions are all invalid. Unfortunately many otherwise well trained and well informed scientists with no expertise in behavior genetics have taken them seriously. These criticisms must, therefore, be considered seriously, if only briefly. Bouchard (1982a, 1982b, 1983, 1987) has dealt in detail with what he calls the pseudoanalysis of the MZA twin literature by Farber, Kamin, and Taylor (see also Fulker, 1975; Jackson, 1975; Mackintosh, 1975; Scarr, 1976). The following discussion draws from these sources. Pseudoanalysis is defined by Bouchard (1982a) as follows:

> The data are subgrouped using a variety of criteria that, although plausible on their face, yield the smallest genetic estimates that can be squeezed out. Statistical significance tests are liberally applied and those favorable to the investigator's prior position is emphasized. Lack of statistical significance is overlooked when it is convenient to do so, and multiple measurements of the same construct (constructive replication within a study) are ignored. There is repeated use of significance tests on data chosen post hoc. The sample sizes are often very small, and the problem of sampling error is entirely ignored. (p. 190)

Following up on numerous, casual analyses by Kamin (1974), Taylor (1980) carried out a "systematic" analysis designed to discredit the MZA data. It should be noted that his reanalysis was *not* conducted blindly. That is, classification of twins into groups separated late or early in life; reunited or not reunited in childhood; reared by relatives or nonrelatives; and reared in environments of strong similarity, or weak similarity was done with knowledge of the twins' IQ. These groupings appear to be simple and nearly dichotomous, but they are not; it is quite possible for systematic bias to affect the classification process. In addition, the sample sizes within classes are tiny and the reclassification of one case can have a profound effect on a correlation. In order to avoid controversy over the classification of cases, Bouchard (1983) accepted Taylor's classification of cases and simply asked what would happen to the conclusions if the appropriate correlation (intraclass, as opposed to double entry used by Taylor) and the alternate tests used in the studies examined by Taylor were analyzed (constructive replication, Lykken, 1968).

According to Taylor (and many others):

> The similarity in educational, socioeconomic, and interpersonal environments, referred to here as social environment, is a central reason why monozygotic twins regarded in the professional literature as separately raised reveal similar IQ scores. MZ twin pairs who have had similar social environment (such as similar schooling) have similar IQs, and twin pairs who have relatively different social environments (especially different schooling) have different IQs. (p. 92)

The data are shown in Table 2.3. Taylor's classification yields a weighted average correlation of .85 for twins reared in strongly similar environments and .46 for those reared in minimally similar environments (a difference of almost .40). The analysis, using the more appropriate intraclass correlation, yields

Table 2.3.   Comparison of MZA Double Entry and Intraclass Correlations for Twins Reared in Two Types of Social Environments and Intraclass Correlations for Constructive Replication

| | Environmental Classification | | | | | |
| | Strong Similarity | | Minimal Similarity | | All cases | |
| Study and test | r | N | r | N | r | N |
| --- | --- | --- | --- | --- | --- | --- |
| Computed by Taylor—Double Entry Correlations | | | | | | |
| Shields (raw scores) | .89 | 27 | .45 | 10 | .77 | 37 |
| Newman et al. (S–B) | .91 | 12 | .36 | 7 | .67 | 19 |
| Juel-Nielsen (W–B) | .56[a] | 7 | .63[b] | 5 | .62 | 12 |
| Weighted Average | .85 | 46 | .46 | 22 | .72 | 68 |
| Same Cases as Above—Intraclass Correlation | | | | | | |
| Shields (raw scores) | .89 | 27 | .50 | 10 | .77 | 37 |
| Newman, et al. (S–B) | .92 | 12 | .43 | 7 | .68 | 19 |
| Juel-Nielsen (W–B) | .61 | 7 | .69 | 5 | .64 | 12 |
| Weighted Average | .86 | 46 | .52 | 22 | .72 | 68 |
| Weighted Average NF&H and Juel-Nielsen | .81 | 19 | .54 | 12 | .66 | 31 |
| Constructive Replication, New Tests, Same Cases—Intraclass Correlation | | | | | | |
| Newman et al. (Otis) | .91 | 12 | .50 | 7 | .74 | 19 |
| Juel-Nielsen (Raven) | .27 | 7 | .98 | 5 | .77 | 12 |
| Weighted Average | .67 | 19 | .70 | 12 | .75 | 31 |

[a]Taylor reports .66. The correct double entry value is .56.
[b]Taylor reports .50. The correct double entry value is .63.
(From Bouchard, 1983; Reprinted with permission of Ablex Publishing Corp.)

figures of .86 and .52 (a still large difference of .34). The findings, however, totally fail to replicate when the alternate tests used in the Newman, Freeman, and Holzinger (1937) and Juel-Nielsen (1980) studies are employed in the analysis (Shields' scores are based on two tests and no independent replication was available). The finding even slightly reverses itself. Twins reared in minimally similar environments show a correlation of .70, hardly different from the overall correlation of .72 for the entire sample. Clearly, Taylor's hypothesis is totally refuted. The implausible correlations of .89, .91, and .98 in the table should warn any alert reader that these results are due to capitalizing on large chance variations that are a consequence of very small sample sizes.

According to Taylor, "Reunion prior to testing is clearly a potential source of environmental similarity, to which any similarity in IQ can at least in part, be attributed" (p. 88). It should be made clear that having been reunited in childhood is not the same as having lived together continuously until leaving one's family after being reunited. As Taylor puts it, "After their initial separation from either one or both of their natural parents, they were brought back together, either into a single family under the same roof, or by means of frequent visits to their respective adoptive families'' (p. 87).

Table 2.4 shows the result of Taylor's analysis and the Bouchard analysis. Taylor finds that, on average, the twins who were reunited yield a weighted average correlation of .84 while those not reunited yield a correlation of .53, a difference of .31 in favor of his hypothesis. The use of intraclass correlations yields values of .85 and .57 respectively. If we look only at the Newman, Freeman, and Holzinger (1937) and Juel-Nielsen (1980) data the numbers are much the same (.82 and .56). This finding does not, however, replicate very well. The constructive replication yields values of .82 and .68. The value of .68 for twins not reunited certainly does not differ materially from the value of .72 for all twins combined. Being reunited in childhood could, at best, explain only a small fraction of the similarity.

Taylor hypothesized that twins having been reared by relatives should be more similar than those reared by nonrelatives. Table 2.5 displays the analysis of

**Table 2.4.  Comparison of MZA Double Entry and Intraclass Correlations for Twins Classified by Taylor as Reunited or Not Reunited in Childhood and Intraclass Correlations for Constructive Replication**

| | Reunion Classification | | | | | |
|---|---|---|---|---|---|---|
| | Reunited | | Not Reunited | | All cases | |
| Study and Test | r | N | r | N | r | N |
| Computed by Taylor—Double Entry Correlations | | | | | | |
| Shields (raw scores) | .86[a] | 27 | .55[a] | 10 | .77 | 37 |
| Newman et al. (S–B) | .87 | 11 | .51 | 8 | .67 | 19 |
| Juel-Nielsen (W–B) | .67 | 6 | .51 | 6 | .62 | 12 |
| Weighted Average | .84 | 44 | .53 | 24 | .72 | 68 |
| Same Cases as Above—Intraclass Correlation | | | | | | |
| Shields (raw scores) | .86 | 27 | .59 | 10 | .77 | 37 |
| Newman et al. (S–B) | .88 | 11 | .56 | 8 | .68 | 19 |
| Juel-Nielsen (W–B) | .72 | 6 | .57 | 6 | .64 | 12 |
| Weighted Average | .85 | 44 | .57 | 24 | .72 | 68 |
| Weighted Average NF&H and Juel-Nielsen | .82 | 17 | .56 | 14 | .66 | 31 |
| Constructive Replication, New Tests, Same Cases—Intraclass Correlation | | | | | | |
| Newman et al. (Otis) | .82 | 11 | .64 | 8 | .74 | 19 |
| Juel-Nielsen (Raven) | .82 | 6 | .73 | 6 | .77 | 12 |
| Weighted Average | .82 | 17 | .68 | 14 | .75 | 31 |

[a]Taylor transposed his correlations for Shields raw scores and transformed scores. These are the double entry correlations for the raw scores reported by Taylor in his appendix.
(From Bouchard, 1983; Reprinted with permission of Ablex Publishing Corp.)

**Table 2.5.   Comparison of MZA Double Entry and Intraclass Correlations for Twins Classified by Taylor as Definitely Related or Not Related and Intraclass Correlations for Constructive Replication**

| | Rearing Classification | | | | | |
| | Definitely Related | | Not Related[a] | | All cases | |
| Study and Test | r | N | r | N | r | N |
| --- | --- | --- | --- | --- | --- | --- |
| | Computed by Taylor—Double Entry Correlations | | | | | |
| Shields (raw scores) | .83 | 29 | .45 | 8 | .77 | 37 |
| Newman et al. (S–B) | .66 | 11 | .66[b] | 8 | .67 | 19 |
| Juel-Nielsen (W–B) | .56 | 8 | .59 | 4 | .62 | 12 |
| Weighted Average | .75 | 48 | .56 | 20 | .72 | 68 |
| | Same Cases as Above—Intraclass Correlation | | | | | |
| Shields (raw scores) | .84 | 29 | .50 | 8 | .77 | 37 |
| Newman et al. (S–B) | .69 | 11 | .69 | 8 | .68 | 19 |
| Juel-Nielsen (W–B) | .60 | 8 | .67 | 4 | .64 | 12 |
| Weighted Average | .77 | 48 | .61 | 20 | .72 | 68 |
| Weighted Average NF&H and Juel-Nielsen | .65 | 19 | .68 | 12 | .66 | 31 |
| | Constructive Replication, New Tests, Same Cases—Intraclass Correlation | | | | | |
| Newman et al. (Otis) | .73 | 11 | .75 | 8 | .74 | 19 |
| Juel-Nielsen (Raven) | .57 | 8 | .81 | 4 | .77 | 12 |
| Weighted Average | .66 | 19 | .77 | 12 | .75 | 31 |

[a]Taylor uses the heading "Possibly related" which I believe is misleading.
[b]Taylor reports .76 for Newman, et al. This figure is a typographical error. I have replaced it with the correct value of .66. The weighted average consequently changes from .61 to .56.
(From Bouchard, 1983; Reprinted with permission of Ablex Publishing Corp.)

these data for this moderator variable. The results require no discussion as they parallel the finding for similarity in social environment very closely. The initial analysis supports the hypothesis, but the replication actually reverses the initial finding with twins having been reared by nonrelatives being more similar than those reared by relatives.

Taylor conducted a similar analysis of MZA twins who were separated late (>6 months) vs. those separated early (<6 months). The results suggested that age of separation has no effect on IQ similarity. Interestingly enough, the constructive replication did show an effect. Given that the results were inconsistent it was concluded that there was little real evidence for an effect.

Before leaving these data it is appropriate to question the plausibility of most of what Taylor has done as well as to question the reasonableness of his proposed explanations. Consider the purported correlation of .84 for twins reared apart but reunited in childhood; we are expected to believe that contact between the twins caused the similarities: yet out of 69 correlations reported for siblings reared together during all of their formative years (Bouchard & McGue, 1981, see below), the average correlation is .47, only 1 is larger than .84 and it is an outlier based on a tiny sample. Yet Taylor, like Kamin and others, is willing to believe that twins reared apart and partially reunited can easily become as similar as identical twins reared together all their lives! Furthermore, it is difficult to see why DZ twins are not far more similar than they are and why psychologists have had so much difficulty enhancing IQ over all these years (Spitz, 1986a, 1986b).

Farber (1981) has made similar phenomenally implausible claims based on her analysis of the MZA data. Farber used two methods of estimating the effect of contact between the reared apart twins. When the effect of contact, estimated by these methods, is removed from the MZA correlations, figures of .45 and .48 are obtained for the female MZA twins and figures of .48 and .60 are obtained for the male MZA twins. She therefore claims:

> It appears that environmental factors associated with degree of contact between twins account for approximately 20 to 25 percent of the variance in IQ scores. If G-E correlation were taken into account (our analysis assumes no G-E correlation), as well as other factors such as prematurity, selection procedures, and so forth, the correlation or heritability estimates would be even lower than the approximately 48 percent suggested here. (p. 196)

This conclusion depends, in large part, upon a remarkable sex by separation interaction. For the sexes combined, with separation partialed out, the correlations yielded by the two methods are .67 and .76 (no effect due to separation). Farber does note that "combining subsamples of males and females obscures differences that are present and may give a misleading impression of normality and high heritability" (p. 197). She fails, however, to unpack an important assumption underlying this conclusion. *Her results can only be true if the environment works in opposite directions for males and females.* We do, however, find a recognition of this assumption in Appendix E of her book: "In these tables the tendency for those pairs who experienced the greatest degree of contact to have the least difference in IQ scores, i.e., to be most similar in IQ, is readily observed for females. The opposite trend is noted for males." Is it at all plausible that degree of contact is an environmental variable that changes the IQs of female in one direction and the IQs of males in another direction? There is *no* evidence in the psychological literature to remotely support such a conclusion. It seems far more probable that existing differences in IQ and other differences related to IQ might influence whether males and females remain in contact. The possibility that the findings are due to chance is even more likely. Note that Taylor (1980) also made strong claims for a reunion effect and ignored sex differences. Both approaches cannot be true and neither position makes psychological sense. These analyses clearly highlight the danger of picking out so-called plausible environmental effects and pseudoanalyzing the data. Bouchard's (1983) detailed criticisms of Taylor's work has yet to be refuted or cited by critics of the MZA data (cf. Lewontin, Rose, & Kamin, 1984; Schiff & Lewontin, 1986).

## Recruitment Bias

Recruitment bias, particularly in twin studies, has been a serious concern of investigators in the IQ domain for some time (cf. Lykken, McGue, & Tellegen, 1987). Tambs, Sundet, Magnus, and Berg (1989) have shown that bias in genetic and environmental parameters based on twin studies that depend on recruitment is likely to be very small for questionnaire data on education, socioeconomic status, and other variables highly correlated with IQ, as well as for IQ itself. More recently Neale, Eaves, Kendler, and Hewitt (1989) have shown that under conditions that characterize participant recruitment (i.e., soft selection, where the probability of including a pair varies over the range of the character), biased estimation may be less of a problem than previously thought.

## Reliability

Correlations between relatives should be compared with reasonable reliability and stability estimates, rather than with a correlation of 1.00. The reliability and stability coefficients of even well developed, individually administered intelligence tests are not as high as many people believe. Parker, Hanson, and Hunsley (1988) report an estimated reliability (internal consistency) of .87 (95% confidence interval of .86.–88) for the Wechsler Adult Intelligence Scale, based on 12 studies and 1,759 subjects, and an estimated stability (retest) of .82 (95% confidence interval of .73–.88), based on four studies of 93 subjects. Retherford and Sewall (1988) recently reported a retest correlation of .81 for 336 students for the Henmon-Nelson test (a group IQ test) administered in the freshman year and readministered in the sophomore year. They also reported a split-half reliability of .89 and an alternate form reliability of .89. It would seem that the highest possible correlation in a study of MZ twins with a reasonably sized sample would be about .89. The median correlation for identical twins reared together in the review by Bouchard and McGue (1981) is .86. As shown below, three recent studies of adult identical twins reared together (the only such studies in existence) yield a correlation of .88. The correlations for adult identical twins reared together are unquestionably very close to their theoretical maximum.

## Mistaken Ideas about Genetic Influences on Behavioral Traits

Considerable confusion exists regarding the relative role of heredity and environment with respect to their influence on IQ. This may be explained by a failure to distinguish between distal and proximal dimensions and levels of explanation

(Mayer, 1982, 1988). Rushton (1988) has developed a diagram, shown in Figure 2.4, which is informative in this regard.

Distal forces are shown at the far left. Evolutionary forces encoded in our DNA have clearly shaped the nature of our species. Species-specific characteristics constitute a very large part of our genetic heritage. We are, however, polymorphic at a very large number of loci. These genetic differences underlie a significant part of our diversity as individuals. They also constitute the basis for asserting that individuals carry inherited differences, a phenomenon that can be empirically studied. Choice of terminology at this point leads to considerable controversy. It is sometimes asserted that the terms "inherited" or "genetic predispositions" imply that behavior is in our genes (Lewontin, Rose, & Kamin, 1984). This is a patently incorrect interpretation. Genes are biochemical codes that influence organismic development. *There is no behavior in our genes.* All development occurs in an environmental context and behavioral development occurs to a large extent in social environments. The extent to which these environments impact upon behavioral development is an empirical question that can be approached in a number of ways. The behavior genetic approach attacks questions such as: (a) To what extent does genotypic variation correspond to variations in behavior? (b) Do genotypes interact with environment? (c) What is the form of the interaction? (d) Is gene expression variable over the course of development? (e) What is the nature of the gene action? These questions do not address the problem of the level of a trait in a population, or why the trait even exists in the species. Figure 2.4 also shows that behavior in specific situations is impacted by the situation. That is, an individual comes to a situation with some enduring characteristics that influence how he or she will perceive and experience the situation. These factors will jointly determine behavior at that point in time. Genetic factors are antecedent explanatory factors. They are not in conflict with behavioral explanations based on reinforcement schedules, social learning theories, or cultural processes. The relevant influence of each type of explanation and how it interacts (or does not interact) with other influences is an empirical question in every instance.

## The Generalizability of Estimates of Genetic Influence

The argument that heritability estimates of IQ are specific to populations and cannot be generalized from one population to another has the status of a central dogma. Heritability is a characteristic of a population located in a particular range of trait-relevant environmental circumstances. One can nevertheless ask how generalizable are heritability estimates? Horn, Loehlin, and Willerman (1981), using the data from the Texas adoption study, showed that estimates of heritability and common environment did not differ meaningfully across half-samples generated by splits at the mean on SES and parental IQ. Sundet, Tambs, Magnus, and Berg (1988) have reported an interesting secular trend in the

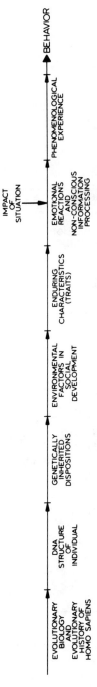

**Figure 2.4.** The distal-proximal dimension and levels of explanation in social behavior. When explanations move from distal to proximal, controversy does not ensue, whereas the converse is not always true. (From Rushton, 1988; Reprinted with permission of Allan R. Liss, Inc.)

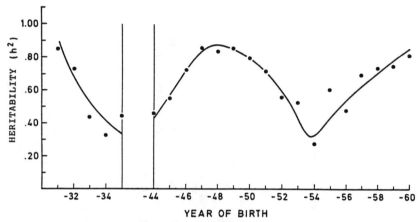

Figure 2.5.   Heritability as a function of year of birth derived from Norwegian twin data. (From Sundet, Tambs, Magnus, & Berg, 1988; Reprinted with permission of Ablex Publishing Corp.)

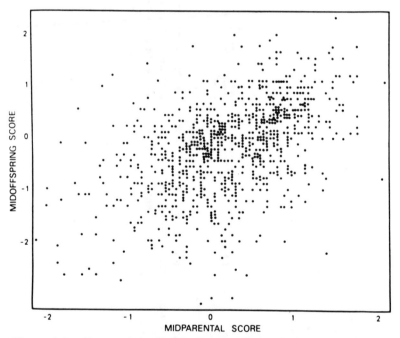

Figure 2.6.   Scatterplot of mid-offspring first principal-component scores, based on Hawaii-Battery, as a function of mid-parental scores. (From Vogler & DeFries, 1983; Reprinted with permission of Plenum Publishing Corp.)

heritability of IQ based on twin data gathered from the Norwegian Armed Forces files. The data are displayed in Figure 2.5.

The authors report that they are at loss to explain the striking dip from about 1950 to 1954. The secular trend in heritability is not necessarily an entirely different question from the well known secular trend in IQ (Flynn, 1984; 1987; Lynn, Hampson, & Mullineux, 1987). Teasdale and Owen (1989), using data from a large representative sample of Danish draftees, showed that this trend may be continuing to the present and is not due to a ceiling effect. They find the increase to be largely concentrated among the lower intelligence levels with no evidence of gain at the higher levels.

In the absence of scalar effects and genotype-environment interactions, the regression of mid-offspring on mid-parent IQ should be linear under the hypothesis of polygenic inheritance. A number of studies have addressed this issue. Horn, Loehlin, and Willerman (1982) and Reed and Rich (1982) have suggested the presence of nonlinearity. Vogler and DeFries (1983), however, using the first principal-component of the Hawaii Battery (which was administered to a very large normal sample) were unable to detect nonlinearity of regression of mid-offspring on mid-parent scores either within the full sample or within a variety of subgroupings. Their data shown in Figure 2.6 can be interpreted to support the conclusion that heritability is constant across the ability continuum. The question of generalizablity of heritability deserves a great deal more attention.

## GENETIC INFLUENCES ON IQ

### Viewing all the Evidence at Once—Model Fitting

As pointed out earlier, model fitting is a powerful method for simultaneously treating a large number of kinships and testing hypotheses about the underlying structure of genetic and environmental influences on behavior. The rigor of model fitting forces the investigator to be very explicit about the assumptions underlying the model being tested.

Loehlin (1989) has recently fit a variety of informative path models to the Bouchard and McGue (1981) summary of the IQ literature shown in Figure 2.7. The most straightforward model that can be formulated for this data set is shown in Table 2.6. This model allows tests for a genetic effect ($h^2$), dominance ($d^2$), common environmental effect for twins ($C_T^2$), common environmental effect for siblings ($C_S^2$), and common environmental effect for parents and offspring ($C_p^2$). Assortative mating is also incorporated into the model. This model failed to fit the data ($\chi_5^2 = 13.75, p < .02$). Loehlin proceeded to ask: Are different results obtained if one allows the direct and indirect estimates of heritability to differ? Direct estimates are those involving reared-apart relatives and consist of the first three equations in Table 2.6. The result is an acceptable fit ($\chi_4^2 = 9.18, p > .05$). The estimates are $h^2$ (direct) $= .41$, $h^2$ (indirect) $= .30$, $d^2 = .17$, $C_T^2 =$

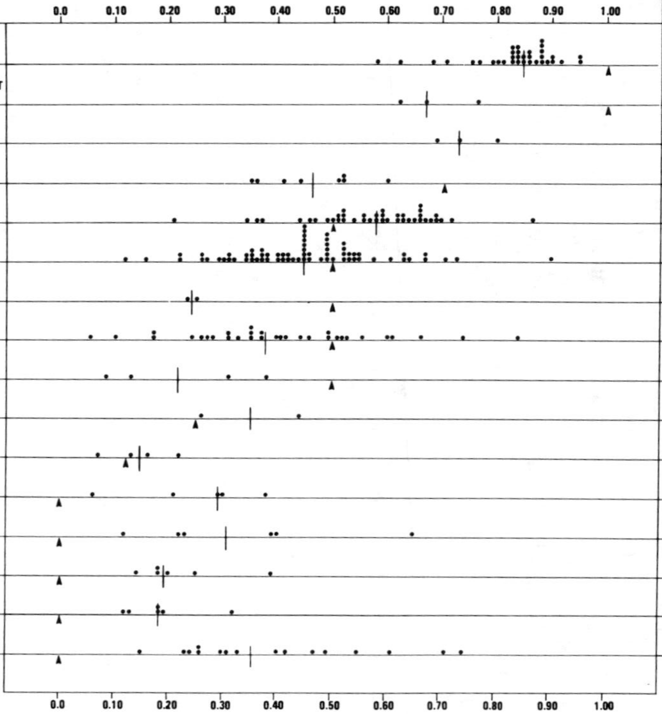


| | NO. OF CORREL-ATIONS | NO. OF PAIRINGS | MEDIAN CORREL-ATION | WEIGHT-ED AVER-AGE | $X^2$ (d.f.) | $X^2$ ÷ d.f. |
|---|---|---|---|---|---|---|
| MONOZYGOTIC TWINS REARED TOGETHER | 34 | 4672 | .85 | .86 | 81.29 (33) | 2.46 |
| MONOZYGOTIC TWINS REARED APART | 3 | 65 | .67 | .72 | 0.92 (2) | 0.46 |
| MIDPARENT–MIDOFFSPRING REARED TOGETHER | 3 | 410 | .73 | .72 | 2.66 (2) | 1.33 |
| MIDPARENT–OFFSPRING REARED TOGETHER | 8 | 992 | .475 | .50 | 8.11 (7) | 1.16 |
| DIZYGOTIC TWINS REARED TOGETHER | 41 | 5546 | .58 | .60 | 94.5 (40) | 2.36 |
| SIBLINGS REARED TOGETHER | 69 | 26,473 | .45 | .47 | 403.6 (64) | 6.31 |
| SIBLINGS REARED APART | 2 | 203 | .24 | .24 | .02 (1) | .02 |
| SINGLE PARENT–OFFSPRING REARED TOGETHER | 32 | 8433 | .385 | .42 | 211.0 (31) | 6.81 |
| SINGLE PARENT–OFFSPRING REARED APART | 4 | 814 | .22 | .22 | 9.61 (3) | 3.20 |
| HALF-SIBLINGS | 2 | 200 | .35 | .31 | 1.55 (1) | 1.55 |
| COUSINS | 4 | 1,176 | .145 | .15 | 1.02 (2) | 0.51 |
| NON-BIOLOGICAL SIBLING PAIRS (ADOPTED/NATURAL PAIRINGS) | 5 | 345 | .29 | .29 | 1.93 (4) | 0.48 |
| NON-BIOLOGICAL SIBLING PAIRS (ADOPTED/ADOPTED PAIRINGS) | 6 | 369 | .31 | .34 | 10.5 (5) | 2.10 |
| ADOPTING MIDPARENT–OFFSPRING | 6 | 758 | .19 | .24 | 6.8 (5) | 1.36 |
| ADOPTING PARENT–OFFSPRING | 6 | 1397 | .18 | .19 | 6.64 (5) | 1.33 |
| ASSORTATIVE MATING | 16 | 3817 | .365 | .33 | 96.1 (15) | 6.41 |

**Figure 2.7.** Familial correlations for IQ. The vertical bar in each distribution indicates the median correlation; the arrow, the correlation predicted by a simple polygenic model. (From Bouchard & McGue, 1981; Reprinted with permission of the American Association for the Advancement of Science)

**Table 2.6.  Equations for Model Fitting to Bouchard
and McGue's (1981) Summary IQ Data**

| Equation | Mean correlation | Number of pairings |
|---|---|---|
| $r_{MZA} = h^2 + d^2$ | .72 | 65 |
| $r_{SA} = .5h^2(1 + h^2m) + .25d^2$ | .24 | 203 |
| $r_{POA} = .5h^2(1 + m)$ | .24 | 720 |
| $r_{MZT} = h^2 + d^2 + c_T^2$ | .86 | 4,672 |
| $r_{DZT} = .5h^2(1 + h^2m) + .25d^2 + c_T^2$ | .60 | 5,333 |
| $r_{ST} = .5h^2(1 + h^2m) + .25d^2 + c_S^2$ | .47 | 26,473 |
| $r_{POT} = .5h^2(1 + m) + c_P^2$ | .42 | 8,433 |
| $r_{ANT} = c_S^2$ | .29 | 345 |
| $r_{AAT} = c_S^2$ | .34 | 369 |
| $r_{PAT} = c_P^2$ | .19 | 1,491 |

Note: MZ = monozygotic twins; A = reared apart; T = reared together; DZ = dizygotic twins; S = biological siblings; PO = parent and biological offspring; AN = siblings, one adopted and one biological; AA = siblings, both adopted; PA = parent and adopted child; $h^2$ = heritability; $d^2$ = genetic dominance; $c^2$ = shared environment; T = twins; P = parent and child. Data from Bouchard & McGue (1981), with corrections (Bouchard, personal communication, June 14, 1988).

(From Loehlin, 1989; Reprinted with permission of the American Psychological Association.)

.39, $C_S^2 = .27$ and $C_P^2 = .22$. A test of the hypothesis that $h = d = 0$ (no genetic effect) results in a very poor fit, as does a test of the hypothesis $C_T = C_S = C_P = 0$ (no common environment). A test of the hypothesis that MZ and DZ twins have different common environments fails to yield a better fit than the model with direct and indirect $h^2$'s. On the other hand, the hypothesis that the common environment is the same for sibs as for twins can be rejected. Loehlin speculates that the reasons direct and indirect estimates of $h^2$ differ may be because some features of family interaction "may serve to attenuate the effects of genes in creating resemblance among family members." One process of this type called "coercion towards the biosocial norm" has been suggested by Cattell (1982, p. 323). A culture might, for example, invest more resources in enhancing the abilities of less able individuals than in enhancing the abilities of more able individuals. This concept applies equally well within families. The less able child might absorb a greater proportion of the families' resources than the more able child. This is an excellent example of a behavior-genetic analysis pinpointing the importance of specific types of environmental studies. Chipuer, Rovine, and Plomin (1990) have analyzed the same data set in a somewhat different manner.

## Evaluating Direct Estimates of Heritability

For many people the most persuasive evidence that intelligence is influenced by genetic factors comes from data on identical twins reared apart. Three major studies in the literature have already been discussed from the point of view of bias, and the model underlying their use has been presented in Figure 2.2. It should be clear from the previous discussion that identical twins reared apart pose a natural experiment and like all such experiments are subject to contamination and/or artifacts. The twins are not literally separated at birth, randomly assigned to homes, and evaluated as adults prior to any social contact. Such procedures would be necessary if a real experiment were being conducted, but such an experiment would be unethical. In addition, the twins share a prenatal experience. The critical question is: To what extent do plausible mitigating factors contaminate the evidence provided by such twins? The analyses previously discussed suggest that the evidence in favor of a sizable genetic influence has not been refuted. The results of the three studies of identical twins reared apart are shown in Figure 2.7. The weighted average IQ correlation of .72 is a direct estimate of the broad heritability and thus includes all effects due to additive genes, dominance and epistasis.

The entire world literature on the IQ correlations between MZA twins including recent data from the Minnesota Study of Twins Reared Apart (MICTAR) is shown in Table 2.7 taken from Bouchard et al. (1990). The MICTAR study includes three different estimates of IQ and clearly replicates the previous studies. As previously shown placement cannot explain the similarity of the

**Table 2.7.   Sample Sizes and Intraclass Correlations for All IQ Measures and Weighted Averages for Four Studies of MZA Twins**

| Study and Test Used (Primary/Secondary/ Tertiary) | N for each Test | Primary Test | Secondary Test | Tertiary Test | Mean Multip Test |
|---|---|---|---|---|---|
| Newman et al. (1937) (Stanford-Binet/Otis) | 19/19 | .68 ± .12 | .74 ± .10 | — | .71 |
| Juel-Nielsen (1980) (Wechsler-Bellevue/ Raven) | 12/12 | .64 ± .17 | .73 ± .13 | — | .69 |
| Shields (1962) (Mill-Hill/Dominoes) | 38/37 | .74 ± .07 | .76 ± .07 | — | .75 |
| Bouchard et al. (1990) (WAIS/Raven-Mill-Hill/ First Principal Component) | 48/42/43 | .69 ± .07 | .78 ± .07 | .78 ± .07 | .75 |

Note: The MZA correlation of .77, reported by the late Sir Cyril Burt and questioned for authenticity following his death (4), falls within the range of findings reviewed here.

(From Bouchard et al. 1990; Reprinted with permission of the American Association for the Advancement of Science.)

MZA twins in this study. In addition the authors demonstrate that neither pre- nor postreunion contact contribute to similarity in IQ.

At the time of the Bouchard and McGue (1981) review no studies of dizygotic twins reared apart had been reported. Since that time one such study has appeared (Pedersen, McClearn, Plomin, & Friberg, 1985). The authors report a correlation of .52, based on 29 pairs of twins, for the first principal component of a variety of special mental abilities, with degree of separation partialled out. Assessments of the effects of age of separation and degree of separation failed to explain the correlation. Indeed, when significant effects due to these factors were found they consistently operated in a counterintuitive direction.

The Bouchard and McGue (1981) paper included only two very early studies of full siblings reared apart. From a genetic point of view, these individuals are equivalent to dizygotic twins reared apart. The participants in these studies were quite young: 12.7 years old in the Freeman, Holzinger, & Mitchell (1928) study and 11.8 years old in Hildreth (1925). The weighted average correlation for the 203 pairs (two studies) was .24. These data had a strong impact on the results of Loehlin's analysis discussed above. A recent adoption study using subjects from the Danish adoption register (Teasdale & Owen, 1984) reports data on reared-apart full siblings and half-siblings, as well as unrelated individuals reared together and full sibs reared together. These individuals had been adopted at an early age (median age of transfer to adoptive home = 5 months) and were tested between 18 and 26 years of age on the same adult intelligence test used for draft board evaluation. The correlations were .52 ($N = 73$) for full siblings reared together, .47 ($N = 28$) for full siblings reared apart, .22 ($N = 64$) for half-siblings reared apart, and .02 ($N = 24$) for unrelated individuals reared together. The data were fit with a variety of biometric models. A simple additive model fit well and neither specific nor shared environmental factors were significant. A model that allowed estimation of the effects of dominance and assortative mating did not yield significant effects with these modest sample sizes.

The correlation of .02 for unrelated adult individuals reared together is quite striking as it is a direct estimate of the effect of shared environment on IQ. The only other IQ correlation for unrelated adults reared together is $-.03$ (Scarr & Weinberg, 1978).

Plomin and Loehlin (1989) suggest that age is unlikely to cause the higher heritabilities derived from direct estimates. They did not, however, properly test this hypothesis. Consider the available twin data. Figure 2.8 shows MZ and DZ correlations and Falconer heritabilities for five age periods. The MZ correlation appears to peak at about 16–20 years, but there are very little data on adults (three studies). Restricting attention to adult data (the average age of participants is 18 years or older), the pattern of findings for unrelated individuals, siblings, and DZ twins and MZ twins, reared apart and together, is striking. The results are shown in Figure 2.9.

The sibling and DZ twin correlations are probably somewhat inflated, relative to the MZ correlations, due to assortative mating variance. It can therefore be

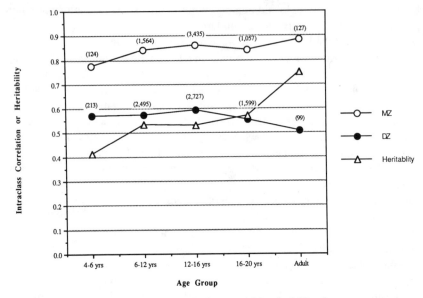

**Figure 2.8.    MZ and DZ correlations and heritability by age groups.**

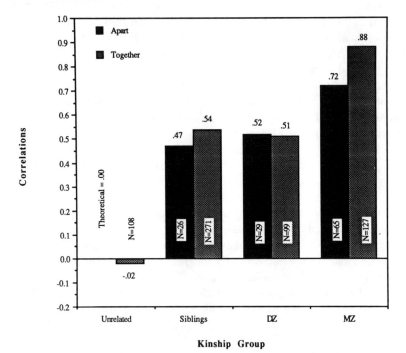

**Figure 2.9.    Correlations for adult samples and four kinship groups
reared apart and together.**

argued that when artifacts due to differential developmental factors and transient common environmental factors are controlled, by dealing with mature individuals living on their own, the results of the two kinds of studies reasonably agree. Most importantly, however, this analysis underlines the paucity of data on adult samples. The study of genetic and environmental factors influencing IQ has been almost exclusively focused on children.

## What Kind of Gene Action?

The classical Falconer (1960) twin method of estimating heritability assumes that genetic variance is additive. More powerful methods, however, applied to large samples detect additional sources of variation. As indicated below, how much variance is ascribable to additive and other sources reflects the model chosen. Choice of model is at least partially dictated by the available data set (Eaves, Last, Young, & Martin, 1978; Rice, Cloninger, & Reich, 1980a). Additive variance is the variance upon which selection operates. The amount of additive variance is consequently sometimes thought to say something about the evolutionary history of a trait (Henderson, 1986; Thiessen, 1972). The amount of additive variance available for a trait can sometimes be surprising. The following description of a selection experiment by Crow (1988) gives a flavor of what can be found experimentally. The chart accompanying the description is even more striking, but is not reproduced here.

> This experiment was started in the 19th century, prior to the rediscovery of Mendel's laws. After nearly 90 generations the oil content in the line selected for increased amount is almost five times (and 20 standard deviations) above the starting value. There is not a hint that genetic variability is running out, despite the fact that the original selected group consisted of only 12 ears. Whether mutation during the process has played a significant role is an unanswered question. (p. 1149)

Grayson (1989) has made a forceful quantitative argument which invokes emergenic processes (Lykken, 1982; Li, 1987), that ordinary twin studies resting on the untestable assumption that most of the genetic variance is additive (within such a limited design), overemphasize the role of genetic factors and underemphasize the influence of shared environmental factors. Hewitt (1989) has properly pointed out that twin studies, in and of themselves, cannot provide conclusive evidence regarding the role of any specific genetic processes. Twin data must be analyzed in association with other designs that more directly assess such possible underlying mechanisms (cf. Eaves, 1988).

Given the extremely large sample sizes, Loehlin's (1989) analysis implicates dominance as a source of variance in the IQ distribution. The Chipuer, Rovine, and Plomin (1990) analysis of the same data also suggest nonadditive variance. We should note, however, that these models are not the only ones that can be fit to these data. Individual studies have virtually no chance of estimating dominance (Martin, Eaves, Kearsey, & Davies 1978; Heath, Kendler, Eaves, & Markell, 1985). A more direct way to determine if dominance is a source of variance in a trait is to analyze the effects of inbreeding (Jinks & Fulker, 1970). If genetically related individuals mate and produce children those children are said to be inbred. A coefficient of inbreeding can be calculated to express the degree of inbreeding. The closer the degree of relatedness of the mating individuals the higher the coefficient of inbreeding used to characterize their children. If a metric trait is characterized by directional dominance, inbreeding will produce an increase in the variance and a decrease in the mean (Falconer, 1981). In order to adequately demonstrate inbreeding depression in human populations, it is necessary to have a control or outbred group with which to compare the inbred group. Selection of an appropriate control group is crucial to the outcome of the study. Even in what appeared to be a highly homogeneous community (the island of Hirado in Japan) Schull and Neel (1972) showed correlations between socioeconomic factors and inbreeding effects in their data, that is, the higher the inbreeding, the lower the SES. Unless such factors are controlled by matching or by regression analysis, inbreeding effects on IQ may be overstated. Several small studies using relatively subjective procedures have demonstrated inbreeding depression, but they will not be reviewed here (Book, 1957; Ichiba, reported by Schull & Neel, 1965, p. 275; Slatis & Hoene, 1961). Cohen, Block, Flum, Kadar, and Goldschmidt (1963) reported a modest study of immigrant Jews from Kurdistan that included 13 percent first-cousin marriages. Thirty-eight cousin children were compared on the Wechsler verbal scales with 47 control children from families matched for parental age, age differential, occupation, and standard of living. The authors suggest that it is possible that cousin families adhered more strictly to traditional patterns of life and this interfered with their children's school adjustment. This is an example of a possible bias that may creep into an inbreeding study. The mean IQs of the two groups were not, however, significantly different (77.1 ± 1.7 vs. 80.9 ± 1.5), and the inbreeding effect was as predicted and the same for all seven subtests. The fact that all subtests were influenced reflects the fact that virtually all metric traits were influenced by inbreeding (see below).

The most comprehensive and careful studies of inbreeding have been carried out by Schull and Neel (1965, 1972) in Japan. As leaders of the genetics group of the Atomic Bomb Casualty Commission, they observed the high incidence of cousin marriages in Japan. In collaboration with a group of Japanese scientists (geneticists, pediatricians, psychologists, dentists, etc.), they conducted two extensive studies. The first study focused on Hiroshima and Nagasaki. The second study focused on the island of Hirado. The IQ data presented here represent only a fraction of that collected.

In the Hiroshima and Nagasaki studies (Schull & Neel, 1965), only the Hiroshima subjects were given an IQ test; the Japanese WISC (Kodama & Shinagawa, 1953) and for that sample the digit span subtest was not administered. Both samples, however, completed the Maze portion of the WISC. School performance data were also gathered for both samples. Subjects were selected at random from a pregnancy register. Subsequent analysis of the data revealed a significant SES difference between the inbred and control groups. Failure to control for SES would have resulted in an overestimate of the inbreeding effect on virtually all measured variables.

Table 2.8 shows the SES corrected WISC data for the Hiroshima study with reference to degree of inbreeding depression on the WISC subtests as a percentage of the outbred mean on the assumption of 10% inbreeding (slightly greater than the first cousin marriage). Notice that as in the Cohen et al. (1963) study, all subtests are depressed. In addition, the magnitude of these effects is in the same range as that for metric traits under an equivalent amount of inbreeding in a variety of animals (cattle, pigs, sheep, poultry, mice, fruit flies; cf. Falconer, 1960, p. 249). Table 2.9 presents additional data gathered from the Hiroshima sample. School performance is more heavily influenced by inbreeding than weight and height.

The Hirado study (Neel et al., 1970) was quite similar to the Hiroshima and Nagasaki studies. In addition to focusing on the effect of consanguinity of parents on children's IQ, the researchers also asked: What is the effect of being born to an inbred parent? The answer to this question was "none." There was no evidence that the inbreeding of a parent diminished the intelligence of the child. These results were consistent with the results of an earlier study that had addressed itself to the same question (Schull, 1962).

**Table 2.8.    The Inbreeding Depression in WISC Performance per 10% Inbreeding as a Percentage of the Outbred Mean. Data for Hiroshima only.**

| Subtest | Predicted outbred mean[a] | | Depression per 10% $F$[b] | Depression as percent outbred mean |
|---------|-------|---------|------|------|
|         | Males | Females |      |      |
| Information | 11.62 | 11.21 | −0.9499 | 8.1–8.5 |
| Comprehension | 12.39 | 12.12 | −0.7424 | 6.0–6.1 |
| Arithmetic | 11.84 | 12.11 | −0.6025 | 5.0–5.1 |
| Similarities | 11.40 | 11.91 | −1.1575 | 9.7–10.2 |
| Vocabulary | 10.35 | 9.86 | −1.1551 | 11.2–11.7 |
| Picture completion | 11.71 | 10.63 | −0.6560 | 5.6–6.2 |
| Picture arrangement | 11.54 | 11.27 | −1.0728 | 9.3–9.5 |
| Block design | 11.24 | 10.99 | −0.5975 | 5.3–5.4 |
| Object assembly | 10.83 | 9.94 | −0.6298 | 5.8–6.3 |
| Coding | 11.54 | 12.27 | −0.5314 | 4.3–4.6 |
| Mazes | 12.30 | 12.09 | −0.6525 | 5.3–5.4 |

[a]Estimated for a child of 120 months of age and a socioeconomic status of 20.
[b]Estimated from the pooled observations.

(From Schull & Neel, 1965; Reprinted with the permission of Harper & Row Publishers.)

**Table 2.9.  Comparison of the Average Control Child with the Average Child of First Cousins. Hiroshima Data Standardized to Age 120 Months with the Confounding Effects of Socioeconomic Status Removed.**

| Characteristic | Sex | Average control child | Average offspring of first cousins | Inbreeding effect | Percent change with inbreeding |
|---|---|---|---|---|---|
| Weight | Male | 265.9 | 263.1 | 2.34 | 0.9 |
|  | Female | 263.5 | 259.9 | 2.34 | 0.9 |
| Height | Male | 1297.2 | 1291.0 | 4.73 | 0.4 |
|  | Female | 1298.1 | 1291.0 | 4.73 | 0.4 |
| Maze test scores | Male | 17.92 | 17.50 | 0.34 | 1.9 |
|  | Female | 16.98 | 16.52 | 0.34 | 2.0 |
| **School Performance** | | | | | |
| Language | Male | 3.09 | 2.95 | 0.10 | 3.2 |
|  | Female | 3.28 | 3.10 | 0.10 | 3.0 |
| Social Studies | Male | 3.17 | 3.04 | 0.09 | 2.8 |
|  | Female | 3.14 | 2.98 | 0.09 | 2.9 |
| Mathematics | Male | 3.21 | 3.04 | 0.13 | 4.0 |
|  | Female | 3.19 | 2.99 | 0.13 | 4.1 |
| Science | Male | 3.29 | 3.11 | 0.13 | 4.0 |
|  | Female | 3.16 | 2.95 | 0.13 | 4.1 |
| Music | Male | 2.94 | 2.78 | 0.12 | 3.6 |
|  | Female | 3.34 | 3.14 | 0.12 | 3.6 |
| Fine Arts | Male | 3.09 | 2.95 | 0.10 | 3.2 |
|  | Female | 3.40 | 3.23 | 0.10 | 2.9 |
| Physical Ed. | Male | 3.28 | 3.13 | 0.13 | 4.0 |
|  | Female | 3.27 | 3.09 | 0.13 | 4.0 |

From Schull & Neel, 1965; Reprinted with the permission of Harper and Row Publishers.

In the Hirado study no statistically significant effects due to inbreeding with respect to height, IQ (as measured by the Tanka-Binet a group-administered IQ test), and school performance were found. Nevertheless, *a depression similar in magnitude to that of the Hiroshima and Nagasaki studies was found for all the above variables*. The authors concluded that, "failure to achieve significance in the present study is interpreted as a result of the smaller number of observations rather than a qualitative difference in the effects."

One aspect of this study is worth emphasizing. The correlation between SES and degree of consanguinity for the rural part of their sample was positive. Failure to introduce a correction in this data would thus have underestimated the consanguinity effect. The positive correlation between SES and consanguinity in

Hirado is not an artifact and reflects a social practice of the sample. Schull and Neel (1972) and Schull, Nagano, Yamamoto, and Komatsu (1970) should be consulted for a thorough discussion of this issue.

Bashi (1977) studied the effects of inbreeding on the intelligence test performance and the achievement test performance of fourth- and sixth-grade Arab children in Israel who were the offspring of first-cousin and double first-cousin marriages. The children were drawn from a national sample of children, from a population in which the rate of consanguineous marriages was 34%. Both groups were compared to a representative sample of children from unrelated parents. Given that consanguineous marriages are encouraged in this population the various groups in the design had very similar levels of SES and the slight bias was in the direction unfavorable to detecting an inbreeding effect. The results, however, supported the conclusion that there was a small and consistent inbreeding effect on all tests for both grades. Double first cousins scored below first cousins who scored below the noninbreed controls. In addition, as expected from genetic theory there was a tendency toward higher variance in the double first cousin group in 13 of the 16 possible comparisons.

Kamin (1980) has criticized most studies of inbreeding. His approach is the same type of pseudoanalysis characteristic of his other writings. For example, the failure to find statistical significance for differences is taken to mean there is no effect, even when findings are consistent across multiple measures, subgroups within the study, and across numerous studies. If an SES variable might explain the results, it is interpreted as an explanation of the results. If SES cannot explain the results, then the measure is not considered an acceptable measure because internal validity evidence is not presented even though the SES measure is fully specified and is composed of all the components ordinarily used in such measures. One is simply left with an ad hoc analysis of studies which, if taken together, clearly support the hypothesis under investigation. As Jackson (1975) pointed out in his review of Kamin's earlier work, if Kamin's approach to data were applied to the evidence in favor of an environmental influence on IQ, it would be very difficult to demonstrate such an effect. Regarding control for SES, Schull and Neel (1965) pointed out that;

> Other measures of socioeconomic standing or "home environment," might remove more or less variation than that removed here. However, it is moot at what point one begins to confuse cause with effect since an important and inseparable element of the "home environment" is the child's as well as the parent's genetic constitution. Thus, a socially deprived home environment may merely testify to a genetic endowment inadequate to cope with the exigencies of life rather than to some environmental effect presumably invariant with genotype. (p. 295)

Evidence in favor of this position has accumulated since that time. To quote Scarr and Weinberg (1978), "Burks (1938) estimated that genetic differences among the occupational classes account for about 2/3 to 3/4 of the average IQ difference among the children born into those classes. Our studies support that conclusion.'' These conclusions flow from the fact that parental environmental characteristics such as education and occupational standing show very modest correlations with adoptive children's IQ, *especially when the children are assessed in late adolescence* (cf. Table 2.2, column 3). It is the case, however, that the subjects of studies of inbreeding have been fairly young and thus still show common family environmental influences. In any event one cannot simply assume that matching or regression procedures undercorrect.

Agrawa, Sinha and Jensen (1984) recently reported an inbreeding study of the Raven Matrices using a sample of Indian school boys whose parents were first cousins ($N = 86$). A control group ($N = 100$) with essentially the same mean and standard deviation for SES was obtained for comparison purposes. The correlation between SES and Raven scores was $-.11$ in the inbred group and .039 in the noninbred group, quite different to what is found in Western societies (Bouchard & Segal, 1985). Both raw scores and scores adjusted by multiple regression for age and SES were compared. In both instances, the inbred group scored lower on the Raven Matrices. The differences was slightly more than half a standard deviation. There was in addition, significantly greater variability among the inbred than noninbred group as predicted by genetic theory.

Afzal (1988) studied the effects of inbreeding on a sample of Muslim children (9–12 years old) using an Urdu translation of the WISC-R. An outbred group of 390 from a suburban area and an outbred group of 358 from a rural area were compared to inbred groups from the same area ($N = 300$ and 266 respectively). The inbred were all children of first-cousin marriages. The inbred group in both the suburban and rural areas scored significantly lower than the comparable outbred group on all subtests as well as Verbal, Performance, and Full Scale IQ. The effects were rather large compared to previous studies. The authors were unable to gather sufficient data on SES to carry out a thorough analysis of its effects. They do assert that the occupational homogeneity of the sample was such that they did not believe SES was an important confounding factor. Nonetheless, this study should be interpreted with caution.

The studies of inbreeding depression have been carried out on a large number of different ethnic groups using a large number of different measures of ability. This makes such studies far more persuasive than they might be otherwise (cf. Daniels, Plomin, McClearn, & Johnson 1982; Hay, 1985, p. 240; Jensen, 1983).

The inbreeding literature supports the contention that IQ is under polygenic control and is characterized by directional dominance. Jensen (1983) has carried out an extensive analysis of the Schull and Neel inbreeding results with the purpose of exploring the correlation between the ''g'' factor and inbreeding depression. Jensen used a variety of factor analytic strategies to avoid possible charges that his results were dependent on a particular strategy. All methods yielded essentially the same results. The correlation for the ''g'' factor, however computed, with inbreeding depression was about .70 (statistically significant).

The correlation for the verbal factor, whether computed as a hierarchical factor (Schmid-Leiman orthognalization) or a rotated Varimax factor, with inbreeding depression was about .58 (statistically significant) and the correlation with the performance factor was about .40 (not statistically significant).

## How Many Loci?

There has been very little research done on the question of the number of loci involved in intelligence. Jinks and Fulker (1970) in their classic presentation of the biometric model fitting approach suggest between 22 and 100 loci, but admit that this is very much an open question. The number of loci is not known for any human polygenic trait.

## Sex-Limitations/Linkage?

Figure 2.10 from Bouchard and McGue (1981) shows the familial correlations for IQ organized by male and female pairings. There is little evidence in that figure to support the conclusion that genetic or environmental factors function differently for males and females. The same was found to be true when same-sex and opposite-sex pairings were compared.

## JOINT GENETIC-ENVIRONMENTAL INFLUENCES ON IQ

### Developmental Process

There is a constant transaction between an organism (genotype) and its environment during development. Genes are biochemical codes. In order to influence behavior genes must be expressed. The expression of the genes that influence each and every trait depends on a wide variety of regulatory mechanisms. Genotypes are very complex and contain the potential to develop into many phenotypes (Ginsburg & Laughlin, 1971). With the exception of identical twins every genotype is unique. Development in individual organisms often has the appearance of smooth continuity but in fact development occurs in spurts and lags. Genes have a temporal dimension such that they turn on and off. The most persuasive evidence available to demonstrate temporal genetic influences on IQ comes from the longitudinal twin data gathered by Ronald Wilson and his colleagues over the course of the Louisville Longitudinal Twin Study (Wilson, 1983). Some of these data are shown in Figure 2.11 below.

Each box in Figure 2.11 contains the developmental profile of a pair of twins (repeated measures of mental ability gathered over time). A flat line would represent the continuous acquisition of mental skills at the rate characteristic of

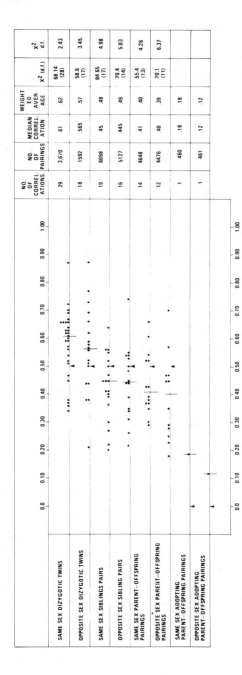

**Figure 2.10.** Familial correlations for IQ organized by opposite-sex and same-sex pairings. (From Bouchard & McGue, 1981; Reprinted with permission of the American Association for the Advancement of Science)

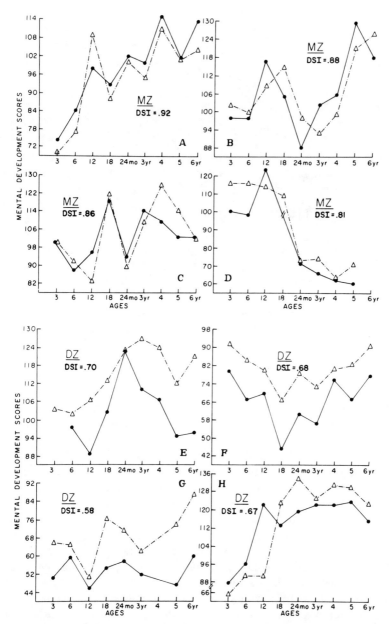

**Figure 2.11.   Trends in mental development during early childhood for four MZ pairs and four DZ pairs. (From Wilson, 1978; Reprinted with permission of the American Association for the Advancement of Science)**

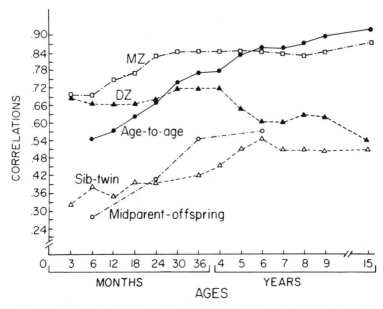

**Figure 2.12.  Mental development correlations for MZ twins, DZ twins, twin-sibling sets, parent-offspring sets; and for each child with itself, age to age. (From Wilson, 1983; Reprinted with permission of the Society for Child Development)**

children of the same age. The four boxes at the top contain data for MZ twins and the four boxes at the bottom contain data for DZ twins. The four pairs of MZ twins show quite different profiles of development, but there is a high degree of concordance for each pair. Pair A shows a pattern of spurts with occasional lags. At no point does the pair fall below previous achievements. Pair D shows a continuous pattern of losing ground relative to peers. The four pairs at the bottom of the table show some concordance as would be expected from individuals who share half their genes in common on average by descent. The developmental synchronies index (DSI) reflects the goodness of fit between the two curves and can be used to quantify the relative similarity of the two groups. Wilson (1978) has presented data of the same sort representing the resemblance between twins and siblings. Another striking demonstration of the expression of genetic similarity in a trait over this is shown in Figure 2.12.

This figure shows twin, sibling, and midparent-offspring correlations as well as age-to-age correlations from three months to 15 years. The patterns are striking. MZ and DZ twins start out quite similar in degree of resemblance. The MZ twin pairs move up towards an eventual correlation in the mid-80s. The DZ twin pairs move down toward a correlation in the mid-50s. This pattern is essentially the same one shown in Figure 2.8 for the assemblage of data gathered from the larger twin literature. The sib-twin correlations start out quite low, but move toward the same target as the DZ twins. The midparent-offspring correlations follow the same path as the sib-twin correlations. Observe that all patterns tend to plateau at about age 6 to 7 years. Change after this point occurs, but is very gradual. This body of evidence strongly suggests that heritability increases with age. Can this hypothesis be confirmed with other data?

The results of the most relevant adoption study, the Colorado Adoption Project (CAP), do not support this conclusion. This project is described in Plomin and DeFries (1985) and Plomin, DeFries, and Fulker (1988). The most recent and thorough analysis of the IQ data is reported in Phillips and Fulker (1989). The CAP data consisted of 247 adoptive families [Biological parents (280 mothers, 58 fathers), Adoptive parents (245 mothers, 239 fathers), Adoptive probands (246), Adopted unrelated siblings (54), biological offspring of adoptive parents (33)] and 246 nonadopted families [Control parents (240 mothers, 241 fathers), Control probands (246), Control siblings (93)]. A longitudinal factor model was fit to these data (ages 1 through 7). Cultural transmission was explicitly modeled as a shared environmental effect and the model incorporated assortative mating and selective placement. The resulting heritabilities for the five ages were .49, .73, .50, .52, and .37. The shared environmental variances were .11, .05, .11, .09, and .23. As the authors point out, these data do not indicate clearly increasing heritability across time. The data do yield a picture of increasing genetic correlations between childhood and adult IQ that are probably responsible for the increasing biological parent-offspring resemblance observed in the data. The authors interpret these findings as "the persistence of time-specific genetic effects" (p. 651). They also suggest that unshared environmental effects do not persist developmentally. A number of features of the twin data are thus confirmed but increasing heritability is not.

### Reaction Range—Genotype × Environment Interaction

As indicated above, the genotype of an organism is specified in its DNA as a biochemical code. The phenotype of an organism is specified by the actual measurement of the trait under consideration at any given point during the life span. If there has been no environmental variation related to the trait under consideration, then all differences between organisms raised in such circumstances are genetic in origin. The mean value of the trait will reflect the ability of that specific environment to foster the trait. A different fixed environment may variously affect trait expression. To the extent that a trait varies in expression across environments, it has a reaction range. When two or more genotypes can be compared, the interaction between environments and genotypes can be examined.

Unfortunately human environments can only be very crudely categorized with respect to features that influence IQ (Bouchard & Segal, 1985; Willerman, 1979). Figure 2.13a shows a simple hypothetical reaction range curve.

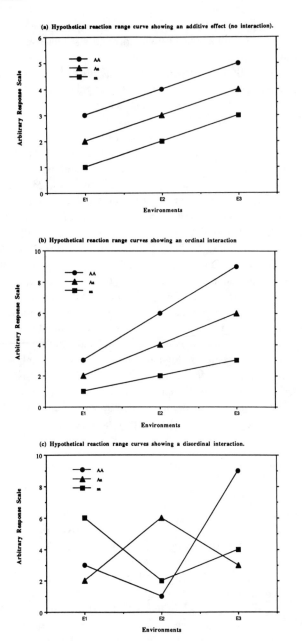

**Figure 2.13. Illustrations of three kinds of genotype x environment interaction.**

There are three hypothetical genotypes, AA, Aa, and aa. The vertical axis shows responses on an arbitrary scale. The horizontal axis indexes the overall quality of three trait-relevant environments. Under adverse conditions none of the genotypes do very well. This reflects the fact that any organism requires an environment of minimum quality to grow and prosper. As the quality of the environment improves all genotypes respond favorably. The pattern is one of parallel lines indicating that there is no interaction between the genotypes and the environment. Environments and genotypes both act in an additive fashion.

Figure 2.13b shows a more complex reaction range curve. This fan-shaped figure indicates that there is an ordinal interaction between genotypes and the environment. The three genotypes respond differentially with some improving much more than others. The genotypes do not, however, change their ranking. Figure 2.13c shows a very complex reaction range curve, implying that different genotypes respond quite differently in different ranges of environmental quality. In this instance, no level of the environment is optimal for all genotypes. This is the type of interaction generally implied when critics of human IQ studies argue that interactions can be quite complex (e.g., Schiff & Lewontin, 1986, p. 172). For human beings, this latter type of interaction appears more plausible if we conceive of the various points on the horizontal axis as representing different types of environments. Imagine that E1 is an environment that emphasized visual learning, E2 is an environment that emphasized verbal learning, and E3 is an environment that emphasized spatial learning. Imagine also that genotype AA is more responsive to spatial learning, genotype Aa is more responsive to verbal learning, and genotype aa was more responsive to visual learning. The real issue at stake is whether or not it is reasonable to believe that the world works this way. The argument is certainly plausible, but is it true? The question is so plausible that educational psychologists have spent millions of research hours exploring this hypothesis under the heading aptitude x treatment interactions (ATIs). The experimental work actually involves phenotype x treatment interactions rather than genotype x treatment interactions, as it is not possible to specify genotypes for abilities. The results of such studies fill numerous volumes (cf. Cronbach & Snow, 1975) and it would not be appropriate to attempt to review that literature here. It is possible nevertheless to report that aptitude x treatment interactions of sufficient magnitude to warrant practical implementation in school settings remain to be demonstrated. Effective interactions in education have been very difficult to demonstrate.

Some critics of the IQ literature (Feldman & Lewontin, 1975) have argued that the possible existence of complex interactions makes the analysis of the main effects of genes and environment futile. The assertion is true, but irrelevant, it explains everything and nothing. "Everything in the world can be explained by factors about which we know nothing" (Urbach, 1974b, p. 253). As Rao, Morton, and Yee (1974, p. 357) have pointed out, "Since armchair examples of significant interactions in the absence of an additive effect are pathological and have never been demonstrated in real populations, we need not be unduly concerned about interaction effects. The investigator with a different view should publish any worthwhile results he may obtain.''

What about simple ordinal interactions? The existence of ordinal interactions has been widely speculated about in the literature. A study by Cooper and Zubeck (1958) has been widely cited in this regard (cf. Plomin et al., 1990). Two strains of rats (dull and bright) were raised in three environments (enriched, normal for laboratory rats, and restricted). Under restricted conditions, both strains made many and about the same number of errors when tested for problem-solving ability on the Hebb-Williams maze. This is sensible because the bright strain may have had an insufficient opportunity to develop its genetic potential. Under normal conditions, the two strains show the difference they were bred to display. Under enriched conditions the bright strain does not improve over normal conditions, but the dull strain does, such that both strains perform equally well. If the implications of this model experiment could be generalized to humans it would have dramatic implications. Enrich the environment and everyone would have equal IQs. The model is, unfortunately, extremely misleading. First, the authors of the article themselves suggest that the results may be artifactual because ''the ceiling of the test may have been too low to differentiate the animals, that the problems may not have been sufficiently difficult to tax the ability of the brighter rats'' (p. 162). The type of data presented by Cooper and Zubeck as well as other animal behavior geneticists illustrating complex interactions is probably not generalizable to humans for a simple genetic reason: The demonstration of complex interactions is heavily dependent on the use of inbred strains. Henderson (1972) and Hyde (1974), using samples of inbred strains in diallele cross studies, have shown that the inclusion of hybrids greatly reduces both environmental treatment effects and genotype x environment interactions. The reason for this is that hybrids are probably buffered from environmental influences (cf. Hyde, 1973). Inbred strains are genetic anomalies, particularly with respect to polygenic traits and are unrepresentative of their species (see Kovach & Wilson, 1988, for a recent discussion of this question in the context of a selection and backcross study). It is important to recognize that natural selection does not apply to traits. What is selected for is reproductive fitness. If a mutation occurs and is favorable, it is favorable because it affects fitness. It does this by being incorporated into a ''complex'' of genes that control fitness. Inbreeding destroys such complexes and creates strains with low levels of fitness. Falconer (1960) pointed out one of the dangers of generalizing from inbred strains to hybrid animals (not to mention hybrid human beings):

> The greater sensitivity of inbred individuals to environmental sources of variation was mentioned earlier in Chapter 8. This phenomenon interferes with the experimental study of changes in variance, and until it is better understood, we cannot put much reliance on the theoretical expectations concerning variance being manifest in the observable phenotypic variance. (p. 265)

Henderson (1990) and Crow (1990) have also commented in an informed manner on the problem of generalizing from animal studies to human studies.

Plomin, DeFries, and Loehlin (1977) have provided a framework for beginning to unravel genotype-environment interaction in human data. They also clearly make the distinction between *interactionism*, the idea (accepted by everyone) that it takes both a genotype and an environment for an individual organism to grow and develop, and genotype and environment *interaction* in the statistical sense described above. They analyzed several unsatisfactory data sets from adoption studies to illustrate the method and suggest that "the use of adoption data to screen for genotype-environment interaction is an unusually promising tool for the more refined analysis of environmental effects in psychology (p. 317)."

Two adoption studies have since been subjected to the appropriate analysis. The first is the Colorado Adoption Project (Plomin et al., 1988). The results were disappointing. The authors concluded "Although few systematic interactions have been found, they are perhaps sufficiently interesting to motivate further research in this difficult area. The results are so meager that they do not suggest hypotheses as to the form or substance of interactions" (p. 249). These conclusions apply to all traits included in the study, not just mental development and IQ.

The second study is a French adoption study (Capron & Duyme, 1989). This study is a full cross-fostering design which crosses IQ and SES. That is, children

**Table 2.10.  IQ of Adopted Children**

|  |  | SES of adoptive parents High A+ | SES of adoptive parents Low A− |  |
|---|---|---|---|---|
| SES of biological parents | High B+ | $n$ = 10 $\bar{x}$, 119.60 $\sigma$, 12.25 Range, 99–136 | $n$ = 8 $\bar{x}$, 107.50 $\sigma$, 11.94 Range, 91–124 | 113.55 |
|  | Low B− | $n$ = 10 $\bar{x}$, 103.60 $\sigma$, 12.71 Range, 91–125 | $n$ = 10 $\bar{x}$, 92.40 $\sigma$, 15.41 Range, 68–116 | 98.00 |
|  |  | 111.60 | 99.95 |  |

An analysis of variance (unweighted means) on full IQ scores indicates significant effects of both biological and adoptive parents SES. Effect of adoptive parents' SES, ($F(1, 34)$ = 7.31; $P$ = 0.010), mean difference 11.6 IQ points in favour of children adopted by high SES parents. Effect of biological parents' SES, ($F(1, 34)$ = 13.02; $P <$ 0.001), mean difference 15.5 IQ points in favour of children born to high SES parents. The interaction for these two factors is not significant ($F(1, 34)$ = 0.011). Nevertheless, a partial analysis of B−/A− and B−/A+ subjects is warranted since a directional hypothesis based on results of a previous study[3] can be formulated. The results show a partial effect for the adoptive parents' SES on the IQ of B− children: $t(18)$ = 1.773; $P <$ 0.05, one-tailed $t$-test.

From Capron & Duyme, 1989; Reprinted with the permission of Macmillan Ltd.

of high SES parents were adopted into both high and low SES homes and children of low SES parents were adopted into both high and low SES homes. Cases were obtained from adoption agency files. The full results are shown in Table 2.10.

It can be seen from the analysis presented in the table that the interaction is not significant. The sample size is, however, very small and the test lacks power. The detection of significant interactions of even large size will require large samples (cf. Wahlsten, 1990, and commentaries). The difference between having been reared in a high SES family, as opposed to a low SES family, is 12 IQ points on the French version of the WISC-R. McGue (1989), in a commentary on the article, notes that adoptees with high SES biological parents score 15 IQ points higher than adoptees with low-SES biological parents. While the original authors avoid a genetic interpretation of these data, McGue points out that such an interpretation for most of the 15 IQ points is fully justified in the context of all that is known about genetics and IQ. The participants in this study average 14 years of age. It will be interesting to follow their intellectual progress once they leave their rearing families.

### Genotype-Environment Correlation

Genotype-environment correlation means that there is differential exposure of genotypes to trait-relevant environments. The most clear-cut example would be children with special talent (e.g., music or math) being exposed earlier and more intensely to environments that enhance their skills. It should be noted that this is actually a phenotype-environment correlation; until genotypes can be characterized, this is the only type of correlation that can be studied. Plomin, DeFries, and Loehlin (1977) distinguish between passive genotype-environment correlation, reactive genotype-environment correlation, and active genotype-environment correlation. The example cited above is of the passive genotype-environment correlation type in which the parent imposes the environment independently of the child. A reactive genotype-environment correlation is one elicited by the individual. A hypothesized explanation of the high IQ correlation for MZA twins which involved people reacting to the twins along a continuum of brightness because of their appearance was previously discussed. The hypothesized treatment is elicited by the individuals and is, therefore, a reactive form of genotype-environment correlation. As was asserted this is a difficult hypothesis to confirm. An active genotype-environment correlation arises when an organism seeks an environment with specific features such that corresponds to his or her genetic predisposition. As pointed out in the discussion of differences between direct and indirect estimates of heritability, there is the possibility of negative genotype-environment correlations. The example given was "coercion to the biosocial norm."

Loehlin and DeFries (1987) have compared some possible methods of estimating passive $r_{GE}$ from adoption data. The path models shown in Figure 2.14

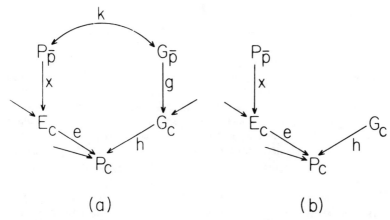

**Figure 2.14. Path diagram of ordinary nonadoptive families (a) and adoptive families (b). $G_{\bar{p}}$, $P_{\bar{p}}$ = average parental genotype and phenotype for a trait, k = correlation between them; $G_c$, $E_c$, $P_c$ = child's genotype, environment,and phenotype; x, e, g, h = causal paths. (From Loehlin & DeFries, 1987; Reprinted with permission of Plenum Publishing Corp.)**

provide a frame of reference. The model for adoptive families assumes no selective placement on the trait in question. Passive $r_{GE}$ is shown in nonadoptive families, via the path *xkg* connecting $E_C$ to $G_C$. There is no similar path in adoptive families.

One way of detecting $r_{GE}$ is to compare the variances of $P_C$ for both families, since $r_{GE}$ should enhance the variance of ordinary families to the extent of $2r_{GE}$. This method yields estimates between .69 and $-.04$ for four studies, centering around .25. Only one study yields negative estimates.

A second method is to estimate $r_{GE}$ from parent-child correlations. This method requires a number of assumptions not discussed here. The method yields estimates between .07 and .23, centering around .15. This latter estimate is considered to be more precise because of the small range of estimates. The authors, however, go on to show that measurement error has a large impact on the estimate of $r_{GE}$ and that correction for measurement error yields a figure of .30.

Plomin, DeFries, and Fulker (1988) have applied both of the above methods to the analysis of the Colorado Adoption Project data. They found a decreasing effect from age 1 to 4 using the variance method (11%, 15.6%, 2.8%, and 1.7%) and a very small nondecreasing effect using the parent-offspring method (2%, 3%, 4%, and 4%).

Studies using other methods have estimated passive $r_{GE}$ in the range of .24 (Jencks et al., 1972; Appendix A), 0.0 to .36 (Rao, Morton, & Yee, 1976) and .14 to .19 (Rice, Cloninger, & Reich, 1980b). It is important to recognize that the $r_{GE}$ cannot exceed the sum of the genetic and environmental variances (Jensen, 1976).

Loehlin and DeFries (1987) point out that a sizable $r_{GE}$ would have interesting implications from the point of view of evolutionary theory:

> Suppose that a mother's intelligence affects the efficiency with which she teaches her children and that intelligence is partially heritable and positively related to relative fitness. There will be a GE correlation present, since the children receiving favorable genes will also experience a more favorable environment. Although natural selection would occur directly for the IQ phenotype, indirect selection of IQ's contribution to the mother's teaching skills would also take place—a form of kin selection, since the genes of the mother are selected in part on the basis of their contribution to the fitness of her offspring. (p. 264)

This topic deserves a great deal more empirical attention. Unfortunately, very large sample sizes will be required to deal with the problem satisfactorily.

### Genotype × Environment Covariance—How Do Genotypes Create Environments?

It bears repetition that there are no known genes for particular behavioral traits. In addition, it is unlikely that any complex behavioral phenotype would be influenced by only one or a few genes. This situation creates difficulty for the behavior genetic theorist. Scientific explanation consists of the specification of the precise mechanism underlying a phenomenon. We know that height is largely under genetic control, but this is a descriptive fact if it is based solely on twin and family studies. We know, in a much more important theoretical sense, that height is under genetic control when we can specify the entire developmental biochemical pathway from genes to structure. The fundamental goal of scientific explanation is the specification of mechanisms—how things happen. With respect to human intelligence we know of almost no such mechanisms.

What might such mechanisms look like? McGue and Bouchard (1989) have suggested that two competing, but not necessarily incompatible, approaches have been proposed to deal with this question. The first is called the innate neurological structure (INS) theory. The second is called the experience producing drive (EPD) theory.

INS theory proposes that genetic influences upon IQ are largely mediated by inherited differences in the structure and function of the brain and central nervous system. Reed (1984), for example, has argued that there may be considerable genetic variability in the genes specifying "transmission proteins." He has shown that, in mice, nerve conduction velocity and residual latency (delay at the neuromuscular junction) are heritable (Reed, 1988a, 1988b). Speed of information processing has also been related to intelligence (McGue, Bouchard, Lykken, & Feuer, 1984; McGue & Bouchard, 1989; Vernon, 1987). Two studies have shown that the covariation between intelligence and speed of cognitive processing has a common underlying biological mechanism (Ho, Baker, & Decker, 1988; Baker, Vernon, & Ho, 1991).

EPD theory, named after Hayes (1962) who coined the term *experience-producing drives*, proposes that individuals do not inherit specific neurological or psychological (intellectual) structures. Instead individuals inherit propensities to engage in different types of activities. The result is that extended practice with particular activities results in the formation of stable psychological structures (abilities, in the case of intellectual structures). EPD theory builds on the observations that a great deal of animal behavior can be best understood in terms of drives that have evolved to fit particular environmental niches. Such drives are powerfully adaptive in rigidly defined environments. They can be manipulated by environmental contingencies (operant schedules), but drift in the direction of species typicality when reinforcement contingencies are relaxed (Breland & Breland, 1961). Examining the entire body of evidence with respect to genetic and environmental influences on IQ with such a frame of reference in mind would appear to be a fruitful enterprise.

A recent, well-elaborated version of EPD theory is the genotype $--\!>$ environment theory of Scarr and McCartney (1983). This theory suggests that genotypes guide experiences (genotypes both push and restrain activities) with environments largely maintaining psychological structures but not creating them anew during development. Upon the discovery that a wide variety of attitudinal data show a significant genetic influence and knowing that the evidence for genetic effects on personality and abilities was very strong Martin et al. (1986) suggested:

> [G]eneticists and social scientists have misconceived the role of cultural inheritance and that individuals acquire little from their social environment that is incompatible with their genotype. In no way does our model minimize the role of learning and social interaction in behavioral development. Rather, it sees humans as exploring organisms whose innate abilities and predispositions help them select what is relevant and adaptive from the range of opportunities and stimuli presented by the environment. The effects of mobility and learning, therefore, augment rather than eradicate the effects of the genotype on behavior. (p. 4368)

## Assortative Mating

As Figure 2.7 shows there is a sizable correlation between mates for IQ. Such a correlation can arise in a several ways. Spouses may select each other on the basis of similarity on the observable characteristics (active phenotypic assortment). On the other hand, spouses may be similar simply because individuals marry individuals with similar backgrounds (both are of the same social class, both are in or are not in college, etc.). This latter process is called social homogamy. Heath and Eaves (1985) argue that this process is likely to involve mostly environmental similarity with respect to IQ (matching is indirect), while active phenotypic assortment may involve greater genetic similarity (matching is more direct). A third possibility is that spouses select each other on the basis of genetic similarity (Rushton & Nicholson, 1988). We will not discuss this possibility here; it is a variant of active phenotypic assortment. To the extent that mating is assortative on a trait under some degree of genetic influence there will be an increase in the genetic variance (Jensen, 1978). Furthermore, if the trait is heritable and is associated with differential fertility gene frequencies will change over time (Crow & Felsenstein, 1968; Rice, Cloninger, & Reich, 1980a). This is an example of how a cultural practice may interact with genetic processes in a manner that has important consequences. There is unquestionably assortative mating variance for IQ, but the accurate estimation of its magnitude remains unresolved (Heath & Eaves, 1985).

A question sometimes asked about spousal correlations is, are they due to initial assortment or to convergence over time? Mascie-Taylor (1989) has presented indirect evidence that most assortative mating is due to initial assortment. Mascie-Taylor and Vandenberg (1988) have also shown that if propinquity variables (school type, family size, locality, social class of parents, years of education, etc.) are partialed out of spouse correlations most, but not all, assortative mating is explained. Nagoshi, Johnson, and Ahern (1987) using a design that involves the spouses of siblings, showed that spouse correlations for verbal ability were mostly due to social homogamy. None of these studies comes close to resolving this issue. This is, however, an active area of research (Buss, 1989; Epstein & Guttman, 1984; Heath, Kendler, Eaves, & Markell, 1985; Heath, Eaves, Nance, & Corey, 1987) and we can expect to see much work in the future.

## CHROMOSOMAL INFLUENCES ON IQ

### The Nonnormality of IQ Distributions

It is widely believed that the distribution of intelligence test scores is largely normal. It is occasionally supposed that a relatively normal distribution of IQ scores is evidence of the biological nature of intelligence. Neither belief is correct. As Micceri (1989) has shown, the normal curve is a highly improbable creature. Indeed a wide variety of statistical tools have been designed to detect multiple sources of etiology on the basis of the nonnormality of distributions. Since the time of Binet the excess of cases at the lower tail of the distribution have been of concern. A proportion of individuals with low IQs are characterized by stigmata.

The explanation of the elevated lower tail of the IQ distribution is encompassed by what has come to be called the two-group theory of mental retardation (Vandenberg, 1971; Zigler, 1967). This theory asserts that there is (a) a group of severely retarded children, with IQs below 50, characterized by central nervous system damage, some of whom show stigmata, who derive from families distributed across the SES spectrum and who have few affected relatives; and (b) a group of mildly retarded children (IQ 50–69) who generally have no pathological signs (no stigmata), tend to be of low SES, and have many affected relatives.

Nichols (1984) demonstrated this dichotomy with cases from the National Institute of Neurological and Communicative Disorder and Stroke Collaborative Perinatal Project (Borman, Nichols, & Kennedy, 1975). Figure 2.15, taken from Nichols (1984), shows the IQ distribution for siblings of severely retarded and mildly retarded individuals. These data are based on white children only. The data on black children are somewhat more complex. As expected from the two-group theory the siblings of the severely retarded distribute themselves in a relatively normal fashion around a mean of 105. In this case none of the siblings is retarded. This indicates that the severely retarded cases are sampled from a normal population and are retarded for quite specific reasons unrelated to the normal distribution of IQ. The siblings of the mildly retarded are distributed over the entire range of IQ with a mean of about 85 (the bimodality is due to the small sample sizes and is unrelated to SES, sex, or siblings' IQ (cf. Murphy, 1964). This indicates that siblings are drawn from the full range of an IQ distribution with a low mean and that the mildly retarded individuals are retarded largely because they come from the lower tail of the distribution of IQs.

### Human Chromosomes

Human cytogenetics began in the mid-1950s when Tjio and Levan (1956) established that the number of human diploid chromosome was 46 instead of the

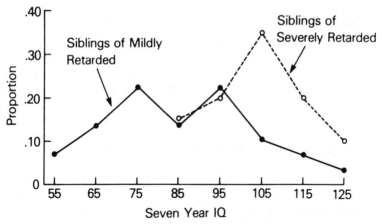

**Figure 2.15.   IQ distribution for siblings of severely retarded (IQ,<50) and mildly retarded (IQ, 50–69) white children. (From Nichols, 1984; Reprinted with permission of Plenum Publishing Corp.)**

widely believed 48. Lejune, Gautier, and Turpin (1959) soon reported that Down's syndrome was due to trisomy-21. In addition there are a number of different types of Down's syndrome (Hay, 1985). Ford, Miller, Polani, Almeida, and de Briggs (1959) and Jacobs and Strong (1959) then described the Turner and Klinfelter syndromes. Since the mid-1950s a large number of chromosomal disorders have been discovered (Gorlin, 1977). In this chapter we can only deal briefly with a few of the major disorders.

### Trisomy-21 or Down's Syndrome

Trisomy-21 or Down's Syndrome is an autosomal aneuploidy. That is, it involves the presence of three autosomal chromosomes, rather than two, and the sex chromosomes are not involved. The incidence of the disorder is about 1 in 700 newborns. The rate increases dramatically with the age of the mother after age 35 years (Penrose & Smith, 1966). Down's syndrome results in mental retardation, but there is considerable variability of outcome (Cowie, 1970; Connolly, 1978). Both males and females show ability decrements with age, with males consistently scoring 5–7 points below females. The specific mechanisms by which trisomy-21 influences intellectual abilities is unknown. It is, however, of interest to note that variability of outcome affects other characteristics besides intellectual abilities. Shapiro (1975) has shown that a wide variety of traits are differentially influenced (e.g., palatal dimensions and dermatoglyphics). In addition, there appears to be greater male vulnerability. Shapiro has proposed a hypothesis of generalized amplified instability of development in Downs' Syndrome cases. He argues:

> No unique physical abnormalities occur in DS. Rather, it is the frequency, intensity and multiplicity of anomalies that are characteristic. The concept of decreased developmental homeostasis resulting in greater displacement from "normal" developmental pathways in DS population suggests that many if not most of the "characteristic" findings involve those traits that are least buffered in the species in general. These traits are less buffered in normals as well, but buffering is generally sufficient in individuals with balanced genomes to prevent the constellation of deviations found in DS.

### Sex Chromosome Aneuploidies

*Turner's Syndrome.* The chromosomal complement of this syndrome in half the cases is 45, XO (only a single X chromosome is present, instead of two XX chromosomes as in a normal female, or one X and one Y chromosome as in a normal male; the 0 indicates the missing chromosome). In the remainder of cases the chromosomal constitution is 45, XO/XX mosaicism (most of these cases are due to the loss of an X chromosome during embryonic development), or various abnormalities of the X chromosome pair (e.g., deletion of part of one of the X chromosomes). The incidence of 45, XO is about 1 in 3,000 births. The vast majority of cases conceived (98%) do not survive (Mittwoch, 1973). The individual with this syndrome is a female with rudimentary gonads, failure to develop secondary sexual characteristics, and webbing of the neck. Expression of the syndrome is highly variable and many individuals are diagnosed only because of infertility.

Turner's Syndrome highlights the complexity of chromosomal disorders in an interesting way. In this instance there are stigmata, but there is no mental retardation. Turner's cases do, however, show a characteristic deficit in spatial ability, and directional sense (Money, 1968; Rovet & Netley, 1980, 1982), resulting in lower Performance IQ scores then Verbal IQ scores. With respect to stigmata, however, Garron (1977) could not find an association between any single somatic malformation or the presence of a number of malformations, and lower general intelligence. Money and Granoff (1965) report similar results.

*Klinefelter's Syndrome.* Males with more than one X chromosome (e.g., XXY, XXXY, XXYY, XXXYY, etc.) are affected with Klinefelter's Syndrome. The incidence of this syndrome is about 1 in 1,000 newborn males. Such individuals, however, represent nearly 1% of males institutionalized for retardation, epilepsy, or mental illness. The degree of retardation increases with the number of excess X chromosomes (Moor, 1967). It has been suggested that all disorders involving an extra sex chromosome are associated with poor speech and language development (Pennington & Smith, 1983). Males with 47, XXY are reported to be less active, less assertive and more susceptible to stress relative to controls (Stewart, Bailey, Netley, Rovet, & Park, 1986).

*Females with extra X Chromosomes (XXX).* This group of individuals includes any female with more than two XX chromosomes. In the normal female, one X chromosome is partially inactivated in each somatic cell. This X-inactivation was hypothesized by Lyon (1961) and is called the Lyon hypothesis. Proper staining of the nucleus of a cell yields a small chromatin body (Barr body) near the inner surface of the membrane for a normal female. Normal males do not have a Barr body; the number of Barr bodies is one less than the number of X chromosomes. This staining technique allows the detection of excess X chromosomes in both males and females. An XXXYY male would, for example, have two Barr bodies. Most females with extra chromosomes have 47, XXX karyotypes (trisomy-X). Karyotypes of up to 49, XXXXX have been found (Sergovich, Uilenberg, & Pozsonyi, 1971). The incidence of trisomy-X is about 1 in 1,000 births, with these individuals being overrepresented in institutionalized populations (Stewart, Netley, & Park, 1982). Individuals affected by this disorder however, are not especially distinctive and expression is very variable. One-fourth are essentially normal with the remainder varying in degree of developmental and congenital problems (Tennes, Puck, Bryant, Frankenberg,

& Robinson, 1975; Gorlin, 1977). Netley (1983) compared Wechsler Intelligence Scale for Children-Revised (WISC-R) scores for 45, XO and 47, XXY and 47 XXX children and showed that the Verbal IQ of the 47, XXY and 47 XXX cases is impaired relative to Performance IQ, whereas in the case of the 45, XO individuals, Performance IQ is impaired relative to Verbal IQ.

Netley (1983), upon reviewing the data on sex chromosome abnormalities, concludes that "the concept of disturbed growth rates may provide a useful focus for future investigations into the origins of developmental disorders in verbal and nonverbal abilities" (p. 192).

*Males with an extra Y chromosome (XYY).* The discovery of the Male 47, XYY syndrome led to a great deal of controversy in the mid-1960s when it was reported that such individuals were prone to violent behavior. These individuals are 10–15 cm taller than average. A careful study by Witkin et al. (1976) using the Danish draft board records, karyotyped the tallest 16% of all males born between 1944 and 1947. They located 12 XYYs and 16 XXYs. While the XYYs had more criminal records and were more likely to be incarcerated than the XXYs, they did not commit more violent crimes. The XYYs also had lower ability scores on the draft board test, relative to the XXYs. The authors concluded: "The elevated crime rate of XYY males is not related to aggression. It may be related to low intelligence" (p. 547).

## Fragile X Syndrome

According to Nussbaum and Ledbetter (1987), "The syndrome of X-linked mental retardation with fragile X is one of the most important and perplexing discoveries in modern genetics. This syndrome is common and affects nearly 1 in 2,000 males" (p. 109). The syndrome is fascinating to geneticists because of its complexity. Its mode of transmission is not fully understood. Nussbaum and Ledbetter (1987) question whether it should be classified as a chromosomal disorder, arguing that it "represents a single gene, or more complex mutation associated with a chromosomal marker" (p. 111). The problem of characterization remains unresolved (Barnes, 1989). Fragile X was discovered in 1969 (Lubs, 1969) in a family that showed what appeared to be an X-linked form of mental retardation. Some of the males in this family had an inducible fragile site on the long arm of the X chromosome. An inducible fragile site is a location on a chromosome than can be induced to break when cultivated in the proper medium. It usually appears as a constriction in the chromosome. Fragile site expression is dependent on the type of medium used for cell culture and detection of the process is a classic example of serendipitous discovery in science (Sutherland, 1977). Other fragile sites exist, but fragile X is, at this point, the only one associated with mental retardation.

Fragile X males are characterized by mild mental retardation. Down's Syndrome alone accounts for more cases of mental retardation. Fragile X males are characterized by specific stigmata (prominent forehead and jaws, large ears, hands, testes, and feet). Expression is highly variable, however, and many cases are of normal intelligence (Hay & Loesch, 1989; Loesch et al., 1987). Expression of the trait varies by tissue type within the individual. A significant portion of heterozygote females show reduced IQ and the disorder can be transmitted through phenotypically normal males. According to Neri et al. (1988) about 2% of the male residents of schools for the mentally retarded have fragile X. This condition, thus, explains a significant fraction of the excess of mentally retarded males observed in the population.

## SUMMARY

Human mental ability can be productively conceived as a hierarchical structure of approximately 10 primary abilities (first-order factors) with three major peaks: General Visualization, Fluid Intelligence, and Crystallized Intelligence (second-order factors). Fluid Intelligence is virtually synonymous with the General Intellectual factor "g" (third-order factor). Correlations between primary abilities subsumed by different second-order factors are unavoidable and probably represent biological and environmental complexities that underlie the developed phenotypic abilities measured by mental ability tests.

In order to draw reliable inferences from the large body of kinship data on the general intellectual factor the data must by subjected to metaanalytic procedures and dealt with as a whole by fitting systematic models. Ad hoc criticism of individual studies (pseudoanalysis) is no longer a viable strategy. This is because most of the criticisms that drive this approach to the analysis of IQ data have been refuted, or can be subjected to systematic analysis using meta-analytic techniques.

The evidence regarding genetic influence on intelligence, when viewed as a whole, overwhelmingly supports the conclusion that genetic factors are the single most important source of variation. Genes are the distal causes of a great deal of variation in IQ. The research front has now moved well beyond this question. The focus of attention is now on questions such as: What kind of gene action is at work? How do genes drive developmental process? What type of genotype x environment interactions are important in the development of intelligence? How and to what extent do genotypes create environments? What is the role of assortative mating? Most of these questions address proximal questions of how nature and nurture work together in the development of a phenotype— nature via nurture as opposed to nature versus nurture. These questions have proven to be very difficult to answer, but they represent a clear challenge to the next generation of behavior geneticists.

## REFERENCES

Afzal, M. (1988). Consequences of consanguinity on cognitive development. *Behavior Genetics, 18*, 583–594.

Agrawa, N., Sinha, S. N., & Jensen, A. R. (1984). Effects of inbreeding on Raven Matrices. *Behavior Genetics, 14*, 579–585.

Baker, L. A., Vernon, P. A., & Ho, H. Z. (1991). The genetic correlation between intelligence and speed of information-processing. *Behavior Genetics, 21*, 351–367.

Barnes, D. M. (1989). "Fragile X" syndrome and its puzzling genetics. *Science, 243*, 171–172.

Bashi, J. (1977). Effects of inbreeding on cognitive performance. *Nature, 266*, 440–442.

Bloom, B. (1964). *Stability and change in human characteristics.* New York: Wiley.

Book, J. A. (1957). Genetical investigation in a north Swedish population: The offspring of first cousin marriages. *Annals of Human Genetics, 21*, 191–221.

Borman, S. H., Nichols, P. L., & Kennedy, W. A. (1975). *Preschool IQ: Prenatal and early developmental correlates.* Hillsdale, NJ: Erlbaum.

Bouchard, T. J., Jr. (1982a). [Review of Identical twins reared apart: A reanalysis]. *Contemporary Psychology, 27*, 190–191.

Bouchard, T. J., Jr. (1982b). [Review of The intelligence controversy]. *American Journal of Psychology, 95*, 346–349.

Bouchard, T. J., Jr. (1983). Do environmental similarities explain the similarity in intelligence of identical twins reared apart? *Intelligence, 7*, 175–184.

Bouchard, T. J., Jr. (1987). The hereditarian research program: triumphs and tribulations. In S. Modgil & C. Modgil (Eds.), *Arthur Jensen: Consensus and controversy* (pp. 55–75). London: Falmer International.

Bouchard, T. J., Jr., Lykken, D. T., McGue, M., Segal, N. L., & Tellegen, A. (1990). Sources of human psychological differences: The Minnesota study of twins reared apart. *Science, 250*, 223–250.

Bouchard, T. J., Jr., & McGue, M. (1981). Familial studies of intelligence: A review. *Science, 212*, 1055–1059.

Bouchard, T. J., Jr., & Segal, N. L. (1985). Environment and IQ. In B. J. Wolman (Ed.), *Handbook of intelligence: Theories, measurements, and applications* (pp. 391–464). New York: Wiley.

Breland, K., & Breland, M. (1961). The misbehavior of organisms. *American Psychologists, 16*, 681–684.

Burks, B. S., & Tolman, R. (1932). Is mental resemblance related to physical resemblance in sibling pairs? *Journal of Genetic Psychology, 40*, 3–15.

Buss, D. M. (1989). Sex differences in human mate preferences: Evolutionary hypotheses tested in 37 cultures. *Behavior and Brain Sciences, 12*, 1–49.

Capron, C., & Duyme, M. (1989). Assessment of effects of socio-economic status on IQ in a full cross-fostering study. *Nature, 340*, 552–554.

Carroll, J. B. (1988). Cognitive abilities, factors and processes. *Intelligence, 12*, 101–109.

Caruso, D. R. (1983). Sample differences in genetics and intelligence data: Sibling and parent-offspring studies. *Behavior Genetics, 13*, 453–458.

Cattell, R. B. (1982). *The inheritance of personality and ability: Research methods and findings*. New York: Academic Press.

Chipuer, H. M., Rovine, M. J., & Plomin, R. (1990). LISREL modeling: Genetic and environmental influences on IQ revisited. *Intelligence, 14,* 11–29.

Cohen, T., Block, N., Flum, Y., Kadar, M., & Goldschmidt, E. (1963). School attainments in an immigrant village. In E. Goldschmidt (Ed.), *The genetics of migrant and Isolate populations*. Baltimore: Williams & Wilkins.

Connolly, J. A. (1978). Intelligence levels in Down's syndrome children. *American Journal of Mental Deficiency, 83,* 193–196.

Cooper, R., & Zubeck, J. (1958). Effects of enriched and restricted early environments on the learning ability of bright and dull rats. *Canadian Journal of Psychology, 12,* 159–164.

Cowie, V. A. (1970). *A study of the early development of mongols*. Oxford: Pergamon.

Cronbach, L. J., & Snow, R. E. (1975). *Aptitudes and instructional methods: A handbook for research on interactions*. New York: Irvington.

Crow, J. F. (1988). [Review of Proceedings of the second international conference on quantitative genetics]. *Science, 242,* 1449–1450.

Crow, J. F. (1990). How important is detecting interaction? *Behavior and Brain Sciences, 13,* 126–127.

Crow, J. F., & Felsenstein, J. (1968). The effects of assortative mating on the genetic composition of a population. *Eugenics Quarterly, 15,* 85–97.

Daniels, D., Plomin, R., McClearn, G., & Johnson, R. C. (1982). ''Fitness' behavior and anthropometric characteristic characters for offspring of first-cousin matings. *Behavior Genetics, 12,* 527–534.

Eaves, L. J. (1982). The utility of twins. In V. E. Anderson, W. A. Hauser, J. K. Penry, & C. F. Sing (Eds.), *Genetic basis of the epilepsies*. New York: Raven Press.

Eaves, L. J. (1988). Dominance alone is not enough. *Behavior Genetics, 18,* 27–33.

Eaves, L. J., Eysenck, H. J., & Martin, N. G. (1989) *Genes, culture and personality: An empirical approach*. Academic Press: New York.

Eaves, L. J., Last, K., Martin, N. G., & Jinks, J. L. (1977). A progressive approach to non-additivity and genotype-environmental covariance in the analysis of human differences. *British Journal of Mathematical and Statistical Psychology, 30,* 1–42.

Eaves, L. J., Last, K. A., Young, P. A., & Martin, N. G. (1978). Model-fitting approaches to the analysis of human behavior. *Heredity, 41,* 249–320.

Epstein, E., & Guttman, R. (1984). Mate selection in man: Evidence, theory and outcome. *Social Biology, 31,* 243–278.

Eysenck, H. J., & Kamin, L. J. (1981). *The intelligence controversy*. New York: Wiley.

Falconer, D. S. (1960). *Introduction to quantitative genetics*. London: Longmans.

Falconer, D. S. (1981). *Introduction to quantitative genetics* (2nd ed.). London: Longmans.

Farber, S. (1981). *Identical twins reared apart: A reanalysis*. New York: Basic Books.

Feldman, M. W., & Lewontin, R. C. (1975). The heritability hang-up. *Science, 190,* 1163–1168.

Flynn, J. R. (1984). The mean IQ of Americans: Massive gains 1932 to 1978. *Psychological Bulletin, 95,* 29–51.

Flynn, J. R. (1987). Massive IQ gains in 14 nations: What IQ test really measure. *Psychological Bulletin, 101*, 171–191.

Ford, C. E., Miller, O. J., Polani, E. E., Almeida, J. C., de., & Briggs, J. H. (1959). A sex-chromosome anomaly in a case of gonadal dysgenesis (Turner's syndrome). *Lancet, 1*, 711–713.

Freeman, F. N., Holzinger, K. J., & Mitchell, B. C. (1928). The influence of environment on the intelligence, school achievement and conduct of foster children. *Yearbook of the National Society for the Study of Education, 27*, 219–316.

Fulker, D. (1975). [Review of The Science and Politics of IQ]. *American Journal of Psychology, 88*, 505–519.

Garron, D. C. (1977). Intelligence among persons with Turner's syndrome. *Behavior Genetics, 7*, 105–127.

Gazzaniga, M. S. (1989). Organization of the human brain. *Science, 245*, 947–952.

Ginsburg, B. E., & Laughlin, W. (1971). Race and intelligence, what do we really know? In R. Cancro (Ed.), *Intelligence: Genetic and environmental influences* (pp. 77–87). New York: Grune & Stratton.

Glass, G. V., McGaw, B., & Smith, M. L. (1981). *Meta-analysis in social research.* Beverly Hills, CA: Sage.

Gorlin, R. J. (1977). Classical chromosomal disorders. In J. J. Yunis (Ed.), *New chromosomal syndromes.* New York: Academic Press.

Grayson, D. A. (1989). Twins reared together: Minimizing shared environmental effects. *Behavior Genetics, 19*, 593–604.

Grotevant, H. D., Scarr, S., & Weinberg, R. A. (1977). Patterns of interest similarity in adoptive and biological families. *Journal of Personality and Social Psychology, 35*, 667–676.

Gustafsson, J. (1984). A unifying model for the structure of intellectual abilities. *Intelligence, 8*, 179–203.

Hay, D. A. (1985). *Essentials of behavior genetics.* London: Blackwell.

Hay, D. A., & Loesch, D. Z. (1989). Fragile-X: The new challenge in intellectual disability. In N. W. Bond & D. A. T. Siddle (Eds.), *Psychobiology: Issues and applications* (pp. 561–572). North-Holland: Elsevier.

Hayes, K. J. (1962). Genes, drives, and intellect. *Psychological Reports, 10*, 299–342.

Heath, A. C., & Eaves, L. J. (1985). Resolving the effects of phenotype and social background on mate selection. *Behavior Genetics, 15*, 15–30.

Heath, A. C., Eaves, L. J., Nance, W. E., & Corey, L. A. (1987). Social inequality and assortative mating: Cause or consequence. *Behavior Genetics, 17*, 9–17.

Heath, A. C., Kendler, K. S., Eaves, L. J., & Markell, D. (1985). The resolution of cultural and biological inheritance: Informativeness of different relationship. *Behavior Genetics, 15*, 439–465.

Hedges, L. V. (1987). How hard is hard science, how soft is soft science? *American Psychologist, 42*, 443–455.

Hedges, L. V., & Olkin, I. (1985). *Statistical methods for meta-analysis.* New York: Academic Press.

Henderson, N. D. (1972). Relative effects of early rearing environment and genotype on discrimination learning in the house mice. *Journal of Comparative and Physiological Psychology, 79*, 243–253.

Henderson, N. D. (1986). Predicting relationships between psychological constructs and genetic characters: An analysis of changing genetic influences on activity in mice. *Behavior Genetics, 16,* 201–220.

Henderson, N. D. (1990). Why do gene-environment interactions appear more often in laboratory animal studies than in human behavioral genetics? *Behavior and Brain Sciences, 13,* 136–137.

Hewitt, J. K. (1989). Of biases and more in the study of twins reared together. *Behavior Genetics, 19,* 605–608.

Hildreth, G. H. (1925). The resemblance of siblings in intelligence and achievement. *Teacher's College, Columbia University Contributions to Education,* No. 186.

Ho, H., Baker, L. A., & Decker, S. N. (1988). Covariation between intelligence and speed of cognitive processing: Genetic and environmental influences. *Behavior Genetics, 18,* 247–261.

Horn, J. L. (1985). Remodeling old models of intelligence. In B. J. Wolman (Ed.), *Handbook of intelligence: Theories, measurements, and applications.* New York: Wiley.

Horn, J. M., Loehlin, J. C., & Willerman, L. (1981). Generalizability of heritability estimates for intelligence from the Texas Adoption project. In L. Gedda, P. Parisi, & W. Nance (Eds.), *Twin research 3: Part B. Intelligence, personality and development* (pp. 17–19). New York: Alan R. Liss, Inc.

Horn, J. M., Loehlin, J.C., & Willerman, L. (1982). Aspects of the inheritance of intellectual abilities. *Behavior Genetics, 12,* 479–516.

Hunt, E. B. (1983). On the nature of intelligence. *Science. 219,* 141–146.

Hunter, J. E., Schmidt, F. L., & Jackson, G. B. (1982). *Meta-analysis: Cumulating research findings across studies.* Beverly Hills, CA: Sage.

Hyde, J. S. (1973). Genetic homeostasis and behavior: Analysis, data and theory. *Behavior Genetics, 3,* 233–245.

Hyde, J. S. (1974). Inheritance of learning ability in mice: A diallel-environment analysis. *Journal of Comparative and Physiological Psychology, 86,* 116–123.

Jackson, D. N. (1975). [Review of The science and politics of IQ]. *Science, 189,* 1078–1080.

Jacobs, P. A., & Strong, J. A. (1959). A case of human intersexuality having a possible XXY sex determining mechanism. *Nature, 183,* 302–303.

Jencks, C., Smith, M., Acland, H., Bane, M. J., Cohen, D., Gintis, H., Heyns, B., & Michelson, S. (1972). *Inequality.* Basic Books: New York.

Jensen, A. R. (1976). The problem of genotype-environment correlation in the estimation of heritability from monozygotic and dizygotic twins. *Acta Geneticae Medicaie et Gemellogiae, 25,* 86–89.

Jensen, A. R. (1978). Genetic and behavioral effects of nonrandom mating. In R. T. Osborne, C. E. Noble, & N. Weyl (Eds.), *Human variation: The biopsychology of age, race, and sex* (pp. 51–105). New York: Academic Press.

Jensen, A. R. (1983). Effects of inbreeding on mental-ability factors. *Personality and Individual Differences, 4,* 71–87.

Jinks, J. L., & Fulker, D. W. (1970). Comparison of the biometrical genetical, MAVA, and classical approaches to the analysis of human behavior. *Psychological Bulletin, 73,* 311–349.

Juel-Nielsen, N. (1980). *Individual and environment: Monozygotic twins reared apart.* New York: International Universities Press. (Reprint of the original 1965 publication).

Kamin, L. J. (1974). *The science and politics of IQ.* Potomac, MD: Erlbaum.

Kamin, L. J. (1980). Inbreeding depression and IQ. *Psychological Bulletin, 87,* 469–479.

Kodama, H., & Shinagawa, F. (1953). *WISC Chino shindan kensaho [The WISC Intelligence Test].* Tokyo: Nihon Bunka Kagakusha.

Kovach, J. K., & Wilson, G. (1988). Genetics of color preferences in quail chicks: Major genes and variable buffering by background genotype. *Behavior Genetics, 18,* 645–661.

Lejune, J., Gautier, M., & Turpin, M. R. (1959). Etude des chromosomes somatiques de neut enfants mongoliens. *C. R. Academie Sciences (Paris), 248,* 1721–1722.

Lewontin, R. C., Rose, S., & Kamin, L. J. (1984). *Not in our genes: Biology, ideology, and human nature.* New York: Pantheon Books.

Li, C. C. (1987). A genetic model for emergenesis: In memory of Lawrence H. Snyder, 1901–86. *American Journal of Human Genetics, 41,* 517–523.

Loehlin, J. C. (1987). *Latent Variable Models: An introduction to factor, path, and structural analysis.* Potomac, MD: Erlbaum.

Loehlin, J. C. (1989). Partitioning environmental and genetic contributions to behavioral development. *American Psychologist, 44,* 1285–1292.

Loehlin, J. C., & DeFries, J. C. (1987). Genotype-environment correlation for IQ. *Behavior Genetics, 17,* 263–277.

Loehlin, J. C., & Nichols, R. C. (1976). *Heredity, environment and personality: A study of 850 sets of twins.* Austin: University of Texas Press.

Loesch, D. Z., Hay, D. A., Sutherland, G. R., Halliday, J., Judge, C., & Webb, G. C. (1987). Phenotypic variation in male-transmitted fragile X: Genetic inferences. *American Journal of Medical Genetics, 27,* 401–417.

Lubs, H. A. (1969). A marker X chromosome. *American Journal of Human Genetics, 21,* 231–244.

Lykken, D. T. (1968). Statistical significance in psychological research. *Psychological Bulletin, 70,* 151–159.

Lykken, D. T. (1982). Research with twins: The concept of emergenesis. *Psychophysiology, 19,* 361–373.

Lykken, D. T., McGue, M., & Tellegen, A. T. (1987). Recruitment bias in twin research: The rule of two-third. *Behavior Genetics, 17,* 343–362.

Lyon, M. F. (1961). Gene action in the X-chromosomes of the mouse (Mus musculus L.). *Nature, 190,* 372–373.

Lynn, R., Hampson, S., & Mullineux, J. C. (1987). A long-term increase in the fluid intelligence of English children. *Nature, 328,* 797.

Macintosh, N. J. (1975). [Review of The Science and Politics of IQ]. *Quarterly Journal of Experimental Psychology, 27,* 672–686.

Marshalek, B., Lohman, D. F., & Snow, R. E. (1983). The complexity continuum in the radex and hierarchical models of intelligence. *Intelligence, 7,* 107–127.

Martin, N. G., Eaves, L. J., Kearsey, M. J., & Davies, P. (1978). The power of the classical twin design. *Heredity, 40,* 97–116.

Martin, N. G., Eaves, L. J., Heath, A. C., Jardine, R., Feingold, L. M., & Eysenck,

H. J. (1986). Transmission of social attitudes. *Proceedings of the National Academy of Sciences, USA, 83,* 4364–4368.

Mascie-Taylor, C. G. N. (1989). Spouse similarity for IQ and personality and convergence. *Behavior Genetics, 19,* 223–227.

Mascie-Taylor, C. G. N., & Vandenberg, S. G. (1988). Assortative mating for IQ and personality due to propinquity and personal preference. *Behavior Genetics, 18,* 339–345.

Mayer, E. (1982). *The growth of biological thought: Diversity, evolution and inheritance.* Cambridge, MA: Belknap Press.

Mayer, E. (1988). *Towards a new philosophy of biology.* Cambridge, MA: Belknap Press.

McGue, M. (1989). Nature-nurture and intelligence. *Nature, 340,* 507–508.

McGue, M., Bouchard, T. J., Jr., Lykken, D. T., & Feuer, D. (1984). Information processing abilities in twins reared apart. *Intelligence, 8,* 239–258.

McGue, M., & Bouchard, T. J., Jr. (1989). Genetic and environmental determinants of information processing and special mental abilities: A twin analysis. In R. J. Sternberg (Ed.), *Advances in the psychology of human intelligence* (Vol. 5). Hillsdale, NJ: Erlbaum.

Micceri, T. (1989). The unicorn, the normal curve, and other improbable creatures. *Psychological Bulletin, 105,* 156–166.

Mittwoch, V. (1973). *Genetics of sex differentiation.* New York: Academic Press.

Money, J. (1968). Cognitive deficits in Turner's syndrome. In S. G. Vandenberg (Ed.), *Progress in human behavior genetics* (pp. 27–31). Baltimore: Johns Hopkins University Press.

Money, J., & Granoff, D. (1965). IQ and the somatic stigmata of Turner's syndrome. *American Journal of Mental Deficiency, 70,* 69–77.

Moor, L. (1967). Niveau intellectuel et polygonosomie: Confrontation du caryotype et du niveau mental de 374 malades dont le carotype comparte un excess de chromosomes x ou y (Intellectual level and polyploidy: A comparison of karyotype and intelligence of 374 patients with extra x or y chromosomes). *Revue de Neuropsychiatrie infantile et d'Hygiene Mental de l'Enfance, 15,* 325–348.

Murphy, E. A. (1964). One cause? Many causes?; The argument from the bimodel distribution. *Journal of Chronic Diseases, 17,* 301–324.

Nagoshi, C. T., Johnson, R. C., & Ahern, F. M. (1987). Phenotypic assortative mating vs. social homogamy among Japanese and Chines parents in the Hawaii family study of cognition. *Behavior Genetics, 17,* 477–485.

Neale, M. C., Eaves, L. J., Kendler, K. S., & Hewitt, J. K. (1989). Bias in correlations from selected samples of relatives: The effect of soft selection. *Behavior Genetics, 19,* 163–170.

Neel, J. V., Schull, W. J., Yamamoto, M., Uchida, S., Yanase, T., & Fujiki, N. (1970). The effects of parental consanguinity and inbreeding in Hirado, Japan. II. Physical development, tapping rate, blood pressure, intelligence quotient, and school performance. *American Journal of Human Genetics, 22,* 263–86.

Neri, G., Opitz, J. M., Mikkelsen, M., Jacobs, P.A., Daviews, K., & Turner, G. (Eds.). (1988). X-linked mental retardation 3. (Special issue). *American Journal of Medical Genetics, 30.*

Netley, C. (1983). Sex chromosome abnormalities and the development of verbal and nonverbal abilities. In C. L. Ludlow & J. A. Cooper (Eds.), *Genetic aspects of speech and language disorders* (pp. 179–195). New York: Academic Press.

Newman, H. H., Freeman, F. M., & Holzinger, K. J. (1937). *Twins: A study of heredity and environment.* Chicago: University of Chicago Press.

Nichols, P. L. (1984). Familial mental retardation. *Behavior Genetics, 14,* 161–170.

Nichols, R. C. (1978). Twin studies of ability, personality, and interests. *Homo, 29,* 158–173.

Nussbaum, R. L., & Ledbetter, D. H. (1986). Fragile X syndrome: A unique mutation in man. *Annual Review of Genetics, 20,* 109–145.

Parker, K. C. H., Hanson, R. K., & Hunsley, J. (1988). MMPI, Rorschach, and WAIS: A meta-analytic comparison of reliability, stability and validity. *Psychological Bulletin, 103,* 367–373.

Pedersen, N. L., McClearn, G. E., Plomin, R., & Friberg, L. (1985). Separated fraternal twins: Resemblance for cognitive abilities. *Behavior Genetics, 15,* 407–419.

Pennington, B. F., & Smith, S. D. (1983). Genetic influences on learning disabilities and speech and language disorders. *Child Development, 54,* 369–387.

Penrose, L. S., & Smith, G. F. (1966). *Down's anomaly.* London: J & A. Churchill.

Phillips, K., & Fulker, D. W. (1989). Quantitative analysis of longitudinal trends in adoption designs with applications to IQ in the Colorado Adoption Project. *Behavior Genetic, 19,* 621–658.

Plomin, R. (1986). *Development, genetics, and psychology.* Hillsdale, NJ: Erlbaum.

Plomin, R. (1989). Environment and genes: Determinants of behavior. *American Psychologist, 44,* 105–111.

Plomin, R. (1990). The role of inheritance in behavior. *Science, 248,* 183–188.

Plomin, R., & DeFries, J. C. (1985). *Origins of individual differences in infancy: The Colorado adoption project.* New York: Academic Press.

Plomin, R., DeFries, J. C., & Fulker, D. W. (1988). *Nature and nurture during infancy and early childhood.* Cambridge: Cambridge University Press.

Plomin, R., DeFries, J. C., & Loehlin, J. C. (1977). Genotype-environment interaction and correlation in the analysis of human behavior. *Psychological Bulletin, 84,* 309–322.

Plomin, R., DeFries, J. C., & McClearn, G. E. (1990). *Behavioral genetics: A primer (2nd ed.).* New York: Freeman.

Plomin, R., & Loehlin, J. C. (1989). Direct and indirect IQ heritability estimates. *Behavior Genetics, 19,* 331–342.

Rao, D. C., Morton, N. E., & Yee, S. (1974). Analysis of family resemblance. II. A linear model for familial correlation. *American Journal of Human Genetics, 26,* 331–359.

Rao, D. C., Morton, N. E., & Yee, S. (1976). Resolution of cultural and biological inheritance by path analysis. *American Journal of Human Genetics, 28,* 228–242.

Reed, S. C., & Rich, S. S. (1982). Parent-offspring correlations and regressions for IQ. *Behavior Genetics, 12,* 535–542.

Reed, T. E. (1984). Mechanism for heritability of intelligence. *Nature, 311,* 417.

Reed, T. E. (1988a). A neurophysiological basis for the heritability of vertebrate intelligence. In H. J. Jerison & I. Jerison (Eds.), *Intelligence and evolutionary biology.* Heidelberg: Springer-Verlag.

Reed, T. E. (1988b). Narrow-sense heritability estimates for nerve conduction velocity and residual latency in mice. *Behavior Genetics, 18*, 595–603.

Retherford, R. D., & Sewell, W. H. (1988). Intelligence and family size reconsidered. *Social Biology, 35*, 1–40.

Rice, J., Cloninger, C. R., & Reich, T. (1980a). Multifactorial inheritance with cultural transmission and assortative mating. I. Description and basic properties of the unitary models. *American Journal of Human Genetics, 30*, 618–643.

Rice, J., Cloninger, C. R., & Reich, T. (1980b). Analysis of behavioral traits in the presence of cultural transmission and assortative mating. *Behavior Genetics, 10*, 73–92.

Rovet, J., & Netley, C. (1980). The mental rotation task performance of Turner's syndrome subjects. *Behavior Genetics, 10*, 437–443.

Rovet, J., & Netley, C. (1982). Processing deficits in Turner's syndrome. *Developmental Psychology, 18*, 77–94.

Rushton, J. P. (1988). Epigenic rules in moral development: Distal-proximal approaches to altruism and aggression. *Aggressive Behavior, 14*, 35–50.

Rushton, J. P. (1989). The generalizability of genetic estimates. *Personality and Individual differences, 10*, 985–989.

Rushton, P. J., & Nicholson, I. R. (1988). Genetic similarity theory, intelligence and human mate choice. *Ethology and Sociobiology, 9*, 45–57.

Scarr, S. (1976). [Review of The science and politics of IQ]. In *Contemporary Psychology, 21*, 98–99.

Scarr, S. (1987). Three cheers for behavior genetics: winning the war and losing our identity. *Behavior Genetics, 17*, 219–228.

Scarr, S., & McCartney, K. (1983). How people make their own environments: A theory of genotype − − > environment effects. *Developmental Psychology, 54*. 424–435.

Scarr, S., & Weinberg, R. A. (1978). The influence of family background on intellectual attainment. *American Sociological Review, 43*, 674–692.

Schiff, M., & Lewontin, R. (1986). *Education and class: The irrelevance of IQ genetic studies*. Oxford, England: Claredon Press.

Schull, W. J. (1962). Inbreeding and maternal effects in the Japanese. *Eugenics Quarterly, 9*, 14–22.

Schull, W. J., & Neel, J.V. (1965). *The effects of inbreeding on Japanese children*. New York: Harper and Row.

Schull, W. J., & Neel, J. V. (1972). The effects of parental consanguinity and inbreeding in Hirado, Japan. V. Summary and interpretation. *American Journal of Human Genetics, 24*, 425–453.

Schull, W. J., Nagano, H., Yamamoto, M., & Komatsu, I. (1970). The effect of parental consanguinity and inbreeding in Hirado, Japan. I. Stillbirth and preproductive mortality. *American Journal of Human Genetics, 22*, 239–62.

Sergovich, R., Uilenberg, C., & Pozsonyi, J. (1971). The 49, XXXXX chromosome constitution: similarities to the 49, XXXXXY condition. *Journal of Pediatrics, 78*, 285–290.

Shapiro, B. L. (1975). Amplified developmental instability in down's syndrome. *Annals of Human Genetics, 38*, 429–437.

Shields, J. (1962). *Monozygotic twins brought up apart and brought up together*. New York: Oxford University Press.

Slatis, H. M., & Hoene, R. E. (1961). The effect of consanguinity on the distribution of continuously variable characteristics. *American Journal of Human Genetics, 13,* 28–31.

Snyderman, M., & Rothman, S. (1988). *The IQ controversy: The media and public policy.* New Brunswick, NJ: Transaction Books.

Spitz, H. H. (1986a). *The raising of intelligence: A selected history of attempts to raise retarded intelligence.* Hillsdale, NJ: Erlbaum.

Spitz, H. H. (1986b). Preventing and curing mental retardation by behavioral intervention: An evaluation and some claims. *Intelligence, 10,* 197–207.

Sternberg, R. J. (1983). Components of human intelligence. *Cognition, 15,* 1–48.

Sternberg, R. J. (1985). Human intelligence: The model is the message, *Science, 230,* 1111–1118.

Stewart, D. A., Bailey, J. D., Netley, C. T., Rovet, J., & Park, E. (1986). Growth and development from early birth to midadolescence of children with X and Y chromosome aneuploidy. *Birth Defects: Original Article Series, 22,* 119–182.

Stewart, D. A., Netley, C. T., & Park, E. (1982). Summary of clinical findings of children with 47, XXY, 47, XYY, and 47, XXX karyotypes. *Birth Defects: Original Article Series, 18,* 1–5.

Sundet, J. M., Tambs, K., Magnus, P., & Berg, K. (1988). On the question of secular trends in the heritability of intelligence test scores: A study of Norwegian twins. *Intelligence, 12,* 47–59.

Sutherland, G. R. (1977). Fragile sites on human chromosomes: demonstration of their dependence on the type of tissue culture medium. *Science, 197,* 265–266.

Tambs, K., Sundet, J. M., Magnus, P., & Berg, K. (1989). No recruitment bias for questionnaire data related to IQ in classical twin studies. *Personality and Individual Differences, 10,* 269–271.

Taylor, H. F. (1980). *The IQ game: A methodological inquiry into the heredity environment controversy.* New Brunswick, NJ: Rutgers University press.

Teasdale, T. W., & Owen, D. R. (1984). Heredity and familial environment in intelligence and educational level—a sibling study. *Nature, 309,* 620–622.

Teasdale, T. W., & Owen, D. R. (1989). Continuing secular increase in intelligence and a stable prevalence of high intelligence levels. *Intelligence, 13,* 255–262.

Tellegen, A., Lykken, D. T., Bouchard, T. J. Jr., Wilcox, K. J., Segal, N. L., & Rich, S. (1988). Personality similarity in twins reared apart and together. *Journal of Personality and Social Psychology, 54,* 1031–1039.

Tennes, K., Puck, M., Bryant, K., Frankenberg, W., & Robinson, A. (1975). A developmental study of girls with trisomy X. *American Journal of Human Genetics, 27,* 71–86.

Thiessen, D. D. (1972). *Gene organization and behavior.* New York: Random House.

Tjio, H. J., & Levan, A. (1956). The chromosome numbers of man. *Hereditas, 42,* 1–6.

Urbach, P. (1974a). Progress and degeneration in the "IQ Debate" (I). *British Journal of the Philosophy of Science, 25,* 99–135.

Urbach, P. (1974b). Progress and degeneration in the "IQ Debate" (II). *British Journal of the Philosophy of Science, 25,* 235–259.

Vandenberg, S. G. (1971). What do we know today about the inheritance of intelligence and how do we know it? In R. Cancro (Ed.), *Intelligence: Genetic and environmental influences.* New York: Grune & Straton.

Vernon, P. A. (Ed.). (1987). *Speed of information-processing and intelligence.* Norwood, NJ: Ablex.

Vogler, G. P., & DeFries, J. C. (1983). Linearity of offspring-parent regression for general cognitive ability. *Behavior Genetics, 4*, 355–360.

Wahlsten, D. (1990). Insensitivity of analysis of variance to heredity-environment interaction. *Behavior and Brain Sciences, 13*, 109–161.

Waller, N. G., Kojetin, B. A., Bouchard, T. J., Jr., Lykken, D. T., & Tellegen, A. (1990). Genetic and environmental influences on religious interests, attitudes and values: A study of twins reared apart and together. *Psychological Science, 1*, 138–142.

Willerman, L. (1979). Effects of families on intellectual development. *American Psychologist, 34*, 923–929.

Wilson, R. S. (1978). Synchronies in mental development: an epigenetic perspective. *Science, 202*, 939–984.

Wilson, R. S. (1983). The Louisville twin study: Developmental synchronies in behavior. *Child Development, 54*, 298–316.

Witkin, H. A., Mednick, S. A., Schulsinger, F., Bakkestrom, E., Christiansen, K. O., Goodenough, D. R., Hirschorn, K., Lundsteen, C., Owen, D. R., Philips, J., Rubin, D. B., & Stocking, M. (1976). Criminality in XYY and XXY men. *Science, 193*, 547–555.

Zigler, E. (1967). Familial mental retardation: A continuing dilemma. *Science, 155*, 292–298.

# Chapter 3

# Genetic Contributions to Intellectual Development in Infancy and Childhood*

## Lee Anne Thompson

Department of Psychology
Case Western Reserve University
Cleveland, OH

## INTRODUCTION

Intelligence has captured the interest of behavioral geneticists since the late 1800s when Galton first studied the inheritance of mental abilities. To date, more behavioral genetic studies of IQ have been conducted than for any other human behavioral trait. Although behavioral geneticists have over the years conducted many studies including of infants and young children, recent years have provided a great deal of new and exciting findings for the first part of the lifespan. A

* This chapter was written while the author was partially supported by a grant from NICHD (HD21947-02).

contributing factor has been the birth of the interdisciplinary field, developmental behavioral genetics, which explores genetic and environmental influences on individual differences. A key concept in the field is that of genetic change across the lifespan. Behavior changes rapidly during the early years of life, providing a wonderful opportunity to study the interplay of genetic and environmental contributions.

The goal of this chapter is to provide an overview of behavioral genetic research on intellectual development during infancy and childhood. The chapter opens with a brief description of behavioral genetic research designs and then turns to a review of the literature. The primary focus is on recent and ongoing studies, as excellent complete reviews already exist (Plomin, 1987; Plomin, 1986; Scarr & Kidd, 1983). The secondary emphasis is to illustrate the usefulness and power of behavioral genetic methodology for understanding the process of development. Multivariate analyses and latent variable modeling have proven to be particularly useful. Behavioral genetic research during infancy and childhood is accumulating rapidly and this chapter also attempts to predict future directions that the field may take.

## Overview of Behavior Genetic Designs

Human behavioral genetic research involves the use of naturally occurring populations to control for genetic similarity among individuals. The three basic designs most commonly used are the family, twin, and adoption studies. Each of the designs is briefly described; however, an in-depth explanation of the designs and their assumptions can be found in Plomin, DeFries, and McClearn (1990).

*Family studies.* Family studies compare parents and their offspring and siblings to each other. Parents and their children share 50 percent of their additive genetic variance as well as shared family environmental influences. Siblings share on average 50 percent of their additive genetic makeup, 25 percent dominance variation, and shared family environment. Although the family design does not allow genetic and environmental variance to be estimated separately, familial resemblance is a prerequisite for the operation of genetic influences. Genetic and shared family environmental influences cause family members to be similar to each other; nonshared or specific environmental influences cause differences among family members. If family members do not resemble one another, then neither genetic nor shared family environment can be important.

Estimates of familiality (family resemblance) are typically calculated by regressing offspring scores on parent scores or by correlating one sibling with another. Assortative mating can inflate estimates of familiality when parents are similar to each other for a trait of interest. Spouse correlations are used to estimate assortative mating. For instance, people mate assortatively for height;

tall women and men tend to marry each other. If the parents are highly similar, then the single parent/offspring relationship becomes inflated because the relationship includes not only the genetic similarity between that parent and their child, but also a portion of the genetic similarity between the child and the other parent. However, if the parents' scores are averaged creating a midparent score, then assortative mating is no longer an issue (Falconer, 1973). The regression of the midparent score on the offspring score estimates 100% of the additive genetic variance plus shared family environmental influences.

*Twin studies.* Twin studies are more powerful than family studies in that genetic effects can be separated from the environment. The design is based upon the fact that identical twins (MZ) share 100 percent of their genetic makeup and fraternal twins (DZ) only share on average 50 percent of their genes. If a given trait is genetically influenced, then identical twins should resemble each other to a greater extent than fraternal twins; the identical twin correlation should be greater than the fraternal twin correlation. Heritability ($h^2$) represents the portion of variance due to genetic effects and can be estimated by subtracting the fraternal twin intraclass correlation from the identical twin correlation and doubling the difference. Identical twin similarity is due to both shared genes and shared environment. Shared or common family environmental influences ($e_c^2$) can be estimated by subtracting $h^2$ from the identical twin correlation. Nonshared or within-pair environmental influences ($e_w^2$) create differences between members of a twin pair; because MZ twins are completely genetically identical, within-pair differences must be caused by environmental influences. Nonshared environment can be estimated by subtracting the MZ twin correlation from 1.0; of course, any error variance would also be contained in this term. As a numerical example, if identical twins correlate .80 and fraternal twins correlate .50, then,

$$h^2 = 2(.80 - .50) = 2(.30) = .60,$$
$$e_c^2 = .80 - .60 = .20, \text{ and}$$
$$e_w^2 = 1.00 - .80 = .20.$$

The twin design assumes that environmental influences are shared to the same extent across the two twin types. Although the validity of this assumption has been challenged, studies have failed to show that the assumption has compromised twin study results for major areas of interest such as intelligence and personality (Plomin et al., 1990).

*Adoption studies.* The adoption design also allows genetic and environmental effects to be separated and is one of the most powerful designs available for studying human behavior. The design compares an adopted child to biological parents who do not share any of the environmental experiences with the child, and with adoptive parents who do not share any genetic similarity with the child. If the child resembles biological relatives, then genetic influences are implicated.

If the child resembles the adoptive relatives, then the effects of shared family environment are operating. Adoption designs also allow unrelated siblings reared together to be studied. Pairs of related and unrelated siblings can be used to estimate genetic and environmental influences in much the same way that twin data is used, except that unrelated siblings do not share any of their genes and related siblings share on average 50 percent of their genetic makeup.

Two major factors must be assessed in adoption studies for the design to be valid; they are the age of placement and selective placement. Adopted children should be separated from their biological parents at birth or shortly thereafter. If the child has contact with biological mother or father, then the estimates of genetic influence will be inflated. Selective placement, the matching of adoptive parents to biological parents, must also be assessed. Under selective placement, both genetic and environmental influences may be overestimated. If genetic influences are important, the adoptive parent/adoptive offspring relationship will be inflated and the effect of shared family environment will be overestimated. If shared environmental influences are important, the biological parent/offspring relationship will be inflated and the estimate of genetic influence will also be too large.

Although behavioral genetic designs are based on the genetic similarity of individuals, they provide the best opportunity to study the effects of the environment. In fact, the field of behavior genetics may hold more promise for understanding the environment than genetic effects. This chapter, however, is directed at understanding genetic influences on intellectual development and will not discuss the many behavior genetic studies of environmental influences, a topic that would require an entire chapter by itself.

## INFANCY

For the most part, developmental psychologists have not been as interested in individual differences during the infancy period as they have universals of development. The general lack of individual differences research can be traced to two main factors. First, individual variation is less marked in infancy than later in life because of the highly canalized nature of infant development. Second, behavioral differences among infants are difficult to measure reliably and accurately. Recent years have seen a shift in interest with greater attention paid to behavioral variation as researchers began to improve their methods of assessing early individual differences. Beginning in the 1970s behavioral genetic studies of infancy also began to emerge with a primary focus on cognitive abilities.

Currently there are four large ongoing studies which provide family, twin, and adoption data on cognitive development in infancy. Each of these four important studies will be briefly described below.

*Louisville Twin Study (LTS).* The oldest of the three studies, the LTS began in the 1950s and continues today (Wilson 1983). Twins are first tested at 3 months of age and are followed every 3 months during the first year, every 6 months during the second and third years, and yearly until they reach 9 years of age. The twins receive their last testing at 15 years of age. During infancy, the primary tests administered are the Bayley Scales of Infant Development through 24 months of age, and the Stanford-Binet at 30 and 36 months of age. The study includes close to 500 pairs of twins. In addition to the twins, whenever possible both older and younger siblings of the twins were also included in the study.

*Colorado Adoption Project (CAP).* Beginning in 1975, biological mothers were recruited through two Denver area adoption agencies. All of the biological mothers, about 25 percent of the biological fathers and both adoptive parents of all of the adopted children were tested on a 3-hour battery of cognitive and personality tests. In addition to the adoptive families, matched control families were also selected for testing based on sex of the child, father's age and occupation, and the number of children in the family. Currently, the sample consists of 245 adoptive families and 245 matched control families. Initially, the children in the CAP were tested twice during infancy at 1 and 2 years of age. The children are then followed longitudinally at 3, 4, and 7, phone interviews and tests are conducted at 9, 10, and 11, and plans are being made for subsequent testing until each child can be tested at age 16 years on the same battery that the parents initially received. Whenever possible, a younger sibling in both the adoptive and nonadoptive families is also included in the study. Beginning in 1982, the infants recruited into the study received the Fagan Test of Infant Intelligence (Fagan & Shepherd, 1986) at 5 and 7 months of age in addition to the rest of the testing. The infant tests administered at 1 and 2 years include; the Bayley Scales of Infant Development, Bayley's Infant Behavior Record, the Sequenced Inventory of Communication Development, maternal interviews, and videotaped assessments. Details about the CAP and extensive data analyses in infancy are reported in Plomin and DeFries (1985).

*The Colorado Infant Twin Project (TIP).* The TIP began in 1985. Currently the study includes over 200 pairs of twins tested at 7, 8, and 9 months of age. The twins receive a wide variety of tests which will be described later, but each test was selected as a possible predictor of later intelligence. Both parents of the twins also receive extensive cogniti·e testing, including the Wechsler Adult Intelligence Scale and a shortened form of the adult battery of cognitive tests used in the CAP. Further information on the TIP can be found in DiLalla et al. (1990).

*MacArthur Longitudinal Twin Study (MALTS).* Beginning in 1986 parents of infant twins were contacted through the Division of Vital Statistics of the Colorado Department of Health. All twins selected were to be full term and of appropriate birth weights. The final sample consisted of over 200 sets of twins. Each twin pair was seen twice at 14, 20, 24, and 36 months of age and assessed on a variety of temperament and cognitive measures. The primary focus of the study was on individual differences in change and continuity during the second year of life in the areas of temperament, cognition, and emotion (Plomin, Campos, et al., 1990).

## Cognitive Development—Conventional Infant Tests

*Twin and sibling studies.* There are only two twin and nontwin sibling studies of infant cognitive development aside from the four studies described above. Twin and sibling data from the Collaborative Perinatal Project (Nichols & Broman, 1974) and sibling data reported by McCall (1972). The results from these two studies are summarized in Table 3.1, and generally concur with the results reported in the LTS and CAP.

Bayley Mental Development Index (MDI) scores from the LTS indicate almost no genetic influence on individual differences in cognitive function during the first year-and-a-half of life and little influence from 18 to 30 months of age (Wilson, 1983). Within-pair correlations are substantial but identical twins are not significantly more similar than fraternal twins. In fact, the twin correla-

**Table 3.1. Twin and Sibling Studies of Infant General Cognitive Ability**

| | | Correlation | | | |
|---|---|---|---|---|---|
| *Study* | *Age in months* | *Identical Twins* | *Fraternal Twins* | *Related Siblings* | *Unrelated Siblings* |
| McCall (1972) | 6 & 12 | | | .24 (142) | |
| | 6, 12, 18 & 24 | | | .40 (142) | |
| Nichols & Broman (1974) | 8 | .55 (110) | .55 (205) | .22 (4,347) | |
| Wilson (1983) | 3 | .66 (72) | .67 (90) | | |
| | 6 | .75 (81) | .72 (101) | | |
| | 9 | .67 (73) | .51 (84) | | |
| | 12 | .68 (89) | .63 (92) | | |
| | 18 | .82 (92) | .65 (113) | | |
| | 24 | .85 (88) | .65 (115) | | |
| | 30 | .88 (72) | .79 (93) | | |
| | 36 | .88 (104) | .79 (125) | .38 (74) | |
| Plomin, DeFries, & Fulker (1988) | 12 | | | .37 (82) | .03 (67) |
| | 24 | | | .42 (70) | .12 (61) |

tions are greater than the age-to-age correlations for the same child; each twin predicts his co-twin's score better than the child himself at a later age. The mean twin correlations across 3, 6, 9, and 12 months of age are .69 and .63 for identical and fraternal twins respectively. In contrast the same correlations across 18, 24, 30, and 36 months are .84 and .71. The pattern of correlations suggests that environmental factors are a strong determinant of twin similarity at these early ages with genetic influences beginning to play a small role after 18 months. Nontwin sibling correlations are also available for some of the ages. It is most striking that the siblings resemble each other significantly less than the fraternal twins, thus suggesting that twins share environmental effects unique to twin pairs. Examples of such effects may be testing artifacts, each twin is tested on the same day, sibling tests are separated by at least a year; or perhaps more likely, twins share perinatal effects and are subject to perinatal problems more often than are singletons.

Another informative approach for studying cognitive development through twin data is to chart longitudinal changes or "spurts and lags" for individual twin pairs. These longitudinal profiles can be used to compute trend correlations for identical and fraternal twins. Figure 3.1 illustrates the pattern of change across three age groupings in the LTS. Trend correlations were computed (Wilson, 1983) for a combination of the 3,6,9, and 12 months Bayley MDI

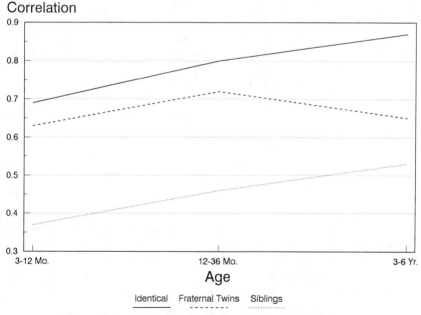

Figure 3.1.   **Louisville Twin Study trend correlations**
**Data from Wilson, 1983.**

scores at .69 and .63 for identical and fraternal twins, respectively. Although these correlations show that twins are very similar in their developmental patterns, no genetic influence is indicated during the first year. Mental development scores at 12, 18, 24, and 36 months were correlated .80 for identical and .72 for fraternal twins ($p < .05$ for the difference between the correlations), indicating that genetic factors begin to exert an influence during the second and third years of life. After the infancy period, combining across IQ at 3, 4, 5, and 6 years yields correlations of .87 for identical and .65 for fraternal twins. These trend results suggest that genetic factors become increasingly important after infancy through the transition into early childhood, but once again implicate the role of shared family environment for the substantial twin similarities observed. The trend analyses for 35 pairs of infant siblings also support the previous single-age correlations in that they are significantly lower than the fraternal twin trend correlations during infancy. The 3-, 6-, 9-, and 12-month correlation is a .37 and the 12-, 18-, 24-, and 36-month correlation is .46. However, the sibling trend correlation (.55) for early childhood is similar in magnitude to the fraternal twin correlation (.65), thus further implicating the effect of perinatal influences that begin to wash out after infancy (Wilson, 1983).

The role of genetic influences on Bayley MDI scores during the first two years of life appear at best minimal in the LTS. Furthermore, development patterns of continuity and change, although very similar for twins, also appear to be unaffected by genetic factors. In contrast to the LTS, a small sample of related and unrelated siblings from the CAP show strong genetic influence for Bayley MDI scores at 12 and 24 months of age (see Table 3.1). The related sibling correlations of .37 and .42 at 12 and 24 months respectively are comparable to other infant sibling correlations in the literature.

Interestingly, recent results from the TIP and MALTS twin studies differ somewhat from those reported in the LTS. For 264 twin pairs at 12 months and 155 twin pairs at 24 months, heritability estimates are .50 and .24, and shared environmental influences are .15 and .55, respectively (Cherny, Cardon, Fulker, & DeFries, 1992). The sample at 3 years of age is still small—62 twin pairs—and the estimates of .30 and .43 for heritability and shared environment are not significant. Although the results appear to differ markedly between the two samples, particularly for the 1-year-olds, Cherny et al. attribute the differences to sampling fluctuations.

Another recent report on a preliminary sample of 14-month-old twins (100 MZ and 100 DZ) from the MALTS examined the interrelationships between the Bayley Mental Development Index and three specific cognitive ability measures comprised of a word comprehension test, a sorting task, and a memory for location task (Whitfield, Cherny, Fulker, & Reznick, 1992). The Bayley and the word comprehension task were both significantly heritable. The four measures did not share a common genetic factor. In other words, each of the measures appear to be influenced by separate genetic influences. This report is particularly interesting however, because measures of specific cognitive abilities during the first two years are scarce, and few multivariate genetic studies of the structure of mental abilities in this early age group have been conducted.

*Adoption studies.* Turning now to results from the CAP, parent/offspring resemblances are examined for 1- and 2-year Bayley MDI scores and parental general cognitive ability. In general the overall results are comparable to other adoption studies involving parent/infant comparisons (Plomin, 1987). Table 3.2 summarizes these studies.

Nonadoptive parent/offspring resemblance estimates familiality or an upper-limit estimate for both genetic and environmental influences; biological parent/offspring resemblance directly estimates the impact of genetic effects, and adoptive parent/offspring resemblance indicates environmental influence. Again genetic influences appear to be minimal during the first year and slightly more important during the second year of life. However, the effect of parent/offspring shared environment also appears to be quite small. Maximum-likelihood model-fitting analyses allow these correlations to be simultaneously analyzed providing a more powerful approach to detect and explain small relationships. These analyses support a genetic hypothesis at 12 months and a combined effect of genes and shared family environment at 24 months of age (Fulker & DeFries, 1983). Plomin (1987) summarizes that about 20% of the variance in Bayley MDI

**Table 3.2.  Adoption Studies of Infant General Cognitive Ability**

| Study | Age in months | Relationship | (N) | Correlation |
|---|---|---|---|---|
| Snygg (1938) | 12–14 | biological mothers | (227) | .08 |
| Skodak & Skeels (1949) | 12–24 | biological mothers | (39) | −.01 |
| Casler (1976) | 9 & 15 | biological mothers | (145) | .09 |
| | 21 & 27 | biological mothers | (145) | .11 |
| Plomin & DeFries (1985) | 12 | biological | | |
| | | mothers | (176) | .12 |
| | | fathers | (41) | .29 |
| | | adoptive | | |
| | | mothers | (177) | .12 |
| | | fathers | (169) | .00 |
| | | nonadoptive | | |
| | | mothers | (157) | .04 |
| | | fathers | (157) | .09 |
| | 24 | biological | | |
| | | mothers | (176) | .06 |
| | | fathers | (41) | .38 |
| | | adoptive | | |
| | | mothers | (177) | .10 |
| | | fathers | (169) | .08 |
| | | nonadoptive | | |
| | | mothers | (157) | .22 |
| | | fathers | (157) | .21 |

Adapted from Plomin (1986).

scores is determined by genetic influences and about 10 percent of the variance can be accounted for by family environment shared by parents and infants.

Finding rather small parent/offspring correlations is not surprising. The interpretation of parent/offspring results requires a slightly different perspective than twin analyses. When twins and/or siblings are tested at the same age using exactly the same measure, it is clear that the resulting heritability and environmentality estimates pertain directly to the trait measured. However, in the case of parents and infant offspring, individuals are tested at drastically different ages on very different measures. When heritability estimates are obtained directly from these comparisons, isomorphism is assumed for the trait in question. This assumption may not be valid, especially for infant intelligence where the predictive power of the infant tests appears to be quite low especially during the first 12 months of life. The discovery of parent/infant resemblance becomes that much more remarkable, because in the case of the biological parent/offspring comparison, it requires not only that genetic influences be important in infancy and in adulthood but that there be some degree of genetic continuity between the two ages. Genetic continuity will be discussed later in the chapter.

The results outlined thus far have only involved general cognitive ability in infancy and in adulthood. The CAP data set can also be used to explore specific cognitive abilities and the process of differentiation in cognitive development (Plomin & DeFries, 1985). Four specific ability factor scores are available for each of the parents in the CAP representing Verbal and Spatial abilities, Perceptual Speed, and Memory. Bayley MDI scores relate only to parental general intelligence, not to these four factors. The next step taken was an attempt to isolate specific cognitive components from the items in the Bayley. Lewis (1983) reported on Spatial, Verbal, and Memory/Imitation scales derived from factor analyses of the Bayley items. These factors were created for the CAP infants and then compared to the parental factor scores as well as to general intelligence (Thompson, Plomin, & DeFries, 1985). Again, however, the results indicate that Bayley factors that relate to adult intelligence only relate to general intelligence and not to the specific abilities. These results suggest that infant intelligence is a global, undifferentiated ability, but this hypothesis requires further exploration. Perhaps specific abilities in infancy are very basic and are therefore not captured by the Bayley in enough detail to indicate differentiation. Similarly, perhaps the parental measures are themselves too complex to relate to specific infant skills. Further research is required to explore these issues.

*Language acquisition.* During the transition from infancy into childhood one of the most important cognitive developments is the acquisition of language skills. Communicative development has been traditionally approached through a universal perspective yet individual differences are marked (Hardy-Brown, 1983). Behavioral genetics research has made important contributions toward the understanding of the origins of individual differences in the rate of communicative development.

Studies from the CAP have yield some particularly interesting results. Infants in the CAP received the Bayley at 12 and 24 months of age, which contains many verbal items, a maternal report of the size of the infants vocabulary is recorded at 18 months, and the infants received the Sequenced Inventory of Communication Development (SICD) at 24 and 36 months of age.

Baker (1983) conducted a path analysis of verbal and nonverbal Bayley clusters at both 12 and 24 months of age. Parent/offspring results support the results discussed previously involving the Bayley factors (Lewis, 1983): Verbal and nonverbal Bayley clusters do not differentially relate to parental verbal and nonverbal skills. This pattern of results continues to suggest that infant cognitive skills are general and undifferentiated. Furthermore, genetic analyses suggest that the same genetic influences are operating to determine individual differences in verbal and nonverbal abilities at 12 months. At 24 months, the amount of genetic overlap is still large but suggests that some genetic differentiation begins to occur during the second year of life (Plomin & DeFries, 1985).

Although the Bayley does contain many verbal items, an entire test devoted to measuring communicative competence might allow a more accurate assessment of individual differences. Thompson and Plomin (1988) report a series of analyses involving the SICD at 2 and 3 years of age in the CAP. When the SICD was compared to measures of general cognitive ability, Bayley at 2 years and Stanford-Binet at 3 years, and other verbal measures, word diary at 18 months and a separate verbal ability test at 3 years, the SICD was significantly correlated with all of the measures. However, the SICD was more highly correlated with general cognitive ability than with specific verbal tests.

Sibling correlations were also examined for the SICD. Although the sample size was small, related and unrelated sibling comparisons are interesting because they provide direct estimates of heritability and shared family environmental influences. Adoptive sibling pairs are genetically unrelated and any resemblance found between members of unrelated pairs must be due to shared family environment. Nonadoptive sibling pairs are on the average 50 percent genetically similar and also share the same rearing environment. The heritability of a trait can be estimated from sibling data as it is estimated from twin data (Plomin et al., 1989) by subtracting the unrelated sibling correlation (shared family environment estimate) from the related pair correlation and doubling the difference. For 70 pairs of related siblings and 56 pairs of unrelated siblings at year 2, the SICD correlations were .29 and .08 respectively, yielding an estimate of .42 for heritability at age 2. At three years, the 53 related pairs and 50 unrelated pairs were correlated at .21 and .10 providing an estimate of .22 for heritability. These results suggest that genetic influences are important for differences in the rate of language acquisition in infancy and early childhood.

Thompson and Plomin (1988) also explored parent/offspring resemblance for parental IQ and specific cognitive abilities as compared with offspring SICD scores. Although the SICD did relate to both IQ and verbal ability in the parents, the SICD/verbal relationship dropped out when IQ was controlled for, suggesting that communicative ability in infancy may be a good representation of general cognitive ability. Parent/offspring model-fitting analyses provide estimates of genetic and environmental influences on the "longitudinal" relationship between SICD and parental IQ. The results from these analyses yield small but significant estimates for genetic influence at age 2 ($h^2 = .19$) and a slightly higher estimate at age 3 ($h^2 = .38$).

In slightly larger sample, 73 adoptive and 83 nonadoptive sibling pairs, Julian, Braungart, Fulker, Defries, and Plomin (1992) report in an update on the CAP sample a multivariate analysis of the SICD scores. They found that approximately 50% of the variance in SICD scores at both ages 2 and 3 can be attributed to genetic influences and only about 2% to shared family environment at age 3. They also report that genetic influences appear to be important in mediating continuity in language acquisition from age 2 to 3 as indicated by greater cross-sibling longitudinal correlations in the nonadoptive pairs as compared with adoptive pairs.

The language measures discussed thus far have been widely used and are reliable but sample from a limited window of infant behavior as they assess language from a global perspective. Measures including detailed assessments from naturalistic observations may provide greater understanding of how communicative development is influenced by genes and by specific aspects of the environment. In a detailed analysis of language development, Hardy-Brown and Plomin (1985) examined a subsample of 50 adopted and 50 nonadopted CAP infants at 1 year of age. The assessment of the infants included analyses of videotapes involving mother/infant interactions during unstructured, semistructured, and structured situations. The variables that emerged from the videotaped situations included: total vocalizations, vocal and physical imitation, syllable structure, communicative gestures, true words, and others. The videotape variables were combined with Bayley communication items and the word diary measure. A first unrotated principal component accounting for 29 percent of the variance of all of these measures was used as an index of infant communicative behavior.

When the first principal component was related to parent IQ, the nonadoptive mother and father and the biological mother comparisons were significant, thus, strongly implicating genetic influences. Adoptive infants did not resemble their adoptive parents. Also of interest is the lack of relationship between the infant measure and parental specific abilities; again, general cognitive ability appears to be the most important determinant.

Although the adopted infants' communicative ability did not relate to adoptive parents' IQ, some aspects of the language learning environment were found to be important. Maternal variables that were assessed from the videotaped interactions included: total vocalizations, sentence types, vocal imitation of the infant, contingent vocal responding, mean length of utterance, and others. Other measures of the home environment thought to be important for language development were also assessed such as time reading books with the infant, presence of older siblings, and parental education and occupation. Although not as strong as the genetic effects, two interesting relationships emerged, nonadoptive and adoptive mothers' imitation of infant vocalizations and time spent reading books with the infant. Despite the small size of the environmental effect and the relatively small number of influential variables, these findings are important because they are estimates of "pure" environmental effects. Reports of significant effects of maternal interaction variables on infant behavior may in fact be indirectly determined by genetic factors unless the mother/child pairs are unrelated as in the CAP.

The acquisition of language skills has proven to be a fruitful area of study for behavioral geneticists. Adoption study results including sibling comparisons and parent/offspring comparisons indicate that genetic influences are an important determinant of early individual differences in communicative development. Furthermore, the results also suggest that it may be possible to identify specific environmental variables that affect the process of language acquisition.

*Infant information processing.* The combined results from the LTS and the CAP are very important and represent the best attempts to study genetic and environmental influences on infant cognitive development to date. However, the measurement of infant intelligence is not an easy task and advances in test development have been made in the last decade that may shed further light on the etiology of individual differences in infant intelligence. Research on infant visual attention has led to a whole new approach to cognitive development in infancy. In particular, measures of visual novelty preference and habituation have been found to be predictive of later intelligence (Fagan & McGrath, 1981; Lewis & Brooks-Gunn, 1981; Rose & Wallace, 1988; Bornstein & Sigman, 1986) more so than conventional infant sensorimotor tests such as the Bayley. An information processing approach has been taken to explain this continuity; visual attention measures tap basic information-processing abilities such as encoding, discrimination, categorization, and memory. All of these abilities are important for performance on intelligence tests later in life (Fagan & Singer, 1983).

Beginning in 1982, the remaining infants recruited into the CAP were administered an early version of the Fagan Test of Infant Intelligence (FTII; Fagan & Shepherd, 1986) at 5 and 7 months corrected age. The FTII uses a paired-comparisons paradigm to measure visual recognition memory through infants' preferences for novel stimuli. Each of the infants received four problems of abstract patterns and photographs of faces at 5 months of age and six problems of photographs of faces at 7 months of age (Thompson, 1989). A total of 41 adopted infants and 95 nonadoptive infants were tested. In general, the 5-month novelty preference did not relate to midparent general cognitive ability. The 7-month novelty scores yielded midparent/infant regressions of .20, .19, and .16 for biological, adoptive and nonadoptive parents, respectively. Although the samples are small, the results are encouraging. In general both the adoptive parent/infant and the biological mother/infant correlations are higher than with the 12-month Bayley MDI scores, thus indicating more continuity mediated both by genetics and by environmental influences.

The infants tested in the CAP were followed longitudinally at 12, 24, and 26 months. Follow-up results for 113 of the infants were reported by Thompson,

Fagan, and Fulker (1991). The follow-up tests allowed novelty preference to be compared not only to later IQ, but to later language and specific cognitive skills. A composite novelty score formed from 10 items administered across the 5- and 7-month-old test sessions was significantly correlated with Binet IQ at 36 months of age was not related to Bayley MDI scores at 12 and 24 months of age. Interestingly, novelty preference related more strongly to later Language, Verbal, and Memory tests than to Spatial Ability and Perceptual Speed. The results suggest that infant novelty preference relates to receptive language and memory skills as well as general intelligence. However, the complexity of the cognitive processes involved in the infant and early childhood measures may be too great to paint a clear picture in terms of continuity in information processing. For example, early language skills may represent specific processing skills that are also important for infant visual novelty preference performance. Conversely, early language ability may be a strong indicator of general intelligence. In other words, if novelty preference is determined by "g", then the strength of the correlation between novelty preference and later tests will be determined by their "g" loadings. However, the relationship between novelty preference and later memory ability appears to support the theory that novelty preference may represent a subset of cognitive processing abilities. Unfortunately, subject recruitment ended in the CAP in 1985 limiting the sample size for the early infancy measure.

The interesting results generated in the CAP involving infant novelty preference prompted the development of the Colorado Infant Twin Project (DiLalla et al., 1990). The study began in 1985 and currently involves over 200 pairs of infant twins and their parents. The primary goal of the study was to identify infant measures that are predictive of adult intelligence through the use of a midparent/midtwin design. In terms of additive genetic variance, the midparent (the average of both parents' IQ scores) to offspring correlation is the same as the longitudinal correlation for the same individual tested in infancy and in adulthood. Therefore, the design is like an "instant" longitudinal study and allows immediate validation of the infant measures. Using a midtwin score (the average of both twins' test scores) rather than a single offspring's score increases the reliability of the infant measure, similar to testing the same individual twice. An added advantage of the twin design is that estimates of heritability and shared family environmental influences can also be calculated for all of the infant measures. The twins have also been followed longitudinally; thus, further testing both the predictive validities of the measures and the power of the midparent/midtwin design as a longitudinal model.

Each of the infant measures used in the TIP was selected to be predictive of later intelligence as indicated by previous developmental research. Twins were tested at 7 and 9 months corrected age in their homes on a 1.5-hour battery of tests summarized in Table 3.3.

When the infants were 8 months corrected age, families were tested at the Institute for Behavioral Genetics where infants received a test of visual expectations developed by Haith (Haith, Hazen, & Goodman, 1988). Haith's measure allows the assessment of both a complex visual attention measure—the anticipation of stimulus location—and a relatively simple cognitive processing measure—reaction time. During this visit, parents were also tested. They were

Table 3.3.  Summary of Infant Measures from the Colorado
Infant Twin Project

| Test | Description | Measure |
|---|---|---|
| Fagan Test of Infant Intelligence (Fagan & Shepherd, 1986) | | |
| Immediate: | 10 novelty preference problems | Mean Novelty Preference |
| Delayed Fagan: | same 10 novelty problems, 30 minutes later using 50 percent of the original familiarization times | Mean Delayed Novelty Preference |
| Lateralization: | | |
| Forced choice of hand | 6 trials retrieving a toy through a hole in a shield | Hand Preference |
| Reaching | 6 trials reaching for a toy placed on a tray | Hand Preference |
| Holding (adapted from Caplan & Kinsbourne, 1976) | two identical toys placed in each hand, length of holding time recorded for each hand | Holding Ratio |
| Orientations | videotape of infant's response to an audiotape of 10 different sounds (dog bark, car horn, etc.) | Percent Trials Oriented |
| Vocalizations: | | |
| tester rating | tester records number of different syllable sounds emitted during the test session | Number of Different Vocalizations |
| Bayley Items: (Bayley, 1969) | | |
| bell | infant responds to a bell ring | Pass/Fail |
| rattle | infant responds to a rattle | Pass/Fail |
| mirror | infant responds to mirror image | Pass/Fail |
| paper play | infant manipulates paper | Pass/Fail |
| Bayley's Infant Behavior Record (Bayley, 1969) | tester rating of infant's test-taking behaviors | Composites representing: Affect/Extraversion, Activity & Task Orientation |
| Visual Expectation (Haith, Hazen & Goodman, Reaction 1988) | videotape of the infant's eye movements in response to a right-left alternating stimulus | Baseline Time, Percent Anticipation, Shift between Targets |

administered the Wechsler Adult Intelligence Scale (WAIS) and a shortened version of the CAP adult battery of specific cognitive abilities (DeFries, Plomin, Vandenberg, & Kuse, 1981). The parental measures provided two indices of general cognitive ability, WAIS IQ and the first unrotated principal component from the CAP battery (CAP IQ). Lengthy descriptions of each of the infant measures will not be given, but can be found in the report by DiLalla et al. (1990).

Midparent/midtwin analyses are available for 208 twin pairs. Each of the infant measures in the form of a mean twin score was regressed onto mean parental WAIS IQ and CAP IQ. Eighteen of the 62 regressions were significant at the 5 percent level and 54 were positive. The best predictors were the FTII, Haiths's Visual Expectation Test, Vocalizations and the IBR scales. Table 3.4 summarizes the results for these predictive measures.

Table 3.4 also presents the correlations between the infant tests and IQ at 3 years of age. The best predictors of parental IQ were also predictive of 3-year-old Binet IQ; thus, verifying the predictive power of the measures and of the midparent/midtwin approach. The infant measures were also entered into a multivariate stepwise regression to predict later IQ and parental IQ. The intercorrelations among the predictors were in general low but two interesting clusters

**Table 3.4.   Midparent/midtwin regressions and longitudinal midtwin correlations between infant measures and IQ**

| | Midparent | | Midtwin |
|---|---|---|---|
| Infant Measure | WAIS IQ (N) | General Intelligence (N) | 3-Year Binet (N) |
| Fagan Test of Infant Intelligence | | | |
| Composite of 7 and 9 month | .24* | .22* | .32* |
| | (200) | (200) | (51) |
| Visual Expectation Test | | | |
| Baseline Reaction Time | .17* | .18* | .47* |
| | (110) | (110) | (33) |
| Percent Shifts Between Targets | .24* | .20* | .29* |
| | (135) | (135) | (36) |
| Vocalizations | | | |
| 7 months | .17* | .13* | -.28* |
| | (175) | (175) | (40) |
| 9 months | .19* | .10 | .17 |
| | (177) | (177) | (44) |
| Infant Behavior Record at 9 months | | | |
| Affect/Extraversion | .20* | .07 | .30* |
| | (194) | (194) | (51) |
| Task Orientation | .19* | .08 | .28* |
| | (194) | (194) | (51) |

*$p < .05$
Adapted from DiLalla et al. (1990).

emerged. The FTII and Visual Expectation Test measures correlated among themselves and the Vocalization and IBR measures formed the second cluster. The two clusters were not correlated with each other. This clustering may indicate that infant intelligence has two important areas. The first area may represent information-processing skills and the second area may reflect temperamental qualities that mediate the infant's interactions with the environment. Additional research is needed to explore this idea.

As mentioned earlier, the use of the twin design allows the estimation of genetic and environmental influences on the infant measures. These analyses are in progress for the current sample in the TIP. However, preliminary analyses (Thompson, 1989) indicated higher estimates of heritability were operating on infant information-processing measures than had been found previously with conventional infant cognitive tests. A model-fitting analysis describing these results will be presented later in this chapter.

## CHILDHOOD

Dramatic changes in cognitive behavior occur as the infant becomes a child. Intelligence tests administered during early childhood finally begin to resemble adult intelligence tests; the predictive power of the tests begin to reach acceptable levels by the age of 3 years. Both twin and adoption studies suggest that genetic influences play an increasingly important role from the transition into childhood through the early school years.

### General Cognitive Ability

*Twin and sibling studies.* The Louisville Twin Study again presents the most complete data set for the development of general cognitive ability during childhood (Wilson, 1983). The twin correlations are presented for every year separately from age 3 to age 9. The Stanford-Binet is administered at age 3, the Wechsler Preschool and Primary Scale of Intelligence at ages 4, 5, and 6, and the Wechsler Intelligence Scale for Children (WISC) at age 7, 8, and 9. Figure 3.2 illustrates the twin and sibling correlations; the picture is striking in that the identical twin correlations remain stable and very high (.83—.88) across the 6-year period while the fraternal twin correlations systematically drop from a high of .79 at 3 years to about the same level as the sibling correlations by age 7. This pattern of correlations, an increase in the difference between identical and fraternal twin correlations, yields an increase in the estimate of heritability. In fact, by age 7 the twin correlations produce an estimate of .50 which is similar in magnitude to estimates from adult twin data. The sibling correlations over the same time period increase from .38 to .55. At ages 8 and 9, the fraternal twin correlations rise again slightly, although not significantly, perhaps reflecting the impact of the early school years.

Correlation

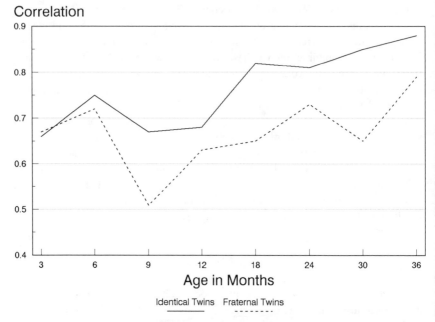

Age in Months

Identical Twins    Fraternal Twins

**Figure 3.2.    Louisville Twin Study longitudinal correlations
Data from Wilson, 1983.**

Additional twin and sibling studies are presented in Table 3.5. The four twin studies report twin data for large age ranges as opposed to separate ages; thus, clouding the developmental picture somewhat. Koch (1966) used the Primary Mental Abilities test and Segal (1985) used the WISC-R; both studies indicate substantial genetic influences. The other two studies (Garfinkle & Vandenberg, 1981; Foch & Plomin, 1980) use the Raven's Progressive Matrices test and suggest very little or no genetic influence. Plomin (1986) cautions, however, that the age-corrected Raven's scores have low reliability and may attenuate the twin correlations.

Thompson, Detterman, and Plomin (1992) report on the Western Reserve Twin Project which includes 148 identical and 135 fraternal twin ranging in age from 6 to 12. For a composite measure of general cognitive ability, heritability is estimated at .50 and shared environment at .42. These estimates seem to agree quite well with the LTS, thus, lending further support to the idea that early school environment may be affecting twin resemblance.

Studies including both related and unrelated siblings are also reported in Table 3.5. The earliest studies report data from unrelated sibling pairs only. Freeman et al. (1928) and Leahy (1935) report correlations of .25 and .08 respectively. The Freeman, Holzinger, and Mitchell correlation may be larger because of the substantial selective placement that was operating in that study. Two more recent studies (Scarr & Weinberg, 1977; Horn, Loehlin, & Willerman, 1979) report similar results for related and unrelated sibling pairs that suggest the importance

Table 3.5.   Summary of Twin and Sibling Studies of Childhood IQ

| | | Correlation | | | |
|---|---|---|---|---|---|
| Study | Age | Identical Twins | Fraternal Twins | Related Siblings | Unrelated Siblings |
| Freeman, Holzinger, & Mitchell (1928) | 2–22 | | | | .25 (112) |
| Leahy (1935) | 5–14 | | | | .08 (35) |
| Koch (1966) | 5–8 | .79 (35) | .45 (36) | | |
| Scarr & Weinberg (1977) | 4–16 | | | .42 (107) | .33 (187) |
| Horn, Loehlin, & Willerman (1979) | 3–26 | | | .35 (40) | .26 (236) |
| Foch & Plomin (1980) | 6–9 | .26 (51) | .44 (33) | | |
| Garfinkle & Vanderberg (1981) | 4–7 | .57 (137) | .48 (72) | | |
| Wilson (1983) | 3 | .88 (104) | .79 (125) | .38 (74) | |
| | 4 | .83 (105) | .71 (120) | .45 (61) | |
| | 5 | .85 (129) | .66 (131) | .56 (88) | |
| | 6 | .86 (139) | .59 (141) | .54 (110) | |
| | 7 | .84 (116) | .59 (119) | .55 (45) | |
| | 8 | .83 (146) | .66 (138) | .44 (126) | |
| | 9 | .83 (85) | .65 (86) | .53 (58) | |
| Segal (1985) | 5–13 | .85 (69) | .42 (35) | | |
| Plomin, DeFries, & Fulker (1988) | 3 | | | .35 (54) | .32 (50) |
| | 4 | | | .24 (43) | .23 (43) |

of both genes and shared family environment. However, the age ranges in these studies
were again quite large, limiting the developmental interpretation of the results. Finally, the most recent report on siblings in the CAP (Plomin, DeFries, & Fulker, 1988) suggest little genetic influence at ages 3 and 4, but significant genetic influence at ages 1 and 2 (see Table 3.1). Taken at face value these results appear to be in direct contradiction to the twin results. However, the differences may at least be partially explained by several factors. First, the CAP sibling sample is small and may not be able to reliably detect the modest level of genetic influence at this age. Data from the LTS yield heritability estimates of only .18–.24 at ages 3 and 4. Second, infant twin data may be particularly sensitive to the shared effects of perinatal factors, thus, increasing early twin resemblance for identical and fraternal twins alike. Sibling relationships would not be affected in this manner.

*Adoption studies.* Turning now to parent/offspring comparisons from adoption studies, Table 3.6 presents a summary of all adoption studies where actual IQ was assessed in the parents. The Skodak and Skeels (1949) study that directly assessed the biological mother/adoptive child relationship agrees with the results from the twin studies that suggest an increase in genetic influence from early to middle childhood. With the exception of the Freeman et al. (1928) study, the early adoption studies concur that genetic influences are in part mediating the relationships between child and adult IQ. Again, the Freeman et al. results must be interpreted with caution due to substantial selective placement.

The more recent studies, particularly the Texas Adoption Project (TAP; Horn et al., 1979; Horn, 1983) and the Colorado Adoption Project (CAP; Plomin & DeFries, 1985; Phillips & Fulker, 1989) clearly suggest the importance of genetic influences. The CAP also shows a definite trend for an increase in genetic influences from age 3 to age 7 where the biological mother/adoptive offspring correlation rises from .18 to .37. However, both the TAP and the CAP report nonadoptive parent/offspring correlations that are lower than the biological parent/offspring estimate that does not logically follow genetic "rules." Plomin (1986) discusses several possibilities for these results including genotype-environment correlation and chance. Currently the issue is not resolved and more research, particularly on the effects of the environment is required.

In summary, twin and adoption studies generally indicate that genetic influences are important for childhood intelligence. Furthermore, the few studies that provide data points separately by age suggest strongly that genetic influences increase from early to middle childhood. The developmental process will be further explored in a later section of this chapter.

## Specific Cognitive Abilities and Information Processing

Behavior geneticists have also begun to explore aspects of intelligence not sufficiently captured by one global index or IQ. Are specific intellectual abilities influenced differently by genetic and environmental factors? The answer to this

Table 3.6.  Summary of Adoption Studies of Childhood IQ

| Study | Age | Biological Mothers | Adoptive Parents | Nonadoptive Parents |
|---|---|---|---|---|
| Burks (1928) | 5–14 | | .13 (200) | .46 (100) |
| Freeman, Holzinger, & Mitchell (1928) | 2–22 | | .32 (255) | .27 (40) |
| Leahy (1935) | 5–14 | | .14 (194) | .46 (194) |
| Snygg (1938) | 3–5+ | .11 (300) | | |
| Skodak & Skeels (1949) | 4 | .28 (63) | | |
| | 7 | .35 (63) | | |
| Fisch, Deinard, & Chang (1976) | 4 | | .07 (94) | .35 (50) |
| | 7 | | .08 (94) | .26 (50) |
| Scarr & Weinberg (1977) | 4–16+ | | .19 (111) | .37 (142) |
| Horn, Loehlin, & Willerman (1979) Horn (1983) | 5–7 | .36 (169) | | |
| | 5–9 | | .15 (188) | .20 (66) |
| Plomin & DeFries (1985) | 3 | .18 (186) | .15 (186) | .14 (151) |
| | 4 | .22 (162) | .15 (162) | .15 (138) |

| | | Biological | Adoptive | | Nonadoptive | |
|---|---|---|---|---|---|---|
| | | mother | mother | father | mother | father |
| Phillips & Fuller (1989) | 7 | .37 (139) | −.05 (139) | .11 (136) | .17 (137) | .17 (138) |

question during the infancy period was no, as discussed earlier. However, measurement limitations are not as severe in childhood, and differences begin to emerge.

Very few behavioral genetic studies of childhood have used tests designed to assess specific cognitive abilities. For the most part, subtest scores from IQ tests have been used to represent specific skills. Mittler (1969) presented twin correlations for subtests of the Illinois Test of Psycholinguistic Abilities. The sample consisted of 28 pairs of identical twins and 64 pairs of fraternal twins; all were

4-year-olds. Mittler interpreted the results as indicating greater genetic influence for visual and motor channels, and less genetic influence for auditory and vocal channels. Plomin (1986) however, suggests that the results indicate that verbal measures show substantial genetic influence and memory measures show very little genetic effects. Another study reported by Munsinger and Douglass (1976) also found substantial genetic influence on childhood verbal measures. Plomin and Vandenberg (1980) reanalyzed data from Koch (1966) consisting of twin correlations for the Primary Abilities Subtests scores. All four scales—Verbal, Perceptual, Quantitative, and Spatial—showed significant genetic influences.

Three twin studies have been reported for Wechsler subtests. A summary of the estimates of heritability and shared family environment are reported in Table 3.7. In general, genetic influences appear to be important for the majority of the subtests, particularly verbal subtests, across all three studies. The magnitude of the estimates vary a great deal, however, across studies and subtests. For the most part, the Wilson (1975) study indicates greater estimates of shared family environment. The Segal (1985) study suggests higher genetic influences. The LaBuda, De Fries, and Fulker (1987) study yields lower genetic influences than does Segal, but for the most part shows negligible effects of shared environment, thus implicating nonshared or specific environmental influences. The differences

Table 3.7.  Summary of estimates of genetic and shared family environmental influences on Wechsler subtests from childhood twin studies ($h^2$ = heritability and $c^2$ = shared family environment)

| | | Studies | | | | |
|---|---|---|---|---|---|---|
| | | Wilson (1975)[a] | | Segal (1985)[a] | | Labuda, DeFries, & Fulker (1987)[b] |
| | N | (50 MZ, 34 DZ) | | (69 MZ, 35 DZ) | | (79 MZ, 64 DZ) |
| Subtest | | WPPSI $h^2$ | $c^2$ | WISC-R $h^2$ | $c^2$ | WISC-R $h^2$ | $c$ |
| Information | | .60 | .21 | .82 | .00 | .54 | .1 |
| Similarities | | .31 | .43 | .94 | .00 | .33 | .1 |
| Arithmetic | | .26 | .39 | .80 | .00 | .43 | .0 |
| Vocabulary | | .42 | .29 | .72 | .06 | .51 | .1 |
| Comprehension | | .36 | .44 | .44 | .21 | .29 | .0 |
| Picture Completion | | .86 | .00 | .00 | .32 | .25 | .1 |
| Block Design | | .50 | .18 | .84 | .00 | .24 | .4 |
| Picture Arrangement | | — | — | .16 | .17 | .26 | .1 |
| Object Assembly | | — | — | .68 | .00 | .15 | .2 |
| Coding | | — | — | .56 | .12 | .47 | .2 |
| Animal House | | .84 | .00 | — | — | — | — |
| Mazes | | .32 | .29 | — | — | — | — |
| Geometric Design | | .94 | .00 | — | — | — | — |

[a]Estimates based on twin correlations reported in the studies.
[b]Actual estimates reported in the study.

across studies may be a reflection of the slightly different age groups represented; Wilson had 5- and 6-year-olds, Segal had 5- to 13-year-olds with an average age of 8, and LaBuda et al. had 7- to 16-year-olds with an average age of 12.5. Perhaps the effect of shared family environment decreases as children begin their formal education, and nonshared family environmental influences increase as children become adolescents. A longitudinal study across this entire age range is required to plot the yearly changes in the proportion of genetic and environmental estimates.

Three twin studies have been reported where tests of specific cognitive abilities were used. Foch and Plomin (1980) studied 51 pairs of identical and 33 pairs of fraternal 5- to 12-year-old twins (average age was 7.5). Surprisingly, the study found little genetic influence; verbal and spatial measures indicated slight genetic effects while perceptual speed and memory showed no genetic influence. Developmental changes in genetic and environmental influences were also examined in this sample (Ho, Foch, & Plomin, 1980) but little evidence for change was found. Genetic and environmental contributions remained relatively stable across the age range represented in the study. A separate study of 4- to 7-year-old twins (Garfinkle & Vandenberg, 1981) also found evidence for genetic influences on verbal but not memory tests. Perceptual speed and spatial ability were not measured in this study.

In contrast to the other two studies, the third study (Thompson, Detterman, & Plomin, 1990) found significant genetic influences for four specific cognitive ability scales, Verbal, Spatial, Perceptual Speed and Memory. The twins in this analysis were 7- to 12-year-olds with an average age of 9.8, who were administered a battery of specific cognitive abilities tests taken from the adult and childhood battery used in the CAP. Each scale used in the analysis was formed by summing two standardized age and sex-corrected test scores. Table 3.8 summarizes the findings. Although Memory shows the least amount of genetic influence, Spatial ability provides the highest estimate of heritability. Shared family environment does not appear to be important for these measures.

**Table 3.8.** **Estimates of genetic and shared family environmental influences for childhood specific cognitive abilities**
($h^2$ = heritability and $c^2$ = shared family environment)

| Study | Age | Verbal $h^2$ | Verbal $c^2$ | Spatial $h^2$ | Spatial $c^2$ | Perceptual Speed $h^2$ | Perceptual Speed $c^2$ | Memory $h^2$ | Memory $c^2$ |
|---|---|---|---|---|---|---|---|---|---|
| Thompson, Detterman & Plomin (1989) | 7–12 | .48 | .12 | .75 | .03 | .60 | .11 | .41 | .02 |
| Cyphers, Fulker, Plomin, & DeFries (1989) | 3 | .35 | .06 | .40 | .02 | .26 | .03 | .33 | −.02 |
| | 4 | .16 | .11 | .48 | −.01 | .48 | −.05 | .00 | .01 |
| | 7 | .50 | −.02 | .50 | −.02 | .30 | .00 | .31 | .02 |

Adoption data from the CAP involving a similar battery of tests were reported for 3-, 4- and 7-year-old adoptive and nonadoptive children (Cyphers, Fulker, Plomin & DeFries, 1989), The results, which are also reported in Table 3.8, were fairly consistent across the three ages; genetic influences were important for Verbal and Spatial abilities but not for Perceptual Speed and Memory. Shared family environment was not important for any of the abilities.

As cognitive psychologists have turned to information-processing theory to further understand intelligence, behavioral geneticists have begun to explore this area of individual differences as well. To date, there is only one childhood twin study of information processing available, but more are sure to follow in the near future. Thirty pairs of identical and 30 pairs of fraternal twins ranging in age from 8 to 18 years of age (Ho, Baker, & Decker, 1988) received four Rapid Automatic Naming tests and two Colorado Perceptual Speed tests; both sets of tests are thought to measure speed of information processing. A factor analysis yielded two factors, Rapid Automatic Naming (RAN) and Symbol Processing Speed (SPS). The results from this study found significant genetic influence on both the RAN and SPS variables ($h^2$ = .52 and .49 respectively). common environmental influences were important only for the SPS variable ($c^2$ = .28).

In summary, behavioral genetic research on specific cognitive abilities during childhood suggest that genetic influences are important, especially for Verbal and Spatial abilities. Some of the discrepancies across studies may be due to developmental changes that either reflect actual maturational change in the etiology of different abilities or maturational influences on the emergence of distinct abilities. A third possibility may be due to the adequacy of the measures used to index abilities; Verbal and Spatial measures may be more accurate and reliable than traditional measures of Memory and Speed of Processing. Further studies looking at age to age changes are required to disentangle these possibilities.

## Scholastic Achievement

Starting school is a highly significant life event for a young child. School performance in this society is highly valued. Understanding genetic and environmental influences on achievement may have important implications for education. However, very few behavior genetic studies of scholastic achievement have been conducted for the early school years. An early study (Hildreth, 1925) found sibling correlations of .65 and .58 for IQ and achievement, respectively, in one study, and .31 and .42 in another study. Sibling relationships, however, are due to the combined effects of genetic and environmental influences.

A recent report (Thompson, Detterman, & Plomin, 1991) examined achievement scores for 146 pairs of identical twins and 132 pairs of fraternal twins. The twin correlations for Reading, Math, and Language scores yield heritability estimates of .27, .17 and .19 and shared family environment estimates of .66, .73 and .65 respectively. Unlike specific cognitive abilities, achievement tests show substantial shared family environmental influences. The results from this study are preliminary but the results are important because they suggest that scholastic achievement may be more sensitive to aspects of the common family environment than are cognitive abilities.

In the same twin sample, Petrill and Thompson (1992) analyzed the achievement measures for differential contributions of genetic and environmental influences on achievement across gender. The overall pattern of findings was one of higher heritabilities in females and higher shared environmental influences in males. The effect was consistent across all measures except mathematics in two separate achievement test batteries (Wide Range Achievement Test and the Metropolitan Achievement Test; MAT); however, it only reached significance for the MAT reading scale. One possible explanation for this effect is the finding that teachers pay more attention to boys in the classroom (Sadker & Sadker, 1985). Boys, in general, demand and receive much more feedback from teachers than girls; thus, teachers may be creating a source of environmental variance that girls do not experience.

### Reading Disability and Mental Retardation

Most behavioral genetic research on intellectual development has focused on normal development. Recently, however, researchers have begun to assess the etiology of disorders using behavioral genetic approaches. Typically, pathology (presence or absence of) is a categorical variable and can only be analyzed in terms of identical and fraternal twin concordance rates. However, when a disorder can be measured as a continuous variable, more informative analyses can be conducted. A multiple regression analysis of selected twin data proposed by DeFries and Fulker (1985) has been used in a study of reading disability and a study of mental retardation with interesting results.

A sample of 64 identical and 55 fraternal twins where at least one member of each pair was classified as reading-disabled by the following: a score of at least 90 on either the Verbal or Performance subscales for the WISC-R, no evidence of neurological problems and designation as affected through a discriminant function analysis which included scores on three subtests of the PIAT (Reading Recognition, Reading Comprehension, and Spelling), the WISC-R Coding-B and Digit Span subtests, and the Colorado Perceptual Speed test (DeFries, Fulker, & LaBuda, 1987). A matched control group of 45 identical and 33 fraternal twin pairs were also included in the analyses.

The reading-disabled probands had mean reading scores of more than a standard deviation below the population mean. If genetic influences contribute to reading ability, then the cotwins of the probands in identical twins pairs should score more poorly than the cotwins of probands in fraternal twins pairs. If genetic influences are not important, then cotwins in both identical and fraternal pairs should show similar levels of reading skill. In regression terms, identical cotwins should show less regression to the mean of the general population then fraternal cotwins if the disorder is heritable. Further analyses comparing the control twins with the affected twins allow the hypothesis of differential genetic and environmental influences across groups to be tested.

The multiple regression analysis indicated quite strongly that reading disability has a genetic etiology. About 30% of the reading deficit in the probands can be attributed to heritable factors. In an earlier report (LaBuda, DeFries, & Fulker, 1986), shared family environment was not significant for either group of twins. There was also no evidence for differential contributions of heritability and shared family environment operating across the reading disabled and control groups. However, the sample may still be too small to reliably detect modest group differences and the authors plan to test the hypothesis of differential heritability further as the sample grows.

Several recent papers from the Colorado Reading Project have explored genetic and environmental influences on the covariance of specific cognitive processes and reading ability. Using the multiple regresssion approach developed by DeFries and Fulker (1985), Olson, Wise, Conners, Rack, and Fulker (1989) analyzed phonological and orthographic coding deficits in a sample of twins selected for deficits in reading recognition. The bivariate heritability estimate for phonological coding was .93, and the estimate for orthographic coding was a nonsignificant $-.16$. These findings indicate that virtually the same genetic factors are affecting deficits on reading recognition and phonological coding, and deficits on the orthographic coding measure are largely due to environmental influences.

Forsberg and Olson (1992) explore the possible pathways of genetic influence on the phonological-decoding deficits found in the Colorado Reading Project. When the proband was selected for scoring 1.5 standard deviations and below on a variety of nonreading performance measures, the co-twins' phonological decoding was observed for differential regression to the population mean for MZ and DZ twin pairs. Significant genetic covariation was found between phonological-decoding deficits and phoneme segmentation, phoneme deletion, rapid naming, WISC-R digit span, and verbal tests from the WISC-R. Significant shared-environment covariation was found by rhyme generation.

Wadsworth, DeFries, Pennington, and Olson (1992) found that approximately 80% of the relationship between reading ability and verbal short-term memory is due to common genetic influences in the Colorado Reading Project. Furthermore, they applied reciprocal causation analyses and determined that differences in reading performance caused differences in verbal short-term memory.

In a twin study of cognition, the multiple regression technique outlined above was used to explore the genetic etiology of mental abilities, in particular, mental retardation (Thompson, Detterman, & Plomin, 1992). The study included 148 pairs of identical twins and 135 pairs of fraternal twins. The twins all received a large battery of intelligence and achievement tests and the first unrotated principal component of these tests was used to represent general cognitive ability.

One of the main goals of this study was to oversample at the high and low ends of the ability distribution. Special attention was paid to locating twin pairs where one or both members were mentally retarded. The total sample was double-entered and the lowest-scoring member of each pair was designated as the proband. The results indicate that cognitive ability has higher heritability for high ability groups, and lower heritability for the low ability groups. Shared family environment also lessens in importance as ability level increases. However, the authors urge caution in interpreting the results because the sample is still relatively small. If the results are replicated, it is clear that they may have important implications for theory and practice in education and psychology.

## MODELS OF DEVELOPMENT

This chapter has thus far outlined genetic and environmental contributions to individual differences in intellectual functioning during infancy and childhood. However, the results have been presented at separate ages or summarized across ages painting a static picture of individual differences. The appeal of developmental behavioral genetics is the dynamic nature of the approach. Delineating and dissecting behavioral changes and continuities across development will provide a more accurate and complete picture of the complexities involved. In this section empirical examples of genetic continuity and change, genetic correlations, and cross-domain relationships will be explored.

### Genetic Continuity

Twin data can estimate heritability and the effect of environmental influences at specific ages. Profile analyses from the LTS have illustrated the usefulness of longitudinal twin data for outlining continuities and changes across the period of infancy in terms of genetic influences. Parent/offspring adoption data provide estimates of genetic and environmental continuity from infancy to adulthood. As shown in the previous section each of these correlational analyses has been informative. However, a model-fitting procedure involving maximum-likelihood estimation would allow the twin and adoption data to be analyzed simultaneously, and would have greater power to detect relationships. Furthermore, model-fitting approaches require explicit specification of the genetic model and also allow alternative models to be accepted or rejected by comparing differences in goodness-of-fit estimates. DeFries, Plomin, and LaBuda (1987) developed a model that allows the simultaneous analysis of twin and adoption data.

The DeFries et al. model is primarily concerned with estimating the extent to which stability in cognitive development is determined genetically. Central to genetic stability is the concept of the genetic correlation (Plomin, 1986). A genetic correlation represents the overlap in genetic variance for the same trait at two different ages. For instance, in the case of the biological parent/adopted infant comparison, phenotypic (observed) resemblance requires that the trait be genetically influenced both in infancy and in adulthood, and that some of the same genetic influences be operating at both ages. Therefore, the phenotypic correlation between a biological parent and their adopted away offspring can be expressed as follows:

$$r_{pc} = .5h_c h_a r_G,$$

where $r_{pc}$ is the parent/offspring correlation, $h_c$ and $h_a$ are the square root of heritability in childhood and adulthood, respectively, and $r_G$ is the genetic correlation from childhood to adulthood. Figure 3.3 illustrates the biological parent/offspring relationship assuming a genetic correlation of one on the left and allowing for genetic change on the right. To the extent that the genetic correlation is less than one, genetic change is implied. As can be seen from the third equation, the phenotypic correlation could be relatively small and the amount of genetic overlap ($r_G$) could still be substantial. Similarly, genetic influences operating in childhood could be minimal but if the same genes are influential in

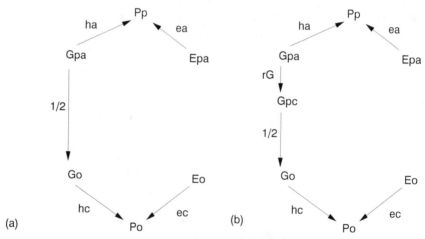

**Figure 3.3.    Path diagrams illustrating genetic continuity and genetic change.**

(a) Assumes that the genetic correlation is equal to 1, the same genes are influencing the trait in adulthood and in childhood.
(b) Allows for genetic change to be operating by estimating the genetic correlation ($r_G$). $P_p$, $P_O$ = phenotypes of the parent and child; $G_{Pa}$, $G_{Pc}$, $G_O$ = genotypes of the parent as an adult and as a child and of the offspring; $E_{Pa}$, $E_O$ = environments of the parent and of the child; $h_a$, $h_c$ = square root of the heritability of the trait in adulthood and in childhood; $e_a$, $e_c$ = path coefficients for the effect of the environment in adulthood and in childhood; ½ = the degree of genetic resemblance between a single parent and their offspring in the absence of assorative mating; $r_G$ = genetic correlation between the trait in adulthood and in childhood.

adulthood, the genetic correlation would be quite large. For example, the reported correlation between biological parents general cognitive ability and their adopted-away infants' Bayley scores is around .10 (Plomin & DeFries, 1985). Infant twin data from the LTS yield an estimate of about .15 for the heritability of Bayley scores. Adult twin data estimate the heritability of adult IQ to be about .50. Using these estimates in the third equation provides an estimate for the genetic correlation between infant Bayley scores and adult IQ of .75 (DeFries, Plomin, & LaBuda, 1987). Although genetic correlations can be simply estimated from the third equation, the equation does not allow for either assortative mating or selective placement, both of which if significant would have a large impact on the results.

The DeFries et al. model is applied to Bayley MDI scores from the LTS (Wilson, 1983) and the CAP for ages 1–4 years, to CAP parental general cognitive ability, and to published adult twin correlations (.86 and .62 for adult identical and fraternal twins, respectively; Loehlin & Nichols, 1976). The model provides a through test of the twin and adoption data in that genetic correlations are modeled explicitly, the effects of both assortative mating and selective placement are accounted for, and a parameter for special twin environmental effects is provided.

Table 3.9 summarizes their results, selective placement is negligible at all four ages, as is the impact of shared environmental influences as transmitted from parents to offspring. However, shared twin environment does have a large impact on twin similarity for cognitive development during the first four years. In other words, contemporaneous experiences and age-linked events play an important role for twin similarity early in life. Heritability estimates increase with age from .10 at age one to .26 at four years of age. The estimate of genetic stability, the genetic correlation parameter, also increases with age, .67, .85, .79, and .90 at ages 1–4, respectively. However, when the significance of the parameter estimates are tested through a series of reduced models, the goodness-

**Table 3.9.    Summary of the parameter estimates for genetic stability in cognitive development in the CAP**

| | Childrens' Age in Years | | | |
| Parameter | 1 | 2 | 3 | 4 |
|---|---|---|---|---|
| assortative mating | .22 ± .05 | .20 ± .05 | .22 ± .05 | .23 ± .06 |
| special environment (adult twins) | .83 ± .02 | .83 ± .02 | .82 ± .03 | .82 ± .03 |
| special environment (child twins) | .80 ± .03 | .87 ± .02 | .91 ± .01 | .87 ± .02 |
| adult heritabilities | .74 ± .04 | .73 ± .04 | .74 ± .04 | .74 ± .04 |
| child heritabilities | .32 ± .25 | .41 ± .11 | .43 ± .07 | .51 ± .09 |
| genetic correlations | .42 ± .50 | .61 ± .33 | .56 ± .28 | .75 ± .27 |

Adapted from DeFries et al. (1987).

of-fit does not change appreciably when heritability and the genetic correlation are dropped at one year of age, thus indicating that genetic influences are not significant for Bayley MDI scores during the first year of life.

The overall results from the DeFries et al. model-fitting analysis are striking in that substantial genetic stability is found to be operating for cognitive ability from the age of two years on into adulthood. It appears as if many of the same genes that are acting on cognitive development during the latter part of infancy and on into early childhood are also important for cognitive ability in adulthood; yet, heritability is low during infancy and increases with age. Are these results theoretically compatible? DeFries and Plomin (Plomin, 1986; Plomin & DeFries, 1985) propose an amplification model for cognitive development. The model predicts that the effects of a set of genes acting in infancy play a cumulative, increasingly important role across age, Genetic effects create relatively small differences in infancy that become magnified with age. The amplification model also appears to explain physical development and possibly some aspects of temperament as well (Plomin, 1986).

Results from the Texas Adoption Study also support the amplification model. Children were originally tested when they were 3 to 14 years old (Horn et al., 1979). Ten years later, 258 adopted children and 93 biological children from 181 families were tested again. IQ scores were available for the biological mothers and the adoptive parents. Loehlin, Horn, and Willerman (1989) used a model-fitting approach to determine if genetic and environmental influences increased, decreased, or remained stable across development. The model included estimates of assortative mating, selective placement, genotype-environment correlations, and a measure of socioeconomic status. The model-fitting results fit nicely with the results obtained by DeFries et al. The effect of shared family environment decreased with age and changes in genetic expression appeared to continue throughout adolescence. Unfortunately, because a wide range of ages were included, it is not possible to accurately determine the ages at which the greatest amount of change occurs. As Loehlin points out, the results go against many commonly held notions, namely that genes are operating at birth and environmental influences increase and accumulate with age. The results from the two studies just described suggest that just the opposite is true.

Eaves, Long, and Heath (1986) propose a model that describes development in terms of genetic and environmental effects that either remain constant over time or are occasion-specific. The model accounts for the cumulative impact of the phenotype at each age on the subsequent phenotype while allowing for additional genetic and environmental factors to come into play at each age. The model can test various hypotheses about the course of development. Eaves et al. explain that different longitudinal patterns of correlations among relatives can imply the nature of gene and environment action. For instance, if the same genetic effects are persistent and cumulative over time, heritability will increase and environmental effects will diminish. Conversely, in a model where environmental effects are made continuous and cumulative, genetic effects may decrease. Twin data from the LTS was fit to The Eaves et al. model and they conclude that continuity in cognitive development and increasing heritability reflect the action of a single set of genes throughout development, and that shared family environmental influences change over time but have a some degree of lasting effect on cognitive development; however, development, in this study, has the upper limit of 15 years of age. Several previous studies have suggested that during late adolescence the effect of shared family environment decreases sharply (Loehlin, Willerman, & Horn, 1988). The Eaves et al. results support the results obtained with the models previously discussed (DeFries et al., 1987; Loehlin, Horn, & Willerman, 1989).

At a practical level, substantial genetic stability from infancy to adulthood seems counterintuitive. After all, the behaviors involved in cognition differ dramatically across development. Genetic stability does not necessarily assume isomorphism for the cognitive processes involved. The genetic effects in infancy and in adulthood may be manifested as different behaviors. DeFries and Plomin give as an example, "For instance, 'childhood genes' might affect rate of language acquisition, whereas 'adult genes' might affect symbolic reasoning." However, it is also possible that the same basic processes are involved while the level of measurement differs. As discussed earlier, new measures of infant visual attention provide an excellent example of this alternative explanation.

The DeFries et al. paper did not find evidence for genetic effects on Bayley MDI scores during the first year of life. Would a different pattern of results emerge if predictively valid measures of infant intelligence were used instead? Infant 7- and 9-month-old visual novelty preference and parental general cognitive ability scores from a combination of 41 adoptive, 95 nonadoptive families, and 83 twin families was analyzed with an adaptation of the DeFries et al. model (Thompson, 1989). Although the analyses are preliminary due to the small sample sizes involved, the results are promising. Heritability estimates for visual novelty preference during he first year of life greatly exceed the estimates previously found for Bayley MDI scores and estimates of shared family environment as well as special twin environment are low. A moderate estimate for the genetic correlation is also found at .32. Additional twin family data are currently available and the analyses will be repeated. Meanwhile, the results are promising and strongly suggest that both continuity and change are operating at the process level for cognitive development and that the continuity form early infancy to adulthood is in part genetically mediated.

Several recent reports have continued to address the question of increasing genetic influences during early childhood. An extension of the Eaves et al. model was applied to CAP data without the addition of the LTS twin correlations (Phillips & Fulker, 1989). The analysis included data from 493 families in the CAP where biological, adoptive, and nonadoptive parent/offspring comparisons as well as related and unrelated sibling pairs were analyzed simultaneously using a maximum-likelihood pedigree procedure. The offspring were tested at 1, 2, 3, 4, and 7 years of age.

Unlike the previously discussed studies, relatively high heritabilities were found for the infant years. The estimates of $h^2$ were .49, .73, .50, .52, and .37 for ages 1, 2, 3, 4, and 7, respectively. Also, the heritability estimates appear stable, in contrast to the pattern of increasing heritabilities found in other studies, and a steadily decreasing pattern of the effect of new genetic variance was evident. The estimates of new genetic variance decreased from .47, .50, .19, .09, to .04 from 1 to 7 years. In other words, very little new genetic variance is added after 3 years of age. Furthermore, shared family environmental influences were not significant.

Using an elegant longitudinal hierarchical model of development, Cardon (1992) explored CAP sibling and parent offspring data for specific cognitive abilities when the children were 3, 4, 7, and 9 years of age. Verbal, spatial, perceptual speed, and memory abilities show a pattern of a decreasing impact of general genetic factors and an increasing impact of specific genetic factors over time. It appears that for these abilities, genetic influences become more differentiated during the transition from early to middle childhood.

Combining data from (342 to 278) singletons, (103 to 43) related, and (87 to 32) unrelated sibling pairs from the Colorado Adoption Project at ages 1, 2, 3, 4, 7, and 9 years, and (201 to 92) identical and (175 to 75) fraternal twin pairs from the MacArthur Longitudinal Twin Study at 1, 2, 3, and 4 years, Cherny (Cherny & Fulker, 1992) fit a developmental model to assess continuity and change in general cognitive ability from infancy through middle childhood. The model indicates that there is strong genetic continuity across these ages with some new genetic variation entering in at ages 2, 3, and 7. This model, however, assumes that cognitive measures across this wide range are isomorphic. As has been pointed out earlier in this chapter, the infant measures may not be reflecting general cognitive ability as it is defined later in life. The new genetic variance at ages 2 and 3 may simply be reflecting the increasing predictive validity of the tests at those ages.

The developmental models discussed thus far have looked at development through increases and decreases in traits measured across time. As Waldeman, DeFries, and Fulker (1992) point out, growth curves may more accurately reflect the continuous nature of development. Using a regression approach, Waldeman et al. fit a growth curve model to parent-offspring IQ data from the CAP when the children were 1, 2, 3, and 4 years old. Interestingly, the primary developmental influence on both mean IQ and IQ development was derived from shared family environment. Using the same data set and a simpler approach involving a multiple-group design in EQS, Loehlin (1992) found that shared family environment influenced IQ level but not slope.

At present, it is difficult to reconcile the differences between the last studies discussed and the previous results. However, there are several major differences between the data sets used. Both the DeFries et al. model and the Eaves et al. model relied quite heavily on the same data set, twin data from the LTS, to estimate their infant and childhood parameters. As discussed earlier, nontwin data suggest more genetic influence during the early years. Phillips and Fulker also warn that their estimates of shared family environmental influences are somewhat unreliable due to the small sample of siblings from which the estimates were obtained. Also, the results reported by Loehlin, although they rely only on adoption data, include a wide age range, extending well into early adulthood. Phillips and Fulker used data from children in infancy and childhood. The CAP is a longitudinal study and data will be available at later ages in the near future. Longitudinal data are crucial for a detailed understanding of changes in genetic and environmental influences with age.

To summarize and interpret the results presented in this section, data from several studies indicate that genetic influences that are affecting intelligence at least by two years of age and perhaps earlier continue to operate on into adulthood; furthermore, genetic influences increase with age and the effect of shared family environment appears to decrease. However, in terms of an exact picture of the timing of genetic and environmental continuities and changes across development, the answer remains unclear.

## Cross-Domain Relationships

Thus far, this chapter has focused on analyses within domains. Behavioral genetic methodology can also explore the etiology of cross-domain relationships. Genetic correlations assess not only the overlap of genetic effects for the same trait across age, but can also be used to assess the overlap of genetic effects for different traits. Doubling the difference between identical and fraternal twin cross correlations (twin As score on trait 1 correlated with twin Bs score on trait 2) yields an estimate of the genetic contribution ($h_1 h_2 r_G$) to the phenotypic relationship (Plomin, 1986; Plomin & DeFries, 1979). Data from related and unrelated sibling pairs can be used in exactly the same fashion. For example, given that language acquisition is an important ongoing process during late infancy and early childhood, to what extent is the relationship between early communication development and infant cognitive development mediated by the same genetic factors? Sibling data from the CAP suggest that the genetic correlation between SICD scores and Bayley MDI scores at two years of age is substantial (Thompson & Plomin, 1988; Thompson et al., 1988). The related and unrelated sibling cross-correlations are .31 and .13, respectively. Doubling the difference yields an estimate of .36 for the genetic chain of paths, $h_1 h_2 r_G$. Substituting actual estimates for the heritability of 2-year-old SICD and Bayley also derived from sibling correlations, .46 and .61 respectively, allows the genetic correlation to be directly estimated at .68.

Although the bivariate approach used above is relatively straightforward and can be useful when a single variable best represents each trait, many times behaviors are more accurately characterized by a set of variables and a multivariate approach may be a better choice. The cross-domain relationship between achievement and cognitive measures is a good example of this situation. Understanding the interrelationships between cognitive ability and scholastic achievement is an extremely important educational issue, yet we know very little about the links between these domains (Plomin, 1986). Thompson, Detterman, and Plomin (1991) applied a multivariate model-fitting approach to specific cognitive abilities and school achievement measures in a sample of 146 identical and 132 fraternal twin pairs. The measures for the most part were moderately intercorrelated. A multivariate genetic analysis proposed by Fulker, Baker, and Bock (1983) was used. The model examined genetic and environmental influences through a components of covariance approach. LISREL IV (Joreskog & Sorbom, 1978) was used to fit the model to the data and obtain maximum-likelihood estimates.

The results for the individual measures indicated that while genetic influences were important for both cognitive abilities and achievement measures, shared family environment only affected achievement. Furthermore, the interrelationship between ability and achievement was mediated almost entirely by an overlap in genetic influences. The genetic correlations among the ability and achievement measures were quite high ranging from .61 to .77. These results suggest that when ability-achievement discrepancies are found within individuals, the discrepancy is due to environmental influences. The results again need to be interpreted with caution due to the small sample, but the implications from this first multivariate genetic study of achievement and cognition during the early school years are exciting.

A separate study involving data from the CAP analyzed the genetic and environmental mediation of the relationships between the Peabody Individual Achievement Test Reading Recognition subtest and Wechsler-R Full-Scale, and Verbal and Performance IQ (Cardon, DiLalla, Plomin, DeFries, & Fulker, 1990). As in the Thompson et al. (1991) study, the achievement–IQ relationship was mediated by substantial genetic correlations and small environmental correlations. Additionally, the Reading Recognition and Verbal IQ genetic correlations were much larger than the Reading/Performance IQ genetic relationship.

The multivariate analysis just described has been used in many other behavioral genetic studies. The approach enables the researcher to dissect the interrelationships among observed characteristics and to understand them in terms of genetic and environmental correlations.

## Genetic Mediation of the Environment

Although this chapter does not in general address behavioral genetic research on the environment, one series of studies will be briefly described; the series explores genetic mediation of environment-development relationships (Plomin, Loehlin, & DeFries, 1985). Although the idea of genes influencing the environment sounds paradoxical, it is not hard to see how parental traits that are in part genetically determined contribute to environmental variables. For instance, the number of books in the home is correlated with parental IQ, and is frequently used to estimate the level of intellectual stimulation provided by the home environment; yet, offspring IQ is also correlated with parental IQ. This effect is an example of passive genotype-environment correlation as described by Scarr and McCartney (1983). Adoptive families provide estimates of the environment-development relationship unconfounded by such genetic effects. While examining the correlations between indices of the home environment such as Caldwell

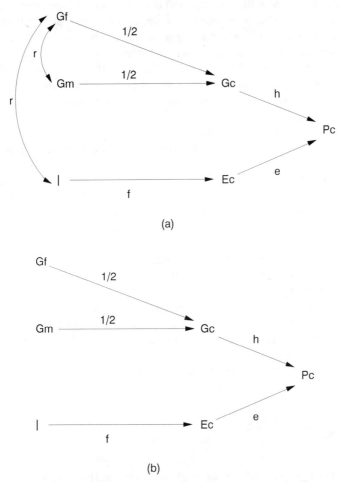

(a)

(b)

**Figure 3.4   Genetic mediation of environmental effects.**

(a) Nonadoptive Families
(b) Adoptive Families
$P_c$ = child's phenotype; $G_c$, $G_f$, $G_m$ = genotype of the child, father and mother; $E_c$ = child's environment; I = measure of the environment; f, e, h, ½ = path coefficients
Adapted from Thompson et al. 1985.

and Bradley's (1978) Home Observation for Measurement of the Environment (HOME) and the Family Environment Scale (FES; Moos & Moos, 1981), and measures of infant cognition and temperament, Plomin et al. discovered that correlations in nonadoptive homes in the CAP were sometimes significantly higher than those in adoptive homes. They examined 113 environment-development relationships in both adoptive and nonadoptive families. Of these, 34 were significant at the .05 level in either the adoptive or nonadoptive family, and 28 of the 34 were greater in the nonadoptive family; 12 of the 28 were significantly greater. In nonadoptive homes, genetic resemblance between parents and their children enhances the relationship between aspects of the home environment and child development. Figure 3.4 illustrates genetic and environmental influences on the correlation between child measures and measures of the environment in adoptive and nonadoptive homes. Although the Plomin et al. findings implicate parental characteristics as the mediating factor for the environment-development relationships, specific parental characteristics were not identified. Furthermore, genetic mediation appears to increase from age 1 to age 4 (Rice, 1987).

A recent application of an extension of the Plomin et al. model found significant genetic mediation of environment-development relationships for 7-year-old children also in the CAP (Coon, Fulker, DeFries, & Plomin, 1990). Interestingly, the assessments of the home environment were taken when the children were 1 and 2 years of age; these assessments were significantly correlated with WISC-R IQ scores collected five years later. The same measures, the HOME and the FES, were used in this application. Only two of the measures indicated direct environmental impact on child's cognitive ability; the FES activity-recreation scale had a negative relationships and the HOME organized environment scale had a positive relationship. The other environment-development relationships were all mediated genetically. As one example, the HOME total score taken at 2 years of age correlated .31 with 7-year IQ. The model-fitting results indicated that over half of this relationship was due to genetic mediation. Plomin (1986) suggests that future studies should focus on the determination of specific parental characteristics that contribute to the HOME index and further use of adoptive families to identify "pure" environmental influences.

## CONCLUSION

As evidenced by the volume of work reviewed in this chapter, behavioral genetics has contributed a great deal to our understanding of intellectual development during infancy and childhood. This final section summarizes the findings reviewed in the chapter thus far, and then suggests possible avenues for future research.

## Summary of Results

1. Twin data from the Louisville Twin Study and parent-offspring data from the Colorado Adoption Project suggest that genetic influences are minimal for conventional infant tests of intelligence during the first year of life and gradually increase after that. Sibling data from the Colorado Adoption Project, and twin data from the TIP and MALTS however, suggest more genetic influence during the early years.

2. New measures of infant information processing, particularly visual novelty preference, reflect higher parent-offspring resemblance during the first year of life than do conventional infant tests.

3. Colorado Adoption Study results involving both parent-offspring and sibling comparisons indicate that genetic influences are an important determinant of early individual differences in communicative development. Furthermore, the results also suggest that it may be possible to identify specific environmental variables that affect the process of language acquisition.

4. Twin, sibling, and adoption studies clearly indicate the importance of genetic influences on general intelligence during the early childhood years. In general, the data also suggest that genetic influences continue to increase from early to late childhood.

5. Specific cognitive abilities appear to emerge by three to four year of age. Again, genetic influences are important, possibly more so for Verbal and Spatial abilities as opposed to Perceptual Speed and Memory. Changes in the impact of shared and nonshared family environment also appear to occur with age; shared family environment decreases in importance and nonshared family environment increases in importance. Scholastic achievement appears to be more affected by shared family environment than are specific cognitive abilities.

6. In general, developmental models support the notion that genetic influences increase from infancy through childhood and shared family environmental influences decrease. Furthermore, substantial genetic stability is implicated; the genes that are influencing intelligence early in life continue to influence intelligence later in life. However, several reports have suggested that shared environment may be influential in the analysis of parent/offspring data through the use of growth curves.

7. Results from the Colorado Adoption Project suggest that environment-development relationships can be mediated to a large extent by genetic influences. Indices of the home environment are not only measuring "pure" environment, but also reflect parental genetically determined characteristics.

## Implications for Future Research

The field of behavioral genetics has just begun to be accepted into mainstream developmental psychology. Already, the merging of the two fields has resulted in advances that neither field could have obtained alone, and further collaboration will inevitably lead to further advancements. However, several specific research areas may be particularly fruitful.

Behavioral genetic methods and sophisticated modeling approaches are limited by the level of measurement. Behavioral genetic research will benefit from newly developed infancy measures. The use of the visual processing measures in the CAP and TIP is a good example, but should be just the beginning. Recent work in psychophysiological variables in infancy may yield particularly interesting results if collected within a behavioral genetic design. Whenever behavioral genetic studies have gone beyond routine standard assessment, new and interesting results have emerged.

While behavioral geneticists will benefit from newly developed tests, test development efforts can take advantage of behavioral genetic approaches as well. The TIP has illustrated the usefulness of the midparent/midtwin design as an "instant" longitudinal study with the purpose of test validation. Predictive validities and longitudinal continuities can be assessed and used to revise instruments.

Recent advances in the measurement of adult intelligence can be used to study intellectual development through a behavioral genetic design. Detterman et al. (1988) has recently devised a battery of elementary cognitive tasks that measure adult intelligence in terms of basic cognitive processes. Although, research has indicated that infant intelligence is undifferentiated, perhaps basic processing indices in adulthood would allow a finer grained analysis. Comparison of elementary cognitive tasks in parents with newer infant information processing measures may allow the identification of specific processing abilities in infancy.

Clearly the verdict is still out on the exact timing of changes in the proportion of genetic and environmental influence on intelligence across development. Additional longitudinal twin and adoption data is required to clarify the developmental process of change. Furthermore, adding measures of information processing and measures of scholastic achievement to twin and adoption studies may allow a more detailed picture of how genetic and environmental influences are operating on intellectual abilities. Elementary cognitive tasks may shed light on the exact links between achievement and cognitive ability during the childhood period. Perhaps basic processing abilities will account for the genetic correlation between achievement and ability, while higher order processing is more affected by environmental influences.

The interesting results obtained on reading disability and mental retardation using the multiple regression technique developed by DeFries and Fulker (1985) should spur interest in the study of intellectual disabilities that can be classified along a continuum. This approach may be applied to other learning and possibly language disabilities. Although, twin samples for specific disorders are difficult to identify and recruit, the practical implications of such research are immense.

Another finding with important practical implications is that of more shared family environmental influence for scholastic achievement than for cognitive abilities. Realizing that ability-achievement discrepancies may be to a large extent environmentally based should encourage investigators to identify specific environmental factors that are mediating the discrepancy.

Greater understanding of genetic variation can only benefit individual differences research. This chapter has found important collaborative efforts between behavioral genetics and developmental psychology toward the study of intellectual development during infancy and childhood. The future promises to hold more exciting discoveries.

## REFERENCES

Baker, L. A. (1983). *Bivariate path analysis of verbal and nonverbal abilities in the Colorado Adoption Project.* Unpublished doctoral dissertation, University of Colorado, Boulder.

Bayley, N. (1969). *Manual for the Bayley Scales of Infant Development.* New York: Psychological Corporations.

Bornstein, M. H., & Sigman, M. D. (1986). Continuity in mental development from infancy. *Child Development, 57,* 251–274.

Burks, B. (1928). The relative influence of nature and nurture upon mental development: A comparative study of foster parent-foster child resemblance and true parent-true child resemblance. *Twenty-Seventh Yearbook of the National Society for the Study of Education, 27*(1), 219–316.

Caldwell, B. M., & Bradley, R. H. (1978). *Home observation for measurement of the environment.* Little Rock: University of Arkansas.

Caplan, B., & Kinsbourne, M. (1976). Baby drops the rattle: Asymmetry of duration of grasp by infants. *Child Development, 47,* 532–534.

Cardon, L. R. (1992, July). *A longitudinal hierarchical model of development with application to specific cognitive ability data from the Colorado Adoption Project.* Paper presented at the 22nd Annual Meeting of the Behavior Genetics Association, Boulder, CO.

Cardon, L. R., DiLalla, L. F., Plomin, R., DeFries, J. C., & Fulker, D. W. (1990). Genetic correlations between reading performance and IQ in the Colorado Adoption Project. *Intelligence, 14,* 245–257.

Cardon, L. R., & Fulker, D. W. (1991). Sources of continuity in infant predictors of later IQ. *Intelligence, 15,* 279–293.

Casler, L. (1976). Maternal intelligence and institutionalized children's developmental quotients: A correlational study. *Developmental Psychology, 12,* 64–67.

Cherny, S. S., Cardon, L. R., Fulker, D. W., & DeFries, J. C. (1992). Differential heritability across levels of cognitive ability. *Behavior Genetics, 22,* 153–162.

Cherny, S. S., & Fulker, D. W. (1992, July). *Continuity and change in general intelligence from ages 1 through 9 years.* Paper presented at the 22nd Annual Meeting of the Behavior Genetics Association, Boulder, CO.

Coon, H., Fulker, D. W., DeFries, J. C., & Plomin, R. (1990). Home environment and cognitive ability of 7-year-old children in the Colorado Adoption Project: Genetic and environmental etiologies. *Developmental Psychology, 26,* 459–468.

Cyphers, L. H., Fulker, D. W., Plomin, R., & DeFries, J. C. (in press). Cognitive abilities in the early school years: No effects of shared environment between parents and offspring. *Intelligence.*

DeFries, J. C., & Fulker, D. W., (1985). Multiple regression analysis of twin data. *Behavior Genetics*, *15*, 467–473.

DeFries, J. C., Fulker, D. W., & LaBuda, M. C. (1987). Evidence for a genetic aetiology in reading disability of twins. *Nature*, *329*, 537–539.

DeFries, J. C., Plomin, R., & LaBuda, M. C. (1987). Genetic stability of cognitive development from childhood to adulthood. *Developmental Psychology*, *23*, 4–12.

DeFries, J. C., Plomin, R., Vandenberg, S. G., & Kuse, A. R. (1981). Parent-offspring resemblance for cognitive abilities in the Colorado Adoption Project: Biological, adoptive, and control parents and one-year-old children. *Intelligence*, *5*, 245–277.

Detterman, D. K., Mayer, J. D., Caruso, D. R., Legree, P. J., Conners, F., & Taylor, R. (1988). *The assessment of basic cognitive abilities in relationship to cognitive deficits*. Manuscript submitted for publication.

DiLalla, L., Thompson, L. A., Plomin, R., Phillips, K., Fagan, J. F., Haith, M. M., Cyphers, L. H., & Fulker, D. W. (1990). Rapid screening of infant predictors of preschool and adult IQ: A study of infant twins and their parents. *Developmental Psychology*, *26*, 759–569.

Eaves, L. J., Long, J., & Heath, A. C. (1986). A theory of developmental change in quantitative phenotypes applied to cognitive development. *Behavior Genetics*, *16*, 143–162.

Falconer, D. S. (1973). *Introduction to quantitative genetics* (2nd ed.). New York: Longman.

Fagan, J. F., & McGrath, S. K. (1981). Infant recognition memory and later intelligence. *Intelligence*, *5*, 121–130.

Fagan, J. F., & Shepherd, P. A. (1986). *The Fagan Test of Infant Intelligence: Training manual*. Cleveland, OH: Infantest Corporation.

Fagan, J. F., & Singer, L. T. (1983). Infant recognition memory as a measure of intelligence (pp. 31–78). In L. P. Lipsitt (Ed.), *Advances in infancy research* (Vol. 2, pp. 32–78). Norwood, NJ: Ablex.

Fisch, R. O., Bilek, M. K., Deinard, A. S., & Chang, P. N. (1976). Growth, behavioral, and psychologic measurements of adopted children: The influence of genetic and socioeconomic factors in a prospective study. *Behavioral Pediatrics*, *89*, 494–500.

Foch, T. T., & Plomin, R. (1980). Specific cognitive abilities in 5- to 12-year-old twins. *Behavior Genetics*, *10*, 507–520.

Forsberg, H., & Olson, R. (1992, July). *Heritable deficits in phonological awareness, rapid-naming, and short-term memory skills are linked to disabled readers' heritable deficits in phonological decoding*. Paper presented at the 22nd Annual Meeting of the Behavior Genetics Association, Boulder, CO.

Freeman, F. N., Holzinger, K. J., & Mitchell, B. (1928). The influence of environment on intelligence, school achievement, and conduct of foster children. *Twenty-Seventh Yearbook of the National Society for the Study of Education*, *27* (1), 103–217.

Fulker, D. W., & DeFries, J. C. (1983). Genetic and environmental transmission in the Colorado Adoption Project: Path analysis. *British Journal of Mathematical and Statistical Psychology*, *36*, 175–188.

Fulker, D. W., Baker, L. A., & Bock, R. D. (1983). *DATA ANALYST: Communications in Computer Data Analysis*, *1*, 5–8.

Garfinkle, A. S., & Vandenberg, S. G. (1981). Development of Piagetian logico-mathematical concepts and other specific cognitive abilities. In L. Gedda, P. Parsi,

& W. E. Nance (Eds.), *Twin research 3: Intelligence, personality, and development* (pp. 51–60). New York: Liss.

Haith, M. M., Hazen, C., & Goodman, G. S. (1988). Expectation and anticipation of dynamic visual events by 3.5-month-old babies. *Child Development, 59*, 505–529.

Hardy-Brown, K. (1983). Universals and individual differences: Disentangling two approaches to the study of language acquisition. *Developmental Psychology, 19,* 610–624.

Hardy-Brown, K., & Plomin, R., (1985). Infant communicative development: Evidence from adoptive and biological families for genetic and environmental influences on rate differences. *Developmental Psychology, 21*, 378–385.

Hildreth, G. H. (1925). *The resemblance of siblings in intelligence and achievement.* New York: Columbia Teachers College.

Ho, H., Baker, L. A., & Decker, S. N. (1988). Covariation between intelligence and speed of cognitive processing: Genetic and environmental influences. *Behavior Genetics, 18*, 247–261.

Ho, H., Foch, T. T., & Plomin, R. (1980). Developmental stability of the relative influence of genes and environment of specific cognitive abilities in childhood. *Developmental Psychology, 16*, 340–346.

Horn, J. M. (1983). The Texas Adoption Project: Adopted children and their intellectual resemblance to biological and adoptive parents. *Child Development, 54*, 268–275.

Horn, J. M., Loehlin, J. C., & Willerman, L. (1979). Intellectual resemblance among adoptive and biological relatives: The Texas Adoption Project. *Behavior Genetics, 9*, 177–207.

Joreskog, K. G., & Sorbom, D. G. (1978). *LISREL IV: Analysis of linear structural relationships by the method of maximum likelihood.* Chicago: National Educational Resources.

Julian, A. J., Plomin, R., Braungart, J. M., Fulker, D. W., & DeFries, J. C. (1992, July). *Genetic influences on communication development: A sibling adoption study of two- and three-year olds.* Paper presented at the 22nd Annual Meeting of the Behavior Genetics Association, Boulder, CO.

Koch, H. L. (1966). *Twins and twin relations.* Chicago: University of Chicago Press.

LaBuda, M. C., DeFries, J. C., & Fulker, D. W. (1986). Multiple regression analysis of twin data obtained from selected samples. *Genetic Epidemiology, 3*, 425–433.

LaBuda, M. C., DeFries, J. C., & Fulker, D. W. (1987). Genetic and environmental covariance structures among WISC-R subtests: A twin study. *Intelligence, 11*, 233–244.

Leahy, A. M. (1935). Nature-nurture and intelligence. *Genetic Psychology Monographs, 17*, 236–308.

Lewis, M., & Brooks-Gunn, J. (1981). Visual attention at three months as a predictor of cognitive functioning at two years of age. *Intelligence, 5*, 131–140.

Lewis, M. (1983). On the nature of intelligence: Science or bias? In M. Lewis (Ed.), *Origins of intelligence: Infancy and early childhood* (pp. 1–24). New York: Plenum.

Loehlin, J. C. (1992). Using EQS for a simple analysis of the Colorado Adoption Project data on height and intelligence. *Behavior Genetics, 22*, 239–246.

Loehlin, J. C., & Nichols, R. C. (1976). *Heredity, environment, and personality.* Austin: University of Texas Press.

Loehlin, J. C., Willerman, L., & Horn, J. M. (1988). Human behavior genetics. *Annual Review of Psychology*, *39*, 101–133.

Loehlin, J. C., Horn, J. M., & Willerman, L. (1989). Modeling IQ change: Evidence from the Texas Adoption Project. *Child Development*, *60*, 993–1004.

McCall, R. B. (1972). Similarity in developmental profile among related pairs of human infants. *Science*, *178*, 1004–1005.

Mittler, P. (1969). Genetic aspects of psycholinguistic abilities. *Journal of Child Psychology and Psychiatry*, *10*, 165–176.

Moos, R. H., & Moos, B. S. (1981). *Family Environment Scale manual*. Palo Alto, CA: Consulting Psychologists Press.

Munsinger, H., & Douglass, A. (1976). The syntactic abilities of identical twins, fraternal twins, and their siblings. *Child Development*, *47*, 40–50.

Nichols, P. L., & Broman, S. H. (1974). Familial resemblance in infant mental development. *Developmental Psychology*, *10*, 442–446.

Olson, R., & Forsberg, H. (1992, July). *Genetic and shared-environment influences on deficits in word recognition and component coding skills*. Paper presented at the 22nd Annual Meeting of the Behavior Genetics Association, Boulder, CO.

Petrill, S. A., Thompson, L. A., & Detterman, D. K. (1992, July). *The effect of gender upon heritability and common environmental estimates in measures of scholastic achievement*. Paper presented at the 22nd Annual Meeting of the Behavior Genetics Association, Boulder, CO.

Phillips, K., & Fulker, D. W. (1989). Quantitative genetic analysis of longitudinal trends in adoption designs with application to IQ in the Colorado Adoption Project. *Behavior Genetics*, *19*, 621–658.

Plomin, R. (1986). *Development, genetics and psychology*. Hillsdale, NJ: Erlbaum.

Plomin, R. (1987). Developmental behavioral genetics and infancy. In J. D. Osofsky (Ed.), *Handbook of infant development* (2nd ed., pp. 363–414). New York: Wiley-Interscience.

Plomin, R., Campos, J., Corley R., Emde R. N., Fulker, D. W., Kagan, J., Reznick, J. S., Robinson, J., Zahn-Waxler, C., & DeFries, J. C. (1990). Individual differences during the second year of life: The MacArthur Longitudinal Twin Study. In J. Colombo & J. Fagen (Eds.), *Individual differences in infancy: Reliability, stability, prediction* (pp. 431–455). Hillsdale, NJ: Erlbaum.

Plomin, R., & DeFries, J. C. (1979). Multivariate behavioral genetic analysis of twin data on scholastic abilities. *Behavior Genetics*, *9*, 505–517.

Plomin, R., & DeFries, J. C. (1985). *Origins of individual differences in infancy: The Colorado Adoption Project*. New York: Academic Press.

Plomin R., DeFries, J. C., & Fulker, D. W. (1988). *Nature and nurture during infancy and early childhood*. New York: Cambridge University Press.

Plomin R., DeFries, J. C., & McClearn, G. (1990). *Behavioral genetics: A primer* (2nd ed.). San Francisco: W. H. Freeman and Company.

Plomin, R. Loehlin, J. C., & DeFries, J. C. (1985). Genetic and environmental components of 'environmental' influences. *Developmental Psychology*, *21*, 391–402.

Plomin R., & Vandenberg, S. G. (1980). An analysis of Koch's (1966) Primary Mental Abilities test data for 5- to 7-year-old twins. *Behavior Genetics*, *10*, 409–412.

Rice, T. (1987). *Multivariate path analysis of cognitive and environmental measures in the Colorado Adoption Project*. Unpublished doctoral dissertation, University of Colorado, Boulder.

Rose, S. A., & Wallace, I. F. (1988). Visual recognition memory: A predictor of later cognitive functioning in preterms. *Child Development, 56,* 843–852.

Sadker, M., & Sadker, D. (1985). Sexism in the schoolroom of the 80's. *Psychology Today, 19,* 54–57.

Scarr, S., & Kidd, K. K. (1983). Developmental behavior genetics. In P. H. Mussen (Ed.), *Handbook of child psychology (4th ed.): Vol. 2. Infancy and developmental psychobiology* (pp. 345–433). New York: Wiley.

Scarr, S., & McCartney, K. (1983). How people make their own environments: A theory of genotype environment effects. *Child Development, 54,* 424–435.

Scarr, S., & Weinberg, R. A. (1977), Intellectual similarities within families of both adopted and biological children. *Intelligence, 1,* 170–191.

Segal, N. L. T. (1985). Monozygotic and dizygotic twins: A comparative analysis of mental ability profiles. *Child Development, 56,* 1051–1058.

Skodak, M., & Skeels, H. M (1949). A final follow-up of one hundred adopted children. *Journal of Genetic Psychology, 75,* 85–105.

Snygg, D. (1938). The relation between the intelligence of mothers and of their children living in foster homes. *Journal of Genetic Psychology, 52,* 401–406.

Thompson, L. A. (1989). Developmental behavioral genetic research on infant information processing: Detection of continuity and change. In S. Doxiadis (Ed.), *Early influences shaping the individual* (pp. 67–84). Plenum Press.

Thompson, L. A., Detterman, D. K., & Plomin, R. (1991). *Scholastic achievement and specific cognitive abilities in 7- to 12-year-old twins. Psychological Science, 2,* 158–165.

Thompson, L. A., Detterman, D. K., & Plomin, R. (1992. July). *Differences in heritability across groups differing in ability, revisited.* Paper presented at the 22nd Annual Meeting of the Behavior Genetics Association, Boulder, CO.

Thompson, L. A., Fagan, J. F., & Fulker, D. W. (1991). Prediction of specific cognitive abilities at 36 months from infant novelty preference. *Child Development, 62,* 530–538.

Thompson, L. A., Fulker, D. W., DeFries, J. C., & Plomin, R. (1988). Multivariate analysis of cognitive and temperament measures in 24-month-old adoptive and nonadoptive sibling pairs. *Personality and Individual Differences 9,* 95–100.

Thompson, L. A., & Plomin, R. (1988). The sequenced inventory of communication development: An adoption study of two- and three-year-olds. *International Journal of Behavioral Development, 11,* 219–231.

Thompson, L. A., Plomin, R., & DeFries, J. C. (1985). Multivariate genetic analysis of 'environmental' influences on infant cognitive development. *British Journal of Developmental Psychology, 4,* 347–353.

Wadsworth, S. J., DeFries, J. C., Pennington, B. F., & Olson, R. K. (1992, July). *Reading performance and verbal short-term memory: A twin study of reciprocal causation.* Paper presented at the 22nd Annual Meeting of the Behavior Genetics Association, Boulder, CO.

Waldeman, I. D., DeFries, J. C., & Fulker, D. W. (1992). Quantitative genetic analysis of IQ development in young children: Multivariate multiple regression with orthogonal polynomials. *Behavior Genetics, 22,* 229–238.

Whitfield, K. E., Cherny, S. S., Fulker, D. W., & Reznick, J. S. (1992, July). *A multivariate analysis of cognitive measures at 14 months: The MacArthur Longi-*

*tudinal Twin Study*. Paper presented at the 22nd Annual Meeting of the Behavior Genetics Association, Boulder, CO.

Wilson, R. C. (1975). Twins: Patterns of cognitive development as measured on the WPPSI. *Developmental Psychology, 11*, 126–139.

Wilson, R. C. (1983). The Louisville Twin Study: Developmental synchronies in behavior. *Child Development, 54*, 298–316.

# Chapter 4

# *Physical Correlates of Human Intelligence*

**Arthur R. Jensen**

School of Education
University of California,
Berkeley

**S. N. Sinha**

Department of Psychology
University of Rajasthan
Jaipur, India

## INTRODUCTION

One of the oldest commonly held beliefs is that there is an association between mental and physical traits in humans. This belief is much older than the history of psychology as an empirical discipline. Indeed, the notion of correlations between physical and mental characteristics can be traced back at least as far as the ancient Greeks. Aristotle is credited with formalizing the theory of physiognomy, though it was not until psychology became established as an independent discipline and began trying to imitate the natural sciences that the relationship between physical and mental traits became the subject of empirical investigation and objective measurement.

It may seem rather surprising, in retrospect, that so many studies were conducted along this line of inquiry during the early history of psychology. Yet specialists in a young science often show particular zeal and pride in applying their methods to the debunking of long-held popular beliefs, and certainly most of the early studies in this realm reported negative results. Negative findings were evidently so easy to come by, and so readily, even eagerly, approved by psychologists, that computing correlation coefficients between mental and physical measurements became a popular area of psychological research in the first quarter of this century, and, for a time, it seems that findings of significant correlations between physical and mental characteristics were generally less prized than the demonstration of nonsignificant correlations.

The many names associated with this early research have been largely forgotten, probably because, in the history of science generally, little lasting credit or honor is granted to investigators whose only contribution has been to demonstrate, however correctly or convincingly, that some particular null hypothesis could not be rejected. This is not to say, however, that the generalized debunking attitude with respect to correlations between physical and mental traits has had no lasting effect. Its legacy endures in the prevailing conviction among present-day psychologists that, with the exception of certain pathological conditions in which mental defect and physical anomalies clearly occur together, the null hypothesis best summarizes the association between physical and mental traits. Clearly, the real problem is not so much whether this conclusion, as a generality, will ultimately be proven right or wrong, but whether the attitude that has been sustained by such a sweeping negative generality has hindered behavioral scientists' inquiring spirit to winnow the chaff from the grain in this broad question.

One important landmark in the history of this subject is Donald G. Paterson's *Physique and Intellect* (1930). In this work, Paterson assembled and critically reviewed virtually all the studies concerned with the association between physical and mental measurements completed prior to 1930. About two-thirds of Paterson's 300-page review examined various physical correlates of intellectual abilities; the remaining one-third of his monograph concerned physical correlates of temperament, or personality traits. Among the main physical correlates of mental ability (usually general intelligence, as indexed by IQ) critically examined in Paterson's review were stature (height and weight), cranial measurements, morphological indices (e.g., height-weight ratio), anatomical and physiological age (as indicated by skeletal development, eruption of permanent teeth, and onset of puberty), and physical health and fitness. In his time, Paterson was respected as a highly competent and sophisticated methodologist in psychometrics and differential psychology. These strengths, combined with his scholarly thoroughness, his meticulous accuracy in reporting, and his consistently objective critical acumen, make it practically unnecessary to reexamine the numerous studies reviewed in *Physique and Intellect*.

The one justifiable criticism that might be leveled at Paterson's effort is that he too, like so many of his contemporaries, was somewhat overly imbued with a zeal for debunking popular myths, thereby incurring the risk of overworking the then-favored null hypothesis. Despite Paterson's evident caution in appraising the results of each study, one gets the impression that if he had to risk drawing the wrong conclusion, because of obvious weaknesses or uncertainties in a particular study, he much preferred to risk making what statisticians term a Type II error (i.e., accepting the null hypothesis when it is false) than to risk making a Type I error (i.e., rejecting the null hypothesis when it is true). The recently developed methodology of meta-analysis (Glass, McGaw, & Smith, 1981) and its various applications to substantive questions in psychology have already demonstrated that the properly *aggregated* statistical results of a large number of studies may yield a quite different conclusion from that arrived at by examining each study separately and then summarizing their results in terms of a ''box score,'' reporting the frequencies of significant and nonsignificant statistical tests. For example, a dozen independent studies may all show a nonsignificant correlation between variables $x$ and $y$, and we might conclude that the null hypothesis ($\rho_{xy} = 0$) is true, or more correctly, that we cannot reject it. But if all of these independent and separately nonsignificant correlations are consistently positive (or consistently negative), the probability that the true correlation is zero is at most $(1/2)^{12}$ or .0002. This simple example of a meta-analysis shows our previous conclusion to be a Type II error. But scarcely anything resembling meta-analysis was in the air in Paterson's day.

Although Paterson's *Physique and Intellect* remains a valuable reference, its net influence in psychology has been generally to discredit the idea that there are significant physical correlates of intellect and to dampen interest in research on this topic. Such was probably not Paterson's aim, yet his frequent reference to correlations which, even when statistically significant, were ''too low to be of practical value,'' served to warn psychologists and the general public that physical appearance and anthropometric measurements could not be substituted for psychometric techniques, in the assessment of intelligence and temperament. During Paterson's time, this was probably a needed and beneficial point to emphasize, but such emphasis unfortunately detracted interest from the possible theoretical significance of discovering particular physical correlates of mental abilities. In general, it can be said that Paterson seemed constantly to imagine a kind of straw-man hypothesis of supposed *strong* correlations between physical and mental measurements, and he could always show, rightly, that his review of the existing evidence completely discredited any such hypothesis. For many readers, and some authors of psychology textbooks, Paterson's largely negative conclusions were generalized beyond the qualifications of his actual statements to include virtually all hypotheses about physical and intellectual traits. Much the same kind of fate befell Sir Francis Galton's early conjecture that certain simple laboratory tasks involving discrimination and reaction time would reflect individual differences in intelligence. The notion remained in its popularly discredited status among psychologists for more than half a century before modern investigators finally discovered that Galton was right, or at least mostly right, after all (Vernon, 1987).

It can be said in Paterson's defense, however, that the quality of a great many of the studies he reviewed, in terms of their poor methodology, would hardly encourage rejection of the null hypothesis, even when their results were statistically significant! From a methodologist standpoint, most of the studies prior to 1930 form a depressing picture. The research standards of psychology and psychometrics during that era were shockingly weak. This was the general condition, with only rare exceptions. Study after study yields no truly interpretable results, so lacking in essential information are the published reports. The effects of restriction of variance on the correlation coefficient seemed wholly unknown to most early investigators, and attenuation of correlations by errors of measurement was hardly better known. Because of inadequate reporting of results and weak or inappropriate statistical analyses of the data, much investigative effort yielded little dependable knowledge. Too many, if not most, of these early studies now appear disgracefully inept by present-day standards of behavioral research.

### Theoretical Significance of Physical and Mental Measurements

The theoretical significance of correlations between physical and mental traits is, of course, an issue that can be properly addressed only after detailed investigation of the empirical facts. Yet certain a priori considerations would seem to afford an incentive for such investigation.

From a purely theoretical standpoint, we need not take much heed of the caveat, so frequently reiterated in the literature, that the correlation between some physical and some mental measurement is too low to be of any "practical significance." Certainly, no one expects to substitute the observation of physical characteristics for the administration of psychometric tests. On a purely theoretical basis, what is more, only quite small correlations between most single physical traits and a complexly determined behavioral trait, such as intelligence, are expected to be the rule, trait variation due to multiple factors being unlikely to show a large correlation with any single causal factor. Hence, even rather small correlations, provided they are statistically significant and, more importantly, are consistently replicable, are of theoretical interest, especially if the intercorrelations among a number of physical and psychometric variables show a consistent pattern. Theoretical interpretation depends upon a network of intercorrelations. Thus, any single correlation, however reliable, can hardly be expected to do more than to spark interest in further inquiry as to its causes and links within a larger correlational network of organismic variables.

To discover a reliable correlation between a psychometric variable, say, intelligence, and some physical characteristic is to point up the intriguing fact that a test devised strictly for measuring a particular behavioral trait is also actually measuring something more, and something apparently very different from the trait originally targeted for measurement. Such correlations pose an important theoretical challenge in that they seem to suggest that there is some greater, more substantial significance and causal underpinning to the behavioral trait expressly measured by the test. Test scores, in other words, apparently measure something more than the elicited behavior that meets the eye or that can be fathomed merely in terms of the item contents of the test. An adequate theory of intelligence should be expected to explain such correlations, if not in precise detail in every case, at least in principle.

Reliable correlations between physical and psychometric variables may also provide clues to the causes of individual variation in mental abilities. All correlations, however, are not of equal value for this purpose, regardless of their magnitude. Some correlations may be the result of relatively short-term environmental influences, such as differences in nutrition, which may simultaneously affect two or more distinct characteristics. Other correlations may be the result of cross-assortative mating for two genetically independent traits, both of which happen to be valued by mating partners in a particular culture. Still other correlations may be the result of a long evolutionary process involving the natural selection of genetically conditioned coadapted traits, or genetic characteristics that have more often than not simultaneously met the same fate in the sieve of natural selection during the evolution of different human populations. The existence of such a mechanism as a possible cause of correlations between physical traits and intelligence, of course, depends upon the validity of the biological view of intelligence, that is, that intelligence has arisen through the same processes that gave rise to other biological properties. Hence, it is subject to the same evolutionary pressures as other biological traits and may play the same evolutionary role as is played by other biological traits. One must reasonably question the extent to which "biological intelligence," here conceived as a product of evolution, is the same intelligence as that which is measured by psychometric tests of mental ability, in which individual differences are expressed on some norm-referenced scale, such as the IQ scale. Analysis of various biological correlates of IQ affords one more avenue of approach to this question, in addition to the methods of quantitative genetical analysis. The many applications of genetic analysis to psychometric variables, particularly IQ, now leave virtually no doubt that a substantial part of the total variance in psychometric intelligence is attributable to genetic factors and their covariation with environmental influences. Genetic analysis by itself, however, cannot elucidate the chain of causality between genes and behavior or explain why individual differences in some superficially dissimilar phenotypic characteristics are correlated with one another. To tackle such questions, research must advance on a broader front than is possible by means of genetic methodology alone. Genetic analysis nevertheless must play an essential role in the theoretical interpretation of

intercorrelations among physical and behavioral variables, as becomes immediately obvious when we examine the various possible causes of correlation
between phenotypic characteristics.

## Causes of Correlation

The most amazing feature of the research literature on correlations between
mental and physical traits is that, until very recently, virtually no attention was
paid to the various *causes* of correlations or to the fact that different types of
correlations have quite different theoretical significance. We are not here referring to the different statistical techniques for expressing the degree of association, but to fundamentally different types of correlation with respect to their
cause. Although the early literature frequently voices the familiar dictum that
correlation does not necessarily imply causation, the causes of correlations are
never considered at all in this early work. Part of the reason for this neglect
seems to be that all organismic variables, physical and mental alike, have been
treated merely as statistical predictors; research has been oriented toward the
comparative validity of physical and mental measurements for predicting socially
significant behavior. If correlations are viewed as a means of pragmatic prediction, there need be no concern as to their causal underpinnings. Moreover,
because the prevailing attitude of psychological researchers on this topic has
been to favor the null hypothesis and to discredit the age-old belief in physical
characteristics as dependable clues to mental traits, there has been no need to
enquire as to the causes of such correlations, which were usually found to be
either statistically nonsignificant or too small to be of practical predictive value
in any case.

This unfortunate failure to recognize different types of causes of correlation
has resulted in a dearth of the kinds of evidence in studies of physical-mental
associations that are crucially needed to permit scientifically interesting inferences from the correlations that are actually found to exist. The theoretically
important questions about the observed correlations are hardly ever asked. In
order to bring such questions to bear on the research evidence surveyed here, it is
necessary first to define the various types of correlation and assign them a
consistent terminology.

*Environmental correlation.* An environmental correlation is defined as a
correlation between two (or more) distinctly measurable phenotypic characteristics for which the cause of the correlation exists entirely in the environment and
for which there is no genotypic counterpart of the observed or phenotypic
correlation. Environmental correlation can exist between characteristics of varying degrees of heritability or between heritable and nonheritable traits. The
higher the broad heritability (i.e., the proportion of variance in phenotypes
attributable to variance in genotypes) of both traits, however, the greater, in

general, is the likelihood that the phenotypic correlation also reflects some degree of genetic correlation. But this is not always or necessarily the case. Consider, for example, a hypothetical population in which, because of some peculiar custom, brunettes are nutritionally favored during the growth period, and blondes are nutritionally deprived, so that brunettes grow up to be of generally greater stature than blondes, thereby creating a purely environmental correlation between hair color and stature, despite the fact that the heritability of both traits remains very high. In such a case, the correlation between hair color and stature could be reduced to zero in a single generation by merely equalizing the nutrition of blondes and brunettes.

Similarly, an environmental correlation can arise between traits because of selection of an individual on one trait as a basis for differential training on some other trait. Many gender differences in our society are clear examples of this phenomenon. Gender, for example, shows opposite correlations with knowledge of cooking and knowledge of auto mechanics. These are strictly environmental correlations due to differences in sex-role acculturation. The possession of the ability known as "absolute pitch," a highly heritable trait, is correlated with musical knowledge and skill, because children who are discovered to have absolute pitch are more apt to be singled out for music lessons and parental pressure to pursue music study seriously.

Experimentally, of course, particular environmental correlations will not hold up from one generation to the next if the environmental conditions are changed, even when there is no change in the mating system across generations. Conversely, if there is no change in the environment across generations, environmental correlations will persist despite changes in the mating system. This is one of the operational distinctions between environmental correlation and genetic correlation.

*Genetic correlation.* Genetic correlation between distinct characteristics or traits is a considerably more complex matter than environmental correlation, not only because the causal agents—the genes—are unobservable, but also because there are several distinctive types of genetic correlation which can be easily confused with one another in their phenotypic effects. These various types can usually be distinguished, however, by means of certain analytic techniques.

Genetic correlation is a generic term that refers to any correlation between phenotypic traits in which the correlation (or some proportion of the covariance between the traits) is the result of one (or some combination) of several distinct genetic mechanisms. The main types of mechanisms are: (a) *Simple genetic correlation* due to (i) correlated social stratification of two or more genetically conditioned traits in the population, or (ii) cross-assortative mating for two or more genetically conditioned traits ("genetically conditioned" refers to a phenotypic character with a heritability greater than zero); (b) *Pleiotropy,* or the effect of a single gene on two or more characters; (c) Genetic *linkage*, as a result of genes that affect different phenotypic characters being located on the same chromosome, usually with their loci in close proximity to each other; and (d) *Supergenes*, a special kind of linkage.

*Simple genetic correlation.* This type of correlation, first described by Karl Pearson (1909, 1931), results from the common assortment of genes in a population through correlated stratification of two or more traits. In this type of correlation there is no inherent or causal connection between the traits or the genes for the traits. If most of a population were divided between two religions, for example, and if membership in the one required that members have brown eyes and tall stature, and membership in the other required members to have blue eyes and short stature, a simple genetic correlation between stature and eye color would be observed among successive generations. There would be nothing intrinsic or necessary about this correlation; the relationship might just as well have been reversed, with brown eyes associated with short stature and blue eyes with tall stature. Correlated stratification of traits in this fashion may result because of seemingly arbitrary cultural mores, or because the two traits are, in some sense, "synergistic" for economic success in a particular culture, as when certain traits so complement each other as to enhance a person's chances of attaining higher socioeconomic status. On this basis, for example, we might expect some degree of positive correlation between intelligence and physical stamina, because both characteristics give their possessor an advantage in almost any kind of competition. Note that selection acts on phenotypes, which in the case of many adaptive physical and behavioral traits will be complex and hence polygenic. Selection therefore will affect *groups* of genes, which will therefore be intercorrelated. If survival in a particular society were to depend upon success in hunting, for example, one can reasonably suppose that a genetic correlation would arise between the constituents of hunting ability—visual acuity, motor coordination, tracking, and running—since all of these are selected simultaneously. The same pattern of genetic associations would not be found in a population whose survival depended upon food gathering or agriculture.

We can represent genetic correlations of various types by simple diagrams in which distinct genetic factors are indicated by circles labeled $G$ and phenotypic traits are indicated by squares labeled $x$, $y$, and $z$ (for different traits). *Causal* correlation is indicated by arrows; noncausal correlation is indicated by curved lines, a solid curved line indicating a within-families correlation, a broken curved line indicating a between-families correlation. In terms of this scheme, a *simple genetic correlation* is represented in Figure 4.1. Note that this type of correlation is only a *between-families* correlation. The absence of a within-families correlation rules out all other types of genetic correlation. By *between-families* correlation, we mean simply that the correlation is entirely dependent upon the association of traits $x$ and $y$ among persons from different families. (The term "family" is used here in the genetic sense, as a cohort of full siblings, and does not include the parents.) As fully explicated elsewhere (Jensen, 1980b), when measures of variables $x$ and $y$ are obtained on sets of siblings in $N$ numbers of families, the between-families correlation between $x$ and $y$ is the correlation between the $N$ pairs of means of the siblings within each family on variables $x$ and $y$. The within-families correlation between $x$ and $y$ is the correlation between the sibling differences on $x$ and the sibling differences on $y$. (This correlation therefore cannot in the least reflect differences between families.)

When genes for distinct traits become segregated together because of common assortment of the genes in the population, the resulting simple genetic correlation will exist only between families. In accordance with Mendel's law of independent segregation of the parental genes in the process of gametogenesis, each sibling in the family receives a random assortment of the segregating genes; this random assortment of segregating genes precludes any *within*-families correlation between traits. (Segregating genes are those that are polymorphous, that is, two or more different alleles [i.e., different forms of the gene], producing variation in the gene's phenotypic effect, can exclusively occupy the gene's locus on the chromosome. All trait variation within a species is the result of segregating genes; nonsegregating genes do not contribute to individual variation.) Hence, the finding of a *within*-families correlation necessarily indicates some type of genetic correlation other than what we have termed *simple* genetic correlation.

Simple genetic correlation may also arise from *cross-assortative mating* for two traits. If women who deviate positively from the population mean on trait $x$ mate with men who deviate positively from the mean on trait $y$, the result will be that their offspring, on average, will deviate positively from the mean on *both $x$* and $y$, and these traits will then be correlated in the population—a simple genetic correlation. Again, this would be a *between*-families correlation only, since independent segregation of the parental genes for $x$ and $y$ prevents a correlation

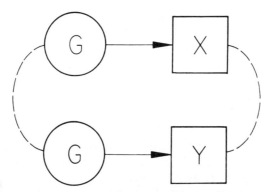

**Figure 4.1.   Path diagram of a simple genetic correlation between two distinct phenotypic traits, X and Y, each conditioned by a different gene (G). Arrows represent a causal connection; broken lines represent a between-families correlation.**

between $x$ and $y$ among siblings. Indeed, the sine qua non for a simple genetic correlation between traits is the absence of a within-families correlation in the presence of a between-families correlation. In this respect, however, a simple genetic correlation may be mimicked by a purely environmental correlation, assuming the traits in question are at least moderately susceptible to environmental deviations of the kind and magnitude that prevail in the population. Social class and cultural differences in factors that can affect physical or behavioral traits will cause between-family correlations but not within-family correlations between traits; this is because such environmental factors generally represent differences between families but not within families. One can think of certain exceptions, however. Differential rearing of boys and girls, for example, could create a within-families environmental correlation between sex and those traits susceptible to the differences in rearing. This also suggests the fact that both genetic and environmental correlations for two (or more) traits may coexist, and may even be of opposite direction, thereby canceling each other, wholly or partially. Thus an observed phenotypic correlation represents the *net effect* of genetic and environmental correlations, although one or the other may predominate for any particular pair of traits.

Falconer (1960, Chapter 19) presents methods for estimating the genetic and environmental components of the phenotypic correlation between two characters. These methods have been applied successfully to the study of correlated characters in farm animals, such as milk-yield and butterfat-yield in cows and body length and backfat thickness in pigs. But such methods are exceedingly limited in their applicability for the analysis of phenotypic correlations between human traits, particularly when one or both traits are behavioral in nature. There are two main reasons for this limited applicability. First, there is the fact that these methods only permit analysis of the phenotypic correlation into two components: (a) a component due to correlated *additive* genetic deviations (i.e., "breeding values"), and (b) a component due to correlated environmental deviations *plus* correlated nonadditive genetic deviations. Phenotypic correlation between traits with considerable nonadditive genetic variance (i.e., high broad heritability but relatively low narrow heritability), therefore, cannot be analyzed in a way that is of main interest for our present purpose, that is, into a wholly genetic component and a wholly environmental (or nongenetic) component. (This consideration is of little importance to animal breeders, who are mainly interested in the breeding values [i.e., additive genetic deviations] that contribute to trait variance.) Second, there is the fact that the method of analyzing phenotypic correlations cannot practicably take account of the degree of genotype-environment correlation for each of the traits in question, and behavioral traits especially are likely to show some degree of genotype-environment correlation. For example, children who are genotypically favored for superior intelligence are more likely than less favored children to grow up in an environment that stimulates intellectual development.

The scientific interest in correlated traits that show *between*-families but not *within*-families correlation is largely of a sociological or cultural nature, regardless of whether the correlation is mainly genetic or mainly environmental. Such correlations reveal nothing about the essential nature of each of the correlated traits per se or about their causal underpinnings. The only interest is in why different values of the two traits have become simultaneously stratified in the population, thereby creating a between-families correlation. This can be an interesting question in its own right, the answer to which may reveal something about the relative social valuation of various traits and their organization within a particular culture. Exclusively between-families correlations, being largely cultural products (even if entirely due to simple genetic correlation), will be less consistent across different cultures than correlated traits showing both between-families and within-families correlation. This latter type of correlation is most probably indicative of pleiotropy.

*Pleiotropic correlation.* Pleiotropy is the effect of a single gene upon two (or more) distinct characters; if the gene is segregating, the two characters are affected simultaneously, and the resulting correlation between them is termed a *pleiotropic correlation*. A pleiotropic correlation between traits $x$ and $y$ is illustrated in Figure 4.2. The correlation $r_{xy}$ may also be mediated by a causal chain of one or more other pleiotropic effects of a gene, acting as an intermediate causal effect between the gene and the phenotypes of interest (in this case, $x$ and $y$) see for example, Figure 4.3.

A pleiotropic correlation always exists within families as well as between families, as indicated by the solid and broken curved lines in the preceding figures. If variation in each character ($x$ and $y$) is attributable to only a single segregating gene and there are no other sources of variation, then, of course, the

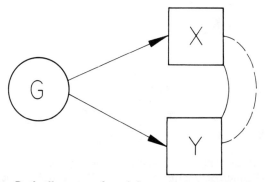

**Figure 4.2.   Path diagram of a pleiotropic correlation between two distinct phenotypic traits, X and Y, each influenced by one and the same gene(s) (G). Arrows represent a causal connection; curved broken line is a between-families correlation; curved solid line is a within-family correlation.**

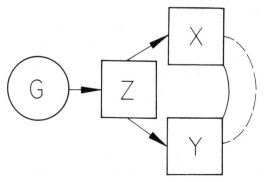

Figure 4.3.   A pleiotropic correlation between phenotypes X and Y, where a single gene (G) conditions a phenotypic characteristic, Z, which in turn affects traits X and Y. Arrows represent causal connections; solid curved line is a within-family correlation; broken curved line is between-families correlation.

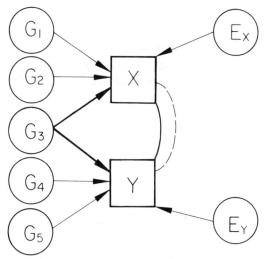

Figure 4.4.   Path diagram illustrating how a pleiotropic correlation between two distinct polygenic traits, X and Y, is attenuated by sources of variance attributable to uncorrelated genes ($G_1$, $G_2$, $G_4$, $G_5$) and uncorrelated environmental effects, $E_x$ and $E_y$. The pleiotropic correlation is attributable to a single gene ($G_3$) in the polygenic system. Arrows represent causal connection; curved solid line is a within-family correlation; curved broken line is a between-families correlation.

correlation will always be perfect ($r_{xy}$ = 1). If the characters are polygenic, however, the pleiotropic correlation can take any value between 0 and ±1, depending upon the number of other nonpleiotropic genes contributing to the total genetic variance in either one or both traits, and also depending upon the proportion of nongenetic variance in the traits. A single pleiotropic gene affecting two polygenic traits of relatively low heritability may cause only a very small pleiotropic correlation between the traits, as illustrated in Figure 4.4, in which $E_x$ and $E_y$ represent independent environmental effects on traits $x$ and $y$.

Pleiotropic correlations can be either positive or negative, and they may be obscured, or completely obliterated, by either simple genetic correlation or environmental correlation acting in the opposite direction to the pleiotropic correlation. The pleiotropic effect on one of the traits may be detrimental to fitness, yet the effect on the correlated trait may be especially beneficial, so that the *net* effect is beneficial to fitness, or if the two traits together are *synergistically* beneficial, the pleiotropic gene will be maintained at some equilibrium frequency in the population.

A pleiotropic correlation between a highly heritable physical character and a behavioral trait, especially when the physical character has no phenotypically discernible functional relationship to the behavioral trait or is even negatively (i.e., unbeneficially) correlated with the behavioral trait, affords strong evidence that genetic factors play a role in the behavioral trait—evidence that is entirely independent of the usual quantitative-genetic methods for estimating the heritability of a trait from twin correlations or other kinship correlations.

A pleiotropic correlation is distinguished from a simple genetic correlation by the fact that a pleiotropic correlation exists within families as well as between families, whereas a simple genetic correlation exists only between families. Selection for one trait in a breeding experiment will result in a directional change in a pleiotropically correlated trait as well. Also, siblings reared apart will show the same correlation between two traits as siblings reared together if the correlation is pleiotropic, whereas an environmental correlation between traits will usually be smaller for siblings reared apart than for siblings reared together. When a highly heritable physical trait is found to be correlated (within and between families) with a behavioral trait, the most likely cause of such a correlation is pleiotropy. Evidence for pleiotropy is ipso facto evidence for a genetic component in the behavioral trait.

*Linkage.* When the genes for two distinct characters are carried on the same chromosome, they are said to be linked—the degree of linkage being directly related to the proximity of their loci. Mendel's law of independent or random segregation of genes does not hold in the case of linked genes, which have a greater-than chance probability of segregating together, and hence, of being transmitted together from parent to offspring, and siblings have a greater-than chance probability of being concordant for the two characters. Because of the mechanism of *crossing-over* in the process of gametogenesis, however, linkages are broken up and genes are recombined on homologous chromosomes, the rate of recombination being directly related to the distance between the genes' loci. Hence, the linkage between any two closely linked genes gradually diminishes from one generation to the next, approaching a "linkage equilibrium." Therefore, in a stable population, that is, a population which is not outbreeding with other populations, linkage will not be a cause of correlation between traits in the population as a whole; this is true for both within-families and between-families correlations.

Linkage, however, can cause some degree of correlation between characters in the first generation after a mixture of different breeding populations, but the (within- and between-families) correlation will decrease in each subsequent generation at a rate inversely related to the closeness of the original linkage. For correlated polygenic traits, linkage would account for such a small fraction of the covariance as to be virtually undetectable, as there would be completely independent segregation for the vast majority of polygenes affecting the trait. Hence, the genetic aspect of within-families correlations between traits is most likely to be pleiotropic.

Although linkage can result in only transiently correlated characters in populations derived from crosses between divergent strains, linkages between characters can be established within separate families by analysis of family pedigrees of the two characters over two or more generations. Unfortunately, the methodology of such linkage analysis is practically limited to two gene loci and hence would not be suitable for polygenic traits in which single genes each contribute only a small fraction of the trait variance. If linkage analysis should discover a linkage between some single gene character, such as a blood antigen, and a presumably polygenic trait, such as IQ, this finding would strongly suggest a "major gene" effect on IQ: that is, most of the IQ variance would have to be attributable to a single gene, with perhaps only a small number of genes (polygenes) slightly modifying its expression. (Polygenes are structurally no different from any other genes; they are merely a number of genes, on the same or different chromosomes, each producing similar and slightly more or less equal phenotypic effects.) Such a "major gene" for general intelligence has been hypothesized (Weiss, 1978), but the evidence for it is exceedingly weak in our opinion.

Thus far we have been discussing only linkage of autosomal genes (i.e., genes located on any of the chromosomes that do not determine sex). Sex-linkage and X-linkage are a quite different matter. In these cases, we are dealing with genes carried on the sex chromosomes. But we are concerned only with the genes on the X chromosomes, which are expressed phenotypically as an X-linked character. (In humans there are very few genes on the Y chromosome besides those that determine sex.) A character that occurs with different frequencies or different average phenotypic values in males and females is often referred to as sex-linked. A female parent can transmit an X-linked trait to her sons or daughters, but a male parent can transmit an X-linked trait only to his daughters. This creates a distinctive pattern of correlations for mother-daughter, mother-son, father-daughter, father-son, same-sex, and opposite sex siblings. All of these correlations are close to 1/2 for autosomal genes, but some will depart markedly from 1/2 in the case of X-linked genes: for example, the theoretical value of the father-son correlation is zero. If an X-linked gene is dominant, the phenotypic character it controls will appear with greater frequency in females; if the gene is recessive, the phenotype will be expressed more frequently in males. A trait that can be conclusively shown to have these distinctive characteristics of parent-offspring and sibling correlations and sex differences in frequency or central tendency is thereby proven to have a genetic basis. A behavioral trait for which X-linkage has been claimed is spatial visualization ability (Bock & Kolakowski, 1973), though the evidence for this claim is not entirely consistent (Bouchard & McGee, 1977). X-linkage has been claimed for some part of the variance in general intelligence (Lehrke, 1978), but the reported evidence for this hypothesis seems far from conclusive.

*Supergenes.* When particular combinations of different genes are especially favored by selection relative to other genetic combinations, they tend to become linked and to resist the process of crossing-over (which breaks up linkages) through the chromosomal mechanisms of inversion and translocation, processes which are themselves subject to genetic selection. The genetic suppression of crossing-over hence allows the formation of complexes of genes which are said to be *coadapted* to one another and which tend to be transmitted from one generation to the next as a unit, termed a *supergene* (Dobzhansky, 1970, Chapter 5). The process of chromosomal *inversion* during gametogenesis acts to resist crossing-over and recombination of linked genes so as to preserve favorable gene linkages. Different combinations of genes, coadapted for relatively optimal fitness in particular environments, form different supergenes in various strains of a species which are adapted to different habitats. The cross-breeding of such strains with different complexes of linked coadapted genes breaks up linkages through crossing-over, and results in recombinations of genes that are less favorably adapted to the habitat of either strain.

Practically all of our knowledge of supergenes maintained by inversions is derived from studies of various strains of Drosophila, other insects, and mice and rats (Dobzhansky, 1970, pp. 146–151). For technical reasons we need not explicate here, the detection of inversions is presently either difficult or impossible in many organisms, including humans. This fact, however, does not contradict the presence of supergenes in such organisms or diminish their potential theoretical significance. But it does mean that supergenes may often be practically undistinguishable from pleiotropy as a cause of correlated characters. Within some segment of the population, supergenes, like pleiotropy, would produce both within-family and between-family correlation between characters. The importance of inversions that maintain supergenes in humans remains speculative, for, as Dobzhansky (1970) notes "it is by no means certain that inversion polymorphism is absent or even rare in human populations" ( p. 150).

## Cautions in Research on Physical-Mental Correlations

Several general cautions should be noted in evaluating reported findings of associations between mental and physical traits.

*Unreplicated findings and Type I error.* In studies involving psychometric testing, it not infrequently happens that certain physical measurements are also available on the same group of subjects, for whatever reason, even when there has been no prior research plan to investigate associations between the psychometric and physical measurements. The researcher often calculates correlation coefficients among all of the available variables, but may report only those which are large enough to be statistically significant or to look "interesting." Nonsignificant, nondescript, or inconsistent correlations are more apt to be left unreported. This tendency disposes toward Type I error (i.e., rejection of the null hypothesis when it is in fact true) with respect to reported correlations between physical and mental traits. Hence, a reported correlation, however significant, should be regarded with some suspicion if it has not been independently replicated. In this field, at least, independent replications are much more convincing evidence for the reality of a phenomenon than is statistical significance per se. One should also note whether a study has been explicitly designed to test a particular hypothesis or whether a reported finding merely represents the adventitious by-product of investigating some other phenomenon; published reports of such adventitious findings are more liable to Type I error.

*Meta-analysis and the risk of Type II error.* The other side of the coin is the risk of Type II error (i.e., accepting the null hypothesis when it is in fact false). Undoubtedly much more frequent than Type I error in psychological research generally, Type II error is especially common in the literature on physical correlates of mental abilities. This type of error is most likely to occur when the true correlation is relatively small and investigators employ samples that are not large enough to give the null hypothesis a fair chance of rejection. Replications of the study under similar conditions merely reinforce and perpetuate the Type II error. Reviewers of the literature who merely report "box scores" of the number of studies with statistically significant and nonsignificant results draw conclusions which further entrench the Type II error as supposedly reliable psychological knowledge. The remedy for this condition is a meta-analysis of all the reported results, that is, a statistical assessment of the entire set of results, regardless of their authors' conclusions as to their significance or nonsignificance

(Hunter, Schmidt, & Jackson, 1982). The consistency of direction of the reported correlations (or other measures of association) in addition to their sample
sizes and the associated statistical $p$ values (probabilities) can be used, along with
information as to attenuating factors such as unreliability of measurement and
restriction of variance, to determine the overall statistical significance of the
composite results and to estimate the true unattenuated value of the correlation in
a specified population.

*Dependence of correlation on the normal-defective saddle-point.* A
"saddle-point" is a region in the total frequency distribution of a variable, in
which there is overlap of the underlying distributions of two essentially different
populations. In the distribution of IQ, the saddle-point falls in the region between
about IQs 50 to 70—the region of maximum overlap between the distribution of
biologically normal variation of intelligence and the distribution of IQs of the
mentally deficient, whose deficiency is often attributable to some specific defect.
The causes of such defects are most commonly mutant or recessive major gene
effects (e.g., phenylketonuria, galactosemia, Tay-Sachs, microcephaly), chromosomal anomalies (e.g., Down's syndrome, Kleinfelder's syndrome), and
brain damage due to prenatal or postnatal trauma or disease. When the bivariate
frequency distribution for a mental-physical correlation coefficient spans the
normal-defective saddle-point, the resulting correlation may not be generalizable
to the normal population; indeed, the analogous correlation may be zero (or even
opposite in sign) when calculated for the normal population only. Hence, the
theoretical interpretation of a correlation will be dependent upon the degree to
which it depends upon the saddle-point. Some quite substantial correlations fall
to near zero when they are calculated for the part of the bivariate distribution that
lies beyond the saddle-point. Failures to replicate correlations in independent
studies are often the result of the presence or absence of a saddle-point in the
various samples. The effect of the saddle-point is usually apparent from inspection of the correlation scatter-diagram, but this source of information is seldom
obtained by investigators and is rarely provided in published reports. Without
such information, the generalizability of any correlations based on samples that
include mentally deficient subjects should be questioned. Both the magnitudes
and causes of correlations between physical and mental variables within the
biologically mentally defective population can be quite different from the biologically normal population. Generally speaking, therefore, it is methodologically
unsound to combine samples of the two populations in a correlational study.

*Spurious index correlations in pre-adult samples.* Both mental and physical
variables show developmental changes with chronological age; consequently, in
a sample that ranges in age, the correlation between the variables of interest may
be due to this factor alone. The relationship of both variables to age should be
analyzed for linearity of their regression on age. If the regressions do not differ

significantly from linear, age (in months) should be partialed out of the correlation. When the relationship to age is nonlinear, the nonlinear components should be partialed out by means of a stepwise multiple regression analysis, in which successive powers of age (in months) are entered as the independent (predictor) variables ahead of entering the physical variable as the final independent variable, with the dependent variable being the psychometric score. Increasing powers of age (i.e., $age^1$, $age^2$, $age^3$, etc.) are entered stepwise into the multiple regression equation until the increment in $R^2$ is nonsignificant (at any desired level of confidence $\alpha$), as determined by the usual $F$ test. The age-partialed correlation between the physical and psychometric variables, in this case, is the square-root of the *increment* in $R^2$ resulting from the final-step entry of the physical variable in the multiple regression equation. (That is, the final increment in $R^2$ is the proportion of variance in the psychometric variable associated with the physical variable independent of age.) In many studies, possible nonlinear correlations between age and the variables of interest have not been ruled out, and some of the correlation between the variable of interest may be due to nonlinear age effects that remain after the simple partialing-out of the linear effect of age.

It should not be assumed that the use of age-standardized psychometric scores, such as the IQ, obviates the need for partialing age out of the physical-mental correlation. Although the age-standardization procedure necessarily causes IQ to be uncorrelated with age in the standardization sample, IQ may in fact be correlated with age in a particular study sample. Also, even if IQ, or any other age-standardized psychometric variable, has zero correlation with age, this fact does not obviate the need to partial out age from the correlation between the psychometric variable and the physical variable (physical measurements are usually not age-standardized). If an age-standardized score, $x$, is uncorrelated with age, $a$, and if $a$ is correlated with variable $y$, the zero-order correlation between $x$ and $y$, that is, $r_{xy}$, is not the same as the partial correlation between $x$ and $y$ with age held constant (i.e., $r_{xy \cdot a}$), as some studies have erroneously assumed. The age-partialed correlation in this case is always larger than the zero-order correlation, that is $r_{xy \cdot a} = r_{xy}/\sqrt{1 - r_{ya}^2}$.

*Correlations within and between populations.* A correlation found to exist between different traits within populations cannot be generalized to differences in the mean values of the traits between different populations, even if the very same size of correlation between the traits exists *within* each of the populations. In other words, knowing the regression of trait Y on trait X *within* populations does not permit any inference about the regression of the means of trait Y on the means of trait X in different populations, such as males and females and different racial groups. Whether the regression is the same or different between populations as within populations is a question that can be answered only by empirical investigation and not by logical inference. For example, the regression of body weight on height in the male population cannot predict the mean difference in weight between men and women from information on the mean height of each sex. The regression of weight on height is different for males and females. The same caveat applies to any correlated traits within any two or more populations.

## Limitations of the Present Review

We have attempted to survey virtually the entire literature on physical correlates of mental ability in humans, but have set several limitations which exclude topics that are less germane to our primary focus of interest, which is physical-mental correlations that have arisen in normal populations as a result of (a) environmental correlations (i.e., a single environmental factor affecting both physical and mental development), (b) genetic correlations between physical and mental traits due to (i) common segregation of genes through simultaneous selection on two or more traits, (ii) cross-assortative mating for two or more traits, and (iii) pleiotropy (i.e., the property of genes by which they affect two or more traits). We recognize that environmental and cultural factors may be involved in all of the above types of environmental and genetic correlation.

We have excluded consideration of relatively rare exogenous environmental factors that can affect intellectual performance, such as pathological conditions, or brain damage, or the effects of various drugs and toxic substances, or drugs that temporarily facilitate neural efficiency. These drug effects have been reviewed by Cattell (1971, pp. 198–204), who concludes that *"except for people in diseased or subnormal conditions,* no artificial drug has appeared that is capable of significantly increasing fluid general intelligence or bringing more than momentary improvements in crystallized intelligence . . ."* (p. 201).

Also, we are not concerned here with trait intercorrelations that depend upon the "saddle-point" between normal variation in intelligence and mental defect, or with rare genetic or chromosomal syndromes that display both physical and psychological anomalies. These conditions and their causes have been thoroughly treated in a classic work by the British geneticists Penrose and Haldane (1969). Correlated effects due to disease and trauma are also excluded.

Our focus is on mental *abilities,* particularly general intelligence, to the exclusion of other psychological traits. The term "IQ" is here used generically for scores on any psychometric tests that experience has shown to be predominantly loaded on the $g$ factor common to all complex tests of cognitive ability, including standard tests of intelligence. Special abilities are identified as such.

The purpose of this chapter is to provide an overview and guide to the literature concerning what seem to be certain more or less general and enduring correlations between physical factors and mental abilities in the population. Our intention is to be critically comprehensive rather than exhaustively encyclopedic. When other satisfactory reviews are available, we cite them and indicate their conclusions rather than citing all the original articles reviewed therein.

## GROSS ANATOMICAL CORRELATES OF INTELLIGENCE

### General Body Size

Numerous studies have found correlations between body size, as measured by height and weight, and ratings on psychometric assessments of general intelligence, or IQ. The fact that the correlation between height and weight is close to .70 within homogeneous age-groups indicates a large common factor—general body size. Hence, consistent or substantial differences between the correlations of height and weight with intellect are virtually nonexistent. What small differences exist can mostly be accounted for by sampling error. Various investigators have rationalized the particular (but inconsistent) differences they observed in various ways. Penrose and Haldane (1969, p. 36), for example, explained the higher correlation of weight ($r = +.324$), than of height ($r = +.154$), with intelligence in a sample of criminals as the result of weight's being a more comprehensive measurement of body size than any linear measurement, such as stature. They cite a factor analytic study (Burt & Banks, 1947) of body measurements in adult males, which showed that weight had the highest correlation of any measurement with the general factor reflecting overall body size. On the other hand, Tanner (1969) has argued that weight is a poor measure of body size because it is so affected by fat; he claims that the true relationship underlying the correlation of IQ with the dimensions of height and weight is the correlation between IQ and general body size. In this case, the ideal correlation to be sought is the correlation of IQ with factor scores on the general factor derived from the factor analysis of a comprehensive set of body measurements, including height and weight. Unfortunately, there is no evidence in the literature that such an analysis has ever been done. Short of this, other approaches are to use partial and multiple correlations. These methods are not applicable to most of the correlations reported in the literature, however, as published reports often fail to give one or two of the three zero-order correlations (i.e., height × IQ, weight × IQ, and height × weight) required to calculate the partial or the multiple correlations. In some cases sample sizes are too small for significant statistical resolution of the various components of covariance revealed by partial and multiple correlations when two of the zero-order correlations are generally very small to begin with. When the differences between the zero-order, partial, and multiple correlations are within the margin of sampling error (say, the 95% confidence interval), of course, no validity can be claimed for comparisons of these statistics. Provided the data and sample sizes have permitted such calculations, however, we have presented them. Also, insofar as possible, we have presented all correlations accompanied by their 95% confidence interval (i.e., $r + 1.96SE_r$); if this confidence interval does not subtend zero, the correlation is significant at $p < .05$ by a two-tailed test.

*Correlation in adults.* The correlation of height and weight with IQ is less complexly determined and more easily interpretable in adults than in children. Studies of adults and studies of children therefore should be dealt with separately. In adults, the correlation is not confounded with individual differences in the growth rates for physical and mental development. In young adults, moreover, stature and mental test scores are not confounded with age, so the correlation between these variables requires no statistical correction for age differences, as is required for correlations obtained in children or elder adults.

Sir Francis Galton, the first scientist to comment on the positive relationship between stature and intelligence, noted in his famous work *Hereditary Genius* (1869, p. 321) that men of genius tend to be above average in height and weight. This finding arises from the fact, now well established, that the positive relationship between body size and intelligence extends over the entire range of both variables. (Certain genetic and endocrine anomalies found at both extremes of stature account for the only exceptions.) Even among the mentally retarded, all with IQs below 70 or 75, there is a positive correlation between body size (height and/or weight) and IQ (Penrose & Haldane, 1969, p. 36; Whipple, 1914, pp. 70–72). The mentally retarded, on average, are shorter and lighter than the nonretarded population, although there is great overlap between retarded and normal groups in height and weight. At the other extreme, it has been noted that groups which are selected for superior mental ability, such as university students, are above the general average of their age peers in height and weight (Tanner, 1969).

Paterson's (1930) comprehensive review of the research literature before 1930 gives a frequency-weighted mean of all the correlations ($r$) for which there were no apparent shortcomings in the data or its statistical treatment, as mean $r = + .12$ for height and IQ, and mean $r = + .15$ for weight and IQ. Samples of university men, who are considerably more homogeneous as a group than men in general with respect to both IQ and social class of origin, show an average correlation of $+ .10$ between height and IQ.

Large-scale studies of adult samples since Paterson's 1930 review are scarce, but results of the few such studies available are fairly consistent. These studies, as reported in Tanner's (1969, p. 188) review, in addition to more recent studies by Susanne (1979) and Passingham (1979), are summarized in Table 4.1. The unit-weighed mean $r = + .218$. The $N$-weighted mean $r = + .229 \pm .04$. (The procedure for computing the 95% confidence interval for the $N$-weighted mean of a number of correlation coefficients based on independent samples is given in Table 4.2, footnote b.) The correlations in these more recent studies are significantly higher than the average of those reported for older studies by Paterson (1930). This is of interest, because in the populations represented by

### Table 4.1.  Correlation (r) Between Height and Intelligence Test Scores in Adult Samples

| Study | Sample | N | r[a] |
|---|---|---|---|
| Husén (1951) | Swedish conscripts | 2250 | +.22 ± .04 |
| Schreider (1956) | French conscripts | 566 | +.29 ± .08 |
| Scott, Illesley, & Thomson (1956) | Aberdeen women | 270 | +.24 ± .02 |
| Udjas (1964) | Norwegian conscripts, age 20 | — | +.16 |
| Susanne (1979) | Belgian conscripts, ages 17–25 | 2071 | +.179 ± .04 |
| Passingham (1979) | English men, ages 18–75 | 212 | +.12 ± .13[b] |
| Passingham (1979) | English women, ages 18–75 | 203 | +.14 ± .14[c] |

[a]Pearson r given with 95% confidence interval.
[b]With age partialed out, r = +.13.
[c]With age partialed out, r = +.15.

these studies, there has been a general improvement and trend toward social-class equalization of the health and nutrition factors affecting physical and mental development—factors often proposed to explain observed correlations between body size and intelligence. The cogency of such explanations is, of

### Table 4.2.  Correlation[a] (with 95% Confidence Interval) between Height and IQ in British Children

| Study | Age Group | N | r |
|---|---|---|---|
| Scottish survey | 11.0–11.9 years | 6490 | +.25 ± .02 |
| London survey | 10 and 11 years | 4000 | +.23 ± .03 |
| National survey | 8 years | 2864 | +.14 ± .04 |
| National survey | 11 years | 2864 | +.14 ± .04 |
| National survey | 15 years | 2864 | +.12 ± .04 |
| N-Weighted Mean | | | +.193 ± .10[b] |

[a]Age (in months) partialed out of correlations.
[b]The 95% confidence interval for the combined samples is computed as follows:

$$s_r^2 = \frac{\Sigma[N_i(r_i - \bar{r})^2]}{\Sigma N_i},$$

where $s_r^2$ is the N-weighted variance of r across samples.
   $N_i$ is the sample size for a single sample.
   $r_i$ is the correlation obtained in a single sample.
   $\bar{r}$ is the N-weighted mean of all sample values of $r_i$.
Then the estimated standard error of $\bar{r}$ is

$$SE_{\bar{r}} = \sqrt{s_r^2 - \frac{(1 - \bar{r}^2)^2 K}{\Sigma N_i}},$$

where $K$ = number of samples.
The 95% confidence interval, then, is $r \pm 1.96 SE_r$

course, weakened by these findings. If the stature × IQ correlation were primarily the result of social inequalities in health care and nutrition, one should predict a decrease in the correlation obtained in studies of contemporary adult populations as compared with correlations obtained prior to 1930. The observed increase in correlation, however, is consistent with the hypothesis that there has been an increase in assortative mating for both height and intelligence, a topic to be discussed in later sections on socioeconomic status and the between-family and within-family correlations of body size with IQ. An opposite trend, however, has been reported for data obtained in Denmark, in the largest study ever made of the height × intelligence correlation (Teasdale, Sørensen, & Owen, 1989). A virtually random sample of 43,979 Danish males, all 18 years of age, were obtained from draft board records, which contained measurements of height and scores on tests of intelligence and scholastic achievement. The data were divided into five cohorts according to the year of birth, between the years 1939 and 1967. The overall mean correlation between height and IQ is .231 ± .012 (99% confidence interval). (For height × educational achievement, mean $r$ = .253; the multiple $R$ of both IQ and achievement with height is .265.) The $r$ = .231 is remarkably close to the $N$-weighted mean $r$ = .229 of the earlier studies summarized in Table 4.1. But the more important feature of the Danish study is the quite regular and highly significant secular decrease in the height × IQ correlation, from .269 in the 1939–43 cohort to .195 in the 1964–67 cohort. There is a linear decrease in the $r$ of .03 per decade (the correlation between year of birth and the height × IQ correlation is − .90). A similar secular trend is seen for the height × achievement correlation. For Danish males born during the period 1939 to 1967 there was a highly significant increase in height (measured at age 18 years) of 4.3 cm, or approximately 1.1 cm per decade. The study's authors interpret these findings as follows:

> The decline in height differences between groups varying in intelligence and educational level is probably to be attributed to changing social factors, perhaps specifically a greater homogeneity of nutritional conditions across different social classes. It is notable, however, that the decline in group differences, and in the corresponding correlations, appears to have been more pronounced among those generations who were in their infancy during the 1940's. The decline thereafter has been less pronounced. It remains, therefore, to be seen whether such differences will disappear, particularly as the secular increases in height appear to be ending— Danish draft board records show the average height of males to have remained virtually stable at about 180 cms. for almost the last ten years. (p. 1293)

Given the indicated trend, we would predict that the height × IQ correlation would remain stable at about $r$ = .20, being maintained in a nutritionally homogeneous population by a simple genetic correlation due to both assortative and cross-assortative mating for height and intelligence.

*Nonlinearity of the height × ability correlation.* Assuming normal distributions of height and general mental ability, or *g*, a linear correlation (Pearson *r*) of + .20 between these variables implies that the tallest 2 percent and the shortest 2 percent would deviate, on average, one half of a standard deviation above or below the mean of the total distribution of *g*. A significant discrepancy from this prediction would indicate nonlinearity of the regression of *g* on height, and would imply that the Pearsonian correlations most commonly reported in the literature to some degree underestimate the true relationship between height and *g*. The difficulty in examining this possibility is that a very large and representative population sample would be required to demonstrate with confidence a relatively small departure from linearity.

A recent study (Teasdale, Owen, & Sørensen, 1991) addressed this question with analyses based on a very large ($N = 71,528$) and highly representative sample of men in Denmark, aged 18 to 26 (mean 19.7) years. On a composite measure of general ability, the mean of the shortest 2 percent of this huge sample fell approximately two-thirds of a *SD* below the overall mean, but the tallest 2% were only slightly more than one-half of a *SD* above the mean. A plot of intellectual ability as a function of height shows a very slight but highly significant departure from linearity, such that when a quadratic term (i.e., height$^2$) was included in the regression equation, the increment over linear correlation is highly significant ($p < 3 \times 10^{-73}$!). Although the authors analyzed their data in a rather complex way, using canonical correlations, here we can express their essential results in terms that more easily permit direct comparison with all the previous studies we have reviewed based on simple correlations. With geographical region of origin and year of birth statistically controlled, the simple linear correlation (Pearson *r*) between height and mental ability is + .2207. The multiple correlation, adding a quadratic component, with both height and height$^2$ as the independent variables, is .2215. Although the slight difference between these correlation coefficients is undoubtedly reliable, given the enormous sample size, its theoretical meaning may seem hard to imagine. The authors suggest that some proportion of very short individuals may have been subjected to factors that are detrimental to both physical growth and mental development, a hypothesis which accords with a review (Skuse, 1987) of studies of short-stature persons that claims evidence of some "minimal impairment" in this group.

*Correlation in children.* It was proposed by the noted anthropologist Franz Boas (1895) that the correlation between intelligence and body size in children arose from individual differences in the rate of growth and development; growth rate was assumed to affect both body size and intelligence. This *co-advancement* theory, as it was known, also assumed that as the rate of development decreased as children grew older, the correlation between body size and IQ should decrease to zero by adulthood. Boas supposed there was no relationship between stature and mental status after maturity. Boas's co-advancement theory now has at least four strikes against it: (a) the size = IQ correlation is found to be at least as high, or even slightly higher, in adults than in children; (b) a longitudinal study (Bayley, 1956) of children from ages 7 to 21 years showed high positive correlations (between .30 and .50) between height and intelligence scores at every age but found a nonsignificant *negative* relationship between mental and physical advancement *rates;* (c) although there are *within*-family differences (i.e., differences between siblings) in rates of physical and mental development, the evidence indicates that there exists no *within*-family correlation between IQ and height or weight; and (d) the correlations of height and weight with IQ (IQ measured at age 4 years) are virtually constant between the ages of 4 months and 4 years and between 8 years and 15 years of age (see Tables 4.2 and 4.3) no such constancy over these age ranges would be expected, because physical and mental growth rates are very negatively accelerated from infancy to maturity, and the sizes of the IQ × height (or weight) correlations do not appear to change systematically with the changing average differences in physical and mental growth rates throughout the course of development.

Three of the largest studies of the correlation between height and IQ in children, conducted in England and Scotland and described by Tanner (1969), are summarized in Table 4.2. The best estimate of the mean and the 95% confidence interval for the overall population value of the correlation is + .193 ± .10. A similar significant correlation was found between height and Raven Matrices scores in 98 third-grade Mexican children in Guadalajara (Pardo, Diaz, Hernandez-Vargas, & Hernandez-Vargas, 1971).

The largest American study with data relevant to this question is the Collaborative Perinatal Project of the National Institute of Neurological Disease and Stroke (an agency of the National Institutes of Health), which conducted a longitudinal investigation of 26,760 children from birth to 4 years of age (Broman, Nichols, & Kennedy, 1975). One hundred and seventy prenatal, perinatal, and early developmental variables, including Stanford-Binet IQ at age 4, were assessed in this study. Reported correlations between IQ at age 4 and height and weight measured at birth, 4 months, 8 months, 1 year, and 4 years are shown in Table 4.3. The correlations fluctuate very little with age. The correlations of height and weight with intelligence do not differ significantly at any age. The partial correlations indicate that weight (independent of height) has a slightly larger correlation with IQ than does height (independent of weight). Although higher levels of SES are underrepresented in this sample, the correlations shown in Table 4.3 probably do not appreciably underestimate the correlations between IQ and height or weight in the total population, because there is no restriction of range in IQ as compared with Stanford-Binet norms. The Collaborative Sample's IQ standard deviation is about 16.5 for whites and 13.9 for blacks.

The Pearson $r$, however, somewhat underestimates the true correlation of IQ with height and weight, because of nonlinear regression of IQ on the physical variables. The 4-year data, shown in Figure 4.5, are fairly typical. The higher Pearson $r$s (in Table 4.3) for blacks, as compared with whites, is clearly due to

Table 4.3. Zero-Order, Partial, and Multiple Correlations between Stanford-Binet IQ (I) at Age 4 Years and Height (H) and Weight (W) Measured at Various Ages

| | Sample Size[a] | | | | Correlation[b] | | | | | | | | | | | |
|---|---|---|---|---|---|---|---|---|---|---|---|---|---|---|---|---|
| | Height | | Weight | | White | | | | | | Black | | | | | |
| Age | White | Black | White | Black | $r_{HW}^c$ | $r_{IH}^d$ | $r_{IW}^d$ | $r_{IH·W}$ | $r_{IW·H}$ | $R_{I·HW}$ | $r_{HW}^c$ | $r_{IH}^d$ | $r_{IW}^d$ | $r_{IH·W}$ | $r_{IW·H}$ | $R_{I·HW}$ |
| Birth | 11,937 | 14,292 | 12,199 | 14,536 | 71 | 07 | 08 | 02 | 04 | 082 | 74 | 12 | 12 | 05 | 05 | 129 |
| 4 months | 11,278 | 13,446 | 11,235 | 13,476 | 62 | 09 | 11 | 03 | 07 | 113 | 68 | 14 | 16 | 04 | 09 | 165 |
| 8 months | 4,427 | 5,368 | 4,436 | 5,381 | 66 | 10 | 10 | 05 | 05 | 110 | 66 | 16 | 14 | 09 | 05 | 166 |
| 1 year | 10,826 | 13,161 | 10,826 | 13,155 | 64 | 11 | 11 | 05 | 05 | 121 | 61 | 13 | 14 | 06 | 08 | 151 |
| 4 years | 9,966 | 12,227 | 9,953 | 12,287 | 68 | 11 | 12 | 04 | 06 | 126 | 71 | 14 | 16 | 04 | 09 | 164 |
| Mean[e] | 9,686.8 | 11,708.8 | 9,729.8 | 11,767.0 | 664 | 095 | 104 | 036 | 054 | 109 | 686 | 135 | 144 | 051 | 074 | 153 |

[a]From Broman, Nichols, & Kennedy (1975), Appendix 3, Table 1. Decimals omitted. The zero-order correlations of IQ with height or weight are corrected for attenuation, based on IQ reliability of .83 (see Broman et al., p. 37). The partial and multiple correlations are based on the disattenuated zero-order correlations. All the zero-order correlations ($r_{HW}$, $r_{IH}$, $r_{IW}$) are significant at $p < .001$. The 95% confidence interval for all zero-order, partial, and multiple correlations (except those at age 8 months) is $r \pm .02$; for those at 8 months, it is $r \pm .03$.

[b]

[c]From Broman et al., Table 9.2, p. 126.

[d]From Broman et al., Appendix 4, Table 1.

[e]$N$-weighted mean, using Fisher's $z$ transformation of $r$.

the greater linearity of the regression of IQ on height and weight in blacks than in whites. The shortest and lightest children contribute disproportionately to the correlation, which therefore would be markedly reduced if the smallest children within each age group were excluded. However, a significant relationship of IQ to height and weight has been found at every level of IQ.

A sample of 594 of Terman's gifted children, selected for Stanford-Binet IQs of 140 or above, showed the following correlations of Stanford-Binet mental age with height and weight, holding chronological age constant (Terman, 1926, p. 168):

|  | Boys ($N = 312$) | Girls ($N = 282$) |
|---|---|---|
| Height: | .219 ± .11 | .211 ± .12 |
| Weight: | .051 ± .11 | .035 ± .12 |

The Harvard Growth Study (Dearborn, Rothney, & Shuttleworth, 1938) is a large longitudinal study of the correlation between physical and mental measurements obtained on the same group of children at yearly intervals between the ages of 7 and 18 years. The correlations are based on about 500 boys and 700 girls; a small percentage of the children was not measured every year, however, so the sample sizes for the obtained correlations vary slightly from year to year. Because the groups were very homogeneous in age at each measurement period, the correlations of height and intelligence with age are so small that partialing age out of the correlation between height and intelligence would not make an appreciable difference. The reliability of the intelligence measures varies slightly but unsystematically from year to year, averaging about .80. (The height-intelligence correlations could be corrected for attenuation by dividing them by the square root of the reliability, i.e., about .90, which increases the correlation by about .02 to .04.) Table 4.4 shows the zero-order uncorrected correlations between height and intelligence at every year of age between 7 and 18 years, for girls and boys. The most striking feature seen in Table 4.4 is the rather consistently lower correlation between height and intelligence in boys than in girls. (Boys' mean $r = .227$, $SD = .036$; girls' mean $r = .287$, $SD = .054$.) We can think of no plausible explanation for this correlation difference between the sexes. Another developmental study (Brucefors et al., 1974), based on 202 children, found a positive correlation between physical and mental growth *rates* over a much shorter age range for boys (4 weeks to 2 years) than for girls (2 to 8 years), resulting in a slightly higher correlation for girls, although the correlation for boys remains significant throughout the entire period of the study, from 4 weeks to 8 years.

The fact that the correlations for both sexes in the Harvard Growth Study are generally larger than those found in the other studies is probably attributable to the greater heterogeneity of the sample, which was obtained in Boston in the 1930s. The authors present evidence that the large proportions of children of

Northern and Southern European heritage in this population contributes to the height-intelligence correlation, as those of Northern European extraction measure taller and obtain higher intelligence test scores, on average, than those of Southern European extraction. In this population, for both girls and boys, the size of the correlation between height and intelligence shows a slight curvilinear (inverted U) relationship to age (see the correlations in the principal diagonal in Table 4.4).

The data of the Harvard Growth Study have been recently subjected to a number of sophisticated statistical analyses by Humphreys, Davey, and Park (1985) in an effort to understand better the nature of the height × IQ correlation. They confirm the overall correlation of about + .2 and the slight, but apparently real, sex difference in the correlation, for which they offer no explanation. However, a cross-lagged correlation analysis, which analyzes the changes in the correlation between height and intelligence when each variable is measured at *different* ages, showed that, for girls, individual differences in height predict individual differences in IQ measured several years later, which suggests a common causal factor in girls' development that affects individual differences in height earlier than in intelligence. The same effect shows up to a much slighter degree in boys, for whom the cross-lagged height × IQ correlations remain relatively more constant across all age intervals. In both sexes, but especially in girls, early height predicts later intelligence better than early intelligence predicts later height. Humphreys et al. state:

> Changes in biological functioning, whatever the causes may be, are not expected to have an immediate effect on intelligence behaviors. The intelligence measured by a standard test is a behavioral repertoire that is acquired over time. A biological deficit of less than traumatic proportions could affect future acquisitions but not the current repertoire. Thus intelligence would lag behind growth. (p. 1477)

Another interesting finding of this analysis by Humphreys et al. (1985) results from the different correlations obtained between IQ and *sitting* height as compared with *standing* height. The difference between the two height measurements, of course, reflects leg length. It turns out that virtually all of the height × IQ correlation is attributable to leg length. The correlation between sitting height and IQ, when standing height is partialed out, is either zero (for boys) or negative (for girls); but partialing sitting height out of the correlation between standing height and IQ has scarcely any effect for either sex. For girls, sitting height is negatively correlated with IQ; the girls' highly positive correlation between standing height and IQ is entirely attributable to individual differences in leg length! We can think of two speculative interpretations of this phenomenon: (a) Nutritional differences affect both mental and physical development, but the growth of the long bones of the legs is much more affected by nutritional factors than is the growth of other somatic features. (b) There is cross-assortative mating

Table 4.4. Correlations (Decimals Omitted) between Height and Intelligence Measured at Yearly Intervals from Age 8 to Age 17 for Girls and Boys (in Parentheses). (From Dearborn et al., 1938.)

| Height at Age | Intelligence at Age (Yrs.) | | | | | | | | | |
|---|---|---|---|---|---|---|---|---|---|---|
| | 8 → | 9 → | 10 → | 11 → | 12 → | 13 → | 14 → | 15 → | 16 → | 17 → |
| 8 | 31 (21) | 31 (17) | 35 (28) | 38 (24) | 41 (25) | 33 (19) | 32 (19) | 34 (21) | 32 (20) | 25 (14) |
| 9 | 30 (20) | 32 (21) | 34 (29) | 38 (26) | 40 (27) | 35 (24) | 33 (23) | 35 (24) | 32 (24) | 25 (16) |
| 10 | 29 (20) | 31 (20) | 33 (27) | 37 (24) | 39 (27) | 33 (24) | 32 (22) | 33 (22) | 32 (23) | 25 (15) |
| 11 | 27 (19) | 29 (20) | 31 (27) | 35 (25) | 38 (28) | 32 (25) | 30 (23) | 32 (24) | 32 (24) | 25 (28) |
| 12 | 28 (19) | 29 (20) | 29 (26) | 33 (25) | 37 (28) | 32 (25) | 30 (22) | 32 (25) | 31 (24) | 25 (17) |
| 13 | 27 (19) | 29 (20) | 28 (26) | 31 (24) | 34 (29) | 31 (24) | 29 (21) | 30 (25) | 30 (22) | 23 (17) |
| 14 | 25 (20) | 27 (20) | 26 (26) | 30 (24) | 33 (28) | 29 (25) | 28 (21) | 28 (24) | 27 (22) | 24 (18) |
| 15 | 22 (18) | 25 (20) | 22 (26) | 29 (25) | 31 (28) | 27 (25) | 26 (22) | 26 (25) | 24 (23) | 23 (18) |
| 16 | 20 (16) | 24 (19) | 21 (27) | 27 (25) | 30 (28) | 25 (26) | 24 (23) | 23 (25) | 22 (24) | 22 (18) |
| 17 | 17 (13) | 21 (16) | 16 (25) | 23 (24) | 25 (28) | 21 (26) | 19 (22) | 18 (23) | 18 (22) | 21 (18) |

between IQ (of men) and leg length (of women), resulting in a simple (between-families) genetic correlation between IQ and leg length in the offspring generation. A longstanding Western cultural stereotype of the attractive female (from the male viewpoint) is the long-legged female exemplified in the Petty-girl "calendar art." Beauty contestants—Miss America, Miss Universe—are notably tall and relatively long-legged compared to the average woman. Of course, these two hypotheses are not mutually exclusive; both could contribute to the observed phenomenon.

*IQ, body size, and socioeconomic status (SES).* The correlation between IQ and SES, as indexed by education, occupation, and income, is so well established and well known as to scarcely call for documentation. In school-age children the correlation averages about + .40, ranging from about .25 to .55 in various samples; in adults, the correlation is considerably higher, averaging about + .65 and ranging between about .55 and .75 (Eysenck, 1979; Jensen, 1973, 1980a; Tyler, 1965).

There is also a low but reliable positive correlation between body size (height or weight) and SES (Dearborn et al., 1938; Schreider, 1967; Tanner, 1966, 1969; Whipple, 1914, p. 70). Also, Schreider (1967) found that there is a negative correlation between the average height in different occupations and the standard deviation of IQs within those occupations; in other words, taller occupational groups (which also have higher average IQs) show smaller variability in IQ than shorter occupational groups.

The correlations between height and SES (correlations are not given between weight and SES) found in the Collaborative Study by Broman et al. (1975) are typical of those found in other studies of children, yet are much more reliable because of the large sample sizes. These are most easily summarized in terms of Figure 4.6. SES and IQ are correlated with height to about the same degree; partialing out each variable, of course, lowers the correlation, but not by very much. (Significant differences between zero-order and partial correlations are indicated by arrows.) The partial *r*s are all significant, indicating that both IQ and height are independently correlated with SES, which in this study is a composite index based on the head of household's education, occupation, and income. That IQ is correlated with body size independently of SES is further shown by the fact that a correlation of nearly the same magnitude also exists within broad SES categories, as shown in the study by Broman et al. (1975) and summarized in Table 4.5. These comparisons are especially important from a theoretical standpoint, because they make it implausible that environmental factors often associated with SES, such as nutrition and health care, could be major causal factors in the association between IQ and body size. The correlations *within* SES categories are barely smaller than the correlations in all of the SES categories combined. (Compare the within-SES correlations in Table 4.5 with the correlations for the combined SES groups at age 4 years in Table 4.3.)

Tanner (1969, pp. 194–198) has pointed out that height, considered indepen-

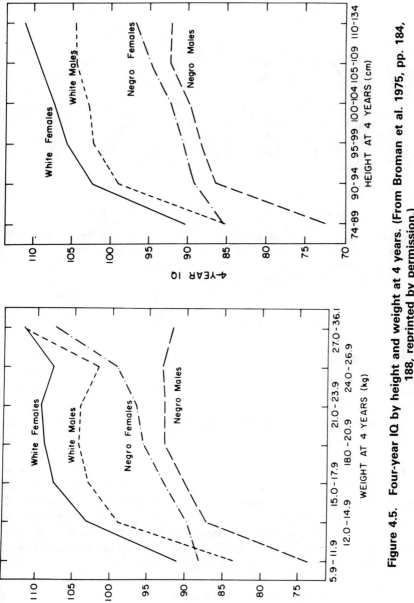

Figure 4.5. Four-year IQ by height and weight at 4 years. (From Broman et al. 1975, pp. 184, 188, reprinted by permission.)

169

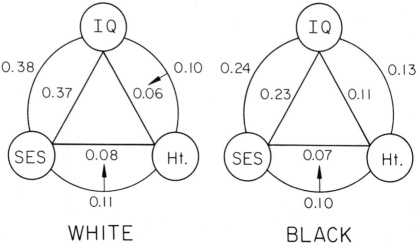

WHITE                    BLACK

**Figure 4.6.** Zero-order correlations (curved lines) and partial correlations, with the third variable partialled out (straight lines) between age-4 Stanford-Binet IQ, age-4 height, and socioeconomic status. The 95% confidence interval for all correlations is $r + .02$. Arrows indicate the partial correlations which are significantly ($p < .05$, one-tailed test) smaller than the corresponding zero-order correlation. Whites $N = 9,790$; blacks $N = 12,064$. (Zero-order correlations from Broman et al. [1975].)

dently of SES and family origin, is positively related to social mobility. An analysis of this phenomenon by Schreider (1964) shows that among all women born into any given social stratum (as indexed by father's occupation), the taller women, on average, move upwards in their own occupational status and marry men of higher status, whereas shorter women, on average, move in the opposite direction. Examples of this relationship between height and social mobility may be seen most clearly in Figures 4.7 and 4.8 from Tanner (1969, pp. 196–197). (Note: The obvious drafting error in Tanner's figure [p. 197], viz., the reverse ordering of husband's occupation, has here been corrected in Figure 4.8.) The trends shown in Figures 4.7 and 4.8 are most likely mediated by the association between height and intelligence, for intelligence is even more markedly related to social mobility than height per se. However, the significant partial correlation between SES and height, with IQ held constant, suggests that height (or general body size) makes some slight contribution to social mobility independently of the association between height and IQ. If the data represented in Figure 4.7 are at all typical of other studies, husband's occupational status is highly correlated (about .65) with husband's IQ; hence, there is here a strong implication of positive cross-assortative mating for wife's stature and husband's intelligence. The genetic effect of cross-assortative mating for two heritable traits is to bring about a genetic correlation between the traits in the offspring generation, due to the

**Table 4.5. Mean and Standard Deviation of 4-Year Stanford-Binet IQ and the Correlations[a] of IQ (I) with Height (H) and Weight (W) Measured at Age 4 Years in White and Black Samples[b]**

| | 4-Year IQ | | | | 4-Year Height | | 4-Year Weight | |
| | White[c] | | Black[c] | | White | Black | White | Black |
| SES | Mean | SD | Mean | SD | $r_{IH}$ | $r_{IH}$ | $r_{IW}$ | $r_{IW}$ |
|---|---|---|---|---|---|---|---|---|
| Upper 25% | 110.9 | 16.5 | 97.7 | 14.3 | .08 ± .03 | .12 ± .05 | .10 ± .03 | .10 ± .05 |
| Middle 50% | 101.3 | 15.1 | 92.0 | 13.5 | .06 ± .03 | .10 ± .02 | .07 ± .03 | .13 ± .02 |
| Lower 25% | 95.6 | 15.0 | 88.0 | 13.2 | .12 ± .06 | .14 ± .03 | .11 ± .06 | .15 ± .03 |

[a]Correlations given with 95% confidence intervals.
[b]Data from Broman et al. (1975), Tables 10.24 (p. 185) and 10.26 (p. 189).
[c]Total sample size: Whites = 9,790; Blacks = 12,064.

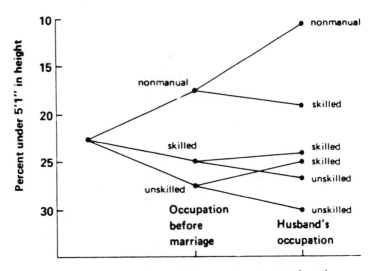

Aberdeen primiparae born to skilled manual workers

Figure 4.7.    Percentage of daughters (of skilled manual workers) under
5'1" tall taking nonmanual, skilled, and unskilled manual jobs and
marrying men in nonmanual, skilled-manual, and unskilled manual
occupations. (From Tanner, 1969, p. 196.)

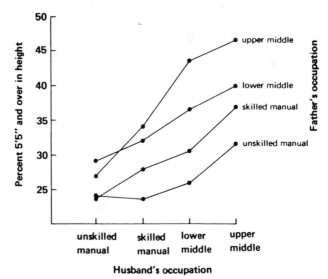

Figure 4.8.    Percentage of British women 5'5" and over in height
according to occupations of father and husband. (From Tanner,
1969, p. 197.)

common assortment of the independently segregating genes that affect each trait, a correlation that is manifested in the population as a correlation *between* families, but not *within* families. This interpretation of the correlation between intelligence and body size would be substantiated by studies which analyze the population correlation into its *between*-families and *within*-families components.

*Between- and within-family correlations of body size and intelligence.* There are studies reported in the literature which directly address the question of whether the body size × intelligence correlation observed in the population exists *within* as well as *between* families. Noting Terman's (1926) finding that gifted children, IQs of 140 and above, are taller and heavier and have generally better physiques than their agemates of average IQ, Laycock and Caylor (1964) decided to investigate this association in terms of between- and within-family correlation, by comparing "gifted" children with their "nongifted" siblings on a number of physical dimensions. They defined "gifted" to include IQs over 120 on the Stanford-Binet or over 130 on the California Test of Mental Maturity. In a large sample of gifted children of school age, they found that one in six had an older or younger sibling whose IQ was lower by 20 points or more. By these criteria, 81 pairs of gifted children and their nongifted siblings were selected for study. The gifted group had a mean IQ of 141.1, $SD = 13.5$; their nongifted siblings' mean IQ was 108.8, $SD = 10.8$. Thus the gifted and nongifted groups differ in IQ by 2.64 standard deviation units. The correlations between siblings in height ($r = .52 \pm .22$) and in weight ($r = .46 \pm .22$) are very typical of other studies, while the sibling correlation for IQ ($r = .68 \pm .22$) is higher (though not significantly so) than the $r$ of .49, which is the average of all sibling correlations for IQ reported in the literature (Paul, 1980). Measurements of height, weight, shoulder width, and leg circumference, standardized for age and sex, were obtained on all subjects. The gifted children and their nongifted siblings showed no significant differences on any of the physical measurements. Such differences as were observed are all very small and nonsignificant, but are all in the direction that favors the gifted. The difference between gifted and nongifted siblings in height, for example, amounted to .059 $SD$, and for weight, .073 $SD$. This small disparity in these highly intercorrelated physical measurements is most likely due to sampling error and a possible slight error introduced by the study's dependence on age-standardized measurements. A more ideal, but scarcely practicable, method would have been to measure each pair of siblings at exactly the same age. (The use of same-sex fraternal, i.e., dizygotic, twins for this type of study would completely obviate the problem of age differences between full siblings, as dizygotic twins are full siblings, genetically speaking, born at the same time.)

These results are highly consistent with the hypothesis that the correlation between body size and IQ exists only between families. Laycock and Caylor (1964) attribute the positive correlation between physical and mental measurements to superior home care of gifted children and their siblings; in other words, they hypothesize an environmental correlation. While this possibility cannot be ruled out, the very high broad heritability of stature (close to .95 in industrialized societies) and the substantial broad heritability of IQ (close to .70) would make it seem more likely that the association between IQ and stature is mainly a genetic correlation due to both assortative and cross-assortative mating for intelligence and stature, for which the average coefficients of assortative mating (i.e., correlation between mates) are about .45 and .30, respectively (Jensen, 1978).

The second study (Husén, 1959) compared the between-family (BF) and within-family (WF) correlations between height and IQ in samples of MZ and DZ male twins. Since both traits show substantial heritability, one should expect a difference in the ratio of BF/WF correlations for MZ and DZ twins if there is a WF genetic correlation between height and IQ. In that case the DZ WF height × IQ correlation should be larger than the MZ WF correlation, because in MZ twins all of the WF correlation would have to be environmental, while in DZ twins both genetic and environmental factors would contribute to the WF height × IQ correlation. Husén found no significant difference (in fact, it was slightly opposite to the theoretical prediction) between the WF correlations (relative to the BF correlations) obtained in the two types of twins. This finding is consistent with the absence of a within-family genetic correlation, and hence the absence of pleiotropy, between height and intelligence.

The third study (Jensen, 1980b) of within-family correlations is based on pairs of siblings from 1,495 white families and 901 black families in grades 2 to 6 (ages of about 7 to 12 years) in California schools. In all cases, the pair of siblings in each family nearest in age and enrolled in grades 2 to 6 was selected for study. In addition to measurements of height and weight, test scores were obtained on Verbal, Nonverbal, and Pictorial IQ (Lorge-Thorndike), Vocabulary, Reading Comprehension, and Short-Term Memory. All test scores as well as all height and weight measurements were age-standardized; score standardization was based on data for an entire school district with approximately 8,000 pupils. Correlations of height and weight with the seven mental tests were calculated *between* families and *within* families. The results clearly show that the correlation between the physical and mental measurements exists only *between* families, for which the average correlation is + .10 ± .04 (significant at $p <$ .01), whereas the average *within*-family correlation is a nonsignificant + .02 ± .04.

The fourth study (Nagoshi & Johnson, 1987) examined BF and WF correlations between height and general intelligence (scores derived from the first unrotated principal component of 15 diverse mental tests, here referred to as $g$) in full siblings in the Hawaii Family Study of cognition. (Other analyses from the same Hawaii study, yielding highly similar results, are given by Baker, 1983.) The height × $g$ correlations were computed separately between and within brother pairs, sister pairs, and brother-sister pairs. For Americans of European ancestry (AEA) ($N = 467$), the mean BF correlation between height and $g$ is +

.17 ± .09; the mean WF correlation is + .07 ± .09. For Americans of Japanese ancestry (AJA) ($N$ = 144), the mean BF correlation is + .10 ± .16; the mean WF correlation is − .02 ± .16. (The 95% confidence interval is given with each $r$.) These results are consistent with the hypothesis that the height × intelligence correlation is only a between-families phenomenon. In the AEA parents there was a significant cross-correlation between height and intelligence, but there was no significant correlation in the AJA parents, which might account in small part for the lower height × $g$ correlation in the AJA than in the AEA offspring. The overall height × $g$ correlation (averaged for males and females) in the AEA parents ($N$ = 1959) is + .14 ± 4.04; for their offspring ($N$ = 768), + .10 ± .07. The corresponding correlations in the AJA parents ($N$ = 766) and offspring ($N$ = 321) are + .13 ± .07 and + .05 ± .11, respectively. The consistently higher height × $g$ correlation in the parent than in the offspring generation suggests some environmental factor, perhaps nutrition, is largely responsible for the height × $g$ correlation, assuming that the offspring generation has grown up under more homogeneous environmental conditions than their parents did, which seems a reasonable assumption.

*Family size and birth order.* Height and weight, like intelligence and SES, are negatively related to family size (see Tanner, 1969, for a good review of this evidence). All of these correlations are mediated by social class. Family size per se has virtually no causal effect on height, weight, or intelligence. A study of over 20,000 high school graduates in the United States showed that family size (i.e., number of siblings) accounted for four percent of variance in IQ; but when SES and race were controlled, family size and birth order together accounted for less than half of one percent of the IQ variance (Page & Grandon, 1979). The negative relationship of family size to IQ is clearly due to differences *between* families in other factors besides family size. Evidence from other studies supports the same conclusion. (For a comprehensive review, see Ernst & Angst, 1983.) The largest study of the relationship between height, intelligence, and family size, by Belmont, Stein, and Susser (1975), is based on a total sample of 234,837 Dutch conscripts tested at 19 years of age. Height measurements and scores on Raven's Standard Progressive Matrices were both transformed to a common scale ($z$ scores) and plotted as a function of family size (total number of children), with the result shown in Figure 4.9. Birth order is also negatively related to both height and intelligence, as shown in the left-side panel of Figure 4.10. But when height and intelligence are plotted as a function of birth order separately for each size of family, so as to unconfound the correlated variables of family size and birth order, we see (as shown in the right-side panel of Figure 4.10) that intelligence is still related to birth order, whereas height shows no consistent relationship to birth order. The right-side panel of Figure 4.10 indicates the expected result if the negative relationship between birth order and intelligence is a *within*-family (as well as between-families) correlation, in contrast to height, which is unrelated to birth order *within* families. This finding

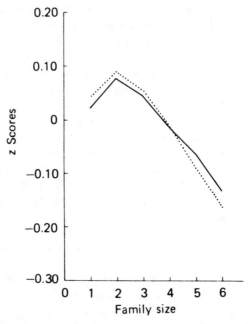

**Figure 4.9.   Height (solid line) and intelligence (broken line) by family size. (From Belmont, Stein, & Susser, 1975.)**

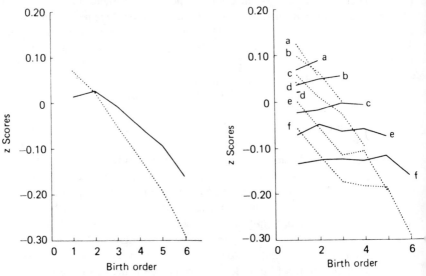

**Figure 4.10.   Height (solid line) and intelligence (broken line) as a function of birth order when (left panel) family size is confounded with birth order, and (right panel) birth order and family size are unconfounded. (From Belmont et al., 1975.)**

of Belmont et al. (1975) is consistent with the failure to detect a significant within-families correlation between height (or weight) and intelligence in the previously described studies by Laycock and Caylor (1964) and Jensen (1980b). This is not to say that we believe the apparent birth-order effect on IQ shown by Belmont et al. is a direct causal effect of birth order per se. The observed effect is artifactual in the sense that it can be attributed to uncontrolled variables in the composition of the sample which are correlated with both IQ and birth order. An exceptionally thorough critical review of the literature on birth order and IQ, including the study by Belmont et al., points out these sampling artifacts and arrives at the following conclusion:

> In extremely *large and representative samples* IQ differences by birth order approach zero when [social] background variables are appropriately controlled. . . . The comparison of *sibs within the same sibship* excludes interfamilial differences and is of paramount importance for assessing whether birth order differences in IQ between unrelated sibs are within- or between-family differences. Among sibs within the same sibships birth order differences [are] near zero. Where they appear, they amount to 1 or 2 IQ points and are either sample-specific or due to disregarding the fact that when sampling younger sibs, those of large, narrowly spaced sibships are more likely to be included. (Ernst & Angst, 1983, p. 49)

*Contradictory evidence.* We have found only one study (Burks, 1940) that would appear to contradict our general conclusion that the correlation between body size and IQ exists between families but not within families. Yet the seeming contradiction is probably more apparent than real. In a group of 20 pairs of monozygotic twins, Burks obtained the correlations between the intrapair differences in IQ and the intrapair differences in several physical measurements. (The IQ and physical measurements are based on the average of measurements taken yearly over a period of several years [median of 7 years] between the ages of 3 to 11 years; this averaging has the effect of increasing the reliability of the composite mental and physical measurements used to obtain the intrapair difference correlations.) These correlations, with their 95% confidence intervals, are shown in the first column of Table 4.6. These are within-family (more precisely, within MZ twin-pair) correlations and, at least for height, trunk length, and iliac width, are much higher than the usual between-family correlations of IQ with any physical traits. These quite large intrapair-difference correlations would seem to be inconsistent with the finding of many other studies that show negligible within-family correlations between IQ and measurements of body size. However, the fact that the correlations in Burks' study are based on MZ twins explains the apparent contradiction. Any differences between MZ twins, which have identical genotypes, necessarily arise exclusively from nongenetic, or environmental, causes. The fact that the nongenetic variance *within* pairs is very small relative to the variance *between* pairs (which is due to both genetic and nongenetic factors) is shown by the extremely high correlation between twins on IQ and on the physical measurements (see second column of Table 4.6). The very small within-pair differences, perhaps arising from inequalities of the prenatal intrauterine environment, can affect both mental and physical development and hence can be quite substantially correlated *within* pairs, even though these particular environmental effects contribute probably as little as 1 percent to 3 percent of the total individual differences variance in either IQ or the body-size measures. In other words, the use of MZ twins eliminates the main source (i.e., the genetic component) of the within-family variance found with full siblings, who have only about half of their genes in common. The small amount of nongenetic variance, relative to the genetic variance, that could enter into within-family IQ × physical trait correlations based on full siblings would be almost completely swamped by the uncorrelated (within-family) genetic components of the mental and physical traits. Hence the results of Burks' study are what we should expect if the hypothesis is correct that the observed correlation between IQ and body size exists *between* families and not *within* families, as a consequence of a between-families simple genetic correlation between the traits. Note that the overall correlations in Burks' sample between *individual differences* in IQ and physical measures (last column in Table 4.6) are in the same range as those in most other studies. The real importance of Burks' study is that it shows that some part of the (IQ) difference between MZ twins is attributable to aspects of the environment which also affect physical growth and therefore are not entirely of a psychosocial nature.

**Table 4.6.   Correlation (and 95% Confidence Interval) of IQ and Anthropometric Measurements in Monozygotic Twins[a]**

| Trait | Correlation between Intrapair IQ Difference and Intrapair Difference in Physical Trait[b] | Correlation between Twins[c] | Correlation between IQ and Physical Trait[d] |
|---|---|---|---|
| IQ | | .95 ± .06 | |
| Height | .47 ± .35 | .96 ± .06 | .17 |
| Weight | .12 ± .43 | .98 ± .03 | −.02 |
| Leg Length | .11 ± .43 | .92 ± .09 | .29 |
| Trunk Length | .40 ± .38 | .98 ± .03 | .08 |
| Iliac[e] | .41 ± .38 | .89 ± .12 | −.11 |

[a]From Burks (1940, pp. 89–90).
[b]Based on average intrapair differences of 20 MZ pairs of both sexes.
[c]Based on 10 pairs of male MZ twins of ages 9 years 7 months to 10 years 6 months.
[d]Based on 21 males (members of 11 twin pairs), ages 9 years 7 months to 10 years 6 months. Confidence intervals not computed because of the high intrapair correlations on these traits.
[e]For a single measure of the iliac taken beyond age 12 years 6 months, the correlation with IQ drops to −.04 ± .46.

*Causal factors.* If the correlation between body size and intelligence is an exclusively between-families correlation and does not exist within families, as the preponderance of the evidence suggests, it necessarily follows that the correlation is not pleiotropic, but that it is instead the phenotypic expression of either a genetic correlation or an environmental correlation, or some amalgam of both. The fact that the correlation is found within every level of social class, in groups with little or no variation in nutrition or other health factors, in addition to the extremely high heritability of stature and the moderate heritability of intelligence, makes it more likely that a genetic correlation, rather than common environment or correlated environmental factors affecting both size and intelligence, is the principal cause of the phenotypic body size $\times$ intelligence correlation. This correlation would seem to be maintained at a "steady-state" level of close to $+ .20$ in the young adult population, most probably as a result of assortative and cross-assortative mating for stature and intelligence in every generation. Men and women tend to choose mates of similar stature (with an assortative mating coefficient of about $+ .20$) and even more similar intelligence (coefficient of about $+ .40$), with the result that genes for both traits are assorted together in the offspring. Although it is easy enough to understand homogamy for these two traits, it seems somewhat more difficult to account for the existence of cross-assortative mating for stature and intelligence. Two hypotheses are suggested: (a) social class propinquity, that is, the greater probability of mating within, rather than outside of, one's own social class, plus the fact that social classes differ statistically in stature and intelligence, and (b) both high intelligence and tall stature tend to be valued as personal qualities in our culture and there is some degree of "tradeoff" between these qualities in mate selection.

We have found only one other type of explanation for the stature $\times$ IQ correlation. A positive relationship has been noted between stature and vanillyl mandelic acid (VMA) level in the urine (Henrotte, 1967). VMA is a breakdown product of catecholamine metabolism. As catecholamines are neurotransmitters involved in states of arousal, tone of awareness, and alertness, they may also be related to intelligence. It is on this basis that Henrotte suggests the hypothesis that the correlation between stature and the intelligence levels of different occupational groups is a result of differences in catecholamine metabolism. Unfortunately, the study does not distinguish between-families and within-family correlations of VMA level with stature. One would expect such a correlation to exist within, as well as between, families, possibly as a pleiotropic effect, that is, as the result of a gene affecting both catecholamine metabolism and stature. The apparent absence of a within-family correlation between height and intelligence, however, is inconsistent with the hypothesis that both stature and IQ are *causally* related to VMA. It is possible, of course, for there to exist a pleiotropic correlation between VMA and intelligence, and a (noncausal) genetic correlation between stature and intelligence. If such is the case, one would predict a within-family correlation between VMA level and intelligence and only a between-family correlation between VMA level and stature. This prediction would seem more likely than the reverse, because of the known connection between VMA and neuronal activity. What is clearly needed is a sibling study of the correlation between VMA and intelligence.

*Height-weight ratios and indices.* Early students of the body size × intelligence relationship, finding only very small correlations of the primary measurements of height or weight with mental test scores, hoped to discover some nonadditive combination of bodily measurements that would yield a more impressive correlation. Combinations of various ratios were tried, such as weight/height$^2$, weight/height$^3$, sitting height/height, height–chest girth + weight, and so forth. The results of these efforts have been reviewed by Paterson (1930, pp. 166–169), who reports that none of the indices yielded significant correlations with intelligence. The correlations based on compound measures were no larger, and often smaller, than those found for simple measurements of height or weight. The correlation of the height/weight ratio with IQ in 206 high school seniors and college freshmen was an unimpressive + .10 ± .14, for example (Paterson, 1930, p. 167). Yet given the relatively small samples used in most of these studies, the 95% confidence intervals for most of the correlations are between $r ± .17$ and $r ± .20$. We have not found any correlational studies making use of such compound physical indices reported in the literature since Paterson's review.

*Obesity and IQ.* Although weight, being highly related to general body size, is positively correlated with IQ, obesity (defined as 20% or more overweight for sex, age, height, and build) has been found to be *negatively* correlated with IQ in adults (Kreze, Zelina, Juhas, & Garbara, 1974). The negative correlation is much higher in women than in men. The percentages of women in the lower and upper quartiles of IQ who were classified as obese are 41.4% and 10.7%, respectively. The corresponding percentages for men are 17.0% and 9.3%. The inverse relationship between IQ and obesity is most likely mediated by a third variable—social class, which is positively correlated with IQ and negatively correlated with obesity (Goldblatt, Moore, & Stunkard, 1965). The hypothesis that the *negative* correlation between obesity and social class in Western European and North American populations reflects different cultural norms associated with social class is further supported by the finding of a *positive* correlation between obesity and social class in India (Siddamma, 1978).

Children 6 to 7 years of age who are overweight (a weight/height ratio above the group median) performed significantly less well than underweight children on 15 Piagetian conservation tests involving the conservation of number, volume, matter, length, and weight; the overweight group scored lower than the underweight group in conservation performance even when IQ was controlled (Ewert, 1977). The author attributed the results to the greater susceptibility of the overweight subjects to cue salience, that is, they were more field-dependent as compared with the relatively field-independent underweight subjects. There is no evidence on this effect *within* families.

## Head and Brain Measurements

The early literature on the relationship of head and brain measurements to intelligence, and even the treatment accorded to this topic in present-day psychology textbooks, affords little indication of the surprisingly complex technical problems that have made it difficult for scientists to agree as to the precise nature of this relationship. The most we can attempt here is to point out these technical problems and summarize the present state of the best available evidence, such as it is.

*Interspecies comparisons of brain size.* The apparent differences between various species of animals in what people commonly think of as the capacity for intelligent behavior, and the perceived relationship of such species differences to differences in brain size, are among the observations that have tempted both scientists and laymen to inquire whether individual differences in brain size among humans are correlated with individual differences in psychometric intelligence. The question has also been raised whether various racial groups among the species Homo sapiens differ in brain size, and whether such differences are reflected in the observed racial differences in psychometric intelligence.

In the five million years of human evolution, from Australopithecus to Homo sapiens, the brain has almost tripled in size, despite the anatomic and metabolic disadvantages of larger brain and head size. The chief advantage of a larger brain, in terms of natural selection, is the greater capacity it confers for complex adaptive behavior. Development of the cerebral cortex, the association areas, the frontal lobes, and, in general, those parts of the brain not directly involved in autonomic and sensory-motor functions, is related to the complexity of behavioral capacities such as perceiving, learning, reasoning, problem solving, and language. Hence, the question persists concerning the relationship between differences in brain size (or its correlate, head size) and intellect.

In considering this relationship among a wide range of mammalian species differing greatly in overall body size, brain size must be regarded in relation to body size, that is, allometrically. The size of every bodily organ is allometrically related to total body size, and a very high correlation exists between body weight and mean brain weight across species. For 93 species of mammals, varying in size from mouse to elephant, the correlation between the means of body and brain weight is .976; among only 15 species of primates the correlation is .973 (Armstrong, 1983). This high correlation, which represents a true functional relationship, and not just a statistical association, results from the fact that much of the brain serves vegetative and sensorimotor functions, and that the number of neurons subserving these functions is directly related to body size, or, more specifically, to the total surface area of the body. The high brain-body size correlation is also reflected in the extremely high correlation between body size and the cross-sectional area of the foramen magnum, an opening in the skull through which the spinal cord passes. Because all but a dozen or so cranial nerves pass through the foramen magnum, this measurement is useful as an index of the total sensory-motor input-output of the animal's brain. The size of the medulla, a measurement that has been used as an alternative index of sensory-motor input-output (Passingham, 1975), is also strongly correlated with body size.

But it is the amount of brain tissue in excess of that part that is predictable from body size and subserves purely vegetative and sensory-motor functions that is most apt to be related to the animal's capacity for developing complex behavior.

This "excess" brain tissue in various species is measured from the regression of brain weight on body weight. In practice, the log of brain weight is plotted as a function of the log of body weight for a large number of mammalian species. The regression equation relating log brain weight to log body weight serves as a baseline for comparing various species on the amount of brain tissue above (or below) the amount predicted on the basis of body size. (Instead of the regression line, the principal axis of the plotted log brain weight by log body weight is recommended by some investigators.) The amount of deviation from the common regression line (or the principal axis) for the mean of any particular species has been termed an *encephalization index* (Jerison, 1973, 1982). This residual brain mass has been expressed mathematically with various modifications and refinements by different investigators (Passingham, 1975), but all such indices are essentially intended to express the degree of encephalization or development of the neocortex, especially that part of the brain that serves complex behavioral capacities, over and above the neural mass associated with general mammalian functions and closely related to overall body size.

The importance of the encephalization index for behavioral science derives from its close relationship, as contrasted with that of overall brain size, to the varying information-processing capacities manifested by different species. Degree of encephalization is found to be related to objective measures of animal intelligence such as "curiosity" (as measured by responsiveness to novel objects) and the speed of acquiring discrimination learning sets, which shows a rank-order correlation of +.96 with an index of encephalization (ratio of neocortex to medulla) among nine species of primates (Passingham, 1975). It is noteworthy that speed of acquisition of discrimination learning sets is also correlated with psychometric intelligence in children (Harter, 1965). On the basis of such evidence, Jerison (1982) claims this encephalization index as a measure of the "biological intelligence" of various species.

Jerison (1982), however, makes the important point that the high degree of relationship between encephalization and biological intelligence across different species does not hold up for individual differences or even for subspecies (or racial) differences within a major species. As Jerison expresses it, the intraspecies relationship of encephalization to behavioral capacity shows none of the orderliness of the interspecies picture. According to Jerison, "Individual variation, the source of microevolution, seems to be decoupled from interspecific variation, which represents the effect of macroevolution'' (p. 743). Not all expert opinion agrees with Jerison on this point, however. In a review of Jerison's major work (*Evolution of the Brain and Intelligence*, 1973), Holloway (1974) dissents from Jerison's position as follows:

> If there is no regular relationship obtaining within the species between brain and body weights, and between brain weight and information-handling capacity, what are the driving forces or evolutionary dynamics that produce the lawful relationships between species or between higher taxa? Somewhere, there is a hiatus in explanations which claim a set of biological (functional) relationships at supraspecies taxon levels but deny such a relationship within the biological unit (the species) undergoing evolutionary change. (p. 679)

Yet, only a slight (but significant) degree of statistical relationship is found between brain-size indices and measures of intelligence *within* any species, including modern Homo sapiens. It would appear, then, that the biological basis of intraspecies individual differences in intelligence probably resides much more in the fine structure of the neocortex (such as the amount of branching and the number of interconnections between neurons) and in the chemistry of neurotransmitters, than in the gross anatomy of the cerebrum. Nevertheless, we are still left with some small but significant correlation between brain size and psychometric intelligence in humans. Because of a number of technical difficulties, however, the precise value of this correlation remains arguable.

*Measurements of brain size.* The primary problem in the study of brain size and intelligence in humans is the measurement of brain size itself. As Van Valen (1974) notes, there is no study reported in the literature prior to 1974 that directly correlates brain size, as measured by weight, volume, or even cranial capacity, with intelligence test scores. With one exception (Willerman, Schultz, Rutledge, & Bigler, 1989), all existing studies are based on *estimates* of brain size or cranial capacity derived from external measurements of the head. The question naturally arises as to the validity of such estimates as measures of brain size. Studies based on direct measurements of excised brains or cranial vault capacity have had to depend on such rough estimates of intelligence as years of schooling or occupational level, as determined from death records. Another serious problem in this line of research is emphasized by Passingham (1979, p. 255), the author of a recent study of brain size and intelligence, who reports that there are no studies based on truly representative samples of the general population. Although Passingham does seem to have overlooked one excellent study by Susanne (1979) that is based on a highly representative sample of young men in Belgium, his point is well taken. In general, the use of nonrandom samples would tend to bias the data to some unknown degree toward a restriction of variance in the variables of interest, the variance of intelligence being most likely affected, with the inevitable result of some diminution of the obtained correlation.

Studies of the validity of external head measurements as estimates of direct brain measurements find correlations between the two variables in the range of .60 to .70 (Van Valen, 1974, p. 423). Head circumference is the most commonly used measure in correlational studies with IQ. Yet, in a study of Jørgensen, Parison, and Quaade (1961, cited by Van Valen, 1974, p. 423) of 89 persons, the correlation between brain volume and head circumference is only $+.50 \pm .21$. Two other studies of the same variables cited by Van Valen (1974, p. 423) give correlations of $+.55 \pm .10$ and $+.36 \pm .14$.

Linear measurements of the skull taken internally and externally are much more highly correlated with one another than are brain volume and head circumference. Hoadley and Pearson (1929) obtained internal × external correlations of $+.78$ for cranial length and $+.88$ for cranial breadth. The $N$-weighted mean of eight coefficients of correlation between direct measures of cranial capacity and linear measurements of the external size of the cranium was reported as $+.66 \pm .08$ (Macdonnell, 1904). Somewhat higher correlations have been found between external head circumference and internal skull diameter and volume measured from X-rays (Bray, Shields, Wolcott, & Madsen, 1969; MacKinnon, Kennedy, & Davies, 1956).

In studies based on living subjects, IQ is usually correlated with head circumference (taken with a tape measure) or with linear dimensions of the head (measured by calipers). When linear dimensions are taken, an estimate of brain capacity may be derived from head length, width, and height measurements, in accordance with a formula devised by Lee and Pearson (1901). Their formula (No. 14, 1901, p. 252) estimates brain volume in cubic centimeters as follows:

For men: Brain cm$^3$ = .000337($L$ − 11 mm)($W$ − 11 mm)($H$ − 11 mm) + 406.01, where $L$, $W$, and $H$ are length, width, and height in millimeters. For women: Brain cm$^3$ = .0004(L − 11 mm)(W − 11 mm)(H − 11 mm) + 206.6. The amount of 11 mm is subtracted as representing the average thickness of scalp and skull. Scalp thickness varies slightly with the amount of body fat, and this, of course, adds to the error of measurement. Brain weight in grams may then be estimated by multiplying the results obtained from Lee's formula by 0.87. (Brain weight is estimated from the *direct* measurement of cranial capacity by an equation given by Baker [1974, p. 429]: Brain weight [grams] = 1.065 cm$^3$ − 195. Cranial capacity is measured directly by measuring, in a graduated cylinder, the amount of buckshot or mustard seed required to fill the skull.)

The main point of all this is that correlations between brain size and intelligence based on living persons for whom IQs are obtainable suffer attenuation from several sources between the external measurements at the surface of the scalp and the brain itself. Head size is far from perfect as a correlate of brain size and may even be correlated to some extent with total body size independently of brain size. If it is assumed that external measurements of head size ($h$) are correlated with intelligence ($i$) only through their relationship with brain size ($b$), then it can be proved mathematically (see Van Valen, 1974, p. 423) that the correlation between head size and intelligence can be expressed as $\rho_{ih} = \rho_{ib}\rho_{bh}$, and the correction for attenuation of $\rho_{ih}$ as an estimate of $\rho_{ib}$ is, of course, simply $\rho_{ih}/\rho_{bh}$. For our purpose, a measure of overall body size should be partialed out of $\rho_{ih}$ and $\rho_{bh}$, as we are interested in determining the degree of association between intelligence and that part of the variance in brain size which is independent of general body size.

Measurements of intelligence are also attenuated, with reliability in the best IQ tests generally ranging between .90 and .95. In addition, most IQ tests measure other factors of ability besides $g$, the general intelligence factor common to all complex cognitive tasks. As true scores from most ordinary IQ tests are correlated between .80 and .90 with $g$, moreover, it follows that the correlation between obtained scores and $g$ falls somewhere between .75 and .88.

Age differences may also attenuate the correlation between head measurements and IQ, as brain size decreases relatively more after age 25 than does head size. Actual brain weight decreases some 100 grams or more between ages 25 and 80. There is an average negative correlation of about $-.20$ between brain weight and age between ages 25 and 80 (Ho et al., 1980a). When corrected for general body size (as measured by total body surface area) the correlation between brain weight and age (between 25 and 80 years) is $-.117 \pm .10$ for white men (Ho, Roessman, Straumfjord, & Monroe, 1980b). Hence, without proper correction for age differences, the head size × IQ correlation will be attenuated to some slight degree in samples of variable age; this effect is so slight between ages 18 and 60 (Ho, Roessman, Straumfjord, & Monroe, 1980a, 1980b), however, as to be of negligible impact when body size is statistically controlled. (Adult height is correlated negatively with age approximately $-.15$ to $-.20$.)

As may be seen in Figure 4.11, which shows the distribution of directly measured brain weights of 733 English men (Passingham, 1979), the distribution of brain size in adult humans roughly approximates the normal, or Gaussian, curve, although this distribution is not completely symmetrical around its mode. A similar-shaped distribution for 505 unselected European men, ages 21 and over, is shown in Figure 4.12. A normal curve has been fitted to both sets of data in Figures 4.11 and 4.12, and a chi-square test shows a close degree of approximation to normality, with neither set of data deviating significantly (at the 5% level) from the normal curve. A larger set of data is provided in a study by Miller (1926), in which cranial capacity (estimated by Lee's formula) was obtained on 4,012 school boys ranging in ages 7 to 17. We have age-standardized the cranial capacity measurements by converting them to $z$ scores within each one-year age interval. The distribution of cranial capacities (age controlled) does not differ significantly ($p > .05$) from the normal distribution fitted to these data. In every study, the departures from normality, though not statistically significant in

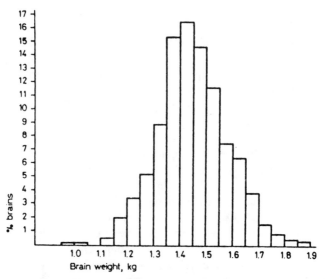

Figure 4.11. Histogram of brain weights (in kilograms) for 733 English men. (From Passingham, 1979, p. 261.) When a normal curve is fitted to these data, with $\overline{X} = 1.442$ kg, $SD = .134$ kg, a chi-square test of the goodness of fit of the data to the normal curve gives $\chi^2 = 28.7$, with 18 $df$, $.05 < p < .10$; i.e., the data depart significantly from normality at $p < .10$, but not at $p < .05$.

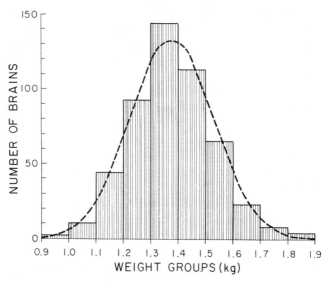

Figure 4.12. Histogram of brain weights of European men aged 21 and over. (From Baker, 1974, p. 430.) A normal curve has been fitted to these data, with $\overline{X} = 1.379$ kg, $SD = 0.151$ kg. The data do not differ significantly from the normal distribution ($\chi^2 = 11.60$, $df = 9$, $p < .30$).

186

separate studies, consist of greater relative frequencies in both the lower and the higher extreme tails of the distribution.

In view of the rather small correlation between brain size and IQ, it is arguable whether the approximately normal distribution of brain weights (and cranial capacities) has any more theoretically important connection with the similarly normal distribution of IQs than have the approximately normal distributions of many other somatic dimensions having no intrinsic relationship to mental ability, such as stature.

*Brain size and body size.* Because body size is correlated with both brain size (or head size) and IQ, it acts as a confounding factor in the correlation between these two variables. If it is assumed that a part of the variance in total brain size is correlated with body size independently of intelligence and a part is correlated with intelligence independently of body size, then the calculation of a partial correlation between brain size and IQ, with body size partialed out, makes theoretical sense. This is exactly what is done in the case of interspecies comparisons, for which brain size shows a close relationship to assessments of intelligence only when body size is controlled. The same reasoning can be applied within a species, despite certain theoretical complications which are illustrated here in terms of simple diagrams showing the possible ways in which correlation might arise between head size (*H*), brain size (*Br*), body size (*Bo*), and IQ. Two of these possibilities, which may be regarded as rival hypotheses, are shown in Figure 4.13.

Solid lines represent intrinsic or causal correlations (with direction of causation left unspecified); dashed lines represent adventitious or noncausal correlations. Figure 4.13a depicts the null hypothesis, that is, the hypothesis that no intrinsic correlation exists between brain size and IQ; the adventitious correlation shown in this figure is due to the fact that both variables are correlated with body size—brain size being causally correlated with body size and IQ being adventitiously correlated. The one part of this hypothesis for which we have already reviewed the evidence and found it fairly conclusive is the adventitious correlation between IQ and body size. Figure 4.13b represents the counterhypothesis, showing an intrinsic correlation between brain size and IQ. (Intrinsic correlation between brain, body, and head size are assumed to be quite reasonable, and so remain the same in Figures a and b.) The hypothesis represented in Figure 4.13b would be ruled out definitively if the brain × IQ correlation *within* families could not be shown to be statistically significant; such evidence, of course, would preclude the possibility of an intrinsic correlation between brain size and IQ, as seen in the case of the body-size × IQ correlation.

The head-size × IQ correlation is more problematic if head size is viewed as a proxy for brain size. The imperfect correlation between head size and brain size attenuates the correlation, and if the within-families zero-order correlation between head size and IQ is low to begin with, partialing body size out of the head size × IQ correlation could result in such a small partial *r* that only a very large sample could make the null hypothesis convincing. We examine the evidence on this point later on. But first we should get some idea of the other correlations shown in Figure 4.13, that is, the correlations of body size with head size and brain size, because these are needed for partialing body size out of the IQ × brain-size (or head-size) correlation. The best justification for partialing out body size is the likelihood that some portion of the brain is more highly correlated with body size, and some portion is more highly correlated with intelligence. If this is true, the essential correlation between brain size and IQ should be revealed most clearly when body size is statistically controlled. Evidence shows that this is more than mere likelihood. When the brain is dissected into three portions—cerebral hemispheres, cerebellum, and pons plus medulla—all three portions are found to be positively correlated with body size; but the portion of the brain showing the lowest correlation with body size is the same portion in which the higher mental functions are known to be localized—the cerebral hemispheres (Marshall, 1892).

Table 4.7 summarizes studies prior to 1980 on the correlations of brain and head measurements with body height and weight in adult samples. The first three correlations are undoubtedly inflated as a result of their being computed on a combined sample of males and females; the inclusion of both genders in a sample of this kind has the effect of approximately doubling the correlation. The unit-weighted mean of same-sex correlations between *brain weight* and *body weight* is only +.21. This is lower than the mean correlation of +.31 between

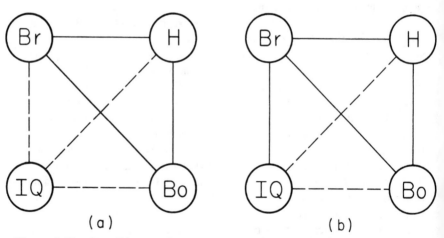

( a )                    ( b )

**Figure 4.13.  Possible correlations between brain size (Br), head size (H), body size (Bo), and intelligence (IQ). Solid lines indicate causal or functional connections, broken lines are correlations without functional relationship. Panel *a* represents a nonfunctional correlation between brain size and IQ; panel *b* represents an intrinsic or functional relation between brain size and IQ.**

**Table 4.7. Correlations between Head and Brain Measurements and Body Size (Height and Weight) in Various Adult Samples**

| Source | Sample | Variables Correlated | Correlation[a] |
|---|---|---|---|
| Passingham (1979, p. 258) | 212 men, 213 women, English, ages 18–75 years | Cranial capacity estimated from Lee formula — height | .62 ± .10 |
| Passingham (1979, p. 258) | 212 men, 213 women, English, ages 18–75 years | Cranial capacity estimated from Lee formula — height (age partialed) | .623 ± .10 |
| Passingham (1979, p. 258) | 212 men, 213 women, English, ages 18–75 years | Cranial capacity estimated from Lee formula — body weight | .57 ± .10 |
| Passingham (1979, p. 262) | 734 Englishmen | Brain weight — height | .31 ± .07 |
| Passingham (1979, p. 262) | 305 English women | Brain weight — height | .20 ± .11 |
| Passingham (1979, p. 262) | 1039 English adults, 18–75 years | Brain weight — height | .45 ± .06 |
| Passingham (1979, p. 262) | 1039 English adults, 18–75 years | Brain weight — height (age partialed) | .406 ± .06 |
| Passingham (1979, p. 262) | 290 English adults, 18–45 years | Brain weight — height | .39 ± .11 |
| Passingham (1979, p. 262) | 290 English adults, 18–45 years | Brain weight — height (age partialed) | .386 ± .11 |
| Passingham (1979, p. 262) | 198 English men, 18–45 years | Brain weight — height | .20 ± .14 |
| Passingham (1979, p. 262) | 92 English women, 18–45 years | Brain weight — height | .12 ± .21 |
| Passingham (1979, p. 262) | 1039 English adults, 18–75 years | Brain weight — body weight | .26 ± .06 |
| Passingham (1979, p. 262) | 290 English adults, 18–45 years | Brain weight — body weight | .36 ± .11 |
| Schreider (1966) | European adults | Brain weight — height | .25 ± .30 |
| Whipple (1914, p. 82) | Oxford male students | Head length — height | .31 |
| Whipple (1914, p. 82) | Cambridge male students | Head length — height | .28 |
| Whipple (1914, p. 82) | 3000 criminals | Head length — height | .34 ± .03 |
| Whipple (1914, p. 82) | Oxford male students | Head width — height | .14 |
| Whipple (1914, p. 82) | Cambridge male students | Head width — height | .15 |
| Whipple (1914, p. 82) | 3000 criminals | Head width — height | .18 ± .03 |
| Susanne (1979) | 2071 Belgian men, 17–25 years | Head circumference — height | .355 ± .04[b] |

[a]Correlation coefficient given with 95% confidence interval when the available information permits its exact computation.

[b]This correlation is not given in Susanne's article, but can be calculated from the given zero-order correlations between (a) head circumference and IQ, (b) height and IQ, and (c) the partial correlation between head circumference and IQ with height partialed out.

externally measured *head length* and *body height*. Head width is less correlated (mean $r = .16$) with height than is head length. Whenever possible, given the available information, the factor of age has been partialed out of these correlations. As can be seen, however, this partialing out of age has very little effect on the zero-order correlations.

The most recent, and in many ways the best, data on these relationships are provided in a study by Ho et al. (1980b). Conducted at the Institute of Pathology, Case Western Reserve University, this study offers a distinct advantage, in that all brain weights were obtained under uniform procedures for excising and weighing. Brains with any abnormalities known to affect brain weight were excluded. The subjects in this study varied in age from 25 to 80 years. The obtained correlations between brain weight and body measurements are shown in Table 4.8. It makes sense neurologically that, more than either body height or body weight, body surface area should be highly correlated with brain weight; this is because every square millimeter of the entire body surface is neurologically represented in the sensory cortex of the brain. (Body surface area [in square meters] = body weight [in kilograms]$^{0.425}$ × height [in centimeters]$^{0.725}$ × 0.007184.) Theoretically speaking, therefore, body surface area would seem to be the best variable to partial out of correlations between brain (or head) size and IQ. We note that the multiple correlation of height and weight with brain weight is a close approximation to the correlation between body surface area and brain weight.

In young children, head and body measurements are more highly correlated than in adults, even when age is controlled; this is probably because of individual differences in physical growth rates which are reflected in both head and body size. Some excellent data on the correlation of head circumference with body height and weight in white and black children from birth to 4 years are shown in Figure 4.14 (from Broman et al., 1975). The consistent decrease in the correlation between birth and 4 years probably continues slightly beyond 4 years, but the 4-year correlations appear to be closely approaching the asymptotes of the functions relating the magnitude of the correlations to age. We cannot explain

**Table 4.8. Correlations[a] between Brain Weight and Body Measurements in White and Black Males and Females[b]**

| Sample | N | Body Height | Body Weight | Body Surface Area |
|---|---|---|---|---|
| White Males | 414 | .20 ± .10 | .24 ± .10 | .27 ± .10 |
| Black Males | 225 | .20 ± .13 | .15 ± .13 | .20 ± .13 |
| White Females | 388 | .24 ± .10 | .23 ± .10 | .29 ± .10 |
| Black Females | 218 | .15 ± .13 | .10 ± .13 | .14 ± .13 |
| Mean[c] | | .204 ± .05 | .196 ± .05 | .241 ± .05 |

[a]Correlations given with 95% confidence interval.
[b]From Ho et al., 1980b.
[c]N-weighted mean.

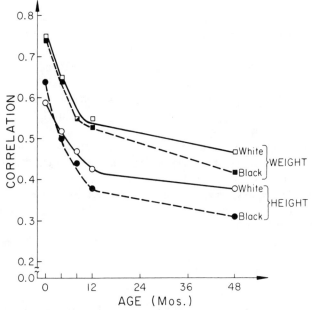

**Figure 4.14. Correlation of head circumference with height and weight at various ages in white and black children. (Data from Broman et al., 1975, Table 9.2, p. 126.) The 95% confidence interval for all correlations is $r \pm .02$ except at age 8 months, which is $r \pm .03$.**

why the correlations should be significantly, and substantially, lower for blacks than for whites; certainly, these lower values are not attributable to differences in variance in any of the correlated variables, as the variances of whites and blacks are nearly identical on every variable considered (Broman et al., 1975, Table 1, p. 174).

When *mean* cranial capacity (as estimated by Lee's formula, from measurements of the length, width, and height of the head of living persons) is obtained for a number of groups, and is correlated with *the mean* body weight of the groups, thereby eliminating individual variation, the resulting correlation is extremely high. Such data were obtained for 38 categories of military personnel in several different countries (NASA, 1978); the correlation between mean cranial capacity and mean body weight for these 38 groups was found to be +.937.

*Head size, brain size, and IQ.* Interest in the relationship between brain size and intelligence is at least as old as the history of psychology. Objective statistical evidence on the subject was not possible until after the turn of the century, however, when Binet, in 1905, invented the first demonstrably valid test of intelligence. Until then, the only evidence of an association between brain size and ability in humans had been based on the cranial measurements and brain weights of deceased famous men of generally acknowledged intellectual distinction, such men as Gauss and Kant, among others. Some of these data are shown in Table 4.9. The mean brain weight of this group is 1,607 g($SD = 282$), which is about 1.3 standard deviations above the mean brain weight (1,410 g, $SD = 152$) of a large random sample of European men. Although most of these specimens were clearly larger than the average volume or weight of male human brains, these data are regarded as hardly more than presumptive evidence of an association between brain size and ability. They leave much to be desired in terms of scientifically worthy evidence. Quite apart from the extremely small sample size, any one of a number of methodological problems—including marked differences in age and cause of death, as well as lack of uniformity in methods of removing, preserving, and weighing the brain specimens themselves—would serve to vitiate these antique curios as reliable scientific evidence. Some idea of the many problems of reliability posed by such data is provided by Baker (1974, pp. 429–432).

The earliest general review of the relation of skull size to intelligence that we have found is that of Whipple (1914, pp. 79–91). But aside from studies by Pearson (1906) and Pearl (1906), which were based on quite large samples, the studies prior to 1914 are hardly worth mentioning. Even the large-scale studies by Pearson and Pearl, based on subjective ratings of intelligence and college grades rather than objective test scores, leave much to be desired. Whipple's conclusions were much like those subsequently expressed by Paterson in a thorough and careful review published in 1930, by which time it was possible to include a few studies that were somewhat superior, methodologically, to those reviewed by Whipple (1914). Paterson concluded that most observed correlations between intelligence and head size fall within the range of .10 to .20, although the $N$-weighted mean of all the correlations available at that time was

**Table 4.9.    Brain Weight (in Grams) of Ten Famous Men[a]**

| Name | Field | Age of Death[b] | Brain Weight |
|------|-------|-----------------|--------------|
| Bismarck, Otto von | Statesman | 83 | 1807 |
| Broca, Paul | Anatomist | 56 | 1424 |
| Byron, George | Poet | 36 | 1807 |
| Cuvier, Georges | Naturalist | 63 | 1820 |
| France, Anatole | Novelist | 80 | 1017 |
| Gauss, Karl F. | Mathematician | 78 | 1492 |
| Kant, Immanuel | Philosopher | 80 | 1631 |
| Schumann, Robert | Composer | 46 | 1413 |
| Thackeray, Wm. M. | Author | 52 | 1658 |
| Turgenev, Ivan, S. | Novelist | 65 | 2000 |
| Whitman, Walt | Poet | 73 | 1282 |

[a]From various sources (Baker, 1974; Cattell, 1971; Cobb, 1965).
[b]The correlation between age of death and brain weight in this sample is $-.238$

+ .20. Paterson noted that the reported correlations, though small, were always positive and clearly not due to chance. He also suggested that these reported correlations, because they are often based on samples that are restricted in range of intelligence (groups of university students, for example), may well underestimate the true correlation in the population. It now appears that Paterson may have been a bit carried away by his general mission of debunking popular myths concerning associations between physique and intellect, however. In his summary of conclusions, he writes as follows:

> Although inadequate statistical methods characterize most of the research studies and although no satisfactory standardized method of measuring head size is adopted in them, it can be said with considerable assurance that whatever positive correlation exists must be of a low order. . . . It appears that variation in head size is a function of race, sex, and family stock. It does not vary between individuals in correspondence with intellect. (Paterson, 1930, pp. 122–123)

It was this overwhelmingly negative conclusion which was to be perpetuated in psychology text books for more than half a century. An unwarranted conclusion in 1930, it is today flatly wrong in light of the best available evidence. As Cattell (1971) has remarked,

> Some of this was the sheer hubris of the specialist out to debunk any popular idea. Students were taught that there is no correlation of head size with intelligence; that some of the largest heads are those of hydrocephalic imbeciles (the head being enlarged by the disease process); and that men of genius have been known to have subaverage brain weight, e.g., the case of Anatole France. (He died at eighty with a somewhat subaverage brain weight [1,017 g, which is about 2.6σ below the average of European males], conceivably due to the usual shrinkage of weight which occurs with age.) (p. 178)

It is certainly true, and has long been acknowledged by all serious students of the subject, that, except at the pathological extremes of microcephaly and hydrocephaly, head size (or brain size) is practically useless as an indicator of intellect in individuals. As Cobb (1965) has noted, an extremely wide range of brain size, extending almost ± 3σ from the mean, is compatible with normal mental functioning. Brains as small as 800-900 grams (as compared with the average of 1,300-1,400) have shown normal intellect, and even nanocephalic dwarfs with brains of less than 700 g can converse fluently (Cobb, 1965, p. 558). Obviously, other features of the brain besides sheer size must account for all but a very small part of the variance in biological intelligence in humans.

We have found only one older study (Miller, 1926) which was not picked up in Paterson's (1930) comprehensive review. This study was based on the head measurements (and estimated cranial capacity) of 176 adult male prisoners, variously identified as mentally retarded, borderline, or normal, and more than

4,000 Tasmanian school boys. Significant differences in mean cranial capacity were found between the three mental levels and between age-matched pupils in academically select and nonselect schools. Unfortunately, no control for body size was provided, no tests of intelligence were used, and no correlation coefficients were reported. While these results do contribute additional evidence of some positive association between head size (or estimated cranial capacity) and a roughly assessed level of mental ability, therefore, they are not very informative for our purpose. Questions of intelligence aside, however, this study presents what is probably the most solid and precise data we have seen on the growth of estimated cranial capacity over the age-range from 7 to 17 years; these data are summarized in Figure 4.15.

Since Paterson's (1930) review, several valuable studies have appeared. Van Valen (1974) has reviewed virtually all the published studies prior to 1974. Van Valen reasons that the obtained partial correlation between head size and IQ, with body size partialed out, is attenuated by two factors—the imperfect measurement of intelligence and the far-from-perfect correlation between external head measurements and actual brain size as measured by volume or weight. In addition, Van Valen makes the reasonable assumption that cranial capacity ($c$) as estimated from external head measurements (controlled for body size) is corre-

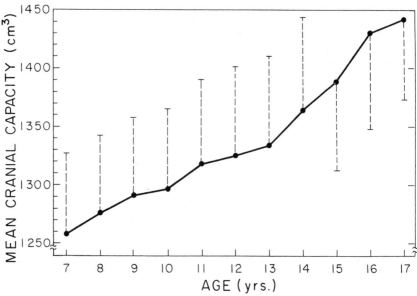

**Figure 4.15.** Mean estimated (by Lee's formula) cranial capacity in cm³ of 4012 Tasmanian (Caucasian) school boys from ages 7 to 17 years. The vertical dashed lines indicate ± 1 standard deviation. These are not longitudinal data; each age is a different group, with average $N$ = 565. (Drafted from data presented in Miller, 1926, Table 7, p. 30.)

lated with IQ ($i$) solely by way of brain size ($b$). Under this assumption, $\rho_{ic} = \rho_{ib}\rho_{bc}$, and so $\rho_{ib} = \rho_{ic}/\rho_{bc}$. Using the best available estimates of $\rho_{ic}$ and $\rho_{bc}$ and correcting for the attenuation of the intelligence measures, Van Valen concludes that the best estimate we now have of the correlation between brain size and intelligence in humans is about + .3. He sees this correlation as related to the increase in human brain size, noting that brain size "has increased dramatically and at an unusually high rate in human evolution" (p. 420). Van Valen also argues that there is a direct effect of brain size on intelligence and that "natural selection on intelligence at a current estimated intensity suffices to explain the rapid rate of increase of brain size in human evolution" (p. 417).

The most important studies cited in Val Valen's (1974) review, as well as those which have appeared since then, are summarized in Table 4.10. A problem with some of these correlations is that stature is not controlled. In Table 4.10, the $N$-weighted means are given for the head-size × intelligence correlation without stature being controlled and with stature controlled (in parentheses). Another problem with many of the correlations is that they are based on samples selected for superior intelligence, and hence, tend to underestimate the true correlation in the general population. For this reason, the large study by Susanne (1979) is probably most important. Susanne's subjects were a random sample of 2,071 drawn from a population of 43,452 young men eligible for military service in 1963 in Belgium. According to Susanne, the age and socioeconomic and geographic distribution of the sample was representative of the Belgian male population in general and was free of serious pathology. Subjects' ages ranged from 17 to 25 years, with a mean of 19.53 years. An overall intelligence measure, derived by averaging standardized scores obtained on five psychometric tests, afforded a highly reliable measure of general mental ability. Susanne's study employed 11 different measurements of the head and face. Only the correlation of the composite intelligence test score with cranial perimeter (head circumference) is shown in Table 4.10; before and after partialing out stature, the correlations are + .242 and + .194, respectively.

The appreciably lower correlations found in the recent studies by Swan and Miszkiewicz (no date) and by Passingham (1979) may be to some extent attributable to the fact that these studies sampled both males and females, a practice which tends to attenuate correlations of this kind, as we have seen. Such attenuation is probably overcome to some unknown degree by partialing out stature. As a general rule, however, correlations involving any body measurements should be calculated separately for males and females.

Following Van Valen, we can estimate the correlation between brain size and intelligence from the $N$-weighted means of the correlations between height ($h$), cranial size ($c$), brain size ($b$), and "IQ" ($i$). We assume virtually perfect reliability of the physical measurements, so there is no correction for attenuation. "IQ" is assumed to have a reliability of .90, which is typical, and correlations involving IQ are accordingly corrected for attenuation. Using the $N$-weighted

**Table 4.10. Correlations between Head Size and Intelligence Reported in Various Studies**

| Source | Subjects | N | Measure | Correlation[a] | Controlled Variables |
|---|---|---|---|---|---|
| Pearson (1906) | Random | 4486 | Subjective ratings | .11 ± .03 | Age, sex |
| Pearson (1906) | University students | 1011 | Grades | .11 ± .06 | Age, sex |
| Pearl (1906) | Soldiers | 935 | Subjective ratings | .14 ± .06 | Age, sex |
| Murdock & Sullivan (1923) | Random | 595 | IQ tests | .22 (.19)[b] ± .08 | Age, sex |
| Reed & Mulligan (1923) | University students | 449 | Grades | .08 ± .09 | Age, sex, body size |
| Sommerville (1924) | University students | 105 | IQ tests | .10 ± .19 | Age, sex |
| Porteus (1937) | School children | 200 | IQ tests | .20 ± .14 | Age, sex |
| Schreider (1968) | Random? | 80 | IQ tests | .08 ± .22 | Age, sex |
| Schreider (1968) | Random? | 71 | IQ tests | .12 ± .23 | Age, sex |
| Robinow (1968) | Children, ages 3–13 years[c] | 300 | IQ tests | .18 (.09)[b] ± .11 | |
| Swan, Haskins, & Douglas[d] | School children | 547 | IQ tests | .11 ± .08 | Age |
| Swan & Miszkiewicz[e] | School children (grades K–12) | 843 | IQ tests (PMA total) | .075 to .084 (.05)[b] ± .07 | Age |
| Passingham (1979) | English adults (18–75 years) | 415 | Wechsler Total IQ | .13 (.03)[b] ± .10 | Age |
| Susanne (1979) | Random Belgian men, ages 17–25 | 2071 | "IQ" (mean of 5 tests) | .242 (.194)[b] ± .04 | Sex, height |
| _N_-weighted Mean | | | | .142 ± .065 (.135 ± .06)[f] | |

[a] Correlation with 95% confidence interval.
[b] Correlation in parentheses is with stature partialed out.
[c] These are longitudinal data from the Fels Research Institute. Stanford-Binet IQs at ages 3, 6, 9 years, Wechsler at 13 years. The unit-weighted mean $r$ is given; its $SD$ across ages is .078.
[d] Reported in Cattell (1982, Table 2.10, p. 38).
[e] Unpublished paper, not dated.
[f] In parentheses, the _N_-weighted mean of only those correlations for which body size (stature) is partialed out (total $N = 4,673$).

mean correlations (corrected for attenuation when involving IQ) as the best available empirical estimates of the true correlations, we can estimate the correlation between brain size (*b*) and IQ (*i*), as shown in Figure 4.16. The formula for theoretically estimating the correlation between brain size and IQ should be used only with the partial correlations, that is, only when height has been partialed out of all the correlations before they are entered into the estimation formula; thus

$$r_{bi\cdot h} = r_{ci\cdot h}/r_{cb\cdot h} = .135/.445 = .303,$$

which is our best estimate of the correlation between intelligence and brain size, as independent of stature, or body size. If we use only the disattenuated partial correlation ($r_{ic\cdot h} = .205$) from Susanne's (1979) study as the basis for estimation, we get $r_{ib\cdot h} = .205/.445 = .460$ as the estimated correlation between intelligence and brain size. The weak link in the estimation procedure is the empirical correlation between external cranial size and brain size. The mean $r_{bc}$ used here is based on only three samples, but this is the best we can do with the available evidence. If we use the largest value of $r_{bc}$ that we can find in the

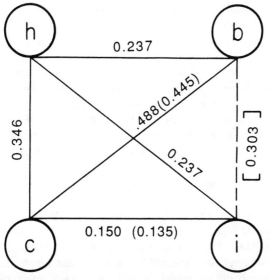

**Figure 4.16**  *N*-weighted mean correlations (IQ correlations are corrected for attenuation) between height (*h*), external cranial size (*c*), brain size (*b*), and IQ (*i*). Solid lines indicate empirical correlations; the dashed line is a theoretically estimated correlation. Partial correlations, with *h* partialed out, are shown in parentheses. The correlation $r_{bi\cdot h} = .303$ is theoretically derived, following Van Valen (1974), from the formula
$$r_{bi\cdot h} = r_{ci\cdot h}/r_{cb\cdot h} = .135/.445 = .303.$$

literature, it is .57 (Van Valen, 1974, p. 423), which, with height partialed out, becomes $r_{bc \cdot h}$ = .535. Using the value in the estimation, along with Susanne's disattenuated partial correlation $r_{ic \cdot h}$ = .205, we get $r_{ib \cdot h}$ = .205/.535 = .383 as the correlation between brain size and intelligence, independently of stature. In any case, if Susanne's study is considered to yield the best determination of $r_{cb \cdot h}$ that we now have, it seems safe to say that the correlation of brain size with intelligence is not less than .2 and may be considerably higher, depending on the size of $r_{bc \cdot h}$, which is not yet very firmly established by the present evidence.

The first (and, as yet, the only) *in vivo* study of the brain-size × intelligence relationship based on the direct measurement of brain size (rather than estimation from external head measurements) was made possible by the technique of magnetic resonance imaging (MRI), which permits, in effect, a 3-dimensional picture of a person's brain, from which precise measurements can be obtained by computer. This method completely overcomes the attenuation of the brain × IQ correlation that results from estimating brain size from external indices which are imperfectly correlated with actual brain size because of individual variation in thickness of the skull and tissues surrounding the brain. Using MRI, Willerman, Schultz, Rutledge, and Bigler (1989) compared two groups of non-Hispanic white college students whose total SAT scores were either high ($\geq$ 1350) or low ($\leq$ 940) and whose Wechsler IQs were $\geq$ 130 or $\leq$ 103. In the total group ($N$ = 40), brain size, adjusted for body height and weight, was correlated $r$ = .51 ($p <$ .01) with IQ. Corrected for the increased IQ variance because of selection of extreme groups, the correlation drops to $r$ = .35, which may be regarded as the "best estimate" of the brain-size × IQ correlation in the general population of healthy people in this age group. This correlation is slightly, but not significantly, higher than Van Valen's (1974) "best estimate" of $r$ = .30, based on external measurements of the head. Further studies using MRI should soon yield definitive answers regarding the relationship of IQ to brain size, but more importantly, MRI will permit study of the correlation of specific brain structures with psychometric abilities.

*IQ and head circumference in young children.* In a longitudinal study, Broman et al. (1975) reported correlations between Stanford-Binet IQ obtained at age 4 years and head circumference measured at birth, 4 months, 8 months, 1 year, and 4 years of age, in very large samples of whites ($N \simeq$ 10,000) and blacks ($N \simeq$ 12,000). The zero-order correlations are shown in Table 4.11, along with the partial correlations controlling for height and weight measured at each age. Unfortunately, the correlations ($r_{CH}$, $r_{CW}$, $r_{HW}$, given in Table 9.2 of Broman et al. 1975) required for computing the partials were not reported separately for males and females, and so in our Table 4.11 we have had to present only correlations based on the combined sexes. This pooling of male and female data very clearly attenuates the partial correlations, as can be seen from the within-sex correlations ($r_{IC}$) of IQ and head circumference (last 2 columns of Table 4.11) as compared with the substantially lower zero-order correlations

Table 4.11. Zero-Order Correlations[a] (Corrected for Attenuation[b]) and First-Order and Second-Order Partial Correlations [Height (H) and Weight (W)] between Stanford-Binet IQ (I) at Age 4 Years and Head Circumference (C) at Various Ages

| Age | White (N ≅ 10,000) | | | | | Black (N ≅ 12,000) | | | | | Mean Within-Sex $r_{IC}$[b] | |
| | $r_{IC}$ | $r_{IC \cdot H}$ | $r_{IC \cdot W}$ | $r_{IC \cdot HW}$ | 95% Conf. Int.[d] | $r_{IC}$ | $r_{IC \cdot H}$ | $r_{IC \cdot W}$ | $r_{IC \cdot HW}$ | 95% Conf. Int.[d] | White | Black |
|---|---|---|---|---|---|---|---|---|---|---|---|---|
| Birth | .088 | .061 | .046 | .044 | ±.018 | .110 | .043 | .031 | .011 | ±.017 | .120 | .121 |
| 4 months | .121 | .088 | .065 | .060 | ±.019 | .110 | .045 | .006 | .001 | ±.017 | .181 | .154 |
| 8 months | .121 | .085 | .080 | .057 | ±.030 | .132 | .067 | .064 | .053 | ±.027 | .186 | .175 |
| 1 year | .132 | .094 | .086 | .081 | ±.019 | .110 | .065 | .041 | .036 | ±.017 | .197 | .154 |
| 4 years | .165 | .134 | .123 | .120 | ±.020 | .132 | .093 | .070 | .069 | ±.018 | .213 | .143 |
| Mean[c] | .124 | .092 | .078 | .073 | | .117 | .061 | .039 | .030 | | .177 | .160 |

[a]From Broman et al. (1975), Table 1, Appendix 4, and Table 9.2 (p. 126).
[b]Correlation for attenuation based on Stanford-Binet test-retest reliability of 0.83 (see Broman et al., p. 37); reliabilities of physical measures are assumed to be 1.00.
[c]N-weighted mean.
[d]All four corrrelations at each age have the same confidence interval.

199

($r_{IC}$) for the combined sexes. Because the correlations used for partialing out height or weight may be spuriously inflated by any sex difference in these variables, the partial correlation between IQ and head circumference could be severely affected by amalgamation of the sexes. Hence, the partial correlations in Table 4.11 are best regarded as lower-bound estimates of the true correlation between IQ and head circumference.

The important conclusion that can be safely drawn from Table 4.11 is that all of the partial correlations are positive and (except for blacks at birth and 4 months) all are statistically significant (at 4 years, $p < .001$ in each racial group). It should also be noted that the correlations at ages 1 year and 4 years are in very close agreement with those of Robinow (1968, see our Table 4.10), who found a correlation (with age and sex controlled) of .18 (.09 with height partialed out) between IQ and head circumference in 300 children between ages 3 and 13. A graph of IQ plotted as a function of head circumference shows some nonlinearity of the relationship, which is therefore somewhat underestimated by the Pearson $r$. The plot for age 4 years, shown in Figure 4.17, is quite typical. The correlation between head size and IQ appears to increase with age, although there are not adequate data to establish this as a fact. In a representative sample ($N = 2023$) of North-Central United States children (94% Caucasian), Stanford-Binet IQ measured at age 7 years showed zero-order correlations with head circumference at birth, 1 year, 4 years, and 7 years of .08, .17, .22, and .23, respectively; all are significant beyond the .001 level of confidence (Fisch, Blick, Horrobin, & Chang, 1976).

**Within-family correlation between head size and IQ.** The fact that correlations between head size and IQ remain positive and significant when body size (height and weight) is controlled is proof that the head × IQ correlation is not entirely attributable to the correlation of both variables with a common factor— body size. But this evidence is not itself proof of an intrinsic, that is, functional or causal, connection between brain size and IQ. It is possible that the correlation between IQ and brain size (with body size controlled) might be only a nonintrinsic, or between-families, correlation, assuming there were common selection, or cross-assortative mating, for IQ and that part of the variance in brain size which is independent of body size. Although this theoretical possibility intuitively seems unlikely, it can be rigorously ruled out only by the finding of a *within-family* correlation between IQ and brain size (or head size as an attenuated proxy for brain size).

We have searched the literature for evidence of a within-family correlation between head size and IQ and have found only one study (Clark, Vandenburg, & Proctor, 1961). Unfortunately, the sample in this study is too small to provide a statistically adequate test of the obtained correlations. The evidence is based on 37 pairs of like-sex dizygotic twins; dizygotic twins are genetically equivalent to full siblings, but provide the added methodological advantage of being exactly the same age, thus obviating the need for age-standardization of measurements.

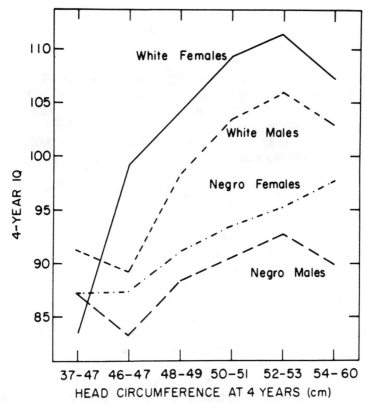

Figure 4.17.   Four-year Stanford-Binet IQ plotted as a function of head circumference. Sample sizes: white males = 5046, white females = 4684; black males = 5964, black females = 6065. (From Broman et al., 1975, p. 186.)

The subjects were junior and senior high school students in Michigan. The within-family (i.e., within-pair) correlation (computed separately for males and females and averaged) between head circumference and IQ (based on Raven's Progressive Matrices, the Chicago Test of Reasoning Ability, and the Chicago Test of Verbal Ability) is + .03 ± .33 (95% confidence interval); with height and weight partialed out, the correlation becomes + .10. (The within-family correlation between IQ and the cross-sectional area of the head is − .09 ± .33, and remains the same with height and weight partialed out.) As these correlations are based on within-pair difference scores, they are more seriously attenuated than ordinary correlations. None of these within-family correlations is significant. Because of the small sample on which these correlations are based, however, we must conclude that it remains an open question whether a correlation between head size and intelligence (with body size controlled) exists within families.

In hopes of getting a better resolution to this question, Jensen (1987) obtained the between-family (BF) and within-family (WF) correlations between $g$ factor scores (derived from a large battery of psychometric tests of mental abilities) and head size in MZ and DZ twins. All of these measurements are tabled in the appendix of a book by Osborne (1980). The variables of sex, age, and race were regressed out of both the test scores and head measurements. Multiple correlations ($R$) were calculated between the three head-size measurements (length, width, and circumference) as the independent variables and $g$ as the dependent variable. The BF and WF multiple correlations for the 82 pairs of MZ twins and the 61 pairs of DZ twins are:

$$\text{MZ BF } R = + .39, p < .01$$
$$\text{MZ WF } R = + .17, p > .05$$
$$\text{DZ BF } R = + .15, p > .05$$
$$\text{DZ WF } R = + .28, p > .05$$

The within-individual (i.e., all twins treated as singletons, with total $N = 286$) multiple $R = + .30, p < .01$. The MZ data strongly suggest that the $g \times$ head-size correlation is largely genetic and that environmental factors contribute little or nothing to the correlation, probably because they have no effect on head size, at least in a population that has not suffered malnutrition. The DZ WF correlation of $+ .28$, which falls just short of significance at the .05 level, suggests an intrinsic correlation between head size and $g$. Since a larger correlation would hardly be expected, in view of the $R = + .30$ ($p < .01$) for the entire sample of MZ and DZ twins treated as singletons, a much larger sample of DZ twins (or full siblings) will obviously be needed for a rigorous test of the WF correlation between head size and $g$ (or IQ). It is a crucial test, however, because without it we cannot really be certain that there is a truly intrinsic, or functional, relationship between head size (or brain size) and mental ability.

*Social class differences in brain size.* As there is a correlation between socioeconomic status (SES) and IQ (Eysenck, 1979, Chap. 7), we might expect a corresponding correlation between head or brain size and SES. SES is usually indexed by occupational status, and many years ago sociologists and anthropologists reported average differences in head size and other body measurements between men in various occupations, with those in the higher-status occupations, in general, averaging larger values on the physical measures (e.g., Hooton, 1939; Sorokin, 1927). We now have somewhat better data, based on much larger samples and more satisfactory measurements.

An important distinction in this context is between a person's SES of origin, which is the SES attained by the person's parents, and attained SES, which is the level of SES attained by the person in adulthood. Correlations of IQ, head size, and other variables with SES of origin are always considerably smaller than with attained SES. For example, the average correlation between IQ and SES of origin is between .30 and .40, whereas the correlation between IQ and attained SES, or occupational level, is between .50 and .70 in various studies (Jensen, 1980a, Chap. 8).

The largest set of data (approximately 10,000 white and 12,000 black children) showing a correlation between head circumference and SES of origin, as indexed by a composite of family income and the amount of education and occupational status (10 categories) of the head of household, is reported by Broman et al. (1975). These data are summarized in Table 4.12. Small but significant correlations are seen in both racial groups between SES and head circumference, even when height is held constant. Control for height also controls for the possible influence of nutritional factors, both prenatal and postnatal, associated with SES. However, head growth is less vulnerable to nutritional deprivation than total body growth (Robinow, 1968).

A relationship between directly measured brain weight and occupational level is reported by Passingham (1979). Persons (734 men and 305 women) were classified according to occupation, or, in the case of women, according to husband's occupation, into one of three categories, which we have labeled *high* (professional), *middle* (skilled workers and tradesmen), and *low* (semiskilled and unskilled workers). The occupational groups for the total sample were matched on age, and there were no significant differences between the three groups in cause of death or in ratings of edema of the brain. The three groups were compared (separately within each sex) by analysis of variance on brain weight and on a "brain index," which is the antilog of the deviation of log brain weight from the linear regression line of the regression of log brain weight (g) on log height (cm). This index of brain size is independent of body height, showing a correlation of only $-.01$ with height and .03 with body weight in both men and women, who do not differ significantly on the brain index ($t = 0.26$, $df = 1,034$, $p = .795$). Thus this brain index fulfills essentially the same purpose as the encephalization index of Jerison (1973).

An analysis of variance shows that, for men, the three occupational categories differ significantly ($F = 6.97$, $df = 663$, $p < .01$) in mean brain weight and in mean brain index ($F = 3.904$, $df = 663$, $p < .05$). For women, none of the

**Table 4.12. Zero-Order and Partial Correlations (Height Controlled) between Head Circumference and Socioeconomic Status of Origin[a]**

| Age[b] | White (N ≃ 10,000) | Black (N ≃ 12,000) |
|---|---|---|
| 8 months | +0.11 (.08)[c] ± .03[c] | +0.11 (.04)[c] ± .03[d] |
| 1 year | +0.14 (.11) ± .02 | +0.08 (.05) ± .02 |
| 4 years | +0.16 (.13) ± .02 | +0.11 (.05) ± .02 |

[a]Data from Broman et al. (1975).
[b]These are longitudinal data, the same children being measured at each age.
[c]Height-partialed correlations in parentheses.
[d]95% confidence interval for both the zero-order and partial correlations.

mean differences between categories was significant for either brain weight or brain index, although with one exception they were in the expected direction. It should be noted that the women were classified by husband's occupation. The low correlation between husband's occupational level and wife's intelligence, which is probably not higher than about $+ .3$, would greatly attenuate the mean differences between the categories in brain size for women. In other words, husband's occupational level is a rather poor proxy for the wife's own level of intelligence, and therefore the nonsignificance of the category differences in mean brain size for women should not be surprising.

As we have been expressing relationships in terms of correlation coefficients throughout this review, we have used the means and standard deviations given by Passingham (1979, Table VII, p. 264) to compute the point-biserial correlation ($r_{pb}$) between dichotomized occupational levels and brain size (brain index, which holds height constant, and brain weight). We have also calculated the $t$ test of significance of each $r_{pb}$ and have determined the exact one-tailed $p$ values corresponding to each $t$. As can be seen in Table 4.13, for men, the High vs. Middle and High vs. Low occupational categories are very significantly differentiated with respect to both brain weight and brain index. Assuming that the correlation between occupational category and brain size is mediated solely by the correlation of each variable with intelligence, and assuming a correlation of .50 between intelligence and men's occupational category, the significant correlations for the brain index in Table 13 are consistent with an inferred correlation of about .24 to .28 between intelligence and brain size (independent of body size).

*Race differences in brain size.* Throughout the history of investigation of this subject, the prevailing notions at any given time and place seem to have shifted about more as a result of social and political attitudes than as a result of the actual scientific evidence. It is interesting, for example, that all editions of the *Encyclopædia Britannica* subsequent to the 18th edition (1964) have omitted any reference to one racially distinguishing characteristic of black people of African origin claimed in earlier editions, namely, "a small brain in relation to their size." Yet a preponderance of the evidence has been consistent with the position taken in earlier editions, and no contradictory evidence had been brought to bear in the meantime. The prevailing sociopolitical zeitgeist of the 1960s, however, abjured all evidence that could possibly be construed as suggesting a biological, rather than exclusively cultural, basis for the well established black deficit in psychometric intelligence. One frequently cited article by Tobias (1970), a South African anatomist and anthropologist, offered some reassurance for this position by arguing that the quality of the evidence, as of 1970, did not permit clear-cut rejection of the null hypothesis with respect to black-white differences in brain size, provided differences in body size and other possible artifacts were taken into consideration. Based entirely on studies of postmortem brains per se, Tobias's critique ignores all of the much more

Table 4.13. Point-Biserial Correlation ($r_{pb}$) between Dichotomized Occupational Categories (High, Middle, Low)[a] and Brain Size, with t Tests and Exact (One-Tailed) Probability (p)[b]

| Contrast | Men | | | | | | Women | | | | | |
|---|---|---|---|---|---|---|---|---|---|---|---|---|
| | Brain Weight | | | Brain Index | | | Brain Weight | | | Brain Index | | |
| | $r_{pb}$ | t | p | $r_{pb}$ | t | p | $r_{pb}$ | t | p | $r_{pb}$ | t | p |
| High-Middle | .144 | 2.81 | .002 | .118 | 2.49 | .006 | .089 | 1.10 | .135 | .112 | 1.10 | .135 |
| High-Low | .188 | 2.93 | .002 | .140 | 2.88 | .002 | .025 | 0.27 | .393 | .015 | 0.17 | .432 |
| Middle-Low | .054 | 1.27 | .101 | .023 | 0.53 | .298 | −.064 | −0.87 | .807 | −.098 | −1.29 | .901 |

[a]Sample sizes: For men: High = 98, Middle = 291, Low = 278; for women: High = 49, Middle = 97, Low = 72.
[b]Correlations and t tests calculated from data in Passingham (1979, Table VII, p. 264).

205

plentiful evidence of cranial measurements and focuses exclusively on the shortcomings and ambiguities of a number of studies of the autopsied brains of blacks and whites. Without question, there are numerous potentially biasing factors (Tobias lists 14 in all) when comparisons are made between brain weights (or volumes) obtained from different studies, for example, the level at which the brain is severed from the spinal cord, the presence or absence of covering membranes, the type of chemical preservative used, the length of time between removal and weighing, the temperature during preservation, as well as age and cause of death. Clearly, such a large number of uncontrolled factors would likely increase random errors of measurement, or unreliability, and hence obscure or attenuate the statistical significance of any true differences between racial groups. What seems most unlikely, however, is that such error factors should consistently produce a *racial* bias in brain weights. Tobias's argument is severely weakened by the fact that the brain weight (or volume) differences between the races are in close agreement with well established measures of cranial volume directly obtained from skulls, which are not subject to the same measurement errors listed by Tobias in the case of autopsied brains. Internally measured cranial capacity sets the upper limit of brain size, which is very highly correlated with cranial capacity, as brain growth creates tension on the cranial suture lines, causing bone deposition and growth of the skull.

   In any case, virtually all of the methodological deficiencies cited by Tobias (1970) have been avoided in a recent large-scale comparative study (Ho, Roessmann, Straumfjord, & Monroe, 1980a) of brain size in blacks and whites. In this study, weights of fresh brains, excised under uniform conditions, were obtained over a five-year period at the Institute of Pathology at Case Western Reserve University in Cleveland, Ohio. Brains showing any pathology (lesions, tumors, hemorrhage, infarct, or edema) were excluded from study. The study sample consisted of 1,261 autopsy cases in a general hospital (222 black females, 228 black males, 395 white females, 416 white males). Ages ranged from 2 to 80 years, with a mean age of 60 years for both blacks and whites. The overall results are shown in Table 4.14. The average brain weights for blacks of both sexes is between 7 and 8 percent lower than the average for whites; expressed in standard deviation units, this is about $0.8\sigma$. The differences are significant; for men, $t = 9.51$, $df = 642$, $p < .001$; for women, $t = 6.23$, $df = 615$, $p < .001$. The sex difference within each race is somewhat larger than the race difference between blacks and whites; note, however, that sex difference is more strongly a function of differences in body size between the sexes, whereas the racial groups show comparatively little difference in body size, as measured by height, weight, and total body surface area. The black women in this study are slightly larger, in fact, than the white women. As can be seen in Figure 4.18, the race difference in brain size is not significantly present at birth and becomes increasingly evident in early childhood, being well established by six years of age, after which the difference remains about the same throughout life.

**Table 4.14. Mean and Standard Deviation of Brain Weight (g) of White and Black Men and Women[a]**

| Group | Men | | Women | | Diff. | % Diff.[b] | Diff./SD[c] | r_pbs[e] |
|---|---|---|---|---|---|---|---|---|
| | *Mean* | SD | *Mean* | SD | | | | |
| White | 1,392 | 130 | 1,252 | 125 | 140 | 10.1 | 1.10 | 0.49 |
| Black | 1,286 | 138 | 1,158 | 119 | 128 | 10.0 | 0.99 | 0.44 |
| | | | | | | | | |
| Difference | 106 | | 94 | | | | | |
| % Diff.[b] | 7.6 | | 7.5 | | | | | |
| Diff./SD[c] | 0.80 | | 0.77 | | | | | |
| r_pb[d] | 0.36 | | 0.35 | | | | | |

[a] Data from Ho et al. (1980a), Table 1. (*N*s = 416 white males, 228 black males; 395 white females, 222 black females.)

[b] % Diff. = 100 (larger mean − smaller mean)/larger mean.

[c] The difference expressed in units of the average standard deviation ($\overline{SD}$) of the two groups. $\overline{SD} = [(N_1 s_1^2 + N_2 s_2^2)/(N_1 + N_2)]^{1/2}$, where *N* is sample size, *s* is standard deviation, and subscripts 1 and 2 refer to each group.

[d] Point-biserial correlation between race and brain weight.

[e] Point-biserial correlation between sex and brain weight.

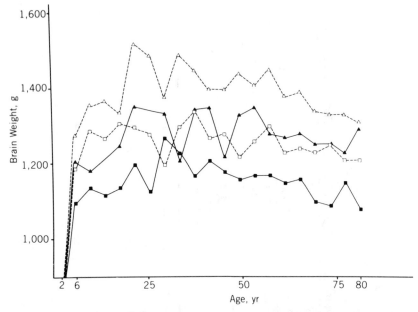

**Figure 4.18.** Mean brain weight of white males (open triangle), black males (solid triangle), white females (open square), black females (solid square). Brain weight is plotted at midpoint of each 4-year age interval, for example, point at 6 years represents average brain weight of all cases between 4 and 8 years. (From Ho et al., 1980a.)

In another publication based on the same data, Ho et al. (1980b) explicitly examined the racial difference in brain weight in relation to body size (height, weight, body surface area). When body size is held constant, the overall racial difference in mean brain weight is reduced to $0.48\sigma$, as compared with the unadjusted difference of $0.79\sigma$. The adjusted difference remains highly significant ($p < .001$), however. Differences in brain weight between the sexes, when adjusted for body size, are much smaller and less clearcut. White women's brains are heavier than white men's, and the reverse is true for blacks. In summarizing their findings on racial differences, Ho et al. (1980b) offer the following general conclusions:

> Our first report (Ho et al., 1980a) indicated that the brain weight is higher for white men than for black men, and higher for white women than for black women. The result is the same when the brain weight is adjusted to the body height, weight, and surface area. The absolute brain weight of black men is heavier than that of white women, but is heavier for white women than for black men when adjusted for height, weight, or body surface area. All the differences in brain weight between the white and black populations are statistically significant when adjusted for any of the body dimensions, except for that between white and black men, when adjusted for body weight. (p. 645)

A more recent article by Ho, Roessman, Hause, and Monroe (1981) analyzes the brain weights of white and black (total $N = 782$) newborn infants, aged 1 to 29 days, in relation to gestational age, body weight, and sex. No significant sex or race differences were found for full-term infants, although among premature infants, whites showed significantly heavier brain weight. Because a significant race difference in brain weight was manifested only in premature infants, Ho et al. suggest that the difference between the races found in their previous study of adult brain weights is best explained by environmental factors implicated in prematurity and low birthweight, both of which have a higher incidence in the black than in the white population. We take exception to this interpretation, for several reasons. First, many types of individual differences in physical (and mental) characteristics that emerge during the course of development are not present at birth. Many important genetic influences have the quality of time capsules, with effects that are not manifested until later stages of the individual's development. For example, the absence of a sex difference in brain weights in infancy and the later appearance of a sex difference is explainable as a difference in developmental growth rates approaching different asymptotes at maturity by the two sexes, and it requires no extraneous causal factors for explanation. Certainly, there is no compelling reason to believe that those differences which are fully manifested at maturity must necessarily be incipiently manifested at birth.

Second, the difference between whites and blacks in prematurity rates is far from being large enough to account for the brain-size difference at maturity, even if it is assumed that prematurity and low birth weight retard brain development much more severely in blacks than in whites. The National Center for Health Statistics reports a prematurity rate of 6.4% for white babies and 13.22% for black babies (Reed & Stanley, 1977). Let us assume, for the sake of argument, that the effect of prematurity on whites is negligible, but that the effect on blacks is to reduce their brain weight throughout their entire development into adulthood. Let us assume that in the absence of prematurity the distribution of brain weight is just the same for blacks as it is for whites. Given these assumptions, the mean brain weight of adult blacks should be a weighted composite of the brain weight of those 13.22 percent who were born premature and those 86.78 percent who were born mature and therefore would have the same average brain weight as white adults. Ho et al. (1980a, Table 1) report the mean brain weight for whites as 1,323 g and for blacks as 1,223 g. Thus, according to our assumptions, $.1322x + .8678(1,323 \text{ g}) = 1,223 \text{ g}$, where $x$ is the mean brain weight of blacks who were premature. Solving for $x$, we get 567 g as the average adult brain weight of those blacks who were born premature. This low brain weight is obviously completely out of bounds; it is much less than the brain weight of true microcephalic imbeciles (Penrose & Haldane, 1969, p. 174), and the very lowest brain weights among the 450 blacks analyzed by Ho et al. (1980a) were only slightly less than 900 g. Therefore, the assumptions we made as the basis for arriving at the virtually impossible figure of 567 g—assumptions in accord with the suggestion of Ho et al. that the greater rate of prematurity in blacks may account for the racial difference in adult brain weights—constitute a reductio ad absurdum disproof of their argument.

Finally, if the higher prematurity rate in blacks appreciably affected adult brain weight, and if, in the absence of prematurity, the distribution of brain weights in blacks were assumed to be the same as in whites, then we should expect negative skewness of the distribution for blacks as well as a larger standard deviation. In fact, as can be seen in Figure 4.19, the distributions of brain weights for black males and females are quite symmetrical (as are the white distributions), and the standard deviations of brain weights for whites and blacks (146 g and 144 g, respectively) do not differ significantly ($F = 1.03$, $df = 811/450$, $p > .05$).

Perhaps the most impressive study of population differences in cranial capacity (and by inference, brain size), based on virtually all of the extant measurements of endocranial volume found in the world literature (numerous studies comprising over 20,000 specimens) is the work of Beals, Smith, and Dodd (1984). They have quite conclusively shown that endocranial volume and cranial morphology vary according to the climatic conditions under which different populations have evolved in different parts of the globe, the main variable being distance from the equator. Linear regressions of cranial capacity on degrees north or south latitude on different continents show slopes of about 2.5 to 3.1 $cm^3$ increase in cranial capacity per degree of distance from the equator. Racial differences in cranial capacity appear merely as incidental correlates of their different long-term geographic-climatic distributions on the earth. The sex-

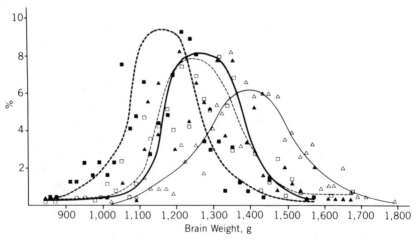

**Figure 4.19. Distribution of brain weight in white men (open triangle, thin line), black men (solid triangle, thick line), white women (open square, thick dashes), and black women (solid square, thick dashes). (From Ho et al., 1980a.)**

combined mean cranial capacities (in cm³) of the specimens from the continents of Asia, Europe, and Africa, for example, are 1,380 (SD = 83), 1,362 (SD = 35), and 1,276 (SD = 84), respectively (Beals et al., 1984, Table 2, p. 306). The precise degree to which these differences in mean cranial capacity are reflected in psychometric measures of mental ability remains highly problematic, and a proper consideration of the relevant evidence is beyond the scope of this chapter.

## Anatomical Age and Mental Age

Individual differences in rates of both physical and mental growth are well established. The question of interest in the present discussion, however, is whether mental growth rate is correlated with growth rate as indexed by physical characteristics.

Paterson's (1930) review of the relevant evidence showed that rate of physical maturation, as indexed by the degree of ossification of cartilage in the bones of the wrist and by the eruption of permanent teeth, is correlated about + .10 with Binet Mental Age, with chronological age controlled. Indeed, even various aspects of physical maturation are not highly correlated. Hence, there is little functional unity in rates of physical and mental growth.

More recent studies are consonant with these conclusions, and provide additional information which explains the low correlations (around + .10) which are usually found between indices of physical and mental maturity. The main factor is socioeconomic status; when it is held constant, the correlations are close to zero. Physical and mental growth rates are both positively correlated with SES. However, no direct causal connection between growth rates and SES per se should be inferred.

*Age of menarche.*    The age of first menstruation, or menarche, is one index of rate of physical maturity in girls which shows a low significant correlation with IQ, particularly in older studies (pre-1940). For example, data from the Harvard Growth Study (Dearborn et al., 1938), based on children born in the late 1920s and early 1930s, show a correlation of about − .20 between age of menarche and IQ. The basis of the correlation appears to be that age at menarche is correlated with social class; higher SES girls begin menstruating earlier (Tanner, 1963). Later studies have also shown a decrease in the correlation between SES and age of menarche; but there remains a negative correlation between menarche and family size (Dann & Roberts, 1969; Douglas, 1966; Nisbet & Illesley, 1962). As family size is negatively correlated with IQ, not causally, but because both variables are correlated with certain social background factors, it mediates most of the small remaining correlation between IQ and age of menarche. But even with SES and family size controlled, there is still found to be some slight IQ superiority of early over late maturing children (Nisbet & Illesley, 1963). The slight relationship between rates of physical and mental maturity is most probably a *between*-families correlation. We have found no evidence for a *within*-family correlation, although no studies have obtained the necessary data for determining a within-family correlation.

*Puberty praecox.*   Precocious puberty, a condition due to the abnormally premature development of the gonads and the sex hormones, provides a natural experiment on the effects of puberty on mental growth independent of chronological age. Occurring at any age in the period from early childhood to just before the age of normal puberty, puberty praecox has marked accelerating effects on overall physical development, reflected in height and weight, muscular development, strength, ossification of metacarpal and carpal bones, closure of epiphyseal junctures, body hair (especially pubic hair), and genitalia, which become equal in development to those of normal adults, and secondary sexual characters. Is this marked acceleration of physical maturation reflected also in an acceleration of mental maturation? The answer is afforded by a review of 62 cases of puberty praecox on which there was evidence concerning mental development as well as physical development (Stone & Doe-Kulmann, 1928). The authors concluded that "there is no evidence for genuine mental precocity regularly associated with any glandular disturbance underlying puberty praecox. Most probably, the rate of mental development is either unaffected by the glandular disorder or is retarded" (p. 393).

Two highly detailed longitudinal developmental studies of girls with puberty praecox were made by Gesell (1928). In these two cases, menstruation began at 3 years, 7 months and at 8 years, 3 months. The girls were observed over a period of several years after the onset of puberty and were periodically subjected to physical and mental measurements. The results are quite clear: Although these girls physically manifested all of the features of puberty, with mature primary and secondary female sexual characteristics, their mental development was normally consistent with their chronological age and reflected not at all their precocious physical maturation. Gesell's (1928) conclusion:

> The nervous system, among all the organs of the body, manifests a high degree of autonomy, in spite of its great impressionability. It is remarkably resistant to adversity, even to malnutrition. This relative invulnerability gives it a certain stability in the somatic competition between the organ systems. *It tends to grow in obedience to the inborn determiners, whether saddled with handicap or favored with opportunity.* For some such biological reason, the general course of mental maturation is only slightly perturbed by the precocious onset of pubescence. (p. 409)

## OCULAR VARIABLES

### Myopia

*Myopia*, or nearsightedness, is a visual deviation in which light rays entering the eye reach their focal point at some distance before the retina. This condition is part of a continuum which includes *emmetropia* (normal vision, with focal point on the retina), and *hyperopia* (farsightedness, with focal point falling beyond the retina). Positive and negative deviations from perfect emmetropia are continuously and symmetrically distributed in the general population of adults, forming a rather markedly leptokurtic bell-shaped curve, as compared with the normal, or Gaussian, distribution (François, 1961; Sorsby, Benjamin, Davey, Sheridan, & Tanner, 1957). Individual differences on this dimension are mainly the result of differences in the refractive power of the lens, but are also affected by differences in the axial length of the eyeball and corneal refraction. Hence, to the extent that hereditary factors may be involved, the overall variation in refraction is most probably polygenic.

The general consensus among contemporary researchers on myopia has been that genetic factors are strongly involved (François, 1961; Karlsson, 1973, 1974, 1975a, 1975b, 1976; Sorsby, Sheridan, & Leary, 1962; Sorsby & Fraser, 1964, 1966; Waardenburg, Franceschetti, & Klein, 1963). Although the evidence for the inheritance of myopia is now substantial, the exact mechanism of inheritance is not yet firmly established. However, few geneticists, if any, still favor the hypothesis proposed by early investigators that myopia is a single-gene, or Mendelian, character. Two facts demand a polygenic model of the total variance in refractive error: (a) the refractive error underlying myopia is a continuous variable with a slightly skewed leptokurtic frequency distribution; and (b) at least three separate but correlated optical factors involving the cornea, lens, and axial length of the eye from the cornea to the retina contribute to the refractive error that makes for myopia. A segregation analysis specifically aimed at testing the single-gene model found no support for it (Ashton, 1985b). However, a number of studies of family pedigrees and studies based on monozygotic (MZ) and dizygotic (DZ) twins, siblings, and other kinships are impressively consistent with a model of polygenic inheritance involving both additive and nonadditive (recessive) effects (Furusho, 1957; Karlsson, 1974, 1975b, 1976; Sorsby et al., 1957, 1962; Sorsby, Leary, & Fraser, 1966; Sorsby & Fraser, 1964; Wold, 1949; Young, 1958). Heritability analysis of the MZ and DZ twin data suggests that additive genetic effects account for almost 50% of the variance in ocular refraction, and additive plus nonadditive genetic factors account for most of the variance. There is no direct evidence that myopia is causally dependent on nearwork or reading or other scholastic activity. Moreover, the nearwork hypothesis seems to be contradicted by the fact that myopia occurs with comparable frequency in both literate and nonliterate populations (Post, 1982) and is as frequent in persons with Down syndrome as in other persons from the same population (Lowe, 1949).

*Correlation with intelligence.* The massive evidence now leaves no doubt that myopia is positively correlated with IQ and with its behavioral correlates, particularly scholastic achievement. A positive relationship between myopia, or nearsightedness, and mental ability was first documented in a European population more than a century ago (Cohn, 1883, 1886). Since then, the positive correlation between myopia and various measures of intelligence and scholastic aptitude and achievement has been substantiated by numerous studies (Ashton, 1985a; Baldwin, 1981; Benbow, 1986a, b; Benbow & Benbow, 1984; Douglas, Ross, & Simpson, 1967; Dunphy, 1970; Grosvenor, 1970; Heron & Zytoskee, 1981; Hirsch, 1959; Karlsson, 1973, 1975a; McManus & Mascie-Taylor, 1983; Young, 1963). The degree of relationship between myopia and mental ability in the general school population, as estimated in three large studies (Ashton, 1985a; Hirsch, 1959; Karlsson, 1975a), when expressed as a coefficient of correlation, is between about .20 and .25, which is equivalent to an IQ difference of about 6 to 8 points between myopes and nonmyopes. A study by Karlsson (1975a), based on 2,527 California high school seniors, found a difference of 8 IQ points on the Lorge-Thorndike IQ test between pupils wearing correctional lenses for myopia ($N = 377$) and nonmyopes ($N = 2,150$). The largest study, by Rosner and Belkin (1987), based on a national sample of 157,748 Israeli Jewish males, aged 17–19 years, recruited for military service, found a strong positive association of myopia with measures of intelligence on both verbal and nonverbal tests and also with years of schooling independent of intelligence.

A recent study of 5,943 myopic and 9,891 nonmyopic 18-year-old men examined for military service in Denmark provides further information on the form of the relationship between mental ability and myopia (Teasdale, Fuchs, & Goldschmidt, 1988). The measurements of myopia in terms of the power (in diopters) of the correcting lens required ranged from mild to severe. The overall intelligence test score differences between myopes and nonmyopes corresponds to approximately 7 IQ points and is, of course, highly significant. Figure 4.20 shows the prevalence of myopia as a function of total scores on a 45-minute group intelligence test consisting of subtests measuring verbal, numerical, spatial, and logical reasoning abilities. Figure 4.21 shows the relation of myopia to educational level (in years of schooling). The authors note that if reading were the cause of the association of myopia with intellectual ability, one should expect a stronger correlation of myopia with *education* than with *intelligence*. (The correlation between these variables was $+.572$.) Yet both variables are equally related to myopia, and each variable is related to myopia independently of the other, as was found also in the large study by Rosner and Belkin (1987).

The largest intelligence and educational differences occur between myopes and nonmyopes, while differences in degree of myopia beyond 2 to 3 diopters account for relatively less of the variance in abilities, as shown in Figure 4.22. The nonmyopic group differs significantly from all myopic groups from mild to severe; and groups with degrees of myopia beyond 2 diopters show no significant differences in intelligence test scores or level of education.

**Within-family correlation between intelligence and myopia.** The correlations in all of the studies reviewed so far are only evidence of a *between-families* (BF) relationship between myopia and IQ. There are only two studies reported in the literature that specifically looked at the *within-family* (WF) correlation,

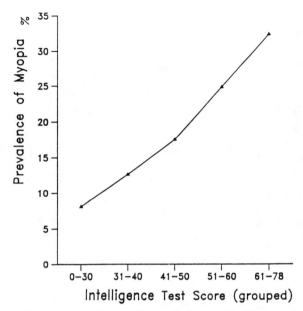

**Figure 4.20.    Prevalence of myopia in relation to intelligence test score. (From Teasdale et al., 1988.)**

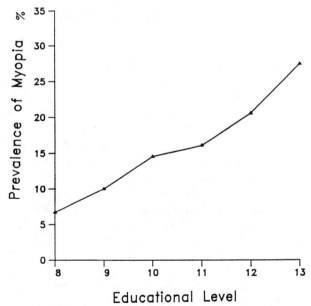

**Figure 4.21.    Prevalence of myopia in relation to educational level. (From Teasdale et al., 1988.)**

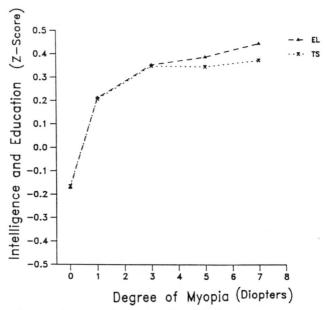

**Figure 4.22. Standardized (z) intelligence test score (TS) and educational level (EL) in relation to degree of myopia measured in diopters. (From Teasdale et al., 1988.)**

which, if significant, would be consistent with the hypothesis of a pleiotropic relationship.

In a study by Benbow (1986b; see also Benbow & Benbow, 1984) of extremely precocious students (the 417 most academically gifted youths selected from over 100,000 gifted students identified in a talent search covering the entire United States), it was discovered that over 50% of the mathematically precocious (and even more of the verbally precocious) were myopic, while fewer than 5% were hyperopic, as compared with about 15–20% of myopes in the general high school population. Myopia in the precocious group was determined by questionnaires mailed to their parents, who were also asked to report on the presence of myopia in any siblings of the precocious probands; 36% of the siblings were reported to be myopic, which is a significantly smaller percentage than the 53% of precocious probands who were reported to be myopic. Among the parents of the extremely precocious, 55% reported being myopic. The greater incidence of myopia in the parents than in their gifted children (55% vs. 53%) is most likely attributable to the increase in myopia with age. Although the Benbows did not measure the IQs of the gifted probands' siblings or parents, it seems safe to infer from simple regression considerations that the IQs of the siblings and parents were lower, on average, than the IQs of the highly selected sample of gifted youngsters. Hence we would conclude that these data indicate a WF correlation between mental ability and myopia.

The WF correlation between myopia and general mental ability was investigated more precisely by Cohn, Cohn, and Jensen (1988), who measured myopia directly as a continuous variable in a group of 60 gifted students (average age about 15 years) and their full siblings. The gifted (G) and their nearest-in-age siblings (S) differed $0.92\sigma$ (equivalent to 14 IQ points) on the Raven Matrices (Standard and Advanced forms combined). The G and S groups also differed significantly ($p < .05$) in degree of myopia (measured as refraction error) in both eyes, the G being more myopic, with an average effect size of $0.39\sigma$.

This study, along with the Benbow (1984), leaves little doubt that there is a WF correlation between myopia and mental ability. Cohn et al. consider alternative hypotheses to account for the WF correlation, and conclude that pleiotropy is the most plausible explanation. (A finding of no difference in degree of myopia between the gifted and their nongifted siblings would clearly contradict pleiotropy.) The two alternative hypotheses, which find little supportive and considerable contradictive evidence in the literature, are that (a) genetically determined myopia leads to a preference for close work and studiousness, which in turn leads to higher performance on IQ tests; and (b) genetically and environmentally conditioned higher IQ leads to a preference for reading and studiousness, which in turn strains the eyes, causing myopia. The second link of the first hypothesis lacks plausibility because it posits a weak cause (studiousness) for a large effect in the case of intellectually gifted and their siblings, who differ almost one standard deviation on a test of intelligence that does not involve reading comprehension or bookish knowledge. No one has yet demonstrated any environmental intervention that will raise the IQ by anything near one standard deviation (Spitz, 1986). Hence the second hypothesis seems more plausible than the first, although it must be recognized that the evidence is quite inconclusive that reading, near-work, or studiousness are among the causes of myopia, and most modern investigators have discounted this "near-work" hypothesis of the relation between IQ and myopia.

## Eye Pigmentation

We have found only three studies of the relation between eye color (i.e., pigmentation of the iris) and intelligence. These studies leave much to be desired methodoligically and none can be considered compelling.

In connection with the Harvard Growth Study, Estabrooks (1929) compared the IQs of four subgroups of large samples of students from grades 6 through 8 in three school systems in New York and Massachusetts: blue-eye and brown-eye, and light-hair and dark-hair, with each pigmentation group divided by sex. All subjects were Caucasian of North European extraction. In the New York sample, the blue-eyed children's IQs were 3 to 4 points higher than those of the brown-eyed children. Because this effect was confounded with age in this sample (the younger children had both higher IQs and a greater frequency of blue eyes), Estabrooks argued that pigmentation increased with age in childhood and he attributed the eye color × IQ correlation to age differences. In the Massachusetts study, all of the subjects were of about the same age (8 years), and there was no relationship between pigmentation and IQ as measured by five different group IQ tests.

Riley (1978) compared the SAT scores of 85 Caucasian college undergraduates, ages 18 to 19, who were classified by self-report as having blue eyes or brown eyes. Despite considerable heterogeneity of the SAT scores, their relation to eye color was virtually nil, and far from even borderline significance ($t < 1$). Nor was the variance of IQ related to eye color.

A study of 122 college undergraduates found correlations between eye color (rated on a 12-point scale from very light $-1$ to very dark $-12$) and scores on the Verbal and Spatial subtests of the Differential Aptitude Tests of $-.21$ and $-.19$, respectively; both are significant ($p < .05$). Because both abilities are related to eye color, it suggests that the correlation is actually with the $g$ factor common to both abilities, but this hypothesis was not tested nor does the article present the necessary correlations for the required test (Gentry, Polzine, & Wakefield, 1985). In the same study, two other genetic markers (ability to curl the tongue into a tube shape and a yes-no taste test for phenylthiocarbamide [PTC]) also showed significant ($p < .05$) correlations (about .18) with both Verbal and Spatial test scores. Because no information at all is given about the degree of ethnic heterogeneity of the subject samples, these correlations can support no really interesting interpretation. In all three of the studies reviewed here, it seems to be totally unrecognized by their authors that the only type of correlation between eye pigmentation (or any other genetic markers) and mental ability that would be of more than trivial interest from a genetic standpoint is a within-family correlation, which would indicate either genetic linkage or, more probably, pleiotropy. At best, between-family correlations can only provide a clue of which genetic variables to investigate for the presence of a within-family correlation.

## BLOOD CORRELATES

Two main classes of blood correlates of mental ability have been studied: (a) antigen polymorphisms, or blood types, and (b) blood serum chemistry, particularly serum urate level. Aside from the fact that they both require the drawing of blood samples, these two classes of variables call for quite different research methods, and they differ markedly in their theoretical implications for study of the biological basis of individual differences in ability.

### Blood Polymorphisms

Classification of individuals by blood group (also known as blood type) is based on various antigens, or specific enzymes, in the blood. Each antigen is attributable to a polymorphic gene, that is, a gene whose particular chromosomal locus can be occupied by two or more alternate forms of the gene, known as alleles. Hence, identification of the various forms of a particular antigen provides a phenotypic marker for a single gene. Over 70 such antigens have been discovered in human blood, some 30 of which are rather commonly used in genetic research. The ABO and Rhesus (Rh) systems of antigens are best known and most widely used, mainly because of their importance in blood transfusion.

The fact that blood antigens correspond to single genes makes them especially valuable in the genetic analysis of other genetic traits. Linkage analysis may show that variance in a given trait (or some fraction of its variance in the case of a polygenic trait) is conditioned by a gene (or genes) located on the same chromosome as the gene for a particular blood antigen. Establishing a genetic linkage between a given trait and a single-gene marker is a large step beyond merely demonstrating the heritability of the trait. Linkage analysis can ultimately lead to the precise chromosomal locus of the gene that affects the phenotypic trait. One of the major tasks awaiting future research in behavior genetics is the linkage analysis of various phenotypic within-family correlates, both behavioral and physiological, of mental abilities. The success of such an endeavor will probably depend as much on the componential analysis of abilities and the measurement of elementary cognitive processes with the techniques of mental chronometry (Jensen, 1985) as on the methodology of quantitative genetics.

*Pitfalls.* There are two major methodological pitfalls that were unrecognized by some earlier researchers in this field: (a) the capitalization on chance, or random variation, in the use of multiple regression techniques, and (b) reliance on between-family data, which capitalizes on what is referred to in population genetics as "heterogeneity of population structure" or "population stratification" (Thomson & Bodmer, 1975). These terms refer to the fact that most natural populations are a composite of a number of genetically differentiated subpopulations, arising from immigration or invasions, and are maintained by social stratification and assortative mating. Such differentiation is often long-standing and not recognizable from superficial appearance. Different traits which are not at all correlated *within* subpopulations but which differ *between* subpopulations will be correlated in the *combined* subpopulations. But such correlations due to population heterogeneity are utterly trivial from the standpoint of understanding the causal nature of the correlated traits. Certain subpopulations, even within the same major racial classification, are known to differ in the relative frequencies of blood groups. To the extent that the subpopulations also differ in mental abilities, for whatever cause, it should be possible to find correlations between blood groups and abilities in any large sample randomly drawn from a composite of different subpopulations. The obtained correlations, however, will most likely not be replicable in some other population sample.

Both of these pitfalls are clearly demonstrated in an early study (Osborne & Suddick, 1971), which showed multiple correlations ($R$) between a number of blood types and three mental test factors ranging from .45 to .77, in white ($N =$

54) and black ($N = 42$) samples. The observed $R$ for 18 predictors (blood types) in the white sample was .69, which is not significant at the .05 level. By selecting from the 18 blood types five that were the best predictors, the $R$ was still large (.58) *and* significant ($p < .05$) for this small number of predictors. This *a posteriori* procedure of selecting a subset of predictors from a much larger set of predictors that in toto is not significant, of course, capitalizes on chance and is a well-known statistical fallacy. This was pointed out by Owen (1972), who attempted to replicate these results using the same set of predictors and regression weights on a similar population sample. The observed sample $R$ of .28 was totally nonsignificant for an $N$ of 84, and the estimated population correlation (i.e., the shrunken $R$) was a mere .08. The failure to replicate the large but fallacious correlations of the original study is not at all surprising. But even if such a study had been analyzed correctly and showed a significant and substantial correlation which could be replicated in other samples from the same population, the finding would still be trivial, because correlation due merely to population heterogeneity simply cannot be ruled out in this type of study. The reason that such a correlation is regarded as trivial is that no scientifically interesting inferences can follow from it.

Another instructive example is the significant ($p < .001$) correlations of .06 and .07 between IQ and the ABO blood types and Rh factor found in the total sample ($N = 26,760$) of white and black children studied by Broman, Nichols, and Kennedy (1975, p. 279). But there were no significant correlations *within* either the white or black samples, even though correlations as small as .02 would be significant beyond the .001 level for such large samples. This can only mean that the observed correlations of IQ with the ABO and Rh systems are attributable to the genetic heterogeneity of the combined black and white samples, which have different gene frequencies for these blood groups.

***Between-families studies of the ABO groups.*** The ratio of A to (O + B + AB) blood type frequencies was found to differ by social class in two districts in England (Beardmore & Karimi-Booshehri, 1983). The social class differences in A/(O + B + AB), with the upper classes having the highest frequencies of A type blood, were consistent in the two separate locales and in males and females. The well-established correlation between social class and IQ makes it reasonable to hypothesize that the correlation between social class and blood type comes about through their mutual association with IQ. The authors of this study favor linkage or pleiotropy to explain their finding, arguing that the two regions studied have different invasion and immigration histories and that generations of social mobility would have homogenized originally different gene pools. If their conclusion is correct, other studies in different populations should reveal a correlation between the ABO system and IQ. As noted previously, no correlation between ABO and IQ was found in very large white and black samples (Broman et al., 1975).

A study of the residents of seven English villages found significant correlations between Wechsler IQ and the ABO system ($A_2 > 0 > A_1$), but the correlation is confounded by IQ differences between locally born residents and immigrant residents—again a case of population heterogeneity (Gibson, Harrison, Clark, & Hiorns, 1973). A later study in much the same locales, with larger samples, found no significant correlation of ABO with IQ when "localness" was controlled, but turned up two other significant blood group correlations with Wechsler Performance IQs—the Kell ($p > .05$) and Haptoglobin (Hp) ($p < .001$) markers (Mascie-Taylor, Gibson, Hiorns, & Harrison, 1985). The Hp correlation was entirely attributable to the Block Design subtest, and Kell was associated only with Performance IQ. The test specificity of these correlations leads the study's authors to suggest that the relationship is probably not a result of population heterogeneity. The correlations remained significant when sex, localness, social class, village, birth order, family size, and handedness were statistically controlled. Six other blood groups (ABO, MNS, Rh, PGM, ADA, and Tf) showed no significant correlations with mental test scores. But the significant correlations (Kell and Hp) will remain of little interest until they can be replicated in different populations, and the possibility of their representing pleiotropy or linkage could be investigated only by a within-families study. The study by Mascie-Taylor et al. (1985) did find a within-family difference in Haptoglobin types between male siblings who were downwardly mobile in social class and those who remained in their father's social class. This one within-family correlation would seem to make Haptoglobin worthy of further study in relation to the spatial visualization factor manifested in the Wechsler Block Design subtest, with which it showed the highest correlation.

*Blood-type homozygosity.* The Haptoglobin (Hp) groups, however, showed no significant correlations with any of the 15 tests, including 5 tests of visual-spatial abilities, used in the large Hawaii Family Study of Cognition (Ashton, 1986). A total of 18 different blood polymorphisms and 15 diverse tests of mental abilities turned up about the same number of significant ($p < .05$) correlations as would be expected by chance alone, with a total $N = 4,469$. However, another kind of relationship between blood polymorphisms and tests of verbal and spatial abilities was discovered at a high level of significance ($p < .001$). (Speed and memory factors did not show this relationship.) This was the individual's overall amount of homozygosity on all 18 blood groups, that is, whether the alleles for any particular blood group were the same (homozygous) or different (heterozygous). Because each allele at a given locus is contributed by a different parent, the homozygous condition suggests less hybridization, but more important, it suggests a lower probability of maternal-fetal incompatibility of blood antigens. It was found that increasing homozygosity, based on the number of homozygous polymorphisms among the 18 that were tested, was significantly correlated with higher test scores for verbal and spatial abilities. This relationship was found in both Caucasian and Asian samples, and in the parent and offspring generations, so it appears to be a genuine phenomenon. Although the mental test variance accounted for by zygosity in this study is exceedingly small, it could amount to a considerable effect over a much greater number of genetic loci. Ashton (1986) estimates that the effects of zygosity at 50 loci could account for 7.5% of the variation in verbal and spatial abilities. (The common ability factor here is most likely *g*.) The mechanism by which zygosity can affect cognitive development is explained by Ashton as follows:

> The advantage of being homozygous is most evident in immunological tolerance expressed during grafting or transplanting. A developing fetus is a special kind of graft in which the fetus is potentially incompatible with the maternal genotype at all polymorphic loci. . . . [A] reasonable biological hypothesis is that antigenic incompatibility exists at many loci and is expressed through subtle effects during brain development *in utero*. The more homozygous an individual is, the less developmental deficit is incurred. (p. 528)

***Rh factor and fetal development.*** The one blood polymorphism that has long been known to have an effect, under certain conditions, on brain development and intelligence is the Rhesus, or Rh, factor, which can result in antigenic incompatibility between the mother and fetus. Rh incompatibility, known in its clinical forms as kernicterus of hemolytic disease of the newborn, can occur when the mother is Rh-negative (*dd*) and the father is Rh-positive (DD or Dd). The Rh-negative offspring are safe, as they are compatible with the mother. The Rh-positive offspring are at risk, because they are antigenically incompatible with the mother, who builds up antibodies to attack the "foreign" fetus. This maternal immunization against an Rh-positive fetus generally has little if any detectable effect on the fetus in the first pregnancy, because the mother's immunization is not sufficiently developed. The build-up of antibodies continues to increase after delivery, and with each subsequent pregnancy the Rh-positive fetus is at increased risk, often requiring a complete blood exchange transfusion at the time of birth in order to maintain the neonate's viability or to lessen brain damage.

The behavioral effect of this condition on mental development varies from very slight retardation to idiocy, although the technique of exchange transfusion greatly improves the prognosis (Penrose & Haldane, 1969, pp. 237-239). A Finnish study of 43 youths, 17 to 19 years of age, who were Rh incompatible with their mothers and had required postnatal replacement transfusions, were compared with 43 matched controls and were found to perform less well than the controls in general intelligence, visual-motor coordination, and scholastic achievement (grade-point average, attention, and concentration). Degree of deficit was positively related to the length of delay after birth in the neonate's being given an exchange transfusion (Wuorio, 1974).

Penrose and Haldane (1969, p. 238) cite other studies that lead them to suspect that maternal-fetal incompatibility in other blood groups, particularly the ABO system, might have similar, though less pronounced, effects on fetal viability and mental development. More recently, another geneticist, Karlsson (1978), wrote:

Blood group incompatibilities, involving both the Rh factor and the ABO system, are known to cause progressively greater damage to the fetus as the number of pregnancies increases. Presumably there are additional factors of this type, which still have not been discovered. (p. 182)

The slight negative correlations between birth order and IQ which show up significantly only in studies of very large groups (Ernst & Angst, 1983) could be a reflection of the effects of such antigenic incompatibilities. The importance of this phenomenon in terms of its contribution to the nonheritable component of IQ variance has not yet been adequately investigated.

*Within-family studies.* As previously emphasized, the study of within-family relationships between genetic polymorphisms and mental ability is the only methodology that can potentially establish genetic linkage, pleiotropy, or an intrinsic, or directly causal or functional, connection between different traits. The method has been applied in only a few studies of the blood-ability relationship.

Bock, Vandenberg, Bramble, and Pearson (1970) compared the within-pair variances of Wechsler Verbal IQ for 526 DZ twins classified as concordant or discordant on each of four blood groups systems: ABO, MNSS, Rh, and Duffy, or Fy. Discordance only for Rh and Duffy showed increased within-pair variance in Verbal IQ, with Rh showing the stronger effect. The authors interpret this result as evidence for linkage between the blood-group loci and a major gene that enhances verbal intelligence. Other plausible explanations have not been ruled out, such as maternal incompatibility with Rh-positive, or linkage of Duffy with Rh (both loci are on the same chromosome), or pleiotropy. In any case, the fact that DZ twins who are discordant for certain blood groups show greater differences in IQ, as compared with DZs who are concordant for the same blood groups, seems worthy of much further investigation. If the phenomenon replicates, a definitive explanation of it would be of great importance.

In an attempt to replicate the findings of Bock et al. (1970), Rose, Procidano, Conneally, and Yu (1979) examined full-sib pairs who were concordant ($N = 56$) and discordant ($N = 74$) on six different blood groups, including Rh and Duffy. Only Rh discordance showed a greater within-pair variance on Wechsler Vocabulary, but the effect is only suggestive and not significant ($p = .12$). Because of the polygenic nature of complex mental abilities, and the linkage of only one or very few genes with any single blood group marker, the effect of sibling discordance on ability for any one marker gene would necessarily be quite small if there were linkage, and hence a very large sample of sibling pairs would be needed to detect linkage with a high level of confidence.

*X-linkage.* So-called sex-linkage, which is usually linkage occurring on the X chromosome, of which females normally inherit two X chromosomes (i.e., XX) and males only one (i.e., XY), is easier to detect by studies of male full siblings than is autosomal linkage, simply because males possess but a single X chromosome. The required data consist of a large number of sets of three male full siblings in which only two members of the set are concordant for a given genetic marker, such as a blood group antigen. Degree of similarity on another trait (in this case mental ability) is compared within male sib-pairs that are either concordant or discordant for the X-linked marker gene. If there is X-linkage between the marker gene and the trait of interest, the brothers who are concordant for the marker gene will be more similar on the trait than are the brothers who are discordant for the marker.

Because of the well-established sex difference in the cognitive style known as field-dependence and in spatial-visualization ability, it was hypothesized that the genetic component of these variables is X-linked. The hypothesis was tested, with the male siblings method described above, in an exemplary study by Goodenough et al. (1977), using a known X-linked blood group, $X_g(a)$. The hypothesized linkage effect was found at a significant level for the two measures (Rod-and-Frame, Embedded Figures) of field-dependence, but in none of the six tests of spatial-visualization ability could the null hypothesis be rejected. Brothers who were identical in $X_g(a)$ blood group were more similar to each other in degree of field dependence than brothers who differed in $X_g(a)$. The authors conclude:

> If the result can be cross-validated . . . the conclusion that a gene on the X chromosome is involved in the development of field dependence would appear to be established. Whether an individual carries the $X_g(a^+)$ gene or not has no known consequence of any importance to him. Certainly neither he nor his associates can detect that fact. If field dependence is transmitted in association with $X_g(a)$, then it would appear difficult to account for such a finding except by appeal to an X-linked model. (p. 383)

The number of identified genetic markers with known loci on specific chromosomes is constantly increasing, a fact which should make it more productive in the future to conduct linkage studies of various mental ability factors. The success of such an effort would counter the common complaint that, despite the great many studies showing high heritability for mental abilities, not a single specific gene has been identified as related to normal variation in mental ability.

## Serum Uric Acid

Belief in an association between gout and eminence dates back to antiquity. This belief first gained more than mere anecdotal status when Havelock Ellis (1904), in his study of a large, representative sample of intellectually eminent Britishers, actually discovered a much higher incidence of gout than is found in the general population. The question naturally arises why gout—a painful inflammation usually of the joint in the big toe—should be associated with notable intellectual achievement.

Gout is the direct result of inflammation due to the formation of uric acid crystals in a joint. Uric acid is the end product of the metabolism of purines, which are constituents of animal proteins and fats. Uric acid is excreted in the urine and is carried in low concentrations in the blood as serum urate, or serum uric acid (SUA). At higher concentrations, SUA forms crystals which are deposited in the joints, most commonly of the big toe, which cause the painful inflammation known as gout.

Interestingly, in all other mammals except man and the higher apes, uric acid is not the end product of purine metabolism. In other mammals, the enzyme uricase oxidizes uric acid to allantoin, which is excreted as the end product of this metabolic chain. In the course of evolution, the higher apes and man lost the capacity for synthesizing uricase, with the result that uric acid was the end product of purine metabolism.

More interestingly, the molecular structure of uric acid is highly similar to that of caffeine, which is a central nervous system stimulant. (High serum uric acid level is also related to faster reaction times, as is caffeine.)

These observations led Orowan (1955) to hypothesize that the uric acid in the blood, SUA, as an endogenous stimulant to the brain, contributed to the evolution of human intelligence by the constant cortical arousal caused by this stimulant. Orowan's hypothesis prompted behavioral scientists to look for mental correlates of SUA. Correlational studies are entirely feasible, as SUA can be quite reliably measured, is quite stable in adults, and shows a wide range of individual differences. The distribution of SUA has a higher mean, larger standard deviation, and is more platykurtic in men than in women (Mikkelsen, Dodge, & Valkenberg, 1965). Proportionally fewer women than men have high levels of SUA. The sex difference is not evident until puberty. SUA then increases more for men, reaching a peak between ages 20 and 24 years, after which there is a gradual decline and plateau. After menopause, women's SUA increases gradually to about the SUA level of men in their fifties.

Genetic factors are implicated in individual differences in SUA. Studies of MZ and DZ twins, of MZ twins reared apart, and of parent-offspring regression indicate heritability coefficients around .30 to .40 (Mueller et al., 1970). The fact that the distribution of SUA is a slightly skewed unimodal curve is consistent with polygenic inheritance.

Orowan's hypothesis gave rise to a large and complex literature on the behavioral correlates of SUA. Fortunately, most of this literature has been excellently and thoroughly reviewed by Mueller, Kasl, Brooks, and Cobb (1970). The 122 references in their article will not be cited here. We will cite only the more recent studies, not included in the Mueller et al. review, in connection with our summarization of the findings in the earlier review that are most germane to the present chapter. A more extensive catalog of the literature related to behavioral aspects of SUA is provided by Stevens (1973).

It should be realized that the causal nature of the observed behavioral correlates of SUA is still obscure. Although there is evidence that the experimental manipulation of uric acid level in rats is significantly related to their maze learning and retention (Essman, 1970), a direct causal connection between SUA and behavior has not yet been established in humans. Many different hypotheses have been suggested to explain the correlation of SUA with behavioral variables: direct neural stimulation affecting certain cognitive processes, increased drive or motivation, effects of other chemical products in the metabolic process ending in uric acid, environmental factors that affect both SUA and behavior, and brain activity that yields uric acid as a product.

*Ability correlates of SUA.* There is a significant positive correlation between SUA levels and mentally retarded/nonretarded treated as a dichotomous variable, but the SUA correlation with IQ (or psychometric *g*), though significant, is quite small. Also, groups with higher than average IQ (e.g., Ph.D.s, medical students, business executives) show higher levels of SUA than the average for the general population. But such groups, of course, also differ from the average in many other ways besides their above-average intelligence.

When we look at the correlations of SUA level with IQ itself, however, the result is less impressive, suggesting that other factors besides IQ per se are probably involved in the elevated SUA levels of professional groups. We note that in the three largest studies, with a total $N = 1104$, the $N$-weighted mean Pearson $r$ is only $+.085$ (unit-weighted mean $= +.093$), which is significant beyond the .01 level. In 149 high school students, the $r$ was $+.10$ (Kasl, Brooks, & Rodgers, 1970), which is nonsignificant for this sample size, but highly consistent with other reported correlations. (We have not come across any negative correlations, but of course there is a greater risk of failure to report negative or inconsistent results.)

As most of the correlations reported in the literature are Pearson $r$ (i.e., a linear correlation), it was suggested that the SUA × ability relationship may actually be nonlinear—an inverted U—and hence is grossly underestimated by the Pearson $r$ (Stevens & Cropley, 1972). This very reasonable hypothesis merits examination. Unfortunately, the one study that attempted to demonstrate the hypothesized nonlinear relationship between SUA level and level of mental ability, with the latter decreasing beyond some optimal level of SUA, yielded equivocal results, showing a significant nonlinear trend on only two out of the four different *g*-loaded tests administered to 115 male university students (Stevens, Cropley, & Blattler, 1975). The hypothesized inverted-U relationship of ability to SUA remains unsubstantiated, but the evidence is also far too inadequate to dismiss it.

*Cognitive styles and SUA.* On the hypothesis that elevated SUA level is related to high ambition, acceptance of conventional goals, and high drive for achievement, it was predicted that SUA level would *be negatively* related to a cognitive style known as "divergent thinking" (Cropley, Cassell, & Maslany, 1970). Divergent thinkers are claimed to be relatively unconcerned about strict observance of rules, and are more impulsive, unconventional, and willing to take risks than are persons who are characterized as "convergent" thinkers, who excel in typical IQ tests, do well in school, and succeed in conventional occupations. The prediction was significantly borne out, but only for the male subjects, in the study by Cropley et al. (1970). Divergent thinking was measured by the Wallach and Kogan battery; convergent thinking by Thurstone's Primary Mental Abilities Test. Male (but not female) high "divergers" showed significantly *lower* SUA levels. There was no significant relationship of SUA to the convergent thinking measures. In another study, of men only, with superior methodology, such as control of diet and exercise (which can affect SUA), Kennett and Cropley (1975) again found a significant inverse relationship between SUA level and divergent thinking, and virtually no relationship with convergent thinking. These findings seem to suggest that SUA levels may be more related to certain personality variables than to intellectual ability per se. The personality variables may simply be influential in intellectually demanding pursuits.

*Achievement and SUA.* If an elevated level of SUA acts as a cortical stimulant, like caffeine, we should expect its main effect to be manifested not in higher intelligence per se, but in a higher level of activation of cognitive functions which would lead to greater *achievement* for any given level of intelligence. This, in fact, is what is most commonly reported in the literature on the behavioral correlates of SUA. The evidence most strongly substantiates the positive association of SUA with achievement in mentally demanding pursuits. In a study of 149 male high school students, SUA level was most notably correlated with *over*achievement, defined as level of achievement (indexed by school grade-point average) adjusted for IQ (Kasl, Brooks, & Rodgers, 1970). SUA level was also positively related to students' number of extracurricular activities. When university faculty ($N = 144$) were rated on overall level of achievement, the ratings were correlated $+.50$ with SUA level (Mueller & French, 1974). Among nontenured faculty, the chief criterion for promotion to tenure—number of publications—was correlated $+.37$ with SUA level.

The relation between SUA and achievement seems well established for males, but too few females have been subjects in SUA studies to warrant any conclusion about SUA and achievement in women.

*Socioeconomic status and SUA.* The cortical stimulant nature of SUA and its relation to achievement has suggested the hypothesis that elevated SUA level would be related to upward social mobility, as indexed by level of education and occupation. Numerous studies have found evidence for this hypothesis, although at least one study (not included in the extensive review by Mueller et al., 1970) showed no relation of socioeconomic status to SUA level (Acheson, 1969). SUA is correlated with the dichotomous variable "school drop-out/persistence in school." It is related to ratings of ambition and "need for achievement," and shows a substantial correlation with "achievement orientation behavior" in professional groups.

One large study (total $N = 1500$) contrasted professionals and executives, on the one hand, with farmers and unskilled workers, on the other, and found, on average, a higher SUA level in the former than in the latter group (Dodge & Mikkelsen, 1968). Perhaps the most interesting feature of this study is that SUA was measured also in the wives of the men in these contrasting occupational groups, and there was no difference in their average SUA levels. This suggests that the differing levels of SUA by occupation in the males is probably not attributable to possible social class differences in dietary habits or general lifestyle, which would presumably be shared by the wives.

## MISCELLANEOUS VARIABLES

Our literature search has turned up a number of other physical variables that studies have found to be related to mental ability. But the studies are single or very few for each variable, and hence afford an inadequate basis for conclusions or theoretical interpretation. Some, however, are probably promising for further research and should be cited in this review. Replication, of course, is essential for these variables to accrue scientific interest. Some of the correlations are merely opportunistic—calculated from sets of physical and mental measurements that were originally obtained for other purposes. Hence, the reported correlations, though significant, are considerably more liable to Type I Error than are correlations found in studies specifically designed to test a particular hypothesis. With this caveat, we mention these studies only briefly.

*Vital capacity.* The maximum amount of air that can be expired from the lungs, which is related to stature, age, and physical fitness, showed correlations of +.23 and +.29 with mental test scores (Schreider, 1968; Whipple, 1914).

*Handgrip strength.* Related to intellectual level and efficiency in various aged samples (total $N = 2000$) of healthy males and females (Clement, 1974).

*Facial features.* Judges' ratings of intelligence from photographs of faces of regular students are correlated (about .20) with teachers' assessments of the subjects' intelligence (Burt, 1919), and with intelligence test scores (Kiener & Keiper, 1977). The latter study details the specific facial characteristics that discriminate significantly between the 14 most and the 14 least intelligent among 84 women students.

*Hair color.* In 1100 Swedish school children, IQ was positively related to darkness of hair, and the mean IQ of red-haired pupils was slightly below average and significantly fewer went on to high school (Lundman, 1972).

*Basal metabolic rate.* High (+.6 to +.7) correlations with IQ were found in two studies ($N$s = 90 and 200) of children, ages 5 to 16 years (Hinton, 1936, 1939), but no significant correlations between BMR and IQ were found in a study of 87 adolescents (Shock & Jones, 1939), or between BMR and scholarship in six studies of college students (Yarbrough & McCurdy, 1958). The studies of children suggest a sharp drop in the BMR × IQ correlation after about age 10; the relationship may be an early developmental phenomenon and, in view of the large correlation reported by Hinton, warrants further investigation.

*Masa intermedia.* This mass of neural tissue connects the two halves of the thalamus. It is absent in about one-third of men and one-fourth of women. In a group of 74 adult neurological patients there was a significant difference in the means of the Wechsler-Bellevue Performance scales of men who possessed the *masa intermedia* and those who did not, the latter scoring *higher* (Landsdell, Davie, & Clayton, 1972). Strangely, among those in whom the *masa intermedia* was present, there was a *positive* correlation ( + .43, $p < .01$) between the size of the *masa intermedia* and Performance scores. The use of magnetic resonance imaging, with neurologically normal persons, should be able to verify these puzzling relationships if they are generalizable beyond the particular study sample.

*Asthma and other allergies.* Intellectually precocious children, especially those with exceptional mathematical reasoning ability, show a much higher incidence of allergies of various kinds than is found in the general population. Some 55% of verbally and mathematically precocious students suffer from allergies, in contrast to about 10 percent in the general population (Benbow, 1986a, 1986b; Benbow & Benbow, 1986). The authors relate this highly significant finding to a hypothesis of Geschwind and Behan (1982) to the effect that immune disorders (and left-handedness, also more prevalent in the precocious) are related to fetal exposure to high levels of testosterone or high sensitivity to testosterone. Testosterone slows development of the left hemisphere, which may lead to enlargement of the right hemisphere, which is presumably involved in the kind of spatial-visualization ability that is often correlated with exceptional mathematical reasoning ability. Whatever the merits of this hypothesis, the essential empirical finding seems an important one in view of the fact that the relation between allergies and precocity is a *within*-family correlation. The incidence of allergies is 15 to 20% higher among the precocious probands than among their parents and siblings.

*Phenylthiocarbamide (PTC) tasting ability.* PTC, a synthetic chemical, is of interest to geneticists because the ability of individuals to taste this chemical (which is unpleasantly bitter if it can be tasted) is due to a single Mendelian dominant gene. About 70 percent of European and Asian populations are "tasters." Hence, PTC tasting ability is frequently used in determining the zygosity of twins and as a genetic marker. Two independent studies, with $N$s = 122 and 141, have both found that nontasters score significantly higher than tasters in $g$ and spatial ability, with correlations about .20 (Gentry, Polzine, & Wakefield, 1985; Mascie-Taylor, McManus, McLarnon, & Lonigan, 1983). PTC showed no correlation (-.04) with a test of clerical speed and accuracy, which has a minimal loading on $g$.

*Tongue-curling ability.* Whether or not a person can curl the tongue into a tube shape behaves like a single-gene Mendelian trait and hence can be used as a genetic marker in studies of linkage and pleiotropism. There seems little likelihood of assortative mating or cross-assortative mating with intelligence for this character, although there remains the possibility of population heterogeneity for both traits and a consequent between-families correlation. In a study of 122 unrelated college undergraduates (hence between-families), tongue-curling ability was found to be positively and significantly ($p < .05$) correlated with verbal reasoning ($r = +.18$) and spatial reasoning ($r = +.20$), but not with clerical speed and accuracy ($r = .03$) (Gentry, Polzine, & Wakefield, 1985). As the authors correctly point out,

> The smaller size (about .20) of the significant correlations between genetic markers . . . and intelligence . . . does not detract from their importance. Indeed if the markers are genetically simple and the psychological variables are genetically complex, small correlations would be expected to occur and can be expected to point the way to specific genetic contributors to personality and intelligence. (p. 113)

However, we emphasize again that such correlations can have no causal status unless they are established in a within-families study. If the variables are significantly correlated within families, then the appropriate studies can be done to determine whether the correlation is attributable to linkage disequilibrium or to pleiotropy.

## SUMMARY AND CONCLUSIONS

The massive evidence of significant correlations between scores on psychometric tests of mental ability and a wide variety of physical traits shows beyond a reasonable doubt that the population variance on standard mental tests reflects latent traits that are profoundly enmeshed with organismic variables in complex ways.

The causes of the relationship between individual differences in mental ability, on the one hand, and individual differences in anatomical, physiological, serological, and biochemical characteristics, on the other, are both numerous and different for various physical traits. Hence, the causal nature of the correlation between mental and physical traits is often unique and must be studied separately in each physical trait for which such correlation is found. This kind of analysis is further complicated by the fact that some of the physical traits that are correlated with mental ability are themselves correlated with one another. The causal pathways therefore do not yield easily to analysis.

The nature of the association between mental and physical traits can be classified in several ways that are useful theoretically. These systems of classification are not all completely independent or mutually exclusive, and any particular correlation can be classified in various ways.

The association between a mental and a physical trait can be (a) *functional*, or intrinsic, and closely related to the biological mechanisms directly involved in the mental activity, such as brain anatomy and biochemistry; or it can be (b) a *nonfunctional*, or indirect, by-product of a long chain of other causes, often reflecting cultural values, such as the nonfunctional relationship between intelligence and physical stature.

Another system of classification is the distinction between (a) significant correlations that occur *within* families (i.e., correlation between different traits among full siblings), and (b)) correlations that are essentially zero *within* families but significantly greater than zero *between* families. The first classification (i.e., (a)) is more likely to include functional or intrinsic relationships (i.e., (a) above), while the second classification (i.e., (b) is more likely to include the nonfunctional types of relationships (i.e., (b) above).

Within each of these categories, there are still other types of correlation between mental and physical traits.

*Within-family* correlations are most often explained in terms of

1. *genetic linkage* (i.e., the genes for different traits having loci in close proximity on the same chromosome), but this correlation is detectable only in family pedigree studies or in genetically heterogeneous populations that are still in a state of linkage disequilibrium for the traits in question
2. *pleiotropy* (i.e., one gene that affects the development of two phenotypically distinct traits)
3. a *structure-function* relationship whereby performance is directly dependent on a particular physical structure or biochemical mediator; and
4. *exogenous* (not heritable) prenatal or postnatal factors that affect siblings differentially with respect to the parallel development of both mental and physical traits.

*Between-family* correlations (when accompanied by zero within-family correlations) are most often explained in terms of

1. *genetic heterogeneity*, or genetic stratification, of the population with respect to certain mental and physical traits, making them correlated in a random sample from such a composite of genetic subpopulations
2. *selective mating* for each of two genetically independent traits, usually because the particular physical and the mental traits both happen to be valued in a given culture, for whatever reason
3. *assortative mating* for each of two distinct traits
4. *cross-assortative mating* for both traits, that is, a tradeoff between a particular trait in one mate for a different trait in the other mate (e.g., intelligence and stature), usually because in the particular culture both traits are perceived as desirable
5. *common environment*, that is, factors (e.g., nutrition, ordinary childhood diseases, and the like) that generally affect all of the siblings within a family

but may differ between families, and which simultaneously affect both mental and physical development.

The origins of exclusively *between*-family correlations must be sought in the immediate environment (e.g., nutritional differences, health-care standards) and in the cultural factors that determine mating preferences.

The origins of *within*-family correlations, particularly pleiotropy and linkage, are more obscure and probably must be sought in the evolutionary history of a given population. There may be little or no evident rhyme or reason to a particular correlation due to pleiotropy (e.g., the positive correlation between myopia and intelligence) or to linkage. But pleiotropy originates through genetic mutation, which is a random phenomenon, and so the effects of mutation are essentially random and without rhyme or reason. However, the pleiotropic mutations that endure in a population do so through selection, by virtue of the increment in overall Darwinian fitness conferred by the *net* adaptive effect of the two or more phenotypic expressions of the pleiotropic gene. Hence there need not be any obvious or inherently "logical" or psychologically explainable connection between the distinct phenotypic characteristics that are correlated pleiotropically. Their continued existence in the population, however, indicates that, adaptively, their net effect (i.e., the algebraic sum of their separate positive or negative effects) has, so to speak, passed the test of natural selection in terms of fitness. A good case can be made that psychomteric *g*, the main latent trait measured by conventional intelligence tests, has evolved as a fitness character during the course of human evolution.

The significant associations between mental ability and physical traits which are the most securely established by research are all quite low—their true or error-corrected values are virtually all represented by correlation coefficients between about .10 and .40.

*Stature* (general body size, height, and weight) shows correlations with IQ averaging close to +.20. This correlation is now so strongly established by such massive evidence that further demonstrations of it would seem pointless. It appears to be a between-families type of correlation, most likely attributable to assortative and cross-assortative mating for stature and intelligence, and probably also to shared nutritional and health factors within families.

*Brain-size* correlations with IQ, controlling for overall body size, differ depending on the precision with which brain size (or the encephalization quotient, which controls for body size) is measured. IQ is correlated with external head measurements between +.10 and +.20, with intracranial volume about +.25 to +.30, and with direct *in vivo* measurement of the brain by means of MRI, about +.35. This is probably a structure-function type of correlation, but this point has not yet been adequately researched to draw any compelling conclusion.

*Age of menarche*, a developmental variable, is correlated with IQ about − .20.

*Myopia* shows a within-family correlation with IQ, which is consistent with the hypothesis that the well-established population correlation of about + .20 to + .25 between IQ and myopia is pleiotropic.

*Blood groups* lend themselves to genetic linkage studies when significant within-family correlations are found between particular blood groups and mental abilities. Research in this vein so far has turned up little, but there is some evidence, surely in need of replication, that certain blood groups may be linked to particular ability factors other than *g*, such as spatial visualization. There is stronger evidence that *maternal-fetal blood antigen incompatibility*, particularly in the Rh and ABO systems, is probably related to the afflicted offspring's mental development, although only some very small proportion of the total population variance in IQ is likely to be accounted for by this factor. *Serum urate* (uric acid in the blood) level is correlated only about + .10 with IQ, but shows considerably higher correlations with various achievement indices, suggesting that it acts as a cortical stimulant affecting intellectual drive more than level of intelligence per se.

Also reviewed briefly were a number of other claimed physical correlates of IQ based on single or very few studies and for which any scientifically worthy conclusions must await replications. Reports in the literature of particular physical correlates of mental ability, when not the main aim of a systematic program of research, are probably more prone to Type I error than might be expected for other findings in the general behavioral science literature.

## REFERENCES

Acheson, R. M. (1969). Social class gradients and serum uric acid in males and females. *British Medical Journal, 4*, 65–67.

Armstrong, E. (1983). Relative brain size and metabolism in mammals. *Science, 220*, 1302–1304.

Ashton, G. C. (1985a). Nearwork, school achievement, and myopia. *Journal of Biosocial Sciences, 17*, 223–233.

Ashton, G. C. (1985b). Segregation analysis of ocular refraction and myopia. *Human Heredity, 35*, 232–239.

Ashton, G. C. (1986). Blood polymorphisms and cognitive abilities. *Behavior Genetics, 16*, 517–529.

Baker, J. R. (1974). *Race*. New York: Oxford University Press.

Baker, L.A. (1983). Familial contributions to the correlation between height and general intelligence (Abst.). *Behavior Genetics, 13*, 526–527.

Baldwin, W. R. (1981). A review of statistical studies of relations between myopia and ethnic, behavioral and physiological characteristics. *American Journal of Optometry and Physiological Optics, 58,* 516–527.

Bayley, N. (1956). Individual patterns of development. *Child Development, 27,* 45–74.

Beals, K. L., Smith, C. L., & Dodd, S. M. (1984). Brain size, cranial morphology, climate, and time machines. *Current Anthropology, 25,* 301–330.

Beardmore, J. A., & Karimi-Booshehri, R. (1983). ABO genes are differentially distributed in socioeconomic groups in England. *Nature, 303,* 522–524.

Belmont, L., Stein, Z. A., & Susser, M. W. (1975). Comparison of associations of birth order with intelligence test score and height. *Nature, 255,* 54–56.

Benbow, C. P. (1986a). Physiological correlates of extreme intellectual precocity. *Neuropsychologia, 24,* 719–725.

Benbow, C. P. (1986b). Physiological correlates of extreme intellectual precocity. *Mensa Research Journal, 21,* 79–89.

Benbow, C. P., & Benbow, R. M. (1984). Biological correlates of high mathematical reasoning ability. In G. J. DeVries, J. P. C. DeBruin, H. B. M. Nylings, & M. A. Corner (Eds.), *Sex differences in the brain—their relation between structure and function. Progress in Brain Research, 61,* 469–490.

Benbow, C. P., & Benbow, R. M. (1986). Biological correlates of high mathematical reasoning ability. *Mensa Research Journal, 21,* 54–78.

Boas, F. (1895). On Dr. William Townsend Porter's investigation of the growth of the school children of St. Louis. *Science, New Series, 1,* 225–230.

Bock, R. D., & Kolakowski, D. (1973). Further evidence of sex-linked major-gene influence on human spatial visualizing ability. *American Journal of Human Genetics, 25,* 1–14.

Bock, R. D., Vandenberg, S. G., Bramble, W., & Pearson, W. (1970). A behavioral correlate of blood-group discordance in dizygotic twins. *Behavior Genetics, 1,* 89–98.

Bouchard, T. J., Jr., & McGee, M. G. (1977). Sex differences in human spatial ability: Not an X-linked recessive gene effect. *Social Biology, 24,* 332–335.

Bray, P. F., Shields, W. D., Wolcott, G. J., & Madsen, J. A. (1969). Occipitofrontal head circumference—An accurate measure of intracranial volume. *Journal of Pediatrics, 75,* 303–305.

Broman, S. H., Nichols, P. L., & Kennedy, W. A. (1975). *Preschool IQ: Prenatal and early developmental correlates.* Hillsdale, NJ: Erlbaum.

Brucefors, A., Johannesson, I., Karlberg, P., Klachenberg-Larsson, I., Lichenstein, H., & Svenberg, I. (1974). Trends in development of abilities related to somatic growth. *Human Development, 17,* 152–159.

Burks, B. S. (1940). Mental and physical developmental patterns of identical twins in relation to organismic growth theory. In G. W. Whipple (Ed.), *Intelligence: Its nature and nurture* (Part II, 39th Yearbook of the NSSE). Bloomington, IL: Public School Publishing Co.

Burt, C. (1919). Facial expression as an index of mentality. *Child Study, 12,* 1–3.

Burt, C., & Banks, C. (1947). A factor analysis of body measurements for British adult males. *Annals of Eugenics, 13,* 238–256.

Cattell, R. B. (1971). *Abilities: Their structure, growth, and action.* Boston: Houghton Mifflin.

Cattell, R. B. (1982). *The inheritance of personality and ability.* New York: Academic Press.

Clark, P. J., Vandenberg, S. G., & Proctor, C. H. (1961). On the relationship of scores on certain psychological tests with a number of anthropometric characters and birth order in twins. *Human Biology, 33,* 163–180.

Clement, F. J. (1974). Longitudinal and cross-sectional assessments of age changes in physical strength as related to sex, social class, and mental ability. *Journal of Gerontology, 29,* 423–429.

Cobb, S. (1965). Brain size. *Archives of Neurology, 12,* 555–561.

Cohn, H. (1883). *Die hygiene des auges in den schulen.* Vienna: Urban und Schwarzenberg.

Cohn, H. (1886). *The hygiene of the eye in schools* (W. P. Turnbull, Trans.). London: Simpkin, Marshall.

Cohn, S. J., Cohn, C. M. G., & Jensen, A. R. (1988). Myopia and intelligence: A pleiotropic relationship? *Human Genetics, 80,* 53–58.

Cropley, A. J., Cassell, W. A., & Maslany, G. W. (1970). A biochemical correlate of divergent thinking. *Canadian Journal of Behavioural Science, 2,* 174–180.

Dann, T. C., & Roberts, D. F. (1969). Physique and family environment in girls attending a Welsh college. *British Journal of Preventive and Social Medicine, 23,* 65–71.

Dearborn, W. F., Rothney, J. W. M., & Shuttleworth, F. K. (1938). Data on the growth of public school children. *Monographs of the Society for Research on Child Development, 3,* 1.

Dobzhansky, Th. (1970). *Genetics of the evolutionary process.* New York: Columbia University Press.

Dodge, H. J., & Mikkelsen, W. M. (1968). Association of serum uric acid scores with occupation: Male heads of households in Tecumseh, Michigan, 1959–1960. *Journal of Occupational Medicine, 10,* 402–407.

Douglas, J. W. B. (1966). The age of reaching puberty: Some associated factors and some educational implications. In British Postgraduate Medical Federation, *The scientific basis of medicine, annual reviews* (pp. 91–105). London: University of London, Athlone.

Douglas, J. W. B., Ross, J. M., & Simpson, H. R. (1967). The ability and attainment of short-sighted pupils. *Journal of The Royal Statistical Society, 130,* 479–503.

Dunphy, E. B. (1970). The biology of myopia. *New England Journal of Medicine, 283,* 796–800.

Ellis, H. (1904). *A study of British genius.* London: Hurst & Blackett.

Ernst, C., & Angst, J. (1983). *Birth order: Its influence on personality.* New York: Springer-Verlag.

Essman, W. B. (1970). Purine metabolites in memory consolidation. In W. Byrne (Ed.), *Molecular approaches to learning and memory* (pp. 307–323). New York: Academic Press.

Estabrooks, G. H. (1929). Intelligence and pigmentation of hair and eyes in elementary school children. *American Journal of Psychology, 41,* 106–108.

Ewert, O. M. (1977). Obesity and attainment of conservation skills. *Zeitschrift für Entwichlungspsychologie und Pädagogische Psychologie, 9,* 1–9.

Eysenck, H. J. (1979). *The structure and measurement of intelligence*. New York: Springer-Verlag.

Falconer, D. S. (1960). *An introduction to quantitative genetics*. New York: Ronald Press.

Fisch, R. O., Blick, M. K., Horrobin, J. M., & Chang, P. N. (1976). Children with superior intelligence at 7 years of age. *American Journal of Diseases of Children, 130*, 481–487.

François, J. (1961). *Heredity in ophthalmology*. St. Louis: C. V. Mosby.

Furusho, T. (1957). Studies on the genetic mechanism of shortsightedness. *Japanese Journal of Ophthalmology, 1*, 185–190.

Galton, F. (1869). *Hereditary genius: An inquiry into its laws and consequences*. London: Collins.

Gentry, T. A., Polzine, K. M., & Wakefield, J. A., Jr. (1985). Human genetic markers associated with variation in intellectual abilities and personality. *Personality and Individual Differences, 6*, 111–113.

Geschwind, N., & Behan, P. (1982). Left handedness: Association with immune disease, migraine, and developmental learning disorder. *Proceedings of the National Academy of Sciences, 79*, 5097–5100.

Gesell, A. (1928). Precocious puberty and mental maturation. *27th Yearbook of the National Society for the Study of Education, 27*(1), 399–409.

Gibson, J. B., Harrison, G. A., Clark, V. A., & Hiorns, R. W. (1973). IQ and ABO blood groups. *Nature, 246*, 498–500.

Glass, G. V., McGaw, B., & Smith, M. L. (1981). *Meta-analysis in social research*. Beverly Hills, CA: Sage.

Goldblatt, P. E., Moore, M. E., & Stunkard, A. J. (1965). Social factors in obesity. *Journal of American Medical Association, 192*, 1039–1044.

Goodenough, D. R., Gandini, E., Olkin, I., Pizzamiglio, L., Thayer, D., & Witkin, H. A. (1977). A study of X chromosome linkage with field dependence and spatial visualization. *Behavior Genetics, 7*, 373–387.

Grosvenor, T. (1970). Refractive state, intelligence test scores, and academic ability. *American Journal of Optometry and Archives of the American Academy of Optometry, 47*, 355–361.

Harter, S. (1965). Discrimination learning set in children as a function of IQ and mental age. *Journal of Experimental Child Psychology, 2*, 31–43.

Henrotte, J. G. (1967). A possible biochemical interpretation of the relation between height and some psychological variables for socio-professional groups. *Revue de la Société de Biomeitrie Humaine, 2*, 47–56.

Heron, E., & Zytoskee, A. (1981). Visual acuity and test performance. *American Journal of Optometry and Physiological Optics, 58*, 176.

Hinton, R. T., Jr. (1936). The role of the Basal Metabolic Rate in the intelligence of ninety grade-school students. *Journal of Educational Psychology, 27*, 546–550.

Hinton, R. T., Jr. (1939). A further study of the role of the Basal Metabolic Rate in the intelligence of children. *Journal of Educational Psychology, 30*, 309–314.

Hirsch, M. J. (1959). The relationship between refractive state of the eye and intelligence test scores. *American Journal of Optometry and Archives of the American Academy of Optometry, 36*, 12–21.

Ho, K-C, Roessmann, U., Straumfjord, J. V., & Monroe, G. (1980a). Analysis of brain weight. I. Adult brain weight in relation to sex, race, and age. *Archives of Pathology and Laboratory Medicine, 104,* 635–639.

Ho, K-c, Roessmann, U., Straumfjord, J. V., & Monroe, G. (1980b). Analysis of brain weight. II. Adult brain weight in relation to body height, weight, and surface area. *Archives of Pathology and Laboratory Medicine, 104,* 640–645.

Ho, K-c, Roessmann, U., Hause, L., & Monroe, G. (1981). Newborn brain weight in relation to maturity, sex, and race. *Annals of Neurology, 10,* 243–246.

Hoadley, M. F., & Pearson, K. (1929). On measurement of the internal diameter of the skull in relation *I* to the prediction of its capacity, *II* to the 'pre-eminance' of the left hemisphere. *Biometrika, 21,* 85–123.

Holloway, R. L. (1974). On the meaning of brain size. Review of "Evolution of the brain and intelligence" by H. J. Jerison. *Science, 184,* 677–679.

Hooton, E. A. (1939). *The American criminal* (Vol. 1). Cambridge, MA: Harvard University Press.

Humphreys, L. G., Davey, T. C., & Park, R. K. (1985). Longitudinal correlation analysis of standing height and intelligence. *Child Development, 56,* 1465–1478.

Hunter, J. E., Schmidt, F. L., & Jackson, G. B. (1982). *Meta-analysis: Cumulating findings across studies.* Beverly Hills, CA: Sage.

Husén, T. (1951). Undersokninger rorande sambanden mellan somatiske for hallanden och intellektuell prestations formaga. *Militar. Halsovand, 76,* 41–74.

Husén, T. (1959). *Psychological twin research.* Stockholm: Almqvist & Wiksell.

Jensen, A. R. (1973). *Educability and group differences.* New York: Harper & Row.

Jensen, A. R. (1978). Genetic and behavioral effects of nonrandom mating. In R. T. Osborne, C. E. Noble, & N. Weyl (Eds.), *Human variation.* New York: Academic Press.

Jensen, A. R. (1980a). *Bias in mental testing.* New York: Free Press.

Jensen, A. R. (1980b). Uses of sibling data in educational and psychological research. *American Educational Research Journal, 17,* 153–170.

Jensen, A. R. (1985). Methodological and statistical techniques for the chronometric study of mental abilities. In C. R. Reynolds & V. L. Willson (Eds.), *Methodological and statistical advances in the study of individual differences.* New York: Plenum.

Jensen, A. R. (1987). *Twins: The puzzle of nongenetic variance.* Paper presented at the 17th annual meeting of the Behavior Genetics Association, Minneapolis, MN.

Jerison, H. J. (1973). *Evolution of brain and intelligence.* New York: Academic Press.

Jerison, H. J. (1982). The evolution of biological intelligence. In R. J. Sternberg (Ed.), *Handbook of human intelligence.* Cambridge: Cambridge University Press.

Jørgensen, J. B., Parison, E., & Quaade, F. (1961). The correlation between external cranial volume and brain volume. *American Journal of Physical Anthropology, 19,* 317–320.

Karlsson, J L. (1973). Genetic relationship between giftedness and myopia. *Hereditas, 73,* 85–88.

Karlsson, J. L. (1974). Concordance rates for myopia in twins. *Clinical Genetics, 6,* 142–146.

Karlsson, J. L. (1975a). Influence of the myopia gene on brain development. *Clinical Genetics, 8,* 314–318.

Karlsson, J. L. (1975b). Evidence for recessive inheritance of myopia. *Clinical Genetics*, 7, 197–202.

Karlsson, J. L. (1976). Genetic factors in myopia. *Acta Geneticae Medicae et Gamellologiae*, 25, 292–294.

Karlsson, J. L. (1978). *Inheritance of creative intelligence*. Chicago: Nelson-Hall.

Kasl, S. V., Brooks, G. W., & Rodgers, W. L. (1970). Serum uric acid and cholesterol in achievement behaviour and motivation: 1. The relationship to ability, grades, test performance, and motivation. *Journal of the American Medical Association, 213*, 1158–1164.

Kennett, K. F., & Cropley, A. J. (1975). Uric acid and divergent thinking: A possible relationship. *British Journal of Psychology, 66*, 175–180.

Kiener, Von F., & Keiper, E. (1977). Some correlates between facial cues and intelligence. *Homo, 28*, 40–45.

Kreze, A., Zelina, M., Juhás, J., & Garbara, M. (1974). Relationship between intelligence and relative prevalance of obesity. *Human Biology, 46*, 109–113.

Landsdell, H., Davie, J. C., & Clayton, J. (1972). Masa intermedia: Possible relation to intelligence. *Neuropsychologia, 10*, 207–210.

Laycock, F., & Caylor, J. S. (1964). Physiques of gifted children and their less gifted siblings. *Children, 63*, 63–74.

Lee, A., & Pearson, K. (1901). Data for the problem of evolution in man. VI: A first study of the correlation of the human skull. *Philosophical Transactions of the Royal Society of London, 196*, 225–264.

Lehrke, R. G. (1978). Sex linkage: A biological basis for greater male variability in intelligence. In R. T. Osborne, C. E. Noble, & N. Weyl (Eds.), *Human variation: The biopsychology of age, race, and sex*. New York: Academic Press.

Lowe, R. F. (1949). The eyes of Mongolism. *British Journal of Ophthalmology, 33*, 131–174.

Lundman, B. (1972). Anthropological, sociological, and psychological investigations of Swedish school children. *Mankind Quarterly, 12*, 189–212.

Macdonnell, W. R. (1904). A study of the variation and correlation of the human skull, with special reference to English crania. *Biometrika, 3*, 191–244.

MacKinnon, I. L., Kennedy, J. A., & Davies, T. V. (1956). The estimation of skull capacity from Roentgenologic measurements. *American Journal of Roentgenology, 76*, 303–310.

McManus, I. C., & Mascie-Taylor, C. G. N. (1983). Biosocial correlates of cognitive abilities. *Journal of Biosocial Sciences, 15*, 289.

Marshall, J. (1892). On the relation between the weight of the brain, and its parts, and the stature and mass of the body in man. *Journal of Anatomy and Physiology, 26*, 445–500.

Mascie-Taylor, C. G. N., Gibson, J. B., Hiorns, R. W., & Harrison, G. A. (1985). Associations between some polymorphic markers and variation in IQ and its components in Otmoor villagers. *Behavior Genetics, 15*, 371–383.

Mascie-Taylor, C. G. N., McManus, I. C., McLarnon, A. M., & Lonigan, P. M. (1983). The association between phenylthiocarbamide (PTC) tasting ability and psychometric variables. *Behavior Genetics, 13*, 191–196.

Mikkelsen, W. M., Dodge, H. J., & Valkenberg, H. (1965). The distribution of serum uric acid values in a population unselected as to gout of hyperuricemia. *American Journal of Medicine*, *39*, 242–251.

Miller, E. M. (1926). *Brain capacity and intelligence* (Monograph Series No. 4). Sydney: Australian Association for Psychology and Philosophy.

Mueller, E. F., Kasl, S. V., Brooks, G. W., & Cobb, S. (1970). Psychosocial correlates of serum urate levels. *Psychological Bulletin*, *73*, 238–257.

Mueller, E. F., & French, J. R., Jr. (1974). Uric acid and achievement. *Journal of Personality and Social Psychology*, *30*, 336–340.

Murdock, K., & Sullivan, L. R. (1923). A contribution to the study of mental and physical measurements in normal children. *American Physical Education Review*, *28*, 209–215, 276–280, 328–330.

Nagoshi, C. T., & Johnson, R. C. (1987). Between- vs. within-family analyses of the correlation of height and intelligence. *Social Biology*, *34*, 110–113.

*NASA Reference Publication 1024*. (1978, July). Anthropometric source book (Vol. 2): A handbook of anthropometric data. Washington, DC: National Aeronautic and Space Administration.

Nisbet, J. D., & Illesley, R. (1963). The influence of early puberty on test performance at age eleven. *British Journal of Educational Psychology*, *33*, 169–176.

Orowan, E. (1955). The origin of man. *Nature*, *175*, 683–684.

Osborne, R. T. (1980). *Twins, black and white*. Athens, GA: Foundation for Human Understanding.

Osborne, R. T., & Suddick, D. E. (1971). Blood type gene frequency and mental ability. *Psychological Reports*, *29*, 1243–1249.

Owen, D. R. (1972). Blood type gene frequency and mental ability: Premature conclusions? *Psychological Reports*, *31*, 835–839.

Page, E. B., & Grandon, G. M. (1979). Family configuration and mental ability: Two theories contrasted with US data. *American Educational Research Journal*, *16*, 257–272.

Pardo, L. C., Diaz, L. A., Hernandez-Vargas, C., & Hernandez-Vargas, J. G. (1971). The relationship between height and intelligence in a group of students in Guadalajara, Jalisco. *Revista Mexicana de Psicología*, *5*, 11–13.

Passingham, R. E. (1975). The brain and intelligence. *Brain, Behavior, and Evolution*, *11*, 1–15.

Passingham, R. E. (1979). Brain size and intelligence in man. *Brain, Behavior, and Evolution*, *16*, 253–270.

Paterson, D. G. (1930). *Physique and intellect*. New York: Century.

Paul, S. M. (1980). Sibling resemblance in mental ability: A review. *Behavior Genetics*, *10*, 277–290.

Pearl, R. (1906). On the correlation between intelligence and the size of the head. *Journal of Comparative and Neurological Psychology*, *16*, 189–199.

Pearson, K. (1906). On the relationship of intelligence to size and shape of head, and to other physical and mental characters. *Biometrika*, *5*, 105–146.

Pearson, K. (1909). *The scope and importance to the state of the science of national eugenics*. London: The [Galton] Eugenics Laboratory Lecture Series.

Pearson, K. (1931). On the inheritance of mental disease. *Annals of Eugenics*, *4*, 362–380.

Penrose, L. S., & Haldane, J. B. S. (1969). *The biology of mental defect*. London: Sidgwick & Jackson.

Porteus, S. D. (1937). *Primitive intelligence and environment*. New York: Macmillan.

Post, R. H. (1962). Population differences in vision acuity: A review, with speculative notes on selection relaxation. *Social Biology, 9*, 189–212.

Reed, D. M., & Stanley, F. J. (1977). *The epidemiology of prematurity*. Baltimore, MD: Urban & Schwartzenberg.

Reed, R. W., & Mulligan, J. H. (1923). Relation of cranial capacity to intelligence. *Journal of the Royal Anthropological Institute, 53*, 322–331.

Riley, J. B. (1978). *The relationship of eye color and intelligence*. Unpublished BA thesis, Hanover College, Hanover, IN.

Robinow, M. (1968). *The relationship between stature, head circumference, and brain size during childhood and adolescence*. Paper presented at the Child Development Section of the Academy of Pediatrics, Chicago, IL.

Rose, R. J., Procidano, M. E., Conneally, M., & Yu, P. (1979). Blood-group discordance and verbal intelligence: Analyses in offspring of MZ twins. *Behavior Genetics, 9*, 478–479.

Rosner, M., & Belkin, M. (1987). Intelligence, education and myopia in males. *Archives of Ophthalmology, 105*, 1508–1511.

Schreider, E. (1956). Taille et capacités mentales. *Biotypologie, 17*, 21–37.

Schreider, E. (1964). Recherches sur la stratification sociale des charactéres biologiques. *Biotypologie, 26*, 105–135.

Schreider, E. (1966). Brain weight correlations calculated from original results of Paul Broca. *American Journal of Physical Anthropology, 25*, 153–158.

Schreider E. (1967). A possible selective mechanism for social differentiation of biological traits. *Revue de la Société de Biomeitrie Humaine, 2*, 67–85.

Schreider, E. (1968). Quelques correlations des testes mentales. *Homo, 19*, 38–43.

Scott, E. M., Illesley, J. P., & Thomson, A. M. (1956). A psychological investigation of primigravidae. II. Maternal social class, age, physique and intelligence. *Journal of Obstetrics and Gynaecology of the British Empire, 63*, 338–343.

Shock, N. W., & Jones, H. E. (1939). The relationship between basal physiological functions and intelligence in adolescents. *Psychological Bulletin, 36*, 642–643.

Siddamma, T. (1978). Obesity and social class. *Mankind Quarterly, 19*, 157–164.

Skuse, D. (1987). The psychological consequences of being small. *Journal of Child Psychology and Psychiatry, 28*, 641–650.

Sommerville, R. C. (1924). Physical, motor and sensory traits. *Archives of Psychology, 12*, 1–108.

Sorokin, P. (1927). *Social mobility*. New York: Harper.

Sorsby, A., Benjamin, B., Davey, J. B., Sheridan, M., & Tanner, J. M. (1957). Emmetropia and its abberations. *Medical Research Council Special Report Series, 293*, 1–42.

Sorsby, A., & Fraser, G. R. (1964). Statistical note on the components of ocular refraction in twins. *Journal of Medical Genetics, 1*, 47–49.

Sorsby, A., Leary, G. A., & Fraser, G. R. (1966). Family studies on ocular refraction and its components. *Journal of Medical Genetics, 3*, 269–273.

Sorsby, A., Sheridan, M., & Leary, G. A. (1962). Refraction and its components in twins. *Medical Research Council Special Report Series, 303*, 1–43.

Stevens, H. A. (1973). A multidisciplinary catalogue of uric acid literature of interest to behavioural scientists. *Perceptual Motor Skills, 36,* 1007–1020.

Stevens, H. A., & Cropley, A. J. (1972). Uric acid and behaviour: A new look at Orowan's hypothesis. *Psychological Reports, 30,* 967–970.

Stevens, H.A., Cropley, A. J., & Blattler, D. P. (1975). Intellect and serum uric acid: An optimal concentration of serum urate for human learning? *Social Biology, 22,* 229–234.

Stone, C. P., & Doe-Kulmann, L. (1928). Notes on the mental development of children exhibiting the somatic signs of puberty praecox. *27th Yearbook of the National Society for the Study of Education, 27*(1), 389–397.

Susanne, G. (1979). On the relationship between psychometric and anthropometric traits. *American Journal of Physical Anthropology, 51,* 421–423.

Swan, D. A., & Miszkiewicz, B. (n. d.). *The relation between two measures of head size and primary mental abilities intelligence test scores among south Mississippi Anglo-Saxon school children.* Unpublished manuscript.

Tanner, J. M. (1962). *Growth at adolescence* (2nd ed.). Oxford: Blackwell.

Tanner, J. M. (1966). Galtonian eugenics and the study of growth: The relation of body size, intelligence test score, and social circumstances in children and adults. *Eugenics Review, 58,* 122–135.

Tanner, J. M. (1969). Relation of body size, intelligence test scores and social circumstances. In P. Mussen, J. Langer, & M. Covington (Eds.), *Trends and issues in child developmental psychology.* New York: Holt, Rinehart, & Winston.

Teasdale, T. W., Fuchs, J., & Goldschmidt, E. (1988). Degree of myopia in relation to intelligence level. *Lancet, 2*(Issue 8624), 1351–1354.

Teasdale, T. W., Owen, D. R., & Sørensen, T. I. A. (1991). Intelligence and educational level in adult males at the extremes of stature. *Human Biology, 63,* 19–30.

Teasdale, T. W., Sørensen, T. I. A., & Owen, D. R. (1989). A secular decline in the association of height with intelligence and educational level. *British Medical Journal, 298,* 1291–1293.

Terman, L. M. (1926). *Genetic studies of genius. Vol. 1. Mental and physical traits of a thousand gifted children.* Stanford, CA: Stanford University Press.

Thomson, E. A., & Bodmer, W. F. (1975). Population stratification as an explanation of IQ and ABO association. *Nature, 254,* 363–364.

Tobias, P. V. (1970) Brain-size, grey matter, and race—Fact or fiction? *American Journal of Physical Anthropology, 32,* 3–26.

Tyler, L. E. (1965). *The psychology of human differences* (3rd ed.). New York: Appleton-Century-Crofts.

Udjas, L. G. (1964). *Anthropometrical changes in Norwegian men in the twentieth century.* Oslo: Universitatsforlaget.

Van Valen, L. (1974). Brain size and intelligence in man. *American Journal of Physical Anthropology, 40,* 417–424.

Vernon, P. A. (Ed.). (1987). *Speed of information processing and intelligence.* Norwood, NJ: Ablex.

Waardenburg, P. J., Franceschetti, A., & Klein, D. (1963). *Genetics and ophthalmology* (Vol. 2). Assen: Van Gorcum.

Weiss, V. (1978). The physiological equivalent of the major gene locus of general intelligence: Discrete individual differences in central processing time of information. *Acta Biologica et Medica Germanika, 38,* 1–4.

Whipple, G. M. (1914). *Manual of mental and physical tests, Part I: Simpler Processes* (2nd ed.). Baltimore, MD: Warwick & York.

Willerman, L., Schultz, R., Rutledge, J. N., & Bigler, E. (1989). *Magnetic resonance imaged brain structures and intelligence.* Paper presented at the 19th annual meeting of the Behavior Genetics Association, Charlottesville, VA.

Wold, K. C. (1949). Hereditary myopia. *Archives of Ophthalmology, 42,* 225–237.

Wuorio, U. (1974). The effect of Rh-immunization on the psychological development of the child. *Annales Universitatis Turkuensis, 132,* 1–79.

Yarbrough, M. E., & McCurdy, H. G. (1958). A further note on basal metabolism and academic performance. *Journal of Educational Psychology, 49,* 20–22.

Young, F. A. (1958). An estimate of the hereditary component of myopia. *American Journal of Optometry, 35,* 337–345.

Young, F. A. (1963). Reading measures of intelligence and refractive errors. *American Journal of Optometry and Archives of the American Academy of Optometry, 40,* 257–264.

# Chapter 5

# Nutrition and Intelligence

## Richard Lynn

*Psychology Department*
*University of Ulster*
*Coleraine, Co. Londonderry*
*N. Ireland*

When the environmental factors determining intelligence are considered people think primarily of cognitive stimulation provided by parents and through education. The Head Start programs designed to raise the intelligence of deprived children concentrated their efforts almost entirely on enhancing cognitive stimulation (Jensen, 1989). It has rarely been considered that nutrition might be a major environmental determinant of intelligence. Nutrition is not even indexed in Sternberg's (1982) 1000-page *Handbook of Human Intelligence*. It is the thesis of this chapter that nutrition is a more important determinant of intelligence than has hitherto been generally recognized. The thesis rests on four propositions to the effect that

1. there is a range of different kinds of evidence indicating a causal effect of the quality of nutrition on intelligence
2. the quality of nutrition is a significant determinant of brain growth and size
3. brain growth and size are themselves significant determinants of intelligence
4. nutritional supplements increase intelligence.

The first sections of this chapter are concerned with the establishment of these four propositions. The next section presents the argument that improvements in nutrition have been the major factor responsible for the increases in intelligence which have taken place in a number of countries during the last half century. Finally, the last section considers the contribution of nutrition to the differences in intelligence between blacks and whites.

## NUTRITION AND INTELLIGENCE

There are several lines of evidence showing an effect of the quality of nutrition on intelligence. The principal problem in demonstrating a causal effect of nutrition on intelligence is that poor nutrition is generally associated with a number of other disadvantageous conditions such as a generally poor environment and possibly poor genotypes for intelligence. It is therefore necessary to isolate the effect of nutrition by providing controls for these confounding influences. There are four principal kinds of study by which this has been done.

1. *Matched control groups.* A good representative study is that of Stoch, Smythe, Moddie, and Bradshaw (1982). Their subjects were 20 marasmic babies from the colored population in South Africa. The babies were matched with 20 well-nourished infants whose mothers were of the same socioeconomic status and had the same mean IQ and head circumference. The two groups were tested at the age of 16 years. At this age the poorly nourished (marasmic) group had a smaller head circumference (51.7 cm vs 54.6 cm) and a lower mean IQ (56.0 vs 73.5). The study suggests that poor nutrition adversely affects both brain size and IQ. It might, however, be possible to object that the control group did not provide a perfect match to the malnourished group. For instance, the control group children came from two-parent families while the malnourished group came largely from one-parent families and there could have been other subtle differences not captured by the matching. These possibilities illustrate the difficulty of obtaining control groups for malnourished children that will satisfy the determined sceptic.

2. *Sibling controls.* A number of studies of the effects of malnutrition on infants have used siblings as controls for the effects of genetic and environmental factors. The methodology is to find an infant suffering from malnutrition and an unaffected sibling and test for intelligence some years later. A study of this type by Birch, Pineiro, Alcalde, Toca and Cravioto (1971) took 37 malnourished infants age 6–30 months suffering from kwashiorkor in Mexico. These and their unaffected siblings were tested with the WISC at the age of approximately 10 years. At this age the malnourished children obtained a mean IQ of 68 and their siblings a mean of 81. The use of sibling controls provides reasonably convincing evidence for a permanent effect of undernutrition on subsequent intelligence,

but even here it is possible to argue that the malnourished sibling has been subjected to other adverse experiences in addition to the poor nutrition.

3. *Adoption studies.* This methodology employs adopted infants who have experienced different nutrition but were reared in the same environments. A good study is that of Winick, Meyer, and Harris (1975) of Korean infants adopted by American parents. One hundred and eleven Korean female babies were classified into three groups of malnourished, moderately nourished, and well nourished on the basis of their height and weight. They were placed with American adoptive parents before the age of 3 years. The mean IQs of the 3 groups at the age of around 10 years were 102 (malnourished), 106 (moderately nourished), and 112 (well nourished), the difference between groups 1 and 3 being statistically significant. A determined critic might argue that the three groups differed genotypically but it seems unlikely that this would be the case and the results are most plausibly explained in terms of a permanently adverse effect of poor nutrition in infancy on subsequent intelligence.

4. *Identical twin studies.* Probably the most persuasive evidence for an effect of nutrition on intelligence comes from studies of identical twins with different birth weights. It is not uncommon for identical twins to have different birth weights. Where this occurs it is normally due to the heavier twin having received better nutrition during the stage of fetal growth from the mother's placenta (James, 1982). Eight studies of this kind have shown that when such twin pairs are intelligence-tested between the ages of 5–15 years the heavier obtains a higher IQ than the lighter. One of the first of these is a little known study carried out in Japan by Takuma (1968). He reported data for 269 MZ twins with a mean birthweight of 2260g. In 106 cases the birthweights were approximately equal to within 100g. But in 80 cases, 30 per cent of the sample, the birthweights differed by more than 300g and in 35 cases by more than 500g. There was a statistically significant tendency for the heavier twin at birth to walk and talk sooner than the lighter and to have a higher IQ at the age of 12 years. The paper does not report figures for the mean IQs of the heavier and lighter twins.

The results of seven studies from the United States and Denmark are summarized in Table 5.1. It will be seen that all the results show that the heavier twin has the higher IQ and there can be no doubt of the overall statistical significance of the effect. The particular interest of these studies is that they isolate the quality of prenatal nutrition as a significant factor affecting later intelligence, since it can be assumed that identical twins would receive the same nutrition after birth. It might be expected that any prenatal deficiency in nutrition would be compensated for in infancy but this is apparently not the case. Prenatal nutritional deficiencies must have permanently damaging effects on the growth of the brain that cannot be compensated after birth. The magnitude of the effect however is quite small, amounting only to 3.4 IQ points.

These four kinds of study indicating adverse effects of suboptimal nutrition on

Table 5.1.    Studies of MZ Twins Where the Heavier Twin at Birth
Obtained a Higher IQ in Childhood. Asterisks Denote Statistical
Significance at *p* < .05.

| Authors | N | Age at Testing | Test | IQ Difference |
|---------|---|----------------|------|---------------|
| Churchill, 1965 | 22 | 5–15 | WISC | 4.3* |
| Kaelber & Pugh, 1969 | 44 | 6–16 | Various | 2.5 |
| Scarr, 1969 | 25 | 6–10 | Draw a Person | 9.0* |
| Babson & Phillips, 1973 | 9 | 13 | WISC Verbal | 8.7* |
| Fujikura & Froehlich, 1974 | 11 | 4 | Stanford Binet | 4.7 |
| Fujikura & Froehlich, 1974 | 15 | 4 | Stanford Binet | 1.9 |
| Henrichsen, Skinhoj, & Andersen, 1986 | 14 | 13 | WISC | 3.6* |

intelligence are together quite strong. But before concluding this section it is
necessary to mention the doubt that has been thrown on this association by the
study of the effects of the Dutch World War Two famine (Stein, Susser, Saenger,
& Marolla, 1972). For six months in the winter and spring of 1944–45 there was
a severe shortage of food in the western Netherlands. The food ration was
reduced to 1144 calories and 34g of protein per day. Males conceived and born
immediately before, during, and after the famine were intelligence-tested approximately 19 years later when they were conscripted into the Dutch army. At
this time there were no IQ differences between these young men and those from
other parts of the Netherlands unaffected by the famine.

Although this study has sometimes been considered to rule out adverse effects
of maternal and early nutritional deficiencies for later intelligence, there are two
reasons why it does not conclusively disconfirm the theory. Firstly, although the
calorie and protein intakes were low the intakes of the essential vitamins,
minerals, and other nutrients may not have been critically lower than in other
parts of the Netherlands. Secondly, the famine was of relatively short duration. It
is possible that women store essential nutrients and can release them during
pregnancy for the use of the fetus during times of shortage. Alternatively, it is
possible that the fetus or young infant can recover from a relatively short period
of suboptimal nutrition. These considerations make the evidence of the Dutch
famine less damaging than has sometimes been supposed to the thesis that the
nutrition received by the fetus or infant is an important determinant of intelligence. Taking the evidence reviewed in this section as a whole it is considered
that there is a strong case that suboptimal nutrition impairs intelligence.

## NUTRITION AND BRAIN GROWTH

The reason that the quality of nutrition is a determinant of intelligence is that the
nutrition received by the fetus and child determines the neurological development of the brain and this in turn affects intelligence. For optimum growth the

brain requires sufficient calories and protein. An inadequate intake of calories leads to marasmus and of protein to kwashiorkor, and both of these can cause mental defect or even death. In addition to calories and protein, there are 45 nutrients which are necessary for the growth and maintenance of the body. These essential nutrients fall into five groups comprising vitamins, amino acids, minerals, trace elements, and other compounds and are set out below:

- Vitamins: A, Bl (Thiamine), B5, B12, C (Ascorbic acid), D, E, K, Folic acid, Nicotinic acid, Pyridoxine, Riboflavin, Biotin, Pantothenic acid.
- Amino Acids: Arginine, Histidine, Isoleucine, Leucine, Lysine, Methionine, Phenylalanine, Threonine, Tryptophan, Valine.
- Minerals: Calcium, Chloride, Magnesium, Phosphorus, Potassium, Sodium.
- Trace Elements: Cobalt, Copper, Chromiun, Iodine, Iron, Manganese, Molybdenum, Zinc, Selenium, Nickel, Tin, Vanadium.
- Other compounds: Polyunsaturated fatty acids, Choline, Inositol.

Thirty-eight of these 45 essential nutrients are known to be necessary for the neurological development of the brain. There is some doubt about the remaining 7 which consist of Molybdenum, Selenium, Nickel, Tin, Vanadium, Chromium, and Vitamin K (Rajalakshmi & Ramakrishnan, 1972).

Insufficient intakes of calories, proteins, or any of these 37 essential nutrients retards the neurological development of the brain. The principal adverse effects on the brain are reductions in brain size, the number of brain cells, the growth of dendrites, and the myelinisation of neurones (Dobbing & Sands, 1985; Dobbing, 1984, 1987). The principal ways in which these adverse effects can be demonstrated are through work on experimental animals, autopsies on undernourished humans, and studies of the effects of suboptimal nutrition on brain size estimated from head circumference. An example of experimental work on animals showing these effects is the study by Clark, Zamenhof, Van Marthens, Grauel, and Kruger (1973). They put pregnant rats on a calorie-deficient diet and found that the offspring had significantly reduced brain weight, DNA, protein content, and thickness of the cerebral cortex.

Similar results have been obtained from autopsy studies of malnourished humans. Brown (1965) reports data for autopsies of 96 malnourished children up to the age of 15 in Kampala compared with 104 adequately nourished children. The brain weight of the malnourished group was 87.6% of that of the adequately nourished group. Further studies reporting that malnourished children have reduced brain size have been reported in Chile, Jamaica, India, and the United States (Winick, Rosso, & Waterlow, 1970; Naeye, Diener, & Dellinger, 1969; Parekh, Pherwani, Udani, & Mukherjee, 1970).

It has also been shown in a number of studies that poor nutrition in pregnant women causes them to have low birth-weight babies (Stein & Susser, 1987). These babies have reduced length and head size, generally measured by head circumference. Head size is correlated at a magnitude of approximately 0.8 with brain size (Brandt, 1978), so that poor nutrition in the mother adversely affects the size of the baby's brain. Small brain size is in turn associated with reduced intelligence (Van Valen, 1974; Lynn, 1989). It has been shown that nutritional supplements given to poorly nourished pregnant women increase the weight and head size of their babies (Stein & Susser, 1987).

The growth of the brain takes place largely prenatally and during early childhood. The normal brain weight at birth is about 350 grams, a little more than a quarter of the brain weight of adults which is about 1,300 grams. By the age of 5 years average brain weight is about 1,200, so that about 90% of brain growth has taken place by this age. Most of the neurological growth of the brain also takes place in the first five years of life, for example, the growth of cells, myelinization of neurones, and development of axons and dendrites (Dobbing, 1984, 1987). These growth processes require a supply of the essential nutrients and if these are suboptimal the neurological development of the brain is impaired. The prenatal stage and the first five years of infancy are therefore the crucial period during which adequate nutrition is necessary for brain growth.

## BRAIN SIZE AND INTELLIGENCE

We have seen that the quality of nutrition is a determinant of intelligence and also of brain growth and size. It remains to be shown that brain growth and size are determinants of intelligence. The simplest measure of brain growth and size is the circumference of the head and hence a positive association between head circumference and intelligence would be expected. I have found 12 studies of the relationship between intelligence and head circumference or of the cephalic index, an alternative measure of head size. All 12 obtained low but statistically significant correlations lying between .10 and .35. The studies, subjects, and the correlation coefficients are as follows: 4,500 British children, $r = .11$ (Pearson, 1906); 1,000 British studies, $r = .10$ (Pearson, 1906); 935 Bavarian soldiers, $r = .14$ (Pearl, 1906); 326 French farmers, $r = .23$ (Schrieder, 1968); 2.071 Belgian conscripts, $r = .13$ (Susanne & Sporoq, 1973); 334 American boys, $r = .35$ (Weinberg, Deitz, Penick, & McAlister, 1974); 26,760 American children, $r = .14$ (Broman, Nichols, & Kennedy, 1975); 600 American children, $r = .18$ (Murdock & Sullivan, 1923); 415 British adults, $r = .14$ (Passingham, 1979); 302 Polish students, $r = .14$ (Henneberg, Budnik, Pezacka, & Puch, 1985); 2,023 American 7-year-olds, $r = .23$ (Fisch, Bilek, Horrobin, & Chang, 1976); 310 British children, $r = .18$ (Lynn, 1989). These correlations are quite low but they should be raised by correction for unreliability of the intelligence tests and of head circumference as a measure of brain size. The consistently positive correlations found in all studies can leave no doubt about the existence of an association between intelligence, the size of the head, and the size of the brain inside the head.

## NUTRITIONAL SUPPLEMENTS

If nutrition is a significant determinant of intelligence, it should follow that nutritional supplements given to poorly nourished pregnant women and to children with nutritional deficiencies should produce IQ increases. There are several studies showing that this is the case. In the United States Kugelmass, Poull, and Samuel (1944) administered nutritional supplements to poorly nourished 0–4-year-olds and obtained an increase of 18 IQ points. Harrell, Woodyard, and Gates (1955) administered supplementary diets of thiamine, riboflavin, niacin, and iron to 1,200 pregnant women of poor economic status in Virginia. Their children were intelligence-tested at the age of 3 and had higher IQs than a matched control group. Oski and Honig (1978) found extensive iron deficiency in a group of 24 infants aged 9–26 months in New York. Half of them were given iron supplements and registered gains in mental and physical development as compared with the remaining half which served as the control groups. Further studies showing increases in intelligence and physical development in anemic children following iron supplements are reviewed by Evans (1985). Increases in intelligence of 3.5 IQ points have also been reported among children deficient in vitamin C following supplementation with orange juice (Kubala & Katz, 1960). Most of these studies have been carried out on infants, but Benton and Roberts (1988) have reported a 9 IQ point gain in nonverbal reasoning among normal 12–13-year-old British children given a multivitamin and mineral supplement over an 8-month period.

## NUTRITION AND THE SECULAR RISE OF INTELLIGENCE

In the last few years it has become clear that the intelligence levels of the populations in a number of economically advanced nations have risen considerably over the course of the last half century. The evidence is reviewed in Lynn and Hampson (1986) and Flynn (1987). Broadly the magnitude of the increase is about 3 IQ points per decade but there are quite wide divergences ranging from increases of about 1 IQ point per decade in some studies to as much as 7 IQ points per decade among military conscripts in the Netherlands over the period 1952–1982 (Flynn, 1987).

One of the interesting features of these secular increases in intelligence is that the nonverbal and visuospatial abilities have been increasing at a faster rate than the verbal and educational abilities. Thus the performance IQ of the Wechsler tests has shown increases of approximately 4 IQ points per decade over the period 1932–1978 in the United States, while the verbal IQ has shown increases of only 2 IQ points per decade (Flynn, 1984). Faster rates of increase of the performance IQs as compared with the verbal have also been found in Japan, France, Austria, and West Germany (Flynn, 1987). These differential rates of increase as between the nonverbal and verbal abilities are picked up using several different kinds of test. In Britain we have found that the mean IQs of 9–11 year olds on Cattell's culture-fair test (a visuospatial and nonverbal reasoning test) have increased by 2.5 IQ points per decade over the period 1936–1986. On the other hand the verbal-educational test used in the Scottish surveys of 1932 and 1947 has registered an increase of only 1.1 IQ points per decade over the period 1932–1986 and vocabulary assessed by the Mill Hill vocabulary scale has increased by as little as 0.5 IQ points per decade over 1943–1979. The rate of increase for Raven's Progressive Matrices in Britain falls between that of the Cattell test and the verbal-educational tests at 1.9 IQ points per decade over the period 1936–1949. The PM is a reasoning test that combines both nonverbal and verbal abilities and hence the rate of increase falls about halfway between the visuospatial culture-fair test and the verbal-educational Mill Hill vocabulary and Scottish survey tests (Lynn & Hampson, 1986; Lynn, Hampson, & Mullineux, 1987; Lynn, Hampson, & Howden, 1988).

Towards the extreme of the verbal-educational abilities stands the American Scholastic Aptitude Test (SAT). This is atypical in showing a decline in means over the period from the early 1960s to 1979 followed by a rise from 1980–1985 (Zajonc, 1986). Here the small increases found in Britain on verbal-educational tests have actually turned negative. Some of this decline and rise of the SAT may be due to secular trends in family size, as Zajonc (1986) argues, although the contribution of this variable appears to be quite small. The cognitive skills tested by the SAT are taught in schools and are probably sensitive to changes in the taught curriculum and also in school students' motivation, as suggested by Jones (1981). These cognitive skills can be usefully described as crystallized educational abilities. There is some evidence for a secular decline in mathematical abilities in Norway (Flynn, 1987) which parallels the decline in the SAT in the United States.

The reasons for the rather considerable secular increases in intelligence have proved a puzzle to students working in this field and no explanation for the increases has yet been offered. The present thesis is that the increases are due virtually entirely to improvements in nutrition. The arguments for this thesis are as follows:

1. In the 1930s substantial proportions of the populations in the economically developed nations obtained suboptional nutrition. In Britain 87% of children had symptoms of rickets due to vitamin D deficiency and 90% had inadequate intakes of calcium (Board of Education, 1931; Orr, 1936). Similar widespread nutritional deficiencies were present in the United States and Japan (Palmer, 1935; Takahaski, 1966). The inadequate nutrition impaired physical growth, height, and neurological development of the brain, and also intelligence, as shown in earlier sections of this chapter.

2. With the considerable increases that have taken place in living standards over the last half-century people have been able to buy more nutritious foods. For instance, in Japan from 1960 to 1980 there were per capita increases of 300% in

meat and dairy products, of 20% in fish, and of 100% in fruit and of 50% in vegetables (Takahashi, 1986).

3. As a result of these improvements in nutrition average heights have increased over the last half-century by approximately 1 standard deviation, i.e. by just about the same amount as intelligence has increased (Van Wieringen, 1978).

4. Increases in head size and brain size of approximately 1 standard deviation have also taken place over the last half-century (Ounsted, Moar, & Scott, 1985). For these reasons it is proposed that the nutrition thesis provides an adequate account of the secular increase in intelligence.

Furthermore, it is doubtful whether any credible alternative theory for the secular increases in intelligence can be formulated. The principal rival theory is that the increases have been due to improvements in cognitive stimulation. There are four principal objections to the cognitive stimulation thesis. Firstly, there is no direct evidence to show that any improvements in the cognitive stimulation of children have taken place over the last half-century and perhaps no particular reason to suppose that any such increases have occurred.

Secondly, improvements in cognitive stimulation would be expected to act more strongly on the verbal and educational abilities taught by parents through games and in conversation and by schools. Yet, as has been noted, the verbal or educational abilities have shown quite low rates of increase. It is the nonverbal and visuospatial abilities that are less subject to cognitive stimulation that have shown the greatest rates of secular increase. The greater rate of secular increase of the nonverbal and visuospatial abilities is explicable in terms of the nutrition theory. For some reason the nonverbal abilities are more vulnerable to nutritional deficits. The evidence comes from two studies of identical twins with differing birth weights. Willerman and Churchill (1967) reported data from 27 such pairs. The twins were given the WISC at a mean age of 9.6 years. The performance IQ of the lighter twin was 5.3 points lower than that of the heavier, but there was only 0.4 points difference on the verbal scale (this difference is statistically significant). A similar result has been reported by Hendrichsen, Skinhoj, and Andersen (1986) for 14 Danish identical twins with different birth weights given the WISC at a mean age of 13 years. There was no difference between the heavier and lighter twins on the verbal scale but a 7.1 IQ point difference in favor of the heavier twin on the performance scale. Further evidence of a similar kind comes from Taub, Goldstein, and Caputo's (1977) study of 38 light birth-weight babies. These babies who weighed less than 2,500 grams (5.5 pounds) at birth were tested with the WISC-R at the age of 8 years. Their verbal IQ was normal but their performance IQ was significantly impaired by approximately 11 IQ points. EEG studies have shown that the right hemisphere, the locus of the visuospatial abilities, is more vulnerable to malnutrition than the left, particularly in the region of the temporal lobe (Bartel, 1976). What these studies suggest is that the poor quality of nutrition in the 1930s exerted a differential depression on the nonverbal and visuospatial abilities measured by the Wechsler performance scale. This is why it is these abilities that have shown the greatest increase as nutrition has improved over the last half-century.

A third argument against a cognitive stimulation theory of the secular increases in intelligence is that the increases have occurred among very young children. The Griffiths scale of mental development is an intelligence test for 0–2 year olds measuring locomotion progress, personal-social behavior, and vocabulary. The test was standardized in Britain in 1950 and in 1980 a nationally representative sample was tested. The mean IQ had risen 10.2 IQ points over the 30-year period, almost exactly the rate of increase of intelligence found for older children and adolescents. Even infants in the first few months of life showed the same accelerated development (Hanson, Smith, & Hume, 1985). Studies in the United States using the Bayley scales of infant development have also shown a similar secular trend of faster motor development among 1-year-old infants over the last half-century (Knoblock, Stevens, & Malone, 1980; Capute, Shapiro, Palmer, Ross, & Wachtel, 1985). These secular increases in motor and mental development among infants in the age range of 6–24 months throw doubt on possible improvements in cognitive stimulation as the factor responsible for the intelligence increases among later age groups. It is questionable whether cognitive stimulation has much effect on the motor development of 1-year-olds. The increases in development quotients at these early ages suggest a secular neurological improvement in brain function and bring us back to nutrition as the most plausible factor responsible for the secular increases in intelligence.

A fourth argument against cognitive stimulation theory is that the beneficial effects of cognitive stimulation on intelligence tend to fade away to nothing some years after the cognitive stimulation has ceased. This has been found in the Head Start programs where the gains of young children do not last into adolescence (Jensen, 1989), and the same is true of the intelligence gains made by children adopted and reared in middle-class families (Scarr, 1984). In contradiction to these fadeouts, the secular gains in intelligence are not merely a temporary acceleration of intelligence among children but are registered among 25–34-year-olds (Wechsler, 1974). This is what would be expected if the increases in intelligence are due to improvements in the neurological development and size of the brain.

There is another possible theory of the secular increase of intelligence that deserves a brief consideration and this is that it could be due to a decrease in inbreeding resulting from increased urbanization and migration. It is known that inbreeding depresses the intelligence of children (Bashi, 1977; Jensen, 1983). However, the magnitude of the depressant effect is relatively small and amounts to only about 4 IQ points in the offspring of first cousins. Furthermore, although inbreeding decreases general intelligence and the verbal abilities, it increases the visuospatial abilities, suggesting the operation of recessive genes for these abilities (Jensen, 1983). Any decrease of inbreeding over the last half-century should therefore have brought about a rise of the verbal abilities and a fall of the visuospatial abilities. Yet, as has been noted, it is the visuospatial abilities which have shown the largest gains over the last half-century. This makes it very doubtful whether any possible decrease in inbreeding can have been a significant factor in the secular increases in intelligence.

## NUTRITION AND BLACK-WHITE DIFFERENCES IN INTELLIGENCE

The mean IQ of blacks is about 15 IQ points lower than that of whites in the United States (Jensen, 1980) and about 10 IQ points lower in Britain (Mackintosh & Mascie-Taylor, 1985). This is about the amount by which mean IQs have increased in the economically advanced nations during the last half-century. If nutrition is the major factor responsible for the secular increase in intelligence it seems reasonable to suppose that nutrition may also make a significant contribution to the black-white difference.

None of the leading students of the problem of the black-white difference in intelligence attaches any credence to the possibility that differences in nutrition make any substantial contribution to the difference in mean IQ (Jensen, 1980; Flynn, 1980; Mackintosh and Mascie-Taylor, 1985; Scarr, 1984). These writers have probably underestimated the effects of poor nutrition on the black-white difference in intelligence. Possibly the best source of data on this question is the Broman, Nichols, and Kennedy (1975) investigation of approximately 14,000 black and 12,000 white mothers and their babies in the United States around the year 1970. The black and white mothers differed by approximately 12 IQ points. The black mothers were approximately representative of the black population for socioeconomic status, but the white mothers were somewhat below the average SES of American whites, so the differences between the two samples understate the true differences in the base populations. During pregnancy 9% of the white mothers and 34% of the black were anemic. This indicates insufficient iron in the diet and is probably representative of general suboptimal nutrition for a number of other essential nutrients. At birth the black infants were on average smaller than the white in terms of weight, length, and head circumference, again indicating a greater prevalence of suboptimal nutrition in their mothers. At the age of 4 years the black children had achieved parity with the whites with respect to weight, height, and head circumference, possibly as a result of the faster maturation rates of blacks which has often been reported. However at the age of 4 years the mean IQs were 91.3 for blacks and 104.5 for whites, a disparity of 13.2 IQ points.

Some indication of the contribution of poorer nutrition in blacks to this difference can be obtained from a comparison of the IQs of the children of anemic and nonanemic mothers. The IQs differed by approximately 3.5 IQ points. This is a fairly small differential and furthermore only about a third of the black mothers were anemic. The results seem to suggest that anemia can only make a small contribution of the order of 1–2 IQ points to the black-white difference in intelligence. There may however be a number of other nutritional deficiencies in blacks not captured in the Broman, Nichols, and Kennedy study and it is possible that the contribution of suboptimal nutrition to the low black IQ may be greater than is generally appreciated.

## CONCLUSIONS

The objective of this chapter has been to establish that nutrition is a more important determinant of intelligence than is generally recognized. It has been argued that there is a variety of lines of evidence to show that the quality of nutrition determines the growth and size of the brain and that these in turn determine intelligence. Improvements in nutrition have probably been the major factor responsible for the increases in intelligence that have taken place in a number of countries over the last half-century, and suboptimal nutrition may well be a more important factor depressing the mean IQ of blacks in the United States, Britain, and elsewhere than has hitherto been appreciated.

There was everything to be said for the objective of the Head Start programs designed to raise the IQs of children of low intelligence. It is generally recognized that the results of these programs have been disappointing and that little permanent increases of intelligence have been obtained (Jensen, 1989). One of the objectives of this chapter has been to establish the reason for these disappointing results. It is because the Head Start people thought it was possible to raise intelligence by cognitive stimulation. This was a mistake. It is quite possible to raise intelligence—this is shown by the 15 IQ point rise that has taken place in many countries over the last half-century. But it seems probable that the way to raise intelligence is not by giving more cognitive stimulation in nursery schools but by providing better nutrition for pregnant women and young children. It is time to think seriously about the practical policies through which this could be achieved.

## REFERENCES

Babson, S. G., & Phillips, D. S. (1973). Growth and development of twins dissimilar in size at birth. *New England Journal of Medicine, 289,* 937–940.

Bartel, P. R. (1976). Findings of EEG and psychomotor studies on malnourished children. In R. D. Griesel (Ed.), *Malnutrition in South Africa.* Pretoria: University of South Africa Press.

Bashi, J. (1977). Effects of inbreeding on cognitive performance. *Nature*, *266*, 440–442.

Brandt, I. (1978). Growth dynamics of low-birth weight infants with emphasis on the perinatal period. In F. Faulkner & J. M. Tanner (Eds.), *Human growth* (Vol. 2). New York: Plenum.

Brown, R. E. (1966). Organ weight in malnutrition with special reference to brain weight. *Developmental Medicine and Child Neurology*, *8*, 512–522.

Benton, D., & Roberts, G. (1988). Effect of vitamin and mineral supplement on intelligence of a sample of school children. *Lancet*, *1*, 140–143.

Birch, H. G., Pineiro, C., Alcalde, E., Toca, T., & Cravioto, J. (1971). Relation of kwashiorkor in early childhood and intelligence at school age. *Paediatric Research*, *5*, 579–592.

Board of Education. (1931). *Committee on adenoids and enlarged tonsils*. London: HMSO.

Broman, S. H., Nichols, P. L., & Kennedy, W. A. (1975). *Preschool IQ*. New York: John Wiley.

Brown, R. E. (1965). Decreased brain weight in malnutrition and its implications. *East African Medical Journal*, *42*, 584–595.

Capute, A. J., Shapiro, B. K., Palmer, F. B., Ross, A., & Wachtel, R. C. (1985). Normal gross motor development: The influences of race, sex and socio-economic status. *Developmental Medicine and Child Neurology*, *27*, 635–643.

Churchill, J. A. (1965). The relationship between intelligence and birthweight in twins. *Neurology*, *15*, 341–347.

Clark, G. M., Zamenhof, S., Van Marthens, E., Grauel, L., & Kruger, L. (1973). The effect of prenatal nutrition on dimensions of cerebral cortex. *Brain Research*, *54*, 397–402.

Dobbing, J. (1984). Infant nutrition and later achievement. *Nutrition Reviews*, *42*, 1–7.

Dobbing, J. (1987). *Early nutrition and later achievement*. New York: Academic Press.

Dobbing, J., & Sands, J. (1985). Cell size and cell number in tissue growth and development. *Archives of Francisco Paediatrics*, *42*, 199–203.

Evans, D. I. K. (1985). Cerebral function in iron deficiency: A review. *Child: Care, Health and Development*, *11*, 105–112.

Fisch, R. O., Bilek, M. K., Horrobin, J. M., & Chang, P. N. (1976). Children with superior intelligence at 7 years of age. *Archives of American Journal of Diseases of Children*, *130*, 481–487.

Flynn, J. R. (1980). *Race, IQ and Jensen*. London: Routledge.

Flynn, J. R. (1984). IQ gains and Binet decrements. *Journal of Educational Measurement*, *21*, 283–290.

Flynn, J. R. (1987). Massive IQ gains in 14 nations: What IQ tests really measure. *Psychological Bulletin*, *101*, 171–191.

Fujikura, T., & Froelich, L. A. (1974). Mental and motor development in monozygotic co-twins with dissimilar birth weights. *Paediatrics*, *53*, 884–889.

Hanson, R., Smith, J. A., & Hume, W. (1985). Achievements of infants on items of the Griffiths scales: 1980 compared with 1950. *Child: Care, Health and Development*, *11*, 91–104.

Harrell, R. F., Woodyard, E., & Gates, A. I. (1955). *The effects of mothers' diets on the intelligence of offspring*. New York: Teachers College.

Henneberg, M., Budnik, A., Pezacka, M., & Puch, A. E. (1985). Head size, body size and intelligence: Intraspecific correlations in Homo sapiens. *Homo, 36*, 207–218.

Henrichsen, L., Skinhoj, K., & Andersen, C. E., (1986). Delayed growth and reduced intelligence in 9–17 year old intrauterine growth retarded children compared with their monozygous co-twins. *Acta Paediatrica Scandinavia, 75*, 31–35.

James, W. H. (1982). The IQ advantage of the heavier twin. *British Journal of Psychology, 73*, 513–517.

Jensen, A. R. (1980). *Bias in mental testing.* London: Methuen.

Jensen, A. R. (1983). Effects of inbreeding on mental-ability factors. *Personality and Individual Differences, 4*, 71–87.

Jensen, A. R. (1989). Raising IQ without raising g. *Developmental Review.*

Jones, L. V. (1981). Achievement test scores in mathematics and science. *Science, 213*, 412–416.

Kaelber, C. T., & Pugh, T. F. (1969). Influence of intrauterine relations on the intelligence of twins. *New England Journal of Medicine, 280*, 1030–1034.

Knoblock, H., Stevens, F., & Malone, A. (1980). *Manual of Developmental Diagnosis.* Hagerstown: Harper and Row.

Kubala, A. L., & Katz, M. M. (1960). Nutritional factors in psychological test behavior. *Journal of Genetic Psychology, 96*, 343–352.

Kugelmass, J. N., Poull, L. E., & Samuel, E. L. (1944). Nutritional improvement of child mentality. *American Journal of the Medical Sciences, 208*, 631–633.

Lynn, R. (1989). A nutrition theory of the secular increases in intelligence: Positive correlations between height, head size and IQ. *British Journal of Educational Psychology, 59*, 372–377.

Lynn, R., & Hampson, S. (1986). The rise of national intelligence: Evidence from Britain, Japan and the United States. *Personality and Individual Differences, 7*, 23–32.

Lynn, R., Hampson, S., & Howden, V. (1988). The intelligence of Scottish children 1932–1986. *Studies in Education, 6*, 19–25.

Lynn, R., Hampson, S., & Mullineux, J. C. (1987). A long term increase in the fluid intelligence of English children. *Nature, 328*, 797.

Mackintosh, N. J., & Mascie-Taylor, C. G. N. (1985). The IQ Question. In *Education for All.* (Cmnd. paper 4-453). London: HMSO.

Murdock, J., & Sullivan, L. R. (1923). A contribution to the study of mental and physical measurements in normal school children. *American Physical Education Review, 28*, 209–215, 276–280, 328–330.

Naeye, R. L., Diener, M. M., & Dellinger, W. S. (1969). Urban poverty: Effects on prenatal nutrition. *Science*, 166, 1206.

Orr, J. B. (1936). *Food, health and income.* London: Macmillan.

Oski, F. A., & Honig, A. S. (1978). The effects of therapy on the developmental scores of iron deficient infants. *Journal of Pediatrics, 92*, 21–25.

Ounsted, M., Moar, V. A., & Scott, A. (1985). Head circumference charts updated. *Archives of Diseases of Childhood, 60*, 936–939.

Palmer, C. F. (1935). Height and weight of children of the depressed poor. *Public Health Reports, 59*, 33–35.

Parekh, U. C., Pherwani, A., Udani, P. M., & Mukherjee, S. (1970). Brain weight and head circumference in fetus, infant and children of different nutritional and socioeconomic groups. *Indian Pediatrics, 7*, 347–358.

Passingham, R. E. (1979). Brain size and intelligence in man. *Brain, Behavior and Evolution, 16,* 253–270.

Pearl, R. (1906). On the correlation between intelligence and the size of the head. *Journal of Comparative Neurology and Psychology, 16,* 189–199.

Pearson, K. (1906). On the relationship of intelligence to size and shape of head, and to other physical and mental characters. *Biometrika, 5,* 105–146.

Rajalakshmi, R., & Ramakrishnan, C. V. (1972). Nutrition and brain function. *World Review of Nutrition and Dietetics, 15,* 35–85.

Scarr, S. (1969). Effects of birth weight on later intelligence. *Social Biology, 16,* 249–256.

Scarr, S. (1984). *Race, social class and individual difference in IQ.* London: Erlbaum.

Schrieder, E. (1968). Quelques correlations somatiques des tests mentaux. *Homo, 19,* 38–43.

Stein, Z., Susser, M., Saenger, G., & Marolla, F. (1972). Nutrition and mental performance. *Science, 178,* 708–713.

Stein, Z., & Susser, M. (1987). Early nutrition, fetal growth and mental function: Observations in our species. *Current Topics in Nutrition and Disease, 16,* 323–338.

Sternberg, R. J. (1982). *Handbook of human intelligence.* Cambridge: Cambridge University Press.

Stoch, M. B., Smythe, P. M., Moodie, A. D., & Bradshaw, D. (1982). Psychological outcome and CT findings after gross undernourishment during infancy: A 20 year developmental study. *Developmental Medicine and Child Neurology, 24,* 419–436.

Susanne, C., & Sporoq, J. (1973). Etude de correlations existant entre des tests psychotechniques et des mensurations cephaliques. *Bulletin Societe Royal Belge Anthropologie et Prehistorie, 84,* 59–63.

Takahashi, E. (1966). Growth and environmental factors in Japan. *Human Biology, 38,* 112–130.

Takahashi, E. (1986). Secular trend of female body shape in Japan. *Human Biology, 58,* 293–301.

Takuma, T. (1968). An experiment on hereditary influence on intelligence by the twin method (in Japanese). *Japanese Journal of Educational Psychology, 16,* 47–50.

Taub, H. B., Goldstein, K. M., & Caputo, D. V. (1977). Indices of neonatal prematurity as discriminators of development in middle childhood. *Child Development, 48,* 797–805.

Van Valen, L. L. (1974). Brain size and intelligence in man. *American Journal of Physical Anthropology, 40,* 417–424.

Van Wieringen, J. C. (1978). Secular growth change. In F. Falkner & J. M. Tanner, (Ed.), *Human growth* (Vol. 2, pp. 445–474). New York and London: Plenum Press.

Wechsler, D. (1974). *WISC-R manual.* New York: Psychological Corporation.

Weinberg, W. A., Dietz, S. G., Penick, E. C., & McAlister, W. H. (1974). Intelligence, reading achievement, physical size and social class. *Journal of Pediatrics, 85,* 482–489.

Willerman, K., & Churchill, J. A. (1967). Intelligence and birth weight in identical twins. *Child Development, 38,* 623–629.

Wilson, D. M., Hammer, L. D., Duncan, P. M., Dornbusch, S. M., Ritter, P. L., Hintz,

R. L., Gross, R. T., & Rosenfeld, R. G. (1986). Growth and intellectual development. *Pediatrics*, *78*, 646–650.

Winick, M., Meyer, K. K., & Harris, R. C. (1975). Malnutrition and environmental enrichment by early adoption. *Science*, *190*, 1173–1175.

Winick, M., Rosso, P., & Waterlow, J. (1970). Cellular growth of the cerebrum, cerebellum and brain stem in normal and marasmic children. *Journal of Experimental Neurology*, *26*, 393–400.

Zajonc, R. B. (1986). The decline and rise of Scholastic Aptitude scores: A prediction derived from the confluence model. *American Psychologist*, *41*, 862–867.

# Chapter 6

# *Intelligence, EEG, and Evoked Potentials*

## *I. J. Deary and P. G. Caryl*

*Department of Psychology*
*University of Edinburgh*
*Scotland*

## INTRODUCTION

The recent interest in what has been termed the biology of intelligence (Mackintosh, 1986; Deary, 1988a) has led to a revitalization of the search for EEG and AEP correlates of cognitive ability. It was not long after Berger's discovery that brain electrical potentials could be measured via scalp electrodes that those psychologists interested in individual differences in intelligence sought EEG variables that correlated with scores on IQ-type tests. The enterprise was begun on little more than the premise that, since IQ tests and EEG traces both have something to do with brain functioning, then aspects of the latter might correlate with the former. A familiar, more detailed hypothesis has been that EEG or AEP indices might confirm the impression that more intelligent subjects are mentally somewhat faster.

The IQ-EEG area has such a long history that review articles were being written in the 1960s (e.g., Vogel & Broverman, 1964), and many present-day psychologists interested in the bases of intellectual functioning have felt able to make pronouncements on the state of the endeavor (Mackintosh, 1986; Howe 1988a, b; Dreary, 1988b). These accounts are brief and selective, and fail to give the reader a full impression of the range or complexity of the work. More extensive accounts cover only specific topics (e.g., Oswald & Roth, 1974) or fall short of providing enough information to allow an evaluation (e.g., Eysenck & Barrett, 1985). This chapter attempts to cover different aspects of IQ-EEG studies in some breadth as well as depth. Five empirical sections describe, largely in chronological order, studies that correlated ability scores and EEG or AEP indices. The first section examines those studies that used nonaveraged EEG or nonaveraged evoked responses as the basis of their analysis. The second section presents studies involving averaged evoked potentials (AEPs); Fourier transformation of AEPs is dealt with in the third section, and the fourth section looks at AEP variability. Because of the focus on measures of AEPs in much recent work on the biology of intelligence, the second and fourth sections are extensive, and form the backbone of the review. The fifth section discusses studies in which measures of brain electrical activity have been correlated with abilities which, although relevant for a discussion of intelligence, are relatively narrow. Because of limitations of space, we have not attempted to include in this section any coverage of the vast literature on the relationship between AEP components such as P300 and simple cognitive tasks. We have attempted to provide a representative survey of the area, emphasizing recent results and techniques, for those interested in human intelligence. We have opted for a style that presents most of the experimental details of each study and then offers comment and, where possible, integration with other studies. The chapter is intended to be an antidote to discussions focusing primarily on a subset of positive or negative IQ-EEG studies and ignoring the rest. Our chronological approach allows us to highlight successful past studies that have not been followed up. By offering a detailed précis of studies we can show that very few may be compared directly, because it is rare to see two studies using the same variables—so-called "failures to replicate" a positive or negative *result* often involve failures to replicate exactly the original methodology. This is not usually due to experimenters' perversity; it is a result of there being innumerable (often apparently equivalent) ways to stimulate (or not) the subject and to record and analyze the EEG, and, as we know, large numbers of IQ tests.

## NONAVERAGED EEG MEASURES

Knott, Friedman, and Bardsley (1942) studied the relationships among alpha rhythm, age, and intelligence in normal children. Because the frequency of the alpha rhythm is 4Hz at 3 months and reaches the adult frequency of 7.5 to 12.5

Hz at 10–12 years, they inquired whether the change was due to mental or chronological age. They studied 49 8-year-olds (in three subgroups with IQ ranges 30–71, 74–102 and 100–171) and 42 12-year-olds (in three subgroups with IQ ranges 56–119, 104–145, 99–153). Using monopolar recording to the mid-occiput, continuous EEG was taken for 5 minutes with subjects' eyes closed. Potential changes falling within the 7.5 to 12.5 Hz range were counted as alpha rhythm potentials, and the number of these falling in 10 randomly selected seconds was averaged to give the alpha frequency. The percentage of time with alpha in a 3-meter sample was termed the alpha-index. Using the Stanford-Binet (and Kahlman-Binet for the lowest IQ levels) ANOVA testing was significant across subgroups of 8-year-olds for both measures. On paired testing of subgroups the upper two differed significantly on alpha frequency and the lower two on alpha index. Correlation between alpha frequency and IQ in 8-year-olds was $+0.50$ ($p < .01$) and that between IQ and alpha index $+0.23$ (ns). In this narrow age range alpha frequency was not correlated significantly with chronological age. Within subgroups correlations revealed that significant alpha frequency-IQ correlations were obtained in the low IQ subgroup ($n = 9$, $r = +0.63$) with the correlations in the other two subgroups being zero. On retesting the EEG of 27 of the 8-year-olds, selected from the three subgroups, the IQ-alpha frequency correlation was $+0.66$.

Twelve-year-olds had mid-occipital as well as midmotor area EEG sampled. Two 30 cm strips of record were examined, one near the beginning and one near the end of the record, and only alpha frequency was recorded. Stanford Binet IQ, taken one year prior to the EEG recording, correlated with alpha frequency at $-0.08$ and $+0.12$ in the motor and occipital areas, respectively. Knott et al. suggest that the difference in correlation between groups could be explained either by sampling error (i.e., the true correlation in both groups is the same, either significantly positive or zero, and one of them is extreme) or by the fact that the EEG has stabilized by age 12 and does not index individual differences in intelligence. However, the authors fail to mention that the significant results in the 8-year-old group were found in an IQ range that was not present in the 12-year-old group, making a comparison impossible.

Shagass (1946) found a correlation of $-0.018$ between scores on the 80-item Royal Canadian Air Force Classification Test and alpha frequency in 1,100 aircrew in training aged 18–33. Alpha frequency was estimated by counting the number of 8 to 13 Hz waves in 10 to 30 separate half second segments of each occipital EEG record. Although most of the subjects were of above-average intelligence and the RCAF test had not been correlated with more standard IQ tests, Shagass argued that beyond a certain age and IQ level there is no correlation between alpha frequency and cognitive ability.

Kreezer and Smith (1950) measured alpha frequency, alpha index, and amplitude in 46 male subjects, with mental ages from 3–10 years, from a school for mental defectives. All subjects were over 16 years of age, and had at least one relative also showing mental deficiency. The Stanford Binet was used to assess intelligence. The authors obtained 10 subjects in each of the mental age bands 7–8, 8–9, and 9–10 years, with fewer in year-bands from 3 to 7 years. None of the correlations with mental age was significant (alpha frequency +0.323, amplitude +0.128, alpha index +0.162), although the first only just failed to reach the significance. Alpha frequency was negatively correlated with chronological age (−0.322, also ns).

Mundy-Castle (1958) correlated alpha frequency and alpha index (the percentage of occipital alpha rhythm greater than 5μV in an EEG strip of 100 seconds) with the Wechsler-Bellevue Intelligence Test scores. The study was post-hoc, the data having been collected for other purposes, and the time between the two procedures was up to 18 months. Of the 34 subjects, whose mean age was 24 years, 23 had or would receive degrees and the mean IQ was 126.5 (range 112–135). Despite these methodological flaws, the alpha frequency-IQ correlations were +0.417, +0.403 and +0.507 for Verbal, Practical, and General IQ respectively, and only one near-zero correlation was in the wrong (negative) direction between alpha frequency and the 11 IQ subtests. Correlations between IQ measures and alpha index were inconsistent, although the correlation with Verbal IQ was +0.333. Mundy-Castle and Nelson (1960) replicated the above findings between alpha frequency and intelligence using a remote South African white laborer group, "the members of which are characterised by a high degree of behavioural uniformity and generally low intelligence." The report has few details, but 96 subjects had 7-site EEG recordings and 55 of these individuals were tested on the Wechsler Adult Intelligence Scale (WAIS; mean 75, SD 15). The correlation between alpha frequency and IQ was +0.34 ($p < .01$), and this was unchanged with age held constant. The study has insufficient detail for critical evaluation, but the finding that 51% of the subjects had abnormal EEGs, mostly bilateral shifting foci from the temporal lobes, adds to the consensus that very low IQ or brain-damaged groups are the easiest in which to demonstrate an EEG-IQ correlation.

Netchine and Lairy (1960) studied the EEG of 209 children (aged 5–12 years) attending hospital EEG departments; their sample included a high proportion of low IQ subjects. EEG frequencies were related to age (2-year bands) and "Q.I." (Binet-Simon, Terman-Merrill, or WISC tests) in the following bands: IQ 75 and below, IQ 75–100, and IQ > 100. Children in the highest IQ group had higher frequency occipital EEG than those in the two lower groups. All three groups showed an increase in mean frequency with age, but in the lowest IQ group, frequencies in the 5–6-year-old members were elevated compared with those of older children in the same group. Percentage of occipital theta activity declined with age, especially in the highest IQ group. The Spearman correlation between occipital EEG frequency and IQ ranged from −0.34 (5–6 years) to +0.38 (11–12 years). Parietal and Rolandic EEG showed similar, but less marked, trends. (The authors also present an index of the amplitude of occipital EEG relative to parietal and Rolandic EEG; this index does not clearly differentiate either age-bands or IQ groups, since it shows nonmonotonic changes with respect to both age and IQ, and so appears to have little to recommend it.) Apart from the trend for increased EEG frequency with increased intelligence, seen previously, the most important result in this study is the aberrant (high-frequency) EEG of the youngest subjects in the very low IQ group.

Vogel, Kun, Meshorer, Broverman, and Klaiber (1969) obtained EEG in 90 mental retardates (45 with abnormal EEG) taken at a mean age of 21.5 years. Mental age was assessed on admission to the institution (mean age 11–12 years), when the EEG was taken (21–22 years), and at the time at which the study of EEGs was conducted (24–26 years). For 45 subjects with normal EEGs, there were significant correlations between alpha frequency and the *gains* in mental age and IQ from admission to the year in which EEG was measured ($-0.59$ and $-0.45$ respectively, $p < .05$), and also with the improvement in educational scale score ($-0.69$, $p < .01$). Although the study is clearly not directly comparable with the others reviewed here, the sign of these correlations involving change in mental age appears to be the opposite of what might be expected. The authors interpret it in terms of an association between *slower* alpha and the "automatisation of behaviour," thus allowing better improvement with practice in those retardates with lower alpha frequency, but the result remains anomalous.

Giannitrapani (1969) extended Mundy-Castle's efforts by recording EEG from 18 subjects, aged 21–45, while at rest and while engaged in mental work (multiplication which was adjusted for each subject to give equivalent difficulty). Recordings were taken from left and right hemispheres over the frontal, temporal, parietal, and occipital areas. For each condition, hemisphere and brain area permutation average EEG frequency was calculated by counting the number of pen deflections in each 5-second period. This was reported to include frequencies from 6 to 50 Hz, and was done independently by two assistants with an interrater reliability of $+0.81$. An alpha index was obtained by examining every fifth second of the right and left occipital traces and recording digitally (1 versus 0) whether alpha activity was present or not. The main results are presented as correlations between WAIS performance, verbal and full scale IQs (range 93–143) and the eight brain area/hemisphere combinations for the two EEG indices.

First, the difference between average EEG frequency in the thinking and resting conditions in the right parietal area correlated at $-0.54$ and $-0.48$ (both $p < .05$) with WAIS performance and FSIQ scores, respectively (i.e., dull subjects showed greater frequency increases than bright subjects, when required to perform mental activity). No other correlations using the thinking minus resting condition differences were significant, but all eight brain area/hemisphere combinations gave negative correlations with Performance IQ (mean $r = -0.30$) while the average correlation with Verbal IQ was $-0.03$.

Second, left-right hemisphere frequency differences were computed for homologous brain areas for both thinking and resting conditions. Again, it was the parietal area and Performance IQ correlation which was highest with correlations of $+0.54$ and $+0.57$ (both $p < 0.05$) for the thinking and resting conditions, respectively. All other frontal, temporal, and parietal correlations except one are positive (range $-0.17$ to $+0.57$, mean $+0.22$), and the occipital correlations are all negative (range $-0.22$ to $-0.54$, mean $-0.38$) with the Performance IQ-resting condition being significant. Giannitrapani undertook a post hoc analysis of the left versus right EEG frequency differences by combining the four brain areas, taking account of the direction of the correlations (i.e., frontal + temporal + parietal − occipital differences), to create a single EEG variable. The average hemispheric EEG frequency difference in the thinking condition correlated at $+0.59$ ($p < 0.05$), $+0.78$ and $+0.72$ (both $p < .01$) with Verbal, Performance and Full Scale IQ scores, respectively. In the resting conditions the respective correlations were $+0.41$, $+0.39$, and $+0.46$ (all ns).

Third, alpha index was correlated with WAIS IQ in the left and right hemispheres for both thinking and resting conditions. Including correlations with both Verbal and Performance IQ, five of the eight correlations were significant (three at $p < .01$) and the range was $+0.38$ to $+0.67$ (mean $+0.54$). Five of the 6 correlations in the thinking condition were significant. Therefore, Giannitrapani's study on a small number of subjects with above average intelligence confirms the impression that the EEG of bright individuals is characterized by a relatively greater amount of high frequency activity. However, the study adumbrates many of the problems of more recent studies which correlate IQ and EEG indices. Although some of Giannitrapani's hypotheses appear well founded— that thinking vs. resting frequency might be important, or that as one hemisphere becomes activated the brighter individual will show increased interhemispheric differences in EEG frequency when homologous areas are compared—others are post hoc, for example, it is not clear why bright individuals should have relatively high frequency differences in the left versus right frontal, temporal, and parietal areas but lower or reversed differences in the occipital area. Also, we see here the potential for huge numbers of correlations to be generated with the possibility of a Type I error sitting uncomfortably beside the possibility of Type II error because of the low number of subjects. Further, the possible confounding influence of age is not addressed in this study. The generation of large numbers of EEG variables is not a problem in itself (in fact, brain localization studies suggest that local differences in brain activity might be revealing), but it becomes so when the variables are not replicated in large-scale studies elsewhere. Nevertheless, Giannitrapani's study deserves credit for anticipating the next development in this area—he suggests that in the future (i.e., post-1969) EEG traces should be digitized to allow Fourier analysis, which would reveal the power spectra of the traces.

Further confirmation of the relatively fast activity of brighter subjects' EEG traces came from Osborne (1969). Sixty subjects, aged 16 to 24, had visual evoked potential traces recorded as they reclined with eyes closed 30 cm from a photic stimulator delivering 75 flashes per second. A subdermal electrode midway between the ear and vertex on the dominant hemisphere was referred to the ipsilateral ear, with a ground electrode in the mid-occipital area. Raw signals, filtered to remove frequencies above 70 Hz and below 1 Hz, were separated into 3 bands, theta (3–7 Hz), alpha (8 to 13 Hz) and beta (14 to 30 Hz). Visual evoked component periods (i.e., peak to peak time in ms) were correlated with 6 subtests of the Revised Beta Examination. Alpha and theta period correlations with ability test scores were low and inconsistent, but the beta correlations were all negative (bright subjects having faster beta activity) and ranged from $-0.19$ to $-0.37$, the correlation with total test score being $-0.39$.

Everhart, China, and Auger's (1974) three experiments offer further evidence for the hypothesis that high IQ subjects have faster nonaveraged EEG activity; in their introduction they add the following caveats: the result is only demonstrable in wide ranges of IQ; the correlations are small; and the results have been constructed into no theory except that EEG and IQ both derive from the brain. Thus frustrated, they decide to study Ertl's "neural efficiency analyser" (NEA) because it represents a theory of sorts. They set out independently to discover whether NEA measures VEPs, and to assess the relationship between NEA estimates and intelligence. They obtain a NEA, but only to find that no one at Neurometrics, Inc. will release a technical manual. The device was supplied with a stimulator which gave 10 ms flashes with an ISI of 400 to 1,600 ms. Their own electronic tests revealed that the device was sensitive to frequency, but not amplitude, and that "Readout A" was, in effect, giving the mean time interval between zero crossings. Moreover, the scalp electrode placement recommended by the inventor—bipolar electrodes 6 cm apart over the right sensorimotor area, parallel with the midline astride C4 in the 10/20 system, with an indifferent electrode on the right earlobe—failed to give a consistent "Readout A" score.

The first of their three experiments used 6 subjects in 8 conditions—eyes open or closed versus attending to auditory stimulus or not, and versus having a light flashing or not. None of these variables had any effect and they concluded that it was the frequency of background EEG that was being measured, not VEPs. They decided to use the NEA with subjects' eyes open, stimulus light off while not attending to another task. Experiment 2 involved 20 female dental assistants aged between 21–27 years who were tested on the WAIS, resulting in very few sub-100 IQs. The correlations between NEA 'Readout A' (note that the time between zero crossings will be the *inverse* of EEG frequency, so negative correlations here would be equivalent to the positive correlations reviewed previously) and Verbal, Performance, and Full Scale IQ were $-0.50$ ($p < .025$), $-0.14$ (ns), and $-0.43$ ($p < .05$), respectively. Experiment 3 tested 47 hospital employees, aged 18 to 63, on NEA and WAIS Verbal IQ in an attempt to replicate the result in experiment 2. This group had one subject with an IQ below 100. Neverless, the correlation was $-0.31$ ($p < .025$).

A more recent study correlating spontaneous EEG and IQ in children (Gasser, Von Lucadou-Müller, Verleger, & Bächer, 1983) illustrates many of the best features of this research, other than large subject numbers. Twenty-five mild mental retardates, with an IQ range of 50–70 and mean age 12.5 years (SD 10 months) and 31 control children were tested. Three minutes of spontaneous EEG was recorded with subjects' eyes closed using 8 unipolar derivations (F3, F4, C3, C4, Cz, P2, O1, O2) of the 10/20 system, and EOG to check for eye movement artifact (handicapped subjects did not show more EOG activity). Bandwidth was 0.16 to 70 Hz and the best (artifact free) 120 seconds of the 3 minutes was digitized at a frequency of 102.4 Hz. EEG was Fourier transformed for all six 20 second epochs in the 120 sec. segment chosen and the epoch with minimum power in the 1.5 to 7.5 Hz band was selected for correlational analysis. The chosen 20 sec. of spontaneous EEG was located to 6 frequency bands, delta (1.5–3.5 Hz), theta (3.5–7.5 Hz), alpha$_1$ (7.5–9.5 Hz), alpha$_2$ (9.5–12.5 Hz), beta$_1$ (12.5–17.5 Hz), and beta$_2$ (17.5–25.0 Hz). In order to examine topographic factors, information from the eight derivations was submitted to a factor analysis to reveal 3 factors; an average EEG factor, a frontal-central versus occipital-parietal derivation factor, and a central-parietal versus frontal derivation factor. IQ tests used were the WISC Verbal subtest (German) and the Columbia Mental Maturity Scale (with an extension in the form of the PSB test for normal children due to ceiling effects).

From the above methodological description (relative and absolute power in 6 frequency bands for eight derivations is being correlated with 2 IQ tests in 2 groups) the reader will see that there are 384 correlations even before topographic indices are examined. Nevertheless, the results are largely coherent and interpretable. Correlations were higher in the mentally retarded group. Because correlations were uniform across derivations, but disparate across bands, the results are presented as average correlations across 8 derivations. For absolute power across 6 bands and 8 derivations, all large correlations were positive and the largest correlations were concentrated in the delta, theta and alpha$_1$ bands for both subject groups. In the theta band the correlations between absolute power and WISC Verbal and CMM were +0.60 and +0.50, respectively, for the retarded group, and +0.34 and +0.30, respectively, for the controls. The general factor theta band results in similar correlations. In the mentally retarded group the mean rank correlation between the IQ tests and absolute power across the delta, theta and alpha$_1$ bands is +0.40 and is +0.22 for the controls. In the alpha$_2$, beta$_1$ and beta$_2$ bands the correlations for both groups are largely between zero and +0.10. When relative power is considered a different pattern emerges. For the mentally retarded group correlations of greater than +0.30 are found with IQ scores in the theta, alpha$_2$, beta$_1$, and beta$_2$ bands (mean $r$ = +0.41) while only the theta and beta$_2$ bands give correlations with IQ of consistently greater than +0.10 in the controls (mean $r$ = +0.23). Gasser et al. also calculate the alpha peak frequency versus IQ correlations for both groups. This is calculated for P2, O2, and O1 derivations and results in near zero correlations in controls, but the mentally retarded group has correlations between +0.26 and +0.56 (mean $r$ = +0.39).

There are very few negative correlations in this study and generally greater power within a band goes with higher IQ. The authors make the point that, in normal children, the alpha frequency is saturated by age 10 and, therefore, correlations with IQ are not expected after that age except in the mentally retarded, as happens here. This painstaking work certainly corroborates the notion that sizeable correlations between spontaneous EEG measures and IQ may be obtained easily in mentally handicapped children. Gasser and colleagues interpret their findings in terms of brain maturation and reckon that, since the maturationally more advanced brains result in higher IQs, the EEG indices are indicators of development and, therefore, the higher correlations are obtained from those frequency bands with the greatest developmental relevance. Once more, this appears to be a largely post hoc formulation and one awaits the same pattern of correlation in a larger study. Also, this developmental hypothesis does not explain why significant IQ-EEG correlations are also found in some of the above studies which tested adults of normal and above-normal IQ. Gasser's subsequent papers extend this analysis. Gasser, Bächer, and Steinberg (1985) demonstrated that the mean reliability for absolute power estimates in the 6 frequency bands studied above was $+0.68$ and for the relative power estimates was $+0.69$. Therefore, the correlations for Gasser et al. (1983) are substantially underestimated, making the results even more significant. Gasser, Jennen-Steinmetz, and Verleger (1987) used data collected from the same subjects approximately 10 months later to examine coherence of EEG both while resting and during a simple 180 sec. picture matching task. In resting EEG, coherence was considerably higher (especially in theta, alpha$_1$ and beta$_2$ bands) in the mentally retarded group, consonant with the idea that progressive differentiation of the brain (which is less complete in the retarded subjects) will reduce coupling between different regions. Unexpectedly for this hypothesis, coherence increased with age; differences between normal and retarded could not be explained simply in terms of developmental lag. Changes in coherence from resting to visual task conditions were complex, and depended on the frequency band, electrode site, and the subject group. The authors did not consider IQ in their analysis.

An article by Thatcher, McAlaster, Lester, Horst, and Cantor (1983) demonstrates the value of the application of coherence measure in analyses of intelligence. Their subjects were 191 schoolchildren, aged 5–16 years, who were tested with a shortened version of the WISC-R (or the WPPSI if under 6 years old), the Wide Range Achievement Test at Level I (ages 5–11) or II (ages 12 and above), plus a laterality test battery. IQ ranged from 150 to 44, with 18 subjects above 130 and 17 below 84; mean IQ was 107.4, SD 17.4.

Nineteen channels of EEG were recorded from electrode placements according to the 10/20 system, referenced to the linked earlobes, with a bandwidth of .5–30 Hz. EOG was also recorded. One minute of artifact-free resting EEG (eyes closed) from the record was digitised at 100 Hz and then processed further to analyze coherence for each frequency band (delta, theta, alpha, and beta) for each of 7 intrahemispheric electrode pairs (7 pairs times 4 frequency bands, making 28 variables), plus 10 interhemispheric electrode pairs (5 in each hemisphere, times 4 frequency bands, making 20 variables in each hemisphere). Amplitude asymmetry (asymmetries in absolute power in each frequency band, that is [left − right]/[left + right], or [posterior − anterior]/[posterior + anterior]) was also calculated for the same 17 inter- and intrahemisphere electrode pairs. Since the age-range covered was wide, the authors applied regression techniques to remove the effects of age and sex before examining coherence and asymmetry measures. These techniques were also important to remove the covariance between variables that is inevitable when so many EEG measures are considered.

Their results show that bright children had lower coherences between different electrode sites, and hence that more differentiated brain activity is associated with intelligence. Twenty-one (75%) of 28 interhemispheric coherence measures, 9 (45%) of 20 left hemisphere coherence measures, and 12 (60%) of 20 right hemisphere coherence measures were significantly related to IQ (at $p <$ .05) after effects of age and sex were removed. Universally, higher coherence was associated with lower IQ. More right hemisphere than left hemisphere coherence variables were significantly related to FSIQ, as were more inter- than intrahemisphere coherence variables, but when the different covariances among the variables were taken into account, the left vs. right hemisphere difference was eliminated. Between hemisphere coherence variables were stronger predictors of IQ than within hemisphere variables.

Analyses of amplitude asymmetry showed that larger asymmetries (left side greater than right) were associated with higher IQ. Interhemisphere and right-side intrahemisphere asymmetries were important in predicting FSIQ; left hemisphere asymmetries accounted for almost as large a fraction of the variance as right hemisphere asymmetries, but did not reach significance in the multiple regression analyses as predictors of FSIQ. (The authors note that right-handed subjects all showed simple linear asymmetries with left > right hemisphere amplitude associated with high IQ. Inclusion of left-handed subjects in some cases converted this simple pattern to a more complex quadratic relationship—high IQ associated with larger asymmetry of hemispheric activity, in either direction, low IQ with zero asymmetry.)

Thatcher et al. (1983) interpret their results cautiously, in terms of a model which suggests that the less differentiated the brain, the less it is able to code information. Similarities in EEG taken simultaneously from different sites indicate lower differentiation, and lower capacity to process information, and hence lower intelligence.

Juolasmaa, Toivakka, Outakoski, Sotaniemi, Tienari, and Hirvenoja (1986) examined EEG measures in 52 patients referred for open-heart surgery, whose intelligence mirrored that in the normal population (WAIS mean FSIQ = 102.7,

SD 13.2). Mean age was 46.6 years, SD 8.2; an important aspect of this work was that age was partialled out in analyses of the relations between cognitive performance and EEG measures (with which it was negatively correlated). EEG channels were T5-C3, T6-C4, P3-O1, and P4-O2; three 10 sec. artifact-free epochs were selected from each channel at each of two recording sessions, and EEG measures were averaged for the two sessions. Measures considered were mean voltage of all EEG frequencies, mean frequency (FFT) of the total EEG, mean frequency of alpha-activity, and percentage of delta, theta, alpha, and beta out of total activity. Psychological measures included a range of WAIS subtests; Wechsler Memory Scale tests (logical memory and paired-associate learning); the Benton visual retention test; and a test battery to identify brain damage.

The authors report positive correlations between mean frequency (of total EEG, and of alpha) and IQ (VIQ, PIQ, FSIQ) and various subtests ranging downwards from +0.48. Thirty-two (19%) of the 168 partial correlations tabulated reach significance at $p = 0.5$ or better. The WAIS vocabulary subtest was positively correlated with alpha-frequency and total-frequency at all four derivations; the WAIS logical memory subtest also correlated positively with both frequency measures at several sites. Overall, there were more significant correlations for right hemisphere derivations.

Breaking down the overall EEG into percentage in different frequency bands showed that percentage theta and delta activity was always negatively correlated with performance (in contrast to the positive correlations for theta in children reported by Gasser et al., 1983, and reviewed above), and that percentage beta was always positively correlated. For percentage alpha, significant partial correlations were generally positive, with the exception of hand tapping (T6-C4) and digit-symbol (P4-O2). Path analyses showed that for VIQ, test performance and memory were related to EEG frequency parameters (with age being of little importance), while for PIQ, age was more important than EEG measures.

Giannitrapani's (1985) book represents by far the most detailed investigation of the relationships among measures of spontaneous EEG and intelligence. The author examined 100 children, 11–13 years of age, with an enhanced proportion of left-handers in the sample. Intelligence was measured by the WISC test, plus a battery of other psychological tests. Sixteen monopolar channels of EEG were recorded, with reference to the combined ears, and 8 sec or 64 sec samples of EEG were digitized at 128 Hz and split into 2Hz wide frequency bands, from 2 Hz to 32 or 34 Hz. EEG was sampled in the initial resting condition; in a variety of conditions involving stimulation or mental activity; and in a second resting condition. (It was notable that correlations of EEG activity with intelligence were in several cases more conspicuous in the Resting II condition than in Resting I, presumably because of after-effects of the earlier active conditions.)

Giannitrapani examines in detail the relationship between EEG power in particular frequency bands, and scores on WISC (and its various subtests) under different task conditions, and at rest. Cross spectra between different sites are also examined. It would be impossible to summarize his evidence in detail here, but the most important feature of his results is the suggestion that activity in *particular* narrow frequency bands may be important for the correlations with intelligence (e.g., 13 Hz rather than the higher amplitude, neighboring dominant alpha-frequency of 11 Hz). A second important feature is the examination of relationships between intelligence and EEG activity at different topographic sites; the danger of this approach, involving fractionation of the frequency spectrum and of brain sites, is of course that the chance of Type I errors is greatly increased, and full evaluation of the results reported by Giannitrapani (1985) must await their replication.

Giannitrapani's book contains a chapter by Liberson that attempts to use the harmonic relationships among frequencies found to relate to IQ scores (13, 17, and 23 Hz) to support the "Law of 3.5" (cf. Liberson, 1989). The inclusion of this argument, in what is otherwise an empirical book, is a pity. Appreciation of D. E. Hendrickson's (1982) empirical results (see section 4) was undoubtedly impeded by their association with an elaborate model (A. E. Hendrickson, 1982) for which there was little direct evidence. It is to be hoped that Liberson's theoretical speculations do not similarly detract from the appreciation of Giannitrapani's important empirical work.

## AVERAGED EVOKED POTENTIALS

Recently, the relationship between intelligence and spontaneous EEG has attracted less attention than that between intelligence and averaged evoked potentials. The brain's electrical response to a simple stimulus contains so much noise that any one recording of an evoked response appears to consist mainly of random fluctuations in electrical potential. However, if many records are time-locked to the onset of the stimulus and an average voltage computed at each time point, then the averaged evoked potential contains characteristic peaks and troughs, the amplitude and latency of which may be measured, and used as indices of the brain's response to environmental stimuli. Much research effort has been put into attempts to reveal the variables which determine, and alter, the amplitude, latency, and appearance of various elements of the evoked potential. It is not the intention of the present authors to cover this work. Suffice it to say that the appearance of peaks and troughs in the AEP has been related to the stages of information processing in the belief that the time-based changes shown in the evoked potential reflect the temporal events involved in stimulus-analysis and decision making.

One of the simplest and most enduring "theories" of the cause of individual differences in intellectual ability is the mental speed hypothesis, which states that brighter individuals have faster thinking processes (Deary, 1986; Brand & Dreary, 1982). Because AEPs appear to offer temporal indices of stimulus processing which are free from the problems of, for instance, reaction time, it is not surprising that AEP indices have been correlated with measures of intelligence. The first attempt to demonstrate such a relationship was made by Chalke and Ertl (1965). The theoretical background to the study is uncomplicated. They reasoned that more efficient brains, as indexed by mental ability testing, should have faster late components—their previous work had indicated that this was true for normal versus cretinous rats! They examined 33 postgraduates, 11 army cadets, and 4 mentally retarded subjects. No mention is made of any IQ-type test, but these subjects are taken to represent "superior," "low average," and "low" ability groups with an age range of 17–41, although the mean age in each group is not stated. Evoking stimuli were 120 short duration bright light flashes at random intervals, and potentials were recorded using bipolar electrodes over the left and right motor areas. Zero crossing analysis (which identifies time points at which a statistically significant excess of single trial responses crosses the baseline in an upward or downward direction, compared to chance levels; Ertl, 1965) was used to analyse AEPs, and within the 500 ms post stimulus epoch five components were detected in most subjects. The superior group, when compared with the low ability group, had significantly faster third (142 vs. 205 ms), fourth (223 vs. 278 ms), and fifth (302 vs. 374 ms) EP components. The superior group was significantly faster than the average ability group on components 4 and 5 and the latter group was faster than the low ability group on components 3 and 4.

From this modest beginning Ertl and Schafer (1969) argued that the speed of higher mental functions, "measured by the latency of sequential AEP components, could be the biological substrate of individual differences in behavioural intelligence." They tested 573 grade 2–8 primary school children on the WISC, PMA, and Otis intelligence tests. Visual evoked potentials over a 625 ms epoch were collected to 400 stimuli, using bipolar electrodes astride C4 grounded to the left earlobe, with a bandwidth of 3 to 50 Hz. Subjects' eyes remained open as they saw bright photic stimuli with an ISI of 0.8 to 1.8 sec. Zero-crossing analysis was used to identify the first four statistically significant peaks for each subject. The mean correlations between the first four EP components and the WISC, PMA and Otis tests were $-0.14$, $-0.29$, $-0.35$, and $-0.33$ respectively. Correlations between any one component and the three ability tests were very similar, presumably due to the large numbers.

The zero-crossing analysis has an obvious defect when one examines the sample AEPs provide in the paper. It is clear that what they call the third peak from a low IQ subject is at a post-stimulus delay of about 200 ms while the third component for a high IQ subject is at about 100 ms, due to the fact that high IQ subjects have an excess of early peaks—a finding noted in passing in their discussion. Therefore, given the more recent and generally accepted method of labeling components by examining a specified time window, it is clear that their discovery, later developed by the Hendricksons (A. E. Hendrickson, 1982; D. E.

Hendrickson, 1972, 1982; Blinkhorn & Hendrickson, 1982) could be that brighter subjects have more complex AEPs rather than shorter-latency components. It is important that the numerical subscripts attached to the peaks derived by zero-crossing analysis are not confused with the P100, N140, P200, P300, and so on, of more conventional AEP analyses. Eysenck (1972) claims in a letter to have replicated these, "correlations of around 0.4 between IQ tests and evoked potential latencies," but gives no details; he is probably referring to the work of Hendrickson (1972) discussed below.

Ertl and Schafer's (1969) study raises the possibility that, apart from the more obvious latency and amplitude measures that may be applied to AEP peaks, it may be AEP variability or complexity that is related to IQ. A further possibility, that the higher IQ subject is characterized by greater neural plasticity, is explored by Dinand and Defayolle (1969), using 16 subjects who were tested on a "test de facteur G." Subjects undertook two simultaneous tasks: one involving logical decision (on the make, color, direction, and power of motor vehicle pictures, which required a manual yes/no response), and one which involved "speaking" when an occasional red stimulus (10%) appeared in a series of white flashes, with ISIs between 850 and 1,250 ms delivered to the right temporal quadrant of the optic field. Few details of AEP collection procedures are given, but they measured the P300 amplitude to potentials evoked by the logical decision task and by the white flashes. The difference between the amplitudes was divided by the mean of the two amplitudes to give the "plasticite des PEV" and this index correlated with "Q.I." at $+0.79$. Given the small number of subjects, the novel AEP index and the fact that the study has never been replicated, this study remains a tantalising curiosity.

Rhodes, Dustman, and Beck (1969) compared visual AEPs in 10–11-year-old children falling into two groups ($n = 20$ in each) selected for high IQ (mean 130, range 120–140) or low IQ (mean 79, range 70–90). IQ was measured with the WISC, and subjects with known brain damage, borderline or abnormal EEG, or emotional disturbance were excluded. Visual AEPs were recorded for series of 100 flashes (interflash interval at least 2 sec, and evidently given in sets of 10) reflected from a white hemisphere in front of the child's head, and children were required to press a microswitch for the fourth and sixth flash of each set to encourage attention, and allow elimination of data in which attention had lapsed. Two sets of VERs were recorded, about 5 min apart, at a first session; in a second session, 2 months later, a further 3 VERs were obtained, one at the original flash setting, and the others at a lower and a higher intensity. VERs were obtained for leads at C3, C4, O1, and O2, referred to the earlobes. The authors measured: amplitude and latency of identified peaks and troughs; the similarity of waveforms between different VER traces to provide evidence of stability over time, and to allow measurement of homogeneity within groups; and they used a map-reading wheel measure of total excursion of the waveform or of parts of it, which anticipated by several years the Hendricksons' "string length" measure discussed in a later section.

Rhodes et al. found clear group differences between VEPs of bright and dull children and provide group schematic VERs which show these well. The map-wheel measure of late components, that is, from the peak of the D wave (P100) to 250 ms, was larger in bright children ($p < .01$, occipital; $p < .05$, central). Amplitudes of D (P100), E (N140) and F (P190) waves significantly differentiated the groups ($p < .05$), and these differences (especially the D–E deflection) were responsible for the differences in the map-wheel measure. For children in both groups, amplitude of the late components was greater for boys than for girls ($p < .05$). In the central area, there was a significant hemisphere by intelligence interaction for DE ($p < .01$) and EF ($p < .05$) excursions; for bright children, the right hemisphere responses were greater than the left while for dull children the difference between hemispheres was minimal. Intensity changes did not modify these group differences.

The only significant latency difference observed was for wave G (N230), which was significantly earlier for bright children at occipital leads ($p < .01$), although at central leads, this wave was *later* in bright children (ns). This is consistent with the evidence from other studies that high and low IQ subjects are most commonly differentiated by ''latency'' measures which confound latency with AEP complexity. Waveform stability over 5 min or 2 months was high in both groups; within-group homogeneity in waveform was greater among the bright group ($p < .05$). Alpha activity was also investigated, and the results went against the idea that these bright-dull differences in VER amplitude could be accounted for in terms of background alpha activity.

The authors point out that although these differences between extreme groups were ''modestly significant,'' the possibility of discriminating bright and dull individuals using the amplitude of the late components of the VER is limited by the large standard deviation within each group. Their pessimism was justified by the results of a subsequent study (Dustman & Beck, 1972; Dustman, Schenkenberg, & Beck, 1976) involving 171 children aged 5–15 with an IQ range of 65 points. Peak latencies and amplitudes were analysed, and results for 114 subjects (mean IQ 88, range 62–133) are tabulated in Dustman et al. (1976). No consistent correlations were discovered for either latency or amplitude measures, centrally or occipitally, leading them to conclude that any AEP-IQ relationship which exists is small and requires selected extreme groups to demonstrate it.

D. E. Hendrickson (1972; procedure described by Hendrickson & Hendrickson, 1980, and by Eysenck, 1973) recorded AEPs from 93 students and nurses (mean age 21 years, range 18–32 years), using electrodes at Cz and T4, with ground to both mastoids. Bandpass was 70 Hz and time constant 0.3 s. Stimuli were 400 ms, 1000 Hz tones, at 60, 80 and 100 dB above the subject's threshold; interstimulus intervals were 4–8 sec, and 60 EPs were averaged for each stimulus intensity. Subjects were required to make an RT response. Intelligence (tested using the AH4) was correlated with component latencies and amplitudes (note that the strict sequential labelling of components raises the problems of associating a particular component with a characteristic latency in all subjects, as discussed earlier for Ertl & Schafer's work). The most important results are tabulated by Eysenck (1973). They show correlations between latency and IQ ranging from $-0.25$ to $-0.50$. Amplitude of the components was also correlated with IQ (correlations ranging up to $+0.45$). On average, correlations were stronger for the verbal component of the IQ test than for the performance component.

In two experiments, Schucard and Horn (1972, 1973) investigated the relationships between AEP indices and crystallized ($G_c$) and fluid ($G_f$) intelligence. Their 1972 study included 108 subjects aged 16–68 years with a wide range of SES and occupations. Eight-channel spontaneous EEG was collected from each subject. AEPs were collected from F4–P4 and F3–P3 while subjects lay supine looking at a disc placed in front of a flashing light with an ISI of 1–4 sec. Subjects received 100 flashes in each of 3 conditions: high extrinsic activation (HEA), where subjects made a RT response to a light which came on 250 ms after the AEP started (AEPs contaminated by flash anticipation were excluded); medium extrinsic activation (MEA), where subjects kept a count of light flashes; and intrinsic activation (IA), where subjects simply attended to the light flashes. AEP 'width' was defined in a 250 ms baseline band prior to stimulus onset. The poststimulus EP deflections had to move at least two-thirds of this width to be called a component. The first 5 AEP peaks and troughs were identified. Therefore, this study, like that of Ertl and Schafer (1969) and Hendrickson (1972) is sensitive to the possibility that high IQ subjects have more numerous early peaks, and falls short of being a standard test of AEP peak latency. Spontaneous EEG was rated by an expert on a scale of 1–6 for alertness.

Cognitive test scores were factor analyzed to give "general intelligence" (G), $G_f$, and $G_c$ and more specific ability scores. Of 300 AEP 'latency' versus ability score correlations, 298 are in the expected direction (brighter subjects have shorter latencies). The range of correlations is $+0.05$ to $-0.31$, with most around $-0.15$. Correlations of 0.195 or greater were $p < .05$. Correlations between G, $G_c$, $G_f$ and the later latencies of the intrinsic activation condition were at the higher end of the range. $G_f$ and $G_c$ correlations were of a similar size. Negative peaks were correlated just as highly as positive peaks with IQ. Few correlations with amplitude measures were significant. EEG arousal ratings were related to short $N_1$ latency but bore no consistent relation to ability scores. The fact that correlations in the IA condition were consistently among the highest led the authors to hypothesize that high IQ subjects are more flexible, in that they are able to relax more easily after a difficult task when required to do so. The authors emphasize that bright-dull differences are demonstrated most easily in long boring tasks. Although this concurs with the correlations found in the IA condition it seems at odds with the negative correlations between subjects' wakefulness reports and general ability ($-0.31$). Their conclusion that "the results of this study indicate that the relationship between latency of the evoked potential and intellectual abilities is a replicable phenomenon and that LAEP may mirror long-term central nervous system differences,'' requires some cautionary comment. Age was not controlled for, and the ability-AEP correlations may be due to age-related factors which are absent from a homogeneous age group. Also, their latency measures are a mixture of latency proper and an indication of the number of peaks in the epoch 250 ms after stimulus exposure. Therefore, the study, like that of Ertl and Schafer (1969), demonstrates that brighter subjects tend to have more identifiable peaks in a shorter poststimulus period when compared with less bright individuals.

Schucard and Horn's (1973) next study focuses on *changes* of AEP amplitude across situations and their relationship at IQ measures. They argue that if subjects are changed from a situation with many inducements to stay alert to a situation which has few, then the subjects move from high amplitude/long latency EPs to low amplitude/short latency EPs. This change, they reckon, represents "flexibility" and is faster in more intelligent subjects because flexibility is part of what fluid intelligence is. Ninety-four subjects were tested on the same ability tests and EEG conditions as above. The order of stimulus conditions was HEA to MEA to IA with 10 minute rests in between. AEPs were collected for a 1 sec epoch starting 250 ms before stimulus onset. When AEP peaks were identified, 9 peak to peak amplitudes were calculated and summed, which in effect gave an average amplitude for the first 500 ms poststimulus. The authors argued that this was a more valid measure than amplitude of any one peak. Three amplitude difference scores were calculated for each hemisphere, but the most crucial to their hypothesis was the amplitude difference between the HEA and IA conditions. The correlations between this measure in the right and left hemispheres and fluid intelligence were $+0.24$ and $+0.25$ respectively. Correlations with crystallized intelligence were in the expected direction, but nonsignificant. Therefore, like Dinand and Defayolle (1969), they argue that change in AEP amplitude from a demanding to a less demanding situation is related to intelligence, in this case to fluid intelligence.

At this stage, then, no straightforward AEP latency measures (as opposed to measures which confound latency and complexity) have correlated significantly with IQ measures. Griesel (1973) tested 109 right-handed males between the ages of 17 and 24 years on a local Mental Alertness Test (including number and letter series, analogies and other reasoning items), the Gottschaldt (embedded) Figures Test, and a test of "rate of information processing," where silhouette stimuli were presented for 750 ms in a perceptoscope and subjects were required to make binary decisions. Resting EEG was recorded for 100 sec at rest using bipolar electrodes at C4-O2. AEPs were collected while subjects saw 25 strobe light flashes with a mean ISI of 4.34 sec, and this was followed with a task-loaded condition where subjects were required to make a RT response to the light flash. Frequency and period of resting EEG were measured by hand, and AEPs were analysed by identifying the latency of the 8 largest peaks falling in specified time windows in the 500 ms after stimulus onset for both task and no-task conditions. Of 57 correlations, only 2 are marginally significant, one in the expected direction and one not. The correlations appear evenly distributed around zero. The authors spend some time going over what might have gone wrong: The wrong tests? Wrong electrode sites? Or too few stimuli? All may be responsible, but the mental alertness test description is enough to make it appear a plausible ability test. Another factor which may have contributed to the uniformly low correlations is the fact that the early peaks (latencies from 28.7 ms upwards) were the "exogenous" stimulus-bound components of the AEP. Moreover, we have seen that previous successful studies have not used the method of identifying peaks in specified time windows.

A further confirmation of the successful correlations between IQ type test scores and latency as measured by time to a given zero crossing was provided by Gucker (1973). Only 17 subjects, aged 8 to 13 and ranging from the 30th to the 99th percentile on either the WISC or the PPVT, were tested. AEPs were collected from the right hemisphere using electrodes anterior and posterior to C3 and C4 in response to 100 light stimuli, with subjects in a dark room with their eyes closed. Stimuli were triggered by the subject's EEG crossing the zero potential line and the dependent variable was the latency to the third post-stimulus zero crossing. The latency (in ms) of this event is not given and the range of other latencies estimated is not stated. Nevertheless, the correlation between the latency to the third significant zero crossing event and IQ percentile was $-0.75$ ($p < .01$).

In 1973, Callaway provided a resumé of work which had attempted to correlate average evoked potential indices and intelligence. He identified two, largely covert, "theories" that drove the research. First, the "psychological bias" theory asserted that AEPs were influenced by the cognitive activity and responses of subjects and, therefore, it would be surprising if AEP indices did not correlate with ability tests. Second, the "neurological bias" theory hypothesized that AEPs were reflecting "fundamental genetic, biochemical or anatomical determinants of intelligence." Callaway (1973) discusses evidence which indicates that AEP latency, amplitude asymmetry, and variability are correlated with IQ measures and, without giving sufficient details to facilitate a critical analysis, discusses work of his own in these areas. Callaway tested 191 naval recruits on 15 "performance measures" and used a bipolar electrode pair like that of Ertl to estimate AEP latency and obtained 14 (11.6%) out of 120 correlations significant at $p < .01$, all negative. Most of the significant correlations were found using the latency of the third positive component, with a latency of about 212 ms.

With regard to amplitude asymmetry Callaway notes results from Dustman and Beck's group, and Lairy and his collaborators, which showed a greater left-right difference in bright subjects, using C4–C3 positions. Callaway develops the finding by Rhodes et al. (1969, see above) by testing 57 subjects in two conditions where AEPs were recorded to light flashes. In the first condition subjects had to make an RT response to occasional dim flashes while AEPs were recorded to the more frequent bright flashes. In the second condition, AEPs were recorded to 100 bright flashes with no task. The correlation between right-left hemisphere asymmetry and intelligence was $-0.18$ (ns) in the task-loaded condition and was $-0.43$ (significant) in the no-task condition, and the correlations were significantly different. Callaway argues that bright and dull subjects perform simple tasks equally well but, "at rest, however, inherent differences are permitted to show themselves and verbally gifted, propositionally inclined subjects then show more asymmetry." The finding is an interesting one but the "hypothesis" appears to be a case of post-hoc assimilation of an unusual result, which warrants attempts at replication.

While discussing AEP variability Callaway mentions his study involving 144 naval recruits who had AEPs collected to 100 tones and 100 flashes which were presented to them while sitting in a dark room. He presents no detailed results but indicates that correlations of around $-0.2$ were found between IQ measures and AEP variability, with the pattern recognition subscale giving the best results. Callaway concludes that all 3 AEP measures—latency, asymmetry and variability—correlate with IQ: latency, because bright subjects become bored with repetitive stimuli, although this appears to be based largely on the work of Shucard and Horn (1972) which does not offer unequivocal evidence for this hypothesis; asymmetry, because bright subjects tend to think in either verbal or propositional terms, for which little convincing evidence is presented; and variability, because bright subjects deal with repetitive stimuli in a more stable fashion than dull subjects, which anticipates the later hypothesis of A. E. Hendrickson (1982). Callaway provides poor references for much of the work he discusses, but his discussions about the origin of AEP patterns—due to ongoing cognitive functioning or neurophysiological differences?—is thought provoking, even if it fails to consider the possibility that ongoing cognitive functioning differences might also have their origins in neurophysiology.

Engel and Henderson (1973) tested 119, 7- and 8-year-old children on an adapted WISC battery (7 subtests) and on the Bender Visual-Motor Gestalt Test. Brain potentials were evoked by 20 to 50 light flashes (until an "interpretable VER" was obtained), triggered by a technician while subjects' eyes were closed. Of 14 symmetrical electrodes applied to subjects, only the averages obtained from the left inion, over a 500 ms epoch, were used in this study. Owing to excess intra- and interindividual variability, no data after 300 ms post-stimulus were used. The latencies of 5 peaks were collected, at mean delays of 61.6 ms, 92.2 ms, 115.4 ms, 155.0 ms, and 215.3 ms. Multiple regression procedures were used to examine the contributions of race, sex, and VER to mental test scores. No significant simple correlations involved VER, and the authors state that they are "unconvinced that VER is related to IQ among subjects without demonstrable neurological involvement." It is notable that this study uses peak latencies rather than zero crossings, and that it uses a relatively small and variable number of stimuli to obtain the AEPs. Nevertheless, it represents an influential negative result obtained after testing a large number of subjects.

Two earlier studies conducted by Engel's group (Butler & Engel, 1969; Engel & Fay, 1972) should be mentioned, if only to indicate that they are not particularly useful in this review. In the earlier study Butler and Engel averaged evoked responses to photic stimuli in 433 newborn babies using 6 electrodes over each hemisphere. Few EEG details are given, save to say that the $N_1$ measure (the beginning of the $P_2$ response) was the index which was correlated with "mental," "gross motor," and "fine motor" scores from the Bayley Scales (tested at 8 months) at $+0.23$, $+0.24$ and $+0.23$, respectively (all $p < .001$). Gestational age had almost identical correlations with the Bayley Scale scores, although when gestational age and birth weight were partialled out the $N_1$ versus 'mental' test score correlation remained significant at $+0.24$. It is notable that the latency versus Bayley test score correlations are positive, indicating that the more developmentally advanced infant at 8 months had a longer photic latency when newly born. It may be that brains which are brighter eventually have a longer initial maturation. It should also be noted that all of the Bayley Scale scores are largely motor measures and do not predict later IQ scores.

In a later study using the same AEP index (the $N_1$ latency at birth, corrected to 40 weeks gestation) Engel and Fay (1972) reported that this measure predicted the articulatory ability, but not the comprehension, of speech in 828 three year olds, and failed to correlate with a short form of the Stanford Binet in 1,046 four year olds.

As in the study by D. E. Hendrickson, discussed earlier, Rust (1975a) used auditory stimuli—binaurally presented 1000 Hz tones lasting 1 sec—to evoke brain potentials. His first study tested 84 male twins, mean age 24.2 years, on the Mill Hill Vocabulary Scale, and collected AEPs to twenty 95 dB stimuli with a 33 ms ISI. In the second study 149 male prisoners and 63 "miscellaneous subjects," mean age 29 and 27 years, respectively, were tested on Raven's Matrices, and AEPs were elicited using the stimuli presented in Study I, and in addition using fifty 55 dB and fifty 70 dB stimuli, with an ISI between 4 and 9 sec. In both studies, bipolar electrodes at Cz and T3 were used and AEPs were recorded for a 500 ms post stimulus epoch. Rust's published AEP traces show clear positive waves at about 100 ms and 200 ms post stimulus (called $P_2$ and $P_3$, respectively) and negative waves at about 100 ms and 400 ms post stimulus (called $N_2$ and $N_3$ respectively). The latencies of these peaks and their amplitudes, obtained by calculating the difference between successive positive and negative points, failed to correlate significantly with IQ in either study. There are small significant positive correlations between self-rated boredom and $N_2$–$P_3$ and $P_3$–$N_3$ amplitudes in study two, but otherwise the AEP-IQ correlations were near to zero. Citing an unpublished report that Ertl could not replicate the Ertl and Schafer (1969) results, and his own and other unsuccessful studies, Rust considers the EEG-IQ relationship as unproven. Of course, there is no consistent record of successful correlations between conventional AEP latencies (as opposed to those identified by zero crossing techniques) and IQ scores; a more likely source of the difference between Rust's results and those of earlier workers is the major difference in details of the stimuli used (stimulus duration, ISIs, etc.) which was due to the fact that in his initial experiment, Rust was also interested in the habituation to stimuli.

Schafer (1982) argued that bright subjects should be the characterized by adaptability, in the sense that they would commit fewer neurones than dull subjects to processing known sensory input, but would show a greater response to unknown stimuli. He examined differences between the total integrated amplitude of the AEP to 60 dB click stimuli delivered under three conditions: (a) periodic—regularly every 2 seconds; (b) self-stimulation—the subject delivered each click by pressing a button, with an attempt to present them "randomly"; and (c) a condition in which clicks were presented irregularly and automatically and, unknown to the subject, the clicks were separated by exactly the same time intervals that the subject had generated himself in condition (b). A control for button press movement artifacts was also included. Schafer's subjects were 109 normal adults (for a subsample of 74, mean WAIS IQ was 118, range 98–135) and 52 retarded adults (mean IQ 37, range 18–68, using various tests as appropriate); both groups were aged about 29 years. For each of the test conditions mentioned above, EPs to 50 stimuli were recorded using a vertex (Cz) electrode, referred to the left earlobe, with ground to the right earlobe. Sampling rate was 500 Hz, and the recording epoch 500 ms.

Schafer presents data on comparisons between normal and retarded groups, but for this review his data on correlations within the normal subjects are more relevant. He constructed a "Neural Adaptability" (NA) index by using the total integrated amplitudes of the AEPs from conditions (a), (b), and (c) as follows (note that the constant scale factor of 50 is included to ensure that all NA scores are positive):

$$NA = [(c) - (b)]/[\text{Average of } (a) + (b) + (c)] + 50$$

For the 74 subjects for whom intelligence test scores were available, the correlations of intelligence with NA were $+0.63$ (VIQ), $+0.44$ (PIQ), $+0.66$ (FSIQ) and $+0.60$ (Peabody PVT). A scatter diagram of NA and IQ showed an empty quadrant: All low adaptability subjects had low IQ, but not all high adaptability subjects had high IQ. In high IQ subjects (IQ = 135 approx.) AEPs in condition (c) were 35–45 percent larger than those from conditions (a) and (b); for low IQ members of this nonretarded group (IQ = 103 approx.) this difference was very small (1–6%). In an earlier report, which deals only with retarded subjects, Jensen, Schafer, and Crinella (1981) had included data on the Neural Adaptability index, and its relationship to specific abilities in the retarded, as assessed from group differences when the sample was dichotomized into high- and low-

NA groups. Word problems show the largest correlation with NA, followed in descending order by Oddity, Comprehension, Definitions, Reading, Categories, and Expressive Function. In his discussion, Schafer (1982) had noted Shucard and Horn's (1973) observation, discussed above, that subjects with high fluid intelligence show greater chances in AEP amplitude across conditions of varying attention. Subsequently, in a short report (Schafer, 1984), he confirmed that habituation of AEPs was also related to intelligence. He tested 47 subjects with a range of WAIS Full Scale IQs from 98 to 142. Vertex EPs were measured to 50 "moderately loud" clicks. Evoked potential habituation was measured as the amplitude difference of the $N_1$–$P_2$–$N_2$ excursion between the first and second 25 stimuli. This measure correlated at $+0.59$ ($p < .001$) with IQ scores. Subjects who had 15% or more EP habituation had a mean IQ of 125, while those with less than 15% habituation had a mean IQ of 114.

Shagass, Roemer, Straumanis, and Josiassen (1981) compared visual, auditory, and somatosensory AEPs in psychiatric patients, and normal controls, differing in intelligence. Intelligence was measured with Raven's Standard Progressive Matrices, using percentile scores, and high and low IQ patient groups ($n = 40$ in each) created by matching patients above and below median Raven's scores for diagnosis, age and sex. Mean RSPM percentile score was 53.6 (SD 30.6). A control group showing a full range of RSPM scores was selected: the mean RSPM percentile score for the 20 controls was 61.1 (SD 27.3). High (7 subjects, RSPM percentile score of 95) and low (7 subjects, RSPM percentile score 50 or below) IQ control groups were created.

Stimuli were: visual, 8 ms duration checkerboard presentation; auditory, 0.1 ms binaural clicks at 50 dB above a constant 75 dB white noise; and somatosensory, 0.1 ms electrical pulses to the left or right median nerves. Stimuli were delivered in randomised order, at ISIs of 1.5 to 2 sec (mean 1.75 sec). 14 electrode sites were used, 6 departing slightly from the 10/20 standard (which we shall refer to as "near C3", etc.), referred to linked ears, and EOG was also recorded. 512 ms AEPs were collected, sampling at 1 ms intervals, for each of two montages of 7 leads plus EOG. 192 responses to stimuli of each kind were averaged, and 4 subaverages (e.g., 1st + 5th + 9th . . . ) were constructed to check reliability of the waveform.

Comparisons were for peak- and trough-latencies, absolute amplitudes (deviations from the epoch mean), and a string length measure of AEP waveform complexity (Hendrickson & Hendrickson, 1980) which will be discussed further in section 4. The mean EPs of patients and controls differed in many respects, and the analysis of data for the patient groups will not be considered here.

Conventional AEP measures of the somatosensory AEP yielded differences between low and high IQ groups, especially in the region of N60 and P185; visual AEPs also showed many areas in which high-low differences were significant. The detailed differences can be best appreciated by inspection of the grand mean AEPs for high and low groups which are illustrated, and will not be presented in detail here. Auditory AEPs yielded few differences, but mean amplitude tended to be higher after 100 ms in high IQ subjects.

Average absolute deviation measures for various subepochs yielded a number of differences between high and low IQ subjects, particularly for VEP. (Since EOG amplitude also differed between groups, EP amplitudes were adjusted for their regression on EOG values before analysis.) For example, for the visual EP at Cz, the correlation between adjusted EP amplitude and RSPM scores of nonpatients ($n = 14$) was $+0.629$ (75–249 ms), $+0.614$ (129–249 ms) and $+0.517$ (74–470 ms), all $p < .05$; the maximum correlations for these epochs were $+0.698$ (near C3), $+0.681$ (near C4), and $+.734$ (near C3) respectively, all $p < .01$, and 6 to 8 of 11 leads achieved significant ($p < .05$ or better) correlations in each of these epochs. For the auditory EP, the correlation at Cz over the whole 40–480 ms epoch was $+0.475$ (ns), and only that for the electrode near C3 ($+0.651, p < .05$) achieved significance. For both visual and auditory AEPs, higher amplitude was associated with higher IQ. For the somatosensory AEP, the pattern of correlations was more complex, and the number of significant values intermediate between the visual and auditory ranges. Early in the somatosensory AEP, high amplitude was associated with low IQ; later in the epoch (the time differing for right- and left-arm stimuli) high amplitude was associated with high IQ.

None of the correlations between string length and RSPM score achieved significance in nonpatients; for the patients, only auditory AEP string length measures achieved significance, and here 7 of 64 measures achieved r-values ranging from $-0.22$ to $-0.31$, that is, in a direction opposite to that predicted by Hendrickson and Hendrickson (1980). For visual AEP, there was a general tendency for high IQ to be associated (at several leads) with stability of wave-shape. For latencies, somatosensory N60 latency was shorter for high IQ subjects, and the visual P200 latency was longer in the high IQ group. No other significant latency difference were found. Since 22 peaks and troughs were considered in the analysis, the number of "significant" latency differences is very close to that expected by chance. The authors note that since the differences between high and low IQ nonpatients are between extreme groups, they probably overestimate the relationships with the full range of IQ.

Auditory, visual, and bimodal (simultaneous auditory and visual stimuli were used to elicit AEPs in a study by Federico (1984). Fifty right-handed Caucasian male navy recruits were tested on the Hidden Figures Test, the Clayton-Jackson Object Sorting Test, the Impulsivity subtest from the Jackson Personality Test, the Tolerance of Ambiguity Scale, the Category Width Scale, the Role Construct Repertory Test, Ekstrom's Vocabulary Test II and Surface Development test, Ekstrom's Nonsense Syllogisms test, the Armed Services Vocational Aptitude Battery and the Gates-MacGinitie Reading Test. Brain potentials were evoked using a black-white checkerboard visual stimulus with an ISI between 1 and 3 sec, 65 dB binaural auditory clicks with the same ISI, or both together. Eight

EEG channels were recorded—F3, F4, $T_3$, T4, P3, P4, O1, and O2—with ground at Pz. AEP variables were the RMS and SD of the waveform amplitudes for a 500 ms post-stimulus epoch. Canonical and product moment correlations were used to analyse the results. Four "significant" canonical correlation results are reported, but only two achieve $p < .05$. One result, which has a $p$ value of 0.011 is a correlation of a combination of right temporal and parietal visual responses in the right hemisphere with a combination of results on the Hidden Figures Test, Clayton Jackson Object Sorting (a negative term in the equation) and the Gates-MacGinitie Reading Test. The other significant canonical correlation results (at $p < .034$) is between a combination of AEP indices derived from bimodal stimuli from temporal and parietal electrodes in the right hemisphere and a combination of results on the Clayton-Jackson Object Sorting Test, the Ekstrom Vocabulary Test II (a negative term) and the Armed Services Vocational Aptitude battery. No satisfactory theoretical formulation of these results is offered, and the study-wise Type I error rate is not given. One particularly odd result is the second significant canonical correlation, where the mental test formula has a verbal ability test as a negative term and the Armed Services Test, which has word knowledge as one of its three subtests, as a positive term.

The product moment correlations, for which the SD of normalized (i.e., transformed to a mean of zero) waveform amplitudes were used, have at least a more consistent direction of correlation. The Surface Development Test (a test of visualization) correlates significantly with AEP amplitude for visual stimuli in the left parietal ($-0.45$, $p < .01$), right parietal ($-0.36$, $p < .01$) and right temporal ($-0.30$, $p < .05$) regions. The emphasis on the right hemisphere and parietal areas in response to visual stimuli concords with our knowledge of brain localization of visuospatial functioning in right-handers. Gates-MacGinitie Reading Test scores correlated $-0.43$ ($p < .01$) with AEP amplitude recorded from the right temporal area using visual stimuli. Ekstrom Vocabulary Test II scores correlated at $-0.28$ ($p < .05$) with amplitude of responses to bimodal stimuli in the right frontal area.

The Hidden Figures Test (measuring field dependence-independence) correlated $-0.23$ ($p < .05$) with AEP amplitude recorded from the left occipital area using auditory stimuli. None of these correlations is easy to interpret; note that the correlations obtained here have a sign opposite to what might be expected from the work of Rhodes et al. (1969) and Shagass et al. (1981), in which greater amplitude was associated with higher IQ. (However, since Federico's "amplitude" measure is the SD of the waveform with mean transformed to zero, it appears to be more correctly described as the square root transform of a *variance* measure. D. E. Hendrickson's variance measure, discussed in a later section, also showed a negative correlation with IQ.) Federico notes that his result is the inverse of that reported in the earlier literature, but fails to provide a convincing explanation. The poor discussion also fails to deal with the problem of Type I error: with 8 electrode sites, 3 stimulus modes, 2 AEP indices (amplitude and standard deviation), and 11 ability tests, there are 528 possible product moment correlations of which only the eight which were significant, admittedly all in the same direction, were reported.

Inconsistencies in the study are worth noting. The following two sentences appear in the results section: "Also, VERP amplitudes elicited in the LH and RH parietal regions and RH temporal region were significantly negatively correlated with SPA [$r(48) = -0.45, p < .01; r(48) = -0.36, p < .01; r(48) = -0.30, p < .05$, respectively];" and "Also, VERP amplitudes in the LH and RH parietal regions were significantly negatively associated with SPA [$r(48) = -0.43, p < .01; r(48) = -0.33, p < .05$, respectively]."

An interesting innovation in the derivation of dependent variables from evoked potential traces has been made by Daruna and Karrer (1984). Their sample and their test of intelligence were poor; they tested 24 undergraduates and used the "intelligence" scale from the 16 PF. However, the novelty of the AEP measures makes their study relevant. Subjects were told to "guess" which of 2 tones, frequent (600 Hz on 80% of trials) or infrequent (2,400 Hz on 20% of trails), would raise on a given trial. EOG was recorded and AEPs were taken from Pz, Cz, Fz, to (a) frequent tones, (b) frequent tones after several other frequent tones and just before rare tones, and (c) frequent tones immediately after rare tones (alternation). Baseline to peak amplitudes were measured for $N_1$, $P_2$, $P_3$ and slow wave at the three scalp positions in response to the three types of stimuli. AEP measures were subject to transformation to give values for the cerebral topography of the peaks, and the differences in topography in different stimulus conditions. Subjects with "high IQs" were found to have a greater change in the $N_1$ linear trend (the difference in amplitude between Pz and Fz) across the scalp from rare to frequent events ($r = -0.647, p < .01$). The authors argue that AEP responses lend themselves to more meaningful interpretation if variables such as probability, event repetition and scalp location are considered, and that IQ is linked to cerebral organization which is linked to topography of AEPs. This is a study with intriguing results and interesting ideas which falls short of being ideal on many counts. Apart from the small sample, homogeneous with respect to ability, and the poor IQ measure, which make a Type II error likely; the number of stimulus types, AEP peaks, electrode sites and their combinations in the form of transforms makes a Type I error likely also.

A thought-provoking comparison of the relative success, in discriminating bright and dull subjects, of studies of quantitative EEG and studies of the latency of AEP components is provided by Gasser, Pietz, Schellberg, and Köhler (1988). These authors examined the same experimental (mildly mentally retarded) and control (nonretarded) groups of children that they used for their quantitative EEG analyses described in the first section, but using visual evoked potential techniques. Details of the subjects have been provided in the previous section. For the present experiment, electrodes were at F3, F4, C3, C4, Cz, P2, O1, and O2, referred to linked earlobes; vertical EOGs were also recorded. The stimuli were high-intensity flashes, 2 m away from the subject's closed eyes, with ISIs in the range 0.627–4.687 sec (mean 1.432 sec). Brain electrical activity was filtered (70 Hz low pass, time constant 1 sec) and digitized at 2.45 ms intervals. VEPs were referenced to a 313 ms prestimulus baseline. The length of the post-stimulus epoch is not specified but appears to be at least 300 ms. Using kernel estimation, latency and amplitude of peaks was quantified: not all peaks were obtained at any site, with occipital electrodes deviating from the rest. The mentally retarded and control subjects differed particularly in the 200–250 ms latency range (normals more negative) and in the latencies of P75, P190, and especially N130 (later in retarded subjects at anterior derivations).

Within the normal group, amplitude and latency of AEP components from N60 to N305 at Cz was generally negatively correlated with WISC Verbal score and PSB (Prufsystem fur Schul- und Bildungsberatung) score. These *rank* correlation coefficients ($n = 31$) were low (PSB-latency: mean $-0.25$, range $-0.55$ to $-0.05$; PSB-amplitude: mean $-0.24$, range $-0.54$ to $-0.07$; WISC Verbal-latency: mean $-0.15$, range $-0.30$ to $-0.05$; WISC Verbal-amplitude: mean $-0.22$, range $-0.62$ to $+0.10$), and only 5 (18%) of 28 were significant at $p = .05$ or better. For this nonretarded group, higher IQ was associated with shorter latency and "more negative" amplitudes, while for the retarded group the pattern of correlations was irregular.

The authors concluded that there is little variation in AEP peak latency and amplitude between normal and retarded children, or in relation to IQ, and the results of spectral analysis of quantitative EEG were more clear-cut and relevant, and had greater test-retest reliability. In this VEP study, multidimensional scaling of the full range of VEP latency and amplitude measurements for consistent peaks separated 14 mentally retarded children from the normals, with 11 retarded children falling in the normative range. A similar analysis of quantitative EEG data had previously identified approximately the same deviant and nondeviant subgroups, implying that the poor showing of the VEP peak analysis in discriminating subjects is not due to the retarded individuals having *normal* VEPs, but "due to the large variability in both groups and to the diversity of deviations among retarded children." This result typifies the generally poor discrimination afforded by conventional latency measures in the studies reviewed in this section.

## SPECTRAL ANALYSIS OF AEPS

If the average evoked response of high-IQ individuals has more peaks and troughs in a shorter space of time, as indicated by the correlations between AEP indices derived from zero-crossing analysis and IQ test results, then analysis of the frequency spectra may provide a more formal way of dissecting the underlying structure of the waveform. Bennett (1968) collected occipital cortex AEPs for a 500 ms epoch in 47 subjects using a photic stimulator. Only 36 subjects had a sufficiently good signal to noise ratio to allow AEP analysis. The Pearson correlation between the "natural frequency of the dominant function" and WAIS IQ was +0.59. Bennett's scatter-plot suggests that this correlation depended strongly on the small proportion of subjects with low IQ (below 95); above IQ 110, there is no clear sign of any relationship. Bennett's report is terse and difficult therefore to evaluate—he makes no formal mention of the age or sex of subjects, and IQ range is not formally described although his figure shows it was considerable. He worked in Weinberg's laboratory, and procedure was presumably similar to that adopted in the study discussed below.

Weinberg's (1969) paper develops further the notion that frequency spectra of the AEP might be related to intelligence. Forty-two subjects, aged 18–39 and with WAIS verbal IQs between 77 and 146, were presented (eyes closed) with 70, 20 ms photic stimuli with a mean ISI of 2 sec. Bipolar recording was used with two electrodes over each hemisphere, one 2.5 cm above the inion and the other 2.5 cm lateral to the midline. EPs were digitized and Fourier analysis used to estimate spectral densities. Frequencies between 2 and 50 Hz were included. There was a positive relationship between overall activity and IQ, with the correlation between mean spectral density and IQ being +0.35 ($p < .05$) and +0.43 ($p < .05$) for the left and right hemisphere respectively. There was a significant correlation between IQ and the variability of the degree to which computed spectral components were in the evoked response, but only for the left hemisphere ($r = +0.43$ ($p < .05$); right hemisphere $r = +0.26$, (ns)). With respect to the importance of individual frequencies, those at 12 and 14 Hz had the highest correlation with IQ (around +0.35). (Subsequently, Giannitrapani (1985, see discussion in section 1) was to find that activity at around this frequency, but especially at 13 Hz, in the ongoing EEG was correlated with IQ.) After about 20 Hz, all the correlations obtained by Weinberg are negative, small, and nonsignificant.

Weinberg's summary of the differences between the AEP traces of high and low IQ individuals is that "low IQ subjects tend to show predominantly low frequency activity, especially with respect to early components of the AER."

Weinberg hypothesizes that the AEP differences reflect subject differences in the state of a "scanner" which is an information processing stage that imposes temporal limitations on the encoding of incoming stimuli, like the sweep of an oscilloscope. Thus, Weinberg proposes that the high IQ individual is distinguished by efficient stimulus encoding, a theory held by others in the field of intelligence research (Brand & Deary, 1982), and that AEPs indexed this efficiency. The following speculation by Weinberg anticipates the work done by Zhang and colleagues (Zhang, Caryl, & Deary, 1989a,b) on inspection time, AEPs and intelligence (see final section): "If such sweeping does occur, and if frequencies within the AER reflect periods of the sweep process, then correlations of frequencies with IQ could be thought of as a procedure for determining the optimal sweep period. This assumes that encoding proceeds more efficiently with individuals of high IQ. The most predictive frequency—the one positively correlated with intelligence to the greatest degree—could reflect the optimal scanning frequency.''

Ertl (1971) undertook a reanalysis of selected 11-year-old subjects' EP records from a tape library of over 1000 cases. One hundred sixty-four subjects were selected on IQ criteria, with group 1 ($n = 93$) having IQ scores of greater than 120 on at least two of the Otis, PMA, and Wisc IQ, and group 2 having IQ scores of less than 85 on at least two of the tests. No details of the photic stimuli are provided. Bipolar recording had been used with electrodes 6 cm apart astride C4 to give a 512 ms post-stimulus epoch, based on a 2 ms sampling resolution. Fourier analysis was carried out over 500 ms with a resolution of 2 Hz, and over 250 ms with a resolution of 1 Hz. Few details of results are given, but Ertl fails to find differences between the groups using average Fourier transform indices. Ertl suggests that, in research into human intelligence, spectral characteristics of the AEP may be ignored.

However, in the subsequent two years Ertl (1972, 1973) retracted this conclusion in two short reports which appear to reanalyze the same data as Ertl (1971), although they arrive at slightly different conclusions. He describes the reason for his change of opinion in the 1973 report, ''on rethinking, I realised (a) that the spectral characteristics of the ER change with time, and (b) that most of the differences between high and low IQ subjects appear to occur in the first 150 ms of the response.'' Therefore, to submit a 500 ms epoch, say, to Fourier analysis was too crude: it might include portions of the post-stimulus response processing which were unrelated to intelligence, and it might include periods with different spectral compositions. Ertl used a sliding time-window technique to take account of the non-stationary characteristics of the EPs. ''Fourier analysis was performed in an 80 ms time window which was incremented in 8 ms steps from 40 to 200 ms following the stimulus.'' One ms steps were examined and frequencies from 12 to 50 Hz were included. High IQ subjects were found to have ''significantly more energy centered in the Fourier transform between 85 and 136 ms following the stimulus at a frequency of 20–32 c/s'' (Ertl, 1972). In his 1973 report Ertl records identical results, save to say that the important frequencies were 18–29 Hz. Ertl's sliding time window introduced a further problem, the large number of statistical comparisons, in the attempt to solve the initial problem of nonstationary characteristics. Also, the window size (80 ms) limited the lowest frequency he could consider to 12 Hz.

The potential importance of the frequency range omitted by Ertl (1972, 1973) is highlighted in a small study carried out by Osaka and Osaka (1980). They tested 8 normal children, age range 12 to 13, with an average Suzuki-Binet IQ of 118 (range 110 to 130), and 8 mentally retarded children, with no neurological deficit, of similar age and an IQ mean of 65.5 (range 54 to 76). Subjects looked at a white screen 1.5 m in front of them and, after 15 minutes of dark adaptation,

100 Xenon flashes lasting 1 ms, with an ISI of 1 sec, were presented. EPs were recorded from midline 3 cm above the inion referred to the left earlobe, and 256 points were sampled per 500 ms epoch. Reliability, which was very good, was tested by running two sessions for each subject with 3 to 5 minutes of rest between sessions. Power spectra were analysed with a Hanning window and a resolution of 2 Hz. The mentally retarded group had relatively low $P_1$–$N_{1/2}$ and $N_2$–$P_2$ amplitudes, and normal children had shorter $N_1$ peak latencies. Sadly, the analysis done on power spectra is impressionistic but revealed that mentally handicapped subjects had a peak at 4 to 6 Hz while bright age-matched children had peaks at 4 and 12 Hz. They report that mentally retarded subjects had lower power high frequency components than normals, and conclude that their results are consistent with Weinberg (1969). Although this study corroborates the possibility that relatively high IQ subjects have increased power at AEP frequency components of above 10 Hz, it has the problems of low subject numbers, inclusion of mentally retarded subjects, and lack of formal statistical analysis that limits its importance.

Some novel indices of AEPs were investigated by Flinn, Kirsch, and Flinn (1977), who tested 64 white females with an IQ range of 69–137, and good 2-year stability on the Lorge-Thorndike test. Subjects were divided into 4 groups of different IQ ranges: below 89 ($n$ = 15), 90–109 ($n$ = 17), 110–129 ($n$ = 24) and > 129 ($n$ = 8). AEPs were collected using bipolar electrodes 6 cm apart, parallel to the midline, using C4 as the midpoint (cf. Ertl's placement). After 5 minutes of dark adaptation subjects, with their eyes open, were presented with 4 runs of 100 photic stimuli. Run 1 was at intensity 4, run 2 at intensity 2, run 3 had the light source covered, and run 4 had the light source at intensity 4. ISI between flashes was 1.6 s, EPs were collected for a 500 ms post-stimulus epoch, and there were 3 minutes between each run.

Fourier transformation was carried out on the records after tapering and padding. The authors examined: spectral amplitude at different frequencies, averaging over 6 Hz bands; average spectral amplitude above and below a "splitting" frequency; bandwidth—the range of frequencies in the spectrum; the frequency at which maximal spectral amplitude occurs; and the average spectral amplitude in various frequency bands, for the first 200 ms of record. In general, high IQ subjects had a wider distribution of power across frequencies, and had higher power at higher frequencies while low IQ subjects had higher power at lower frequencies. Maximum amplitude in frequencies 0–12 Hz was correlated negatively at an average of $-0.37$ ($p < .01$) with IQ in runs 1 and 4, and IQ was correlated positively at an average of $+0.36$ ($p < .01$) with frequencies 30–54 Hz in run 1 only. Correlations with amplitudes at low frequencies were caused by the low IQ subjects being different from the rest, while at the higher frequencies there was steady increase in amplitude from low to high IQ. Similar results were obtained with 'splitting' frequency analysis, with IQ-spectral amplitude correlations in wide bands being negative (consistently around $-0.31$, $p < .05$) for frequencies below the split, and positive (ranging from $+0.31$ to $+0.45$, all correlations significant and usually at $p < .01$) for those above it.

ANOVA performed across the four groups for average spectral amplitude, for the ranges 0 to 20 Hz and 30 to 60 Hz, and for bandwidth, resulted in significant F statistics in all cases, but pairwise comparisons revealed that this was largely due to the lowest IQ group being different from the other groups.

Few significant results were obtained in the control or low intensity runs, but the low intensity run correlations were in the same direction as the high intensity runs and around 0.2. In agreement with Ertl (1971), they failed to find a correlation between IQ and maximum spectral amplitude. Apart from the fact that this subject group was biased towards high IQ, it is difficult to find fault with this careful, well-presented study which confirms and extends the impression that high IQ subjects have greater power in higher frequency components of Fourier-analysed EPs.

We have not reviewed Robinson's (1982a, 1982b, 1989) work in this section, although it might be considered relevant here, because he presents no primary data. It is impossible to infer, with any degree of confidence, what the measured data were for any subject on the basis of the fitted constants whose values he does present (in scatter-plots), and which are based on a model of the visual system involving equivalents of electrical resistance, inductance and capacitance. This illustrates an important point, that the value of new techniques can best be appreciated when older, well-understood techniques are also applied to analysis of the same data, and when the basic data input to both forms of analysis are provided as well as the final results. Clear evidence of the value of comparison of different techniques to the same subject population was provided by the work of Gasser et al. (1988), presented at the end of the second section, and by the work of Sutton and his colleagues discussed in the fifth section.


## EP VARIABILITY, COMPLEXITY, AND "STRING LENGTH"


Variability in the response evoked by identical stimuli was the reason that the technique of time-locked averaging was developed. We have already noted above that there are reports that amplitude variability of the *average* evoked potential is greater in high IQ subjects across hemispheres and across tasks, but variability across individual evoked responses to identical stimuli in the same run has been seen as something to get rid of. Callaway (1979) urged an end to this attitude and stated that EP variability should not be ignored—rather, it should be "invited in by the front door and offered . . . a cocktail." Callaway presented evidence to indicate that individual differences in EP variability are stable across time and are related to maturity, schizophrenic thought disorder, IQ, attention, and so on. Such evidence as he has to back his claims on IQ is not presented fully. Two pilot studies with children ($n = 22$ and $n = 17$) obtained negative correlations between $-0.2$ and $-0.4$ between EP variability and test performance, with age partialled out. Details are missing, but results on the Beery Visual Motor Integration test for small groups separated into "variable EP" and "stable EP" are interesting. When the task was new to the subjects it was not possible to have good performance and variable EPs. After practice on the task almost none of the stable EP group had low task performance, while about 50% of the variable EP group did. Callaway's opinion was that, "EP variability may reflect a more enduring quality of mind than do performance measures."

Callaway mentions another study of his own where 207 white navy recruits were divided into low (87–96) and high IQ (113–133) groups, based on Armed Forces Qualification Test results. Of 64 EP measures, one was a variability measure, and was used as the first variable in a stepwise discriminant function. In a $2 \times 2$ table based on IQ-EP variability the Chi-square was 10.1.

Two of Callaway's impressions—that a no-task EP situation is advantageous in discriminating individuals of different IQ, and that high IQ subjects give more stable responses to "dull," repetitive stimuli—are important elements of the Hendrickson's (Hendrickson & Hendrickson, 1980; A. E. Hendrickson, 1982; D. E. Hendrickson, 1982) "string length" measure of the AEP trace. Theirs is a view of the AEP trace that contains the ideas of Ertl (that high IQ subjects have more significant zero crossings in a given time window), Callaway and Weinberg. The key ideas are that variability (in a single subject) between EPs to the same stimulus is the result of neural transmission error, and that high IQ subjects make fewer neural transmission errors than do low IQ individuals. Therefore, it follows that brain potentials evoked by identical auditory stimuli will be less variable in high IQ subjects, and that the AEP will preserve more of the detail of the individual EPs. In low IQ subjects, owing to transmission infidelity, the brain will produce less similar EPs; when averaged, these will give a trace that has fewer, coarser, excursions.

Shagass et al. (1981) had attempted unsuccessfully to discover the string length differences predicted by the Hendricksons' theory in a comparison of high and low IQ subject groups. In an analysis reviewed in the second section, they failed to find *any* significant differences in string length of AEPs to visual, auditory, or somatosensory stimuli, although a few latency differences, and much larger set of amplitude differences, occurred between groups.

Despite this unpromising precedent, Blinkhorn and Hendrickson (1982) set out to test the idea that "the effect of error is to reduce both the number and amplitude of excursions of the a.e.p. trace." Their eventual subject group was 33 Hatfield Polytechnic undergraduates with a range of Raven's Advanced Progressive Matrices scores from 17 to 35 (approximate mean IQ, 128 to 130). Subjects were under instruction to relax and keep their eyes closed while they heard one hundred, 1000 Hz, 30 ms, binaural, 85 dB tones with an ISI of between 1 and 8 sec. A specially constructed PTT4 amplifier (D.E. Hendrickson,

1982, provides the details and circuit, as well as the rationale for choosing this design) was used and 256 and 512 ms pre- and post-stimulus epochs, respectively, were examined. The dependent variable used for EP measures was the "string length," literally the total length of the AEP trace over a given epoch, calculated as if a string had been placed over the trace and its length measured. Although Blinkhorn and Hendrickson present this as a new measure of the AEP, it had precursors in the "map-wheel" measures in common use in the previous decade (e.g., Rhodes et al., 1969; Buchsbaum, 1974), and with hindsight, it may have been unfortunate that the precedent was not recognized in the intelligence literature. Precursors of the string length measure are discussed at the end of this section.

Correlation between the string length of the 256 ms post-stimulus trace and APM score was $+0.538$ ($p < .001$), while the prestimulus string length versus IQ correlation was $+0.127$ (ns). The correlation was almost identical when a 512 ms post-stimulus string was used. Scores on verbal ability tests, performed on 25 of the same subjects, did not correlate significantly with string length. However, string length is not the same as variability and the authors, without giving details, state that, "none of the variance measures from the various data passes correlated significantly with APM." It may be useful to compare the procedure used by Blinkhorn and Hendrickson with that used by Shagass et al. (1981) who failed to find a significant string length–RSPM correlation. The most striking difference is that Blinkhorn and Hendrickson used stimuli in just one modality, coming at relatively long, unpredictable intervals, while subjects relaxed with their eyes closed. Shagass et al. (1981) used a mixture of visual, auditory, and somatosensory stimuli, presented at shorter and less variable intervals (ISIs 1.5–2 sec) while subjects kept their eyes open and fixated an illuminated point on the TV screen. Clearly, there is considerable potential for these differences in experimental procedure to affect the subject's perception of the task, and in particular to modify the range and nature of background thoughts that subjects engage in during the task. Secondly, Shagass et al. report that they equalized scaling of all individual EPs (presumably to remove overall amplitude differences) before their string length analyses; Blinkhorn and Hendrickson did not do this. Shagass et al. did find differences in average absolute deviation from the epoch mean, as discussed in the second section, which could potentially have produced a difference in string length between high and low IQ groups in their study if scaling had not been equalized.

D. E. Hendrickson (1982) examined string length and a variety of related AEP measures for a large sample of schoolchildren ($n = 219$, average age 15.6 years, SD 1.13). Mean IQ (WAIS) was 107.7 (SD 13.9). Evoked responses were collected from the vertex, with reference to the left mastoid, and with the right mastoid earthed; they were again amplified by the specially built PTT4 amplifier used in the previous study, and recorded on tape for subsequent analysis. Stimuli (to which no response was required) were one hundred, 1,000 Hz, 30 ms, 85 dB tones with 1–8 sec ISIs, as in the previous study. AEPs were calculated from 90 trials (eliminating any which had obvious artifacts, plus an appropriate number of good trials to achieve this figure), and a string length measure, total variance measure, and composite (variance minus string) score were obtained over a 256 ms epoch, and subsequently for a 512 ms epoch. In the first analysis, samples were taken at 1 ms intervals, in the second at 2 ms.

Correlations between total IQ and string length and variance measures were +0.72 and −0.72, ($p < .001$) respectively: the "composite" score correlated −0.83 ($p < .001$) with total IQ. To examine the relative importance of early and late components of the AEP in predicting IQ, the epoch was extended to 512 ms (across a subset of the subjects, $n = 78$); when this was done, correlations fell to +0.47, −0.35 and −0.56 for the string length, variance and "composite" measures respectively, suggesting that the relationship depended primarily on components occurring within the first quarter second after the stimulus. Correlations with VIQ were stronger than with PIQ, and full details of correlations of AEP measures with WAIS subtests are provided in the article.

A second sample for which full WAIS IQs were obtained, 16 court stenographers, was of higher IQ (mean FSIQ 126, SD 11.5) and age (mean 42.4 years). In this sample the AEP measures were also correlated with IQ (string length +0.80, variance −0.66, both $p < .01$), confirming Blinkhorn and Hendrickson's (1982) conclusion about a correlation between the AEP complexity and IQ in subjects of above-average intelligence. However, in a third group with a mean IQ of about 147 (19 members of Mensa, an organization for the very highly intelligent), different results were obtained. In this group (average age 28.7 years, SD 6.54), intelligence was assessed only through Mensa's own test, and correlations of IQ with AEP measures were essentially zero. This result is difficult to interpret; it would not be surprising if a general relationship between AEP complexity and intelligence broke down at the extremes of high or low intelligence, and so the lack of significant correlations in the Mensa sample might be interpreted in this way. Alternatively, with such small numbers in the sample, the chance of a Type II error is considerable. In support of the idea that the increase in complexity of AEPs with intelligence extended into the highest IQ range, average string length and variance scores for the Mensa group differed from the averages for the groups of lower intelligence discussed above, in the way that would be predicted from the within-group correlations.

In a final group of 15 severely subnormal subjects, D. E. Hendrickson attempted to apply string length to measurement at the other extreme of the scale of intelligence. In this group, the ERP records were "qualitatively different" from those obtained with other groups. Correlation coefficients for the various measures and IQ are not presented, but string length is reported as being very high in the subnormal group. This difference may depend on the amplitude differences in AEPs reported, for example, for Down's syndrome individuals (Callner, Dustman, Madsen, Schenkenberg, & Beck, 1978; Dustman & Callner,

1979; Schafer & Peeke, 1982). Rather than pointing to a defect in the string-length measure, the result perhaps illustrates in reverse the often-emphasized point that inclusion of retarded subjects in an analysis of intelligence may change relationships which would be obtained if the analysis had been confined to the normal range.

Vetterli and Furedy (1985) reported that the Hendrickson string measure, "suffers from a unique source of arbitrariness: the magnitude of the correlations obtained depends on the scale used to plot the voltage and time axes in the EP graph. Specifically, the greater the ratio of ordinate to abscissa length, the higher the correlation." D. E. Hendrickson devised a revised string measure (RSM) to get rid of this effect and the authors reexamined the published EP traces by Ertl and Schafer (1969) using the RSM, because the Hendricksons have often presented these traces as independent evidence which corroborates their string-length theory. Vetterli and Furedy employed 3 dependent variables when examining the traces: latency of the third peak, a "speed theory" measure; revised string measure, a Hendrickson "error theory" variable; and mean voltage for the epoch, which captures the amplitude but not the frequency aspect of EP complexity, and which the authors hypothesize should correlate with IQ, according to "error theory."

Twenty of the Ertl and Schafer (1969) traces were used, and one voltage reading was taken every 2.94 ms for a 250 ms epoch. The correlation between IQ and revised string measure was $+0.80$, and between IQ and third peak latency was $-0.92$, both in the expected direction. However, the authors point out that these 20 traces were selected from an original sample of 573, in which the latency-IQ correlation was $-0.35$. The IQ-mean amplitude correlation was $-0.25$, which was non-significant and in the wrong direction. Next, the authors reanalyzed 12 unselected traces from Weinberg (1969), with a 4.35 ms sampling rate and a 250 ms epoch. The two "error theory" variables, revised string length and mean amplitude, correlated at $-0.34$ (ns) and $-0.59$ ($p < .05$) with IQ, both being in the direction opposite to that predicted by error theory. The "speed theory" variable, latency of the third peak, correlated at $-0.66$ ($p < .05$) with IQ, which was in the expected direction. The authors conclude that the older, simpler, speed theory of IQ-EP correlations—that high IQ subjects complete psychological processing faster and that this is indexed by the time of the appearance of EP peaks—receives more support than error theory.

A partly successful attempt to replicate the results of Blinkhorn and Hendrickson was carried out by Haier, Robinson, Braden and Williams (1983). In their summary they note that a review of the EP-IQ correlations indicates that high IQ subjects tend to have more EP components than low IQ subjects, and that failures to replicate the original results by Ertl have tended to ignore Ertl's method of identifying peaks by their order of occurrence. They tested 23 nursing students, mean age 22.1, mean RAPM score 21.4, who sat in a dark room observing light flashes of 4 intensities through a translucent screen. One subject was lost owing to blinking. There was no task; flashes came at 1 per second and there were 64 trials at each intensity. A vertex (Cz) electrode was used, with right ear as reference and frequencies from .04 to 40 Hz were included. Sampling rate was 250/sec over approximately 500 ms and the average trace of 2 sessions in each condition was used. Lengths of the waveform measures—using the sum of absolute differences between adjacent points—for 0–252 ms, 252–508 ms, and 0–508 ms epochs were used as EP dependent variables, as were maximum amplitudes of P100 and P200 excursions relative to mean potential between 0 and 36 ms, and peak to peak amplitude of N140 and P200 excursions. Correlations between the 0–508 ms string lengths and RAPM scores were $+0.29$ (ns, low intensity), $+0.27$ (ns, med-low intensity), $+0.43$ ($p < .025$, med-high intensity), and $+0.50$ ($p < .01$, high intensity). Correlations between RAPM scores and the waveform-length measures for 0–252 and 252–508 ms epochs had a similar pattern. There were no consistent patterns in the low correlations between IQ and P100 amplitude over the four intensities, but P200 amplitude correlated at $+0.18$ (ns), $+0.30$ (ns), $+0.59$ ($p < .005$) and $+0.48$ ($p < .025$), and N140–P200 amplitude correlated at $+0.38$ ($p < .05$), $+0.43$ ($p < .025$), $+0.69$ ($p < .005$) and $+0.57$ ($p < .005$) with IQ over the 4 intensity conditions (ordered as previously). The string length was found to correlate between $+0.74$ and $+0.80$ with P200 and N140–P200 over the different stimulus conditions, and the authors conclude that string length, in their experiment at least, was an epiphenomenon of the N140–P200 excursion. They also concluded that relatively high intensity stimuli were necessary to elicit the IQ-string length correlation.

The same group of researchers (Haier, Robinson, Braden, & Williams, 1984) have used the same EP set-up to examine the temperamental differences between EP augmenters (those subjects with a positive slope when the P100–N140 amplitude difference is plotted against the log of stimulus luminance), and EP reducers (those subjects with a negative slope). Using 11 augmenters and 10 reducers, the former were found to have significantly lower sensation seeking, Psychoticism, Extraversion, and Raven's Advanced Progressive Matrices scores. The latter result is thought by the authors to be due to extraverts being better at "performance" versus "verbal" tasks. Robinson, Haier, Braden, and Krengel (1984) attempted to replicate the N140-P200 amplitude versus IQ correlations using 27 subjects of mean age 27.7 years, with an RAPM range of 15 to 33. Details of EP recording were as described above. All correlations were small and non-significant. Post hoc subject exclusion was performed by omitting all those who differed greatly in age ($n = 5$), and by excluding all those subjects with high EP measurement error ($n = 7$). The remaining 15 subjects' data were included and the correlations between N140–P200 amplitude and RAPM scores for the same intensity levels as above, in increasing order, were $+0.28$ (ns), $+0.18$ (ns), $+0.50$ ($p < .025$), and $-0.15$ (ns). The authors emphasize that this is at best a weak corroboration of their original findings, even with post hoc subject exclusion, and that it may be important only to include homogeneous age samples in such studies.

Two unpublished attempts to replicate the Hendrickson work are mentioned in the literature. In an unpublished honours thesis, Fraser (Caryl & Fraser, 1985) attempted to replicate Hendrickson's ERP procedure, including using the same design of amplifier. Subjects listened to one hundred 30 ms, 85 dB, 1000 Hz sine wave tones (which, in contrast to Hendrickson's work, began and ended abruptly). Intelligence was measured by the AH4 test. The study was marred by high electrode impedence in many subjects; after rejecting subjects with high impedence, the remainder ($n = 10$) showed a string length—AH4 score correlation of $+0.78$ ($p < .01$). Mackintosh (1986) reports an unpublished study conducted with R. G. Adams, R. Armbruster, and O. Bathgate involving 18 subjects, in which the correlation between string length and RAPM score was $-0.33$ (ns) and between string length and Mill Hill Vocabulary score was $-0.34$ (ns). This correlation with RAPM scores differed significantly from that reported by Blinkhorn and Hendrickson (1982).

Finally, Stough, Nettelbeck, and Cooper (1990) have reported a more adequate attempt to replicate Hendrickson's procedure, and have extended her analysis to investigate the part of the post-stimulus epoch on which the IQ-string length correlation depends. Twenty subjects (aged approximately 19 years) were tested on RAPM and WAIS-R, and ERPs were recorded from a vertex electrode in response to 100 sine wave tones. The procedure was modeled on Hendrickson's, save that the tones had negligible rise and fall times, and were presented at 70 dB. String length of the AEP was correlated with WAIS FSIQ at $r = +0.43$ ($p < .05$) over the epoch from 0–250 ms after stimulus onset. String length showed no significant correlation with RAPM scores. Stough et al. were able to refine the epochs over which string length was calculated, and showed that the strongest correlation with VIQ ($r = +0.71$, rising to $+0.86$ after correction for range and test reliability) was obtained from the epoch from 100–200 ms after stimulus onset, in which the $N_1$ component occurs. They suggest that this component, which is implicated in the process of attention to stimuli, may account for their results; but in a post hoc comparison of the first and last 50 trials they were unable to confirm their speculations that, when compared with high IQ subjects, low IQ subjects might show a greater waning in attention—indexed by $N_1$ amplitude. Stough and his collaborators have thus clearly identified as important the period of the post-stimulus epoch that had previously been implicated by Haier and his colleagues in 1983, on the basis of correlations of N140–P200 amplitude with intelligence, and earlier by Rhodes et al. (1969).

A further attempt to replicate the string length-IQ correlation using a different method, was undertaken by Vogel, Kruger, Schalt, Schnobel, and Hassling (1987). They collected data on 3 groups of subjects over two experiments. Experiment 1 involved 236 students, representing 12 percent of a population who had undergone EEG screening and who had one of the following EEG characteristics:

low voltage EEG; monomorphic alpha waves; fronto-precentral groups of beta waves; or beta waves which were mixed diffusely with alpha waves. Experiment 2 included 24 mentally retarded in-patients aged 15–29 and 19, "students and employees of the institute" with a similar age range. IQ-type tests administered to subjects were the Intelligenz-Struktur-Test (with 9 subtests), the Leistungs-Pruf-System, the d2-Aufmerksamkeits-Belastungstest and Raven's Standard Matrices. Brain potentials were evoked by visual stimuli—light flashes at 4 levels of intensity (presented at random)—and auditory stimuli—tones with a frequency of 500 Hz and a duration of 500 ms—with 2 sessions per modality (one of fixed ISI of 1.5 sec., and one of variable ISI of 1 to 2 sec.), and 256 stimuli per session. Electrodes used were F4, Cz, P4, P1, O1, O2, with right ear as reference, and EOG was recorded. An epoch of 700 ms, beginning 100 ms before the stimulus, was sampled at a rate of 333 Hz. Period analysis was used to obtain $P_1$, $N_1$, and $P_2$ latencies, and a method called "oscillation," which sums local maxima and minima, beginning 70 ms after stimulus onset, was used as a similar measure to the Hendrickson string length. In experiment 1, the 45 correlations between "oscillation" indices derived from the 4 visual and one auditory condition, and IQ scores were all nonsignificant. The correlations between peak latency and IQ test scores (again, 45 in all) were all nonsignificant except for one marginally significant at $-0.193$. In experiment 2 there were a few small significant correlations within the groups, but the likelihood of these being chance occurrences is heightened by the lack of EP index differences *between* the two groups, other than the unexpected finding that the controls had longer latencies in one visual condition. The authors' discussion is pessimistic about the possible existence of AEP-IQ correlations, putting great stress on the failure of Engel and Henderson (1973). A very useful table compares their own experimental set-up with that of Haier et al. (1983) and Blinkhorn and Hendrickson (1982). They conclude that EEG set-up differences are not convincing reasons for their failure to obtain significant correlations in the expected direction. However, there are sufficient departures from the Hendrickson methodology to make this a possibility.

It may be that future studies will confirm straightforward correlations between EP variability measures and IQ, but an older study by Shucard and Callaway (1974) suggests that the relationship between these two variables is a complex one, which is evident only in its interaction with other variables in the EP test set-up. They introduce the study by summarizing that amplitude is decreased by ISI reduction, stimulus predictability and decreased attention; and increased by stimulus relevance and importance, and by the reduction in EP variability (i.e., a large amplitude is obtained if waves from any single trial evoked responses are always in phase—a relationship confirmed by Haier et al., 1983). They selected 8 high and 8 low scorers on tests of G, $G_f$, and $G_c$, as in their previous studies, for EP testing. Brain potentials were tested in 2 sessions, 7 days apart, evoked by 1,000 or 1,020 Hz, half-second, 65 dB tones (in 58–60 dB white noise), with an

ISI of 2 sec between tones and 16 sec between blocks of tones. There were two task variables, each with 2 conditions. Presentation was either ordered (blocks of 4 tones with an ISI of 2 sec.), or random (blocks of 1, 2, or 3 tones occurring randomly, that is, subjects were unsure at any time whether a tone would appear in 2 or 16 sec). Subjects were either attending (i.e., listening to the pattern of high and low tones and being rewarded where their record of tones was accurate), or nonattending (reading a magazine article while the tones were being played). Subjects had AEPs collected, twice in each presentation, using vertex to left ear electrodes (Cz–A1) for a 500 ms epoch. Separate averages were calculated for the first two tones in each block. Therefore, AEPs were based on only 15 stimuli, or as little as 10 stimuli in the random condition, as there was no second tone at times.

Average amplitude (mean of 200 time points in the 500 ms) and mean standard deviation of the 200 time points were calculated for 16 different binary variable permutations–intelligence (high vs. low) by ISI (2 vs 16 sec) by attention (yes vs no) by order (ordered vs random). Amplitude was increased by attention to stimuli and uncertainty of stimuli, and first tones in a block evoked larger amplitude responses than second tones. Uncertainty and attention interacted, and both interacted with ISI. There was no main effect for intelligence with respect to amplitude, but it interacted with other variables. Comparisons within conditions across intelligence level yielded 6 out of 16 comparisons (all in nonattending conditions) significant at $p < .05$ and, in general, brighter subjects had greater amplitudes. Therefore, nonattention to stimuli was the most potent variable in distinguishing the high and low IQ groups.

With regard to EP variability, there were main effects for attention and ISI. Intelligence interacted with uncertainty, attention, and ISI. Generally, bright subjects showed less change in variability as a result of change in the experimental conditions. Dull subjects showed a marked reduction in variability when stimuli were random rather than ordered and showed a greater shift in variability in response to second tones in the attending condition. The general, but slight, trend is for low IQ subjects to be less variable, in contrast with other studies. The small number of subjects and stimuli used to obtain AEPs are flaws that make Type II errors likely in this study, but the independent variables used in this investigation, and their interaction, highlight the possibility that intelligence, where it does not present a main effect, may be involved in an interaction.

## Precursors of String Length

A striking discovery, in reviewing the literature for this chapter, was that the Hendrickson string length measure was almost exactly equivalent to the "map-reading wheel" or "CVC" (cumulative voltage change) measures of the waveform which were well established in the literature—the parallel appears to be unknown to those interested in intelligence. For example, Rhodes et al., (1969) applied their map-wheel measure to occipital and central AEPs, and identified the P100, N140, and P200 waves as of primary importance for differentiating bright and dull children, thus anticipating the results of Haier et al. (1983) and Stough et al. (1990) which implicated the area around the N140 component. There is valuable information in the early literature on this area of the AEP. Using a map-wheel measure on VERs from the vertex (Cz) and occiput (O1 and O2), Buchsbaum (1974) showed that heritability was highest for the part of the trace from 116–152 ms. The portion from 168–248 ms, which included P200, showed lower heritability (because of greater similarity in this region of traces from dizygotic twins). Rust (1975b) found that what would now be called the $N_1$ and $P_2$ components of the AER (which he labeled $N_2$ and $P_3$) had high reliability, and that there was a strong genetic component in the amplitudes of excursions that we should term $P_1$–$N_1$, $N_1$–$P_2$ and $P_2$–$N_2$. But, when latencies were considered, this early segment of the AER was not unitary, with what we should term $N_1$ and $P_2$ latencies showing significant between-family environmental variance, absent in $P_1$ and $N_2$ latencies. The results of Lewis, Dustman, and Beck (1972) are less easy to link to the more recent work, since their map-wheel measures are tabulated primarily for right-hemisphere sites, and since they used an age range (4 to 40 years) over which profound variation in map-wheel (string length) measures occurs. They do confirm the high similarities for monozygotic twins in the middle region of the AER, which would be expected if this part of the response reveals inherited individual differences in neural pathways or stimulus processing, although they do not break this region (68–200 ms) down further.

The work of Dustman and Beck's group (Rhodes et al., 1969; Lewis et al., 1972) raises several further issues about application of string length or equivalent measures to the analysis of intelligence.

*Location of electrodes.* Location of electrodes might be important. Rhodes et al. (1969) found that the bright-dull amplitude difference was greater for the right hemisphere. Lewis et al. (1972) found more obvious differences in AER frontally (F4) than centrally (C4), when comparing monozygotic twins with other individuals. Dustman and Beck (1965) found that the similarities among unrelated individuals in VER increased with age at the vertex (thus obscuring individual differences) but decreased with age in the occipital region. There appears to be no evidence to show that use of the vertex will be appropriate for both auditory AEPs (Blinkhorn & Hendrickson, 1982; D. E. Hendrickson, 1982; Stough et al., 1990) and visual AEPs (Haier et al., 1983; Robinson et al., 1984), or that string length at the vertex will be more closely related to IQ than string length measures taken from other sites, and the issue deserves further investigation.

*Sex differences.* Sex differences in amplitude of the P100–N220 map-wheel (string length) measure, for electrodes at C3 and C4, were recorded by Rhodes et al. (1969). Boys had greater amplitude than girls. This difference appears to have shown up in the string lengths recorded by Hendrickson (1982) at the vertex (mean string length from 0–256 ms: boys, 142.950; girls, 134.878), although it received no comment. Schenkenberg (1970) reports that this sex difference is reversed after adolescence, so Hendrickson's 15–16-year-old subjects might be expected to show a smaller difference than would be obtained with younger children.

*Age changes*. Map-wheel (string length) measures of different segments of the VER, AER and SER show important and often complex changes with age. These have been documented most thoroughly in Schenkenberg's (1970) unpublished PhD thesis, but are also discussed by Callner, Dustman, Madsen, Schenkenberg, and Beck (1978), while illustrations of the changes in form of the visual, auditory, and somatosensory AEPs on which these string length changes depend are provided in Dustman, Schenkenberg, and Beck (1976, Fig. 8–16) for ages from 5 to 77 years. Such data should be considered in planning studies of the relation between string length and IQ. For the VER, the pattern of age changes in string length presented by Schenkenberg is complex, and details differ at different electrode sites. Knowledge of variation of string length with age would have allowed Robinson and colleagues (Robinson et al., 1984) to reject, from the outset of their study, volunteers differing significantly in age from the intended subject group, as well as choice of an age when string length was relatively stable. Their post hoc decision to eliminate 5 subjects on an age criterion, before analyzing the correlation between the N140–P200 excursion and IQ, would then have been unnecessary. Similarly, the 250 ms epoch of the AER analysed by Blinkhorn and Hendrickson (1982) and D. E. Hendrickson (1982) appears to contain three elements, when age changes are considered, and the reversal after adolescence of the initial sex differences in string length (as reported by Schenkenberg, 1970) might be an important consideration in designing studies aimed at correlating string length with IQ.

## SPECIAL ABILITIES

This section includes those studies where EEG or AEP indices are correlated with scores on more specific mental abilities, but not the voluminous literature on the relationship between late potentials, such as P300, and psychological processes.

### Spatial Ability

Furst (1976) suggested that those subjects who excel in visuospatial ability tests should have relatively low ratios of right to left hemisphere alpha activity. Sixteen students worked on 20 visuospatial items selected from 3 sources (cube-folding, 3-D mental rotation and paper folding), which were held on cards in front of them, and two-channel (O1 to P3 and O2 to P4, each referred to the ipsilateral earlobe) EEG was recorded while subjects worked on the problems. Ratios of integrated alphas activity across hemispheres were calculated for each 1 sec epoch and the rank correlation between visuospatial ability and lower right hemisphere alpha activity was $+0.546$ ($p < .05$, in the expected direction). However, the baseline alpha asymmetry versus ability correlation was almost the same ($+0.508$, $p < .05$), leading the authors to conclude that those superior on visuo-spatial ability had tonic asymmetry. This is another small pilot study which merits replication in a larger and more representative sample.

Willis, Wheatley, and Mitchell (1979) screened 129 students from a high school math club and geometry class on the Purdue Spatial Visualization Test and the Briggs Handedness Questionnaire. From this pool they obtained 17 right-handed females and 21 right-handed males for the EEG session. EEG was recorded from P3, P4, T3 and T4 leads, referred to Cz, with a forehead ground, and alpha (8–13 Hz) activity was filtered out and its power measured for each channel at 1 sec. intervals. For each of 4 tasks, plus a resting baseline condition, two 30 sec. samples were analysed for alpha power, and the average and SD of these measurements (across the total 60 sec) for each channel, and the mean log ratios of alpha power at corresponding leads between hemispheres (log T4/T3, log P4/P3) and within hemispheres (log T4/P4, log T3/P3) were compared for each task condition.

Of the four cognitive tasks, three were designed to tap different components of performance required by the PSV Test: mental rotation (Rotations); perceptual matching (Perceptions); and analytical processing (Areas). They each involved similar perceptual configurations but different production components, and were based on the same types of configuration as used in the PSV Test. The final task (a control intended to index left hemisphere function) involved items similar to those in the WAIS Similarities subtest, but selected to be low in imagery. Task items were presented on worksheets. Students worked on items of each type for at least 30 sec, on two occasions, while EEG was recorded, and there were also two resting periods (eyes open) in which 30 sec baseline EEG was obtained.

Willis et al. found no differences in left-right log ratios for high- and low-spatial ability groups, for any task. However, on the right side there were temporal-parietal ratio differences, significant only for the Rotations task ($p = .026$), with the overall trend for high (spatial) ability students to show more temporal (as opposed to parietal) activity compared to low-ability students. On the left side, a sex by ability interaction was found. Females showed no ability differences in ratios, but males did so ($p < .023$). The magnitude of the difference was greatest for the Perceptions task (where high ability males showed more parietal activity than low ability males), and varied in direction between tasks.

The result provided little support for the authors' initial view that spatial "reasoning" (as opposed to spatial perception) was a function of the right hemisphere, and would be tapped particularly by the Rotations task.

A sex by ability interaction also appears in the study by Ray, Newcombe, Semon, and Cole (1981). They tested subjects on two visuo-spatial tasks—the

Survey of Object Visualization and Part V of the Guilford Zimmerman ability tests—and obtained 7 subjects in each of four groups: high and low ability males and females. Using band pass filters at 0.5 and 30 Hz, and a sampling rate of 100 Hz, EEG was recorded from parietal electrodes (P3 and P4) on both hemispheres, referred to Cz. During EEG recording subjects examined 8 items from the Object Visualization test. There were 2 minutes between items, subjects gave verbal responses to them and the last 6 were used to record EEG data. The output from each channel was converted to an asymmetry measure. For high spatial ability males ($n = 7$) the correlation between EEG asymmetry and spatial ability scores was $-0.71$ ($p < .05$) for baseline EEG, and $-0.53$ (ns) for EEG during problem solving. For low-ability males the respective correlations were $+0.77$ ($p < .05$) and $+0.56$ (ns); for high-ability females $+0.20$ (ns) and $-0.09$ (ns); and for low-ability females $+0.19$ and $+0.54$ (both ns). The authors conclude that high spatial ability males are able to exclude intrusive thoughts from the left hemisphere, and that for low-ability males a verbal or analytic strategy is used to solve visuospatial problems. No relationship was found between EEG indices and ability in females. It is hardly necessary to add that, had all males been analysed as a single group, the correlation would have been zero, that their hypothesis with respect to low ability males is post hoc, and that correlations based upon an $n$ of 7 have very wide confidence limits.

## Digit Span

Because digit span is a subtest of the WAIS, EEG correlates of digit span are of interest, even when obtained in experiments which do not have the analysis of intelligence as their primary objective. Polich, Howard, and Starr (1983) argued that, since depth electrode recordings indicated that the P300 wave of the AEP might arise from the area of the medial temporal lobe, hippocampus and amygdala, P300 indices should be correlated with memory indices. Ninety-six neurologically normal subjects, aged 5 to 87, were tested on WAIS forward and backward digit span. Brain potentials were evoked by 1,000 or 2,000 Hz binaurally presented 60 dB tones, with a 9.9 ms rise/fall time and 50 ms plateau. Subjects kept count of high (20%) tones, and tones came at 1.1 per second. 200 artifact-free recordings were collected in two independent sessions. AEPs were averaged using a vertex (Cz) electrode referred to linked mastoids, with forehead as ground. Rare and frequent tones were averaged separately, the filter-band pass was 1 to 30 Hz, and the EEG was digitized at 3 ms points over a 768 ms epoch. EOG was not recorded, but trials where EEG was greater than $+/- 45 \mu V$ were rejected. Correlations between $N_1$, $P_2$, $P_{3a}$ (220 to 320 ms) and $P_{3b}$ (300 to 450 ms) and memory scores were $-0.03$ (ns), $+0.11$ (ns), $-0.47$ ($p < .001$) and $-0.36$ ($p < .001$), respectively, that is, those subjects with shorter $P_3$ latencies had better memory scores. When age was partialed out the correlations between $N_1$, $P_{3a}$, and $P_{3b}$ and memory scores were $-0.09$, $-0.52$, and $-0.40$, respectively. The authors speculate that P300 latency may reflect "an individual's capacity to retain recently encoded information for comparison with the new, incoming information."

However, Polich et al.'s attempt to partial out age from their correlations was declared invalid by Surwillo (1984), who pointed out that the partial correlation method assumes a linear function for the P300 versus age and memory versus age relationships whereas, in the extraordinary age range included in the Polich et al. study, the relationship was curvilinear. Polich's (1984) reply to Surwillo's comments is not substantial and the latter's comments, which suggest that age might be the explanatory variable despite partial correlation, appear to be valid. In a later study by Howard and Polich (1985), 24 children, aged 5 to 14 years, and 24 adults, aged 20–40 years were tested exactly as described above (Polich, Howard, & Starr, 1983). P300 latency was measured as the maximum positive amplitude between 225 and 400 ms. The correlation between memory (digit span) and P300 latency was $-0.59$ ($p < .005$) for children and $-0.15$ (ns) for adults. In the group of children memory was significantly correlated with age ($+0.68$, $p < .001$), as was P300 latency ($-0.46$, $p < .025$). Neither of these correlations was significant in adults. In children, the correlation between P300 latency and memory, when age was partialled out, was $-0.43$ ($p < .025$), while the corresponding correlation in adults was $-0.13$ (ns). The small range of digit span scores in adults may account for the lack of correlation in adults. The authors conclude, perhaps rather confidently, that, "the ERP findings of the present study strongly suggest that the primary cause of memory span increase is the improved stimulus processing capacity that occurs with development."

## Specific Learning Disability

A study by Sutton, Whitton, Topa, and Moldofsky (1986) of children with low Loban Language Rating Scale scores but normal intelligence is worth considering because of the possibility that the approach they adopted could be applied more widely in the analysis of intelligence. These authors found little evidence that conventional amplitude/latency measures of AEP peaks, and in particular the P300, could be used to differentiate learning disabled children from matched controls; they present an alternative approach, involving a measure of synchrony in activity between pairs of sites, which appears to combine valuable features of both the quantitative EEG techniques reviewed in the first section, and the time-locked analysis of conventional AEPs, and this technique provided detailed evidence of differences (significant at $p = .001$) between the two groups in specific areas and at specific times after stimulus onset.

Eleven right-handed, learning-disabled children were selected from a larger population on the basis of (a) *normal* intelligence, (b) low Loban Language Rating scale and PIAT Reading Achievement scores, and (c) low teacher estimates of reading achievement, taking into account age, intelligence, and previous schooling. They were matched with 11 controls on the basis of sex, age, and GDAPT scores. Mean age was 7.4 years. Recording was from F3, F4, C3, C4, T3, T4, P3, P4, O1, and O2 with reference to linked earlobes, with a ground lead to the forehead. EOG was also recorded. Filters were set at 0.3 and 35 Hz, and 60 Hz activity was removed after digitization. Records were digitized at 7.8125 ms intervals. Stimuli were a binocular flash, a binaural 90 dB click, and a left wrist tap. 50 stimuli of each sort were presented in a randomised order. 500 ms AEPs, processed in the conventional way and scored blind by an experienced rater, revealed *no* differences in peak latency or amplitude between LD and control children at the chosen level of significance, $p = .001$.

The authors' alternative (synchrony) measure is introduced and described in detail. In essence, it involves—for each time-point of the 500 ms epoch, and for each pair of sites—taking a correlation across trials between the voltages (at the given time point) of the appropriate single trial EPs. After application of the Fisher transform to these correlations, their value could be averaged for each electrode pair. LD children always showed higher correlations (implying more synchrony) between pairs of sites than did controls.

For the visual EP, LD children showed increased synchrony (compared to controls, at $p = .001$) frontoparietally, from 30–40 ms, centroparietally and occipitotemporally from 120–150 ms, and frontotemporally and frontoparietally after 350 ms. LD children were more synchronized in the left parietal area throughout most of the visual EP. For the auditory EP, LD children showed increased synchrony between central, parietal and occipital areas between 50 and 80 ms; after approximately 120 ms, intergroup differences were localized (bilaterally) to the frontotemporal region. Few intergroup differences were found for the somatosensory EP. Left centroparietal differences between LD and control children in the period 250–260 ms were common to al three modalities, and these appeared to reflect specific language disability, since they correlated more closely with Loban Language Rating Scale scores than with any other psychometric measure used.

## Inspection Time

Zhang and his collaborators (Zhang, 1987; Zhang, Caryl, & Deary, 1989a,b) examined AEPs to visual stimuli for differences which were related to the subjects' level of performance on a visual inspection time (IT) task, which had been shown to be related to general intelligence. The IT task emerged from a psychophysical theory developed by Vickers, Nettelbeck, and Willson (1972): they proposed that information from a stimulus is sampled in quanta, implying that a certain minimum time ("inspection time") is required for a reliably correct discrimination to be made. If a stimulus is simple enough, it may require only a single inspection to make an accurate discrimination, but accuracy can never be complete if the stimulus is presented for less that this minimum inspection time, which varies between subjects. In the IT task, stimuli are followed by a backward mask; stimulus duration is under control of the experimenter, and can be reduced until it is below this minimum duration and the subject begins to make mistakes. In practice, it is very difficult to estimate the point at which performance just begins to drop below 100%, and an arbitrary point on the psychometric curve (often 90% or 85%) is chosen as the hit rate at which stimulus duration will be measured. IT has been found to be shorter in bright subjects: Nettelbeck (1987) and Kranzler and Jensen (1989) have reviewed the IT-IQ literature and concluded that the correlation is in the region of $-0.50$. Some authors have suggested that this correlation occurs because IT indexes a basic component of human information processing, or represents neural efficiency (Deary, 1988a; Nettelbeck, 1987). Others suggested that intelligence determines the readiness with which subjects discover and adopt task-specific strategies (Mackenzie & Bingham, 1985; Mackenzie & Cummings, 1986) or the rate at which they become inattentive and careless in the IT task (Mackintosh, 1986).

Zhang et al. (1989a) obtained AEPs to visual stimuli obtained while 16 subjects were engaged in a task in which their visual inspection time was estimated. Stimuli were presented on a LED display; the task required discrimination of the relative length of pairs of illuminated lines (one twice the length of the other) which were followed by a backward mask. Stimulus onset asynchrony was varied (using the PEST algorithm) until target performance (85% correct responses) was achieved, and then retained at this duration for the balance of a minimum 100 presentations. (Because the two-line stimulus was followed immediately by the backward mask, and the combined duration of stimulus plus mask was held constant at 600 ms, variation between stimuli was in the timing of an early change in the form of the illuminated display, rather than the duration of a bright stimulus).

EPs were recorded from a vertex (Cz) electrode, referred to the left mastoid, with ground to the right mastoid, using an intersample interval of 1 ms over a 1,024 ms epoch. The recording epoch began at the onset of a 300 ms warning cue, presented on the same LED display as that used to present the stimuli, starting 500 ms before the IT stimulus. The epoch ended shortly before termination of the mask, and subjects were required to delay their response (a lever-press to indicate the side on which the longer vertical line had been shown) until after mask offset, so that it did not contaminate the AEPs. The subjects were allowed to take their time in coming to a decision, and since the task is one of speeded perception rather than a reaction time task, they were discouraged from responding rapidly.

In experiments eventually published as part of the second paper in this series (Zhang et al., 1989b), Zhang had noticed that subjects who were good at the IT task typically had a more sharply rising onset of the P200 component of the AEP. A new measure termed $P200_T$, which was preferred to gradient because it was not a function of amplitude as well as wave-shape, was defined (Zhang, 1987) and in the present experiment correlated with IT at P $= +0.44$ ($p < .05$, 1 tailed, since it was in the predicted direction). P200 latency correlated with IT at $+0.41$ (ns). When age was partialed out, correlations between IT, and $P200_T$ and P200 latency became $+0.43$ and $+0.55$, respectively.

In the second paper, Zhang et al. (1989b) included the results of two earlier experiments mentioned above, in which $P200_T$ had been observed to correlate with IT. Each was a small sample study ($n = 8$), but both experiments included one comparable condition in which subjects viewed backward-masked stimuli set at their previously determined IT duration; the overall IT-$P200_T$ correlation for this condition, when the results for the two experiments were combined, was $+0.57$ ($n = 16, p < .05$). The main point of these small-sample studies was to establish whether the individual variation in P200 rise-time was an artifact of the presentation to different individuals of discriminative stimuli of different duration, before onset of the mask. Stimuli were therefore presented both at the previously established IT duration, and for much shorter or longer durations. These manipulations failed to affect the $P200_T$ rise-time measure, although P300 amplitude (which provides an index of the subject's confidence in their discrimination) did vary with stimulus duration in the way that would be anticipated as the difficulty of the task was altered.

The $P200_T$-IT correlation in AEPs to IT stimuli was also replicated ($r = +0.645, n = 37, p < .001$) in the main study reported by Zhang et al. (1989b), whose aims were to examine (a) whether the correlation was dependent on the need to attend to the stimuli, and/or (b) the rapid, backward masked nature of the IT stimulus, and (c) whether the $P200_T$ measure correlated with IQ, as well as with IT. For this experiment, the number of subjects was 37 (IT-AEP correlations) or 35 (IQ-AEP correlations), and the IT-IQ (AH5 test) correlation in the subjects was $-0.301$ ($n = 38, p = .05$, one-tailed). The direction and magnitude of the IT-IQ correlation was as predicted from larger studies using this particular undergraduate population, which had an estimated mean IQ of about 124.

The task used was more complex that the conventional IT task, and readers are referred to Zhang's paper for details; essentially, the IT stimulus plus mask was sandwiched in sequence between an initial digit stimulus (presented on the LED display) which told the subject how to treat the IT and subsequent stimuli on that trial, and a response signal which cued the subject's lever press. Trials were of two types. In one type, the subject had to treat the IT stimulus as a discrimination task in the conventional way; in the second, the subjects could ignore the IT stimulus plus mask, *but still looked at it*, since they were awaiting the onset of the response signal (500 ms after mask offset, and appearing on the same LED display) to which a simple RT response was required.

AEPs were collected to the digit stimulus which cued the subject as to the task required on each trial, to attended IT stimuli, and to IT stimuli that could be ignored. Measures of $P200_T$, P200 latency and amplitude, and P300 latency and amplitude, were correlated with IT and IQ. The results showed that, for AEPs to the IT stimulus plus mask, the correlation of the rise-time measure $P200_T$ with IT dropped from $+0.645$ ($p < .001$) in the attended condition to $+0.117$ (ns) in the ignored condition. For the digit stimulus (not requiring a speeded discrimination) the correlation between $P200_T$ and IT was lower ($+0.299$, $p < .05$, one-tailed) than for the IT stimulus, but still significant in the predicted direction. Thus the individual differences indexed by $P200_T$ depended on attention to the stimulus much more strongly than on the requirement for speeded perception. In addition, the $P200_T$ measure for responses to the digit stimulus was correlated with IQ ($r = -0.34$, $p < .05$). With such a complex design, the number of correlations to be taken into account is considerable; a principal components analysis was used to clarify the pattern of relationships among the various AEP measures considered, IT, and IQ. The PCA revealed 3 factors, which were of almost equal importance after varimax rotation, together accounting for 72 percent of the variance. The first was interpreted as a task-specific encoding-speed factor, reflecting processes specific to the IT task rather than those involved in general intelligence; IT, P200 latency and $P200_T$ loaded heavily on this factor. The other interpretable factor was a general speed factor, with intelligence (AH5), as well as IT and the $P200_T$ measure for AEPs to the digit stimulus all loading heavily on it. The remaining factor extracted had loadings from IT, and P200 and P300 amplitudes, and Zhang was unable to interpret it with confidence.

Zhang et al. suggest that simple extrapolation from the view that intelligence involves "mental speed" or "speed of apprehension" to predict that this should imply *shorter latency* of AEP components is inappropriate: in the experiment described, it is not so much the latency of components as the faster *speed of transition* between components representing different stages of the stimulus processing which characterizes the intelligent, or task-successful, subject. Their results implicate the region just before the time of 200 ms after stimulus onset, which had been identified as important for the distinction between bright and dull subjects by Rhodes et al. (1969), Haier et al. (1983), and Stough et al. (1990), as important also for the dichotomy between higher and lower ability on this perceptual task (on which performance is related to intelligence). However, the IT task has the advantage that (in contrast to earlier AEP paradigms, in which subjects are required, e.g., simply to "listen to the tones," where differences in AEP waveforms may reflect what they do with the balance of their attention) the nature of the stimulus processing performed by bright and dull subjects can be kept firmly under experimental control in such a demanding task. The results of Zhang support the view that IT taps individual differences which arise at an early stage of stimulus processing (well before the "decision making" often associated with late components of the AEP, such as P300), but which are none-the-less fundamental to performance on more complex tasks, such as pencil and paper tests of intelligence.

## DISCUSSION

The evidence reviewed in this chapter justifies the following assertions:

1. A variety of measures of EEG and of averaged evoked responses correlate

with intelligence, in adults as well as in children, and in samples with above-average intelligence, as well as in those including retarded subjects. This allows us to dismiss as un-informed those authors (e.g., Howe, 1988a, 1988b) who have questioned whether *any* biological measures can be found which correlate with intelligence once studies involving retarded subjects have been excluded.

2. The factors leading to the observation of substantial correlations between measures of brain electrical activity and IQ are not well understood. There have been unexpected and unexplained failures in some studies to obtain the significant correlations expected from earlier work and, while some of these can probably be attributed to Type II errors, or to failure to replicate procedure and methodology exactly, the critical design features which account for the different results remain to be established. Any theory of the biological basis of intelligence must account for those parameters which determine whether a correlation is observed.

3. Analyses of ongoing EEG (using measures such as power in particular frequency bands, or coherence) have been relatively successful in obtaining significant associations between brain electrical activity and intelligence. Analyses of AEPs have been less successful; correlations between intelligence and component latencies (as distinct from "latency" measures that also depend on waveform complexity), while nonzero and generally negative, do not clearly separate bright and dull subjects in the normal IQ range. Differences in component amplitude have provided a rather clearer separation, and it is probably amplitude differences, as well as those of complexity, which underly the high correlations between string length (map-wheel) measures and IQ. While the highest correlations with intelligence have come from measures such as string length and Schafer's Neural Adaptability Index, both of which provide a gross measure of differences between waveforms, rather than measures such as component latencies which allow the time course of stimulus processing to be charted, recent work by Zhang et al. (1989a, 1989b), Stough et al. (1990), and Sutton et al. (1986) has begun to fill this gap. An important feature of their results is the discovery that differences relatively early in stimulus processing (before 200 ms in the first two cases, and before 260 ms in the third) correlate most strongly with scores on the performance measure of interest. This suggests that the differences detected in the evoked responses reveal differences in stimulus-analysis mechanisms which may cause, rather than being epiphenomena of, the differences in ability. In contrast, results for measures such as Schafer's Neural Adaptability Index merely show that bright subjects divert fewer of their resources to processing an anticipated stimulus than do dull subjects, and this difference in brain activity is as likely to be a consequence of rather than a causes of differences in intelligence.

4. It is unlikely that any single index of brain electrical activity will provide a "biological measure of *g*" which can replace conventional tests of intelligence. Progress in understanding the biological basis of intelligence will come from

acceptance of the fact that the brain is not a homogeneous unit, and from the measurement of the contribution of different areas to performance on particular subtests, in addition to the continued search for single measures which correlate highly with *g*.

5. The recent history of the analysis of the AEP-IQ relationship by workers interested in intelligence has been dominated by the rediscovery (admittedly with lower chances of Type I error) of results previously known in the electroencephalographic literature. Their independent discovery of the importance (for differentiation between bright and dull subjects) of certain epochs of the AEP lends weight to the argument that, despite generally low correlations between latency measures and intelligence and the problems raised by failures to replicate results, there *are* real differences between brain electrical activity in bright and dull subjects.

While quantitative EEG techniques (reviewed in the first section) have yielded clear associations between brain electrical activity and intelligence, they have provided little insight into the causal links between the activity and test performance which underly the association. The differences in electrical activity may be interpreted as *consequences* of differences in intelligence, and the associated differences in mental activity, rather than as giving information about their causation. Giannitrapani (1971) showed that experimentally induced changes in subjects' mental activity produced changes in frequency content of the EEG, and in his large scale study (Giannitrapani, 1985) the greater frequency of significant IQ-EEG correlations in the Resting II condition, compared with Resting I, is evidently a consequence of intelligence-related differences induced in the periods of stimulation and mental exercise that separated these two Resting conditions. Similarly, the evidence, presented in the first section, that brain activity in bright subjects is more differentiated (lower coherence between sites) confirms a reasonable expectation about the basis of their abilities without providing insight into the mechanisms involved. However, the evidence localizing the IQ-related differences to particular electrode sites and *particular frequency bands* now provides a way to examine the issue of causation in more detail, as well as giving the lie to the simplistic equation of higher intelligence, higher 'mental speed' and generally faster brain electrical activity.

One attraction of AEPs as an alternative technique to the quantitative study of EEG has been the possibility of linking particular stages of stimulus processing to the timing of particular AEP components. However, latencies of components in the evoked response to simple stimuli are not highly correlated with intelligence. They have provided little clear information about the nature of processing differences between bright and dull subjects, save (a) to confirm that bright subjects are slightly faster than dull subjects, and (b) that these differences in speed are not cumulative over different stages in processing (i.e., late components do not differentiate bright and dull subjects more clearly than early components, as might be expected if speed differences had had more stages of processing, or a greater time, over which to act). However, several lines of evidence have recently identified a region around P200 as important for differentiating bright from dull subjects, and it is interesting that this is well before the P300 component of the AEP which has often been used as an index of decision-making in the psychological literature. There are other approaches which could be applied to examine such differences; for example, the technique used by Sutton et al. (1986) revealed clear differences in brain activity over particular epochs (between normal and learning-disabled children) which had not been apparent using conventional latency measures of AEP components. Since it provides spatial and temporal localisation of differences between groups, it would be of considerable interest to apply this technique to the comparison between high and low IQ subject groups.

The Hendricksons' string-length measure has shown high correlations with intelligence, and it is of considerable importance to develop a better understanding of the factors determining waveform complexity, and the underlying mechanisms. Data presented by Schenkenberg (1970) show that, while string lengths may be correlated with IQ within age-bands, intelligence-related differences in string length are likely to be confounded with age-dependent ones, in studies where subjects vary widely in age.

There is little direct evidence to support the Hendricksons' suggestion that string length differences between bright and dull subjects are a consequence of the process of averaging (i.e., that the greater inter-trial variation in the timing of peaks, which they postulate for dull subjects, will broaden components and reduce their amplitude in the AEP). Since the ongoing EEG contains more high frequency activity in bright subjects (see first section), it is possible that it is a difference in power at higher frequencies in the raw EEG, rather than an effect of averaging, which accounts for the greater complexity of waveform they observed. One way to assess their interpretation might be to compare (using the FFT) the differentiation of IQ groups in evoked response data before averaging, and also (using the FFT) to compare the AEPs from these data. If it is the process of averaging which eliminates high-frequency components, then high and low IQ subjects would be expected to be better differentiated in the AEP than in the raw EEG.

One of our most striking discoveries, in preparing this review, was the extent to which recent conclusions about the string length measure had been anticipated in earlier work. For example, Rhodes et al. (1969) wrote that, ''The [map-reading wheel] excursion measure of late components (100–250 ms) of both occipital and central VERs were found to be reliably larger for the bright children ($p < .01$, occipital; $p < .05$, central). Much of the excursion difference in the central responses could be attributed to the amplitudes of the D [P100], E [N140] and F [P200] waves, especially the D–E deflection. Each of these measures differentiated the groups significantly.'' Not only did their technique (the map-wheel measure and the later cumulative absolute voltage change [CVC] measure) anticipate precisely the string length measures subsequently used by Hendrickson and Hendrickson (1980) and Haier et al. (1983), but their results identified as important the area of the evoked response that was later identified by Haier et al. (1983), by Stough et al. (1990), and (in a different context) by Zhang et al. (1989a, 1989b) as most relevant to IQ and to inspection time. With independent confirmation of the importance of this area, the question of why some recent studies have failed to observe a string-length IQ correlation becomes one of identifying critical features of experimental design which may enhance or diminish IQ-related variation in string length, particularly around N140.

Although it may be said that authors failing to find a string length-IQ correlation have not employed the "correct" stimulus conditions (cf. Eysenck & Barrett, 1985), such failures might be instructive. Providing that a substantial correlation *has been* obtained, it is of almost as much interest to find a set of experimental conditions in which it *disappears* as to find it continues to reappear as parameters are varied. Contrasting the sets of conditions in which the correlation is present and absent can give us important clues as to the mechanism involved, which would otherwise not be available. At any age, and with any type of stimulus, the question of whether string length measures at a particular site correlate with intelligence is an empirical one. The complexity of the changes in string length with age, for different stimulus modalities and at different electrode sites (Schenkenberg, 1970), is such that it does not appear appropriate to attempt to account for the changes as an index of increasing mental age. (However, it will be interesting to compare the ages at which changes in trend are observed, using Schenkenberg's approach, with those at which Thatcher, Walker, and Giudice, 1987, have reported growth spurts in phase and coherence measures of ongoing EEG.) The variation between electrode sites in these string length changes should be followed up. In addition to using Hendrickson's data to show that string length at the vertex correlates highly with the *g* loading of various tasks (Eysenck & Barrett, 1985; Eysenck, 1986), it would be interesting to extend the analysis to other sites, and to ask how the correlation between the WAIS *subtest* scores and string length varied over the two hemispheres. Giannitrapani's (1985) maps of electrode sites showing significant associations (in terms of auto- or cross-spectrum) between ongoing EEG and WISC subtest score might provide an appropriate framework within which to begin such an analysis of AEP string length.

Our review suggests that the most successful approach in the short term will be atheoretical. In this area, theories have been typically esoteric, and/or have involved mechanisms which do not permit the detailed and testable predictions which would allow a theory to be corrected and refined. Obvious examples possessing these faults are Hendrickson and Hendrickson's (1980) theory of "pulse trains"; Liberson's (1989) "Law of 3.5", which has been linked to "the quantum mechanics of cognitive function" (Weiss, 1987); and the McCulloch "scanning hypothesis" (Weinberg, 1969; Giannitrapani, 1971). Such esoteric or high-level theories, which treat the brain as an undifferentiated unit, must surely have contributed to the scepticism that is still evident about the search for the biological basis of intelligence. It would be surprising if details of neural circuitry did not matter, and our review has shown that effective techniques exist for analysing the relationship between brain electrical activity and test performance, and defining both spatially and temporally the regions of highest correlation. As well as continuing the search for the *single* measure of brain activity correlating most highly with *g*, it is now time for research workers to examine in greater detail the empirical relationships between IQ-test scores and the numerous EEG/AEP measures currently available, with an emphasis on the information they provide about underlying mechanisms of intelligence and its subtypes.

## REFERENCES

Bennett, W. F. (1968). Human perception: A network theory approach. *Nature, 220,* 1147–1148.

Blinkhorn, S. F., & Hendrickson, D. E. (1982). Averaged evoked responses and psychometric intelligence. *Nature, 195,* 596–597.

Brand, C. R., & Deary, I. J. (1982). Intelligence and "inspection time." In H. J. Eysenck (Ed.), *A model for intelligence* (pp. 133–148). New York: Springer.

Buchsbaum, M. S. (1974). Average evoked response and stimulus intensity in identical and fraternal twins. *Physiological Psychology, 2,* 265–274.

Butler, B. V., & Engel, R. (1969). Mental and motor scores at 8 months in relation to neonatal photic responses. *Developmental Medicine and Child Neurology, 11,* 77–82.

Callaway, E. (1973). Correlations between averaged evoked potentials and measures of intelligence. *Archives of General Psychiatry, 29,* 553–558.

Callaway, E. (1979). Individual psychological differences and evoked potential variability. *Progress in Clinical Psychophysiology, 6,* 243–257.

Callner, D. A., Dustman, R. E., Madsen, J. A., Schenkenberg, T., & Beck, E. C. (1978). Life span changes in the averaged evoked responses of Down's syndrome and nonretarded persons. *American Journal of Mental Deficiency, 82,* 398–405.

Caryl, P. G., & Fraser, I. J. (1985, September). The Hendrickson "string-length" measure and intelligence—A replication. Paper presented at Psychophysiology Society Scottish Conference, Edinburgh, U.K.

Chalke, F., & Ertl, J. (1965). Evoked potentials and intelligence. *Life Sciences, 4,* 1319–1322.

Daruna, J. H., & Karrer, R. (1984). Event-related potential correlates of intelligence and personality. *Annals of the New York Academy of Science, 425,* 565–569.

Deary, I. J. (1986). Inspection time: discovery or rediscovery? *Personality and Individual Differences, 7,* 625–631.

Deary, I. J. (1988a). Basic processes in human intelligence. In H. J. Jerison & I. Jerison (Eds.), *Intelligence and evolutionary biology* (pp. 351–362). Berlin: Springer.

Deary, I. J. (1988b). Prospects for the biology of human intelligence. *Human Evolution, 3,* 503–513.

Dinand, J. P., & Defayolle, M. (1969). Utilisation des potentials evoques moyennes pour l'estimation de la change mentale. *Agressologie*, *10* (suppl.), 525–533.

Dustman, R. E., & Beck, E. C. (1965). The visual evoked potential in twins. *Electroencephalography and Clinical Neurophysiology*, *19*, 570–575.

Dustman, R. E., & Beck, E. C. (1972). Relationship of intelligence to visually evoked responses. *Electroencephalography and Clinical Neurophysiology*, *33*, 254 only.

Dustman, R. E., & Callner, D. A. (1979). Cortical evoked responses and response decrement in nonretarded and Down's syndrome individuals. *American Journal of Mental Deficiency*, *83*, 391–397.

Dustman, R. E., Schenkenberg, T., & Beck, E. C. (1976). The development of the evoked response as a diagnostic and evaluative procedure. In R. Karrer (Ed.), *Developmental psychophysiology in mental retardation and learning disability* (pp. 247–310). Springfield, IL: Thomas.

Engel, R., & Fay, W. (1972). Visual evoked responses at birth, verbal scores at three years and IQ at four years. *Developmental Medicine and Child Neurology*, *14*, 283–289.

Engel, R., & Henderson, N. B. (1973). Visual evoked responses and I.Q. scores at school age. *Developmental Medicine and Child Neurology*, *15*, 136–145.

Ertl, J. P. (1965). Detection of evoked potentials by zero crossing analysis. *Electroencephalography and Clinical Neurophysiology*, *18*, 630–631.

Ertl, J. (1971). Fourier analysis of evoked potentials and human intelligence. *Nature*, *230*, 525–526.

Ertl, J. (1972). Fourier analysis of evoked potentials and human intelligence. *Electroencephalography and Clinical Neurophysiology*, *33*, 254.

Ertl, J. (1973). I.Q., evoked responses and fourier analysis. *Nature*, *241*, 209–210.

Ertl, J., & Schafer, E. (1969). Brain response correlates of psychometric intelligence. *Nature*, *223*, 421–422.

Everhart, J. P., China, C. L., & Auger, R. A. (1974). Measures of EEG and verbal intelligence: an inverse relationship. *Physiological Psychology*, *2*, 374–378.

Eysenck, H. J. (1972). Letter. *Science*, *178*, 232–235.

Eysenck, H. J. (1973). *The measurement of intelligence*. Lancaster, England: MTP.

Eysenck, H. J. (1986). The theory of intelligence and the psychophysiology of cognition. In R. J. Sternberg (Ed.), *Advances in the psychology of human intelligence* (Vol. 3, pp. 1–34). Hillside, NJ: Erlbaum.

Eysenck, H. J., & Barrett, P. (1985). Psychophysiology and the measurement of intelligence. In C. R. Reynolds & V. L. Willson (Eds.), *Methodological and statistical advances in the study of individual differences* (pp. 1–49). New York: Plenum.

Federico, P. A. (1984). Event-related-potential (ERP) correlates of cognitive styles, abilities and aptitudes. *Personality and Individual Differences*, *5*, 575–585.

Flinn, J. M., Kirsch, A. D., & Flinn, E. A. (1977). Correlations between intelligence and frequency content of the visual evoked potential. *Physiological Psychology*, *5*, 11–15.

Furst, C. J. (1976). EEG alpha asymmetry and visuospatial performance. *Nature*, *260*, 254–255.

Gasser, T., Bächer, P., & Steinberg, H. (1985). Test-retest reliability of spectral parameters of the EEG. *Electroencephalography and Clinical Neurophysiology*, *60*, 312–319.

Gasser, T., Jennen-Steinmetz, C., & Verleger, R. (1987). EEG coherence at rest and during a visual task in two groups of children. *Electroencephalography and Clinical Neurophysiology*, *67*, 151–158.

Gasser, T., von Lucadou-Müller, I., Verleger, R., & Bächer, P. (1983). Correlating EEG and IQ: A new look at an old problem using computerized EEG parameters. *Electroencephalography and Clinical Neurophysiology*, *55*, 493–504.

Gasser, T., Pietz, J., Schellberg, D., & Köhler, W. (1988). Visually evoked potentials of mildly mentally retarded and control children. *Developmental Medicine and Child Neurology*, *30*, 638–645.

Giannitrapani, D. (1969). EEG Average frequencies and intelligence. *Electroencephalography and Clinical Neurophysiology*, *27*, 480–486.

Giannitrapani, D. (1971). Scanning mechanisms and the EEG. *Electroencephalography and Clinical Neurophysiology*, *30*, 139–146.

Giannitrapani, D. (1985). *The electrophysiology of intellectual function*. Basel: S. Karger.

Griesel, R. D. (1973). A study of cognitive test performance in relationship to measures of speed in the encephalogram. *Psychologia Africana*, *15*, 41–52.

Gucker, D. K. (1973). Correlating visual evoked potentials with psychometric intelligence, variation in technique. *Perceptual and Motor Skills*, *37*, 189–190.

Haier, R. J., Robinson, D. L., Braden, W., & Williams, D. (1983). Electrical potentials of the cerebral cortex and psychometric intelligence. *Personality and Individual Differences*, *4*, 591–599.

Haier, R. J., Robinson, D. L., Braden, W., & Williams, D. (1984). Electrical potentials augmenting-reducing and personality differences. *Personality and Individual Differences*, *5*, 293–301.

Hendrickson, A. E. (1982). The biological basis of intelligence: Part 1: Theory. In H. J. Eysenck (Ed.), *A model for intelligence* (pp. 151–196). New York: Springer-Verlag.

Hendrickson, D. E. (1972). *An examination of individual differences in the cortical evoked response*. Unpublished doctoral thesis, University of London, England.

Hendrickson, D. E. (1982). The biological basis of intelligence. Part II: Measurement. In H. J. Eysenck (Ed.), *A model for intelligence* (pp. 197–228). New York: Springer-Verlag.

Hendrickson, D. E., & Hendrickson, A. E. (1980). The biological basis of individual differences in intelligence. *Personality and Individual Differences*, *1*, 3–33.

Howard, L., & Polich, J. (1985). P300 latency and memory span development. *Developmental Psychology*, *21*, 283–289.

Howe, M. J. A. (1988a). Intelligence as an explanation. *British Journal of Psychology*, *79*, 349–360.

Howe, M. J. A. (1988b). The hazard of using correlational evidence as a means of identifying the causes of individual ability differences: A rejoinder to Sternberg and a reply to Miles. *British Journal of Psychology*, *79*, 539–545.

Jensen, A. R., Schafer, E. W. P., & Crinella, F. M. (1981). Reaction time, evoked brain potentials, and psychometric *g* in the severely retarded. *Intelligence*, *5*, 179–197.

Juolasmaa, A., Toivakka, E., Outakoski, J., Sotaniemi, K., Tienari, P., & Hirvenoja, R. (1986). Relationship of quantitative EEG and cognitive test performance in patients with cardiac vascular disease. *Scandinavian Journal of Psychology*, *27*, 30–38.

Knott, J. R., Friedman, H., & Bardsley, R. (1942). Some electroencephalographic correlates of intelligence in eight-year and twelve-year old children. *Journal of Experimental Psychology, 30*, 380–391.

Kranzler, J. H., & Jensen, A. R. (1989). Inspection time and intelligence: A meta-analysis. *Intelligence, 13*, 329–347.

Kreezer, G., & Smith, F. W. (1950). The relation of the alpha rhythm of the EEG and intelligence level in the nondifferentiated familial type of mental deficiency. *Journal of Psychology, 29*, 47–51.

Lewis, E. G., Dustman, R. E., & Beck, E. C. (1972). Evoked response similarity in monozygotic, dizygotic, and unrelated individuals: A comparative study. *Electroencephalography and Clinical Neurophysiology, 32*, 309–316.

Liberson, W. T. (1989). Contribution to the hypothesis that one of the functions of brain waves is the frequency analysis of the incoming stimuli. *Journal of Clinical Neurophysiology, 6*, 292 (Abstract).

Mackenzie, B., & Bingham, E. (1985). IQ, inspection time and response strategies in a university population. *Australian Journal of Psychology, 37*, 257–268.

Mackenzie, B., & Cummings, S. (1986). Inspection time and apparent motion. *Personality and Individual Differences, 7*, 721–729.

Mackintosh, N. J. (1986). The biology of intelligence? *British Journal of Psychology, 77*, 1–18.

Mundy-Castle, A. C. (1958). Electophysiological correlates of intelligence. *Journal of Personality, 26*, 184–199.

Mundy-Castle, A. C., & Nelson, G. K. (1960). Intelligence, personality and brain rhythms in a socially isolated community. *Nature, 185*, 484–485.

Netchine, S., & Lairy, G-C. (1960). Ondes cérébrales et niveau mental: quelques aspects de l'évolution génétique du tracé EEG suivant le niveau. *Enfance, 13*, 427–439.

Nettelbeck, T. (1987). Inspection time and intelligence. In P.A. Vernon (Ed.), *Speed of information processing and intelligence* (pp. 295–346). Norwood, NJ: Ablex.

Osaka, O., & Osaka, N. (1980). Human intelligence and power spectral analysis of visual evoked potentials. *Perceptual and Motor Skills, 50*, 192–194.

Osborne, R. T. (1969). Psychometric correlates of the visual evoked potential. *Acta Psychologica, 29*, 303–308.

Oswald, W. F., & Roth, E. (1974). Zusammenhänge zwischen EEG- und Intelligenzvariablen. *Psychologische Beiträge, 16*, 1–47.

Polich, J. (1984). On P300 latency and correlational inference. *Psychophysiology, 21*, 710–711.

Polich, J., Howard, L., & Starr, A. (1983). P300 latency correlates with digit span. *Psychophysiology, 20*, 665–669.

Ray, W. J., Newcombe, N., Semon, J., & Cole, P. M. (1981). Spatial abilities, sex differences and EEG functioning. *Neuropsychologia, 19*, 719–722.

Rhodes, L., Dustman, R., & Beck, E. (1969). The visual evoked response: A comparison of bright and dull children. *Electroencephalography and Clinical Neurophysiology, 27*, 364–372.

Robinson, D. L. (1982a). Properties of the diffuse thalamocortical system and human personality: A direct test of Pavlovian/Eysenckian theory. *Personality and Individual Differences, 3*, 1–16.

Robinson, D. L. (1982b). Properties of the diffuse thalamocortical system, human intelligence and differentiated vs integrated modes of learning. *Personality and Individual Differences, 3*, 393–405.

Robinson, D. L. (1989). The neurophysiological basis of high IQ. *International Journal of Neuroscience*, *46*, 209–234.

Robinson, D. L., Haier, R. J., Braden, W., & Krengel, M. (1984). Psychometric intelligence and visual evoked potentials: A replication. *Personality and Individual Differences*, *5*, 487–489.

Rust, J. (1975a). Cortical evoked potential, personality and intelligence. *Journal of Comparative and Physiological Psychology*, *89*, 1220–1226.

Rust, J. (1975b). Genetic effects in the cortical auditory evoked potential: A twin study. *Electroencephalography and Clinical Neurophysiology*, *39*, 321–327.

Schafer, E. W. P. (1982). Neural adaptability: A biological determinant of behavioral intelligence. *International Journal of Neuroscience*, *17*, 183–191.

Schafer, E. W. P. (1984). Habituation of evoked cortical potentials correlates with intelligence. *Psychophysiology*, *21*, 597 (Abstract).

Schafer, E. W. P., & Peeke, H. V. (1982). Down syndrome individuals fail to habituate cortical evoked potentials. *American Journal of Mental Deficiency*, *87*, 332–337.

Shagass, C. (1946). An attempt to correlate the occipital alpha frequency of the encephalogram with performance on a mental ability test. *Journal of Experimental Psychology*, *36*, 88–92.

Shagass, C., Roemer, R. A., Straumanis, J. J., & Josiassen, R. C. (1981). Intelligence as a factor in evoked potential studies in psychopathology. 1. Comparison of low and high I.Q. subjects. *Biological Psychiatry*, *11*, 1007–1029.

Schenkenberg, T. (1970). *Visual, auditory, and somatosensory evoked responses of normal subjects from childhood to adolescence.* Unpublished doctoral thesis, University of Utah, Salt Lake City, UT.

Shucard, D., & Callaway, E. (1974). Auditory evoked potential amplitude and variability - effects of tasks and intellectual ability. *Journal of Comparative and Physiological Psychology*, *87*, 284–294.

Shucard, D., & Horn, J. (1972). Evoked cortical potentials and measurement of human abilities. *Journal of Comparative and Physiological Psychology*, *78*, 59–68.

Schucard, D., & Horn, J. (1973). Evoked potential amplitude change related to intelligence and arousal. *Psychophysiology*, *10*, 445–452.

Stough, C. K. K., Nettelbeck, T., & Cooper, C. J. (1990). Evoked brain potentials, string length and intelligence. *Personality and Individual Differences*, *11*, 401–406.

Sutton, J. P., Whitton, J. L., Topa, M., & Moldofsky, H. (1986). Evoked potential maps in learning disabled children. *Electroencephalography and Clinical Neurophysiology*, *65*, 399–404.

Surwillo, W. W. (1984). P300 latency and digit span. *Psychophysiology*, *21*, 708–709.

Thatcher, R. W., McAlaster, R., Lester, M. L., Horst, R. L., & Cantor, D. S. (1983). Hemispheric EEG asymmetries related to cognitive functioning in children. In E. Perecman (Ed.), *Cognitive Processing in the Right Hemisphere* (pp. 125–146). New York: Academic Press.

Thatcher, R. W., Walker, R. A., & Giudice, S. (1987). Human cerebral hemispheres develop at different rates and ages. *Science*, *236*, 1110–1113.

Vetterli, C. F., & Furedy, J. J. (1985). Evoked potential correlates of intelligence: Some problems with Hendrickson's string measure of evoked potential complexity and error theory of intelligence. *International Journal of Psychophysiology*, *3*, 1–3.

Vickers, D., Nettelbeck, T., & Willson, R. J. (1972). Perceptual indices of performance: The measurement of 'inspection time' and 'noise' in the visual system. *Perception, 1,* 263–295.

Vogel, W., & Broverman, D. M. (1964). Relationship between EEG and test intelligence: a critical review. *Psychological Bulletin, 62,* 132–144.

Vogel, W., Kruger, J., Schalt, E., Schnobel, R., & Hassling, L. (1987). No consistent relationships between oscillations and latencies of visually and auditory evoked EEG potentials and measures of mental performance. *Human Neurobiology, 6,* 173–182.

Vogel, W., Kun, K. J., Meshorerer, E., Broverman, D. M., & Klaiber, E. L. (1969). The behavioural significance of EEG abnormality in mental defectives. *American Journal of Mental Deficiency, 74,* 62–68.

Weinberg, H. (1969). Correlation of frequency spectra of averaged visual evoked potentials with verbal intelligence. *Nature, 224,* 813–814.

Weiss, V. (1987). The quantum mechanics of EEG-brain dynamics and short-term memory. *Biologisches Zentralblatt, 106,* 401–408.

Willis, S. G., Wheatley, G. H., & Mitchell, O. R. (1979). Cerebral processing of spatial and verbal-analytic tasks: An EEG study. *Neuropsychologia, 17,* 473–484.

Zhang, Y. (1987). *A study of the relationships between evoked potentials, inspection time and intelligence.* Unpublished doctoral thesis, University of Edinburgh, U.K.

Zhang, Y., Caryl, P. G., & Deary, I. J. (1989a). Evoked potential correlates of inspection time. *Personality and Individual Differences, 10,* 379–384.

Zhang, Y., Caryl, P. G., & Deary, I. J. (1989b). Evoked potentials, inspection time and intelligence. *Personality and Individual Differences, 10,* 1079–1094.

# Chapter 7

# *Cerebral Glucose Metabolism and Intelligence*

## *Richard J. Haier*

*Dept. of Psychiatry and Human Behavior*
*College of Medicine*
*University of California, Irvine*

Where in the brain is intelligence? Human neuropsychology research reveals that dramatic IQ decreases are not routinely associated with damage to any particular brain lobe or structure. Even frontal lobe psychosurgery produces little impairment in tests of general intelligence (see review by O'Callaghan & Carroll, 1982, pp. 103–105; see also Stuss & Benson, 1983, pp. 437–438). Brain damage often impacts specific abilities, but general processes, like those assumed to underlie intelligence, are less effected. In mental retardation, no brain abnormality is apparent in over 50% of the cases (see review by McLaren & Bryson, 1987). Where the cause of mental retardation is known, often some diffuse abnormality of brain development is implicated. Why does there seem to be no relationship between specific brain damage and IQ? One major limitation for research in this area has been the lack of a way to measure brain function directly in humans. Also, the brain organization coordinating many areas may be more important for intelligence than the functioning of any one area, since complex tasks require performance from more than one part of the brain. The use of different cognitive strategies, each dependent on separate brain areas or on areas integrated differently, may also underlie intelligence differences. Measuring the functional relationships among different brain areas, therefore, is necessary in addition to studying the structural connections among brain areas.

The advent of Positron Emission Tomography (PET) provides a powerful tool for the *in vivo* investigation of brain/intelligence functional relationships. Because PET makes direct measures of function throughout cortical and subcortical areas, it is the latest and most powerful technology for the study of the biological basis of intelligence. This chapter reviews the use of PET to study general intelligence. The area is new and still small, but even the early results reported to date are intriguing. The concept of brain "efficiency" reoccurs throughout the reporting of PET/intelligence data so it is introduced next.

## EFFICIENCY

Researchers investigating the biological correlates of *g* (i.e., the general factor common to many tests of various cognitive abilities first proposed by Spearman) have noted strong associations with reaction time during complex tasks (see Jensen 1985; Jensen, Cohn, & Cohn, 1989; Cohen, Carlson, & Jensen, 1985). Faster reaction time goes with higher intelligence. Vernon (1985) has reviewed this large literature and concluded that a general factor of neural efficiency is a major aspect of psychometric IQ, since faster basic processing reflected by short reaction time characterizes more intelligent subjects. He notes that efficiency can occur at three levels: the speed of processing information, adaptability of allocating limited neural resources, and yet to be identified biological processes (p. 146).

Similarly, Ahern and Beatty (1979) argued for an efficiency model based on their finding of greater task-evoked eye pupil dilation (a sign of increased cognitive capacity used during a cognitive task) in low intelligence subjects. They reasoned that the smaller dilations shown in the high intelligence group indicated less brain effort and more efficient processing. Vernon (1989) has reported recently that nerve conduction velocity measured in the arm is correlated with intelligence in the direction consistent with an efficiency model; the faster the conduction velocity the higher the intelligence. This has not been replicated, however, in all studies (Reed & Jensen, 1991).

Efficiency was a key concept in early evoked potential (EP) research. Chalke and Ertl (1965) found short latencies went with higher IQ and argued that fast minds would have short latencies. Schafer's interpretation of evoked potential correlates of intelligence (Schafer, 1982) also focused on efficiency. He reported that smaller EPs to unexpected stimuli were found in brighter subjects. An index of this "neural adaptability" based on EP's was correlated with IQ ($r = .66$).

For Schafer, neural adaptability implied both the efficient inhibiting of response to insignificant inputs and the vigorous orientation to unexpected stimuli. He suggested that, "A brain that uses fewer neurons (smaller EP amplitude) to process a foreknown sensory input saves its limited neural energy and functions in an inherently efficient manner" (p. 184). Unfortunately, although the EEG/EP and intelligence literature is extensive (and will not be reviewed more fully here), it lacks sufficient methodology standardization and replication of findings to be compelling (see Callaway, 1975; Chapter 6 by Deary and Caryl; Gale & Edwards, 1983). PET provides greater accuracy of anatomic localization, although time resolution, cost, and repeatability of electrophysiological measures are clearly superior (see also Chapter 6). PET studies of intelligence, however, can build on the EEG/EP work.

According to Maxwell, Fenwick, Fenton, and Dollimore (1974), one of the earliest brain efficiency concepts is implied in Thomson's (1939) model of brain function. Thomson proposed that the brain has a large number of components (e.g., neurons), and that cognitive test performance requires a random sampling of the components. For a test of general ability, all the components would be sampled, whereas a test of a specific ability would require sampling a subset of components. On the basis of Thomson's model, Maxwell et al. (1974) factor analyzed 10 subtests of the WPPSI in a sample of 150 7-year-old children. They did separate analyses in the group of children with good reading scores and in the group with poor reading scores. As expected three factors were predominant: a general factor, a verbal factor, and a performance factor. The theory was that a general cognitive factor would reflect a large number of neurons sampled from many brain areas, whereas factors of more specific abilities would reflect subgroups of neurons. Factor loadings were expected to estimate the proportions of neurons involved in the general and the specific factors. Maxwell et al. found that factor score loadings on the general factor were larger in the poor reading group, suggesting that more neurons were involved; in fact the verbal factor was weak in the poor group. The larger loadings on the general factor were seen as compensatory. They concluded that the lower factor loadings on the general factor in the good readers was evidence for brain efficiency. These data are shown in Table 7.1. Maxwell et al. note that their data "proposes the surprising hypothesis that high test scores or efficient cognitive functioning require fewer neurons for its elaboration than is otherwise the case" (p. 280). Detterman and Daniel (1989) and Jensen (personal communication) report findings that replicate Maxwell's important and original (but under cited) work.

These diverse findings, for the most part, are consistent with an association between inefficient brain activity and low psychometric IQ, although much remains to be learned about specific features of brain organization, development, and cognitive ability. For example, Diamond, Scheibel, Murphy, and Harvey (1985) have reported that Albert Einstein's brain showed a statistically smaller neuron:glial ratio in the left area 39 compared to 11 control brains. This area is

Table 7.1. Loadings on Three Factors in Good and Poor Readers
(from Maxwell et al., 1974)

| Tests | Good readers | | | Poor readers | | |
|---|---|---|---|---|---|---|
| | I | II | III | I | II | III |
| 1. Information | 213 | | 702 | 805 | | 165 |
| 2. Vocabulary | 291 | | 532 | 831 | | 026 |
| 3. Arithmetic | 554 | | 281 | 740 | 226 | |
| 4. Similarities | 531 | | 192 | 609 | | 273 |
| 5. Comprehension | 298 | 237 | 619 | 797 | | |
| 6. Animal House | 329 | 327 | | 304 | | 731 |
| 7. Picture Completion | 398 | 448 | | 635 | 297 | 246 |
| 8. Mazes | 224 | 665 | | 491 | 643 | |
| 9. Geometric Design | 298 | 288 | | 393 | 309 | |
| 10. Block Design | 675 | 377 | | 558 | 490 | 292 |

thought to be important to verbal associations and conceptual ability; Einstein's brain apparently had more glial support cells suggesting a "greater neuronal metabolic need" (p. 203) in this area, one of only four areas studied. Alternatively, Einstein's left area 39 might have had fewer neurons that worked more efficiently. The work of Schiebel (1987) suggests that more dendrite complexity may be found in brain areas associated with higher cognitive tasks. Efficiency of function, however, may not be predictable from structural features. This brings us to the use of PET, a functional imaging technique.

## POSITRON EMISSION TOMOGRAPHY

Brain imaging with positron emission tomography (PET) has the capability to survey functional activity throughout the brain. With F-18 deoxyglucose (FDG) as a tracer of glucose metabolic rate, brain work can be quantified. This analytical tool is based on the close coupling of local neural activity and glucose metabolism in normal brain as demonstrated by Sokoloff (1981) using autoradiography with 2-deoxyglucose in animals. It has adequate resolution to view both individual gyri of the cortex and discrete portions of the basal ganglia, limbic system, and other subcortical areas (see Phelps et al., 1979).

PET works in a conceptually simple way. The tracer includes a positron emitter like Fluorine 18 or Oxygen 15. Each emitted positron collides with an electron to produce two gamma rays that travel in opposite directions 180 degrees apart from the point of each positron annihilation. After injection of the tracer and uptake by the brain, the head is placed in a ring of gamma ray detectors (i.e., the PET scanner), and every simultaneous detection at two points in the ring 180 degrees apart is counted.

A large number of these coincidence counts from all points around the ring enter a mathematical reconstruction producing a slicelike view of brain metabolic activity. This is because greater activity requires more glucose use or blood flow which provide greater isotope concentration. For the FDG used in many studies it takes about 30–35 minutes for the brain to use the tracer and be labeled; 0–15 is used to image blood flow and has an uptake period of about 40 seconds. The resulting PET scan shows cumulative brain function over this period. For many complex psychological processes, this cumulative activity over 35 minutes is desirable since it strengthens signal-to-noise effects. Moreover, metabolic rate labeled with FDG can be quantified using the Sokoloff (Sokoloff et al., 1977) model of cerebral glucose use. Note that the subject need not be in the scanner during the uptake period; this allows for increased control and flexibility of the uptake task. Only after the uptake period does the subject move into the scanner, but the scans show brain function during the 30–35 minutes following injection of the isotope tracer not brain activity while lying in the scanner. Because the uptake period is sensitive to the task being performed, PET, by its very nature, is fundamentally a psychological technology.

## PET Studies of Intelligence

PET studies in normals support the efficiency concept, but PET studies in brain damaged patients show opposite effects. Chase et al. (1984) reported PET/FDG data on 17 Alzheimer's patients and 5 normals. They correlated the subjects' WAIS scores with regional cortical glucose use; no subcortical areas were reported. All subjects rested with eyes closed during FDG uptake; the WAIS was administered independently of the PET scan. Data for all 22 subjects were reported together; no separate correlations for the 5 normals were given. In general, verbal WAIS subtests correlated positively with glucose in left hemisphere parasylvian areas, whereas performance scores correlated positively in right hemisphere posterior parietal areas. The digit symbol substitution subtest correlated positively with glucose in the frontal lobes bilaterally. These results (shown in Figure 7.1) were consistent with other earlier regional cerebral blood flow studies in brain damaged patients (Butler, Dickinson, Katholi, & Halsey,1983), indicating more increased flow went with cognitive activation. In other words, the more the brain activity, the better the cognitive performance. However, the Chase et al. study and a similar PET study of seven Alzheimer's patients (Ferris et al., 1980) looked at patients with considerable brain degeneration. The positive correlations with glucose use likely reflect mostly the extent of brain damage and not necessarily the relationship between quality of performance and brain work in the physiological normal brain. This is especially so because the PET scans reported by Chase et al. were done with the subject resting during uptake.

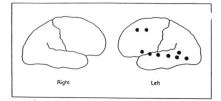

(a) Correlation between Wechsler Adult Intelligence Scale verbal IQ scores and local cerebral metabolic rates for glucose. Closed circles indicate significance at $P <$ .0002.

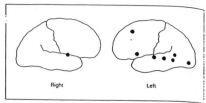

(b) Correlations between scores on vocabulary subtest and local rates of glucose metabolism. Closed circles indicate significance at $P <$ .0002.

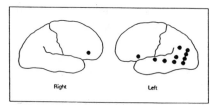

(c) Correlations between scores on arithmetic subtest and local rates of glucose metabolism. Closed circles indicate significance at $P <$ .005.

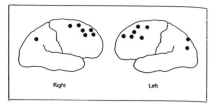

(d) Correlations between scores on digit span subtest and local rates of glucose metabolism. Closed circles indicate significance at $P <$ .02.

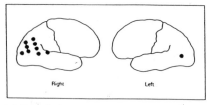

(e) Correlations between Wechsler Adult Intelligence Scale performance IQ scores and local rates of glucose metabolism. Closed circles indicate significance at $P <$ .001.

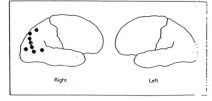

(f) Correlations between scores on block design subtest and local rates of glucose metabolism. Closed circles indicate significance at $P <$ .005.

**Figure 7.1.   PET/glucose data in Alzheimer's patients & controls (from Chase et al., 1984)**

Haier et al. (1988) reported PET/FDG data on eight normal males performing the Ravens Advanced Progressive Matrices (RAPM) during the FDG uptake. Other matched subjects doing the degraded stimulus Continuous Performance Test (CPT) (Neuchterlein, Parasuramam, & Jiang, 1983) and a control task were compared to the RAPM group. The RAPM is a difficult nonverbal test of abstract reasoning, highly loaded on $g$ (Vernon, 1983; Paul, 1986). It was chosen specifically for its relevance to intelligence measurement. A four-way ANOVA (task group × hemisphere × slice level × cortical sector) showed a group ×

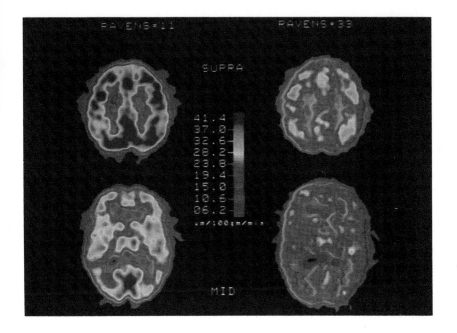

**Figure 7.2.   PET in high and low RAPM scoring subjects
(from Haier et al., 1988)**

hemisphere × cortical sector significant interaction. Post hoc t-tests showed the left posterior portions of the cortex were higher in the RAPM group, consistent with Luria's (1973) model of localization of abstract reasoning. Milner (1964) also indicated that lesions in this area had the largest effects on IQ. However, the major finding of the PET study was that scores on the RAPM were inversely correlated with absolute glucose throughout the cortex; similar correlations did not exist for CPT performance and glucose. The widespread inverse correlations (statistically significant ones ranging between −.72 and −.84; $p<$ .05) were taken to be consistent with neural efficiency theories of intelligence, since high scores on the RAPM went with low cortical glucose use (see Figure 7.2).

This analysis was based on three PET slices (supra-, mid-, and infraventricular) and four equal area cortical peel sectors in each hemisphere for each slice. Although this automated scheme allowed reasonable localization of cortical areas, it is not anatomically exact. A newer system combines all nine PET slices obtained from each person and stereotaxic demarcations of the major lobes and their gyri (see Buchsbaum et al., 1989). This system is an improvement over the system used in the original 1988 report. The 1988 data, therefore, have been reanalyzed with this improved system (Haier et al., 1992a).

The new analyses are shown in Table 7.2. Correlations between absolute glucose use and scores on the RAPM are still negative throughout the cortex, but the anatomically improved analysis now reveals that most of the significant correlations are in the temporal lobes. Areas 18 and 19 in the occipital lobes and the superior frontal cortex also show significant inverse correlations with RAPM scores. The largest lobe median correlation is in the left temporal, and the lowest is in the right superior parietal lobe. This suggests that the more left temporal-based verbal mediation strategies are used, the worse the performance. It may be that high performers on the RAPM use a right parietal strategy. Brain efficiency may partly reflect such a strategy preference (see Haier et al., 1992a). Possibly, a high $g$ score or a high factor loading on $g$ reflects the use of a general verbal strategy, even when a more task specific strategy is optimal. The reanalysis also included ANOVA's which confirmed frontal and temporal involvement for performance on the RAPM.

In a similar PET study, Parks, Loewenstein, and Dodrill (1988) used a verbal fluency test (subjects say all the words they can think of starting with a given letter) during FDG uptake in 16 normals scanned as part of investigations into neuropsychology. Compared to another normal group studied while resting with eyes closed (no uptake task), the verbal fluency task showed increased cortical activation, especially in temporal and frontal lobes bilaterally. Glucose use went up about 23% overall during the verbal fluency task. Like Haier et al. (1988), correlations between glucose and performance of the task were negative. In frontal, temporal, and parietal cortex regions the correlations between glucose and scores on the test were −.54, −.50, and −.54, respectively ($p < .05$). Verbal fluency, like the RAPM, is highly loaded on $g$. It should be noted that this

Table 7.2. Anatomically Refined Analysis of RAPM Data
(Haier et al., submitted) (glucose/RAPM correlations;
$N = 8$, absolute data)

|  | Left | Right |
|---|---|---|
| Frontal cortex | | |
| superior | −.74 | −.76 |
| mid | −.55 | −.58 |
| inferior | −.47 | −.68 |
| precentral | −.34 | −.34 |
| Parietal | | |
| post central | −.55 | −.52 |
| supra marginal | −.49 | −.39 |
| angular gyrus | −.17 | −.14 |
| superior parietal | −.38 | −.12 |
| Temporal | | |
| superior | −.84 | −.85 |
| mid | −.87 | −.83 |
| inferior | −.92 | −.73 |
| posterior | .32 | −.49 |
| Occipital | | |
| area 19 | −.75 | −.72 |
| area 17 | −.60 | −.38 |
| inferior 17 | −.63 | −.60 |
| lateral 18 | −.92 | −.75 |

Note: $r >$: .71 $p < .05$, 2-tailed
.79 $p < .02$, 2-tailed
.83 $p < .01$, 2-tailed

study analyzed relative glucose (area glucose divided by occiput glucose) and used a different way of defining cortical areas than Haier et al., but the results are very similar. Parks et al. also argued that the finding of inverse correlations implied an efficiency theory of cognitive performance.

Berent et al. (1988) reported Wechsler Memory Scale and WAIS-R subtest correlations with subcortical glucose use (right and left averaged together for each structure) in 15 Huntington's patients and in 14 normal controls. PET scans with FDG were obtained during a resting state (no uptake task) and the WAIS had been completed prior to the scan. Correlations were positive in the patient group ($n = 15$), consistent with Ferris et al. and with Chase et al. As noted, this can be interpreted as a relationship to degrees of brain damage and possibly not relevant to functional/intelligence relationships. In the normal controls ($n = 14$), however, almost all correlations were negative and statistically significant for the digit symbol/putamen relationship ($r = -.68, p < .01$). It is of interest that a similar subcortical analysis of the RAPM group reported by Haier et al. (submitted) shows a significant putamen/RAPM correlation bilaterally ( − .80 on the left; − .77 right), replicating Berent et al. on this specific finding (the caudate data are similar as well, although not quite significant in Berent et al.). Berent et al. noted the negative direction as an important observation that suggested further work on the functional relationships among brain areas in normal groups. No cortical data were reported, although inverse correlations between glucose use and WAIS subtests were observed in the normal group (Giordani, 1989, personal communication). Thus, the only 3 PET studies to date reporting data in normals correlating glucose use with intelligence measures find inverse correlations, despite procedural and methodological differences among the studies.

Parks et al. (1989) have reviewed other PET/cognition reports and expanded the efficiency concept. They propose a systems efficiency model of neuro-psychological function with four components: brain chemistry, cortical structural integrity, topographical distribution of neural networks, and strategies of cognition. This model recognizes the importance of the functional relationships among brain areas and the many possible ways efficiency can be attained by a complex system like the brain. Their focus is broader than intelligence, but as empirical data accumulate, especially PET data (see Haier, 1987), the efficiency concept may prove useful for a range of cognitive processes relevant to neuropsychology and intelligence research.

For example, we conducted a study addressing whether complex learning results in lower cerebral glucose use, implying that learning makes brain circuits more efficient. Kintsch (1965) demonstrated that galvanic skin response decreased as items were learned, suggesting that practice decreases processing load of retrieval and increases automatic and efficient processing. In our learning study, each normal subject received FDG while playing a complex computer game for the first time. The game, Tetris, requires visual spatial ability, strategy, and motor coordination. After the first PET scan, the subject practiced the game for 30 to 45 minutes a day for 30–60 days. Performance increased an average of sevenfold. Then each subject was scanned a second time, again receiving the FDG while playing. On the basis of inverse correlations between cortical glucose use and scores on the RAPM, we hypothesized a decrease in glucose from scan one to scan two. The analyses on eight normal male subjects showed less cortical glucose use on the second scan, consistent with the efficiency concept (Haier, Siegel, MacLachlan, Soderling, Lottenberg, & Buchsbaum, 1992). Additional analyses (Haier, Siegel, Tang, Abel, & Buchsbaum, 1992) indicate that the size of the glucose change with learning is correlated with RAPM and WAIS-R scores (high intelligence scores going with biggest glucose decreases). Further, it may also be possible to quantify the relationship between cerebral regional glucose use and mental performance. For example, does the recalling of 5 items use half or twice the glucose in a specific region that recalling 10 items takes? Work in progress at UCI addresses such potential brain/cognition equations.

## PET AND MENTAL RETARDATION

Huttenlocher (1979) demonstrated that synaptic density increases markedly in the first 5 years of life, but then a dramatic decrease occurs throughout the early teen years. This "neural pruning" is a central developmental feature of the normal brain, but its mechanism is largely unknown. Some researchers have speculated that a failure of neural pruning may result in too many redundant synaptic connections and abnormal brain organization. This may be the cause of some cases of mental retardation. Consistent with this idea, Cragg (1975) reported three cases of mental retardation where higher than normal rates of synaptic density were found at autopsy. Huttenlocher (1974) also reports such a case. Together, these observations suggest that individual differences in intelligence, defined as psychometric IQ, may be rooted in individual differences in brain organizational development.

Normal brain development has been studied with PET cross-sectionally in children (Chagani, Phelps, & Mazziotta, 1987). Cerebral glucose use increases with age from birth to about age 5 where the rate is approximately twice that of normal adults. Mirroring the Huttenlocher curve of synaptic density, glucose use falls off dramatically from age 5 through the early teen years. Similar glucose curves were reported for all areas of the brain studied, including frontal cortex. This indicates a close relationship between the development of structure and function.

Would the fall-off in glucose use after age 5 be missing in mentally retarded cases? Only a small number of Down's patients have been studied with PET, and they have higher cerebral glucose use than normals (Schwartz, Duara, Haxby, & Grady, 1983). One case of Down's at an older age showed lower glucose (Schapiro, Ball, Grady, Haxby, Kaye, & Rapoport, 1988), but this may reflect the severe Alzheimer's dementia present. Autism, usually showing decreased IQ, also has been associated with higher than normal glucose use with PET (Rumsey et al., 1985). A number of severely retarded cases have undergone PET at UCLA and most of them, especially those with cerebral palsy, show lower than normal glucose (Chagani, personal communication) as would be expected with brain damage. No complete study of PET and mental retardation in the moderate range or in cases of unknown etiology has been published. We have begun such a study; preliminary analyses show higher glucose use than in controls.

We have recently used FDG and the CPT for scanning a patient with Olivoponto cerebellar degeneration, a disease of the brain stem. This patient's IQ has been declining steadily since diagnosis, consistent with the disease. At the time of the PET scan, the patient had an IQ in the moderately retarded range, down from the normal range assessed five years before. During the FDG uptake, the patient was to do the CPT but the d' was low; the number of total button presses was small and random. Comparisons, therefore, were made not only to our reference group of normals doing the CPT, but also to our reference group of normals in the no-task condition (the subject watches the same stimuli as in the CPT task condition, but receives no instructions regarding a target stimulus or button pressing). Compared to the task group, this patient had cortical relative glucose rates in the normal range; brain stem areas were low. However, compared to the no-task group, the patient showed higher cortical relative rates (2 sd's > the mean) in the inferior frontal lobes and frontal white matter. Of interest, areas of the anterior cingulate gyrus, the putamen, the amygdala, and the mid-corpus callosum also were 2 sds higher in this patient. These values suggest that trying, but failing to do the task, resulted in as much brain activity as normals performing the task well, and in more brain activity than normals not even doing the task. In this case, the brain may be undergoing a kind of compensation for the damaged areas which results in more, inefficient activity.

A major question about mental retardation can be addressed with PET, namely, is mental retardation associated only with brain tissue damage or with abnormal brain organization? In cases where mental retardation results from damage to brain tissue, we would expect glucose to be lower in salient areas. A positive correlation would exist between IQ and glucose use in patients with a range of damage studied. However, if brain organization was different in mental retardation, brain areas not traditionally associated with cognitive ability might be higher than normal, or if diffuse redundancy occurred because of a lack of neural pruning, a negative correlation between glucose use and performance may occur.

We expect that among cases of mental retardation with unknown etiology, widespread, higher than normal, cerebral glucose use will be found, consistent with the efficiency model of intelligence. We also anticipate that the normal neuropsychology-related associations between specific brain areas and specific cognitive functions will not uniformly hold for mental retardation, consistent with the view that brain organization differs in mental retardation. Evidence for either hypothesis would have implications for training and treatment programs.

## CREATIVITY AND EXCEPTIONAL ABILITIES

Another side of the speculative efficiency/neural pruning argument in mental retardation is suggested by the hyperpruning illustrated in Figure 7.3. If a failure of pruning can result in inefficient neural circuitry, overpruning may result in especially efficient function. This could be manifest as high $g$, or if the hyperpruning was confined to a specific brain area or to a critical period of development, exceptional specific cognitive abilities could result. Mathematics, music, foreign language skills, or even the savant type of calculating or calendar computation skills come to mind (see Obler & Fein, 1988). Sex differences in cognitive abilities can also be thought about in this context. An interesting PET

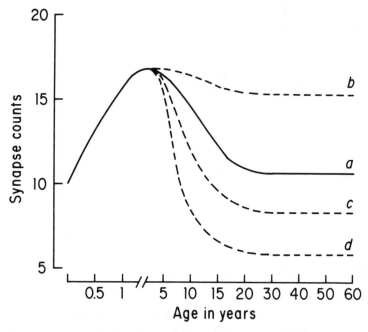

**Figure 7.3. Huttenlocher's synaptic count curve plus hypothetical results of neural pruning failures**

Legend: (a) shows Huttenlocher's curve of synaptic density; (b) shows hypothesized lack of neural pruning in some cases of mental retardation; (c) shows hypothesized over pruning in giftedness; (d) shows hypothesized superpruning in psychiatric disorder.

study, for example, could compare men and women matched for superior SAT math score while they performed math problems during FDG uptake. Such PET data could reveal whether men and women use the same brain areas equally hard or efficiently to do math (see Benbow, 1988). Sex differences and heritability in the pruning mechanism need to be investigated.

It is tempting to continue this speculative train of thought to a possible link between creativity and psychopathology. Andreasen (1987) has reviewed the literature on whether these domains are linked. Her data and other family studies suggest a relationship (see also Coryell et al., 1989). For the argument advanced here, failure or abnormality of the neural pruning mechanism may define the "fine line" between madness and genius depending on the degree or rate of overpruning. Overpruning may result in the high intelligence often associated with creativity, but supersevere hyperpruning may result in psychopathology. Schizophrenia, for example, is associated with lower glucose metabolic rates in the frontal lobes (hypofrontality) and reduced basal ganglia activity as assessed by PET (see review by Buchsbaum & Haier, 1987). Whether this is a result of developmental overpruning or some other damage is not known (see Murray,

Lewis, Owen, & Foerster, 1988). PET data can be useful in testing hypotheses about these seemingly different domains (see also discussion by Chen & Buckley, 1988, and chapter by Waterhouse, 1988).

## CONCLUSIONS

Cerebral glucose studies are few and limited in scope compared to the other intelligence research literatures. Early data appear consistent in supporting an efficiency concept of intelligence, although there are many possible neural routes to efficiency; neural pruning is not the only one and at this point, it is quite speculative. Strategy preferences, as possibly shown in the RAPM data, may reflect another kind of efficiency.

The potential power of PET is great for elucidating intelligence and cognitive processing questions. To the extent that $g$ or specific abilities may be localized (see Gazzaniga, 1989), PET can determine the localization. Moreover, the functional relationship among brain areas can be determined with PET. The pattern of correlations of glucose use among brain areas can be factor-analyzed, or clustered, or treated with other multivariate statistical approaches. In this way, the salient organizational structure for specific brain functions can be identified and compared among groups of interest. Individual differences are particularly amenable to PET, as demonstrated in the RAPM study. Finally, because PET can quantify metabolic rate, a new kind of study is possible where equations between brain energy use and mental performance can be developed and tested. These applications require sample sizes larger than any reported in the PET literature to date. The cost and complexity of PET are formidable, but the benefits for research are so enticing that PET access must be a long-term priority for intelligence researchers.

## REFERENCES

Ahern, S., & Beatty, J. (1979). Pupillary responses during information processing vary with scholastic aptitude scores. *Science, 205,* 1289–1292.

Andreasen, N. (1987). Creativity and mental illness: Prevalence rates in writers and their first degree relatives. *American Journal of Psychiatry, 144,* 1288–1292.

Benbow, C. P. (1988). Sex differences in mathematical reasoning ability in intellectually talented preadolescents: Their nature, effects, and possible causes. *Behavioral & Brain Sciences, 11,* 169–232.

Berent, S., Giordani, B., Lehtinen, S., Markel, D., Penney, J. B., Buchtel, H.A., Starosta-Rubinstein, S., Hichwa, R., & Young, A. B. (1988). Positron Emission Tomographic scan investigations of Huntington's Disease: Cerebral metabolic correlates of cognitive function. *Annals of Neurology, 232*(6), 541–546.

Buchsbaum, M. S., Gillin, C., Wu, J., Hazlett, E., Sicotte, N., Dupont, R. M., & Bunney, W. E. (1989). Regional cerebral glucose metabolic rate in human sleep assessed by positron emission tomography. *Life Sciences, 45,* 1349–1356.

Buchsbaum, M. S., & Haier, R. J. (1987). Functional and anatomical brain imaging: Impact on schizophrenia research. *Schizophrenia Bulletin, 13*, 115–132.

Butler, M. S., Dickinson, W. A., Katholi, C., & Halsey, J. H. (1983). The comparative effects of organic brain disease on cerebral blood flow and measured intelligence. *Annals of Neurology, 13*, 155–159.

Callaway, E. (1975). *Brain electric potentials and individual psychological differences.* New York: Grune & Stratton.

Chen, A. C., & Buckley, K. C. (1988). Neural perspectives of cerebral correlates of giftedness. *International Journal of Neuroscience, 41*, 115–125.

Chase, T. N., Fedio, P., Foster, N. L., Brooks, R., Di Chiro, G., & Mansi, L. (1984). Weschler Adult Intelligence Scale performance: Cortical localization by flurodeoxyglucoseF18-Positron Emission Tomography. *Archives of Neurology, 41*, 1244–1247.

Chagani, H. T., Phelps, M. E., & Mazziotta, J. C. (1987). Positron Emission Tomography study of the human brain functional development. *Annals of Neurology, 22*(4), 487–497.

Chalke, F. C. R., & Ertl, J. P. (1965). Evoked potentials and intelligence. *Life Sciences, 4*, 1319–1322.

Cohen, S. J., Carlson, J. S., & Jensen, A. R. (1985). Speed of information processing in academically gifted youths. *Personality and Individual Differences, 6*, 621–629.

Coryell, W., Endicott, J., Keller, M., Andreasen, N., Grove, W., Hirschfeld, R. M., & Scheftner, W. (1989). Bipolar affective disorder and high achievement: A familial association. *American Journal of Psychiatry, 146*, 983–988.

Cragg, B. G. (1975). The density of synapses and neurons in normal, mentally defective and aging brains. *Brain, 98*, 81–90.

Diamond, M. C., Scheibel, A. B., Murphy, G. M., & Harvey, T. (1985). On the brain of a scientist: Albert Einstein. *Experimental Neurology, 88*, 198–204.

Detterman, D. K., & Daniel, M. H. (1989). Correlations of mental tests with each other and with cognitive variables are highest for low IQ groups. *Intelligence, 13*, 349–359.

Ferris, S. H., DeLeon, M. J., Wolf, A. P., Farkas, T., Christman, D. R., Reisberg, B., Fowler, J. S., MacGregor, R., Goldman, A., George, A. E., & Rampal, S. (1980). Positron Emission Tomography in the study of aging and senile dementia. *Neurobiology of Aging, 1*, 127–131.

Gale, A., & Edwards, J. (1983). Cortical correlates of intelligence. In A. Gale & J. Edwards (Eds.), *Physiological correlates of human behavior* (Vol. 3). London: Academic Press.

Gazzaniga, M. S. (1989). Organization of the human brain. *Science, 245*, 947–952.

Haier, R. J. (1987). The brain is back but is neuropsychology in the future? *Contemporary Psychology, 32*, 236–237.

Haier, R. J., LaFalase, J., Katz, M., & Buchsbaum, M. S. (submitted). Brain efficiency and intelligence: Inverse correlations between cerebral glucose metabolic rate and abstract reasoning.

Haier, R. J., Siegel, B. V., Jr., MacLachlan, A., Soderling, E., Lottenberg, S., & Buchsbaum, M. S. (1992). Regional glucose metabolic changes after learning a complex visuospatial/motor task: A positron emission tomographic study. *Brain Research, 570*, 134–143.

Haier, R. J., Siegel, B., Jr., Nuechterlein, K. H., Hazlet, E., Wu, J., Paek, J., Browning, H., & Buchsbaum, M. S. (1988). Cortical glucose metabolic rate correlates of abstract reasoning and attention studied with Positron Emission Tomography. *Intelligence*, *12*, 199–217.

Haier, R. J., Siegel, B., Tang, C., Abel, L., & Buchsbaum , M. S. (1992). Intelligence and changes in regional cerebral glucose metabolic rate following learning. *Intelligence*, *16*, 415–426.

Huttenlocher, P. R. (1974, March). Dendrite development in neocortex of children with mental defect and infantile spasms. *Neurology*, pp. 203–210.

Huttenlocher, P. R. (1979). Synaptic density in human frontal cortex-developmental changes and effects of aging. *Brain Research*, *163*, 195–205.

Jensen, A. R. (1985). Methodological and statistical techniques for the chronometric study of mental abilities. In Reynolds & Wilson (Eds.) *Methodological and statistical advances in the study of individual differences*. New York: Plenum Press.

Jensen, A. R., Cohn, S. J., & Cohn, C. M. G. (1989). Speed of information processing in academically gifted youths and their siblings. *Personality and Individual Differences*, *10*(1), 29–33.

Kintsch, W. (1965). Habituation of the GSR component of the orienting reflex during paired-associate learning before and after learning has taken place. *Journal of Mathematical Psychology*, *2*, 330–341.

Luria, A. R. (1973). *The working brain. An introduction to neuropsychology*. London: Penguin Press.

Maxwell, A. E., Fenwick, P. B. C., Fenton, G. W., & Dollimore, J. (1974). Reading ability and brain function: A simple statistical model. *Psychological Medicine*, *4*, 274–280.

McLaren, J., & Bryson, S. E. (1987). Review of recent epidemiological studies of mental retardation: Prevalence, Associated Disorders, and Etiology. *American Journal of Mental Retardation*, *92*(3), 243–254.

Milner, B. (1964). Some effects of frontal lobectomy in man. In J. M. Warren & K. Akert (Eds.), *The frontal granular cortex and behavior* (pp 313–334). New York: McGraw-Hill.

Murray, R. M., Lewis, S. W., Owen, M. J., & Foerster, A. (1988). Neurodevelopmental origins of dementia praecox. In P. Bebbington & P. McGuffin (Eds.), *Schizophrenia: The major issue*. London: Heinemann.

Nuechterlein, K. H., Parasuraman, R., & Jiang, Q. (1983). Visual sustained attention: Image degradation produces rapid decrement over time. *Science*, *220*, 327–329.

Obler, L. K., & Fein, D. (Eds.). (1988). *The exceptional brain*. New York: Guilford Press.

O'Callaghan, M. A., & Carroll, D. (1982). *Psychosurgery: A scientific analysis*. New Jersey: George A. Bogden & Son, Inc.

Parks, R. W., Loewenstein, D. A., Dodrill, K. L., Barker, W. W., Yoshii, F., Chang, J. Y., Emran, A., Apicella, A., Sheramata, W., & Duara, R. (1988). Cerebral metabolic effects of a verbal fluency test: A PET scan study. *Journal of Clinical and Experimental Neuropsychology*, *10*(5), 565–575.

Parks, R. W., Crockett, D. J., Tuokko, H., Beattie, B. L., Ashford, J. W., Coburn, K. L., Zec, R. F., Becker, R. E., McGeer, P. L., & McGeer, E. G. (1989).

Neuropsychological "systems efficiency" and positron emission tomography. *Journal of Neuropsychiatry, 1,* 269–282.

Paul, S. M. (1986). The Advanced Raven's Progressive Matrices: Normative data for an American university population and an examination of the relationship with Spearman's *g*. *Journal of Experimental Education, 54,* 95–100.

Phelps, M. E., Huang, S. C., Hoffman, E. J., Selin, C., Sokoloff, L., & Kuhl, D. E. (1979). Tomographic measurement of local cerebral glucose metabolic rate in humans with (F-18) 2-fluoro-2Deoxy-D-glucose: Validation of method. *Annals of Neurology, 6,* 371–388.

Reed, T. E., & Jensen, A. R. (1991). Arm nerve conduction velocity (NCV), brain NCV, reaction time, and intelligence, *Intelligence, 15,* 33–47.

Rumsey, J. M., Duara, R., Grady, C., Rapoport, J. L., Margolin, R. A., Rapoport, S. I., & Cutler, N. R. (1985). Brain metabolism in autism: Resting cerebral glucose utilization rates as measured with Positron Emission Tomography. *Archives of General Psychiatry, 42,* 448–455.

Schafer, E. W. P. (1982). Neural adaptability: A biological determinant of behavioral intelligence. *International Journal of Neuroscience, 17,* 133–191.

Schapiro, M. B., Ball, M. J., Grady, C. L., Haxby, J. V., Kaye, J. A., & Rapoport, S. I. (1988). Dementia in Down's syndrome: Cerebral glucose utilization, neuropsychological assessment, and neuropathology. *Neurology, 38,* 938–942.

Scheibel, A. B. (1987). Valiant Neurons and Inexorable Aging. *Neurobiology of Aging, 8,* 548–549.

Schwartz, M., Duara, R., Haxby, J., & Grady, C. (1983). Down's syndrome in adults: Brain metabolism. *Science, 221,* 781–783.

Sokoloff, L. (1981). Relationships among local functional activity, energy metabolism, and blood flow in the central nervous system. *Proceedings from the Symposium Regulation of the Cerebral Circulation, 40,* 2311–2316.

Sokoloff, L., Reivich, M., Kennedy, C., DesRosiers, M. H., Patlak, C. S., Pettigrew, K. D., Sakurada, O., & Shiniohara, M. (1977). The [14C] deoxyglucose method for the measurement of local cerebral glucose utilization: Theory, procedure, and normal values in the conscious and anesthetized albino rat. *Journal of Neurochemistry, 28,* 897–916.

Stuss, D. T., & Benson, D. F. (1983). Frontal lobe lesions and behavior. In A. Kertesz (Ed.), *Localization in neuropsychology.* New York: Academic Press.

Thomson, G. H. (1939). *The factorial analysis of human ability.* London: University of London Press.

Vernon, P. A. (1983). Speed of information processing and general intelligence. *Intelligence, 7,* 53–70.

Vernon, P. A. (1985). Individual differences in general cognitive ability. In L. C. Hartlage & Telzrow (Eds.), *The neuropsychology of individual differences: A developmental perspective.* New York: C. F. Plenum Press.

Waterhouse, L. (1988). Speculations on the neuroanatomical substrate of special talents. In L. K. Obler & D. Fein (Eds.), *The exceptional brain* (pp. 493–512). New York: Guilford Press.

Chapter *8*

# Biochemical Correlates of Human Information Processing*

### Hilary Naylor
### Enoch Callaway
### Roy Halliday

*University of California, San Francisco
and
San Francisco Veterans' Administration Medical Center*

## INTRODUCTION

The two disciplines of cognitive psychology and neuropharmacology have amassed a considerable amount of data concerning the function of the brain, yet the theoretical accounts of the observations seem to have almost no overlap. We

* The authors wish to acknowledge the assistance of Lovelle Yano, Pamela Walton, Ruth Prael, and Patricia Meek in collecting data and preparing reports that contribute to this chapter. We also wish to thank Dani Brandeis, Linda Davenport, George Fein, Karen Herzig, and Bruce Turetsky for suggestions and critical comments on earlier versions of this manuscript.

**333**

believe that there must be an intimate relationship between neurochemical function and efficiency in the brain and the function of information processing that leads to an efficiency called "intelligence."

We are discussing intelligence in terms of information processing operations rather than intelligence test scores. This view of intelligence is in contrast to the psychometric view, and is one that has emerged in recent years, most closely associated with the work of Sternberg (1977) and Hunt (1983). According to this view:

> Mental behavior should be explained by identifying the processes involved in problem-solving, rather than by producing abstract descriptions of the outcome of thinking. (Hunt, 1983, p. 142)

The goal of our research program over the past few years has been to identify not only the processes involved in problem solving, but also to identify the neurochemical bases of those processes. We seek a marriage of pharmacology and information processing mediated by chronometry as the methodological matchmaker.

The problem is one of finding the synthesis of neuropharmacology and cognition. Many of the mechanisms of chemical change in the brain are well understood; much is known about how humans process information presented in strictly limited laboratory contexts. The purpose of this chapter is to define what specific areas of knowledge from these two disciplines might be most useful in developing a synthesis. We will show how mental operations may be dissected into their component parts, and describe some results of using drugs to simultaneously manipulate both information processing operations and neurotransmitter operations. The use of chronometry will be explained in detail as it pertains both to the parsing of response time and to the timing of brain wave potentials.

## KNOWLEDGE BASES

Neuropharmacology has developed a great body of information regarding neurotransmitter synthesis, uptake, storage, receptor sensitivities, breakdown, and so on. Classification of synapses (inhibitory and excitatory) and receptors (pre- and postsynaptic), and identification of subclasses of receptors for a given transmitter (alpha1, alpha2, and beta noradrenergic) all contribute to this knowledge base.

Cognitive psychology also has a large knowledge base regarding the processing of information from stimulus to response, the transformations that take place, variables that slow or speed transmission, and factors that increase or decrease accuracy.

The link between these two knowledge bases that allows us to build a theory about the biological basis of cognition is the relatively small number of reports on the effects of drugs on information processing. Drugs that selectively change the status of the neurotransmitter systems and produce behavioral changes in information processing tasks allow us to pinpoint the neurochemical basis for isolated cognitive operations.

An important aspect of this approach is the assumption that different neurotransmitters affect different processes. The term "operations" includes an array of complex pharmacological effects by which neurotransmitters act on a variety of neuroanatomical sites and receptor types, with pre- or postsynaptic actions having opposite effects. There is abundant evidence in the animal literature that the control of even relatively simple responses uses information generated in several specific neural systems. Components of these systems appear to be controlled by specific neurotransmitters (Yim & Mogenson, 1986). Studies in animals suggest that, even at global levels, gabaergic, dopaminergic, and norepinephrinergic systems serve different information processing functions. For example, Oades (1985) has speculated on the basis of animal data that the function of norepinephrine is to change the signal to noise ratio of processing systems.

## Models of Cognition

Many models and theories put forward by cognitive psychologists are based on evidence for separate and isolated mental operations. Experimental tests of these theories have rarely included the use of drugs as independent variables, but these theories nevertheless provide a basis for finding links between cognition and pharmacology. Because we are talking in terms of neurotransmitters that speed or slow cognitive operations, this discussion will be limited to models that attempt to account for the *timing* of mental processes. These models are therefore known as *chronometric* models.

*Discrete, serial stages.* A fundamental assumption shared by serial models of information processing is that performance on any task can be accounted for by the operations of separate hypothetical processes. These processes transform information so that an appropriate output can be generated. The current popularity of these models may be traced to a seminal paper by S. Sternberg (1969), in which he described a method of determining the separation of processing stages. The idea of separate stages originated in the last century in the work of Donders, on which Sternberg based his ideas.

Sternberg's model assumes that the time to make a response is the sum of the times taken to complete each of the operations involved in generating that response. The boxes in the diagram in Figure 8.1 represent the processing operations that the organism is presumed to go through in order to respond to a stimulus. The model shows serial, discrete processing with no feedback loops. The additive factors method (AFM) described by Sternberg (1969) provides a research methodology for the discovery of these operations or stages. With this method one can isolate cognitive processes by manipulating variables that

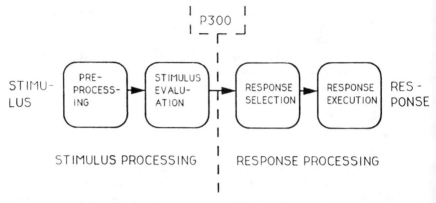

Figure 8.1.   The serial model of human information processing.

change reaction time (RT) and then examine their relative effects on performance. According to the AFM, if two variables influence different processing stages then their effects on RT will be additive. However, if two variables influence a common processing stage, then their joint effects on RT will produce an interaction. Use of this method depends on the following assumptions: unidimensional cognitive processing, strict serial processing between stages, no feedback loops during the reaction process and a constant stage output (i.e., the input and output of each stage is independent of the factors that influence its duration).

Thus, the serial model provides a framework for studying the operation of discrete components of information processing. It assumes that there are a number of component processes that transform information in discrete steps and are governed by different psychological factors. If we hypothesize that some of these processes are sensitive to particular psychoactive drugs then we can design experiments using the AFM to test these hypotheses. The critical idea here is that the interaction between a drug and some task variable localizes the action of the drug to a particular stage. Theoretically, this idea can be used to answer specific questions regarding the specific neurotransmitters involved in these cognition-drug relationships.

*ERPs and serial information processing.* In the mid-1960s, Sutton and his coworkers (Sutton, Braren, Zubin, & John, 1967) discovered that the scalp potentials evoked by sensory stimuli were also sensitive to cognitive variables. These "event-related potentials" (ERP) vary in amplitude and latency depending on the stimulus probability, the subject's expectations about the stimulus, the cognitive demands of the task, the meaningfulness of the stimulus, and other factors (Donchin, 1979).

One of the early motivations for studying the latency of brain event-related potentials in relation to stages of information processing came from some observations showing that RT and the latency of components of the ERP were correlated. The latency of ERP components demarcates where in the flow of information particular effects occur. The latency of the positive component that occurs between 300 and 500 msec (P3), for example, indicates the process of stimulus evaluation (see Figure 8.1). Stimulus evaluation includes the processes of discrimination, feature extraction, identification, and categorization. Thus, if a drug affects both P3 and RT we can assume that its actions occur before the completion of stimulus evaluation. This is not to say that P3 is a manifestation of stimulus evaluation processes but that the P3 is not emitted until the stimulus has been cognitively processed. If a drug affects RT but not P3 then we have evidence that this drug influences response processing. The specific time frame can be deduced by the effects of the drug on the latency of earlier components such as N2, P2, and N1 (see Figure 8.6). ERP latencies, in this context, estimate the timing of processes before the overt response and supplement the behavioral measures.

A landmark experiment in separating the factors that differentially affect P3 was reported by McCarthy and Donchin (1981). In this study stimulus discriminability and response complexity were varied in a choice RT experiment. The stimulus display is shown in Figure 8.2. The subject was presented with a cue

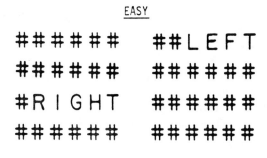

EASY

```
######    ##LEFT
######    ######
#RIGHT    ######
######    ######
```

HARD

```
BHIMHQ    EHGMNI
EMKEKM    LEFTUD
JUEIKE    VNFMKM
KRIGHT    ILUYRM
```

Figure 8.2. Easy and difficult stimuli similar to those used by McCarthy and Donchin (1981).

word followed by a matrix containing the words "right" or "left." The cue informed the subject whether he was to respond with the same or opposite hand as the word in the stimulus array. Stimulus discriminability was varied by embedding the discrimination stimuli in other letters (noise) or in other symbols (no noise).

The results showed that RT increased with both the discriminability and response compatibility manipulations. These effects were additive. However, P3 latency was increased only when the array was noisy, and was not affected by response compatibility. The authors concluded that these interactions provide additional evidence that P3 indexes stimulus evaluation while RT indexes both stimulus evaluation and response selection-execution. This experiment is important because it clearly showed that RT and P3 latency could be dissociated experimentally and understood as manifestations of the activation of different processes.

The McCarthy and Donchin findings were replicated and extended by Magliero, Bashore, Coles, and Donchin (1984). The lack of response compatibility effects on P3 latency has been replicated in several experiments (e.g., Mulder, Gloerich, Brookhuls, Van Dellen, & Mulder, 1984; Fitzpatrick, Klorman, Brumaghim, & Keeover, 1988; Bashore, 1990). Spatial incompatibility is not the only response manipulation that fails to change P3 while changing RT. Callaway (1983, 1984) has used a response manipulation that essentially varies the number of response alternatives (2 or 4 responses). This manipulation significantly increased RT but had no effect on P3 latency in several studies (see Table 8.1).

There are many technical and theoretical issues concerning the recording, measurement, and interpretation of P3 latency (Coles, Gratton, Kramer, & Miller, 1986) that are beyond the scope of this chapter. It is, however, important to note that certain changes in requirements for response processing may vary this component (Ragot & Lesevre, 1986).

Many experiments have shown that the latency of P3 and RT can be dissociated. Further, P3 latency is, at least in some paradigms, primarily sensitive to variables that change stimulus processing and these findings provide a rationale for using it to measure stimulus evaluation independently of RT. If a variable changes the latency of P3, then we can infer that it is acting on pre-P3 processes.

*From serial to parallel.* Modern cognitive psychology has been much influenced by the work of Michael Posner. In his book *Chronometric Explorations of Mind* (1978), Posner describes a unified experimental approach based on observations concerning the time course of human information proeessing. The important thing about this work is the progress it made in linking information processing and psychophysiology. It provides the essential basis for the theme of this chapter, that is, the link between information processing and neuropharmacology.

Although Posner finds that research in the last few years has not supported a

**Table 8.1. Studies with Stimulants and the SE/RS Task**

| Expt # | # of Subjects [and ages] | Drugs and dose | SE/RS task variable × drug Interaction | Max drug effect on RT (ms) | Max drug effect on P3 (ms) |
|---|---|---|---|---|---|
| 1 | 8[30–40] | MP 5, 10, 20 mg | resp.c. [+] | −20 | ns[−5.9] |
| 2 | 12 [20–30] | MP 20 mg | resp.c. [+] | −20 | — |
|  |  | DAMP 10 mg | ... | −24 | — |
| 3 | 16 [21–30] | DAMP 10 mg | ... | −24 | −6.6 |
|  |  | PROP 40 mg | ... | ns[−8] | ns[−7.6] |
| 4 | 270+ [41–60] | PROP 160–400 mg (chronic) | resp.c. | +25 | — |
| 5 | 16 [21–30] | DAMP 10 mg | ... | −27 | ns[−2.4] |
|  |  | PIMO 4 mg | ... | −20 | ns[−1.2] |
|  |  | DAMP & PIMO |  | ns[23] | +8.5 |
| 6 | 6 [21–30] | YOH 30 mg | stim.c. | ns[11] | — |
|  |  | CLON 0.2 mg | stim.c. | +56 | — |
| 7 | 12 [21–30] | DAMP 10 mg | resp.c. | −26 | ns[−13] |
|  |  | YOH 30 mg | stim.c. | ns[−4] | ns[−6] |
|  |  | CLON 0.2 mg | stim.c. | +56 | +26 |

resp.c. = response complexity
stim.c. = stimulus complexity
PIMO = pimozide
PROP = propranolol
YOH = yohimbine
CLON = clonidine

strictly serial-stage view of the internal mental operations involved in information processing, he states that

> these studies have generally used some variant of mental chronometry and serve to strengthen the notion of mental chronometry as a general approach for the study of pattern recognition and mental processing in general. (1978, p. 19)

Posner's research supported the idea of two different kinds of processing systems, one automatic and the other controlled, distinguished by various characteristics related to speed of processing and to other properties of the process. The automatic system operates through psychological pathways that are activated automatically by the presentation of a stimulus. A psychological pathway is defined as the set of internal codes and their connections that are activated. Such pathways are characterized by invariance between the input and the activated codes, and by independence—that is activation of one pathway does not affect the operation of another. Others have called such a system "data-driven" (Norman & Bobrow, 1975).

In contrast to the automatic system, the controlled system requires conscious attention and has a limited capacity. When the resources of this system are directed to a particular input pathway, then there is inhibition of processing of all other input. Such a system is "resource-limited," that is, its operation is not determined by the nature of the input, but by competing demands on the capacity of the processing system.

This "two-process" theory is elegantly illustrated in an experiment reported by Posner and Snyder (1975). They used a cost-benefit analysis to show the difference between automatic and controlled processing. The basic design was to present a single priming item, which is either a signal of the same type to which a subject will have to respond or a neutral warning signal. By manipulating the probabilities that the prime will be a valid cue to the stimulus array, it was hoped that subjects would vary the degree of active attention they committed to the prime. According to the two-process theory, when little processing capacity is committed to the prime, there can be a benefit from automatic pathway activation but no cost for such activation. Conversely, when conscious attention is directed to the prime, there is benefit from both the automatic and the controlled attention, but there is cost on those trials when the prime is not a valid cue. Costs and benefits are calculated by comparing RTs on trials when the cue is either valid or invalid with trials when the cue is neutral. In a letter matching task, the cue is valid if it is the same as the two comparison letters ("same" trial), and invalid if it is different to the two comparison letters. The cue does not predict the outcome of the match, which is either "same" or "different." Figure 8.3 shows the results of this experiment according to the time delay between the prime and the stimulus array. The important point is that the time course of the two processes are different. Benefits accrue rapidly in both the high validity (automatic + controlled processing) and low validity (automatic only), but costs develop more

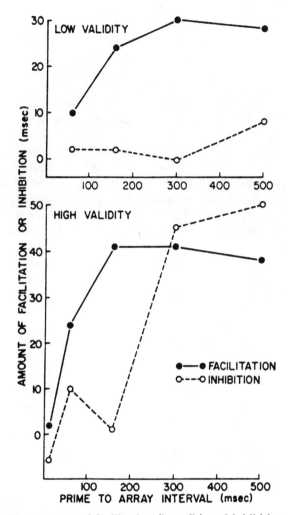

Figure 8.3.   Time course of facilitation (benefit) and inhibition (cost) as a function of prime to array interval for low (upper panel) and high (lower panel) valid primes. (From Posner & Snyder, 1975, Copyright 1975 by Academic Press, reprinted by permission.)

slowly (in controlled processing = high validity) or not at all (in automatic processing = low validity).

A similar distinction to the one between controlled and automatic processing has been made by Anne Treisman (1985; Treisman & Souther, 1985). A general theory of preattentive processing is presented and has ample experimental support. Experimental manipulations allow one to operationally distinguish two systems of processing: parallel and serial systems. The model asserts that without focused attention (that is, when attention is divided over the whole display) only the presence of a unique feature can be detected, not the absence. This is because the target with a unique feature produces unique activity in the relevant feature detectors. The target with an absent feature produces no unique activity. The activity of feature detectors is processed in parallel and automatically—this is called preattentive processing. When the activity of the feature detectors is uniform, the display must be searched serially by focused attention.

Some of the research to be described below has raised the question as to whether changes in neurotransmitter systems (brought about by the administration of psychotropic drugs) change specific stages of information processing in the Sternberg sense. (Some of these stages are named in Figure 8.1.) An alternative hypothesis is that the drug-induced changes (and by inference, the underlying neurotransmitter changes) are in the *mode* of processing rather than in the timing of any processing stage. The distinction between serial and parallel, controlled and automatic, modes of processing is one of the more obvious to be explored in this context.

*Alternative processing constructs.* In addition to the contrast between a mode of processing and a stage of processing approach, there is also a need to take into consideration those noncognitive changes in the organism that may be affected by pharmacological intervention and thus may influence the drug-specific cognitive effects. As Hockey, Coles, and Gaillard (1986) have pointed out, the problem with a purely chronometric model of information processing is that it does not allow for variability in computational characteristics under different environmental or internal states. There has been a traditional separation of emotion and cognition in psychology that makes the integration of current approaches to stress and arousal into the structure of information processing theories very difficult. For example, Sanders (1983) has proposed a model to integrate energetics and processing information. The basic assumption is that the duration of a stage is dependent on the state of the subject as well as the computational demands of the task. He proposes three types of energetical supply: arousal, effort, and activation. Sanders also includes another construct: evaluation. This mechanism would assess the functioning of the arousal and activation mechanisms, and was also a major element in Kahneman's (1973) theory of attentional processes.

We have not included such constructs as attention or arousal in this discussion because attempts to differentiate the effects of drugs on processing states from processing stages have only just begun (Molenaar, van der Molen, & Halliday, 1990). Eventually we hope this approach may allow a development from statements concerning specific drugs to more general statements concerning the systems that mediate these drug effects.

In addition to noncognitive influences on information processing, there is also the possibility that the processing system may be a combination of different processes. Serial models with discrete transmission assume that each stage must finish completely before the next stage can begin. In other words, each stage transmits output only after it is finished, and this transmission occurs at a discrete point in time. Therefore, different stages cannot overlap in time. On the other hand, continuous models allow each stage to transmit its information gradually to the subsequent stage. In these models, which are also known as cascade or continuous flow models, the partial information acquired by a stage will be immediately transmitted to the next stage. Since partial information is transmitted continuously, the different stages within the model can operate with some temporal overlap.

It should be understood that the distinction between discrete and continuous processing is not an "either/or" situation (Miller, 1988). It is quite probable, and consistent with existing data, that information is processed by a combination of these operations, and that different tasks will depend more heavily on one process than another. Within an entire processing system there may be a few points of discrete transmission and several processes within stages operating in parallel.

A processing system that allows for some stages to operate in parallel and for some to be strictly serial is potentially a lot more complex than the system outlined in Figure 8.1, even if the other restrictions that apply to the AFM are adhered to. At this point we have found it most useful to design tasks and experiments that allow the application of the AFM, but to be alert to the possibility that certain kinds of interactions, such as subadditivity, may indicate parallel processing.

## The Neuropharmacological Model

The following paragraphs provide a simplified introduction to neuropharmacological processes and terminology. Readers will find a comprehensive treatment of this field in Cooper, Bloom, and Roth (1986) and in Thompson (1967). Figure 8.4 illustrates the following discussion.

When a neuron communicates with another neuron, it usually does so by releasing neurotransmitters at its junction with another neuron. The junction is known as a synapse. Most psychoactive drugs produce their effects by modifying or imitating the effects of one or more neurotransmitters. This can take place in a variety of ways.

The nerve impulse is propagated to the synapse by a number of interrelated changes that include shifts in electrical potential across the nerve cell membrane, movements of ions into and out of the cell, and alterations of the membrane itself. On arrival at the synapse, the impulse releases stored transmitter into the synapse. The released transmitter may act on receptors and then is usually destroyed outside the cell or taken back up into the cell. In the cell, it may also be destroyed or it may be recycled and reused.

At the receptor, one neurotransmitter may alter the changes produced by another transmitter, and a transmitter's actions may be modified by peptide

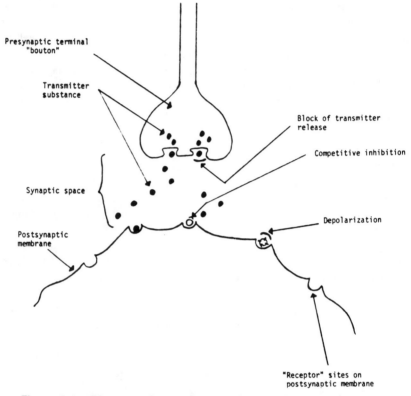

**Figure 8.4.   Diagram of a synapse to show various ways in which synaptic transmission may be blocked. Normal transmission is shown at left. Transmitter release may be blocked, or the receptor site may be occupied by an inactive substance (competitive inhibition). If the receptor site is occupied by a depolarizing substance, the postsynaptic membrane will be permanently depolarized.**

neuromodulators that were waiting at the synapse or coreleased with the transmitter. The receptors for a given transmitter may be inhibitory or excitatory, and in addition may differ in other more subtle ways. They may be postsynaptic, and serve to transmit information between cells, or presynaptic (usually inhibitory) and provide negative feedback to the releasing cell. Receptors are located in the cell membrane, and are coupled to second messenger systems that carry the message into the machinery of the cell. There, such things as protein synthesis may be controlled. Finally the receptors themselves change in response to the amount of transmitter that is present. They up-regulate (increase in density or sensitivity) when there is less transmitter present, and down-regulate when there is more. These changes may be a function of information processing demand, individual differences, diurnal rhythms, practice, diet, and a long list of intervening variables that have to be accounted for in some way.

Support for the idea that the physiology of the brain might be divided into separate systems defined by their neurotransmitters comes from a review by Vanderwolf and Robinson (1981) of different arousal systems. They contrast a cholinergic arousal system with an aminergic system that is activated by stimulants. The aminergic system is supposed to stimulate activities primarily concerned with active, operant, exploratory types of behavior. The cholinergic arousal system is more concerned with receptive, consummatory, automatic behavior. This is at least suggestive of a dimension of information processing running from stimulus to response, with the aminergic stimulants acting more on response selection and cholinergics more on stimulus evaluation.

*Drug effects on neurotransmitters.* There are drugs that act at every step in this complex process, and a given drug may act on more than one of the transmitter systems and on more than one step. Drugs may alter the manufacture or storage of a transmitter. They may change membranes and so modify the propagated impulse and the transmitter release. They may prevent reuptake of the transmitter. They may retard its destruction in the synapse or in the cell after reuptake.

Most important, drugs may bind to a receptor and imitate the transmitter (agonist), block the transmitter (antagonist), or even produce changes opposite to those that the transmitter produces (negative agonist). A drug may be highly selective and act only on one subset of receptors, or it may act on a general class of receptors. For example, nicotine is a cholinergic agonist specific to nicotinic receptors, and physostigmine is a cholinergic agonist that affects all cholinergic receptors (its effect is indirect because it changes the amount of Ach available at the synapse).

Drugs rarely act in a completely simple way. They may not reach all points in a neurotransmitter system equally well. They may have one effect at low dose and the opposite effect at a high dose. This may be due to an excitation of receptors at a low dose which turns into receptor blockade at a high dose, or may be due to presynaptic effects at a low dose and postsynaptic effects at a higher dose. Drugs may also have psychoactive metabolites that may differ between species. Such interspecific differences may lead to incorrect inferences about human responses being drawn from animal studies. Another caveat in making inferences from animal research is that the doses used in animal studies are frequently much higher than those used in studies with humans.

Drug studies offer the best chance of discovering links between cognition and chemistry. Naturally occurring changes, such as are found with age and in disease, allow experiments that cannot be duplicated in the laboratory, and that are of great intrinsic interest. However, the more precise experimenter control of neuropharmacological variables plus the advantages gained from using subjects as their own controls make pharmacological studies very appealing.

## Specific Links Between Cognitive
## and Neuropharmacological Theory

Links between particular neurotransmitters and particular cognitive and/or be-havioral operations have been proposed. Thus, Vanderwolf and Robinson (1981) contrast a cholinergic arousal that supports consummatory and automatic behav-ior with a monoaminergic arousal that supports exploratory and operant behav-ior. This recalls Hess's (1954) ergotrophic and trophotrophic states. Oades (1985) reviews support for the idea that dopamine enhances switching while norepinephrine controls tuning. Soubrie (1986) argues that serotonin controls response delay. All of these share the idea that certain transmitters may not transmit the data being processed but rather carry information about how to process data. Oades uses the analogy of a sound system. The tone and volume controls supply information about how the music should be amplified but carry no information about the music per se. These schemas all include to some degree the appealing if tenuous assumption that a neurotransmiter may have some single macroscopic purpose even though at the microscopic level its actions seem heterogeneous and unrelated.

## STUDIES EXPLORING THE LINKS BETWEEN COGNITION
## AND BRAIN CHEMISTRY

### Methodology

*Reaction time.* The additive factors method (AFM) (Sternberg, 1969) pro-vides a research methodology for the discovery of operations or stages. With this method one can isolate cognitive processes by manipulating variables that change RT and then examine their relative effects on performance. Traditionally task variables have been manipulated, but the same logic can be applied to biological manipulations (i.e., a psychoactive drug). The critical idea here is that the interaction between a drug and some task variable localizes the action of the drug to a particular stage.

For an example of the application of the AFM, consider an experiment reported by Shwartz, Pomerantz, and Egeth (1977). Three factors were varied in a two-choice RT paradigm. The task was to discriminate the direction in which an arrow pointed and to respond by pressing one of two buttons. The first variable was intensity: The arrows were either bright or dim. The second variable was stimulus similarity: The two arrows pointed in either grossly or only slightly different directions. The third variable was stimulus-response compatibility: The subject had to respond by pressing either the button toward which the arrow was pointing or the opposite button.

The results showed significant effects for all three task factors and no interac-tions between them (see Figure 8.5). Interpreting these results in the serial stage

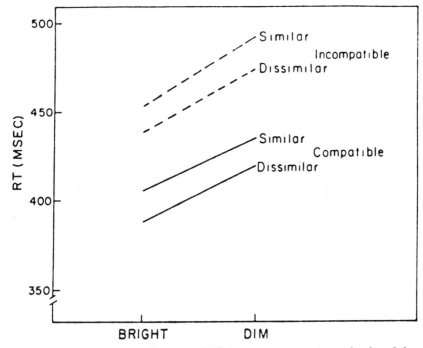

**Figure 8.5.   Mean reaction times (RT) for correct responses in the eight conditions of Experiment 1. (From Shwartz et al., 1977, Copyright 1977 by American Psychological Association, reprinted by permission).**

model leads to the inference that there are three independent processing stages in this discrimination task. Stimulus intensity affects the encoding of the stimulus, stimulus similarity affects a memory comparison stage, and stimulus-response compatibility affects a response selection stage.

*ERP latencies.* Event-Related Potentials (ERP) represent changes in the electrophysiological activity generated by neural tissue in response to some event. The event may be related to the onset of a stimulus (stimulus-related potentials) or to the onset of a response (movement-related potentials). In both cases, the ERP is manifest as changes in voltage and can be detected from scalp electrodes by averaging the EEG activity with respect to the occurrence of an event. As shown in Figure 8.6, these voltage-time fluctuations exhibit a typical series of peaks and valleys. The orderly sequence of these waveforms and their sensitivity to different stimulus-response and task variables suggested that the ERP might reflect the activity of specific information processing activities as they are activated and decay over time. This basic premise has led to the use of the ERP as a tool to study the chronometric properties of human information processes to complement the findings from behavioral and other measures.

Information about the serial position of an experimental effect on information processing is provided by components of the ERP. Certain ERP components

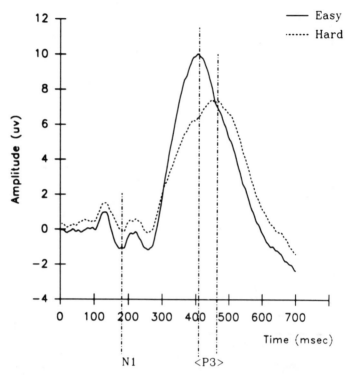

**Figure 8.6. Event related potentials to easy and hard stimuli in the SE/ RS task.**

measure the times taken by subsets of the processes that go into generating the RT. Thus these components provide a method for subtracting times involved in specific processes without changing the task. We will discuss only the P3 component although other ERP components can be used in essentially the same way.

P3 is a positive component occurring between 300 and 600 msec. post stimulus that is sensitive to a variety of cognitive variables. An example of P3 latency change by stimulus task factors can be seen in Figure 8.6 (ERPs to easy-to-discriminate and hard-to-discriminate stimuli). Variations in stimulus parameters, such as defocusing the image, increase the latency of the P3 component. In contrast, changes in response requirements in most paradigms have little effect on P3 latency.

*The RT/P3 relationship.* There are several important reasons for conceptualizing P3 latency and RT in terms of the serial model. A more formal treatment using the AFM has been presented and criticized by Meyer, Osman, Irwin, and Yantis (1988). Using the serial model, the power of AFM can be applied to both RT and P3 and the effects of the manipulations interpreted in terms of specific processing stages. Using both dependent variables also serves to provide a convergent test of an hypothesis when some of the effects are difficult to interpret within an AFM framework. For example, we have frequently found subadditive effects of stimulus and response complexity on RTs (e.g., Naylor, Halliday, & Callaway, 1985). According to the logic of the AFM this interaction means that stimulus and response stages cannot be separated, and therefore one cannot strictly localize the effects of drugs even when they interact with only one of the task variables. However, since stimulus complexity affects only P3, we have converging evidence of at least two processing stages. Without the P3 data these investigators would lose an important "methodological knife" for isolating drug effects in terms of specific component processes.

The use of P3 latency and RT in the context of the serial model also has some methodological implications that assist in the interpretation of data. For example, the ratio of P3 latency to RT is directly interpretable within a serial model. Since P3 measures a subset of the components that generate a response, the ratio of P3 to RT induced by different task, drug, and subject variables can be used to identify where a particular manipulation is acting in the model. For example, if a drug changes P3 and RT equally this would signify that the effects are occurring pre-stimulus-evaluation. If the drug changes RT without changing P3 then the drug is acting post stimulus-evaluation. Using this ratio, Callaway, Halliday, Naylor, and Schechter (1985) showed that scopolamine acted before stimulus-evaluation while Naylor et al. showed that stimulant, methylphenidate, acted after stimulus-evaluation. Ford and Pfefferbaum (1980) used this approach to show that set size effects on RT occurred largely after stimulus evaluation.

## Aminergic Systems

Under the heading "aminergic systems" we will include those neuronal systems whose actions are primarily mediated by norepinephrine, dopamine, or serotonin. Studies of drugs that affect these systems predate current ideas about information processing by many decades, due to the interest in the stimulant drugs that change these neurotransmitters.

The neuropharmacological actions of stimulants are complex and involve several neurotransmitter systems (Moore, 1977). All stimulants reduce appetite and reduce sleepiness, all increase the availability of monoamines—including norepinephrine (NE), dopamine (DA), serotonin, and probably other transmitters. But they may also have different neuropharmacological actions. For example, d-amphetamine and methylphenidate both increase locomotor activity in rats. Pretreatment with reserpine, a drug that depletes the brain of catecholamines, blocks the locomotor effects of methylphenidate but not that of d-amphetamine (Moore, 1977). A serotonin antagonist reduced the lethality of DAMP and MP, but did not affect the lethality of phentermine (Lopataka, Brewerton, Brooks, Cook, & Paton, 1976). MP and DAMP have grossly different effects on the urinary excretion of monoamines and their metabolites

(Zametkin et al., 1985). Other differences among the monoaminergic stimulants are described in Creese (1983).

Behaviorally, stimulants are best known because they improve performance. These improvements are usually attributed to increases in alertness or arousal. Thus, there is also a more or less consistent relationship between stimulant-induced speeding of RT and the apparent alertness of the subject. Stimulants speed RT best when the subject is sleepy, fatigued, and/or bored, and when the task demands are relatively simple (Weiss & Laties, 1962). One of the earliest indications that stimulants might have a specific effect on information processing stages, rather than a general alertness effect, came through studies of the effects of methylphenidate (Ritalin) on hyperactive (ADD) children (Halliday, Callaway, & Naylor, 1983; Halliday, Callaway, & Lynch, 1984). In a visual vigilance task, methylyphenidate (MP) improved the children's performance, that is, speeded response time, with no comparable decrease in P3 latency. This dissociation of RT and P3L was reported (McCarthy & Donchin, 1981) to be the hallmark of separate information processing stages (see pp. 332–334). The specificity of the stimulants' effect was confirmed (Naylor et al., 1985) by showing the interaction between response complexity and stimulant drug dose. Three different stimulants, phentermine (PH), d-amphetamine (DAMP), and methylphenidate (MP), have been used in studies based on the serial information processing model. However, it appears that although all stimulants affect response processing, the specific stage of response processing involved may depend on the stimulant used, as discussed in the next section.

*Effects of stimulants on information processing.* Frowein and coworkers (1981a, 1981b; Frowein, Gaillard, & Varey, 1981c; Frowein & Sanders, 1978) have done considerable work on stimulant effects on information processing during the AFM. The stimulant they used was PH in suppository form, chosen because subjects were tested for a period of 4 to 5 hours requiring a stable plasma concentration of the drug. This proved to be an unfortunate choice because it is one of the most poorly characterized stimulants, and has received little attention since the development of modern receptor physiology (Yelnosky, Panasevich, Borrelli, & Lawlor, 1969).

Response processing was divided into five independent stages: response selection, motor programming, motor initiation, motor adjustment, and response execution (see Figure 8.7). Evidence for the existence of these stages was based on the literature and supported by the AFM. RT, that is, time from stimulus to the first measurable motor response, was sometimes divided into two components: (a) reaction time to initiate the response by leaving a ready key (RT/i), and (b) movement time between leaving the ready key and striking the response key (MT).

Frowein found that PH did not interact with variables affecting stimulus processing, but did interact with factors generally subsumed under response processing. PH consistently speeded MT, the pattern of interaction suggesting that PH speeds the response-execution stage and a temporally prior stage that he

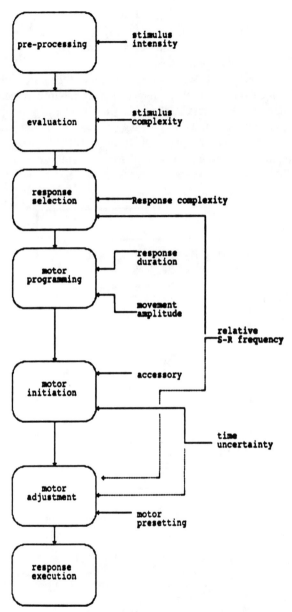

**Figure 8.7. Task variables and inferred stages in the reaction process.**

termed motor adjustment. With respect to response time, these studies provide evidence that the drug changed response processing, they give no compelling evidence concerning the specific stage(s) involved. It may be that response execution and motor adjustment stages are changed by PH, while a more abstract motor program assembly stage is not. The differential weighting of these two processes in the various tasks may explain why RT is speeded on some tasks but not on others. However, this was not explicitly tested, for the tasks sampled a restricted set of response processes.

The apparent action of MP on response processing, as evidenced by its contrasting effects on P3 and RT in hyperactive children, was then tested more explicitly using the SE/RS task (Callaway, 1983; Naylor et al., 1985). This task combined easy and hard stimuli with easy and hard responses to produce four task conditions as shown in Figure 8.8. A target "X" occurred in one of four positions. It was made more difficult to detect by displaying stars in the other 3 positions. In this version, the easy task was to press a key when the target

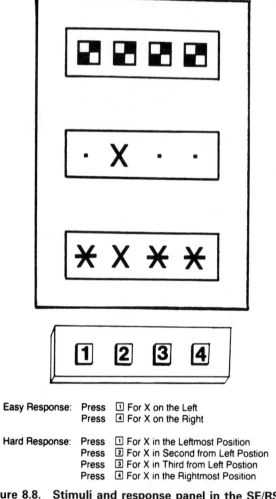

Easy Response:  Press  ① For X on the Left
Press  ④ For X on the Right

Hard Response:  Press  ① For X in the Leftmost Position
Press  ② For X in Second from Left Postion
Press  ③ For X in Third from Left Postion
Press  ④ For X in the Rightmost Position

**Figure 8.8.   Stimuli and response panel in the SE/RS task.**

appeared. For the hard response, one of four keys was to be pressed corresponding to the one of the four positions that the target occupied.

Eight young and eight elderly normal females were tested before and after
placebo and three doses of MP (Naylor et al., 1985). As shown in Figure 8.9, for
the young women, MP speeded RTs although it had no effect on P3 latency. The
maximum dose of MP produced about 30 msec speeding of RT, while the
average change in P3 latency was an insignificant slowing. Stimulus complexity
and drug dose were additive. Response complexity interacted with the drug
effect such that the speeding due to MP was largest in the hard response
condition. The interaction of MP and response complexity indicated that the
stimulant was acting on response processing.

A list of studies using stimulants and variations of the SE/RS paradigm is
given in Table 8.1. The first two experiments used the stimulants MP and
DAMP, the remainder used more specific agonists and/or antagonists. In all
cases stimulants speeded reaction time of young subjects on SE/RS, and in only
one instance did the drug affect P3 latency.

*What neurochemical systems mediate the speeding of RT?* Two approaches to
this question have been taken and each has contributed some new information.
One is to give various blocking agents and determine which one counteracts the
enhancing effects of a particular stimulant. Alternatively, a drug that has specific

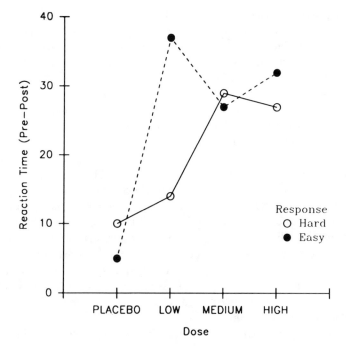

Figure 8.9.   The effect of four doses of methylphenidate (stimulant) on
prepost drug changes in reaction time.

receptor effects can be used to determine whether it behaves like a stimulant. Several experiments with the SE/RS and other tasks have been conducted to try to tease out the neurotransmitter bases of RT speeding with stimulants. In the first experiment (Table 8.1, Exp. 3) the noradrenergic beta receptor blocker propranolol (PROP) was administered following a dose of DAMP (Halliday, Naylor, Callaway, Yano, & Walton, 1987). DAMP speeded RT but this effect was not changed by PROP. The second experiment (Table 8.1, Exp. 4), a study of the chronic effects of hypertensive medication (propranolol), showed that RT was slowed after 1 year's treatment with PROP (160–400 mg per day) and this effect was dose related (Halliday, Perez-Stable, Coates, Gardiner, Hauck, & Hilliard, 1990). RT differences between baseline and three months and one year tests were computed for each stimulus-response condition. PROP has no significant effects at three months. PROP caused a significant (p < .05) slowing of RT at the one year follow-up, and this effect interacted with response complexity. Complex responses were slowed almost twice as much as easy responses.

The third experiment (Table 8.1, Exp. 5) used the dopamine blocker, Pimozide (PIMO), with and without DAMP (Halliday, Naylor, Callaway, Yano, & Walton, 1987). PIMO reduced the speeding of RT by DAMP on the SE/RS but the effects were not significant. However, PIMO alone speeded RT and P3L and this effect interacted with stimulus complexity—a finding that was neither expected nor easily explained.

In an attempt to isolate specific DAMP effects, the fourth experiment (Table 8.1, Exp. 6) used two specifically noradrenergic drugs, clonidine (CLON) and yohimbine (YOH) (Halliday, Callaway, & Lannon, 1989). CLON is an A2 norepinephrine presynaptic agonist that reduces noradrenalin (as measured by a decrease in MHPG, a metabolite of noradrenalin) (Leckman, Maas, Redmond, & Heninger, 1980). YOH is an A2 postsynaptic antagonist. Its effect is to increase sympathetic nerve discharge, with rises in blood pressure and heart rate. It has been found to increase MHPG (Charney & Heninger, 1986a). CLON decreases alertness while YOH increases alertness and to some extent fear and anxiety (Charney & Heninger, 1986b).

The results show that CLON significantly slowed mean RT on the SE/RS task by 56 msec. and had no significant effects on SE/RS errors. The size of the CLON effect was not differentially affected by any of the task variables in the SE/RS. YOH tended to decrease mean RT for both tasks compared to placebo and tended to improve SE/RS accuracy, but this effect was small. However, this experiment also included a task in which the stimuli were sine wave gratings of different frequencies. The processing of spatial frequency takes place at an earlier stage than stimulus evaluation (preprocessing, see Fig. 8.1). The effect of YOH interacted with spatial frequency, indicating an effect at the earlier stage that is not manipulated in the SE/RS task.

The results of experiment 6 make it clear that YOH was not acting in a similar way to DAMP in previous experiments, and that its effect was most likely at the preprocessing stage. Therefore experiment 7 (Table 8.1, Exp. 7) was designed to compare YOH and DAMP, and to use ERP component latencies (both P3 and N1) to evaluate early stimulus processing. The spatial frequency task, SF/LP, has high and low spatial frequency gratings for stimuli, and expectancy is induced by varying the probability of the location (left or right) in which the stimulus will appear. The subject is required to press one button in response to high frequency gratings and the other to low. Thus this task allows the separation of drug effects that are pathway specific (spatial frequency dependent) from those that are attention specific (determined by expectation) (cf. Dunne & Hartley, 1986).

Figure 8.10 summarizes the effects of the three drugs on the SE/RS task. Compared to placebo, DAMP speeded RT. DAMP tended to speed RT for hard responses more than easy, but the effects were not significant. YOH decreased N1 latency, but had no effect on errors, P3 latency or RT. CLON increased RT by 56 msec. None of the drugs had an overall effect on P3 latency. CLON slowed P3 latency more for the easy relative to the hard stimulus. Both DAMP and YOH decreased N1 latency.

The effects of the three drugs on the SF/LP task are summarized in Figure 8.11. DAMP had no effect on RT but CLON slowed RT. The size of this effect was largest for RTs to high spatial frequencies. DAMP and YOH had no effect on P3 latency but CLON slowed both N1 and P3 latency.

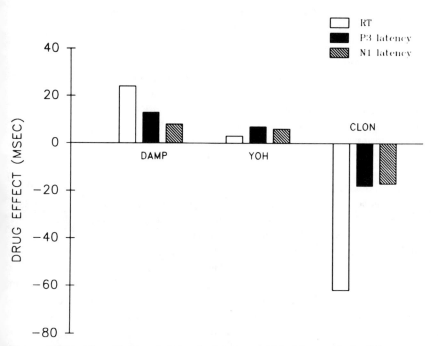

**Figure 8.10.   The effects of d-amphetamine, yohimbine and clonidine on reaction time, P3 latency and N1 latency in the SE/RS task.**

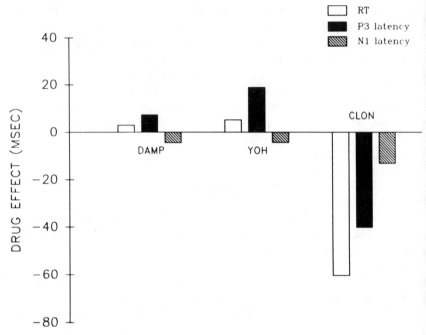

Figure 8.11.   The effects of d-amphetamine, yohimbine and clonidine on reaction time, P3 latency and N1 latency in the SF/LP task.

These findings suggest that these drugs affect different component mental processes that have differing chronological onsets and durations. First consider N1 latency: All three drugs affect N1, CLON increases while DAMP and YOH decrease latency. Independent of drug, N1 is shorter for hard than for easy stimuli, and shorter for low than for high spatial frequency. Thus N1 appears to have two functional components, one sensitive to early stimulus processing, the other a generalized drug-response component that reflects increases in arousal or alertness.

As reported in several earlier studies, DAMP decreased RT and had no effect on P3 latency. Clearly DAMP speeds response processing, although these data do not enable the identification of which particular process is speeded. CLON increased both N1 and P3 latency in both tasks, and it also increased RT more to high spatial frequencies than to low. The interaction of the drug variable with the task variable spatial frequency would suggest the locus of the drug effect to be early stimulus processing (preprocessing). However the lack of such interaction for N1 or P3 contradicts this interpretation. There is clearly some dissociation of the RT and ERP data that allows for some early processes involved in the generation of an RT to fail to appear in the ERP.

*Conclusions from aminergic studies.* The SE/RS task has, with some consistency, shown that DAMP speeds RT but not P3. This suggested to us that response processing is somehow facilitated by DAMP. Unfortunately we have not found any consistent interactions between task variables used in the SE/RS and the drug effect that permitted us to specify the nature of this speeding. Response processing is a broad construct and any particular method for classifying its components will not meet with universal acceptance. However, there does appear to be some agreement that response processes can be divided into those associated with intention and preparation and those involved in the execution of the response. The differential effects of PIMO and DAMP along with their respective interactions with task variables suggests that they are not affecting the same neurochemical systems.

A second purpose of the propranolol and pimozide experiments was to determine if the Beta-adrenergic or Dopamine systems mediated selective aspects of DAMP speeding of information processing. The results of the acute propranolol experiment were negative, indicating that this system is probably not involved. The failure to find a reversal of DAMP effects with PROP is inconsistent with other data showing that PROP does block the euphoria associated with DAMP in humans (Johnsson, 1972) and the hyperactivity induced in rats following injections of monoamines into the nucleus accumbens (Costall, Naylor, & Pinder, 1976). However, the results of the study of chronic propranolol *do* show a slowing of RT after one year of treatment. This supports the idea of a role for the beta-adrenergic system in information processing.

PIMO, in combination with DAMP, tended to reduce RT speeding, but PIMO by itself speeded RT on the SE/RS. It is difficult to specify the nature of this effect, but we note that PIMO is a D1 and D2 dopamine antagonist and that these receptors are postsynaptic. It is possible that differential activation of these receptors may account for the variation in PIMO effects.

In the two studies with CLON and YOH the major finding was that CLON significantly slowed RT in both tasks. There were no interactions between the amount of slowing and any of the task factors. The first study had indicated that YOH interacted with spatial frequency, and thus affected early stimulus processing. This lead to the prediction that YOH would decrease P3 latency. In the second study this prediction was disconfirmed, instead YOH decreased N1 latency.

While these findings need to be replicated we suggest that noradrenergic drugs act on visual information processes that occur relatively early during the encoding of the stimulus. These processes may have to do with the preprocessing of visual information either through feature extraction or in the selectivity of early visual attention (see Meek, Callaway, Merrin, & Juarez, 1989). This suggestion would be consistent with the YOH effect on N1 latency in the spatial frequency task. No task variables in SE/RS manipulate the feature extraction stage (prior to stimulus evaluation) so the effects of YOH and CLON on RT are not differentially affected by either the stimulus or response complexity manipulations.

These results indicate the importance of using both the RT and ERP measures in evaluating drug effects on information processing. If we had measured only RT in the SF/LP task, we would have concluded that the interaction of clonidine and spatial frequency implied that clonidine affects only stimulus preprocessing. If we had measured only ERP latencies we would have concluded that the interaction of clonidine and stimulus complexity for P3 latency implied that clonidine affects stimulus evaluation. Considered together, and in conjunction with the N1 effects, the results indicate a much more complex picture. Firstly, given that the two tasks tap into different aspects of information processing, clonidine must affect more than one stage of stimulus processing. Secondly, given an interaction with stimulus complexity for P3 and not for RT, there must be processes contributing to the appearance of P3 that do not change RT, which implies the existence of overlapping processes, rather than the serial ones shown in Figure 8.1.

## Cholinergic systems

The cholinergic systems of the brain depend on the neurotransmitter acetylcholine for their operation. These systems may be subdivided according to the characteristics of their receptors. The two main classes of receptors are muscarinic and nicotinic. The drug scopolamine (SCOP) is a specific blocker of muscarinic receptors. The effect of SCOP may be reversed by a cholinergic agonist such as physostigmine (PHY) which is an antiacetylcholinesterase, that is, it inhibits the breakdown of Ach at the synapse. It is therefore an *indirect* agonist, not specific to any receptor. On the other hand, arecoline (ARE) is a direct-acting agonist whose effects are primarily muscarinic. Methscopolamine (MSCOP) is a peripheral antimuscarinic that does not pass the blood-brain barrier, and is therefore sometimes used as a placebo for SCOP. On the nicotinic side, nicotine (NIC), the main psychoactive ingredient in tobacco, primarily affects nicotinic receptors. There is no specific antinicotinic blocker analogous to SCOP that is safe to use with human subjects. However, SCOP does appear to have some antinicotinic effects.

In this section we review the muscarinic and nicotinic systems separately, while noting where there appears to be some overlap.

*The Muscarinic System.* Scopolamine, also known as hyoscine, is the psychoactive substance in the plant *Datura stramonium*, or "Jimson weed," recognized for centuries to induce alterations of thought processes and amnesia. This century, scopolamine has been used in obstetrical anesthesia, and in motion sickness remedies. It produces a number of side effects such as dry mouth, paralysis of visual accommodation, and short-term memory impairment. Anticholinergic side effects are present in a variety of psychiatric medications such as drugs used to treat depression.

*Effect of scopolamine on information processing.* The most reliable cognitive effect of SCOP is its interference with verbal memory (Peterson, 1977; Drachman, 1978; Drachman & Leavitt, 1974; Ghoneim & Mewaldt, 1975, 1977; Caine, Weingartner, Ludlow, Cudahy, & Wehry, 1981). The pattern of disruption indicates the effect to be primarily at the encoding stage, although there are a few indications of an effect at the retrieval stage (Beatty, Butters, & Janowsky, 1986; Dunne & Hartley, 1985). In many respects the effect of SCOP is similar to the changes in memory seen with normal aging, that is, on the formation of memory traces or on the transfer of information from short to long term memory (Rusted, 1989). The reduction of cholinergic activity with aging has also been well documented (Bartus, Dean, Beer, & Lippa, 1982).

Our series of studies of the effect of SCOP on information processing began with the observation that elderly subjects have longer P3 latencies and reaction times than younger subjects (Callaway, 1984; Halliday, Callaway, Naylor, Gratzinger, & Prael, 1986). This slowing was isolated to the stimulus evaluation stage of processing by the finding that an increase in stimulus complexity produced more slowing in older than younger subjects. We therefore expected the effect of SCOP on normal young adults to be a slowing of both reaction time and P300, with an interaction with stimulus complexity. The progression of our research program with SCOP is given in Table 8.2.

Twelve women (aged 19–33 years) were tested before and after placebo, 0.6 mg and 1.2 mg oral SCOP (Callaway et al., 1985). On the SE/RS task, SCOP slowed both RT ($p < .02$) and P3L ($p < .05$). There was a tendency for SCOP to slow P3L *less* for difficult stimuli and *more* for easy stimuli ($F = 3.2, p < .09$). RTs to easy stimuli were also slowed more although this interaction was statistically insignificant. The greater effect on easy stimuli is contrary to the prediction that SCOP would imitate age by interacting with stimulus complexity (slow responses to hard stimuli the most). Rather, it suggests that SCOP slows processing before P3 is generated (since it slows P3L) but not at the stimulus evaluation stage where stimulus complexity slows processing. This idea was supported by an interaction of SCOP and SF grating size for P3 latency in a SF discrimination task (Table 8.2).

From these results we concluded that SCOP must act on a processing stage prior to stimulus evaluation, such as preprocessing (see Figure 8.1), and therefore predicted that SCOP would interact with spatial frequency (SF). We designed three tasks to tap different aspects of SF processing: threshold evaluation, simple RT and choice RT. All used sine wave gratings of different frequencies as stimuli. These procedures were designed to show the specificity of SCOP to stimulus preprocessing as opposed to stimulus evaluation. Artificial pupils (1 mm) were used to prevent changes in accommodation and pupil size from influencing the results.

We predicted that SCOP would (a) increase threshold for detection of high SF more than for low; (b) increase the sensitivity of the high frequency channels to contrast; and (c) be interactive with SF and additive with stimulus difficulty.

There were no significant drug effects. All of the task variables performed as expected and at high levels of confidence. The drug data generally run contrary

## Table 8.2.   Summary of Studies with Scopolamine (SCOP)

**2.1 Study 1** (Callaway et al., 1985)
*Rationale:*

| | | | |
|---|---|---|---|
| SCOP: | Slows P3 latency | Age & barbiturates: | Slow P3 latency |
| | Slows some RTs | | Slow RT |
| | Impairs memory | | Impair memory |
| | | | Slow stimulus evaluation |

*Hypothesis:*
SCOP, like age, will impair stimulus evaluation.
*Results:*
SCOP slows responses to Easy stimuli more than responses to Hard stimuli (slows
   both RT and P3 latency);
Increased spatial frequency (SF) slows P3 (acts on pre-processing);
SCOP slows P3 latency for high SF more than low.
*Conclusion:*
SCOP impairs stimulus pre-processing.


**2.2 Study 2**
*Hypothesis:*
SCOP will interact with spatial frequency.
*Results:*
SCOP slows reaction time, but does not interact with spatial frequency under
   conditions of: (a) identification of different spatial frequency gratings; (b)
   constant threshold for different gratings; or (c) discrimination of shape.
*Conclusions:*
SCOP effects are due to peripheral anti-cholinergic changes, therefore the effects
   observed in study disappeared when artificial pupils were used.


**2.3 Study 3** (Brandeis et al., 1988)
*Rationale:*
SCOP impairs performance on vigilance tasks (Warburton, 1987);
SCOP impairs response to high probability stimuli and facilitates responses to low
   probability stimuli (Dunne & Hartley, 1985, 1986);
SCOP and SDAT slow flash VEP and not pattern VEP.
*Hypotheses:*
SCOP slow early VEP components to flashes and to high SF gratings;
SCOP slows High SF/High Prob. responses more than Lo/Hi, Hi/Lo and Lo/Lo;
SCOP slows responses more the greater the processing demand;
SCOP slows responses (RT and P3 latency) to Easy stimuli more than to Hard.
*Results:*
SCOP slows responses (RT and P3 latency) to Easy stimuli more than to Hard;
For hard stimuli, SCOP slows responses to central stimuli more than peripheral;
SCOP interacts with SF for error-rate, not RT.
*Conclusions:*
General: In feature detection, SCOP slows parallel processing rather than serial
   processing.
Alternative: SCOP causes parallel processing to become serial.
Specific: SCOP slows responses to targets defined by absent features more than
   to targets defined by present features.
General: SCOP reduces responsiveness to stimuli at the "center of attention."
Alternative: SCOP produces an increase in RT and P3 latency that is linear with
   respect to display size for the absent-features condition.
Specific: SCOP slows responses to high prob. stimuli at periphery more than to
   low prob. stimuli at fovea.

to the prediction that SCOP would raise thresholds and slow RT to high spatial frequencies. Only in the simple RT task was there even a hint that SCOP slowed RT more with high than with low spatial frequencies. This provides little evidence suggesting a differential effect of SCOP on preattentive processing. At this point the most parsimonious conclusion was that the drug effects found in our 1985 study were due to peripheral changes, that is, in pupil size and accommodation, because we had not used artificial pupils (see Table 8.2).

With no SCOP effect on preprocessing, and reports by others that SCOP reduces stimulus sensitivity in a vigilance task (Wesnes & Warburton, 1983) we felt it important to replicate our earlier findings with SCOP using artificial pupils to control for the peripheral effects of SCOP. This study (Brandeis, Callaway, Naylor, & Yano, 1988; Naylor, Brandeis, Halliday, Yano, & Callaway, 1988; Brandeis, Naylor, Callaway, Halliday, Meeke, & Yano, 1990) was designed to separate the effects of SCOP on attention and SF. Some studies have shown SCOP to impair the processing of high SF stimuli; others have shown SCOP to impair processing of attended information. It is unclear whether distinct or common neural processes mediate these effects. Stimulus specific effects of SCOP included slowing of early ERP components to flashes and slowing of P3 latency to high SF gratings (Callaway et al., 1985), but no slowing to low or medium SF patterns (Bajalan, Wright, & Van der Vliet, 1986). It is possible that SCOP effects on high SF might have an attentional component: High SFs are more difficult to see than low SFs, so more attention might be devoted to high SF processing.

Twelve subjects were tested on four tasks in a pre/post-double-blind placebo/SCOP design. For three of the tasks, the relevant stimuli were either flashes or gratings of high or low SF, and either black and white or colored. Attentional effects were examined by varying location probability and the difficulty of featural integration while using identical stimuli. The fourth task was the SE/RS task. Artificial pupils (1 mm) were used in this study. Results for RT showed that the effects of both stimulus complexity and response complexity were significant and additive. SCOP slowed RT, and this effect interacted with stimulus complexity such that responses to easy stimuli were slowed more than responses to hard stimuli ($F = 7.46$, $p < .02$, Easy stimulus slowing = 65 ms, Hard = 45 ms). This result is a replication of the tendency that was observed in our previous study (Callaway et al., 1985, Easy slowing = 30 ms, Hard = 21 ms).

The P3 identified in this study appears to be the same as that identified as P3 in our earlier study (Callaway et al., 1985). The latency for the Easy stimulus is 428 ms (1985 = 424 ms), for the Hard stimulus, 460 ms (1985 = 445 ms). This component showed a significant slowing with SCOP of 34 ms (1985 = 22 ms), but in this analysis slowing was not influenced by stimulus complexity. N1 has a shorter latency for the hard stimulus (197 ms) than for the easy stimulus (212 ms). It shows an early effect of SCOP, with some 12 ms slowing in the active drug condition (Table 8.2).

Figure 8.12 shows the Pz vs. ears voltage waveshapes from the current and the previous studies (Callaway et al., 1985). Although the waveshapes are quite

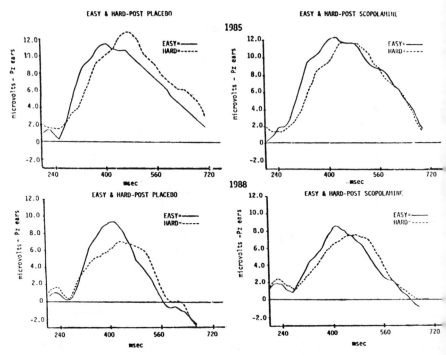

Figure 8.12.   The effect of stimulus difficulty and dose of scopolamine on the P3 component of the event related potential.

similar, they confirm that scopolamine did not reduce the lag between "EASY" and "HARD" stimulus P3 peak in the current study, as it had tended to do in the previous study. It appears that for both studies, scopolamine did not reduce the timing differences between EASY and HARD stimuli during the early, "ascending" portion of P3, and the waveshapes for EASY and HARD stimuli actually begin to diverge somewhat earlier after scopolamine. This comparison suggests that the different results in the two studies are genuine, and that the differential scopolamine effects on EASY and HARD stimuli in the 1985 study emerged after P3 onset, at latencies in excess of 350 ms.

RT and the P3 latency measures replicated the task effects found in previous studies. P3 latency was affected only by stimulus complexity, and RT showed additive increases with stimulus and response complexity. N1 latency was shorter to the hard stimuli than to the easy. This indicates the purely pattern analytic nature of N1, unrelated to cognitive load, that is, more pattern leads to shorter N1 latency.

An analysis of target position effects showed that the outer positions were slower for hard, but faster for easy stimuli. This pattern replicates a study by Mulder et al. (1984). The SCOP effect interacted with both stimulus complexity and position, and Figure 8.13 shows that the "hard" stimuli in outer positions

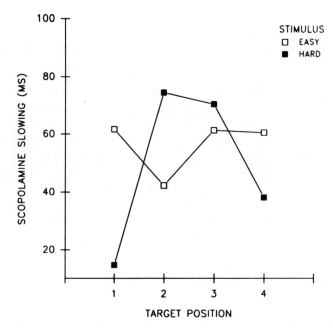

**Figure 8.13.  Scopolamine effect by stimulus position in the SE/RS task.**

are less slowed by SCOP. It seems likely that this position effect is also related to changes from serial to parallel processing. If easy stimuli are processed automatically then all locations should be equally fast (Table 8.2.).

While P3 and RT showed the expected slowing for hard targets, the N1 showed slowing for easy targets. These opposite effects of stimulus complexity on N1 and P3 latency show that processing of easy and hard targets differs on at least two stages and along at least two separable dimensions. N1 latency may index processes related to pattern detection which precede evaluation of target positions.

SCOP slowed RT as well as N1 and P3 map latencies, but only RT was slowed less for hard than for easy targets. This reduced slowing for hard targets held only for the outer display positions. SCOP thus eliminated the position advantage for hard inner targets. This suggests that under SCOP all targets are processed like the hard outer targets in the predrug conditions. The latencies of N1 and P3 indicated additivity between the delays due to SCOP and stimulus complexity. We suggest that SCOP impairs the parallel processing mode for localization of easy targets and that RT reflects this processing mode to a greater degree than does P3. That is, P3 indexes the timing of an alternative, serial, less SCOP-sensitive processing mode.

*Other actions of Scopolamine on information processing.* In addition to the numerous reports of the effects of SCOP on stimulus processing, there have been some suggestions that SCOP affects response processing. For example, SCOP interferes with the Stroop test. This is a measure of response conflict engendered by trying to report out loud the color of ink used to print the name of a different color. For example if the word RED is printed in green ink, it takes more time to report the color (e.g., say green) than to read the word (e.g., say red) or to name the color of a spot. The RT for naming a color used to print a conflicting color name is slower than the RT for naming the color presented as a spot. P3L is the same in both conditions so the effect is not due to slowing of stimulus processing (Duncan-Johnson & Kopel, 1981). Callaway and Band (1958) found that atropine (an anti-cholinergic like scopolamine) had a tendency to increase the Stroop effect. Ostfeld and Aruguette (1962) found SCOP to increase it significantly. Wesnes and Revell (1984) also found that SCOP disrupted performance on the Stroop test, and that NIC reduced the effect of SCOP.

Broks et al. (1988) report that SCOP slowed RT to both valid and invalid targets in primed location tasks in which the time between prime and target (stimulus-onset-asynchrony-SOA) was varied, and also interacted with SOA. According to Posner's two-process theory (see above), RT to valid targets would be the result of the combined effects of automatic and controlled processing, with controlled processing having greater weight at longer SOAs. RTs to invalid targets are slowed if controlled processing in operating but not if only automatic processing is taking place. This interaction suggests that SCOP may change the balance between parallel and serial processing.

*An alternative processing model.* The simple serial model cannot explain the effects of SCOP on the SE/RS task. Since SCOP slows P3 latency, the model has SCOP acting on stimulus processing. That means it is acting either on preprocessing or stimulus evaluation (or both). There is no SCOP × spatial frequency interaction to suggest an action on preprocessing. There is no positive SCOP × stimulus complexity interaction to suggest an action on stimulus evaluation. In fact the interaction we found suggests that there are two different processing operations at work in evaluating the stimuli in the SE/RS task, one of which is more efficient for easy stimuli, the other more efficient for hard stimuli.

These two modes of processing may be the same as those identified by Treisman and Gelade (1980). One is a simultaneous search mode which is not slowed by increasing the number of items to be searched. Targets for simultaneous search must be identified by the presence of a feature. The other is a controlled serial search mode which is slowed when the number of items to be searched is increased. Serial search must be used if the target is identified by the absence of a feature.

The target X in the easy display of the SE/RS task (see Figure 8.8) is identified by the presence of two features (\ and /) that are not present in the other items in the display, the dots. However, in the hard display when the target X is mixed with stars, the target shares features (\ and /) with the distractors, and is defined by the absence of a feature ( + ). It seems plausible that SCOP particularly slows the simultaneous search which is more efficient in the easy stimulus condition. If then the slower serial search required in the hard stimulus condition was relatively SCOP-resistant, the observed results would occur.

*The Nicotinic System.* The U.S. Surgeon General's 1988 report reviewed findings from a large number of studies on the cognitive effects of nicotine and concluded that depriving smokers of nicotine degrades performance and these deficits are reversed following nicotine. These effects have been reported on tasks that tap sustained and selective attention, distractibility, and on cognitive tasks in which neurocognitive processes are indexed by response speed, accuracy, and psychophysiological measures such as the scalp event potential (ERP) and the electroencephalogram (EEG).

There is not a large body of research relating to the chronometric effects of nicotine, but several significant studies have been reported, many by Warburton and his colleagues. They have examined the effects of nicotine (Wesnes, Warburton, & Matz, 1983) and smoking (Wesnes & Warburton, 1983) on rapid information processing, and compared the effects of nicotine to scopolamine (Wesnes & Warburton, 1984; Wesnes & Revell, 1984; Rusted & Warburton, 1989).

Warburton and colleagues have concluded (Warburton & Wesnes, 1985; Warburton, 1987, 1990) that nicotine affects stimulus processing through its effects on the cholinergic mediation of ascending reticular activation pathways. This conclusion is most clearly supported by the study of Edwards, Wesnes, and Warburton (1985) that showed nicotine decreased RT and the latency of the P300 component of the scalp event related potential using a rapid visual information processing task. Since P300 latency has been related to those cognitive processes that underlie the evaluation of stimuli and are independent of response processes, this finding suggests that nicotine may affect some cognitive processes and spare others.

This study is important for two reasons. It is the only report showing that *any drug* decreases the latency of P3. Most studies have found either no effect or a drug-associated increase in latency (see Table 8.1). Secondly, according to the serial model, the decrease in both RT and P3 indicates that nicotine acts on stimulus and not response processes. Unfortunately the authors showed no ERP wave forms, did not record EOG activity, gave no descriptions of their criteria for artifact rejection, recorded only a single EEG lead, and used a crude measure of peak latency that may have underestimated the size of the true latency differences. They also did not have any converging evidence, such as task manipulations, for what theoretical variables P3 reflected in their task. There were also differences in how RT and P3 behaved over time following nicotine (P3 was maximal at 10 min and then declined rapidly while RT was high for both 10 and 20 minutes posttesting).

Another group of studies has looked at the effects of nicotine on deprived smokers and has demonstrated the decrement in performance following deprivation and the improvement in performance following nicotine administration after a period of deprivation.

Snyder and Henningfield (1989) demonstrated an increase in reaction time (RT) following 12 hours of tobacco deprivation in volunteers in a special NIDA clinical ward. A choice RT task was used but the nature of the task was varied to assess serial search, logical reasoning, and digit recall. The stimuli were presented on a computer screen, and the response for all subtasks was a two-choice RT. Relative to a smoking baseline, RTs in all the subtasks were significantly increased after 12 hours of deprivation. In another study by this group (Snyder, Davis, & Henningfield, 1989) nicotine deprived smokers were studied for 10 days on the same computerized RT task. Nicotine deprivation increased RT starting 4 hours post deprivation. This increase peaked around 24 hours and then began to decline. However, even after 10 days of nicotine deprivation subjects still had longer RTs than their baseline measures. The nicotine deprived increase in RT is reversed by nicotine. Snyder and Henningfield (1989) showed that nicotine gum (0, 2, 4 mg) reversed the nicotine deprivation increase in RT and this effect was dose related. Snyder et al. (1989) showed that ad lib smoking after the 10-day deprivation period reduced RT and this effect became more prominent with time over repeated testing in the first 8 hours. In addition, the performance improvements following nicotine gum where not related to changes in subjective mood. These effects were very robust, being obtained in 6–7 subjects, and consistently obtained over different subtasks. Accuracy also changed with both nicotine deprivation and nicotine, but the effects were more consistent for RT.

The contrast between nicotinic and muscarinic activity is less obvious in human studies than in animal studies. Nicotine has regularly been reported to have effects opposite to those produced by antimuscarinics, and, in all cases where it has been tried, nicotine has reversed the effect of an antimuscarinic (Warburton, 1990). It is not necessarily the case that NIC affects the same stage and/or mode of information processing as SCOP. Some of the results described above would indicate that NIC affects stimulus processing. But other reports (Petrie & Deary, 1989) have concluded that NIC affects response processing. An alternative model is that NIC has a general effect on information processing, and thus affects all stages of information processing with no evidence of localization.

## CONCLUSION

The progression outlined in this review has been from the general to the specific. We began with a drug, DAMP, that has broad stimulant effects on the aminergic systems, both dopaminergic and noradrenergic. As it became clear that DAMP's effects, while clearly specific to response processing, were not going to lead to any more detailed parsing of this system, we adopted the use of the specific drugs YOH and CLON. Unexpectedly, these drugs, rather than homing in on the response processes, showed evidence of stimulus-related effects. These results have raised fundamental questions about the interrelationship between ERP latencies and RT, but this does not alter our basic premise that information processing may be chemically parsed.

In our research on the cholinergic system we have relied on a single drug, SCOP, and our efforts have been rewarded by the gradual realization that while the serial model provides a useful basis for designing experiments and determining outcomes, there comes a point where it breaks down and an alternative model may more parsimoniously account for the results. We are at this point now. We do not know if the cholinergic system differentially drives parallel and serial processing, but we do know that we can generate some very specific hypotheses to evaluate this idea. We also have more work to do in contrasting SCOP with cholinergic agonists such as PHY and ARE.

One of the more interesting aspects of this review is that it allows the comparison between drugs that produce similar subjective effects. For example, CLON and SCOP both reduce alertness and arousal, and increase ratings of fatigue (Profile of Mood States [POMS]) (McNair, Lorr, & Droppleman, 1971). However their patterns of effect on performance in the SE/RS task are quite different. SCOP slowed both RT and P3, but interacted with stimulus complexity only for RT. CLON slowed both RT and P3, but interacted with stimulus complexity only for P3. Both drugs slow mean RT and N1 latency by a comparable amount. These effects are not an artifact of the SE/RS task because a recent study reports similar findings with a tracking task. Frith, McGinty, Gergel, and Crow (1989) find that both SCOP and CLON decrease initial performance in a tracking task. But when the subject had to learn a new, more complicated tracking task, SCOP impaired the acquisition of the task but CLON did not. The usefulness of the information-processing approach combining measures of RT and ERP is that differential effects of superficially similar drugs can be clarified.

The goal of this chapter is to demonstrate that the links between cognition and pharmacology can be explored by using low doses of drugs with a normal adult subject population. Both the aminergic and cholinergic sections have reviewed data that support this idea. We have shown that different tasks (SE/RS and SF/LP), different measures (RT and ERP latencies), and different drugs can be used to parse the processing of information according to its neurochemical bases.

If we are unable at this point to say exactly which processes or stages of information processing are driven by which neurochemical systems, we hope we have made it clear that this area of study is only in its infancy. With only a few tasks, measures, and drugs, we have shown that the processing of information breaks down along neurochemical lines. The potential for this method in the arena of mental health is great. In the first instance, the fourth leading cause of death in this country is Alzheimer's disease, a disease in which the first indicators are decline of the higher mental processes, and which appears to be caused by loss of cholinergic neurons. An understanding of the mechanisms of this breakdown using specific tasks and drug probes could lead to the development of remedial treatments.

# REFERENCES

Bajalan, A. A. A., Wright, C. E., & Van der Vliet, V. J. (1986). Changes in the human visual evoked potential caused by the anticholinergic agent hyoscine hydrobromide: Comparison with results in Alzheimer's disease. *Journal of Neurology, Neurosurgery, and Psychiatry, 49,* 175–182.

Bartus, R. T., Dean, R. L., III, Beer, B., & Lippa, A. S. (1982). The cholinergic hypothesis of genatric memory dysfunction. *Science, 217,* 408–417.

Bashore, T. R. (1990). Stimulus-response compatibility viewed from a cognitive psychophysiological perspective. In R. W. Proctor & T. G. Reeve (Eds.), *Stimulus-response compatibility: An integrated perspective* (pp. 183–223). Amsterdam: North-Holland.

Beatty, W. W., Butters, N., & Janowsky, D. S. (1986). Patterns of memory failure after scopolamine treatment: Implications for cholinergic hypotheses of dementia. *Behavioral and Neural Biology, 45,* 196–211.

Brandeis, D., Callaway, E., Naylor, H., & Yano, L. (1988). Cholinergic control of stimulus and attentional processing. Abstract. *Psychophysiology, 25*(4), 425.

Brandeis, D., Naylor, H., Callaway, E., Halliday, R., Meeke, P., & Yano, L. (in press). Scopolamine affects easy to discriminate targets. In C. M. M. Brunig, A. W. K. Gaillard & A. Kok (Eds.), *Psychophysiological brain research.* Tilburg: Tilburg Univ. Press.

Broks, P., Preston, G. C., Traub, M., Poppleton, P., Ward C., & Stahl, S. M. (1988). Modelling dementia: Effects of scopolamine on memory and attention. *Neuropsychologia, 26,* 685–700.

Caine, E. D., Weingartner, H., Ludlow, C. L., Cudahy, E. A., & Wehry, S. (1981). Qualitative analysis of scopolamine-induced amnesia. *Psychopharmacology, 74,* 74–80.

Callaway, E. (1983). The pharmacology of human information processing. *Psychophysiology, 20,* 359–371.

Callaway, E. (1984). Human information processing: Some effects of methylphenidate, age and scopolamine. *Biological Psychiatry, 19,* 649–662.

Callaway, E., & Band, I. (1958). Some psychopharmacological effects of atropine. *Archives of Neurology and Psychiatry, 79,* 91–102.

Callaway, E., Halliday, R., Naylor, H., & Schechter, G. (1985). Effects of oral scopolamine on human stimulus evaluation. *Psychopharmacology, 85,* 133–138.

Charney, D. S., & Heninger, G. R. (1986a). Alpha-adrenergic and opiate receptor blockade. *Archives of General Psychiatry, 43,* 1037–1041.

Charney, D. S., & Heninger, G. R. (1986b). Abnormal regulation of noradrenergic function in panic disorders. *Archives of General Psychiatry, 43,* 1042–1054.

Coles, M. G. H., Gratton, G., Kramer, A. F., & Miller, G. A. (1986). Principles of signal acquisition and analysis. In M. G. H. Coles, E. Donchin, & S. W. Porges (Eds.), *Psychophysiology: Systems, processes, and applications* (pp. 183–221). New York: Guilford Press.

Cooper, J. R., Bloom, F. E., & Roth, R. H. (1986). *The biochemical basis of neuropharmacology.* New York: Oxford University Press.

Costall, B., Naylor, R. J., & Pinder, R. M. (1976). Characterization of the mechanisms for hyperactivity induction from the nucleus accumbens by phenylethylamine derivatives. *Psychopharmacology, 48,* 225–231.

Creese, I. (1983). *Stimulants: Neurochemical, behavioral, and clinical perspectives.* New York: Raven Press.

Donchin, E. (1979). Event-related potentials: A tool in the study of human information processing. In H. Begleiter (Ed.), *Evoked potentials and behavior* (pp. 13–75). New York: Plenum Press.

Drachman, D. A. (1978). Central cholinergic system and memory. In M. A. Lipton, A. DiMascio, & K. F. Killam (Eds.), *Psychopharmacology: A generation of progress* (pp. 651–662). New York: Raven Press.

Drachman, D. A., & Leavitt, J. (1974). Human memory and the cholinergic system. A relationship to aging? *Archives of Neurology, 30,* 113–121.

Duncan-Johnson, C. C., & Kopel, B. S. (1981). The Stroop effect: Brain potentials localize the source of interference. *Science, 214,* 938–940.

Dunne, M. P., & Hartley, L. R. (1985). The effects of scopolamine upon verbal memory: Evidence for an attentional hypothesis. *Acta Psychologica, 58,* 205–217.

Dunne, M. P., & Hartley, L. R. (1986). Scopolamine and the control of attention in humans. *Psychopharmacology, 89,* 94–97.

Edwards, J. A., Wesnes, K., & Warburton, D. (1985). Evidence of more rapid stimulus evaluation following cigarette smoking. *Addictive Behaviors, 10,* 113–126.

Fitzpatrick, P., Klorman, R., Brumaghim, J. T., & Keeover, R. W. (1988). Effects of methylphenidate on stimulus evaluation and response processes: Evidence from performance and event-related potentials. *Psychophysiology, 25*(3), 292–304.

Ford, J. M., & Pfefferbaum, A. (1980). The utility of brain potentials in determining age-related changes in central nervous system and cognitive functioning. In L. W. Poon (Ed.), *Aging in the 1980s: Psychological issues* (pp. 115–124). Washington, DC: American Psychological Association.

Frith, C. D., McGinty, M. A., Gergel, I., & Crow, T. J. (1989). The effects of scopolamine and clonidine on the performance and learning of a motor skill. *Psychopharmacology, 98,* 120–125.

Frowein, H. W. (1981a). *Selective drug effects on information processing.* Doctoral dissertation, Institute of Perception TNO, Soesterberg, The Netherlands.

Frowein, H. W. (1981b). Selective effects of barbiturate and amphetamine on information processing and response execution. *Acta Psychologica, 47,* 105–115.

Frowein, H. W., Gaillard, A. W. K., & Varey, C. A. (1981). EP components, visual processing stages and the effect of a barbiturate. *Biological Psychology, 13,* 239–249.

Frowein, H. W., & Sanders, A. F. (1978). Effects of amphetamine and barbiturate in a serial reaction task under paced and self-paced conditions. *Acta Psychologica, 42,* 263–276.

Ghoneim, M. M., & Mewaldt, S. P. (1975). Effects of diazepam and scopolamine on storage, retrieval and organizational processes in memory. *Psychopharmacologia* (Berl.), *44,* 257–262.

Ghoneim, M. M., & Mewaldt, S. P. (1977). Studies on human memory: The interactions of diazepam, scopolamine and physostigmine. *Psychopharmacology, 52,* 1–6.

Halliday, R., Callaway, E., & Lannon, R. (1989). The effects of clonidine and yohimbine on human information processing. *Psychopharmacology, 99,* 563–566.

Halliday, R., Callaway, E., & Lynch, M. (1984). Age, stimulant drug and practice effects on P3 latency and concurrent reaction time. In R. Karrer, J. Cohen, & P. Tueting ( Eds.), *Brain and information: Event-related potentials* (Vol. 425, pp. 357–361). New York: The New York Academy of Sciences.

Halliday, R., Callaway, E., & Naylor, H. (1983). Visual evoked potential changes induced by methylphenidate in hyperactive children: Dose/response effects. *Electroencephalography and Clinical Neurophysiology, 55,* 258–264.

Halliday, R., Callaway, E., Naylor, H., Gratzinger, P., & Prael, R. (1986). The effects of stimulant drugs on information processing in the elderly. *Journal of Gerontology, 41,* 748–757.

Halliday, R., Naylor, H., Callaway, E., Yano, L., & Walton, P. (1987) What's done can't always be undone: The effects of stimulant drugs and dopamine blockers on information processing. In R. Johnson, Jr., J. W. Rohrbaugh, & R. Parasuraman (Eds.), *Current trends in event-related potential research (EEG Suppl. 40)* pp. 228–234). Amsterdam: Elsevier Science Publishers.

Halliday, R., Perez-Stable, E. J., Coates, T. J., Hauck, W., Gardiner, P., & Hilliard, R. (1990). *Long term use of propranolol may impair specific cognitive functions.* Presented at the Thirtieth Annual Meeting of the Society for Psychophysiological Research, Boston, MA.

Hess, W. R. (1954). *Diencephalon: Autonomic and extrapyramidal functions. Monographs in biology and medicine* New York: Grune and Stratton. (Vol. III).

Hockey, G. R. J., Coles, M. G. H., & Gaillard, A. W. K. (1986). Energetical issues in research on human information processing. In G. R. J. Hockey, A. W. K. Gaillard, & M. G. H. Coles (Eds.), *Energetics and human information processing* (pp. 3–21). Dordrecht: Martinus Nijhoff Pubs.

Hunt, E. (1983). On the nature of intelligence. *Science, 219,* 141–146.

Johnsson, L. E. (1972). Pharmacological blockade of amphetamine effects in amphetamine-dependent subjects. *European Journal of Clinical Pharmacology, 4,* 206–211.

Kahneman, D. (1973). *Attention and effort.* Englewood Cliffs, NJ: Prentice-Hall.

Leckman, J. F., Maas, J. W., Redmond, D. E., & Heninger, G. R. (1980). Effects of oral clonidine on plasma 3-methoxy-4-hydroxyphenylethylene glycol (MHPG) in man: Preliminary report. *Life Sciences, 26,* 2179–2185.

Lopatka, J. E., Brewerton, C. N., Brooks, D. S., Cook, D. A., & Paton, D. M. (1976). The protective effects of methysergide, 6-hydroxydopamine and other agents on the toxicity of amphetamine, phentermine, MDA, PMA, and STP in mice. *Research Communications in Chemical Pathology and Pharmacology, 14*(4), 677–687.

Magliero, A., Bashore, T. R., Coles, M. G. H., & Donchin, E. (1984). On the dependence of P300 latency on stimulus evaluation processes. *Psychophysiology, 21,* 171–186.

McCarthy, G., & Donchin, E. (1981). A metric for thought: A comparison of P3 latency and reaction time. *Science, 211,* 77–80.

McNair, D. M., Lorr, M., & Droppleman, L. F. (1971). *Profile of mood states (POMS).* San Diego, CA: Educational and Industrial Testing Service.

Meek, P., Callaway, E., Merrin, E. L., & Juarez, M. (1989). On the variety of relations between spatial frequency and reaction time. *International Journal of Neuroscience, 45*, 55–69.

Meyer, D. E., Osman, A., Irwin, D. E., & Yantis, S. (1988). Modern mental chronometry. *Biological Psychology, 26*, 33–57.

Miller, J. (1988). Discrete and continuous models of human information processing: Theoretical distinctions. *Acta Psychologica (Amst.), 67*, 191–257.

Molenaar, P. C. M., Van der Molen, M. W., & Halliday, R. (submitted). Energetic effects on the duration of processing stages: Analysis of higher-order moments using an additive neural network representation of Sanders' cognitive energetic model.

Moore, K. E. (1977). The actions of amphetamine on neurotransmitters: A brief review. *Biological Psychiatry, 12*, 451–462.

Mulder, G., Gloerich, A. B. M., Brookhuis, K. A., van Dellen, H. J., & Mulder, L. J. M. (1984). Stage analysis of the reaction process using brain-evoked potentials and reaction time. *Psychological Research, 46*, 15–32.

Naylor, H., Brandeis, D., Halliday, R., Yano, L., & Callaway, E. (1988). Why does scopolamine make "easy" difficult? Abstract. *Psychophysiology, 25*(4) 472.

Naylor, H., Halliday, R., & Callaway, E. (1985). The effect of methylphenidate on information processing. *Psychopharmacology, 86*, 90–95.

Norman, D. A., & Bobrow, D. G. (1975). On data-limited and resource-limited processes. *Cognitive Psychology, 7*, 44–64.

Oades, R. D. (1985). The role of noradrenaline in tuning and dopamine in switching between signals in the CNS. *Neuroscience and Behavior Reviews, 9*(2), 261–282.

Ostfeld, A. M., & Aruguette, A. (1962). Central nervous system effects of hyoscine in man. *Journal of Pharmacology and Experimental Therapy, 137*, 133–139.

Petersen, R. C. (1977). Scopolamine induced learning failures in man. *Psychopharmacology, 52*, 283–289.

Petrie, R. X. A., & Deary, I. J. (1989). Smoking and human information processing. *Psychophysiology, 99*, 393–396.

Posner, M. I. (1978). *Chronometric explorations of mind*. Hillsdale, NJ: Erlbaum.

Posner, M. I., & Snyder, C. R. R. (1975). Facilitation and inhibition in the processing of signals. In P. M. A. Rabbitt & S. Dornic (Eds.), *Attention and performance V*. New York: Academic Press.

Ragot, R., & Lesevre, N. (1986). Electrophysiological study of intrahemispheric s-r compatibility effects elicited by visual directional cues. *Psychophysiology, 23*(1), 19–27.

Rusted, J. M. (1989). Dissociative effects of scopolamine on working memory in healthy young volunteers. *Psychopharmacology, 96*, 487–492.

Rusted, J. M., & Warburton, D. M. (1989). Cognitive models and cholinergic drugs. *Neuropsychobiology, 21*, 31–36.

Sanders, A. F. (1983). Toward a model of stress and human performance. *Acta Psychologica, 53*, 61–97.

Shwartz, S. P., Pomerantz, J. R., & Egeth, H. E. (1977). State and process limitations in information processing: An additive factors analysis. *Journal of Experimental Psychology: Human Perception and Performance, 3*, 402–410.

Snyder, F. R., Davis, F. C., & Henningfield, J. E. (1989). The tobacco withdrawal syndrome: Performance decrements assessed on a computerized test battery. *Drug and Alcohol Dependence, 23*, 259–266.

Snyder, F. R., & Henningfield, J. E. (1989). Effects of nicotine administration following 12 h of tobacco deprivation: Assessment on computerized performance tasks. *Psychopharmacology (Berlin), 97*, 17–22.

Soubrie, P. (1986). Reconciling the role of central serotonin neurons in human and animal behavior. *Behavioral and Brain Sciences, 9*(2), 319–363.

Sternberg, R. (1977). *Intelligence, information processing and analogical reasoning.* Hillsdale, NJ: Erlbaum.

Sternberg, S. (1969). The discovery of processing stages: Extensions of Donders' method. In W. G. Koster (Ed.), *Acta Psychologica 30 Attention and Performance II.* Elsevier: North-Holland.

Sutton, S., Braren, J., Zubin, J., & John, E. R. (1967). Information delivery and the sensory evoked potential. *Science, 155*, 14–36.

Thompson, R. F. (1967). *Foundations of physiological psychology.* New York: Harper & Row.

Treisman, A., & Souther, J. (1985). Search asymmetry: A diagnostic for preattentive processing of separable features. *Journal of Experimental Psychology: General, 114*, 285–310.

Treisman, A. (1985). Preattentive processing in vision. *Computer Vision, Graphics, and Image Processing, 31*, 156–177.

Treisman, A. M., & Gelade, G. (1980). A feature-integrating theory of attention. *Cognitive Psychology, 12*, 97–136.

Vanderwolf, C. H., & Robinson, T. E. (1981). Reticulo-cortical activity and behavior: A critique of the arousal theory and a new synthesis. *Behavioral and Brain Sciences, 4*(3), 459–475.

Warburton, D. M., & Brown, K. (1972). The facilitation of discrimination performance by physostigmine sulphate. *Psychopharmacologia (Berlin), 27*, 275–284.

Warburton, D. M., & Wesnes, K. (1984). Drugs as research tools in psychology: Cholinergic drugs and information processing. *Neuropsychobiology, 11*, 275–284.

Warburton, D. M., & Wesnes, K. (1985). Historical overview of research on cholinergic systems and behavior. In M. M. Singh, D. M. Warburton & H. Lai (Eds.), *Central cholinergic mechanisms and adaptive dysfunctions.* New York: Plenum.

Warburton, D. M. (1987). Drugs and the processing of information. In S. M. Stahl & S. D. Iversen (Eds.), *Cognitive neurochemistry* (pp. 112–133). Oxford: Oxford University Press.

Warburton, D. M. (1990). Psychopharmacological aspects of nicotine. In S. Wonnacott, M. H. A. Russel, & I. P. Stollerman (Eds.), *Nicotine psychopharmacology* (pp. 77–111). Oxford: Oxford University Press.

Weiss, B., & Laties, V. (1962). Enhancement of human performance by caffeine and the amphetamines. *Pharmacological Review, 14*, 1–36.

Wesnes, K., Warburton, D. M., & Matz, B. (1983). Effects of nicotine on stimulus sensitivity and response bias in visual vigilance task. *Neuropsychobiology, 9*, 41–44.

Wesnes, K., & Revell, A. (1984). The separate and combined effects of scopolamine and nicotine on human information processing. *Psychopharmacology, 84*, 5–11.

Wesnes, K., & Warburton, D. M. (1983). Effects of scopolamine on stimulus sensitivity and response bias in visual vigilance task. *Neuropsychobiology, 9,* 154–157.

Wesnes, K., & Warburton, D. M. (1983). Effects of smoking on rapid information processing performance. *Neuropsychobiology, 9,* 223–229.

Wesnes, K., & Warburton, D. M. (1984). Effects of scopolamine and nicotine on rapid human information processing performance. *Psychopharmacology, 82,* 147–150.

Yelnosky, J., Panasevich, R. E., Borrelli, A. R., & Lawlor, R. B. (1969). Pharmacology of phentermine. *Archives of International Pharmacodynamics, 178*(1), 62–77.

Yim, C. Y., & Mogenson, G. J. (1986). Mesolimbic dopamine projection modulates amygdala-evoked EPSP in nucleus accumbens neurons: An in vivo study. *Brain Research, 369*(1–2), 347–352.

Zametkin, A. J., Karoum, F., Linnoila, M., Rapoport, J. L., Brown, G. L., Chuang, L., & Wyatt, R. J. (1985). Stimulants, urinary catecholamines, and indoleamines in hyperactivity. *Archives of General Psychiatry, 42,* 251–255.

*Chapter 9*

# Neural and Hormonal Mechanisms Mediating Sex Differences in Cognition*

### Doreen Kimura and Elizabeth Hampson

*University of Western Ontario, London, Canada*

A major reason for studying sex differences, apart from the intrinsic interest, is that such research provides a systematic means of investigating individual variation in behavior. The information derived from studying sex differences will increase our understanding of the mechanisms for many intellectual or problem-solving behaviors, and thus, how these come to vary across different individuals, male or female.

* This research was supported by grants to the first author from the Medical Research Council and the Natural Sciences and Engineering Research Council, Ottawa, Canada. The second author was the recipient of a predoctoral fellowship from the Medical Research Council and a postdoctoral fellowship from the Natural Sciences and Engineering Research Council.

Reprint requests should be sent to D. Kimura, Dept. Psychology, Univ. Western Ont., London, Canada, N6A 5C2.

* We are grateful to Corinne Toussaint for assistance in data collection, and to Neil Watson for assistance in data analysis and for comments on the manuscript.

Human males and females are known to differ, on average, in their respective intellectual strengths. Women in Western cultures tend to excel on certain verbal abilities, such as fluency, spelling and early articulatory accuracy; tasks on which there are constraints related to the letter or sound to be selected (Maccoby, 1966). They tend also to be better on a function labeled "perceptual speed," which requires rapid scanning to find designated target stimuli or to decide whether two arrays are identical (Harshman, Hampson, & Berenbaum, 1983; Maccoby, 1966). Finally, there are reports that women are better at small-amplitude motor skills, or those requiring motor coordination within personal space (Kimura & Vanderwolf, 1970; Ingram, 1975; Maccoby, 1966; Tiffin, 1968).

Men, in contrast, are better on certain spatial tests, particularly those requiring accurate orientation to the vertical and horizontal (Witkin, Goodenough, & Karp, 1967), or imaginal rotation of stimuli (Sanders, Soares, & D'Aquila, 1982). Another task on which they excel, albeit less obviously spatial, is the disembedding of a simple geometric form from a more complex figure (Witkin et al., 1967). Males are also superior on motor skills requiring accurate targeting of distant stimuli (Jardine & Martin, 1983; Watson & Kimura, 1989, 1991). They also excel on tests of mathematical reasoning (Benbow, 1988). Obviously, when we speak of average differences, it is implicit that there is great overlap between males and females in their performance on such tasks.

Table 9.1 shows the results across different studies in our laboratory, for motor tasks performed in personal and extrapersonal space. Females are significantly better than males in performing isolated finger movements, or hand postures involving such movements. However, their previously reported superiority on speeded fine movement tasks like the Purdue Pegboard (Tiffin, 1968) may in part be related to their smaller hand size (Peters, Servos, & Day, 1990), though Peters et al. have not ruled out a hormonal contribution. Males, in contrast, are superior on throwing accuracy. Both patterns are present at a very early age (Ingram, 1975; Lunn & Kimura, 1989).

Many of these sex differences may be understood within the context of evolutionary pressures for sexual dimorphism in the hunter-gatherer society in which our brains developed (Daly & Wilson, 1983). In this milieu, men had chief responsibility for the hunting of both large and small game, which would select for accurate targeting ability, initially perhaps in simple stone throwing, ultimately in the wielding of larger manufactured weapons. The hunting of large game also required accurate navigational skills, since it took the hunter far from the home base, sometimes for long periods of time (Lovejoy, 1981).

Women in such societies had the primary responsibility for care of small children, and for preparation of food, clothing, and household articles, activities carried on in or near the home base. These activities would be especially demanding of motor skills executed within reach, that is, within personal space. If we can take present-day primitive societies as models, it appears that women

Table 9.1. Sex Differences on Intrapersonal and Extrapersonal
Motor Tasks

| | Children | | | |
| --- | --- | --- | --- | --- |
| Task | Source | Boys | Girls | p |
| Hand Postures (%) | Ingram (1975) | 73.7 | 79.5 | <.05 |
| Throwing (errors/cm) | Lunn & Kimura (1989) | 15.8 | 18.8 | <.04 |
| | Adults | | | |
| Task | Source | Men | Women | p |
| Finger Flexion (%) | Kimura & Vanderwolf (1970) | 48.7 | 52.0 | <.05 |
| Throwing (errors/cm) | Watson & Kimura (1989) | 14.3 | 23.2 | <.01 |

also were the chief contributors to foraging, again typically within sight of the home base, or at most within a distance where landmarks would be favored as navigation cues. The ability to make rapid identity matches might also be differentially selected, since it would be of importance both in detecting small changes in children, and in discriminating edible from inedible food.

Of course, many would argue that men and women are reared quite differently, even in our present Western society, and that this is the chief basis for any differences in cognitive strengths between the sexes. While not denying that differential experience contributes to idiosyncratic cognitive patterns, our task will be to indicate that certain basic biological mechanisms contribute substantially to the established sex differences, and that they are in fact important determinants of individual differences in the broad sense, quite apart from the male/female dichotomy. Moreover, any environmental factors must operate within these biological frameworks, making it problematic to separate experiential influences from physiological ones.

Two chief areas of investigation will be reviewed. One is concerned with sex differences in brain organization and morphology, the other with the role of sex hormones in determining individual differences. Although sex differences in brain organization have been assumed for some time, direct evidence that such variation is systematically related to variation in cognitive function or pattern is meager. This is almost certainly because in the past it has been technically difficult to relate these two functions within an individual. With the invention of noninvasive brain-imaging and recording techniques, information on the relation between brain morphology/physiology and cognitive function will undoubtedly increase.

In contrast, the evidence that sex hormones contribute to cognitive variation is substantial, and much of our chapter is concerned with such hormonal evidence. We do not consider genetic evidence directly, since this topic is covered in other contributions to this volume.

## SEX DIFFERENCES IN BRAIN ORGANIZATION

### Brain Asymmetry and Commissural Connections

There is a generally accepted view in the neuropsychological literature that cognitive functions are more bilaterally represented in females than in males. Although a detailed review of this question is beyond the scope of this chapter, some aspects of the question are pertinent to sex differences in cognitive ability, and these are briefly reviewed. The two major variants of the bilaterality hypothesis are (a) that assignment of particular functions to one hemisphere is less marked in females (Bryden, 1982; McGlone, 1980); and (b) that inter-hemispheric commissural connections are stronger in females, so that each hemisphere normally has better access to the specialized functions of the other hemisphere.

The supposed superiority of women for verbal abilities is explained in this schema by the more bilateral representation of verbal functions. Paradoxically, however, the fact that women show poorer average spatial ability than men has also been attributed to the lesser specialization of the right hemisphere for such functions in women (Bryden, 1979; Witelson, 1976). This would, of course, mean that asymmetric organization is advantageous for spatial ability, while bilateral representation is favored for verbal ability. While such an arrangement is by no means impossible, it will be seen that the evidence in favor of either of these assumptions is sparse. There is, however, evidence in male rodents that the right hemisphere is thicker than the left, while in females there is a nonsignificant trend for the left to be thicker (Diamond, Dowling, & Johnson, 1981). A recent report of an analogous pattern in the human fetus (deLacoste, Horvath, & Woodward, 1991) would lead one to expect that some aspects of asymmetric functioning might also be different in men and women. Only future research can determine what these might be.

It has been reported that the major commissure between the hemispheres, the corpus callosum, is larger in its splenial (most posterior) portion in women than in men (deLacoste & Holloway, 1982; deLacoste, Adesanya, & Woodward, in press) [Note that Witelson (1989) disputes this claim.] While it is always risky to infer function from morphology, the simple inference from the sex difference in the splenium might be that those functions more dependent on the posterior part of the brain are more readily accessible to each hemisphere, through callosal connections, in women than in men. A recent study relating posterior callosum size to verbal fluency in women (Hines, Sloan, Lawrence, Lipcamon, & Chiu, 1988) is thus somewhat paradoxical, since fluency is thought to be more depen-dent on anterior systems (Milner, 1964). Nevertheless, it does suggest that interhemispheric transmission may be a more significant factor for certain cogni-tive functions.

The inference that women's brains are functionally less asymmetrically organized than men's is based on two main lines of evidence: (a) degree of lateralization on various perceptual tests, assumed to reflect degree of cerebral asymmetry, with women more often showing lesser asymmetries than men (Bryden, 1982) ; and (b) the lower incidence of intellectual defects of the kind expected after pathology to one cerebral hemisphere (McGlone, 1980). Most of the latter data derive from standardized tests of intelligence. While such tests are adequate for measuring general intelligence, the subtests typically are not pure enough to allow inferences about coherent cognitive "factors."

Additionally, there is a lower incidence in women of aphasia or outright speech disorders after left-hemisphere damage (McGlone, 1977). If the lower incidence of aphasia after left-hemisphere pathology in women were indeed related to more bilateral speech representation, one might expect a higher incidence of aphasia after right-hemisphere damage in women than in men. In a retrospective review of all right-handed cases with unilateral right-hemisphere damage in a series seen by the first author, 2 of 105 men and 1 of 84 women were aphasic (Kimura, 1987). The incidence is thus under 2 percent for each sex, with no difference between them. It therefore seems improbable that a substantial contribution is made by the right hemisphere in women, to basic speech function as tested in screening for aphasia.

Nevertheless, when we look at more abstract verbal function, of the kind tested by vocabulary, for example, we do find some evidence for a proportionally greater right-hemisphere contribution in women than in men. After right-hemisphere pathology, performance on the Vocabulary subtest of the Wechsler Adult Intelligence Scale is more depressed in women, compared to an age- and sex-matched control group, than is true for men (Kimura & Harshman, 1984). However, this is not true for all verbal functions, nor is the parallel true for any of the subtests of the Performance IQ. The effect of a right-hemisphere lesion on the constructional tests Block Design and Object Assembly is quite comparable in men and women (Table 9.2). Overall analysis of variance shows only a weak trend for a side effect, no sex effect, and no sex X side interaction.

**Table 9.2.   Scores on Constructional Tasks in Males and Females after Unilateral Damage**

| Side | N | Block Design | Object Assembly |
|------|---|--------------|-----------------|
| Left (Males) | 177 | 22.9 (11.1) | 22.7 (9.8) |
| Right (Males) | 105 | 21.2 (14.1) | 20.6 (10.8) |
| L-R | | 1.7 NS | 2.1 NS |
| | | | |
| Left (Females) | 100 | 24.9 (11.9) | 24.3 (11.1) |
| Right (Females) | 86 | 23.0 (12.2) | 22.7 (9.2) |
| L-R | | 1.9 NS | 1.6 NS |

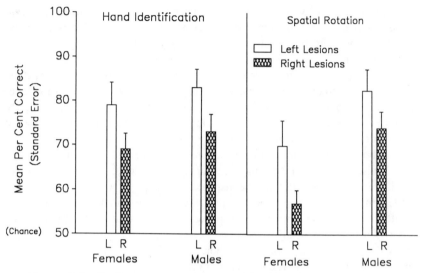

**Figure 9.1.  Performance on two spatial tasks after left- or right-hemisphere damage in males and females.**

One might argue again that tasks such as Block Design and Object Assembly are quite complex, requiring more than spatial analysis for their performance. We have recently been accumulating data on two other tasks of a more purely spatial nature, a Hand Identification task, and a Rotation task. In the Hand Identification task, the subject is shown line drawings of a gloved left or right hand in various orientations, and must point to one of two stuffed gloves in front of him to indicate which is depicted. No naming or any vocal utterance is permitted. (In a second phase of the task, not reported here, the pictures are identified by verbally labeling the hand as left or right.) In the Rotation task, the stimuli to be viewed are actual 3-dimensional block versions of Shepard-Metzler-type designs.[1] Two mirror-image blocks are placed in front of the subject, and a pack of cards, each containing a photograph of one of the blocks must be sorted by placing the photos in front of the appropriate block.

Unlike the constructional tasks above, there is a significant difference overall between groups of patients with unilateral left or right pathology, as indicated by significant effects of side of lesion on both tests (Figure 9.1). However, there is no difference between the sexes in the magnitude of the right-hemisphere decrement, thus no trace of a side X sex interaction. There is only a slight tendency for women overall to be inferior to men on the Hands task, but the effect of sex is significant for the Rotation task ($F = 10.38$, $df = 1.56$, $p < 01$).

---

[1] The Hand Identification and Spatial Rotation tests were constructed and modified with the assistance of Neil Watson and Gerry Stefanatos.

The evidence for sex differences in perceptual asymmetry is more substantial (Bryden, 1982). However, both those findings and the differing incidence of aphasia in men and women after left-hemisphere pathology may be subject to alternative interpretations, related to differing intrahemispheric organization of function between the sexes (see below).

## Sex Differences in Intrahemispheric Organization of Function

Although the incidence of aphasia after right-hemisphere pathology is no higher in women than in men, when one compares anterior and posterior brain damage within the left hemisphere, some clear sex differences emerge. Aphasia occurs significantly less often after left posterior damage in women than in men, but the reverse is true for anterior damage, that is, it more often results in aphasia in women (Table 9.3). The same has been found to be true for cases of global aphasia, which is usually said to occur after widespread damage in the left hemisphere. When it occurs after restricted damage, there is an anterior dependence in women, and a posterior dependence in men (Cappa & Vignolo, 1988; Vignolo, Baccardi, & Caverni, 1986). This increased dependence of speech functions on the anterior system in females may also account for the reduced incidence of aphasia after left-hemisphere pathology. When vascular pathology does not involve the entire hemisphere, it more often spares the anterior than the posterior regions, making it less likely that the critical speech areas in women would be affected.

This sex difference in dependence on anterior and posterior systems is even sharper for manual apraxia, a disorder in motor programming which is a common consequence of left-hemisphere pathology, and is closely associated with aphasia (Kimura, 1983, 1987). Apraxia of this kind has typically been tested in our lab by having subjects copy meaningless movements, or by having them learn and then perform a speeded motor sequencing task (Figure 9.2). Manual apraxia in women occurs almost exclusively after anterior damage, while in men the reverse pattern obtains (Table 9.4). Most of the apraxic males shown in Table 9.4 have pathology involving the left parietal lobe. Thus the greatest functional discrepancy between males and females for speech and praxic function combined appears to be in the parietal lobe. This is consistent also with data from

**Table 9.3.   Incidence of Aphasia in Males and Females after Restricted Left-Hemisphere Pathology**

|  | Anterior Lesions | | | Posterior Lesions | | |
|---|---|---|---|---|---|---|
|  | Total | Aphasic | Nonaphasic | Total | Aphasic | Nonaphasic |
| Females | 14 | 9 | 5 | 30 | 4 | 26 |
| Males | 18 | 5 | 13 | 46 | 19 | 27 |
|  |  | $X^2 = 4.27$ ($p < .04$) | |  | $X^2 = 6.73$ ($p < .01$) | |

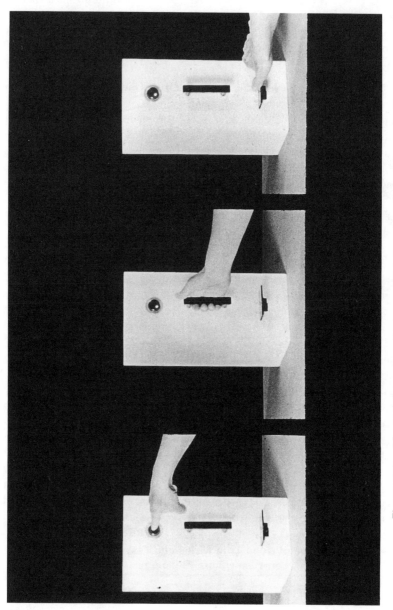

Figure 9.2. Manual Sequence Box, sensitive to manual apraxia, as well to fluctuations in estrogen levels.

**Table 9.4.  Incidence of Manual Apraxia after Restricted Left-Hemisphere Pathology**

|  | Anterior | | | Posterior | | |
|---|---|---|---|---|---|---|
|  | Total | Apraxic | Nonapraxic | Total | Apraxic | Nonapraxic |
| Females | 14 | 10 | 4 | 27 | 2 | 25 |
| Males | 16 | 2 | 14 | 43 | 19 | 24 |
|  | $X^2 = 10.8$ ($p < .001$) | | | $X^2 = 10.7$ ($p < .001$) | | |

misnaming after cortical stimulation, where parietal lobe stimulation results in much less frequent speech disruption in women than in men (Mateer, Polen, & Ojemann, 1982).

A parallel sex difference is found for the right hemisphere, on constructional tasks (Figure 9.3). Women with right anterior pathology are significantly impaired on Block Design and Object Assembly subtests, compared both to women with posterior pathology, and to men with anterior pathology. Men show a reverse trend, but those with posterior pathology differ from those with anterior pathology only in the Object Assembly subtest. This is compatible with the previous evidence that the functional difference between anterior and posterior systems is smaller in males, consistent with the pattern for the left hemisphere/ speech and praxis systems.

Although not shown in the figure, women with right anterior damage are not impaired on the test for manual praxis (Copying Movements), indicating that praxic function, like speech, is no more bilaterally organized in women than in men (Kimura, 1987).

If we reexamine the perceptual asymmetry studies in the light of these anterior/posterior differences, an alternative explanation for the lesser perceptual asymmetries presents itself. That is, the speech systems critical for processing verbal input to the left hemisphere, from the right ear or the right visual field, may be synaptically further from the posteriorly based cortical receiving areas in women. Thus, the difference between left/right ear or visual field may be slightly diminished, due, not to lesser brain asymmetry, but to a different intra-hemispheric organization. It is also possible that better interhemispheric communication exists for posterior areas in women, related to increased callosal size. We need not, however, entirely rule out a sex difference in functional brain asymmetry, particularly for functions dependent on the posterior brain sectors. Precisely what these functions may be in women is still to be determined.

It has been suggested that the anterior/posterior sex difference may be related to the way in which male and female motor skills are organized (Kimura, 1987). In females, small-amplitude movements within personal space, especially involving the distal muscles, are more highly developed. Praxic or motor-

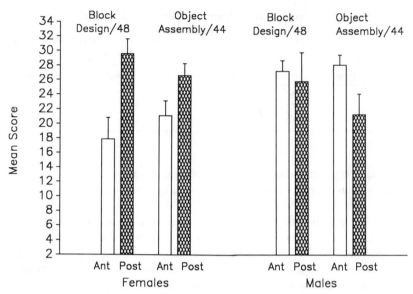

**Figure 9.3. Comparison of effects of "right" anterior and posterior lesions in males and females on two constructional tasks.**

programming control over such functions would be best served by close connections with the motor cortex. In males, praxic function should in theory be coordinated with large-amplitude movements directed at external stimuli, which would best be served by close connections with visual areas. But however plausible this explanation, there may be a more fundamental divergence of brain organization in males and females, since an anterior/posterior sex difference is seen also in rats, in which comparable praxic function does not exist (Kolb, 1990).

We have implied that the difference between male and female motor superiorities, the former directed at external targets and the latter within intrapersonal space, is related to the demonstrated sex difference in brain organization. However, we have no direct evidence that this is the case. What such an hypothesis might predict is that individuals, be they male or female, with praxic function more dependent on posterior regions, would tend to excel at targeting tasks, while individuals with these functions more dependent on anterior regions, would excel at intrapersonal motor skill. No data are available on this point, and it is not clear that it could be tested from lesion data alone. We will, however, outline below some evidence that manual praxic and articulatory functions, known to depend on the left hemisphere in both males and females, are very sensitive to fluctuations in estrogen.

## SEX HORMONE INFLUENCE
## ON NONREPRODUCTIVE BEHAVIORS

### Chronic Hormone Levels

We know, primarily from work in rodents, that fetal gonadal hormones determine whether male or female genitalia will be formed, and also whether sex-appropriate reproductive behaviors will occur in adulthood (Gorski & Jacobson, 1982). Since the latter are under central nervous system control, early exposure to sex hormones must somehow early-wire the brain to achieve lifelong effects on behavior. The effect on behavior of hormonal manipulations is still operative in rats in the immediate postnatal period, when the genitals are already formed. Castrating males in this period, and thus removing the effects of testosterone, will result in an increased incidence of the female sexual response, lordosis, in adulthood. Similarly, exposing females to androgens in this period will result in a higher incidence of mounting in adulthood. These early ''organizational'' effects, as they are called, extend to aggressive and territorial behavior as well, indicating that sex differences in brain organization are by no means limited to reproductive behaviors.

It is therefore reasonable to expect that early sex hormones might also influence problem-solving behaviors. This possibility has recently been investigated in rodents, in a radial-arm maze (Williams, Barnett, & Meck, 1990). Normal male rats perform somewhat better than females rats, and moreover, there are sex differences in mode of responding. Females may use either the landmark cues or the geometric cues in the room, while males prefer the geometric cues. These findings in rats are reminiscent of anecdotal reports in humans that males prefer directional or geometric cues in route finding, while females prefer landmark cues (Miller & Santoni, 1986; Ward, Newcombe, & Overton, 1986). In the Williams study, standard early hormonal manipulation of the kind described above resulted in a reversal of these abilities/preferences in adult male and female rats. This finding suggests that gonadal hormones have a pervasive influence on almost every aspect of sexually dimorphic behavior.

Gaulin and Fitzgerald (1989) propose that the sexual dimorphism found in rodents for spatial ability is based on a differential need for males and females to roam large territories. They find, in studies on several species of voles, that this sex difference obtains only in those species in which the males are polygynous, and thus must maintain larger territories to find females.

In humans, where direct manipulation of gonadal hormones is not possible, one must rely on natural experiments, which sometimes tend to confound hormonal effects with rearing practices. Nevertheless, the evidence suggests that more or less the same mechanisms operate for humans. As in rodents, the female ''default'' form may develop in the presence of an XY genotype, if androgens are not present early in life. Human XX individuals may also be masculinized in the presence of early androgens, to the point of exhibiting male genitalia. Other data indicate that the nervous system and the subsequent behavior are also affected. Thus girls with abnormal exposure to androgen or androgenic compounds tend to be tomboyish (Reinisch, 1981) and to have more masculine toy and game preferences than their unaffected siblings (Berenbaum & Hines, 1992).

Again, problem-solving abilities are not immune to such hormonal influences. Thus, Hier and Crowley (1982) studied a group of men with idiopathic hypogonadotrophic hypogonadism (IHH), and presumably lifelong testosterone deficiency, identified by delayed puberty. They were significantly worse than a group of men with late onset of pathologically reduced testosterone on a number of spatial tests, but not on verbal tests. Short-term androgen therapy did not restore spatial function. Resnick, Berenbaum, Gottesman, and Bouchard (1986) also found that girls with congenital adrenal hyperplasia (CAH), and consequent prenatal exposure to higher-than-normal levels of androgens, were superior to their siblings on spatial tasks. Even the slight exposure experienced in utero by females with male co-twins is apparently effective in enhancing spatial ability (Cole-Harding, Morstad, & Wilson, 1988). Such findings suggest that pre- and perinatal hormonal environments have lifelong effects on intellectual function in humans, just as in nonhumans.

The above studies might seem to suggest that there is a linear relation between androgenization and spatial ability, but this is apparently not the case. Within the *normal* range of androgens, there appears to be a curvilinear relationship, with the optimal level below that of the most androgenic males, but above that of the average female (Petersen, 1976; Shute, Pellegrino, Hubert, & Reynolds, 1983). Shute et al. reported that normal males selected for low plasma testosterone were superior to those at the high end on certain spatial tests; while in females, the reverse was true, that is, highest-androgen females were superior. The low positive correlations found between testosterone levels and performance on spatial tasks in young men (Christiansen & Knussmann, 1987) are compatible with a curvilinear relation, though the data are not presented in such a way as to permit the inference directly.

We have found an effect similar to that of Shute et al., using not the extremes of the group only, but a simple median split to divide all subjects on the basis of saliva testosterone levels[2], again in normal young men and women. The results of such analyses are shown in Figure 9.4. for one spatial test, the Paper Folding test (Ekstrom, French, Harman, & Dermen, 1976). On this test, there is a significant sex by hormone-level interaction, indicating that high levels of testosterone in females, and low levels of testosterone in males, are associated

---

[2] Testosterone levels were determined by radioimmunoassay using a Coat-a-Count kit manufactured by Diagnostic Products Corporation, 5700 West 96th St., Los Angeles. We are grateful to Dr. A. Rees Midgeley, Dr. Jill Becker, and Ms. Monika Naegeli at the University of Michigan, Ann Arbor, for their assistance in obtaining these values.

with superior performance. A composite score for tests on which males normally excel (Shepard-Metzler, Paper Folding, Mathematical Reasoning) shows a similar effect while a composite score for two perceptual speed tasks (Finding a's, Identical Pictures) on which females usually excel, shows no such effect (Gouchie & Kimura, 1991). Shute et al. did not report any data for nonspatial tests, but Christiansen and Knussmann reported fewer significant correlations of testosterone level with verbal than with spatial tests.

The interpretation of all such findings is complicated by the fact that testosterone may exert some of its effects through aromatization to estradiol in the brain (McEwen, 1987). Female brains are thought to be protected from masculinization in early life by alpha-fetoprotein, which sequesters natural estrogen. The suggestion has been made that it is in fact the estrogen level which is related in a curvilinear fashion to spatial ability (Nyborg, 1988). Unfortunately, neither Shute et al.'s study, nor Christiansen and Knussmann's, nor our own, had measures of estrogen. Until we know the levels of all the relevant hormones within one study, such questions cannot be definitively answered.

We must also point out that most such studies have been done in Caucasians, and the conclusions may not be readily generalizable to other races or ethnic groups, in whom chronic hormone levels may be different (Ross et al., 1986; Soma, Takayama, Kiyokawa, Akaeda, & Tokoro, 1975; Tobias, 1966). Possibly related to such hormonal variation is the fact that the typical male superiority for

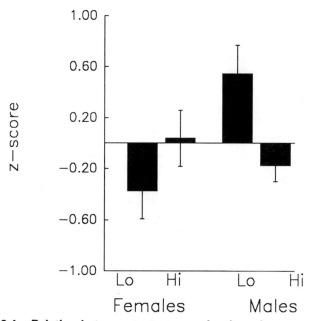

Figure 9.4.   **Relation between testosterone levels and scores on ETS Paper Folding test, in males and females.**

certain spatial tasks apparently does not hold for the Inuit (Berry, 1966), and that the sex difference for mathematical ability is significantly less in Asians (Benbow, 1988). To the extent that the physical and cognitive sexual dimorphism differs across groups, the relation of cognitive pattern to sex hormones may also differ. One would expect that each gene pool will be influenced by different environmental pressures for development of particular abilities in preference to others, as well as for development of sexual dimorphism in such abilities.

## Fluctuations in Hormones

We provisionally assume that the levels of testosterone being measured in our and others' normal young subjects are relatively stable, representing long-term states which differentiate individuals. They may in fact reflect the early organizational effects of gonadal hormones, though we have no way of confirming this. However, it is also known that temporary changes in hormones can affect behavior. This effect has been studied primarily in rodents, with respect to a variety of reproductive and nonreproductive behaviors (Beatty, 1979). There is also a report that a locomotor skill is enhanced in female rats during oestrus, compared with nonestrus, and that such enhancement can be reproduced in ovariectomized females by injection of 17-beta-estradiol into the striatum (Becker, Snyder, Miller, Westgate, & Jenuwine, 1987).

In humans, the regular fluctuations in estrogen and progesterone throughout the menstrual cycle provide another ready means to test effects on cognitive ability. Finding systematic variation in cognitive patterns across the cycle would strengthen the suggestion that intellectual functioning is in part determined by hormonal factors. Other subjects in whom gonadal hormones vary regularly are those on various kinds of hormone therapy—for example, post menopausal women. We tested subjects from both these populations—young women throughout the natural menstrual cycle, and postmenopausal women undergoing hormone replacement therapy—during high and low estrogen phases.

We adopted the simple hypothesis that variations in estrogen might selectively affect abilities on which women normally excel, on the assumption that estrogen somehow contributed to the stable female superiority on such tasks. Predictions for tasks on which males normally excel were less clear, but if anything were expected to show the opposite pattern. We thus chose tests on which either males or females, in turn, had demonstrated a superiority. Table 9.5 lists most of the tests administered. In addition, we employed a more crystallized measure, not sex-sensitive, as an index of general intelligence (Information subtest of the WAIS, Wechsler, 1955).

In the menstrual-cycle population, we compared subjects in the low-hormone phase 3 to 5 days after onset of menstruation, and in either the high estrogen-and-progesterone midluteal phase 5 to 10 days prior to menstruation, or the high

**Table 9.5.   Battery of Cognitive and Motor Tests Completed
by Spontaneously-Cycling Women**

| *Spatial Ability* | *Articulation* |
|---|---|
| Space Relations | Speeded Counting |
| Hidden Figures | Color Reading, Naming |
| Portable Rod-and-Frame Test | Syllable Repetition |

| *Perceptual Speed* | *Manual Speed/Coordination* |
|---|---|
| Identical Pictures | Purdue Pegboard |
| Number Comparisons | Manual Sequence Box |
| Subtraction & Multiplication | Finger Tapping |

| *Verbal Fluency* | *Deductive Reasoning* |
|---|---|
| Oral Fluency | Inference Test |
| Expressional Fluency | |

estrogen peak just prior to ovulation. The latter phase was confirmed by blood assays (Hampson & Kimura, 1988; Hampson, 1990a,b).

The results of the study comparing menstrual and midluteal phases only, for between-subject comparisons, is shown in Figure 9.5. The findings for both studies indicate that, in fact, variations in female sex hormones have different and generally opposite effects on tests which differentiate males and females. The articulatory, complex manual, verbal fluency and some perceptual speed tests, on which women are often superior to men, generally showed enhancement in the high estrogen phase, compared to the low. Tests of spatial ability showed the reverse effect, in that they were depressed for women seen first in the high-estrogen phase compared to those seen in the low phase.

These results were significant in the Figure 9.5 data for composite scores of spatial ability and articulatory ability, in opposite directions (Hampson, 1990b). There was also a strong trend for enhancement of manual coordination in the high phase. An unexpected finding was that estrogen/progesterone also depressed deductive reasoning, although in the study looking at the pre-ovulatory estrogen peak, where only estrogen is raised and progesterone is low, there was no significant effect on this task (Hampson, 1990a).

These findings suggest that estrogen is not having merely a generalized arousing or depressing effect on cognitive function, but rather that the effects are selective. Moreover, they are predictable from a schema that classifies abilities according to whether they favor males or females. Estrogen may well be important in organizing male/female abilities pre- or perinatally, and it appears that this influence is still reflected in adult women throughout the fluctuations of the menstrual cycle. The fact that estrogen has opposite associations with two classes of abilities may mean that estrogen is simultaneously modulating two

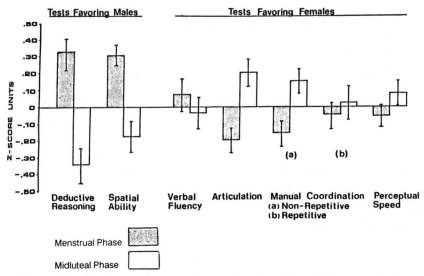

Figure 9.5.   **Performance on various tests in midluteal (high estrogen and progesterone) and menstrual (low hormone) phases of the menstrual cycle.**

neural systems in opposite ways, a paradox noted for rodent behavior (McEwen, 1987). It is also possible that, if "male" abilities and "female" abilities have a tradeoff relationship, then estrogen fluctuations could merely be altering a balance between them, rather than affecting either directly.

The possibility remained that, since the natural fluctuations in the menstrual cycle are accompanied by many other physiological changes related to the endogenous rhythms (including other hormonal changes which might affect the nervous system), the cognitive changes we saw might be secondary to something else. The data from postmenopausal women who were receiving exogenous estrogen provided support for the view that estrogen was sufficient to produce some of these effects (Kimura, 1989). Most of the women we assessed were on estrogen alone, less than a third being on progesterone as well. For the latter, progesterone was administered only in the last few days of the on-therapy phase. All women went off all therapy for a few days at the end of the treatment cycle, and they were therefore all assessed once in the on-estrogen only phase, and again in the off phase.

The results in Table 9.6 indicate that exogenous estrogen has a facilitating effect on the motor and articulatory abilities that were also sensitive to the natural menstrual fluctuations. The effects on perceptual speed are more variable, significant only on *Finding a's* in the between-subjects condition. (Practice effects are often a confound in the within-subjects comparisons, thus they tend to show weaker though very similar effects.) There are no significant changes on the spatial tests.

**Table 9.6. Relation between hormone-therapy phase and performance on various ability tasks**

| | Within Subjects (N = 32) | | | Between Subjects, Session 1 | | |
|---|---|---|---|---|---|---|
| | Low Estrogen Phase | High Estrogen Phase | p* | Low Estrogen Phase (N = 17) | High Estrogen Phase (N = 16) | p* |
| *Motor Tasks:* | | | | | | |
| Manual Sequence Box | | | | | | |
| Time to Acquisition (sec) | 11.8 (5.1) | 10.1 (3.6) | <.04 | 14.0 (3.5) | 10.9 (4.7) | <.05 |
| Post-Acqu. 5 trials (sec) | 7.3 (1.7) | 6.9 (1.8) | <.06 | 8.1 (1.4) | 6.5 (1.4) | <.02 |
| Tongue Twister, | | | | | | |
| 5 criterion trials (sec) | 15.2 (3.3) | 14.3 (3.2) | <.10 | 16.5 (3.1) | 14.5 (2.7) | <.06 |
| *Perceptual Speed Tests:* | | | | | | |
| Finding A's (% correct) | 32.1 (9.9) | 32.3 (8.3) | NS | 28.5 (8.4) | 35.1 (8.9) | <.04 |
| Identical Pictures (% correct) | 54.6 (12.7) | 53.1 (12.1) | NS | 53.8 (12.3) | 51.7 (11.3) | NS |
| *Spatial Tasks:* | | | | | | |
| Card Rotations (% correct) | 43.5 (17.4) | 46.4 (18.4) | NS | 44.0 (15.1) | 41.5 (22.6) | NS |
| Hidden Patterns (% correct) | 42.7 (13.7) | 42.0 (12.9) | NS | 38.7 (11.8) | 39.5 (14.5) | NS |

*Two-tailed probabilities

The effects of estrogen therapy apparently significantly outlast the cessation of therapy, in that raised levels of estradiol in the blood can be detected for several weeks, on a regime very similar to that of our subjects (Hammond & Maxson, 1986). Thus, the difference in plasma estradiol between "on" and "off" phases may be much smaller in the postmenopausal women than in the younger women throughout the menstrual cycle. If so, it suggests that the motor programming/articulatory skills are more sensitive to the effects of exogenous estradiol than are the perceptual speed or spatial skills. Another possibility is that the baseline levels of spatial ability are different in the younger and older women, and consequently the variations in estrogen are having different effects. Unfortunately, we did not have identical spatial tests in the two studies, to enable direct comparison.

### Shifts in Lateralization

The kinds of abilities that show significant sex differences tend to overlap with those that are claimed to depend preferentially on left or right hemispheres. Sex differences in cognitive function have been attributed to differences in asymmetry of hemispheric organization (Geschwind & Galaburda, 1984). It became apparent quite early in our studies on the menstrual-cycle and hormone-therapy fluctuations, that the tasks most enhanced by estrogen were those which were shown from neurological studies to depend on the left hemisphere. To sample possible shifts in hemispheric activity, a dichotic words task (Kimura, 1986) was administered in the menstrual and pre-ovulatory phases of the menstrual cycle. The right-ear advantage was significantly larger in the preovulatory high-estrogen phase of the cycle than in the low-estrogen phase (Figure 9.6). Although both right and left scores changed, the decrement in the left-ear score during the high phase appeared greater than the increment on the right ear (Hampson, 1990). Nevertheless, it is fair to say that there is a shift in relative hemispheric activity during the high-estrogen phase, such that the left hemisphere is facilitated relative to the right.

### CONCLUSIONS

The animal literature suggests that androgens organize the brain pre- and peri-natally for all sexually dimorphic behaviors, including problem-solving behaviors. This appears to be true in humans as in other mammals. Thus, if androgens are present early in life, the brain may somehow be organized to enhance spatial, mathematical, and extrapersonal targeting ability; whereas if they are not present, brain organization appears to favor small-amplitude intrapersonal motor skill, verbal articulation/fluency, and perceptual speed (identity matching). However, the relation between amount of androgen and degree of spatial ability is apparently not linear.

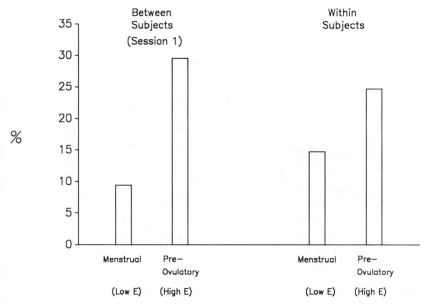

**Figure 9.6.   Magnitude of right-ear superiority across high-estrogen and low-estrogen phases of the menstrual cycle.**

In adult humans, then, some of the intellectual variation from person to person is related to hormonal status. This holds not merely across sexes, but also within males and within females. Moreover, intellectual patterns can vary within an individual as hormone status fluctuates. Experience with the environment must also play some role in the specific problem-solving behaviors we acquire. Perhaps the genetic makeup and the early hormonal organization of the nervous system establish a range within which experience can have an effect.

In rodents, androgens promote the growth of the right cerebral hemisphere relative to the left. In humans, we know that fluctuations in estrogen may be associated with alterations in *functional* brain asymmetry, with left-hemisphere activity relatively enhanced during higher levels of estrogen. Since this is a reversible effect, one might speculate that it is achieved by changing inter-hemispheric inhibition, though other mechanisms are certainly possible.

In humans moreover, we see a strong sex difference in the way in which anterior and posterior regions of the brain are organized for speech, praxic motor, and constructional skills. There is a sharp dependence on the anterior systems for such functions in women, even when controlling visuoconstructional tasks. We have speculated that this organization is related to the differing utilization of external or distance information in conjunction with large-amplitude movements (more developed in males), as compared to intrapersonal and distal motor control (more developed in females).

Individual uniqueness in intellectual pattern can thus be viewed as an intersection between genetic makeup (which we have not discussed), prenatal brain growth, the hormonal status throughout early life and perhaps puberty, and of course the idiosyncratic personal experience that each of us enjoys.

## REFERENCES

Beatty, W. W. (1979). Gonadal hormones and sex differences in nonreproductive behaviors in rodents: organizational and activational influences. *Hormones and Behavior, 12*, 112–163.

Becker, J. B., Snyder, P. J., Miller, M. M., Westgate, S. A., & Jenuwine, M. J. (1987). The influence of estrous cycle and intrastriatal estradiol on sensorimotor performance in the female rat. *Pharmacology, Biochemistry and Behavior, 27*, 53–59.

Benbow, C. P. (1988). Sex differences in mathematical reasoning ability in intellectually talented preadolescents: Their nature, effects, and possible causes. *Behavioral and Brain Sciences, 11*, 169–232.

Berenbaum, S. A., & Hines, M. (1992). Early androgens are related to childhood sex-typed toy preferences. *Psychological Science, 3*, 203–206.

Berry, J. W. (1966). Temne and Eskimo perceptual skills. *International Journal of Psychology, 1*, 207–229.

Bryden, M. P. (1979). Evidence for sex-related differences in cerebral organization. In M. A. Wittig & A. C. Petersen (Eds.) *Sex-related differences in cognitive functioning* (pp. 121–143). New York: Academic Press.

Bryden, M. P. (1982). *Laterality. Functional asymmetry in the intact brain*. New York: Academic Press.

Cappa, S. F., & Vignolo, L. A. (1988). Sex differences in the site of brain lesions underlying global aphasia. *Aphasiology, 2*, 259–264.

Christiansen, K., & Knussmann, R. (1987). Sex hormones and cognitive functioning in men. *Neuropsychobiology, 18*, 27–36.

Cole-Harding, S., Morstad, A. L., & Wilson, J. R. (1988). Spatial ability in members of opposite-sex twin pairs. *Behavior Genetics, 18*, 710 (Abstract).

Daly, M., & Wilson, M. (1983). *Sex, evolution, and behavior*. Boston: Willard Grant Press.

Diamond, M. C., Dowling, G. A., & Johnson, R. E. (1981). Morphologic cortical asymmetry in male and female rats. *Experimental Neurology, 71*, 261–268.

Ekstrom, R. B., French, J. W., Harman, H. H., & Dermen, D. (1976). *Kit of factor-referenced cognitive tests*. Princeton, NJ: Educational Testing Service.

Gaulin, S. J., & Fitzgerald, R. W. (1989). Sexual selection for spatial-learning ability. *Animal Behavior, 37*, 322–331.

Geschwind, N., & Galaburda, A. M. (1984). *Cerebral dominance*. Cambridge: Harvard University Press.

Gorski, R. A., & Jacobson, C. D. (1982). Sexual differentiation of the brain. *Frontiers of Hormone Research, 10*, 1–14.

Gouchie, C. T., & Kimura, D. (1991). The relation between testosterone levels and cognitive ability patterns. *Psychoneuroendocrinology, 16*, 323–334.

Hammond, C. B., & Maxson, W. S. (1986). Estrogen replacement therapy. *Clinical Obstetrics and Gynecology, 29,* 407–430.

Hampson, E. (1990a). Estrogen-related variations in human spatial and articulatory-motor skills. *Psychoneuroendocrinology, 15,* 97–111.

Hampson, E. (1990b). Variations in sex-related cognitive abilities across the menstrual cycle. *Brain and Cognition, 14,* 26–43.

Hampson, E., & Kimura, D. (1988). Reciprocal effects of hormonal fluctuations on human motor and perceptual-spatial skills. *Behavioral Neuroscience, 102,* 456–459.

Harshman, R. A., Hampson, E., & Berenbaum, S. A. (1983). Individual differences in cognitive abilities and brain organization, Part I: Sex and handedness differences in ability. *Canadian Journal of Psychology, 37,* 144–192.

Hier, D. B., & Crowley, W. F. (1982) Spatial ability in androgen-deficient men. *New England Journal of Medicine, 306,* 1202–1205.

Hines, M., Sloan, K., Lawrence, J., Lipcamon, J., & Chiu, L. (1988). The size of the human corpus callosum relates to language laterality and to verbal ability. *Society for Neuroscience Abstracts, 14,* 456.1 (Abstract).

Ingram, D. (1975). Motor asymmetries in young children. *Neuropsychologia, 13,* 95–102.

Jardine, R., & Martin, N. G. (1983). Spatial ability and throwing accuracy. *Behavior Genetics, 13,* 331–340.

Kimura, D. (1983). Sex differences in cerebral organization for speech and praxic functions. *Canadian Journal of Psychology, 37,* 19–35.

Kimura, D. (1986). *Neuropsychology Test Procedures.* London, Ontario: D. K. Consultants.

Kimura, D. (1987). Are men's and women's brains really different? *Canadian Psychology, 28,* 133–147.

Kimura, D. (1989) The effect of exogenous estrogen on motor programming skills in post-menopausal women. *University Western Ontario, Depart. Psychology Res. Bull.,* number 684.

Kimura, D., & Harshman, R. A. (1984). Sex differences in brain organization for verbal and nonverbal functions. In G. J. deVries, J. P. C. de Bruin, H. B. M. Uylings, & M. A. Corner (Eds.), *Sex differences in the brain. Progress in Brain Research* (Vol. 61, pp. 423–441). Amsterdam: Elsevier.

Kimura, D., & Vanderwolf, C. H. (1970). The relation between hand preference and the performance of individual finger movements by left and right hands. *Brain, 93,* 769–774.

Kolb, B. (1990). Prefrontal cortex. In B. Kolb & R. Tees (Eds.), *The cerebral cortex of the rat* (pp. 437–458). Cambridge: MIT Press.

deLacoste, M. C., Adesanya, T., & Woodward, D. J. (new press). New measures of sexual dimorphism in the human brain. *Biological Psychiatry.*

deLacoste, M. C., Horvath, D. S., & Woodward, D. J. (1991). "Possible" sex differences in the developing human fetal brain. *Journal of Clinical & Experimental Neuropsychology, 13,* 831–846.

deLacoste-Utamsing, C., & Holloway, R. L. (1982). Sexual dimorphism in the human corpus callosum. *Science, 216,* 1431–1432.

Lunn, D., & Kimura, D. (1989). Spatial abilities in preschool-aged children. *University of Western Ontario, Department of Psychology Research Bulletin*, No. 681.

Lovejoy, C. O. (1981). The origin of man. *Science, 211*, 341–350.

Maccoby, E. E. (1966). *The development of sex differences*. Stanford: Stanford University Press.

Mateer, C. A., Polen, S. B., & Ojemann, G. A. (1982). Sexual variation in cortical localization of naming as determined by stimulation mapping. *Behavioral and Brain Sciences, 5*, 310–311.

McEwen, B. S. (1987). Observations on brain sexual differentiation: a biochemist's view. In J. M. Reinisch, L. A. Rosenblum, & S. A. Sanders (Eds.), *Masculinity/femininity* (pp. 68–79). New York: Oxford.

McGlone, J. (1977). Sex differences in the cerebral organization of verbal functions in patients with unilateral brain lesions. *Brain, 100*, 775–793.

McGlone, J. (1980). Sex differences in human brain asymmetry: a critical survey. *Behavioral and Brain Sciences, 3*, 215–263.

Miller, L. K., & Santoni, V. (1986). Sex differences in spatial abilities: strategic and experiential correlates. *Acta Psychologica, 62*, 225–235.

Milner, B. (1964). Some effects of frontal lobectomy in man. In J. M. Warren & K. Akert (Eds.), *The frontal granular cortex and behavior* (pp. 313–334).

Nyborg, H. (1988). Mathematics, sex hormones, and brain function. *Behavioral and Brain Sciences, 11*, 206–207.

Peters, M., Servos, P., & Day, R. (1990). Marked sex differences on a fine motor skill task disappear when finger size is used as a covariate. *Journal of Applied Psychology, 75*, 87–90.

Petersen, A. C. (1976). Physical androgyny and cognitive functioning in adolescence. *Developmental Psychology, 12*, 524–533.

Reinisch, J. M. (1981). Prenatal exposure to synthetic progestins increases potential for aggression in humans. *Science, 211*, 1171–1173.

Resnick, S. M., Berenbaum, S. A., Gottesman, I. I., & Bouchard, T. J. (1986). Early hormonal influences on cognitive functioning in congenital adrenal hyperplasia. *Developmental Psychology, 22*, 191–198.

Ross, R., Bernstein, L ., Judd, H., Hanisch, R., Pike, M., & Henderson, B. (1986). Serum testosterone levels in healthy young black and white men. *Journal of the National Cancer Institute, 76*, 45–48.

Sanders, B., Soares, M. P., & D'Aquila, J. (1982). The sex difference on one test of spatial visualization: a nontrivial difference. *Child Development, 53*, 1106–1110.

Shute, V. J., Pellegrino, J. W., Hubert, L., & Reynolds, R. W. (1983). The relationship between androgen levels and human spatial abilities. *Bulletin of the Psychonomic Society, 21*, 465–468.

Soma, H., Takayama, M., Kiyokawa, T., Akaeda, T., & Tokoro, K. (1975). Serum gonadotropin levels in Japanese women. *Obstetrics and Gynecology, 46*, 311–312.

Tiffin, J. (1968). *Purdue Pegboard Examiner Manual*. Chicago: Science Research Association.

Tobias, P. V. (1966). The peoples of Africa south of the Sahara. In P. T. Baker & J. S. Weiner (Eds.), *The biology of human adaptability* (pp. 111–200). Oxford: Clarendon.

Vignolo, L. A., Boccardi, E., & Caverni, L. (1986). Unexpected CT-scan findings in global aphasia. *Cortex, 22*, 55–69.

Ward, S. L., Newcombe, N., & Overton, W. F. (1986). Turn left at the church, or three miles north. A study of direction giving and sex differences. *Environment and Behavior, 18*, 192–213.

Watson, N. V., & Kimura, D. (1991). Nontrivial sex differences in throwing and intercepting: Relation to psychometrically-defined spatial functions. *Personality & Individual Differences, 12*, 375–385.

Watson, N. V., & Kimura, D. (1989). Right-hand superiority for throwing but not for intercepting. *Neuropsychologia, 27*, 1399–1414.

Wechsler, D. (1955). *The Wechsler Adult Intelligence Scale.* New York: The Psychological Corporation.

Williams, C. L., Barnett, A. M., & Meck, W. H. (1990). Organizational effects of early gonadal secretions on sexual differentiation in spatial memory. *Behavioral Neuroscience, 104*, 84–97.

Witelson, S. F. (1976). Sex and the single hemisphere: Specialization of the right hemisphere for spatial processing. *Science, 193*, 425–427.

Witelson, S. F. (1989). Hand and sex differences in the isthmus and genu of the human corpus callosum. *Brain, 112*, 799–835.

Witkin, H. A., Goodenough, D. R., & Karp, S. A. (1967). Stability of cognitive style from childhood to young adulthood. *Journal of Personality and Social Psychology, 7*, 291–300.

# Author Index

# Subject Index

## A

Adoption studies, 40–43, 46, 57, 64, 73–75, 96–98, 99, 103–108, 112–119, 121, 123–127, 130, 245, 252
  placement bias in, 41–43, 56, 75, 98, 112, 123–125
Alzheimer's disease, 321, 322, 326, 367
Aphasia, 379, 381
Apraxia, 381–384
Armed Forces Qualification Test (AFQT), 289
Armed Services Vocational Aptitude Battery (ASVAB), 281, 282
Aufmerksamkeits-Belastungstest, 295
Autism, 326
Averaged evoked potentials (AEPs), 2, 23–27, 259–315, 318, 319, 336–338, 347–367; *see also* Hendricksons' theory
  correlations with specific mental abilities, 298–305
  Fourier transformation of, 260, 264, 266, 285–288
  nonaveraged EEG measures, 260–270, 307
  spectral analysis of, 284–288
  variability in, 260, 272, 276, 277, 282, 288–298

## B

Bayley Infant Behavior Record (IBR), 99, 109–110
Bayley Scales of Infant Development, 99–109, 123–127, 252, 278
Beery Visual Motor Integration test, 289

## B

Behavior genetics, 33–84, 95–133, 219
  developmental behavior genetics, 65–69, 95–133
  environmental correlations, 144, 145, 148, 149, 151, 157, 174, 179
  genetic correlations, 121–128, 132, 145–154, 157, 161, 170, 174, 179
  between and within families correlations, 146–154, 161, 163, 168, 173–180, 187, 200–202, 212, 214, 216–221, 223, 229–233
Bender Visual-Motor Gestalt Test, 277
Benton visual retention test, 269
Biochemical correlates of human information processing, 333–373
Briggs Handedness Questionnaire, 299

## C

California Test of Mental Maturity, 173
Category Width Scale, 281, 282
Cattell's culture-fair test of intelligence, 250
Cerebral glucose metabolism, 27, 317–332
Cerebral palsy, 326
Chicago Test of Reasoning Ability, 201
Chicago Test of Verbal Ability, 201
Clayton-Jackson Object Sorting Test, 281, 282
Columbia Mental Maturity Scale, 266
Creativity, 13, 327, 328

## D

Darwin's theory of evolution, 13, 16, 17, 232
Differential Aptitude Tests, 218

**413**